INFINITE LOOP

INFINITE LOOP

HOW THE WORLD'S MOST INSANELY GREAT

COMPUTER COMPANY WENT INSANE

MICHAEL S. MALONE

AURUM PRESS

To everyone who ever believed the dream

First published in Great Britain 1999 by Aurum Press Limited, 25 Bedford Avenue,
London WC1B 3AT by arrangement with Doubleday, a division of Random House, Inc.

This paperback edition first published 2000 by Aurum Press Limited

A catalogue record for this book is available from the British Library.

ISBN 1 85410 693 7

Book design by Leah S. Carson

Printed and bound in Great Britain
by MPG Books, Bodmin

FOREWORD

It has often been written that Silicon Valley is merely a very large and very wealthy small town in which everyone at some time has worked for, with or against everyone else.

If that is the case, then Apple Computer for me has always been the curious neighborhood just down the street. I have encountered it in some way almost every day of the last quarter century—sometimes just passing by, on other occasions stopping for a visit, but never out of my life. Indeed, so ever present, for good and bad, has Apple been in my life that I gave a second thought to ever beginning this book. The prospect of having to relive the Apple story, with all its hopes and heartbreaks, hypocrisies and disasters, was almost too exhausting to contemplate.

My dealings with Apple Computer began two decades before the company was even founded. I saw a nine-year-old Steve Jobs on the playground of our elementary schoolyard in Mountain View. I even found one of his homework assignments in my papers.

A few years later, having coincidentally moved to Sunnyvale at the same time as Jobs, I watched Steve Wozniak ride up Bernardo Drive on his way home from swim practice. I looked over Woz's primitive adder at the local science fair. For a short time, I was part of the Boy Scouts Explorer post that was one of the roots of the Homebrew Computer Club. And I saw, but didn't recognize, Woz, Jobs and Bill Fernandez (whose father was my Sunday school teacher) as they shopped for parts in Owen Whetzel's hobby shop. A year after that, I saw a lonely—and apparently unremarkable—Apple I on a shelf at the first Byte Shop.

When I was just out of college and working in public relations at Hewlett-Packard, one of my divisions was APD, Woz's employer. And during that period, handling publicity for Dave Barram and Dianne McKenna in their run for Sunnyvale City Council, I stood in the Wozniak living room as Mr. Wozniak cornered Regis McKenna over his concerns about his son and Steve

Jobs. Ten years later, I sat in Barram's office at Apple just days before he was nominated to the Commerce Department.

When I began my journalism career at the *San Jose Mercury News* at the end of 1979, one of my first assignments was to profile a new young company with the absurd name of Apple Computer. I interviewed Jobs and Woz in their chaotic offices just days after their move to Bandley Drive. There I found two bright, if eccentric, young men whom I nevertheless recognized as fellow children of Silicon Valley.

I visited Apple many times in subsequent years, writing about it for the *Mercury News*, the *New York Times* and the *Boston Globe*. I was in the audience, as a stringer for *The Economist*, at the extraordinary Macintosh introduction. Then, broke and hungry, I quit reporting on Apple for several years and went to work writing for it. Writing on an Apple III given to me by Mike Markkula in exchange for ghostwriting an article, I authored one of the many drafts of the notorious 1984 Apple annual report—and saw firsthand both the eerie bond between John Sculley and Steve Jobs and the emotional damage that Jobs was wreaking on the company. I heard the grumbles of the Apple II group as their product was eclipsed by the Mac.

Having been a reporter and a contractor, my third relationship with Apple was as a beggar—that sophisticated version known as an entrepreneur. In the middle of the Sculley era, I spent some time as part of the start-up team of a new Valley company. Like many such teams of the period, we imagined the answer to all our prayers was to convince Apple to become a customer, an investor or a strategic partner (these days, such teams dream of the same deal with Microsoft). For two years, we used every connection we had—Barram, Del Yocam, Debi Coleman and dozens of others—to no avail. Most of the problem lay with our company—it is only now preparing to go public after a decade—but as we sat through endless meetings, being ignored by Apple executives as they jockeyed for power among themselves, it became apparent to us that this was a company in serious trouble, one that had lost the edginess and drive that had once made it great.

In 1996, the world saw what we had seen during those long, posturing meetings: a hollow company that had lost its purpose, a company searching for a charismatic figure to save it. And so, once again a reporter, I found myself in the crush of true believers in a ballroom in San Francisco to hear Gil Amelio describe his plans to turn Apple around—and more important, to see the return of Steve Jobs. Sitting there on the floor, I thought about the distance we had traveled in three decades. We were all now middle-aged fathers, some rich, some mythical, some still just trying to cover their mortgage—as old as our own fathers had been when the personal computing revolution began. Now that revolution seemed to be coming to an end, replaced by new technologies and new products that rightly belong to a younger generation. It had been thrilling and degrading, noble and base—and it would ring down through history.

That was when I knew I had to write the Apple story. The true story that lay beneath the accretion of thirty years of legends and lies. I figured getting all the truth was probably impossible, but at least I could make a start. Apple had defeated every other attempt to capture its story, so I had no illusions. But at least I could stake out a path for that definitive Apple biography that waits to be written by some future generation. For now, here is a look, from inside and outside, at a deeply human institution that is unlike any other, yet is somehow emblematic of America at the end of the twentieth century.

Having covered Apple for a quarter century, I find it impossible to list all the individuals, named and anonymous, who helped in the creation of this book. The sources (see Notes on Sources at the end of the text) number literally in the hundreds. However, I would like to acknowledge several individuals who made important contributions to the actual production of this manuscript.

First and foremost is Roger Scholl, my editor at Doubleday, and his staff. *Infinite Loop* was originally Roger's idea, and during the many long months of waiting for me to meet one missed deadline after the next, he no doubt often wondered what had possessed him. Roger's suggestions were always insightful, and his patience awe-inspiring. Also at Doubleday, I'd like to acknowledge the hard work of attorney Kathy Trager in legal fact-checking.

As always, my agent Don Congdon brought his wisdom and experience to the project, keeping me on track. This time, however, I had the added pleasure of working with Michael Congdon.

In Silicon Valley, my vital right hand was Geoff Baum, columnist for *Forbes ASAP*, co-founder of garage.com and world-class researcher, interviewer and fact-checker. Among Geoff's many contributions were the interviews of everyday Apple employees that provided much of the versimilitude and texture in this book. He also cast his legendary cold eye over my hyperbolics. Eleventh-hour research was provided by David Raymond of *Forbes ASAP*.

Finally, and most importantly, at home I enjoyed tremendous support from my family. Of my seven books, this one was easily the most difficult: endless 3 A.M. nights and groggy days. Through it all my wife, Carol, and my two boys, Tad and Skipper, stood by me, propping me up and keeping me going. To them, as usual, I owe my deepest gratitude.

A final note on technology, because my experience with computers seems to match that of the rest of the consuming public. I wrote my first books, and launched my freelancing career, with an Apple III. Despite its infamy, I loved that computer, using it long after Apple had orphaned it, even after I'd worn away the tops of some of the keys. It was venture capitalist Bill Davidow, when we were writing *The Virtual Corporation,* who finally convinced me to upgrade: to a Macintosh IIsi. I used that computer for three years, but as I began *Infinite Loop,* it started to fall apart. I borrowed an Apple Duo Dock for a while, but that only delayed the decision. It was a dilemma being faced by millions of Apple owners during that dark period in the company's history: Should I spend above-market prices for an inferior Apple machine just out of perhaps misguided loyalty to a company that hadn't really cared about me for a long time? Or should I go over to the dark side, accept the cynical compromises of Windows 95 and do my part to line Bill Gates's already well-gilded pockets?

It was a painful decision. In good times and bad, I had always aligned myself with Apple, the maverick company fighting the good fight against the bureaucratization of personal computers.

But I was tired of passing those endless aisles of Windows programs at Fry's just to get to the few shelves of Apple products. I was tired of paying too much for too little computing power. Most of all, I was tired of being loyal to a company that was so self-centered and arrogant that it seemed to have lost all interest in me as a customer. And so, even as I was writing about the glory days of Apple Computer, I was abandoning the Mac for a Toshiba laptop. It was on this Windows computer that, ironically, I wrote this book.

And yet . . .

These days I find myself again eyeing Apple computers, this time with envy. Not the iMac, Steve Jobs's triumph of image over reality, but the G3 machines—fast, powerful and only a little overpriced. Most of all, I find I miss the excitement of the Little Kingdom . . . especially now that Apple seems to have gotten the magic back. After all, it was always about magic.

—Michael S. Malone
Sunnyvale, California

CONTENTS

Can any poet re-create
a worthy portrait of the great?

—Horace, *Odes* 1:6

1.0 ROOTS

Before and after everything, companies are about character.

Before the first idea, the first money, the first employees, the first distributor, retailer and customer, before the creation of the company itself, there is the character of the founders. Their ambition, talent, creativity and will to succeed are what make them successful entrepreneurs and distinguish them from the millions of people who only dream of creating their own company. Character also distinguishes these rare individuals from the thousands who try to create their own companies but are defeated by the market, competition, bad luck and an unwillingness to do whatever it takes to win.

After the company has grown rich and safe and mature, character tells as well. After the founders have left or died, after the excitement has moved elsewhere along with the best employees, after the company's products and logo and image have grown synonymous with staid and predictable. After hot new firms have appeared on the scene, start-ups that most resemble the company of old, and begin to carve away great chunks of the market. Then once more it is character, in the company's institutional memory, its community and in the philosophy with which the founders imbued it, that may spell the difference between another generation of success, or a slow, ugly corporate death.

Good companies have strong characters. Great companies have heroic characters. The greatest companies of the twentieth century all had extraordinary characters: Royal Dutch Shell, De Beers, Ford, General Motors, IBM, Hewlett-Packard, General Electric, Intel, Microsoft. They weren't necessarily "good" characters. One need only think of De Beers and Shell and their rape of underdeveloped nations, Ford and its crushing of workers early in this century, Microsoft and its alleged monopolistic destruction of the software industry. But they were bold, fearless and consistent. And it was this inner strength that enabled these companies not only to win their early competitive battles but to survive wounds that would (and did) kill their lesser counterparts.

Ford, battered first by GM, and then by the Japanese in the 1980s, struggled and regained its leadership in the 1990s with a new family of brilliantly innovative cars. IBM suffered one of the worst business collapses in the century at the end of the 1980s, then restored itself in just five years. HP slid into complacency and inertia, then somehow righted itself in the 1990s to become the most innovative large company on the planet. During this same period, Microsoft missed the most important technological revolution of the era, the Internet, then accomplished a breathtaking turnabout and gained the leadership of that industry.

Of all the great companies of recent memory, there is only one that seemed to have *no* character, but only an attitude, a style, a collection of mannerisms. It constructed a brilliant simulacrum of character, in the way a man without empathy or conscience can pretend to have those traits. But it was never really there—even though two generations of employees convinced themselves otherwise. It was only when that character was finally tested did the essential hollowness of the enterprise finally stand exposed, and the employees and customers shrieked with betrayal.

This was Apple Computer Inc., and there has never been a company like it. It was founded by two young men, one a genius with no allegiance to any institution but his own mind; the other a protean, inconstant figure who seemed composed of nothing but charm and a pure will to power. The company they built seemed to have everything: great technology, superb products, talented employees, rabidly loyal customers, an arresting vision, even a lock on the zeitgeist. But, like its founders, it lacked character. And because of that, from the first minute of the first meeting of Steve Jobs and Steve Wozniak, a decade before the company's founding, Apple Computer was set on a path from which it could not escape, even after those founders were gone. And that path would in time lead to the company's destruction.

More than any other great company, the seeds of Apple's future glory and its subsequent humiliation were planted long before the company ever began. And bend and prune as it might, Apple Computer could never free itself of its roots.

2.0 SEED

It was Regis McKenna, the Silicon Valley marketing guru, who first saw the horrible truth: "The mistake everyone makes is assuming that Apple is a real company. But it is not. It never has been."

He was too much of a businessman (after all, Apple could prove to be a once and future client) to draw the final inference: "And it never will be."

Nobody alive knew Apple better than Regis McKenna—at least nobody who had been affected by the notorious "reality distortion field" that emanated from Steve Jobs. After fifteen years of handling the company, Regis had remained unwarped and unconverted because no matter how successful Regis McKenna Inc. had become, and no matter how far it had left the publicity game behind for the more rarefied climes of marketing and business development, Regis still remained a PR man at heart. He still upheld the flack's first law: never, ever believe the hot air you put out about your client.

Not that it was easy. When you watched your client land on the cover of *Time* magazine and knew you got the credit for getting him there; when you stood in the convention centers and giant auditoriums and felt the waves of adoration rolling around you; and when the calls came late at night and you heard Jobs the Seducer telling you how much he depended upon you, it would have been so simple to surrender to the undertow, to lose yourself in the Apple Will.

But every time Regis thought of doing so there would be a meeting to remind him that Apple was a kind of collective madness. He would bring in an expert on marketing, or branding, or organizational theory—anything that might give the company some order, some strategic planning, some simulation of real business discipline—and he would watch in dismay as that person was humiliated, ignored or driven away. As for his own advice—well, nobody blew off the mighty Regis McKenna. Instead, they'd listen intently, nodding, foreheads pinched in concentration, even the seraphic Jobs himself making those unreadable and delicate motions with his fingers on the tabletop as if he was taking seriously what Regis was saying . . . and then the Apple Corps would leave the room and never think about Regis's message again.

In the end, after fifteen years advising the company he'd helped to create, McKenna walked away from Apple Computer. And not just from Apple, but from PR itself. Henceforth, the most successful publicist in the history of high technology would dedicate his firm to marketing. "It got to be my cross to bear," he said, looking back at the story of Apple Computer. "I helped create much of the image of Apple. Then I realized that I could help make people famous and have them assume the mantle of greatness, but that I couldn't do anything about the reality behind the story—the flaws and the insecurities and the egos. It just got to the point where I couldn't do it anymore. If it wasn't real, I didn't want to construct it."

So McKenna understood first. And in the years that followed, others, typically after they left the Cupertino kindergarten, caught on as well. Yet what they had learned was somehow inexplicable. It was like coming out of a coma and trying to describe where you've been. Some were bitter, a few amused, most just dazed in a way that could never be brought to focus. Even Regis, a man who had become rich and famous explaining technology and the companies that built it, would hit a wall when describing Apple. After twenty years, he could tell you what Apple was not, but he was at a loss for words telling you what it was. The best he could come up with was "a corporate Woodstock"—which explained everything, and nothing.

Others tried. Michael Moritz, who in 1984 wrote the first and best-known book about Apple, entitled it *The Little Kingdom*, suggesting at once the attractive preciousness of the place, its essential unreality, and the imperial nature of its organization. A few years later, Steven Levy, in his book about the Macintosh, would choose a memorable Jobs phrase, *Insanely Great*, that captured in its near-oxymoronic form two essential characteristics of the company. The pseudonymous Robert X. Cringely, in his entertaining (if suspect) *Accidental Empires*, compared Apple to an episode of *Bonanza*, the Bagwan's Rancho Rajneesh in Oregon and even the suicidal Jonestown.

Yet none of these descriptions, witty as they were, were sufficient to capture the true nature of Apple. It was only later, as the deep undercurrents in the company finally broke the surface that it became apparent that Apple Computer was, in fact, a beautifully constructed story, an elaborate fiction that mixed comedy with tragedy, piled irony upon irony, and then finally, bizarrely, looped back on itself.

And once that became clear, so did the author. Steve Jobs. The truth had always been there in Jobs's knowing little smile.

There are thousands of successful entrepreneurs at work right now, from

Bill Gates to the men and women meeting right now with a start-up team at Denny's, and none of them have written a tale as soaring and arresting as that of Apple. Perhaps no company in history has ever provoked such intense interest, loyalty, love and hate. For the richness of the plot, for the endless dramas, for the sheer *aesthetics* of its story, Apple is unique.

Trip Hawkins, himself an important entrepreneur, and a former Apple manager of market planning, told Cringely, "Steve never knew his parents. He makes so much noise in life, he cries so loud about everything, that I keep thinking he feels that if he just cries loud enough, his real parents will hear and know that they made a mistake giving him up."

That cry was Steve Jobs's hidden goad. With it alone he might have become a poet like his natural sister, or, quite easily, given the pathological parts of his personality, gone into crime—which, in fact, for a short time he did. His great luck was to find himself on the perfect playground for his gifts: the world of Silicon Valley in the 1970s.

2.0.1 COLLISION

Silicon Valley in 1965, at the time when Steve Jobs was attending Monte Loma elementary school in Mountain View, was a tense combination of opposing demographic forces.

Strictly speaking, Silicon Valley didn't yet exist. Sure, Fairchild was there, but it became mythic only in retrospect. If you were to drive down Ellis Street in Mountain View past its headquarters you never would have known that this little company was already changing the world.

Hewlett-Packard, of course, was there. By 1965 it was already more than twenty-five years old. At night, driving up El Camino Real in Palo Alto heading to the young Stanford Shopping Center, you could see its sawtooth roof glowing atop the hill up Page Mill Road. But HP was, and is, as hermetic as a church. If your father worked there, you were embraced within the HP family, you met Bill and Dave and attended the company picnic, and lived in an Eichler home in Palo Alto. Your neighbors were college professors from Stanford, other HPers or engineers and scientists who worked near HP in the Stanford Industrial Park at companies like Varian Corp., Watkins Johnson or Syntex.

But more important than HP was Lockheed Missiles & Space (LMSC), a city in itself rising alongside the Bay next to the Moffett Naval Air Station and NASA's Ames Research Center. Each day at 7 A.M., Lockheed's 25,000 employees would leave their homes in Mountain View, Sunnyvale, Cupertino and Santa Clara—from housing developments that had been built specifically for them by smart developers—and crowded the streets heading east into the morning sun toward the two LMSC gates. And each day at 3:30 P.M., the process would reverse, giving the Valley a distinct work cycle that would dominate the area for twenty years.

More than any other force, Lockheed was the dynamo that made Santa Clara County (the western cities of the South San Francisco Bay from Palo Alto to San Jose) the fastest-growing place in America. Young men, new families in tow, arrived by the scores each day, armed with a GI Bill degree in aeronautical, electrical or mechanical engineering, and looking for a piece of the aerospace future. They bought their ranch-style house—or, if they were adventurous, a Bauhaus-for-everyman Eichler with an atrium—and drove off every morning to build ICBMs for Lockheed.

Those who now call that world stultifying, conformist or retrograde weren't there. It was, in fact, as progressive in its way as any place on earth. The men and women who populated Silicon Valley in the 1960s were optimists. They believed that they were not only constructing the future but creating a perfect world for themselves and their families in the process. They would be famous and rich, have beautiful children and live in a Winterless Paradise and own a modernistic house and collect fine wines—all at the same time.

The betrayal, the depression and the self-doubt only came later, after Lockheed laid off at least one breadwinner on every residential block, after their kids grew their hair long and despised them and, worst of all, after these young men and women of infinite promise became divorced, career-stalled middle-aged men and women with a ceiling on their hopes.

It came after the counterculture revolution, Vietnam and recession, and after Silicon Valley had become a single monolithic urban stretch of high-tech communities thirty miles long and ten miles wide. In 1965, though, these professional communities were still tiny enclaves of (mostly) white, (mostly) Protestant, (mostly) engineers embedded in vast stretches of old Santa Clara Valley: blue-collar, rural, orchard-based, seasonal, immigrant, Catholic.

Mountain View was one of the oldest of Valley communities. Originally the Castro family land grant from Mexico, it was a well-developed farming community by the beginning of the twentieth century. The children and grandchildren of these farmworkers were enjoying the postwar prosperity by moving up to the new suburban housing developments, like the square mile of ersatz Eichlers built by Mackay Homes on the edge of Mountain View along Alma and San Antonio roads hard by the southern tip of Palo Alto.

For the local families that moved into this development in the early 1960s, these homes were the culmination of an assimilationist dream that in some cases reached back a century. It was the family's first toehold in the middle class, thanks to new jobs in auto repair shops, assembly lines and retail stores. Yet they soon found their shiny dreams tarnished by the arrival of new neighbors from the East Coast or the Midwest; arrivistes who drove their foreign cars every Friday night to San Francisco in search of real culture, and who owned not just college diplomas but graduate degrees in unimaginable disciplines like solid-state physics and semiconductor electronics.

For these newcomers, the neighborhood was not a culmination but a flagstone on the path to bigger houses in nicer neighborhoods in Sunnyvale or Cupertino, and then, with luck and some stock options, Los Altos Hills or Saratoga. For now, they merely demanded that the schools improve their facilities, that local stores offer more diverse merchandise and that the constabulary protect their children from the predations of the tougher working-class kids down the street.

It was a situation guaranteed to provoke friction and hostility. The upwardly mobile new Silicon Valleyites saw the natives as uneducated, unsophisticated and slightly dangerous, and the old Santa Clara Valleyites saw the newcomers as arrogant, pushy and, worst of all, a threat to their hard-fought prosperity.

2.1 MOCKINGBIRD

It was in this tense milieu that nine-year-old Steven P. Jobs found himself in 1965. And within this sensitive and often irritating boy the schisms went even deeper.

His father, Paul Jobs, grew up on a farm in Germantown, Wisconsin, dropped out of high school, then knocked around the Midwest in search of work. After Pearl Harbor he made the odd decision, for someone at the landlocked center of the country, to join the Coast Guard. As the war ended, he found himself in San Francisco on a decommissioning ship, and in yet another one of the compulsive moves that would characterize his life, Jobs bet a shipmate that on one of their upcoming leaves he would find himself a wife.

He did just that, on a blind date. Feckless he might be, but Paul Jobs was also a persuasive man; a natural salesman. Unfortunately, he had one disastrous flaw for a salesman. He hated kowtowing to customers. He talked his new wife, Clara, into moving back with him to the Midwest, a decision that ran precisely counter to the great migration of ex-GIs. Needless to say, it was a bad strategy, and after struggling as a machinist and then a used-car salesman, Paul finally, in 1952, caught on to the spirit of the era and he and Clara headed back to San Francisco.

Despite the fact that California wasn't as golden as he expected, and Paul jumped from one lousy job to another—bad-debt collector, car repossessor, loan checker—he and Clara were now feeling suitably stable and settled to start a family. In 1956, they adopted a baby boy, Steven. Five months later, before the adoption legalities were even complete, the family moved to South San Francisco.

There was in Paul Jobs an unusual, though not rare, combination of romanticism, unreality, hard work, ego and self-doubt. He was, in a sense, an entrepreneur who missed his calling, a lone wolf who chafed in every organization in which he worked, who resented being subordinate to anyone, who felt he was destined for important things but always arrived at the station just as the train pulled away, and who was perpetually ashamed about his lack of success. No sooner did he construct a new hopeful reality than it would crash around him and he would set off again.

In 1960, the finance company Paul was working for transferred him to Palo Alto. It was a good place for a man approaching middle age. The economy was booming and jobs were waiting unfilled. As they moved into their new home in Mountain View, it seemed that Paul Jobs had finally made it. Marking this new phase in their lives, Paul and Clara adopted a daughter, Patricia.

Now the Jobs family was in the very embodiment of a Postwar Upward Mobile community. It was as diverse a neighborhood as any the Valley would ever know. On a single block one might find a psychiatrist working at Agnews State Mental Hospital, a high school janitor, a naval officer flying P-3 sub chasers out of Moffett Field, a gardener from the Philippines who worked for the city, a Pakistani PhD in geology analyzing moon rills at NASA-Ames Research Center and a computer scientist who would one day be a vice president of Hewlett-Packard.

In the midst of all this was a brilliant little boy, often distracted, something of a discipline problem and accustomed to being the center of attention. He was the inevitable star of neighborhood home movies, birthday parties and picnics. Not only was young Steven doted upon by his parents but as the years went on he increasingly became the surrogate for his father's frustrated career desires.

The result would likely have been an arrogant chronic overachiever, the kind of obnoxious personality type that fills the senior, but not top, management ranks of Silicon Valley. But there were two other factors at work as well. One was that young Steven, the adopted child, was simply *different* from his family. Where his old man was tough and gregarious, the kind of guy who could repossess cars all week, then spend the weekend rooting around junkyards for parts for the classic cars he rebuilt in his garage, his son was sensitive and withdrawn. The boy was a discipline problem at school, while still managing to have few friends. He would go with his dad to the junkyards, obviously enjoying the dickering, but once they returned home he showed no interest in getting his hands dirty bolting on carburetors and fenders.

Worse, Steven was also a whiner. When he took swim lessons at the Mountain View Dolphins Swim club, one of his classmates, Mark Wozniak (yet more evidence that Silicon Valley has always been a very large small town) would recall: "He was pretty much of a crybaby. He'd lose a race and go off and cry. He didn't quite fit in with everybody else. He wasn't one of the guys." In fact, he was one of the boys, found in every class, who get the stuffing knocked out of them on a regular basis.

Out of place at home and at school, Steven turned to others in the neighborhood for friendship. It was possible in those days to walk down the street on a Saturday morning, past all the open, well-stuffed one-car garages and see the neighborhood men at work on their hobbies. And these extracurricular activities were as diverse as their careers. For every two Paul Jobses installing new lifters on engines there was at least one man surrounded by used oscilloscopes, multimeters, waveform generators, oscillators and all the other detritus of the vacuum-tube age of electronic instruments. Many of these obsolete devices had been lifted out of Dumpsters at the office and were now being put to use on televisions, stereos and, identified by the telltale antenna masts swaying over the house, ham radios.

Steven had just such a neighbor, a Hewlett-Packard engineer. One Saturday, while the boy was desultorily working with his father on a car, this engineer hauled a carbon microphone, a battery and an old stereo speaker out on the driveway, hooked them up and shook the street. Steven's eyes lit up. How does that work? he asked his father. Paul Jobs shrugged. He didn't know. So Steven ran to the engineer's house to ask. From then on, almost every Saturday, Steven stood in a new garage, peppering his new role model with questions.

His son's attention wasn't the only thing Paul Jobs lost. His job, he was convinced, was going nowhere. It didn't help that one by one the professionals among his neighbors began to move away to smarter, more expensive neighborhoods in Palo Alto and Los Altos. Unhappy and desperate, Paul Jobs decided once again to make a career shift. He took courses in his off-time and earned his realtor's license.

It was, in fact, a brilliant move. With the economy surging, the cost of living starting to climb, and one more old cherry orchard being covered by a new housing tract almost by the week, real estate was one of the most lucrative professions in the Valley. Had he stuck with it, Paul Jobs, like many others, might have made himself wealthy over the next twenty years.

Instead, he detested the work, a fact he might have realized long before he got into it. He didn't like making nice to every idiot with a buck in his pocket, he despised the whole phony nature of the profession and, most of all, he really hated not knowing when the next check was coming in. And they came in less and less frequently as his attitude spilled into his work and scared away clients.

The family was now caught in a downward spiral, made worse by the success of everyone around them. To stay afloat, the Jobses had to mortgage their house. Clara even took a part-time job. And when Steven took up swimming, she added babysitting to pay for his fees. Vacations were canceled. The car grew old. And in perhaps the ultimate statement of defeat in 1960s California, when the Jobses' color TV broke it was replaced with a black-and-white version. Eventually, to everyone's relief, Paul Jobs bailed out of real estate. But his only career choice now was to go back to work as a machinist with no seniority. He managed to find a job twenty miles away in San Carlos and the family struggled on.

Steven, now nine years old, watched in despair as the world around him, *his* world, began to crumble. Already alienated from his parents and his schoolmates, he was now, in a way he couldn't fully appreciate, also losing touch with his social class. It came to a head one day in school when his teacher asked a simple astronomy question: "What is it in this universe you don't understand?"

Little Steven Jobs, hovering over a cosmic abyss the teacher couldn't understand, answered abjectly: "Why is my family so broke?"

2.2 Revenge

Although the smartest kid in his class, Jobs became so difficult and obnoxious that he was thrown out of his fourth-grade class. Luckily, another, better, teacher took him in. Years later, Jobs would recall that the teacher found a quick motivational tool for the young man: bribes. Especially money. With the prospect of a payoff down the line, Steven Jobs could do amazing things. So amazing that he skipped fifth grade altogether.

But skipping a grade was both an honor and a curse, because the troubled, socially awkward boy was now a year younger than his classmates. Worse, jumping to sixth grade brought Steven one year closer to Crittenden Junior High School.

Monte Loma was paradise compared to Crittenden. Located in a poor neighborhood a half mile closer to the Bay, drawing from the middle class all the way down to the bottommost economic strata, Crittenden was a school where the daughter of an astrophysicist might sit at a desk next to the deeply disturbed son of a parolee. Fights were a daily occurrence; as were shake-downs in the bathrooms. Knives were regularly brought to school as a show of macho. The year before Steven arrived a group of eighth-grade boys had gone to jail for gang rape. During Steven's seventh-grade year the school lost a wrestling match to Sunnyvale's Mango Junior High and proceeded to demol-ish that school's team bus.

Among the students, there were two ruling elites: the hoods, mostly His-panic, in pointed high-heel shoes, pegged black pants, white shirts, DAs; and a small number of surfers, with long blond hair, knit shirts, baggy pants and deck shoes. Everyone else cowered in fear. And Steven Jobs, a year younger than his classmates and thus the youngest kid in school, a pariah even among the pariahs, was in the sorriest spot of all.

That summer, Steven dreaded September more than anything he'd ever known. Finally, he couldn't stand it any longer. He told his parents that if he had to go back to Crittenden, he would quit school.

What happened then was a turning point in Steven Jobs's life. He wasn't alone in fearing his school. In his neighborhood scores of families, worried about the quality of education and the threat to their children represented by Crittenden, had picked up stakes and moved elsewhere. But these were up-wardly mobile families; most had planned to leave for months, even years, and the quality of schooling proved to be the trip wire.

An even greater number of kids in the neighborhood, when they expressed the same fear, or came home with a split lip and missing lunch money, were told by their less affluent parents to buck up and not be pushed around.

But when Steven Jobs made his ultimatum, the most amazing thing hap-pened: his parents agreed. His family *moved* to a safer, and more expensive, neighborhood in Sunnyvale—despite the fact that they were working extra jobs trying just to stay solvent, despite the fact that it meant an even longer commute for his father and pulled his sister out of elementary school.

This was power. And Steven Jobs learned its lesson.

2.3 SUBURBIA'S CHILD

Sunnyvale, though it abutted Mountain View, was a very different town. Younger than its neighbor, it was part of the giant landholdings of Martin Murphy, Jr., one of the first American pioneers of California.

Sunnyvale had largely grown up north (on the Bay side) of El Camino Real, and many of these older neighborhoods of bungalows and tiny homes were as rough and troubled as the one in Mountain View. Until after World War II, the land south of El Camino consisted of several square miles of orchards and farmland. It was this land that was flattened, asphalted and covered with tract homes, mostly Eichlers, to house the workers of Silicon Valley.

This section of Sunnyvale was one of the first neighborhoods to become part of the new Silicon Valley. The streets were wide, the shopping centers and light poles and sidewalks brand-new, and, because all of the newly planted trees were still saplings, everything was brilliantly lit in a sharp intense light. The city government was progressive, the public safety officers switched back and forth between being cops and firemen and crime was almost nonexistent. Even thirty years later, Sunnyvale would be named the safest city of more than 100,000 citizens in the entire United States.

This was Stephen Wozniak's world. Born in 1952, he had grown up in the stablest of families in the safest of neighborhoods. That very security, while it might temper his ambition, even when the opportunity was put in his hands, would also make him one of the few entrepreneurs in high-tech history to emerge contented from great success.

If Steven Jobs was an odd child who imposed his vision of normalcy upon the world through sheer force of will, Stephen Wozniak was the opposite: a normal kid turned odd by the power of obsession.

It didn't begin that way. Contrary to his later reputation as a nerd, Wozniak was a typical, even athletic, boy. His father had played football while earning an electrical engineering degree at Caltech; and then had spent a year as an entrepreneur, working with a partner in a failed venture to design and sell an automatic stacking machine. After that, now married and with a son, Jerry Wozniak sought out more stable corporate work. Drawn to the aerospace boom, he first found work in San Diego designing weapons, then with Lear in Santa Monica perfecting autopilots. Finally, following the path of thousands of other young engineers, he went to work at Lockheed. The family moved to an Eichler on the Sunnyvale-Cupertino border in a neighborhood that had once been the farm of an entrepreneur of a previous generation, William Wright, Jr., who had pioneered the artesian wells and orchards that transformed Santa Clara Valley from cattle ranches into a sea of fruit trees.

Even as he played Little League baseball and golf on the former orchards with his dad, the zeitgeist was already stalking Stephen Wozniak. History, in the form of computers and Steven Jobs, was about to catch him by the tail.

There is an intersection in Sunnyvale that a cynical person might say embodies everything wrong with life in postwar suburban America. The intersection, of Fremont and Bernardo avenues, is flanked on one side by freeway on- and off-ramps and an overpass which covers a once beautiful stretch of Stevens Creek. The other two corners of the intersection are blank walls hiding two housing developments. Fremont Avenue at this intersection is four lanes wide, with a divider filled with stones. In summer this intersection of cement and asphalt bakes under an unrelenting sun. Except for the crush of cars waiting for lights or racing along the ramps, this intersection is almost completely devoid of life.

And yet, on a given evening in the late 1960s, two men and a boy would have passed one another at this intersection. One was Robert Noyce, racing home from his new company, Intel Corp., to his home in Los Altos. The other man was one of Noyce's employees, Ted Hoff, who happened to live at the intersection in a house directly behind one of those walls. The boy was a teenaged Stephen Wozniak, returning home on his bike from swim practice, his left arm scraped and sore from always having to swim the butterfly stroke in the outside lane.

Thus, the inventors of three of the most important technology products of the century, the integrated circuit, the microprocessor and the personal computer—each made possible by the one that came before—regularly converged on this anonymous and bleak intersection in a seemingly unremarkable suburban city on the edge of a continent.

2.4 Obsession

If the electronics revolution was in the air in Steven Jobs's Mountain View neighborhood, it was the very soil of Stephen Wozniak's corner of Sunnyvale. Essentially everybody in northwestern Sunnyvale and Cupertino worked in the high-tech industry or in a profession that supported it. Jerry Wozniak was a prime example: each morning he drove off to Lockheed to work on a top secret defense project. The other fathers on the street were also engineers, some at Lockheed or NASA. But as the years passed more and more worked for the new local electronics companies that had sprung up after the disintegration of Fairchild.

In this world, the neighborhood children, if they showed any aptitude, soon found themselves immersed in the world of electronics. There were odd jobs they could do for neighborhood men on weekends, such as soldering or helping to test new semiconductor devices bought at local specialty shops. A few of the more ambitious and talented boys (and it was always boys) built simple devices of their own.

And no neighborhood kid showed more aptitude than Stephen Wozniak. By the time he was ten, the neighborhood men recognized that little Stephen was a natural, even a savant, at electronics. In fifth grade, as part of this informal apprenticeship, he was given a voltmeter kit and built it beautifully. A year later, thanks to long hours spent hanging around a neighbor, Stephen built his own 100-watt ham radio station and qualified for an operator's license. He also interconnected his home with those of nearby friends in a crude communications network.

By the time Stephen entered Cupertino Junior High he was so lost in the grip of an obsession with electronics that it resembled a kind of autism. "I was all alone," he would later say. His mother, Margaret Wozniak, a strong-willed, outspoken woman who in later years would call and berate reporters if they wrote anything less than positive about "my Stephen," would remember going into his bedroom and finding the boy so intent on a new project or trade magazine article that she would have to rap him on top of the head to get his attention.

If such behavior wasn't healthy, it sure beat stealing cigarette lighters at Payless or smoking reefers or hiding under the headphones listening to the Rolling Stones or any of the other forms of teen rebellion of the day. "I was lucky," he would later tell *Wired* magazine. "Keys to happiness came to me that would keep me happy for the whole of my life. It was just accidental. I don't know how many people get it. It's like a religion or something that just popped into my head, walking home from school."

Stephen loved what he was doing. Working in the cramped kitchen, making a disaster of the standard Eichler Formica breakfast table, Stephen built an electronic tic-tac-toe game like the one he'd seen in one of his endless electronics magazines. Next he built a prototype robot.

Then came a breakthrough. Stephen had begun a new project: a basic two-function calculator circuit that had become the hot new build-at-home fad among electronics hobbyists. The actual circuit was called an adder-subtractor, which, though Wozniak didn't know it yet, was a board-level version of the same kind of transistor "gate" circuitry on the surface of the new semiconductor logic chips.

With the kind of maniacal focus that now characterized his daily encounter with the world of electronics, Stephen studied the diagram in the magazine over and over . . . until he understood not only how the circuit worked but its underlying *metaphysics*. And with that understanding came the flash of an epiphany.

Now Stephen understood. Electronics could be more than just the manipulation of electricity or radio waves to achieve some physical result. It could create the world itself; becoming thought and memory. It could inhabit a universe of its own devising. And if you knew these basic components, like the adder-subtractor, you could treat them the way a conductor would a string section, calling up this instrument or that or all together. You could create a symphony of effects, a harmony—a music of digital life.

Stephen was so excited that he decided to vault the one-bit adder-subtractor described in the diagram and build a ten-bit parallel (that is, it would carry) adder-subtractor. He built it out of spare parts and with a soldering gun. There were two rows of switches on the bottom, one for addition, the other for subtraction, and a row of lights at the top from which you could read the results of the computation.

Not surprisingly, the adder-subtractor won the Cupertino school district science fair. Thirteen-year-old Stephen Wozniak, on his own, from his own design, had built a computer as powerful as any in the nonmilitary world just twenty-five years before. That alone was incredible, but more important for the future, his design exhibited uncanny elegance and conservation of parts and board space. Young Steve announced to his father that he wanted a Data General Nova, a hot new minicomputer that featured 4K of onboard memory. Jerry Wozniak informed his crestfallen son that such a machine "cost as much as a house." "Well, I'll live in an apartment," Steve replied.

Woz's childhood enchantment wasn't unique. When his protocomputer was entered in the Bay Area Science Fair that year, it earned only third place. This was an era when first place went to teenagers who built homemade Van de Graaff atomic particle accelerators. Even in his neighborhood, Wozniak was hardly alone. Walking the halls of Cupertino Junior High in that era one would have seen perhaps a half dozen kids just like him. Some were ham radio fanatics. Others built nasty electric shockers that could send arcs of blue light from every door of a bank of student lockers.

The luckiest kids were the ones whose fathers had jobs that allowed them to bring home printer-terminals. These heavy, typewriter-sized machines could, with the help of an acoustic coupler into which the family telephone receiver was jammed, talk to a distant mainframe computer. This was heaven itself, especially when you could "talk" to one of those programs that, in rehearsal for some future Turing test, would converse with you by riffing off your own statements. If your dad worked for NASA-Ames you could even sit in the lobby of one of the buildings there and talk to a computer this way for hours—for free! It was amazing. You could feel the power of digital reality, a new life form, through your fingertips.

Each year it seemed there were more and more of these boys who had been inhabited by electronic dreams. Anywhere else—say, up the road in Steven Jobs's neighborhood—they might have been tortured by fellow students for their strangeness. Even at Sunnyvale High School, across town, this was still true. But not in Cupertino, and not at Homestead High. Homestead, upper-middle-class, almost exclusively white and Asian, was instead a kind of sanctuary for the brilliantly dysfunctional. Not only was it among the best schools in the South Bay, it also had the resources to respond to this influx of odd newcomers.

In particular, there was a class at Homestead in electronics taught by John McCollum. It would prove as important to the computer age as Fred Terman's electronics class at Stanford had been for Bill Hewlett and David Packard three decades before. There, at last, Stephen Wozniak's private love and public education could become one.

2.5 HOMESTEADING

From the moment he arrived in McCollum's class, in which he quickly became the shining star, Wozniak's life seemed to take a sidetrack from the rest of mankind. In an obvious way, he seemed to stop developing emotionally like his peers, but instead drifted on in pursuit of his Cyber Circe. The rest of his studies suffered, as did his social life. His classmates would see him all day, in homeroom and other classes, sketching out new circuit designs, absent-mindedly drifting off to conduct rondos and sonatas with the brass, woodwinds and strings of logic chips, memory devices and linear circuits. By the time he finished high school, Woz had designed fifty computers on paper.

Stephen Wozniak, the boy who played golf and swam competitively and watched television, the typical suburban boy, had now become the Woz. The great achievements were still years ahead; and for now the new persona, unadorned by fame, was not a pretty sight.

One characteristic of the new Woz was a singular lack of understanding of human behavior and the boundaries of social etiquette. And nowhere was this more evident than in his practical jokes—a lifelong predilection that took on twisted new forms in the hands of the Woz.

The most celebrated example of this was the bomb scare. Using some old-fashioned, stick-shaped dry cell batteries, some wire and an oscillator chip to produce a reliably loud clicking sound, Woz constructed a pretty good simulacrum of a dynamite device. He put it in a friend's locker and gleefully awaited the result.

He got more than he bargained for: the bomb squad. Evacuated buildings. Hysteria. And the crowning touch: William Byrd, the school principal, rushing up, grabbing the "bomb" and sprinting with it—sweat flying, tie flapping, leather shoes clicking on the cement hallway—out to the football field. There, expecting death at any second, he yanked out the wires.

By most measures, Byrd was a hero. Except one: Stephen Wozniak had made a complete fool of him. Woz somehow never anticipated any of this. He trotted off to the principal's office later that day expecting to receive a math award—and instead was arrested and thrown into juvenile hall overnight. But what is perhaps most telling about this episode is that Margaret Wozniak bailed out her son the next day, all the while screaming at the cops and anyone else in earshot that her son was the suburban equivalent of a political prisoner, that she was surprised he hadn't had a number tattooed on his chest and thrown into San Jose's equivalent of Bergen-Belsen. Stephen's sister Leslie got into the act too, writing an exposé on the affair of the faux bomb in the school newspaper she helped edit.

Despite the troubles at school, which included not just the bomb prank but falling grades in other courses as electronics took over more and more of his life, Woz was also becoming one of the more celebrated students at Homestead. Single-mindedness is not a common trait in high schoolers, and single-mindedness combined with genius appears rarely indeed. Stephen Wozniak was that student. Often those students are hated by their classmates, but the Woz was too friendly (if distracted) to have enemies.

Instead, his classmates mostly just stood back in amazement as the Woz devoured every bit of knowledge in McCollum's class and then begged for more. One of the glories of Silicon Valley, then and now, was the proximity of some of the best minds and technology in the world. McCollum wisely found a school credit internship for the boy at GTE Sylvania, a microwave telephony research facility in Mountain View. Joining Woz there was his closest friend, Allen Baum, the only other kid at school who could remotely keep up with him in electronics.

The two boys were lucky to have landed at Sylvania. In Silicon Valley at this time there were perhaps a dozen mainframe computers. Some, like those at NASA-Ames and Lockheed, were largely inaccessible. Others, like those at Hewlett-Packard, were simply too busy doing payroll and engineering simulations. But Sylvania was a looser place, an R&D lab whose fiberglass bubble dome rose over the surrounding orchards as a South Bay icon.

The mainframe used by Sylvania was nothing special, an IBM 1130 that in the words of one author "was about the size of a refrigerator, shook the floor when it operated, and was so loud that shouting replaced normal conversation." It required punched computer cards for input and had about the same computing power as a modern fifty-dollar handheld video game. But Stephen Wozniak would have sawed off his arm to own it.

High school technical internships in the late 1960s and early 1970s are a rarely noticed factor in the creation of the modern Silicon Valley. Yet these programs, at Ames, Lockheed, Sylvania, the Stanford Linear Accelerator and elsewhere, were of incalculable value to the founders of personal computing; and it is no coincidence that the early organizations in this field had their beginnings at these sites.

Certainly the internship at Sylvania, with the mainframe at hand and friendly scientists more than happy to help a young kindred soul, had a profound effect upon the Woz. He arrived an electrical technician of native genius and left a computer scientist of nearly infinite potential.

Until now, Woz had dealt with electronics as a hardware exercise. You had a problem to be solved and you did so using some configuration of the hardware tools of electronics: the old linear devices like capacitors, oscillators, resistors; discrete devices of more recent vintage like diodes; and the new digital integrated circuits, including ROMs, RAMs and TTL logic. The obvious difficulty in this method—the only method the engineering world had known until recently—was that the more complex the problem, the more complicated the hardware setup needed to address it. In this world, the most gifted engineers were those who could puzzle out novel ways to reduce the number of components by, say, 10 percent. And it was in this particular type of simplification that Woz had shown almost supernatural talent.

The encounter with the Sylvania computer changed Wozniak's life because, thanks to helpful explanations from the scientists and time spent playing with the machine itself, Woz saw, literally in a flash of lights, another, *better* way.

What the scientists showed him was how the compiler of the 1130 worked. Thirty years later, the millions who use a personal computer, whether they know it or not, have a good idea of how a compiler works. When you type in a command, or drag a window across the screen with a mouse, you know that the computer is actually taking this information, converting it in software to a series of instructions in the ones and zeros of binary code, then performing the requisite operations in hardware, then translating the results through software—moving the window, erasing a word, drawing a shape—back onto the screen.

We understand this because Woz taught us. But the teacher himself had to be taught; and the education of Stephen Wozniak took place during those days at Sylvania. The lesson wasn't self-evident. As with most electrical engineers of the era, Woz's notion of data processing was computation, and his image of a computer was a calculator. Thus, the music of electronics he heard in his head, complicated as it was, remained merely a melody, a string of distinct events leading toward a conclusion.

What transformed Wozniak at Sylvania was the realization that there was another world in electronics, *software,* that would make the music infinitely richer and more ambitious through counterpoint, minor chords and repetitive refrains. He learned one of the early computer languages, FORTRAN, and began programming the 1130 to do things he had never before imagined possible. From now on, he would create symphonies.

Again, Woz wasn't the only teenager in Silicon Valley learning about computers. All those boys tapping into distant mainframes through the acoustic modem and terminal Dad brought home from work every Friday night were doing the same thing. Out at NASA-Ames, Foothill Community College taught a course in programming on Saturday mornings that was jammed with students ranging from high schoolers to pensioners. But what made Woz almost unique among the young budding programmers was his already vast experience in circuit design. And even as he was finishing his Sylvania internship, Ted Hoff, that neighbor he passed in the intersection, was working a few miles away at the Intel Corp. plant in Cupertino to create the microprocessor, the electronic device that would bring Woz's two great skills together.

2.6 LIAISON

Woz was a junior at Homestead High when Steven Jobs arrived for his eighth-grade year at Cupertino Junior High four blocks away. There, Jobs soon found a friend and kindred spirit in Bill Fernandez. Fernandez would say, "For some reason the kids in eighth grade didn't like [Jobs] because they thought he was odd." Fernandez didn't follow suit, largely because he and Jobs shared a common passion for electronics.

The two boys would hang out together in Steven's garage, listen to rock and roll, build simple electronics devices and put on cool light shows by ricocheting laser beams off bottles and cans. This garage would later become an object of myth, the spiritual descendant of that most sacred of Silicon Valley sites: the Packard garage in Palo Alto—as if a garage beginning conferred a certain mystical advantage to high-tech companies. In fact, given the mild winters of the Bay Area, the thin sound insulation of most houses and the high flammability of Eichlers in particular, garages were typically the most comfortable, safest and most soundproof places for teenage experimenters to build stuff and crank the music up loud.

Jobs and Fernandez never built anything of importance in that garage—that would come later. Neither, in fact, had much technical acumen. Jobs in particular was just too mercurial to develop any real skill—though he would sometimes show flashes of brilliance.

Fernandez, for all of his shyness, nevertheless was well connected to the neighborhood nerd network. Woz, of course, was already a local legend, and Fernandez knew him slightly. It was Fernandez, halfway in age between Woz and Jobs, who would first bring the two future partners together—creating a friendship that would soon leave him behind.

Steve Jobs's sojourn at Homestead was marked by what can only be called a singular combination of conventional failures and unforgettable victories. Like Woz two years earlier, he took John McCollum's electronics class. But whereas Wozniak had become a class legend, Jobs alienated everyone, then dropped out of the class. Despite this, he still managed to perform one indelible act: unable to get a part he needed at school to finish one of his projects, Jobs simply placed a collect call to the PR department of computer giant Burroughs in Detroit and asked for it. When told by McCollum that a collect call wasn't proper, Jobs reportedly replied, "I don't have the money for the phone call. They've got plenty of money."

Jobs's act of rebellion was well timed. This was the first moment in history that a kid could learn about computers without a classroom or a rich dad. The minicomputer revolution was now in full bloom throughout Silicon Valley. Mainframes were becoming more numerous too, and using them becoming less expensive. It was possible now for a kid to get cheap computer time at numerous locations all over the Valley, including Homestead High's electronics club. Despite having dropped McCollum's class, Jobs maintained a steady attendance at the club. Ames Research Center was doing more educational work all the time; not the least of which was hosting a new Boy Scout Explorer Post dedicated to high tech. The Post would be one of the farm teams of what would be called the Homebrew Computer Club.

Hewlett-Packard too was helping teach young people about electronics.

Stanford professor Fred Terman had trained Bill Hewlett and Dave Packard; now they returned the favor by enabling their engineers to take Stanford graduate courses in HP facilities. Some of these courses and lectures were open to the public, and they regularly drew a young and increasingly scruffy (Fremont Union High School District had by now abandoned its dress code) Steve Jobs. Jobs, as was characteristic of him, was fearless about going up to the speakers afterward and peppering them with questions.

But the most significant event that occurred at this time happened in Santa Clara in a laboratory to which only a handful of people had access. In 1968, Fairchild Semiconductor of Mountain View, the preeminent computer chip company in the world, exploded. A half dozen key employees, all of them in their late twenties and early thirties, walked out, furious at the company's unwillingness to award them stock options and let them get rich off their success. This core group teamed up with the very first high-tech venture capitalists and founded a group of new companies. Their success in turn convinced other Fairchildren to walk out, some to try their own hand at entrepreneurship.

By the mid-1970s the Valley had been seeded with more than fifty new semiconductor companies. Their success turned Santa Clara Valley into Silicon Valley. Then these new firms in turn blew up and scattered even more new companies across the landscape, making Silicon Valley the world's leading technology center.

A few of these firms became very successful and survive to this day, notably Advanced Micro Devices, National Semiconductor (which had the revenge of buying and bulldozing the Fairchild building into dust) and, greatest of all, Intel Corp. Intel was founded by the general manager and the chief technologist of Intel, Robert Noyce and Gordon Moore, respectively, and the two had quickly hired a third, Andrew Grove, Fairchild's top applications scientist.

Intel took off quickly, moving fast to dominate the memory chip market with a new type of semiconductor design called MOS (metal on silicon). In 1970, about the time Stephen Wozniak was graduating from high school, Intel was approached by a Japanese calculator company—calculators being the hottest and most fiercely contested consumer electronics market of the era—named Busicom to develop a new chip set to run its calculators.

Intel was still young enough, and cash poor enough, that it took on the contract, even though it didn't fit with the company's business. The project took so long, more than a year, that Busicom eventually gave up and sold the rights to Intel. And when the finished chip set, called the 4004, finally appeared in 1971, even Intel wasn't sure it wanted to deal with a whole new technology and brand-new market. Eventually, thanks to some strong lobbying by, among others, outside PR consultant Regis McKenna, Noyce, Moore and Grove decided to give the 4004 (which had begun to be called a "microprocessor") a few months' tryout. The rest was history.

But as important as the microprocessor was as a digital electronics device, perhaps even more important was the way it behaved economically. Just about the time his company was announcing the 4004, Gordon Moore took out a sheet of graph paper and plotted out the performance of each of Intel's random-access memory chips to date. To his amazement, the plot points made a straight line, doubling in complexity (speed, performance, etc.) every two years. Moore realized that the line might continue its upward path for decades to come. He was looking at the future of electronics.

His discovery, called Moore's Law ever since, is the defining rule of the chip age, and the metronome of modern life. In accord with that law, the Intel Pentium chip of 1996 was 10,000 times as powerful as the 4004 from twenty-five years before—yet carried the same price.

This performance-to-price curve, unprecedented in the history of commerce, worked the other way as well—and that would prove to be of crucial importance to Steven Jobs and Stephen Wozniak. Moore's Law meant that the same chips of a given performance would also *halve* in price every two years. So the most powerful microprocessor or memory chip in the world in one era would be reduced in price from a few hundred dollars to a few hundred cents in just a few years. And that would make it available to even the poorest Sunnyvale schoolboy.

At this time, the high-end effect of Moore's Law was being felt in the new computer-based "smart" instruments (like programmable mass spectrometers) and the new minicomputers from HP, DEC and Digital Equipment that the two Steves were now encountering in their sojourns around Silicon Valley.

By comparison, the low-end impact of Moore's Law was only now beginning to show sparks. The first consumer product made possible by Moore's Law was the pocket four-function calculator, first introduced by Canon in 1970, but made into a market phenomenon by Texas Instruments two years later. Soon more than forty companies would be vying for that market. Three years after that, TI, Japanese companies Casio and Seiko, and even Intel, kicked off another fad with the introduction of the first digital watches. Millions were sold in a matter of months.

Both of these consumer booms proved fleeting. By the end of the decade, bloody shakeouts had taken place in both industries, prices had been slashed and just a few survivors remained. It was the first glimpse of a pattern of boom and bust that would characterize all hot new consumer electronics businesses thereafter.

But there was a third consumer electronics explosion during this period that would prove far more enduring. About the time Steven Jobs was graduating from Homestead High, a twenty-six-year-old engineer from Ampex was working late nights in his home in Santa Clara in a shop made from the borrowed bedroom of one of his daughters. With $500 in capital, this engineer, Nolan Bushnell, set out to re-create a game he had played on a mainframe computer while a student at the University of Utah.

Bushnell's great breakthrough, the lesson he taught Silicon Valley and the rest of electronics, was that Moore's Law was a design tool. Since you knew where price and performance were going, you could design a product early and then wait, ready to jump, for the curves to cross and the market opportunity to open up. And that's exactly what he did—though not without a few sleepless nights.

The result was Pong. In 1972, Bushnell set up the first of his arcade-type video games in Andy Capp's, a bar operating along the main drag of El Camino Real in one of Sunnyvale's oldest buildings. He prayed as only a good lapsed Mormon can. God apparently listened, but not without playing a practical joke. The next day, the bar's owner called and, to Bushnell's dismay, told him that the damn game had already busted. Bushnell sent his partner, Al Alcorn, down to the joint, prepared to pack it in. He was out of money and out of hope.

But once Alcorn got there, he almost laughed out loud when he saw the cause of the problem: the cardboard box he'd used to collect the players' money was so jammed with quarters that it had backed up into the coin slot. From that moment, Nolan Bushnell realized he was going to become very, very rich.

2.7 CREAM SODA

The years after Wozniak's graduation from high school have always been a difficult time for computer industry fanatics and Apple Computer public relations people to deal with. In the early 1980s, when the excesses of the 1970s were still freshly shared and the myths not yet exposed, it was possible to think of the late-adolescent Woz and Jobs as heroic—or, better yet, antiheroic—mavericks.

Certainly an increasingly mature Apple liked to use that angle, as it justified the various felonies committed by its founders. In fact, the pairing of an increasingly socially retarded genius with a frighteningly precocious narcissist was a dangerous combination. Four years apart in age, the two were, for the next few years, almost equals in emotional development.

Woz, now bearded and long-haired, grew chunkier and more stooped. He was becoming the very embodiment of what happens to a human being who spends his life hunched over a printed circuit board and survives on junk food. Jobs, by comparison, though also long-haired and with the wisps of a beard, was whippet-thin, with all the intensity and mystery of a medieval fanatic.

Wozniak had finished Homestead High in glory. The capstone was scoring a perfect 800 on the math portion of the SAT, the first official recognition of his brilliance. But, as is often the case, the beginning of college also signaled the beginning of payback time for all of the other parts of life Woz had neglected in high school. His father sensed what was coming, and asked his son to stay closer to home, but Woz wanted to go away to school.

Having failed in his dream of going to Caltech, Woz accepted the fallback of the University of Colorado in Boulder. But within months of enrolling there, he dropped out just before flunking out, his only noteworthy accomplishment a series of characteristically juvenile practical jokes: jamming closed-circuit classroom televisions during lectures, blacking out a dorm TV just before the finish of the Kentucky Derby, programming a school computer to print out thousands of lines of FUCK NIXON. Unhitched from a larger purpose, Wozniak became a tiresome jerk.

Finally he returned home, to the relief of his parents, and enrolled at De Anza Community College in Cupertino, a half mile from his old high school. Safe again, Woz buried himself in electronics, haunting local electronics stores and chip "schlockers" who sold obsolete or slightly flawed circuits. With a structure again surrounding his life, Woz also managed to complete the school year with (barely) passing grades.

That summer was one of the best of Wozniak's youth. Baum was back from his first year at MIT and between them the two talked endlessly about electronics. They even found a job together as programmers at a start-up called Tenet, one of the scores of short-lived Valley computer companies of the era. When Baum went back to school, Woz stayed at Tenet, content that he had at last found a place to put all of his private skills to work.

And by this point those skills were formidable. Ever since GTE Sylvania, Woz's heart had been stolen by computers. At night, while still in high school, he would read trade magazines like *Datamation* and *Electronics*, or scrutinize the schematics in manuals like DEC's *Small Computer Handbook,* and then fall asleep dreaming of building his own minicomputer.

But the dream proved difficult to realize. During high school, using the schematics of a minicomputer designed by Varian Corp. up the road in Palo Alto, Woz tried to build one of his own using his growing hoard of chips. He couldn't do it. He understood computer architecture now, but not how to create that architecture using integrated circuits. And though he'd glimpsed the power of software, he still couldn't speak its language.

Then came graduation and the disastrous trip to Colorado. But if Woz's brief sojourn in Boulder had been an academic failure, it was not a technological one. Instead of cutting class to ski like the rest of his classmates, Woz hung around the computer labs, perfecting his fluency in computer languages, especially FORTRAN, and picking up design clues.

Now back at California, working at Tenet, Woz had access to computers every day. Moreover, Allen Baum was sending him photocopies of anything interesting in his classes at MIT. And, most important, there was the charged environment of Silicon Valley itself. Here he could attend trade shows and conferences and science fairs. It was at one such fair that Woz had his next breakthrough. He saw on display a working electromechanical calculator that could perform multiple operations in sequence, emitting intermediate results as it did.

For the era, the calculator was truly kid stuff. But in Woz it awakened a new understanding of how a low-cost computer, built with a microprocessor and other integrated circuits, could perform a string of functions on command. Just to check, Woz converted the design of the device he saw into an electronic schematic.

There it was. The missing philosophical gap in his understanding. He tested his new wisdom against the design of the Data General Nova minicomputer, one of the most powerful machines of the era. He saw it now: a direct cognitive link between that first simple adder-subtractor he'd built six years before and this cutting-edge computer used to design satellite trajectories and track subatomic particles.

It was all of a piece now. The symphony in his head now echoed across the vault of heaven. Woz knew he could do it. He would build a computer of his own. He began to lay out the schematics for one imaginary computer after another, each of them better, more elegant and more efficient than the one that came before. He dreamed of building each one, but the chips he needed were still too expensive to buy on his Tenet salary.

Then, drowned by the recession of 1972, Tenet went belly-up. At the time it seemed the worst thing that could have happened to Stephen Wozniak. After all, there went his daily access to computers. And a salary. But had Tenet survived, Woz might well have stayed on, becoming a lifer, just like his dad at Lockheed. Instead, he was forced out on his own. Now he had not only time to build his computer but the financial incentive to come up with a design that used as few chips as possible.

Toward that end, Jerry Wozniak made his own commitment to his son's obsession—a tacit, and no doubt painful, admission that this was Stephen's destiny in life—by connecting the boy with an old friend who designed integrated circuitry for Fairchild. From this man Stephen learned just which portions of his circuit board design could now be reproduced with silicon at a much lower cost.

With Baum a continent away, Woz settled for another neighborhood kid as a partner: Bill Fernandez, Steven Jobs's friend. It was Fernandez's unlucky fate to be the bridesmaid to history. For now, though, he was just happy to work with a neighborhood legend—so happy in fact that he offered his own family's garage for the work area. Then the two set out in search of parts.

The project took several months. In every spare moment the pair would head for the Fernandez garage, crank up the rock and roll, down endless cans of Shasta cream soda that Mrs. Fernandez bought by the case and worked on the computer. Woz did almost all of the work, laying out the printed circuit board, soldering the chips and testing the circuits. Fernandez's official duty was to construct the timing circuits for the computer's flashing output lights. But his real job was to be a sounding board and companion to the older genius hunched over the table next to him. And his greatest talent was neatness, something Wozniak at this embryonic stage needed more than anything else.

In 1973 the machine, which the two had dubbed the Cream Soda Computer in honor of their life-sustaining refreshment, was nearly completed. Fernandez, knowing he was part of a great event, was ecstatic. So ecstatic that he brought his young friend Steve Jobs over to the garage to see the project.

There is no record of that first meeting in the Fernandez garage. Even the two principals don't recall what they were wearing (though probably T-shirts and jeans) or what they said. But before that chance encounter was over an hour later, Woz and Jobs had already embarked on a fateful partnership.

What was the chemistry? For his part, Jobs would say years later, "He was the only person I met who knew more about electronics than me." This, of course, was utter bullshit, said at a time when Jobs was feeling under assault and had the reality distorter at full throttle. The fact was that there were probably a half dozen men and boys on Steve Jobs's *block* who knew more about electronics than he did.

No, the connection was far more complex than that. The key lay in an odd feature of the relationship that few observers have ever remarked upon: Stephen Wozniak was *four* years older than Steve Jobs; Jobs was just a junior at Homestead while Woz was two years beyond graduation. This was unusual pairing to say the least.

What it does suggest, from Wozniak's side, was how far emotionally he had already fallen behind his contemporaries. Now, in this sixteen-year-old he finally found a peer who could also, if not as deeply, hear the music that played in Woz's own head twenty-four hours a day.

Jobs's perspective was more subtle and, as usual, manipulative. Once again, he had found that helpful engineer down the street—only this time it was even better, because now he could dominate his emotionally underdeveloped partner, pulling him firmly into the Steven Jobs universe.

Mrs. Wozniak called the community newspaper, the *Sunnyvale Scribe/Cupertino Courier*, and convinced it to send out a reporter and a photographer. Woz and Fernandez prepared a demonstration of their invention. But as the reporter scratched out notes and the photographer focused his lens, the Cream Soda Computer, in a shower of sparks and a puff of smoke, blew up.

So did the story. Woz had missed his chance. The next time a Woz computer would meet the press, its inventor would have to more than share the credit.

2.8 COUNTERCULTURAL SCHLOCK

The sixteen-year-old Steven Jobs that Stephen Wozniak met that day in the Fernandez garage had a remarkable combination of childlike selfishness and grown-up bravado. Jobs would later say that had he not become a business tycoon he probably would have been a criminal—an opinion that would not be disputed by many of his old classmates.

Steven Jobs was simply not like anyone else you knew in high school in the early 1970s. There were druggies, there were gifted manipulators of others and there were unbelievably gutsy con men. But no one had all three traits in one person—except Steven Jobs.

The call Jobs made to Burroughs for parts was just the beginning. Not long thereafter, he called Bill Hewlett to hustle parts. Hewlett, a great engineer and an even greater entrepreneur, was at this point one of the most powerful businessmen in America and on the way to becoming a multibillionaire. Forty thousand people reported to him from HP divisions and sales offices in nearly a hundred countries.

It speaks volumes that, even as a teenager, Steven Jobs could detect a soft touch in Hewlett and then contact him directly (and even more volumes that Hewlett would answer the call). Once he had Hewlett on the line, Jobs made his pitch. Remarkably, though also characteristically, Hewlett agreed. The man who would one day give some $50 million to build an engineering building at Stanford in the name of his old professor, was never one to turn down a student. But once Steve Jobs scored, he wasn't about to stop there. He then pitched Hewlett for a summer job at HP. He got that too, ending up on an assembly line at HP's plant in Cupertino building computers. The experience was so compelling that Steven even tried to design a computer of his own—a notion he quickly abandoned as too difficult.

There were other after-school jobs, notably working at an electronics store in Sunnyvale. This job taught Steven the real value of electronic components: how little squares of silicon sand, once etched with a maplike grid of circuitry, could leap in value from a few cents of materials to a hundred dollars or more in market value. He also learned the rhythms of the chip industry—how the periodic cycles of boom and bust created distortions between chip demand and supply that sent prices skyrocketing; how companies would pay outrageous sums for that one obsolete chip that kept their expensive machinery running; and, most of all, how the inefficient distribution process of the semiconductor industry created a lucrative market for middlemen who could find the right chips and bring them together with the right customer.

Long before he graduated from high school, Jobs had already become a journeyman "schlocker," one of the small army of men—some of them legitimate, some criminal, nearly all slightly shady—who brokered rare old chips and popular (and sometimes hot) new ones. Before long, Jobs became something of a phenomenon within this small community as the kid who could wander through the warrens of the big Haltek chip warehouse and score that one critical part, or wander among the broken toasters and bicycle frames of the San Jose Flea Market and find that apparently worthless circuit board that yielded a rare, and profitable, chip when sold to an electronics shop. It was a talent Jobs had developed touring the junkyards with his father, and it put him in good stead with Stephen Wozniak. At this point in his work, with his computer burning itself up, Woz needed Jobs's procuring skills even more than he needed Fernandez's neatness—or even his garage.

Besides, Jobs had a garage too. And soon Wozniak's equipment moved three blocks across the city limits into Los Altos and the Jobs garage. Now Jobs could not only help Woz but keep an eye on him. Woz, happy to have a place to work and a source of parts, couldn't have been happier.

Jobs also appealed to Woz's puerile sense of humor. Woz was always willing to go along on any adventure or practical joke his young friend could devise. And Woz would sometimes enlist Allen Baum, when he was home from school, into the scheme as well. Once, the three persuaded Baum's mother to paint a giant hand giving the finger—they told her it was a Brazilian good-luck symbol—on a sheet tie-dyed in the Homestead colors, which they then hung at the school. Jobs, the only student of the three, was eventually caught and hauled before the principal. Steven's father got him off the hook.

By this point, Woz had enrolled at Berkeley. He would stay less than a year before again dropping out. But his presence at the university gave Jobs an excuse to regularly drive up to the campus. Soon, he was also visiting friends at Stanford as well. Needless to say, Berkeley and Stanford in 1972 were singular places, where predators and purists lived side by side in a kaleidoscope of sin, pharmaceuticals, study and sedition. Despite his now long hair, beard and tie-dyed clothes, the hermitlike Woz, with his 1980s view of technology and 1960s flower power beliefs about human nature, fit in poorly in 1970s Berkeley.

But for high schooler Steven Jobs it was paradise. He might be a pariah in Cupertino, but in Berkeley his behavior was barely eccentric. He could smoke dope and talk the usual epistemological blather all night long with confused undergraduates and sinister grad students. He even took to walking around smoking a pipe, a nice beatnik touch that connected him behaviorally with an even older group of outcasts. It was in this period that Jobs took on the manner, the vocabulary and the mores that would seem paradoxical in later years, when people would ask how someone his age, properly an early yuppie, could have so assimilated the hippie persona, an era he was too young to fully know.

Paul Jobs once found a bag of ground leaves in his son's car and asked what it was. "It's marijuana," Steve replied blithely. Needless to say, his father did nothing. The day when he might have drawn a line, or at least boxed his son's ears, was long past.

The Berkeley experiences proved good for young Steven back at high school as well. His new worldliness got him a girlfriend; pretty, if a bit of a druggie. She met Steven while they were working on a semisecret animated movie that classmates assumed was pornographic. Wozniak never quite understood what Jobs saw in her; but it may have been because he didn't recognize elements of himself. She was a lonely, vulnerable girl trying to make sense of her parents' impending divorce. And Steve Jobs was there to give her life direction.

As for the girl (she has preferred to remain anonymous), she would later say that Jobs "was kind of crazy. I think that's why I was attracted to him."

Jobs's later description of this relationship would sound like the screenplay for a bad psychedelic movie. They would cut class, drink wine and talk about higher things. They dropped acid together for the first time and Jobs found himself standing in one of the area's many piedmont meadows of dried straw grass, conducting the waving stalks as they exploded into a Bach fugue.

2.9 NOTES FROM THE UNDERGROUND

At the beginning of 1972, while Woz was distractedly making his way through Berkeley and Jobs was exploring the delectations of his new girlfriend, an engineer at National Semiconductor named John Draper took the little plastic whistle from a box of Cap'n Crunch cereal, glued closed the third sound hole, then held the device to a telephone mouthpiece.

The first sound he heard was an earsplitting, 2,600-cycle, high A note from the whistle. The second sound was a click on the other end of the phone. From that moment on, the telephone call was free.

Draper, soon to call himself Cap'n Crunch in honor of the source of his little discovery, had been following a hunch. He knew that when the phone company, AT&T, first developed the direct dial system after World War II it had chosen to use multifrequency tones to direct the call and turn tolls on and off. Furthermore, Draper knew that, to save money, Ma Bell had combined these tones and callers' voices on the same circuit. What this told Draper—and a number of other budding phone phreakers around the country—was that if he could duplicate the right tone, *he*, and not the phone company, would be in charge of the call.

It was illegal, of course. But it was also 1972, and Draper, who had done a hitch in the Army working sophisticated radar systems, didn't have much respect for large corporations or their shareholders. Besides, when he left the Army the phone company had offered him a job with a starting salary—$650 per month—that he saw as insultingly low.

The whistle was just the beginning. Soon Draper made himself a celebrity among the growing crowd of fellow phone phreakers by building a "blue box" tone generator to mimic the whole palette of telephone tones. With it he could break through busy signals and pick up engaged conversations (a hobby he dropped after hearing his girlfriend flirt with another man). He could make calls around the world for free. He once even called President Nixon's private White House line to complain (snicker, snicker) about a toilet paper shortage in Southern California.

In late 1971, *Esquire* magazine, as always anxious to stay atop any new fad, wrote an article about Cap'n Crunch and his fellow phreakers. The article had two immediate consequences. First, it alerted the phone company (and scores of prospective phreakers) to this new and felonious phenomenon. Second, it was read by Margaret Wozniak, who, apparently oblivious to the fact that this behavior was criminal, saw kindred spirits among the phreakers to her own little Stephen. She showed the magazine to Woz and his new friend Steve Jobs.

Scales fell from their eyes. For the two boys, phone phreaking combined everything they loved: technology, practical jokes, insider status among the illuminati and an outlaw relationship to the rest of society. They immediately established for themselves two goals: one, find Cap'n Crunch, and two, build their own telephone blue box.

Despite the obvious obstacles, the second proved easier than the first. The phone company had read the *Esquire* article too and systematically set out to retrieve every telephone operating manual in every library in America. Unfortunately, it missed one such manual at the Sunnyvale library. Woz and Jobs found it and soon knew every page by heart.

But the manual only took them part of the way. From it, they learned how the tones worked, but not what they were or how to create them. An initial attempt, which involved building an audio oscillator and capturing the tones it produced on a tape recorder, failed. No matter how carefully the two tuned the oscillator, the combination of variation in its tone and distortion in the tape made the resulting note unreadable by the phone system.

Frustrated by his failure, Woz characteristically regrouped and set about developing a radically new design—this one designed to generate its own digital audio tone. This was an extraordinarily ambitious project for a twenty-year-old working in his dorm room, but it is a measure of Wozniak's genius that he completed the blue box in a matter of weeks. It ran off a 9-volt dry cell battery, and had a little speaker, so that the user merely had to hold it up to a phone and type on the calculator keyboard. On the first attempt, Woz tried to call his grandmother in Los Angeles, but managed instead to reach a wrong number—toll-free—in the small Southern California town of Angelino. Still, it worked.

Finding Cap'n Crunch was more problematic. Draper, like the other phone phreakers, preferred to fly low and out of sight of the authorities. The two boys, anxious to meet their hero, tried to locate him through *Esquire* and through a local radio station on which the Cap'n had appeared, but to no avail. The only way to find Cap'n Crunch was to become like him. Sure enough, as word spread about the Wozniak blue box, John Draper suddenly became accessible.

They met at Woz's dorm room at Cal. Draper, with his wild hair and even wilder eyes, bad teeth and dirty clothes, looked more like a mad monk than a king of electronic crime. "He looked absolutely horrid," Woz would say. But Draper also knew his place. When Woz asked, "Are you Cap'n Crunch?" Draper replied royally, "I am he."

And he was. The Jesus of Phreakdom. In the next couple of hours, Draper opened up the world of phreaking to the pair. Just for fun, Draper made a few toll-free long-distance calls. Next he made a free international call. He called weather forecasts in distant cities. Dial-A-Joke. Each time, he showed his mastery of the technology and, in his mind, of the phone company. Finally, with a showman's touch, Draper stacked a series of calls from one relay to the next, connected them in a single interconnected chain around the country, and rang the telephone across the hall from Woz's room.

After that Cap'n Crunch and his newly recruited apostles retired to a pizza parlor, where Draper studied Woz's blue box and gave some advice for boosting its tone, handed out phone numbers of other phreakers as well as a list of useful codes to unlocking the wonders of Ma Bell, and then warned them to always use a pay phone so as not to be traced. Then he disappeared into the darkness and, it would seem, to the empyrean of telephony.

On the way back to Jobs's house in Los Altos, Steven's worn-out Fiat, as usual, broke down. Abandoning it, the two finally found a pay phone and, in an unusual bit of logic, decided to use their blue box to call Cap'n Crunch and ask for help. Instead, an operator came on the line, and the boys, already jumpy from Draper's warning about being traced, panicked and hung up. Jobs stuffed the blue box in his pocket.

They were just beginning to make a legal phone call when a police car suddenly roared up, and two officers jumped out. Jobs managed to hand the blue box to Wozniak just before the two were run up against a wall and frisked. With their long hair and grungy clothes, Woz and Jobs no doubt looked like a couple of drug dealers taking orders from customers.

Perhaps remarkably in Jobs's case, the cops found no drugs. But they did find the blue box on Woz. When asked what it was, Wozniak replied, "A music synthesizer."

The other cop took the box and studied it. He pointed at an orange button. "What's this?"

"That's for calibration," said Jobs. Woz explained that the box was for synthesizing music via a computer.

"Too bad a guy named Moog beat you to it," said the cop.

"He's the guy who sent us the schematics," replied Steven Jobs.

Convinced that the boys weren't carrying any contraband, the policeman offered to give the two a ride to the nearest gas station.

In retrospect, the parable of the Cops and the Blue Box, a touchstone of the Apple legend, contains many of the defining features of the Jobs-Wozniak story. There is the meeting with a mysterious wizard who gives them the key to a new technology; the funky, breakdown-riven car to provide an earthy touch; the thrill of illicit behavior at the risk of being caught by the authorities; and, most important, *épater les bourgeois*: the clever technical insiders pulling a fast one on the ignorant rubes. The last would become an enduring attitude right up to today's computer hackers.

But on closer look the legend gives a more insightful picture. First there is the telling (and characteristic) moment when Jobs unloads the guilty object on poor Woz. Then there is the clever lying to the cops: Why do it at all? If they had said it was an automatic telephone dialer, the police would still have shrugged. And finally, there is that little comment by the one patrolman about the Moog synthesizer. Apparently, the cops weren't quite the ignorant fools the phreakers wanted them to be—something they would prove the next spring.

There was one other event that occurred that evening. After finally reaching Los Altos in the early hours of the morning, Woz climbed into his own car and drove back to Berkeley. On the way, he fell asleep at the wheel and crashed into a road barrier. Fortunately, he wasn't hurt.

2.10 BLUE OAFS

Their dabble into the world of phone phreaking only made Jobs and Woz anxious for more. Having met the King Phreaker himself, the two began to model themselves after him. They affected code names—Woz was Berkeley Blue, Jobs was Oaf Tobark—and set about learning everything about their new hobby. They talked to other phreaks, read underground phreaker newsletters and experimented. Jobs used the blue box to set up a party at a London hotel; Wozniak showed off to Allen Baum by making a toll-free call to Baum's sister at an Israeli kibbutz.

But the most celebrated of these Adventures in Phreaking was Woz's call to the Pope. It was his first use of Cap'n Crunch's long-distance codes, and Wozniak went for the home run. Pretending to be Henry Kissinger, not only did he reach a papal secretary but that official actually offered to awaken the Pontiff. Terrified, Woz hung up.

Draper's recollection of the event is less factually accurate, but perhaps metaphorically truer: "Woz's first call was to the Pope. He wanted to make a confession."

In a pattern they would follow ever after, Wozniak soon returned to the challenge of improving his creation. Jobs, meanwhile, set out to find ways to sell Woz's creation. "He wanted to make money," Woz would say simply.

Jobs's strategy was a straightforward one: sell the service to students. For one thing, they didn't have enough money for all the calls they wanted to make; and second, they identified with the outlaw idea of blue-boxing. As he would show consistently throughout his career, Jobs was a brilliant marketing idea man—but he was not always a great implementer. With Woz's blue box he correctly identified the market, but had no idea how to reach it. As a result, he and Woz were reduced to knocking on dorm doors, hinting around to the resident what they had, and then inviting him to a demonstration. If this kind of shotgun marketing was hard enough with legal products, it was positively dangerous with felonious goods.

Nevertheless, the two were lucky enough not to get turned in to the feds, and in a few weeks they had enough of a customer base to abandon the high-risk approach and simply service the clients they already had—yet another useful lesson for the future. In short order, they were selling not only the $150 boxes, but a customized service of tape recordings of tones customers regularly used.

Meanwhile, Woz, when he wasn't building boxes, was perfecting their design—a lesson for him on the value of product upgrades. One of his most important innovations was an automatic dialer; thereby enhancing what would one day be called the user interface.

The two budding entrepreneurs also taped a handwritten guarantee on the bottom of each box. Customer service. Thus, Woz and Jobs, with almost no business experience, while breaking the law, managed to devise on their own most of the key operating units of the modern technology corporation.

There was only one problem with their business model: the more successful they became as a blue box manufacturer, the more likely they were to get arrested. Woz, as might be expected, was all but oblivious to the danger. He continued happily along, improving his product, adding upgrades to make it usable in almost any location, trying out new and more outrageous phreaks— such as tapping into an FBI call.

Jobs, on the other hand, was terrified. It was one thing to bluff some cops, another to run an ongoing criminal enterprise. He would always have a gift for sensing a shift in the culture, and he felt it now. The phreaker world, especially Cap'n Crunch itself, was getting too cocky and out of control. It had begun to read its own magazine clippings and convinced itself it was too clever and too cool to be ever taken down by the System. Though the blue box project had by now netted $6,000, and promised to make much more, Steven Jobs started backing away from it and from Stephen Wozniak.

He had good reason to be afraid. Woz's blue box was so good that everybody in the phreak underground knew about it, including the growing army of phone company undercover agents. Meanwhile, General Telephone, tracing Crunch's calls, had turned up, among others, Jobs's home number. The net was closing and Steven sensed it.

The end came, according to Jobs, when he was selling a Woz blue box to a prospective customer in a Sunnyvale pizza parlor parking lot and the other party pulled a gun and robbed him. One may choose whether or not to believe the account, but it was the story Jobs used to extricate himself from the business.

Woz soldiered on, eventually even hiring other people to sell the boxes, and jumping on planes himself to pitch his wares at other UC campuses. In his characteristically honest, touching and softheaded way, Woz continued to split his earnings with the partner who had abandoned him. Also characteristically, he often forgot to go to his nontech classes, and found himself on the brink of expulsion from Berkeley.

In May 1972, as he returned from a FORTRAN programming class, John "Cap'n Crunch" Draper was arrested by federal agents for wire fraud. Given probation, he returned to phreaking. Four years later he was arrested again on the same charges, convicted and sentenced to four months at the federal prison in Lompoc, California. He spent his hard time teaching phreaking to fellow inmates "so they would stop beating me up." By the time he emerged, the computer revolution was underway.

Draper, out of arrogance and enthusiasm, had made the mistake of being too early. In high technology, today's felony is next month's misdemeanor and next year's career path. Had he kept a lower profile he probably would have eventually been hired as a security consultant by the same phone company that busted him.

Instead, his place in history would be as the man who drew the heat off and spared Stephen Wozniak for bigger things.

3.0 SPROUT

About the time Woz was getting in trouble at Berkeley for his grades, Steven Jobs graduated from Homestead High.

In many respects, Jobs had outgrown high school long before. After all, not many high school seniors, even in those heady days, had already been involved in numerous felonies, been traced by the FBI and, by his own account, looked down the wrong end of a gun.

He informed his parents that he planned to rent a cabin in the Santa Cruz mountains for the summer and shack up with his girlfriend. His father, in an almost unprecedented display of determination toward his son, refused to allow him to go.

"Bye," said Steven Jobs, and he walked out of the house.

Like most postgraduation summers, for Steve Jobs the first few weeks of June were lit with a special glow. He and his girlfriend set up house, played guitar, wrote poetry, listened to Bob Dylan records and played host to their regular houseguest, the Woz. It was just like being grown up.

Then Steven's notorious Fiat caught on fire. Paul Jobs, ever willing to help, towed the car home. The young couple, now broke, were reduced to working as greeters at San Jose's decaying Valley Fair Shopping Center dressed in Alice in Wonderland costumes. Woz, also ever willing to help, joined them, despite the fact that his blue box business was quite lucrative. While his girlfriend played Alice, Jobs traded off with Woz the roles of White Rabbit and Mad Hatter, depending upon his mood.

It was the most degrading moment of Steve Jobs's life. He had organized his world like a kingdom, with himself as king and everyone from his parents to his best friend as vassals, and now here he was in a heavy, sweat-stinking, humiliating costume, acting like a damn fool for the entertainment of middle-class parents and their kids. Jobs would later say that after a few hours of this each day, he'd feel like murdering his young audience.

There was still a way out: college. Steven Jobs, who had professed a measure of contempt for higher education, now suddenly embraced it.

In his senior year, like most of his classmates, Jobs had leafed through a pile of college brochures and admission forms. Unlike most of his peers, however, Jobs was less than enthusiastic. He dismissed Cal and Stanford as being too big, too impersonal and, in Stanford's case, too haughty, for his tastes (though years hence he would pose for a collection of Silicon Valley leaders under an arch in Stanford's sandstone quad, thus looking forever like one of the school's most famous grads). He would later say, "Everyone [at Stanford] knew what they wanted to do with their lives. And I didn't know what I wanted to do with my life."

The school that did pique his interest was Reed College, outside of Portland, Oregon. As Steven confirmed during a visit there, Reed had the advantage of being small, five hundred miles from home, and the most radical liberal arts college on the West Coast. As it happened, Jobs was at Cal visiting Woz when his father called to say Reed had accepted him.

His parents preferred for him to get a more traditional education. Moreover, the tuition was prohibitively expensive, given Paul Jobs's salary. But this, of course, was not Steven's concern. Following his proven technique, he informed his parents that if he couldn't go to Reed, then he wouldn't go to college at all. They quickly caved in. They even drove him to Portland—and got into a fight with their son when Steven tried to keep them from taking him on campus. He wanted to create his own entrance, looking like an orphan who'd just arrived from years of bumming around the country and riding the rails.

3.1 FLOATER

Even among the radical schools of the West Coast, Reed was famous for being a kind of counterculture Lourdes. The campus and its environs were a way station for poets, counterculturalists and revolutionaries as they migrated out from the cities and back to the earth. And yet, even Reed College found Steven Jobs to be one of its weirder residents. The adult Steven Jobs, the enigmatic persona that would make him one of the most famous people in the world, was beginning to emerge. There was, as always, the infinite narcissism. But the creepy, off-putting behavior of high school was being transformed into a kind of beguiling willfulness.

This growing charisma was reflected in the people he sought out as friends. One, Dan Kottke, was the son of wealthy New York suburbanites and a National Merit Scholar who had chosen Reed only after being turned down by Harvard. Another was Jack Dudman, Reed's dean of students, and Jobs's latest surrogate father. With each, Jobs would spend long hours in deep conversation.

With Kottke, Jobs talked about Eastern mysticism. The two read endlessly from the corpus of books on Zen Buddhism and yoga then in vogue. Jobs, in particular, was drawn to Zen because of its emphasis upon surrendering the intellect to physical experience.

Steven also made a third friend at Reed, a parolee named Robert Friedland. The importance of Friedland to the creation of the Jobs mystique cannot be underestimated. Friedland had been a major manufacturer of LSD, producing an estimated 30,000 tabs of the hallucinogen before he was arrested and tried. During the trial, Friedland told the judge he shouldn't pass judgment until his honor had tried acid himself. The judge sentenced Friedland to two years in jail.

Paroled early, Friedland arrived at Reed with his counterculture hero's stripes and set about constructing a power base. Dressed in Indian robes, he ran for student body president. He failed, but thereafter cut a mighty figure on campus. He was admired, attended upon, and got to bed any number of pretty coeds.

He happened to be in the middle of doing the last when Steven Jobs knocked on his door selling a typewriter to make some quick cash. As an amazed Jobs looked on, Friedland calmly finished his immediate business, then sat down with the young man. Awestruck, Steven was smitten. He had found his first guru.

This was the education Steven Jobs had come to Reed for. With a few bizarre exceptions—like a dance class he took in hopes of meeting a more perfect mate than his present girlfriend—he slowly dropped each of his classes. This still being the early 1970s, Jobs was allowed to quit school without actually having to leave it. He became a "floater," moving from one unused dorm room to the next as they were occupied or emptied.

In his vision of himself, Jobs was becoming an ascetic, a holy man unencumbered by the burdens of the material world. It was a good strategy, especially after his angry parents finally cut back on their financial support for their college dropout. Steve's hair and beard grew long and ragged, his clothes worn and his feet usually bare. He spent his days reading religious books and meditating, and on Sundays he would hitchhike over to the Hare Krishna temple in Portland, eat the free vegetarian meal it proffered, then gave thanks by placing on the Krishna shrine flowers he'd stolen from neighborhood gardens.

Thanks to a horrifying diet, Jobs began to exhibit the emaciated, crazed look of a true shaman. To perfect that image, he took to staring at people, unblinking, for long minutes on end.

His friends, even Kottke, who shared many of Jobs's philosophical views, became worried about Steven's health and would regularly cook him vegetarian meals. Woz would occasionally drive up to Portland—a fifteen-hour drive in those pre-Interstate 5 days—for a long weekend (Woz wasn't going to class anyway) and come away concerned about his old friend. Jobs seemed not only distant and listless—spending all of his time meditating and reading—but also increasingly secretive. Everyone saw less and less of him, and to this day, there remain holes in this part of Steven Jobs's story.

At the end of the first year, Jobs moved off campus and took a $25-per-month room in town. All but cut off by his parents, he borrowed some money from Reed, then took a job there as a maintenance man for the electrical equipment used to experiment with animals—an interesting job choice for a young man who objected to the slaughter of animals for food.

But the job didn't pay much, and in that miserable, wet, cold, quintessentially Portland winter, huddled in a heatless room in an old down jacket, throwing the I Ching and slurping his Roman Meal, Steven suffered through the most physically difficult time he would ever know. The prince was sick and exhausted, his kingdom reduced to a single, cold rented room. The optimism of two years before was almost gone, but the inexhaustible ego remained.

Studying other primates, he determined, again without any scientific evidence, that mankind's natural diet was fruit. Thus he began a regime of fruit, fasting, occasional drugs and regular, endless lecturing of his friends about the wonderful changes taking place in his body. That Jobs never developed pellagra is a testament to the resilience of youth.

This odd fruitarian phase of Steven Jobs's life would be of interest only as an example of just how dumb college kids can be, if not for the fact that a few years later this fructophagia would prove historic when it came time for Jobs to name his new company.

Whereas Steven had staked his faith on fruit, Robert Friedland, the previous summer in India, had determined, a little more realistically, that the universe was composed of electricity—and nowhere, he claimed rhapsodically, was this "electric atmosphere of love" more charged than in the holy presence of the divine guru Neem Karolie Baba.

Throughout the story of Steven Jobs there are seemingly random events that lead him to change his life just when, pragmatically, it's a helluva good idea to do so. This time, the call of cosmic electricity arrived just as he was at a dead end in his life. And what better place to pursue this universal power grid than in the Mecca of Electricity itself, Silicon Valley? That it also happened to be the place where his best friend, his girlfriend, his parents' kitchen and a well-paying job were waiting was, of course, merely incidental. The goal was to loot the Valley for just long enough to pay for permanent expatriatism in India.

And so Steven Jobs came home.

3.2 THE HP WAY

If Steven Jobs was doing his best to spin out beyond the fringes of normal society, Steven Wozniak was trying to find his way back in.

It was a pattern that would last into middle age. Woz was a hedgehog to Jobs's fox; more stable, feeling deep responsibility for all of his actions and relationships—and, if not as brilliant as his friend, trapped in an obsession that had made him, for good and bad, a genius.

Even when he was breaking the law making blue boxes, Wozniak still included a money-back guarantee with each one. And, of course, he had split his take with the ever-inconstant Steven Jobs. There would always remain in him, whatever the distortions wrought by obsession, wealth and fame, a desire to return to a normal life, to be like his father and his brother, to be just another suburban kid turned suburban adult.

Toward this end, when Wozniak at last accepted the inevitable and dropped out of Berkeley in 1973, the place he went to find work was that most traditional, conservative and family-oriented of Silicon Valley companies, Hewlett-Packard. There he joined his old neighbor and Cream Soda Computer partner Bill Fernandez working at the company's handheld calculator division in Cupertino.

It was an inspired choice. The HP Advanced Products Division was, at the time, the most freewheeling and entrepreneurial of all HP operating units. Staffed by young men and women fresh out of college or from other Valley companies, it had a brashness and risk-taking style that made it something of a scandal within its staid parent company. Within four years all of that would begin to fade as the division moved to Corvallis, Oregon, and lost many of the wilder figures when they chose to stay in the Valley. But within that brief window of time, Woz managed to find the one part of Hewlett-Packard where he could easily fit in.

Just across the street from APD was HP's data systems group, the people who built the company's minicomputers. Though one might imagine that Woz might have been better off there, among the computers and the managers—Paul Ely (Convergent), Ed McCracken (Silicon Graphics), Bill Krause (3Com), and others—who would go on to lead the Silicon Valley computer and networking industry, he was, in fact, better off in calculators at that moment in technological history.

A year before, HP had introduced the HP-35, the world's first scientific calculator. It revolutionized scientific and engineering computation. And that was just the beginning. By the time Woz arrived, APD had introduced the HP-55, the world's first programmable calculator; and was preparing to introduce the company's flagship, the HP-65, programmable by magnetic strips and easily the most influential handheld calculator ever built.

Until the HP-65, calculators and computers, despite their apparent similarity to the layperson, were fundamentally different devices. The calculator's functions were essentially wired into its circuitry. It might do complex calculations blindingly fast, but that was all it could do. Computers, by comparison, were stupid until programmed with software, but then had almost infinite adaptability.

With the HP-65, calculators first moved into the middle ground between the two worlds. It was still a calculator, with a fixed set of functions, but now those functions could be strung together as a series of commands to perform calculations of enormous complexity. Moreover, by virtue of its tiny size, this handheld calculator, unlike its big desktop counterparts, forced a high level of integration of its electronics. In other words, semiconductor chips, including early forms of microprocessors. Thus, the HP-65 was the apotheosis of that multifunction calculator Woz had dreamed of a few years before.

Woz, who was naturally inclined toward finding the most economic and compact solution to any electronics design problem, found in the HP-65 a revelation. "It's got this little chip and serial registers and an instruction set," he would later recall thinking. "Except for its I/O [input/output] it's a computer, the love of my life." Studying the HP-65's design, he got his first clue that it might now be possible to enter that middle ground of computation from the other direction as well.

It was a happy time for Wozniak. He had a secure and legal job at a great company with an old friend, and he was working on an intriguing technology he could learn from. He rented an apartment and, not being a particularly social animal—a coffee shop just a block from his office was in fact one of the great high-tech watering hole/job hopping/technology transfer places of the era—spent his evening playing with a new project: Dial-A-Joke. Each morning as he left for work Woz would turn on his answering machine and read into it a joke using a thick accent.

Of all the businesses Stephen Wozniak started alone, Dial-A-Joke was the most successful. Unfortunately, it was also nonprofit—nobody having figured out a way yet to directly bill for services over the phone—but nevertheless it was a phenomenon. At its peak, Dial-A-Joke averaged 2,000 calls per day. It became the single most frequently called telephone number in the entire Bay Area, and on more than one occasion caused such switching snarls that the phone company asked him to shut it down.

Dial-A-Joke also drew the attention of other organizations as well, notably the Polish-American Congress, which, incensed by the jokes, sent Woz—himself of Polish extraction—a cease-and-desist letter. Woz switched to Italian jokes, waited until the furor died down, then went back to insulting Poles.

Dial-A-Joke would have been a footnote to Woz's career except that one caller, a young babysitter named Alice Robertson, proved so intriguing that the shy Woz, eavesdropping through a headset he often wore, impetuously picked up the receiver and said, "I bet I can hang up faster than you." He did just that—and the intrigued Alice called right back. Five calls and several weeks later, the two finally agreed to meet. Within a year they were married.

The Silicon Valley that Steven Jobs returned to from Oregon had changed subtly, but profoundly, in the two years he had been gone. Intel's microprocessor family had become the technological wonder of its time, the subject of numerous trade magazine articles and provoking a design frenzy across the electronics industry.

Meanwhile, the hottest new company in town was Nolan Bushnell's Atari. Video games were popping out in bars around the country, elbowing pinball machines out of the way and beginning to pull in millions of dollars in revenues, one quarter at a time. An even newer business was starting to make its first appearances on the scene: video game arcades, which eschewed booze or music or anything else to allow the growing population of young, male video game addicts to concentrate solely on their art.

In the meantime, Atari was learning something unexpected: consumer electronics was in many critical ways closer to Hollywood than to Hewlett-Packard. The public had a voracious appetite for video games, but also a short attention span. New and ever more technically impressive games had to be created every few months to keep this thirst slaked.

As a result, Atari and the growing number of firms chasing it were on a continuous search for new creative talent. Because the technology and the market were so new, almost any idea, no matter how off-the-wall, had the potential to be a new home run product . . . after all, who'd have thought electronic Ping-Pong and hungry little yellow dots would capture the minds of 50 million baby boomers?

No one was untouched by the video game wave. Even Woz, having spotted a Pong game in the Cherry Chase Bowling Alley, was hooked. He immediately had gone home and designed a game of his own. Of course, in typical Woz style, whenever a player missed, the words "OH SHIT" would flash on the screen—but the programming was brilliant. For fun, he even showed the game to Atari, which, not surprisingly, instantly offered him a job. Woz said no, thanks, he was happy at HP, and went back to his calculators.

Back in the Valley, Steven Jobs couldn't help but fall under Atari's spell. Soon after arriving in Los Altos, he spotted an employment ad in the *San Jose Mercury News* offering work at Atari designing video games. Though he knew little about the company, and had played no more than a handful of video games in his life, Jobs wanted the position. And when he wanted something, Steven Jobs got it, by whatever means necessary.

In this case, he had to lie through his teeth. When he arrived at the lobby of the Atari building, which happened to be just a couple of blocks from where Jerry Wozniak worked at his desk at Lockheed, Steven Jobs was not a likely candidate for a new job. He was scraggly, impossibly thin and, thanks to a philosophical disagreement with bathing, smelled. He also behaved like a methamphetamine addict, talking so fast—a technique he'd developed in Oregon to intellectually bully people—that he was nearly incoherent to an average human being. The receptionist called upstairs, saying, "We've got this kid in the lobby. He's either a crackpot or he's got something."

Being bizarre was not an impediment to becoming a game designer at Atari. The lab was full of people nearly as strange as Steven Jobs, though none quite as brazen. What did work against Jobs was that he had almost no job experience, much less any real training in electronics.

Still, Jobs had managed to talk his way into an interview with Al Alcorn, now the company's chief technologist. He would just have to bullshit the rest. As he had done in the past, he simply adopted Woz's career as his own. He told the credulous Alcorn that he worked at Hewlett-Packard, that he was part of the HP-35 team and that he could reprogram the HP-45 as a stopwatch.

Alcorn was so impressed he never even checked out Jobs's résumé, but hired him on the spot as a technician for ten bucks an hour.

Jobs's bluffing his way into Atari would later become part of his legend. But what is rarely asked is whether Jobs played the Woz card out of desperation or whether he already knew then that he would exploit his friend's skills.

Either way, Nolan Bushnell's Atari was perfectly suited for Steven Jobs—more so, in fact, than it was for Alcorn. As a lapsed Mormon who had worked the midway at amusement parks as a teenager, Bushnell seemed to be in a hurry to make up for past carnalities lost—and he was doing so in wealthy splendor by hustling millions of kids into his electronic games of chance.

Bushnell was himself a singular figure, the original of the swinging high-tech tycoon that dominated electronics until that archetype was replaced first by the ascetic hippie of Steven Jobs, then by the billionaire nerd of Bill Gates. Bushnell stood six foot four, but looked taller in his corona of curls and bespoke suit. He sported a beard and pipe, drove a Rolls-Royce, held dope-smoking executive staff meetings in hot tubs and code-named new company games after female staffers with the biggest breasts. Like many who followed, Bushnell was half con man, half visionary.

Such a swinging CEO might seem the very antithesis of the younger, self-denying Zen mystic Steven Jobs. But in fact they had much in common—enough so that, in a unique way, Nolan Bushnell served as Jobs's last great role model. After all, in the face of very long odds, Bushnell had managed to create and then successfully rule his own little, but rapidly growing corner of technology. He lived his life according to his own rules, some of them illegal in the surrounding society, and had not only escaped punishment but actually was both celebrated and amply rewarded for his moxie. Bushnell was arrogant, and the world admired him for it. He was mercurial, and people said that was genius. He lied with impunity—sometimes claiming orders he didn't have in order to spur Alcorn and the troops—and his people loved him for it. Bushnell lived his life exactly as he wished, and the world made him rich for doing so.

If Nolan Bushnell could do it, so could Steven Jobs.

3.3 PARIAH

In the chaos that was Atari in the early 1970s, one might imagine that even as bizarre a character as Steve Jobs would have fit right in. In fact, it was just the opposite. His co-workers objected not only to Steve's smell—he still didn't believe in bathing—but to his attitude as well.

In a new start-up company, no matter what your lifestyle, experience or personality, your work must be subordinate to the team itself. This is the essential paradox of entrepreneurship: to become one you must be a rugged individualist, but to succeed as one you must be a team player. The infighting and purges must wait for better times.

Jobs was not, by any stretch, a team player. Worse, he was a backstabber. Bushnell would remember that Jobs was forever calling other Atari technicians and engineers "dumb shits" and claiming he could do their job better—despite the fact that he had little experience or skill, nor ever made much of a contribution to the company. In the end, he was so hated and reviled by his fellow workers, and caused so much workplace tension, that Alcorn moved him to the night shift.

It was, though Alcorn didn't appreciate it at the time, an inspired move. Left to his own devices, Jobs was capable of miracles. There on the night shift, Jobs had lots of time not only to bone up on his electronics—he was a mind-bogglingly fast learner—but to plot his escape. Eventually, an answer presented itself: the new Atari game machines being shipped to Europe were leaking radio waves at just the right frequency to interfere with the reception on European-standard televisions. The first place this problem had appeared was Germany. A call for help came in to Atari headquarters.

Jobs volunteered, knowing that once he got to Europe he could hop his way on to India and Neem Karolie Baba, Friedland's "divine guru." Alcorn, who had refused more bald-faced requests by Jobs for paid trips to India, agreed to let him go. Within days, Jobs had notified his old classmate Dan Kottke to meet him in the subcontinent, packed and was on his way.

In the first of what would be a series of legendary encounters between Steve Jobs and traditional business establishments, Jobs arrived in Germany to face a collection of stunned engineers. What kind of creature is this? they asked themselves. So incredulous were they that for a short time they assumed Jobs was an imposter; they even cabled Alcorn in Sunnyvale to see if there had been a mistake. No mistake, Alcorn replied. I know it's hard to believe, but he's our guy.

The punch line to this story, as to all the Steve versus the Straights stories, is that Jobs actually pulled the job off. Though he had no apparent natural aptitude for electronics, his mind was so quick that he could learn what he needed to know faster than anyone around him. Moreover, for the first time, he displayed a special gift for identifying the critical flaw within a larger working system. In short order, he fixed the problem.

And with that, Steven Jobs took leave of the dumbfounded German engineers and flew off to New Delhi.

Unfortunately, though Neem Karolie Baba may have been divine, he was not immortal. By the time Jobs and Kottke reached his home, having wandered around India and Tibet for a while, the guru was dead. To memorialize him, the two young men stayed in the guru's town, Kainchi, for a month in a rented hut that was happily right next to a marijuana field. They made their own burned offerings to the late guru, one joint at a time.

The one-room hut, though primitive, did come with daily meals prepared by the owners, a family of potato farmers. Soon, showing solidarity with poor Third World people, Jobs was accusing the farmer's wife of cheating him by diluting his water buffalo milk. The woman responded by calling Jobs a criminal.

And so went the summer of enlightenment, suffering from dysentery, haggling in the local market to deny poor farmers a few pennies, shaving his head and smearing himself with ashes.

Eventually, Kottke, whose parents apparently weren't interested in underwriting his subcontinental adventures, ran out of money. Jobs loaned him a few hundred bucks, which let his friend spend a month at a meditation center. Jobs meanwhile wandered about India a little longer, grew increasingly disenchanted with enchantment—he would later say that he learned that Thomas Edison had done more to improve the human condition than all the gurus that ever lived—and went home.

Disenlightenment, however, was not allowed to intrude on a good image. The Jobs who returned to Silicon Valley in late 1974 presented an even more singular appearance than the one who'd left. He was even more emaciated, and he still didn't bathe, but now he wore Indian clothes and his long hair was cut down to stubble. Most of the time his mind seemed a million miles away, as if the demands of quotidian reality could only barely penetrate his higher consciousness.

In time, he wandered back up to Oregon to where his old friend Robert Friedland was now running his newest shtick, the Oregon Feeling Center. There, Jobs signed up for a three-month course in primal scream therapy.

From the perspective of twenty years on, it's hard not to look at all of this quintessentially California-in-the-1970s crackpotism and laugh. But at the heart of all of Steve Jobs's posing, searching and dissembling seemed to be a sad emptiness. And it centered on his adoption and his sense of being unworthy, abandoned and a stranger to this life.

Three months later, Jobs returned once again to the Valley and Atari. He was not especially welcome by his old workmates, and Jobs was soon removed from the day-to-day activities of the firm by being made a consultant.

Why was Jobs rehired by Atari when he returned, more unpleasant than ever, after being gone most of the year? The answer was that Steve had the one champion that mattered: Nolan Bushnell. Entrepreneurs are a different breed, a fraternity of the possessed. They come in many different forms: libertines, ascetics, brainiacs, Scoutmasters and average Joes. But underneath they share a common desire to construct and then control their own world at any cost. As different as Steven Jobs was to Nolan Bushnell, the older man saw in the younger man a secret sharer. He saw in Jobs's bravado, his outlandish and impossible claims to get products ready in a fourth of the time, his dismissal of everyone else as incompetent, a mirror of his own self. And because of that, Bushnell chose to defend Jobs against the revilement of his own staff, even after there was no practical reason to do so.

Before that point was reached, however, Jobs was to make one real contribution to Atari. He did it, as usual, on the back of his friend Stephen Wozniak.

3.4 NOCTURNAL INVENTIONS

Atari in the early days—in fact, right up to its big collapse in 1983—always had a room set up for people to try out its latest video games. It was a perfect market research tool, and on a given day one might find in there a couple of kids, a senior citizen, some young company executives on a lunch break and perhaps a designer enjoying playing his creation as much as any customer.

In all of his wanderings, Steven Jobs had never been out of touch with Stephen Wozniak. Now that he was back in town, he and Woz saw each other regularly. And Woz, not surprisingly, soon gravitated to Atari, where he could see his friend and play the newest games. He became such a fixture in the evenings that he was even allowed to play some of the games as they were being tested on the assembly line. And, as always, even as he played Woz studied each game, learning how it was built and programmed.

It was during this period that Bushnell, perpetually testing his young charge, finally decided to take Jobs up on his claims of superiority and offered him the chance to devise a game of his own, one that, Bushnell stipulated, involved a bouncing ball systematically knocking down a brick wall.

Bushnell, who has never been known as a great manager or motivator, nevertheless perfectly understood what made Steven Jobs tick. At the heart of his offer, Bushnell dangled a financial reward. Payment was to be based not upon delivery of the new game, but on how efficiently it could be manufactured. It is doubtful that Bushnell ever thought Jobs could do the job; but there is no doubt that Bushnell knew that Jobs would somehow get the job done. Jobs, who also understood exactly what Bushnell saw in him, made the outrageous claim that he would design the new game'in just four days.

Jobs's counterparts at Atari knew this was impossible, and many secretly thrilled at the prospect of watching the cocky kid fail. But Jobs for his part knew he had an ace in the hole: after all, Jobs had gotten the Atari job impersonating Wozniak; now he would become a game designer by taking advantage of the real thing.

It helped that Woz was already a regular at Atari in the evenings. And it was not unusual for Jobs to call him away from the video game for a moment to help him on some technical problem or other. So the transition was easy. Now Woz spent only a few minutes each night at the games and the rest at Jobs's workstation. Woz needed no excuse to bury himself in a design project—especially one that put a premium on a solution using the fewest number of chips.

The two young men, as the future would certainly underscore, worked very well together despite all of their personality differences. Jobs was a natural "finder and minder," the guy who could identify and land the big projects and then seduce, cajole and threaten his partners (and later subordinates) to not only get the job done but accomplish far greater things than they could imagine. Wozniak was the critical third leg of the stool, the "grinder," the engineer of extraordinary gifts who was a perfect tool for Jobs, who could utterly submerge himself in the work until it was completed.

Both in recognition of Wozniak's critical (some would later say complete) contribution and no doubt in response to what Woz had done with the blue box profits, Jobs agreed to split the award for the new game, to be called Breakout, with his partner.

Wozniak, thrilled, stayed up for four consecutive nights, going from HP in the afternoon directly to Atari and then, after a short nap and a shower, back to HP in the morning. It was a heroic achievement. Each day, Jobs would look over the accomplishments of his partner from the night before, advance it forward as much as he could, then leave it for Woz to fix his errors and push on again the next night.

3.5 BETRAYAL

In the end, they did it. Wozniak had nearly broken his health and risked his job in the process, but Breakout was done. Jobs delivered it to Bushnell, listened to the chorus of praise and murmurs of resentment, and took it all upon himself with his trademark little smile that managed to combine wry bemusement and an arrogant smirk. And he never once mentioned the contribution of Stephen Wozniak.

Later, when he saw his partner, Jobs informed him about how happy Atari was with their work and counted out $350, Wozniak's half of the $700 bonus Jobs said Bushnell had awarded them for the project. Wozniak was thrilled.

There are moments, even with the most brilliant and carefully constructed personalities, when a single act, once exposed, opens a window into the essential character that lies underneath. And this was such a moment. Steven Jobs had taken advantage of his friend many times in the past. A sympathetic observer might even argue that some of these manipulations were in Wozniak's best interest; that the young man, in the grip of his obsession, needed someone to give him direction.

But this time was different. Jobs had lied. The payment was, in fact, $7,000. It had not been enough merely to exploit his friend, or even enough to take all the credit for the result. Jobs had then gone on to steal most of the award for Wozniak's herculean effort. It was a breathtaking betrayal; a glimpse into the dark center of Steven Jobs's soul.

It was also an extraordinarily risky and brazen move on Jobs's part. Woz was his meal ticket, not to mention one of his few friends, and now he had just put all of that on the line for a few thousand dollars. Until this point in Steve Jobs's story, it is easy to dismiss his behavior as that of a troubled, lonely, spoiled kid. But by the time he reached Atari, Jobs was twenty years old. He had traveled the world, and lived by himself for two years. He was a grown man and his character was established. Nonetheless, he had just betrayed, exploited and robbed his best friend.

One can muse on what would have happened if Jobs's fraud had failed— say, if he had found out a few months later when Alcorn learned who had really built Breakout and again offered Woz a job.

Woz again politely refused Alcorn's offer, saying he preferred to stay at HP. Alcorn, for his part, never knew of the financial deception. But had the $7,000 amount come up, would it have meant the end of the friendship and the stillbirth of Apple Computer?

Perhaps. But then again, if Steven Jobs had been so sure he could lie to and steal from his friend with such impunity, he must have also been sure that if he was caught he could lie his way out of that too. Apple would have happened, no matter what. Jobs would have made sure of it.

After Breakout, with his friend's money in his pocket as well as his own, Jobs again left Atari, to return to Oregon and the spiritual path. This time he landed at the All One Farm, an Oregon commune that specialized in growing organic apples. Here Steven pruned and picked apples and added bulimia to his growing portfolio of strange dietary habits.

Meanwhile, the Breakout experience, the ninety-six hours of pure kamikaze creativity, had rekindled in Wozniak his old spirit of invention. The job at Hewlett-Packard was interesting, paid pretty well ($24,000 per year) for a young man with a limited résumé. It even offered the occasional challenge. But Woz remained, at best, a glorified technician. Those nights at Atari he'd been the Man himself, the creator, who set his own standards and made his own rules. He set out to find something new and interesting to do.

He could not have picked a more perfect time. Something profound was happening out in Silicon Valley, a fundamental shift that Woz, tucked away in the notoriously cocoonlike Hewlett-Packard, had not even noticed.

The metronome of Moore's Law had clicked once again. Microprocessor prices had again fallen, while their power had increased. The hot new Intel chip was now the 8080, the first modern microprocessor and the founding member of what would be the Intel microprocessor family dynasty that dominates electronics to this day.

What made the 8080 particularly compelling was that, unlike its predecessors, the 4004 and 8008, it was not a collection of chips, but a single integrated circuit. That meant it could be designed into almost anything. And it was, from games to minicomputers.

Moreover, now Intel wasn't alone. In Austin, Texas, Motorola's design team had developed a competing chip, the 6800. Meanwhile, Federico Faggin and Masatoshi Shima, two of the men who'd built the first Intel microprocessor, had just left that company and were rumored to be designing their own competing chip at a new company called Zilog in Cupertino. A reborn Fairchild was apparently working on a microprocessor too, as was Texas Instruments. And, in the unlikely location of Norristown, Pennsylvania, a company called MOS Technologies had just announced its own microprocessor, the 6502.

Clearly a movement was underway. The microprocessor was no longer an expensive novelty, but the flagship device of the next high-tech wave — and the sheer number of players building them almost guaranteed prices would soon fall into a range affordable to the average tinkerer.

This wasn't the only movement afoot. Moore's Law worked on computers too. By the time Woz began to look around for a new challenge, Digital Equipment Corp. had cut the price of its PDP-8F minicomputer to just $6,000. That was still a lot of money in 1975, but it was just low enough to tantalize the growing numbers of people who dreamed of owning their own computers.

In the three years since Woz had built the Cream Soda Computer, much had changed in the world of personal computing. Now throughout the country there were scattered pockets of computing enthusiasts numbering perhaps a thousand individuals. They came from all sorts of backgrounds, from the military to the counterculture, the Explorer Post at NASA-Ames to the criminal underground of blue boxes. Even Cap'n Crunch was now playing with computers.

With a population of enthusiasts, personal computing reached its first critical mass: it now constituted a viable market for new products. And between 1972 and 1976 there was a rush of small businesses, typically run by inexperienced enthusiast/entrepreneurs, created to pursue this market.

About the time Jobs and Woz were selling blue boxes, the *People's Computer Company*, a computer enthusiast tabloid, was founded in the Bay Area. In Seattle, Paul Allen and sixteen-year-old Bill Gates founded Traf-O-Data to measure traffic patterns with computer software. And in Santa Cruz, programmer Gary Kildall devised PL/I, the first programming language for the Intel 4004.

By the time Woz finished Breakout, the electronics press was already beginning to talk about a new generation of companies—MITS, Altair, Cromemco, IMSAI—that were offering (or about to offer) hobbyists a whole new world of kits for building their own computers. Kildall, with John Torad, was now offering these same hobbyists a new kind of all-controlling "operating" software for these same machines. And, perhaps most portentous of all, the research arm of Xerox, the Palo Alto Research Center (PARC), was publicly describing a new prototype computer, the Alto, that featured such radical features as display graphics, a new handheld input device called a "mouse" and a technique for networking multiple machines called Ethernet.

Woz, for his part, knew almost nothing of this revolution for which he had been an unknown pioneer. But as he asked around, and read the new magazines, he became more and more intrigued. It was by chance that a workmate at HP learned of Woz's interest in computing and told him about a new group, the Homebrew Computer Club, that was meeting in a suburban garage in Menlo Park. Curious, Woz decided to attend.

The garage belonged to Gordon French, a mechanical engineer, slot car motor builder and budding computer hobbyist. He had been turned on to computers by Fred Moore, who had run a counterculture information service out of the Whole Earth Truck Store, located just a few blocks north of the Stanford campus in Menlo Park. Moore had in turn been introduced to computers by some of his clients, who asked him to help them meet other computerphiles.

The galvanizing event for the creation of Homebrew was the January 1975 issue of *Popular Electronics*. There, on the cover, for the first time anywhere, was a photograph of a true personal computer: the Altair. It was, in fact, an empty box, and a desperate gamble by the president of a fading Albuquerque calculator company called Micro Instrumentation Inc. MITS's president, Ed Roberts, had managed to convince *Popular Electronics* that by the time the issue appeared, his company would actually be able to deliver the $300, Intel 8080-based kit, named, on Roberts's daughter's suggestion, after the planetary destination of one episode of *Star Trek*. Altair made the deadline by a matter of weeks.

Meanwhile, this issue hit like a lightning bolt in computer hobbyist communities from coast to coast. A decade later, journalist T. R. Reid would describe its impact.

Here it finally was: the dream of every computerphile, blue boxer and programmer for nearly a decade. A computer anyone could own. Individual issues, increasingly battered and worn, were passed from one sweaty hand to the next, becoming a sacred text to join the seminal September 1973 issue of *Radio Electronics* that first described a "TV Typewriter."

Realizing the personal computer revolution had finally arrived, French and Moore sent out a flyer to Moore's wide network of computer junkies, phone phreaks, corporate hardware jockeys and anyone else anywhere near the Whole Earth Truck Store who'd ever mentioned computing. It read:

> Are you building your own computer? Terminal? TV Typewriter? I/O device? Or some other digital black box? Or are you buying time on a time-sharing service? If so, you might like to come to a gathering of people with like-minded interests. Exchange information, swap ideas, talk shop, help work on a project, whatever . . .

It was this flyer that was read by an engineer at Hewlett-Packard, who in turn told Stephen Wozniak. Woz contacted Allen Baum and the two agreed to go.

The first Homebrew meeting, held on March 5, 1975, drew thirty-two people from all over the Bay Area. All of them jammed into Gordon French's garage. The high point of that first meeting was a demonstration of a brand-new Altair that Berkeley's *People's Computer Company* had just received from MITS. The room was thrilled at the very sight of this marvel.

The low point came six weeks later with a presentation by Steve Dompier, a Berkeley building contractor who had sent MITS a check for $4,000 asking for "one of everything." What he got back was an apologetic note from the company secretary saying Altair "didn't have all that stuff yet." Dompier, not one to take no for an answer, caught the first flight to Albuquerque—only to discover that mighty MITS was in a little storefront next to a laundromat in a shopping center. Thanks to the *Popular Electronics* article, MITS had been buried in a blizzard of 4,000 orders, of which it had filled just 1,500, and might be able to ship 1,100 more in another month . . . though by then no doubt thousands of more orders would have poured in. In other words, said Dompier, who was the envy of nearly everyone because while at MITS he had spotted a box of parts and bought everything in it, the Homebrew members, even if they ordered today, might not get their Altair for months. And even then it might be incomplete. Later reports from those who did receive their Altairs suggested that the kit was not only very crude—basically a box and a handful of logic and memory boards—but that the Altair memory boards were unreliable.

One might imagine that this would have damped the spirits of the enthusiasts at Homebrew. Instead it did just the opposite. Had MITS produced a complete, reliable, and full-powered computer kit, it might well have scared everyone away. But by being maddeningly incomplete and limited, the Altair left open the door to every entrepreneur who had an idea how to finish it, or at least make it run better. It offered a furtive glimpse of what might be, without being that future itself.

3.6 HOMEBREWING

That first Homebrew meeting and the ones that came after were a revelation to Stephen Wozniak. Lost in the worlds of calculators and video games, he quickly discovered that a new computing subculture had been created since his departure, a world with its own language, heroes and sacred texts. He had a lot of catching up to do. And one of the best ways to do so was to attend the Homebrew meetings, which, thanks to the press of rapidly growing member-ship—numbering several hundred people by the third meeting—moved first to a nearby Victorian house, the Coleman Mansion, and then to an auditorium at the Stanford Linear Accelerator Center.

Though he was still catching up, Woz did enjoy a certain celebrity even in this group, thanks to his blue box career. And the meetings were great fun, thanks to Lee Felsenstein, something of a prophet of personal computerdom, its reigning philosopher, who had taken over as master of ceremonies and shown a surprising gift for running a chaotic but entertaining show. Felsenstein was also the perfect man for the moment; his distaste for structure led to meetings that were half formal presentations and half wild scrambles of people running around getting to know one another. In such an environment, new ideas were tossed about at electronic speed and even the oddest, youngest, or quietest person in the room could get noticed if he had something useful to share.

But even with Felsenstein's charisma, Homebrew soon grew so large that a second, San Francisco branch—which met, oddly, in the Lawrence Hall of Science in Berkeley—was formed. Now, a real computer enthusiast, which Woz had again become, could attend two different personal computing-oriented clubs, and swap ideas with more than a thousand of his peers.

Instead of just an Allen Baum or Steven Jobs off whom to bounce his ideas, Woz now had hundreds of people. As he attended the meetings of the subsequent months, and as he listened to the presentations and swapped ideas, Woz began to soak up not just the technology of personal computing but its gestalt, its wacky mix of Silicon Valley engineering for engineering's sake, Stanford technical phariseeism and Berkeley street Marxism. The personal computer of Homebrew's dreams would combine the coolest design features with the purest individuality, built by enterprises that undermined the predatory world of Big Business, and priced to liberate the common man. It would be not just a personal computer but a revolutionary act.

It wasn't long before Woz had not only caught up with the others but began to move beyond them. He was so quick and skilled with board-level design that soon other Homebrew members began to regard him with a certain awe. For example, one evening Homebrewer Harry Licht was talking to an acquaintance about some parts he had that neither of them knew much about. Harry picked up the phone and called Wozniak. As he listed each product number, Woz instantly responded with that chip's performance specs. When Licht hung up the phone, the amazed visitor asked: Who was that? Oh, said Licht, that's a young kid named Steve Wozniak. He keeps all that information in his head.

Despite its air of self-righteous radical purity, Homebrew contained many members who appreciated the real world of commerce and competition.

They were using Homebrew not only for market and product research but also to scout talent. And these individuals noticed Wozniak too.

The quickest recruiter off the mark was Alex Kamradt of Call Computer, the man looking for someone to build his video terminal with a keyboard. He asked around at one of the meetings who everybody thought was the smartest engineer in the hall. Just about everyone pointed at Stephen Wozniak.

Woz wasn't surprised to be approached. Before Jobs had left town he'd mentioned Call Computer to Woz as an interesting opportunity for their skills. Now here was Kamradt standing before him. But what did surprise Woz was Kamradt's offer: if Wozniak would build him a keyboard video terminal, Kamradt would pay him $12,000 and give him 30 percent ownership in a new subsidiary, Computer Converser, created just to manufacture and market the new invention. Woz didn't even have to quit his day job. And, of particular interest to Woz, he could even work with Call Computer's minicomputer.

This was serious money, half Woz's annual salary at HP. Playing with a real minicomputer was Woz's favorite hobby. And the stock was Wozniak's first glimpse at the real world of entrepreneurial equity. He liked it. A lot.

As he had with the Atari project, Woz quickly set aside every spare minute of his nonworking life to build the new terminal. In one respect, the project was actually retrograde to the events occurring at Homebrew. Whereas the Altair and the other new hobby computers in development were microprocessor-driven and designed to free their owners from dependence upon big computer iron, the purpose of Computer Converser terminal was to do just the opposite: to create a more efficient way for time-share users to communicate with mainframes and thus become even more dependent—and pay Alex Kamradt for that service.

Moreover, at a time when the rest of the hobbyist world was trying to learn more about using microprocessors, Woz was now getting paid to figure out how *not* to use those precious and expensive little chips.

In all, the whole project would have been a distraction to Woz's budding computer career . . . except for one crucial factor. It was that Woz, almost alone among his peers, was devoting his time to designing a complete *system*. The other Homebrewers were buying their Altairs—or, soon, their Cromemcos, IMSAIs and a half dozen others—soldering together the boards and then eagerly jumping into programming. Woz, by contrast, remained buried in the world of hardware, squeezing out every superfluous component to create the most elegant and inexpensive design. And, even more than the computer kit companies themselves, Woz was learning how to link together the main processor with peripherals such as a keyboard and video screen. By purposely not building a kit computer, Wozniak was making himself the best home computer designer in the world.

Woz finished his design and prototype by the end of the summer of 1975. Now he needed to test it. And, as an old blue box master, Woz knew exactly how to test a phone-based terminal. He called his old friend Cap'n Crunch and took his terminal over for a visit and tour of the world's telephone network.

Draper, on probation, but still a year away from his big bust and prison stretch, had taken phone phreaking on to even greater heights than the days when Woz and Jobs had been acolytes. Now he had discovered a target even more exciting than the phone company: the ARPAnet, the nationwide computer network of military, research and academic users. Draper showed Woz the way onto the network and Woz tested out his new design. It worked beautifully, the keyboard and VDT a distinct improvement over the traditional and awkward teletype machine. Woz logged off, thanked Draper and took off to deliver the terminal to Kamradt.

He would not log onto the network again for nearly twenty years, long after it had transformed into the Internet.

In the story of Apple Computer, each of the principal figures makes at least one dreadful mistake that will eventually prove disastrous to the company.

This was Woz's mistake. As it was the first, it was also the most forgivable.

Still, the moment is so tantalizing, the possibilities so infinite, that one just can't help thinking: what if, that day at Cap'n Crunch's, Stephen Wozniak had just played a few more minutes on the ARPAnet? Perhaps he would have seen in his mind's eye that moment, two decades off, when the paths of the Net and the personal computer would intersect. The day when the Net itself, driven by the PC, would create a social and commercial transformation far greater, and far more liberating, than anything imagined by the revolutionaries of the 1960s.

And, having glimpsed that future, perhaps Woz would have then gone home and tried to turn the Computer Converser terminal into a kind of pioneering Net Computer—or short of that, designed his own computers for the Internet Age to come—instead of creating an architecture that would resist the Internet until it was too late.

But that is asking an awful lot of a twenty-four-year-old. Changing the world once is enough to ask of anyone.

In the end, Wozniak delivered the keyboard video terminal to a thrilled Kamradt. But it wasn't long before the majority shareholder realized that only his junior partner understood how the terminal worked, even how to fix it. And when the prototype crashed, as prototypes will do, Kamradt quickly found that Woz, still working full-time at HP and contemplating marriage, wasn't always available to come over to fix the problem. Kamradt, knowing from experience that this was a recipe for disaster should the terminal ever be built in volume, killed the project. And Woz answered forever the question of whether he could have built a great company on his own.

Meanwhile, the young man who would do just that with Woz's help had just returned to Silicon Valley.

3.7 CONVERSANT COMPUTER

Jobs arrived in the Valley just as Woz was turning in the finished terminal. Kamradt, a pretty good judge of people, immediately recognized the power Steven Jobs had over his friend. Despite feeling that Jobs was "pretty unscrupulous," Kamradt approached the young man and asked for his help in handling Woz.

Jobs agreed, once again not telling his friend about the new role, and once again bringing his formidable negotiating skills to bear. Knowing he was the only person who could manipulate the young inventor, Jobs demanded from Kamradt not only money but title (director of the company's terminal division) and even stock.

It wasn't much, but it was a gig. And Jobs even had a subordinate, a contractor named Robert Way, whom he rode so hard that the man eventually quit the project—later calling Jobs "one of the weirdest people I ever met."

But Jobs wasn't concerned, even after Kamradt killed the project, because he'd learned a great truth in his time at Atari and Computer Converser: find a genius, ride his slipstream and wait for your chance. And Wozniak was, amazingly enough, proving to be just such a figure. The good side of that genius had made Jobs money at Atari, and the bad side of it had landed him a job at Computer Converser. Jobs couldn't lose.

The trick, then, was to keep an eye on Woz. Find out where his mind was roving next, then push and prod and cajole him toward that goal, demand the impossible from him and then look for ways to convert the results into money in Jobs's pocket.

It didn't take long for Woz, still bored by Hewlett-Packard, to cast off again on a new project. He was still a regular at Homebrew, and as the months passed, like all the others he could see a pecking order emerge. At the bottom were the computer curious, the gamma goofballs, the guys who'd heard about home kits and were carefully sticking a toe into the water. These were the consumers, the hobbyist hoi polloi who would ultimately buy the creations of others.

Next up the ladder were the bolt-on beta boys. These were the guys who bought the kits currently on the market, like the Altair, and had seen a way to make a buck building aftermarket hardware, such as memory boards, writing operating systems or applications software or selling their services to the gammas.

And at the very pinnacle of the Homebrew world were the alpha inventors. These were the guys who pissed on the Altair, believing they could build a better box. Felsenstein was an ersatz alpha; but his partner Bob Marsh was the real thing, as he would prove with his own new computer company, Processor Technology. So were two Stanford graduate students, Harry Garland and Roger Melen, who had just started Cromemco.

Wozniak looked at these alphas, and as shy as he was, knew he belonged with them. He had built the Cream Soda Computer, designed the greatest blue box, an Atari game, and now the Computer Converser terminal. Nobody at Homebrew had anything close to his credentials. Besides, he couldn't afford an Altair, anyway.

But he still hadn't built a computer that he could prove to the world actually worked. It was time.

So, while Jobs was off at Computer Converser trying to figure out Woz's last design, Wozniak once again went to ground to come up with a new invention. And once again, he took Allen Baum with him.

The first step for the two men was to bring themselves up to date. Almost a half decade had passed since their internship days at Sylvania, and both were convinced that they'd missed an entire technology revolution.

In fact, they were half right. In the years since they'd played on the big, noisy IBM 1130, the world of computing had indeed turned upside down. The new generation of minicomputers, exemplified by the DEC VAX, Data General Eclipse and the HP 3000, were as fast and nearly as powerful as the big iron mainframes, but much smaller and less expensive, and most important, they were real-time machines. You entered in the data, the internal program processed that data and the computer gave you back the results. No more stacks of punched cards awaiting one gigantic "batch" processing. The new minis took your call *right now.*

But the new minis were only half the story. At the other end of the spectrum, Moore's Law had done its work and the first generation of single-chip microprocessors were now on the scene in volume, their prices falling rapidly toward consumer levels. Just a hundred or so bucks now would buy you an Intel 8080 or its near relation, the Zilog Z80, or the exciting new Motorola 6800. And that was just the hottest name. In all, in 1975 there were sixteen major microprocessor manufacturers (including TI, National Semiconductor and Fairchild) selling on the open market, and perhaps an equal number (including IBM and HP) building proprietary microprocessors for their own equipment.

By picking the Intel 8080, Altair had made Intel the microprocessor supplier of choice for the Homebrewers. At the meetings, almost all the new designs were Intel chip-based. But the 8080 was expensive, one chip costing as much as a new stereo or an old Volkswagen. On Woz's salary, and with the prospect of marriage waiting around the corner, he couldn't afford that kind of investment on a device that might short itself out on a random burst of static electricity or a power surge when it was first turned on.

All of this—the prospect of relearning computer architecture, then trying to duplicate those operations with a microprocessor, then determining how to lay out all the supporting chips around that processor for input-output to the video screen, keyboard and memory, the memory boards themselves and a power supply, and *only then* addressing the problem of programming the finished box—was daunting even to the ever-ambitious Wozniak. Baum was even more doubtful.

Then Woz made a happy discovery: microprocessors *were* minicomputers. That might seem obvious; after all, from the beginning microprocessors had been called "computers on chips." But Woz had always assumed that meant that the two were alike only functionally. What he found instead was that organizationally, architecturally, the transistors on the surface of the silicon chip were laid out almost identically to the chips on the motherboards of the refrigerator-sized minis on which Woz and Baum had once played—and, by the same token, in the Cream Soda Computer itself.

What this meant, first of all, was that Woz didn't have to go back and relearn computer science, a task that might have driven away even Wozniak, who, for all his legendary focus, was increasingly being pulled in many different directions by love and work. But even more important, as Woz and only a few others understood, the microprocessor *gave you an architecture.*

This was a crucial breakthrough. Now you didn't have to completely design a new computer from the ground up, beginning with the central processing unit. The microprocessor could be your CPU, and your much simpler task then became finding the best way to construct all the interconnections that enabled the microprocessor to get electrical power and then to drive the external memory boards, disk drive or (in those days) cassette tape player, keyboard and display.

It is interesting to ask in retrospect why this understanding first arose among nerd hobbyists and not with the big established computer companies such as IBM, Burroughs or DEC. One answer is practical: the true microprocessor, in the form of the Intel 8080, was only a couple years old and still comparatively unproven. Giant corporations take longer than that to test new inventions for their usefulness. A second answer is philosophical: big-iron computer guys had built an entire epistemology around mainframe and mini-computers and the MIS departments that ran them. Personal computers in the control of individuals simply didn't fit into this reality. A third answer was technical: in an industry dedicated to constructing machines of ever-greater computing power, the personal computer represented a kind of surrender. Compared to a mainframe it was slow and unreliable, and it couldn't do a thousandth of the important applications—like process a 30,000-employee payroll—a mainframe could. Who needed it? A fourth answer was marketing: established computer companies sold to other companies, most of them man-ufacturers, and had little understanding of, or interest in, the consumer mar-ket. And a fifth answer was bureaucratic: these companies had made billions of dollars in large-scale computing. Many, like Burroughs and Univac, had resisted even minicomputers. Personal computing represented the ultimate apostasy. Most companies felt it was just a novelty, anyway, which would suck millions out of any foolish firm that pursued it, while acting as a distraction to the real business of building big iron. Better to just ignore it and hope it would go away.

In fact, there was one giant company at work building a personal com-puter: Xerox. The computer, designed between 1972 and 1974, was called the Alto and it was not only more advanced than anything being built anywhere else in the world, but with its use of a mouse, a sophisticated language called Smalltalk and a networking scheme called Ethernet, the Alto would remain the world's best personal computer for nearly a decade until the advent of the Macintosh, which more than a little resembled it. But it was the Alto's fate to be designed by Xerox's Palo Alto Research Center—and so, like many PARC inventions before and after, it was released commercially years too late (as the overpriced Star in 1981) and mainly served as useful carrion for other, more aggressive competitors to pick over.

Unlike the thousands of computer professionals at all of these giant firms, Stephen Wozniak understood what the microprocessor made possible. Now all he needed was to score one of those chips.

3.8 REVOLUTION ON THE CHEAP

Obtaining a microprocessor wasn't as easy as it might sound. Like everyone else in the Homebrew Computer Club, Woz coveted the Intel 8080. But not only were they expensive, but with everyone from NASA to Ford ordering them for testing and design, damn hard to get. There was also the year-old Motorola 6800, not as cool as the Intel chip but nevertheless being designed into the new MITS computer kit in Albuquerque and the Ohio Scientific mail-order computer kit. The 6800 was bigger than the 8080, but it was also 5-volt, which made it compatible with existing computer logic chips. Best of all, Woz could buy one for half the price of the Intel chip. Woz already knew the 6800—he'd used it with the Computer Converser terminal—and was comfortable with its design, which in some ways was even better than that of the 8080.

But the deciding factor was the decision by his employer, HP, at the time a major Motorola customer, to offer the 6800 to employees at discount. When Baum brought in that bit of good news, Woz quickly decided upon the Motorola chip.

But soon thereafter another piece of good news reached Woz. The Wescon computer show, at the time the largest gathering of computer manufacturers in the world, would be holding its annual event in San Francisco in just a matter of weeks. Wescon, with its big displays of big computing iron and sea of meandering computer engineers in white shirts, was just the kind of event the computer hobbyists despised and yet couldn't stay away from.

Woz was already planning to go. But what made the trip north an absolute necessity was the announcement that Chuck Peddle, a former Motorola chip guy now with MOS Technologies Inc. of Norristown, Pennsylvania, was planning on using the show to sell a limited number of new MOS 6502 microprocessors—basically a low-budget 6800, designed by some ex-Moto engineers—at the jaw-dropping price of *twenty dollars*. It was unbelievable! It was like selling a Ferrari for the price of a Chevy, a mansion for the price of its garage.

In those purer days before such free-for-alls as CES and Comdex, Wescon, which was held in the underground exhibit space called Brooks Hall in the City Hall plaza, did not allow the grubby business of retail selling on the exhibit floor. So Peddle set up shop, like a dope dealer, in a nearby hotel suite. And it was there that Wozniak found him, paid the twenty bucks to the lady at the door (who happened to be Mrs. Peddle) and dug the cherished 6502 chip out of a glass bowl. It was a brief, but fateful, meeting. Within two years, MOS would be bought by Commodore and Peddle would help that company build the Pet computer and make a serious, if brief, challenge to Apple.

Woz drove home to Sunnyvale with his prize, as excited as he'd ever been. In retrospect, he'd just made his second great mistake. By the time the magnitude of this mistake was apparent, it would be too late for Apple to turn back. Woz himself would be gone from the company as well.

Given what was to come, one can only look back in dismay and wonder what might have happened if Wozniak had not been too broke to buy anything but the 6502. What if he had the money—say, the $3,150 Jobs owed him—to have followed the lead of the other Homebrewers, as he wanted to, and bought an Intel 8080. Instead of building the first great personal computer around a chip from a troubled company that would soon disappear into the bowels of a competitor, Apple would have been working with one of the best-run companies in the world. Instead of being bludgeoned by the team of Intel and Microsoft in the years to come, Apple might have led it in an unbeatable troika. It's entirely possible that in cheating Woz out of thousands of dollars Steven Jobs robbed his own future of billions. He may have hamstrung Apple even before it began.

Woz began work almost from the instant he got home. For the next two months he would immerse himself in the last great solo act of invention in the twentieth century, and put himself in the company of the great lone inventors—Ford, Firestone, Tesla—who had begun it.

3.9 SMALL MIRACLE

There is something almost miraculous in the story of Woz's creation of the Apple I. For someone who until this point had seemed lost and undirected, Woz, perhaps because he was in the grip of the project of his dreams, was suddenly more surefooted in his actions than at any time before or after.

For example, despite what one would expect from a hardware guy with the critical part at last in hand, Woz instead kicked off the project by writing software. In fact, he wrote the first BASIC language program for the 6502. He would later say that he did so because he could "whip it out in a few weeks and zap the world with it"—which he certainly did with his admiring counterparts at Homebrew. But strategically it was exactly the right thing to do. BASIC validated the 6502; it showed not only that this microprocessor could run the kind of programming language needed for a good personal computer, but it also enabled Woz to work backward, designing the hardware to optimize for that language.

It was also a breathtaking achievement. In the entire history of digital electronics there are no more than a handful of examples of hardware designers crossing over to write code, or vice versa. It is the equivalent of a figure skater taking up water polo, and doing both at the Olympic level. And that is one reason why computer folks still speak with reverence and awe of Stephen Wozniak.

But he'd only just started. With the key software out of the way, Woz set to work building the hardware. As one might expect, in his own territory he was even more surefooted. He set about designing a motherboard to hold the central processor (including the 6502) with the minimum number of chips and the maximum number of interfaces to the outside world. Woz took on the board design challenge and passed much of the interface work to the ever-helpful Baum, who later described the experience of creating links for the keyboard, display and memory boards—all within the restrictions of a primitive 8-bit microprocessor—as having wrung the last bit of the fun for him out of computer design.

Woz, by comparison, was having the time of his life. The restrictions created by his limited budget had the same effect as a limited palette sometimes has on a painter: it forced him to find the most economical and most elegant solution to every problem. There was no place for anything extravagant or extraneous. And Woz, whose mind had always bent that way, rose to the challenge. One way he did so was to dip into his employer's supply of parts—not exactly legal, but, given the long-standing attitude of HP toward this behavior as well as the Advanced Products Division's own iconoclastic style, it was not a career-threatening infraction either. But even with these expropriated HP parts, Woz still was ruthless in his design economies.

This decisiveness seemed to spill out into Woz's private life as well—again for perhaps the only time in his life. In the midst of this design madness, trying to build a computer while still holding a full-time job, Woz suddenly decided to make up his mind about getting married to Alice Robertson.

Still, he wasn't so decisive as to simply make a stand. Instead, he decided to be mathematical about it: he would flip three coins. If all three came up heads (a one-in-eight likelihood) he would marry Alice. A rather cold-blooded way to make a decision about love and marriage . . . but a sweet story when one next learns that Woz kept flipping coins until those three heads finally came up. One cannot imagine his erstwhile best friend, or, for that matter, most of the future top executives of Apple, being caught in such a romantic act.

But marriage, once decided, would have to wait. The computer came first, and it was nearly done.

Woz himself, typically, cannot remember the exact date he finished the computer, though it was probably in late November 1975. But also typically, even today he can still describe its design in detail. In one respect, the computer was similar to the other computers being shopped around Homebrew. It was essentially a motherboard full of chips (though, of course, the use of the 6502 was a major departure), a keyboard and, less common, a video display (many computers demanded that the user buy a display somewhere else). To the modern user the computer would look like the remains of a PC ready to take to the recycler, not the beginning of a revolution.

Yet, for all of its similarities to other machines, the experienced homebrewer would have instantly noticed some fundamental differences in Woz's design. For one thing, it was simpler; Woz's genius for design had enabled him to endow his computer with the most elegant architecture anyone had ever seen. And simplicity meant greater reliability, because fewer chips reduced the likelihood of breakdown. It also meant it was cheaper: Woz's design meant not only greater profits at the market's typical selling price, but more important when the competitive crunch came, more room to cut prices while still dancing out of the red.

Of course, pricing strategy was about the furthest thing from Wozniak's mind, but there were people coming into his world who would know just what to do with it—for a while, at least.

The second obvious feature of Woz's computer was its neatness. Neatness, too, often manifested itself in reliability. Whereas many of his current colleagues/future competitors were selling motherboards that looked—with their externally attached wires and kluged together subsystems—less like finished products than like breadboarded prototypes, Wozniak's motherboard was clean; every chip and every other component was snipped and soldered into place. As such, Woz's computer was probably the very first kit machine that could actually be dropped and survive—not so important now with guys who spent their lives reconnecting wires and searching out shorts, but a very big deal when it came to the commercial market.

Finally, a third, and less obvious, feature of the Woz computer—one that would prove decisive in the long run—was that *it actually worked*. Working at HP, Woz had access to one of the company's minicomputers, with which—without HP's permission, of course—he simulated the operation of a 6502 and then ran his programs through it, checking for bugs, infinite loops (where the computation would stick in a logical cul-de-sac, unable to escape, repeating its action over and over again forever) and design flaws. Thus, poor in terms of cash on hand, Woz was incredibly rich when it came to test and measurement tools—richer in fact than all but his most established counterparts such as MITS. With his own native genius, backed by the laboratory resources of one of the electronics industry's greatest companies, Woz could run with the best of them.

By Christmas 1975, Wozniak had finished, tested and debugged his computer. And like a true engineer, the first thing he wanted to do was show everybody what he'd done. Then he wanted to be paid for it, forget it and move on to the next engineering challenge.

So for the next month he went about displaying his brilliance. The first place he showed it was to his own bosses at Hewlett-Packard. As it happened, he wasn't the only Homebrewer at the Advanced Products Division. In fact, he wasn't even the only designer working with the 6502: his workmate Myron Tuttle had also caught Woz's enthusiasm for personal computing, bought his own 6502 from Chuck Peddle and was also during this period racing to build a board-level computer.

But Woz's was finished first, and was clearly superior. So it was agreed that it would be Woz's machine that would be demonstrated to their superiors. So, on a day in early January 1976, Woz, Tuttle and one other young engineer had an informal meeting with their supervisor. The supervisor was impressed, but informed them that it was no go. Tuttle would later recall, "It was one of those informal meetings. It wasn't a big deal. We just sort of asked for five minutes and showed Woz's board. We were told, 'HP doesn't want to be in that kind of market.' "

Out of that meeting would come the myth that hidebound old HP had looked at Woz's revolutionary design and was either too unimaginative or too stupid to get it . . . leaving the brilliant young visionaries to make it on their own. Like most myths, however, anyone who was at APD during that era would have seen an entirely different situation.

HP's Advanced Products Division was, for the moment, as nonconformist and innovative as any place in Silicon Valley. Inside the company itself the division was seen as a collection of wild-eyed radicals not only by HP's very traditional instrument group but also by APD's compatriots across the street in the minicomputer group. Chartered to create perpetually innovative new calculator products, not just for engineers but also for businesspeople, students, even everyday consumers, APD had developed an internal culture that would not be seen again until, well, Apple Computer itself.

And this culture became even more anarchic after the announcement, soon after Woz arrived, that the division would be moving to Corvallis, Oregon. Half the division was excited about going, while the other half planned on staying in the Valley by transferring to another HP division or leaving the company. Either way, almost nothing substantive happened at the division while it awaited the move. Instead, APD's employees, Woz not least among them, spent much of their days playing with their own private projects.

So why turn down Woz's design? It probably had nothing to do with the inventor—HP had gotten into calculators, as well as LED displays, from outsiders with good ideas. More likely, HP was wary of anything purely targeted at consumers, a market that had sunk many an ambitious tech company and in which HP had no particular experience or skill. The company also had an unwritten (and, time would show, shortsighted) rule that there was no way it could make a profit on a computer priced less than $3,000. And if all that wasn't enough, there was the distraction at APD.

On April 28, 1976 (according to a copy in the HP Archives), Wozniak sent a memo to the company requesting a release of the technology. This was followed on March 1 by a carefully drawn schematic of a "Microprocessor System," with a footnote reading: "Apple Computer Co. is a partnership of myself and Steve Jobs founded to market PC boards." Four days later, HP granted the release.

Of course, plodding old HP would have the last laugh. Entering into the PC business late, it nevertheless managed to play off of its strengths—high quality and a strong connection to corporate offices and research labs—and slowly began accumulating market share. Taught by its successes with laser printers (which it also supplied to Apple under the latter company's Laser-Writer title), HP even learned, after a few nasty missteps, how to mass-market to everyday computer owners. Moreover, because of HP's dominance in mini-computers, and later large computer servers and workstations, it was able to link its calculators, personal computers and large computers into giant networked client-server systems for corporations and other institutions.

As a result, in the end HP earned more revenues and profits from the personal computer it had originally turned down than Apple Computer ever did. Just as important, as Apple began to spiral down, HP, after its own stumble, righted itself and became the most successful large company of the era. In 1996, twenty years after Hewlett-Packard turned down what would be the Apple I, HP passed Apple in the personal computer market share. Two years later, Hewlett-Packard was the world's fourth-largest personal computer company, and planning to become the first.

All legends to the contrary, even in high tech the tortoise often beats the hare.

Since HP wasn't interested, in February 1976 Wozniak made the first public showing of his computer at the Homebrew Computer Club.

Despite yet another myth to the contrary, the reaction that night to Woz and his computer was relatively cool. Sure, everyone knew Wozniak was a hotshot computer designer and programmer. And yeah, as Woz handed out copies of the schematics, everyone was impressed by the elegance of the design. *But it was built around a 6502!* By now, everyone who was anyone had already adopted the Intel 8080 architecture, and Homebrew was rapidly turning into a user's group for computers built around Intel chips. What Woz had done was a work of genius, no doubt about it, but it was also a work of apostasy. Either you joined Woz or you joined everybody else—not a tough decision, no matter how slick Woz's computer. Still you could study his schematics and find some new design ideas to steal . . .

There was one person at the Homebrew meetings, though, who was willing to side with Woz. Steve Jobs had been an irregular and indifferent attendee at Homebrew almost from the beginning, more often than not going just to keep Woz company. But, as he buried himself deeper into Woz's terminal for Call Computer, Jobs began to appreciate just how extraordinary his friend really was.

It must have come as something of a shock to Jobs. After all, he had searched the world for a guru, a man of unique knowledge and vision—and that guy turned out to be his goofy childhood friend. Watching Woz at the meeting handing out schematics, Jobs saw what his friend did not: that though their design loyalties lay elsewhere, the Homebrew members held Woz in awe and were more than happy to get hold of his most recent design and deconstruct it for their own uses.

Jobs also knew something else as well: left to his own counsel, as he had been with the Computer Converser, Woz would happily design himself into a corner. But if properly managed and directed, as with Atari's Breakout, Woz could change the world.

So the first and most important step for Jobs was to get Woz back under his wing. The HP presentation, which Jobs had not been privy to, was a dodged bullet. Had HP said yes, Jobs would have been left in the cold. Now Woz, frustrated by the lack of universal acclaim for his invention, was talking about selling the machine to Call Computer. Kamradt, who had returned to the Homebrew meetings to find Wozniak and reenlist his help on the Computer Converser, was entranced by the new Woz design and was trying to recruit the young man back.

That would have to be stopped, and fast. Woz and Jobs were accustomed to talking on the phone nearly every day, usually about the computer and Woz's various pipe dreams for it. Now Jobs sat Woz down and told him what he really thought. It was a terrific invention, but Woz was being utterly unrealistic about it. Not only was he trying to sell it to the wrong people, but by giving away the schematics, Woz was essentially handing over his hard work for free to anyone willing to hold out a hand. It's time to turn this into a real business, said the young man who until recently had publicly eschewed all worldly things; and the first step is to start charging for the damn schematics.

Jobs was never a tactful person, but he had also never before called Woz a fool. Woz listened. Woz would say later, "Steve was the one who thought we could make money. I was the one who designed the computer. I was the one who had attended the Homebrew meetings and I had written the software, but Steve is the one who had the idea we could sell the schematics." He would later add, perhaps a bit ruefully, "Steve was the hustler, the entrepreneurial type."

And Jobs was about to give Woz a first lesson on what that meant.

3.10 FAST LEARNER

Jobs had before him five immediate tasks. One was to redirect Woz's attention away from Kamradt. The second was to convince Woz to join him, legally, in a new business. The third was to create a market for the new computer. The fourth was to build a manufacturing operation. And the fifth was to construct a supply and distribution channel to build and sell the new computer in volume.

This is not an easy task even for an experienced business entrepreneur. It requires a combination of charisma, leadership, promotional talent and sales-manship—not to mention basic business theory. Jobs, the rebel against West-ern Society, whose total (noncriminal) work experience at this point amounted to less than a couple of years and whose entire management experi-ence consisted of supervising one employee for two months, had so far shown little business acumen beyond a capacity for hyperbole with his superiors.

And yet, within five months he had accomplished everything. It was the first indication that Woz was not the only member of the partnership with a kind of genius.

The first two steps were actually the hardest. Woz was happy at Hewlett-Packard. The mother firm of Silicon Valley, with its perfect job security, doughnuts in the morning and one big happy family atmosphere, had em-braced the young engineer in its arms. And Stephen Wozniak, like 25,000 other employees, never wanted HP to let go. His father, after all, was a lifer at Lockheed, and it was with the idea of just such a career that Woz felt most comfortable. Thus, a deal with Kamradt offered the perfect scenario: Woz could keep designing new computers in his spare time, sell them to the Call Computers of the world—which would be more than happy to buy them— and use the bucks to supplement his HP salary.

Jobs used two levers on his old friend. First, he played the money angle, suggesting to Woz that he could make even more money going it alone. Next, he played on Woz's engineer's ego, arguing that Woz would enjoy far greater glory among his peers holding on to the machine. He even hinted darkly that if the computer was sold to Call, it would be mishandled and quickly disappear into the mists of computing history.

Desperate to reel in Woz, Jobs, in a beautiful bit of surrogation, enlisted an Atari engineer he knew named Ron Wayne. Wayne was two years older than Woz, and that maturity gave added weight to Jobs's argument. Wayne, a classic eccentric Silicon Valley bachelor who combined cranky survivalism with a belief in the transcendental power of engineering, tried to appeal to Woz's ego. He pointed out to the young man that few engineers ever made it on their own, that famous designers like Eiffel and Colt had always needed a good business mind behind them. It was, in fact, a very accurate argument, though the description of Steven Jobs as that crucial figure showed either incredible insight or craven self-interest on Wayne's part.

Still, Woz had hesitated. Ironically, it seemed that he had learned too well all those agrarian, proto-Marxist homilies Jobs had been spouting all these years. He was willing to let Jobs and Wayne build the new computer, but Woz wanted to be able to stay at HP and use whatever design tricks he'd learned with the computer as a leverage into a better job in a different division at the giant firm.

No way, thought Jobs and Wayne. The last thing they needed was Woz as their competitor. It took an all-out, and nearly all-night, assault on Woz before, at last—partly out of exhaustion, partly out of not wanting to disappoint his old friend and partly out of his own tangential ambitions—he signed on. The clincher was a compromise: Jobs agreed that Woz could stay at Hewlett-Packard, but he was not allowed to duplicate his computer work there. Wozniak was happy, but Jobs was even more so. That's because Jobs knew that if the new company failed, he wouldn't be responsible for his friend's career, and if it succeeded, Jobs could simply charm Woz into working for the company full-time. And, in the meantime, that was one less salary on the payroll.

In yet another too perfect bit of symbolism, the articles of incorporation for the new company were signed on April Fools' Day, 1976. The founders, who would forever be known as a duo, were in fact a troika.

With Woz, Jobs had the computer, but he still didn't have a business. First he needed to come up with a name. Exactly how he decided upon Apple, probably the most influential new business name of the century, remains, like many facts about the early days of the company, the subject of considerable speculation.

The best-known story, told by Michael Moritz in *The Little Kingdom*, is that the pair were driving up the Peninsula and Jobs, lost in reverie about his days at the commune picking apples, suddenly had a Paul-like epiphany on the road to Los Altos and realized that Apple Computer—rather than other proposed titles such as Executek and Matrix Electronics—was the perfect name for the firm. That's possible, though the stretch of 280 they were driving on hasn't a single fruit tree to spark such a memory. Another story, published elsewhere, says that the trio were sitting around Woz's apartment throwing out ideas and Jobs, in a neat piece of out-of-the-box brainstorming, threw out Apple and found that it trumped every other idea. Yet another story has it that Jobs, a Beatles fanatic, took the name Apple from the Apple Records label of the album he was playing (and it is known that the trio had a few days of worry about a trademark infringement suit from the Fab Four). And at least one old Homestead High classmate would later claim to remember a scurrilous publication by the two called "The Road Apple" (Homestead's nickname was the Mustangs), though naming his new company after horseshit is probably too flip and cynical even for Steven Jobs. This was, after all, about money.

Ultimately, the final decision to name the company Apple was determined by the United States government. In particular, the Securities and Exchange Commission required a name on its new company registration forms. So, finally, when the day came to mail in the form and the entry for company name was still blank, Jobs announced, "Come up with a better name than Apple by five P.M. or that's it."

Whatever the source, it was a brilliant name. Smart, funny, antiestablishment, unforgettable, friendly but hip, the very antithesis of not only the eponymous Fairchild and Hewlett-Packard but also the technophilic Intel and Intersil. Perhaps no company name has ever fit its era so perfectly. The Apple name may have been the Apple Company's biggest strength—and, ultimately, its biggest weakness. Because, like so many things that fit an era so precisely, it became at best an anachronism, and at worst a liability, when that era ended and a new one arrived.

But in 1976, Apple was a killer name. You laughed the first time you heard it, smiled the second time and fell in love with it thereafter. It wasn't just a name, it was the culmination of the Age of Aquarius. It said to tens of millions of baby boomers now cutting their hair and entering the corporate world that they weren't selling out after all, that every time they saw that logo on the computer before them they were still Woodstock warriors, undermining the suits around them, fomenting the revolution from within and, duplicating Steve Jobs's famous knowing smirk, secretly laughing at the absurdity of it all.

4.0 SAPLING

A modern venture capitalist looking at the Apple Computer of April 1976 as a possible investment would have tossed the business plan into the trash.

Sitting up on Sand Hill Road in Menlo Park overlooking the stretch of freeway where Steven Jobs first named Apple Computer, the venture capitalist would look at this motley team with its crude product and see it as just another of the hundreds of doomed new start-ups whose business plans cross his desk each year.

In the years since Apple was founded, Silicon Valley has become the most efficient new-company incubator the world has ever known. In a good year, more than one hundred new companies are founded and funded. In a great year such as 1996, thirty local companies, the creation of similar investments two or three years past, will go public with market valuations of $100 million or more. In such years, the cities of Sunnyvale, Mountain View and Santa Clara together are home to more newly public large companies than all the rest of the United States.

That kind of efficiency is the product of experience and the ongoing perfection of techniques. The modern venture capitalist uses not only a wealth of institutional experience but also highly sophisticated analytical tools to determine whether a new company will be successful, including measuring the quality of the entrepreneurial team, the innovativeness of the product and the potential growth and size of the market. And even with all of this wisdom and skill, a good venture capitalist is lucky to have one new company that eventually goes public out of every five investments. That's why the venture capitalist is very, very selective about the firms in which he or she will invest money.

It is interesting, and telling, that Apple Computer, one of Silicon Valley's greatest entrepreneurial success stories—the company that is emblematic of the power of entrepreneurs, venture capitalists and bankers working together synergistically—would have fit none of the modern investment templates. In fact, it would have fallen so far off the charts as to be unmeasurable.

The Valley's venture capital superstar of the 1990s, John Doerr of Kleiner Perkins Caufield & Byers, has said that the first thing he looks at in evaluating a new start-up is the quality of the team—in his words, each team member should look at the others and ask, "Are these the people I want to be in trouble with for the next five, ten, fifteen years of my life?" Among other features of a start-up team, Doerr looks for experience, a natural leader who is "ruthlessly, absolutely intellectually honest," a technical genius, an intelligent manufacturing and distribution strategy, a good understanding of the customer and a brand-new market with enormous upside potential.

In April 1976, Apple had none of these things. The company was three guys, none of them with much business—or any managerial—experience. The one founder with a real career, Wayne, gave no indication of any entrepreneurial acumen, nor exhibited any leadership skills. The apparent leader, Jobs, was a strange guy with an even stranger lifestyle who had a habit of walking away from employment to wander off to a commune or Indian ashram. He was reputed to have been involved with another of the partners in past criminal activity. And that confederate, the technical guy, while possibly a genius, wasn't even sure he wanted to be part of the company.

The product itself existed only in prototype, and the team didn't have a clue how to build it in volume. And even if they did, they didn't know how to sell it. And even if they knew how to sell the computer, the cold shoulder it had already earned from the largest single organization of potential stakeholders (Homebrew), suggested that the team completely misunderstood the market's desires.

Yet, four months later, that same, apparently doomed, little company had somehow transformed itself into a hot new firm that now easily met all of those criteria it had so recently failed. And the force behind this miraculous transformation was twenty-one-year-old Steve Jobs. The many later, and more public, achievements aside, it was Jobs's finest hour. In sixteen weeks, ferociously learning the rules of business as he lived them, Jobs leaped from a second-rate, indifferent low-level product manager to the most interesting young businessman of the era. And in the process he turned Apple from an impossibility to the early stages of a social phenomenon.

And most remarkable of all, Jobs did all this without for an instant surrendering his announced attitude that commerce would never tarnish his shining soul. That he was now spending his days down in the engine room of capitalism with all the hustlers, door-to-door salesmen and greedy shopkeepers never once seemed to smudge his persona. And this obvious exercise in public

hypocrisy and (perhaps) personal delusion would prove to be Steve Jobs's—
and Apple Computer's—critical competitive edge.

4.1 HIGH FINANCE

Just how Steve Jobs managed to accomplish so much in such a short time is
worth a closer look.

His first step after getting Woz and Wayne to sign on was to divvy up the
firm. Even the most inexperienced modern high-tech entrepreneur knows
enough to establish a valuation for the firm, as well as the number of outstanding shares, then award some fraction of that to the founders and leave
the rest for outside investors. It is a measure of just how primitive was Jobs's
understanding of business and finance that he simply cut up the pie: 10
percent for Wayne, 45 percent each for himself and Wozniak.

Nevertheless, inexperienced as he was, Jobs wasn't stupid. The comparatively tiny percentage for Wayne was not just a recognition that he was little
more than a contractor brought in to persuade Woz but also a signal that he
was going to be a short-timer. The other two stakes were even more illuminating: Jobs, who had essentially contributed *nothing* to Apple Computer to that
moment, nevertheless had made himself coequal to the man who had done
everything. At first glance this might seem a supreme example of Jobs's characteristic selfishness, but as time would show, it was exactly right. Jobs knew that
his critical contribution to the company lay ahead, that without it Apple
Computer would be worth less than nothing, and he had the ego to cast that
fact in equity right away.

With that little exercise in high finance out of the way, Jobs set to work
figuring out how to build the damn machines without killing the three of
them. Woz's original Apple I (as it was now called) was a beautiful piece of
construction, but it also took sixty hours to get all those tiny solders and wiring
interconnects just right. Obviously, taking that much time on each computer
was unthinkable—to sell the results at anything near a competitive price
would earn them less per hour than they did dressed as the White Rabbit and
the Mad Hatter. The only practical solution was to take the basic wiring
scheme and convert it into a printed circuit board (PCB) onto which the
chips could be quickly attached.

But printed circuit boards weren't cheap. At least not the first one. There
was a sizable up-front cost to lay out the wiring diagram artwork and create
the silk screens needed to produce the finished board. Only in volume did

this up-front cost eventually pay for itself, and more. Thus, in shifting to a PCB, the fledgling company was taking its first real financial risk.

Jobs may still have had as much as $5,000 left from the Atari deal, but he kept that hidden from his partner. He did so despite the fact that Woz, now married, was so broke that his landlord, tired of rubber checks, demanded Woz's rent in cash. Instead, Jobs proposed that the two of them each sell something of value, to raise the estimated $1,300 he figured it would cost to design the board. In the end, Woz sold his HP-65 calculator and Jobs his Volkswagen van.

The layout and silk-screening was done by an old officemate of Jobs's at Atari named Howard Cantin. Cantin did the work for the ever-persuasive Jobs at a discount, for cash. As a result, by not asking for a piece of the company, Cantin joined the legions of Silicon Valleyites who didn't take the piece of a new start-up that would turn out to be worth millions.

With the board in hand by mid-June, Jobs next set out to establish a market. By his estimation, the total potential business for the basic board was about one hundred units, most of them to be sold to Homebrewers. At $50 apiece retail, with a cost to produce of just $25, Jobs figured Apple could clear a neat $2,500.

The three men scrambled to build a handful of Apple I's to meet the expected demand. As all of them had other jobs, this meant evenings and weekends at the expense of just about everything else. Then, at the July Homebrew meeting, days after the nation's Bicentennial, Jobs and Woz took the podium at the Homebrew Computer Club and for the first time demonstrated the next great American invention.

The two young men were as simpatico again at this moment as they had been in their blue box days. They were again filling in each other's blanks; once more combining their personalities into a single character that would in time be the Apple business style. Woz took the technical explanation, as always racing through his talk in a nearly mumbled blur of technical data tinged with an inventor's obvious pride. Jobs, for the first time facing his future market, exhibited the irresistible combination of contempt and enthusiasm that would eventually lead millions to follow.

But not that night. The Homebrewers like and admired Woz—he was, after all, one of them—but almost from his first words it was obvious that the Apple I was a product so eccentric in its processor, its design and its software as to belong in an utterly different reality than the 8080/Engineers Only machines on which they had set their fortunes. This sense of difference was only exacerbated when Steve Jobs stepped up to give Apple's marketing presentation. They had noticed Jobs hanging around Homebrew meetings for a couple of months, and most knew he was chummy with Woz, but except for an odd personality and style, he was no doubt one of the multitude carpetbaggers that had recently popped up to cash in on the home computer fad.

It was circle-the-wagons time at Homebrew. Those members who managed to look up from their soldering irons now and then noticed that their precious little club was suddenly under assault from all sides. The Homebrewers had believed, as the Internet pioneers would two decades later, that they could somehow keep their new world free of ambition, greed, hierarchies and profit. They bought into Felsenstein's image of an engineering utopia.

Now that dream was melting fast. In February, a letter from Albuquerque had arrived at Homebrew signed by Bill Gates, listed as general partner of a new company called Micro-Soft. Entitled "An Open Letter to Hobbyists," Gates's missive blasted Homebrew members for copying Micro-Soft's BASIC software instead of paying for it. Copying had, of course, been a standard procedure in the Brave New Homebrew World, part of the easy ethics of the hobbyist universe. Now Gates, still in his teens, was calling them thieves: "As the majority of hobbyists must be aware, most of you steal your software."

This was not only outrageous but almost incoherent to the Homebrewers. How can you steal in a world where everything is shared? It was true, of course, but that didn't make any difference. Now standing in front of them were two guys presenting a nearly turnkey computer that was obviously designed more for Everyman than to impress one's peers.

There was a smattering of applause, a few questions, and then it was over. Lee Felsenstein would famously conclude, "Wozniak might very well be heading for a fall. I thought if he was going to fail he was going to fail big and I wasn't going to step in the way." And thus, as often happens, the intelligentsia, dreaming of touching the masses, turned away just as the tool for the task floated by.

And, once again, commerce, with the same goal but a different motive, kept a steady eye and put out a hand just in time.

4.2 STOREFRONT

Steve Jobs wasn't the only carpetbagger trolling the July 1976 Homebrew meeting. Another was Paul Terrell.

Terrell was the rare combination, for that era, of a computer hobbyist with the soul of a shopkeeper. He has never gotten due credit as one of the greatest visionaries of the electronics age. While the rest of the hobbyists were wanking around selling computer boards to one another, Terrell had the crazy notion that just maybe you could sell these things to regular people. Consumers! And instead of selling fifty, maybe you could sell a thousand, someday maybe even two thousand. Terrell figured this out long before the people who usually get credit for the idea.

In mid-1976 Terrell knew he was on to something special. He had watched a demonstration of the Altair soon after it was introduced, saw the future in its front panel lights and quickly talked his way into a license as the computer's distributor for Northern California. Demand soon proved so strong that Terrell made the jump from distributor to retailer and set up a store on El Camino Real in Mountain View. He called it the Byte Shop—and he dreamed of running a national chain with hundreds of franchise stores.

The role of El Camino in the story of Silicon Valley has never really been described. The original path of the missionaries establishing missions in the late eighteenth century throughout California, El Camino was, by the early twentieth century, the business spinal cord of the San Francisco Peninsula. Well into the 1970s, nearly everything that happened in the electronics industry in Northern California occurred within shouting distance of El Camino Real. Stanford and Santa Clara universities, the Packard garage, Shockley Semiconductor, the first Fairchild building, all lay within blocks of the King's Highway.

By the 1970s and the rise of the great industrial parks of the modern Silicon Valley, the industrial heart of the community moved elsewhere, away from El Camino, which quickly reverted to its old form of small restaurants, car dealerships, bars and tiny retailers. And yet, El Camino still retained a vital role for Silicon Valley that it retains even to this day: as a test lab for the Valley's newest consumer products. It is no coincidence that Andy Capp's Tavern, where Nolan Bushnell first tested Pong, was located on El Camino in Sunnyvale, just across the street from a Radio Shack store and from Olson's Cherries, where Charlie Olson literally sold the fruits of the old Santa Clara Valley.

Where Terrell chose to site his first Byte Shop in Mountain View was no less symbolic. The shop was tucked between cocktail lounges and auto repair shops, across the street from a Mexican restaurant and a few blocks from Clark's hamburgers, where one could see above the fireplace an already fading photo of Steve Jobs's Monte Loma classmates on the 1964 Clark's team in the Mountain View Americans Little League.

Terrell's Byte Shop was impossibly crude by today's standards. A little store with a few shelves containing motherboards and a few Altairs, electric typewriters for printers, a couple of displays, a tiny rack bearing a handful of mimeographed hobbyist newsletters, it offered less merchandise than just the Mouse & Joystick aisle in a modern CompUSA or Fry's. But in the tiny, incestuous world of computer hobbyists in 1976, it was a revelation—*now you could actually go to a store and buy this stuff!*

Not surprisingly, that night at Homebrew, Terrell listened to the Woz and Jobs presentation more intently than did most of the rest of the audience. Here, after all, was a potentially brand-new product line for which the Byte Shop could be the sole distributor. So, as the rest of the crowd thinned out, Terrell went up and met the two entrepreneurs. Jobs in turn immediately did a second private demonstration of the computer, prefacing it with "Take a look at this. You're going to like what you see."

And Terrell did. That is, he liked the computer. He wasn't so sure about Jobs, who struck him as "a guy who could give you a hard time." Still, the computer had some potential. As he had done with others in the previous few months, Terrell told the two young men to stay in touch, gave them his card and left. Maybe they would call; but more likely, faced with the daunting prospect of building a new company, they wouldn't:

So it was with shock late the next morning that Terrell looked up from his work to see a barefoot Steve Jobs strolling into the store. "I'm keeping in touch," he said with his sardonic half smile. Terrell couldn't help but be impressed. The kid was strange, but he had guts. Terrell ordered fifty Apple I's in different configurations for $489 to $589 each, payment in cash on delivery.

Steve Jobs was more shell-shocked than cocky as he walked back out of the shop. The order represented almost $30,000, more than either he or Woz had ever earned in a year's work. He rushed home to tell Wozniak, who was even more overwhelmed. Later Woz would call it the single most important moment in Apple's history. "Nothing in subsequent years," he would say, "was ever so great or unexpected."

Then reality set in. The pair had assumed that Terrell would be buying the new PC boards. Instead, he had demanded assembled computers. Holy shit! How many hours would that take? And worse, how much would it cost to build them before the company saw a penny back?

The answer to the first question was the usual: they would just work their butts off day and night, and charm anyone else they could into helping. But the second question was more difficult to answer. After all, Woz and Jobs had originally planned to sell 100 boards. Now, Terrell's order had turned half of those boards into computers—and that was within less than twenty-fours after first demonstrating the new machine! If the computer was this hot, why not do them all? Jobs might not yet know much about business, but he had a native sense of both economies of scale and of catching a demand wave. He decided to convert all the boards to computers.

But a quick calculation told him that building those hundred Apple I's, including parts and labor, would run about $25,000. That meant a profit of as much as $5,000, or 20 percent pretax. A few years later Apple would walk away from products with a potential for twice that profit, but for now, to the neophyte businessmen, this seemed a spectacular return on their investment.

The only problem was the investment itself. Where were they going to find that kind of money? It was time for Steven Jobs to quickly teach himself yet one more skill: begging.

It didn't start well. A visit to a bank in Los Altos only got him tossed out, and convinced Jobs to try somewhere else besides banks. Next he tried his old employer, the parts warehouse Haltek. He offered owner Hal Elzig an equity participation in Apple (though it is not sure whose stock was to be given up since there were no outstanding shares) in exchange for parts. Elzig turned him down, saying later, "I didn't have any faith in those kids. They were running around barefoot"—an extraordinary remark from a man who employed some of the strangest technogeeks in the Valley.

Even Al Alcorn, Jobs's recent boss at Atari, refused to sell the pair parts unless they paid cash up front.

It is telling that Steven Jobs could not get credit with either of the two most important employers in his career to date. Perhaps they knew him too well. By the same token, in his visit to the bank he had been so many deviations from the norm that getting a loan beggared the imagination. As always a quick learner, Jobs realized he had to find a middle ground—that of people who knew electronics but didn't know him.

The perfect place for that was distributors. They had all the necessary parts, they were used to flaky customers and they had never heard of Steve Jobs or Apple Computer. Needless to say, it was here that Jobs struck gold. At three different parts houses, he was able to get past the initial resistance executives had to his style and manner by using the force of his personality to drive a deal. It took every trick Jobs knew or could improvise. Certainly he wasn't afraid to wave the Byte Shop contract and suggest the doubting supplier call Paul Terrell as a reference . . . which they did, once even interrupting Terrell in the middle of a conference.

All of this proved to be perfect training for Jobs as he went after the closer: Kierulff Electronics. Kierulff was one of the nation's largest electronic distributors, and its operation in Palo Alto was a major supplier to the companies of Silicon Valley. Like so many others, Bob Newton, Kierulff's division manager for the area, wasn't particularly impressed with Jobs ("He was just an aggressive little kid who didn't present himself very professionally"), yet still sat through a demonstration and made a deal with the young man: he would sell Jobs $20,000 in parts, net thirty days (a phrase Jobs didn't understand) without interest.

Had any other young man with Jobs's mannerisms—and there were more than a few of them in Palo Alto in 1976—walked into Bob Newton's office, would he have given them the same deal? Not likely. Steve Jobs had something. Charisma, perhaps, if that elusive word means a preternatural ability to enlist others in one's own single-mindedness. Throughout Steve Jobs's career there have been thousands who have done extraordinary things for him without ever being able later to explain why.

4.3 PAYING THE PRICE

With the Kierulff agreement, Jobs had it all nearly in place. He had a product, orders, suppliers, capital and a small staff. All that was left was manufacturing. He and Woz had originally thought they could do it the old way: no sleep and continuous work until they were done.

But life was beginning to intrude on the two Steves. In particular, Woz was a married man now, and couldn't just take off for a month with his pal anymore. Besides, the HP job could withstand four nights at Atari, but it would be hard to explain four weeks of sleeping at your desk all day.

They tried anyway, using Woz's apartment as the factory. This was a mistake. Alice Wozniak, understandably, was soon furious. Woz and Jobs would go off to Jobs's parents' house or someplace else and work on the Apple I design. Then in odd hours Woz would come home and build. As Alice later told Mike Moritz: "The Apple was consuming all of his time. I saw very little of him. He'd go off to HP and eat something at McDonald's on the way home. He wouldn't get home usually until after midnight. I was going nuts coming home from work and having things on the dining-room table that I couldn't touch."

Faced with this adamantine attitude, the pair for once retreated—this time to the one place that could never refuse them: Jobs's house. Jobs was back living with Mom and Dad, but there still was a spare room in the back that had once belonged to Steve's now married younger sister, Patty. Jobs and Woz took over the room, soon filling it with boxes of components arriving from the various suppliers. The pair built the computers in that bedroom and in Jobs's, where the endless soldering burned grooves into the top of Steve's desk.

But even with this new setup, the pair was falling behind. The thirty-day mark was approaching fast. The two were building computers so fast they were barely able to do much more testing than simply turning on the finished computer to make sure it didn't explode. And that still wasn't fast enough. It soon dawned on Jobs that what his manufacturing model lacked was sufficient labor: there were simply too many chips to stuff into too many slots on too many printed circuit boards for two assemblers to complete in the requisite time. So the ever-inventive Jobs went out and recruited a third worker: his sister Patty.

Patty was the perfect assembler: pregnant, stuck at home, looking to make a little extra money. Jobs offered his sister a buck a board and she soon was settled on the living-room couch of her apartment, the boards on the coffee table before her, the soaps on TV and a phone cradled on her shoulder talking to friends, jamming the rows of little caterpillar-shaped integrated circuits into the holes on the surface of the green place-mat-sized fiberglass printed circuit boards. She wasn't very good at it, with a tendency to jam the chips down when they didn't fit just right—thus bending their little gold legs and setting the stage for future short circuits—but she was cheap, methodical and, most of all, available.

As the thirty-day mark approached, the two Steves sat down to determine a price for a finished Apple I. A retail price, that is. Jobs was already thinking beyond the Byte Shop contract. Woz, ever the innocent, thought the computer should be priced at a fair markup over manufacturing costs. He suggested $300. Had that price stuck, Apple Computer would have been gone by the end of the summer.

Jobs's appraisal was more insightful. He understood, almost instinctively, though perhaps with a little of his Atari experience, what the rest of the electronics industry was only now beginning to appreciate: the market for new tech toys and tools was different from that for most other manufactured goods. You needed to charge a high initial price for the "early adopters," the hardcore techies who would try anything new, to get the profits you needed to pay back the high up-front development costs. Then, as volume went up you cut the price—almost to match Moore's Law—to capture market share and stay ahead of the growing body of competitors. Then you started the process all over again with the next product.

So Jobs essentially doubled Woz's suggested price, then tacked on top of that an 11 percent dealer markup. The result wasn't that much more than what Terrell had offered, so Jobs figured he was in the ballpark. (In fact, Terrell was selling his own brand of computer, the Byte 8, at a 50 percent margin.) And the number, with its satanic overtones, must have appealed to Jobs's sense of humor: $666.66.

4.4 FIRST TEAM

On the thirtieth day, Steve Jobs walked back into the Byte Shop carrying a stack of finished Apple I motherboards, each in a pizza-sized box. The moment Terrell saw the boxes, he knew something was very wrong.

What he had ordered were finished computers. That meant a keyboard. A display. The BASIC programming language either encoded onto a chip on the board or downloadable from an attached cassette. And, if nothing else, for God sakes, it certainly meant a *box* to put the board in. "There was nothing," Terrell would later say.

Terrell at that moment had every right to say, "Are you nuts? Come back when you've fulfilled your end of the deal." After all, he didn't much trust Jobs in the first place and now it looked in every way like the kid was trying to pull a fast one. But then, as so often occurred inside Steve Jobs's reality distortion field, something happened. Terrell took delivery and, as promised, paid Steve Jobs in cash. Apple Computer was now a profit-making enterprise. The company would thank Terrell a year later by making it the first registered Apple retailer . . . then in 1980, when it stumbled trying to expand its franchise nationally, killed the Byte Shop chain by refusing to continue supplying it.

Jobs now had cash in Apple's account and fifty more computers to build and sell. He was still on a roll. Entrepreneurship is, at its heart, a kind of fraud. You begin with nothing more than an idea, and at every step thereafter you must convince employees, customers, supplier, investors and often even yourself that your enterprise is bigger and more sophisticated than it really is. You sell a fantasy of the future as if it was a reality of the present. To investors, your résumé is deeper than it really is, product development further along, customers hungrily lining up in legions, your finances so strong that you hardly need the added money. More than anything, even than the product itself, start-up entrepreneurship is playacting, constructing an elaborate persona in the belief that someday it will be indistinguishable from the real you.

For Steve Jobs, who had been trying on and tossing off images since childhood, this was the most intriguing and exciting role yet. And he took to it as well as anyone before or since. The summer of 1976 was his debut as an entrepreneur. He had begun the summer almost a stranger to personal computing; he would finish it as the best businessman in the industry.

From the day he walked out the Byte Shop with the money he was amazingly adroit. He rented a mail slot in Palo Alto to give Apple an HP-like address. He signed on to a telephone answering service to create the image of a busy corporate headquarters with a receptionist.

Now he needed talent. If Apple was going to keep growing, he needed to begin dividing up tasks and assigning them to new employees. First, after a perfunctory interview, he hired Woz's old friend Bill Fernandez, who'd not been invited to Corvallis with APD and wasn't excited about the prospect of working in the other old, boring divisions of HP. A veteran of the game already, Fernandez shrewdly asked for a contract. He was Apple's first true employee.

Fernandez proved valuable to Apple in those first few weeks in ways the two founders would never know. Owen Whetzel, now a reporter for the *San Jose Mercury-News*, at the time owned a hobby shop at the nearby little Westmoor Shopping Center. He often noticed the three longhairs in the back of the store buying alligator clips and other items. The parts were in fact for the Apple I. But Whetzel assumed they were buying drug paraphernalia (and perhaps dealing) and was preparing to call the cops when he noticed that one of the trio was Bill Fernandez. Since Bill's dad was not only the local Sunday school teacher but also mayor of Sunnyvale, Whetzel let them be.

Next, Jobs signed up an old Reed friend, Elizabeth Holmes, who'd been working as a gem cutter in San Francisco, to handle Apple's books. Holmes, who was paid four dollars per hour, would drive down to Jobs's house once a week and pick up the invoices and bills. She would describe Jobs at the time as "working very, very hard. He was very directed and not very sentimental." The ashramite had already become a hard-nosed businessman.

Finally, Jobs called his old friend Dan Kottke in Oregon and talked him down to Silicon Valley for the summer to help with assembly. The ever-dutiful Clara Jobs put Kottke up on the couch.

The team was now in place, but it was already beginning to splinter. Entrepreneurial teams are volatile aggregations, with often conflicting goals that aren't exposed until placed under stress. Fulfilling the Byte order was one thing: the money was already guaranteed. But now little Apple was embarking on a speculative venture that, should it fail, might place its founders under financial liability. Woz was willing to take that risk; he still had a job. Jobs was too, because Apple was now his company.

But Ron Wayne, fearful of his share of the company's growing financial liabilities, was unprepared to go any further. Steve Jobs and Apple scared him: "I had already learned what gave me indigestion and I was beginning to feel the months running by. If Apple had failed, I would have had bruises on top of bruises. Steve Jobs was an absolute whirlwind and I had lost the energy you need to ride whirlwinds."

It was the classic lament of the corporate soul trapped in an entrepreneurial start-up. It is still heard a hundred times each day in Silicon

Valley and other tech communities throughout the world. Wayne's remark about bruises was telling: a real entrepreneur is hardly slowed, much less bruised, by failure. Had Apple failed that summer, Jobs would have walked away without looking back and without remorse, leaving the broken hearts and angry debtors to work it out among themselves. And he would have been right to do so.

Wayne, stereotypically, wrote the company a heartfelt and exculpatory resignation letter and left to pursue other opportunities. His 10 percent ownership, even diluted by the time of the Apple initial public offering, would have been worth more than $100 million.

Jobs hardly noticed Wayne's departure. By now he had concluded that he could sell the next fifty machines and had decided to build a hundred more beyond that. It was a crazy notion, based on the fact that the Byte Shop had already bought twenty-five, and no doubt would buy many more—not to mention the huge direct sale market out there that Jobs was convinced was already waiting for the Apple Computer. He was, in fact, wrong on every count. Over at the Byte Shop, Terrell was having trouble selling the machines, even after he got a local cabinetmaker to fit the boards into koa-wood cases. And he didn't need the frustration: the Byte Shops, undergoing a rapid expansion, were suffering severe cash-flow shortages. Being stuck with $10,000 in unsalable inventory didn't help matters.

Terrell even went back to Woz and asked him to design an interface to the Apple I that would allow the user to download Woz's BASIC off a cassette player. Woz didn't have enough time to do it, so he contracted a fellow HP engineer in return for royalties. As it turned out, the finished design sucked— bad news for Apple in the short term, good news in the long term in that it might have had to pay millions in profits in perpetuity for that one-time engineering job. Instead, they paid the engineer off with $1,000—a devastating amount at the time—and Woz, with no experience, managed once again to come up with a brilliant solution on his own: an interface board, the size of a Post-it note, that connected from a cassette player into the Apple I motherboard.

Woz had performed another miracle, but it did little to help Apple's sales. The new generation of customers the Byte Shop was pulling in didn't give a damn about the elegance of Woz's design. Far more important was the fact that the Apple I used a 6502 processor instead of the 8080. And that difference was driven home by the week as new computers appeared on the scene and rumors spread that even big companies were now looking into the business.

The machine that exemplified the new competition was the IMSAI 8080, built by a team sixty miles to the north in Marin County. The IMSAI was almost everything the hobby computers were not. Its founder, Bill Millard, was not a techie, but an entrepreneur and a salesman, a man who had once sold IBM computers. Millard didn't give a damn about the nuances of computer hardware, or the Homebrew Computer Club. He just wanted to sell computers and build a healthy business doing so. And he surrounded himself with bright young men, most of them recruited from scary est graduates that populated Marin in that era. They all nodded appreciatively whenever Millard spoke his mantra: "Make a Miracle."

Or steal one. Millard's first idea was to buy MITS, but when Roberts refused, Millard simply hired a computer guru named Bill Killian, ordered some Altairs from Paul Terrell and had Killian reverse-engineer them and come up with an improved copy. That was the IMSAI 8080. It had all the strengths of the Altair—the 8080 chip, BASIC, all of the growing library of Altair software—and fixed some of the glaring weaknesses of the Altair, like a lousy power supply.

The result was a real computer, in a case, that the thousands of electronic engineers and mainframe computer programmers who weren't hobbyists could finally take home and crank up. Not surprisingly, IMSAI became the first personal computer company to sell (with a little book cooking) more than $1 million PCs in a single month.

This was what Apple Computer, with its four guys all but living with the founder's mom and dad in a suburban tract home, were up against. And all of the company's feeble promotional efforts—giving away the interface card and a BASIC cassette, crude ads that read "Byte into an Apple" and "A Little Cassette Board That Works" or a demonstration program on the display Apple I's that printed out on the screen THIS IS AN APPLE COMPUTER—did next to nothing to help. The Apple I's sat on the shelf while the IMSAIs flew out the door.

And the salespeople at the Byte Shops, many of whom thought Jobs was a jerk, didn't go out of their way to help. They watched as Jobs and Kottke, riding the bus up and down the Peninsula, would storm into their stores, making demands and pestering them with endless questions. To the salespeople, these two were a pain in the ass compared to the well-dressed, professional folks from IMSAI, who talked and acted like winners, rather than escapees from a Grateful Dead concert.

Computer consultant Darrell Chambers was working at the time as a clerk at the second Byte Shop, this one in San Jose. "Jobs and this other guy rode up on bikes. I remember the long hair. They were carrying this case made out of cardboard and foam. And they took out what we now call the Apple I and started showing it off to me. It was like 'Hey, this is really cool. Check it out.'

They were just kids like I was, hackers really, and they were absolutely convinced that people would just want to get into their computer.

"But all I saw was just a motherboard. There was nothing to it. Worse, it had a 6502 processor, a toy, when everybody else was using the Motorola 6800 or the Intel 8080, so it wasn't even compatible with what little software there was on the market.

"At the time, all the computers we were selling—the IMSAI, Altair, SWTP (which we called Southwest Toilet Paper)—at least came in a box. Most of them had an S100 interface bus, so they could also be expanded. The Apple didn't have anything going for it except, if I remember, a TV interface.

"So I told them to come back when they'd put the motherboard in a case, changed the processor and added a keyboard. They said, 'Thank you very much,' and left. I remember thinking as they walked away: Apple. What a strange name for a computer. All the other companies had such professional-sounding names. It stuck with me."

And so it went at one shop after the next. Steve Jobs began to panic. When things had been going well, the notion of being a businessman—a new kind of honorable, enlightened Buddhist businessman—had appealed to Jobs. But now after just three months, as the company seemed to be sliding toward oblivion, Jobs began to seriously doubt himself.

With the help of his old girlfriend, Jobs consulted a Zen monk, Kobin Chino, who lived on a ranch in the hills above Jobs's house, for advice. Wouldn't it be better, Jobs asked, if he were to drop this capitalist deceit and head for a monastery in Japan? The monk laughed and told Jobs that he would not find much difference between the two . . . a statement that showed the monk had incredible insight into either the nature of entrepreneurship or the personality of Steven Jobs. Afterward Jobs confided to his old girlfriend that he was afraid that Apple would turn him into a monster.

Jobs even flipped out with his most important client. As Terrell recounted to Moritz: "[Jobs] came flying into the Byte Shop, buzzing at a hundred miles per hour. 'It's the goddamn logo. People think it's horseshit. We've got to change the name. Nobody is going to take it seriously.' " Terrell wisely convinced the frantic young man not to abandon what would be the most famous logo on earth.

Trouble finds trouble in Silicon Valley. When you are on top, everything seems to break your way, but when you slip, the bad news piles on. As if the current marketing problems weren't enough, the too clever price tag began to create its own problems. First a group of Sikhs complained about the demonic nature of the $666.66. Then the hottest movie of the summer proved to be *The Omen*, with its explicit references to the Number of the Beast. Certain Christian Fundamentalist groups, already having convinced themselves that IBM bar code readers were part of a satanic conspiracy to read hidden 666s tattooed on American babies, went out in search of other electronic products bearing strings of sixes. Needless to say, soon the telephones at the answering service and the Jobs house were lit up with rabid callers.

Yet, even as he panicked under this pressure, Jobs once more showed a unique talent that set him in the company of the best executives. As much as he panicked to those outside Apple, inside the company he maintained his composure. When he expressed doubt, it was only about his own role, and then to the introverted and self-contained Fernandez during long walks away from the house. With the troops, he never wavered in his enthusiasm for the project or his apparent optimism that it would succeed. It was a fraud, but an *appropriate* fraud, of the type any successful leader must develop in tough times.

So it was that even as he was expressing doubt about the whole enterprise to others, inside Apple he was not only keeping production moving but even working to expand it. Toward that end, he even approached Allen Baum. Woz had long borrowed a few dollars here and there from Baum whenever he'd found himself in a cash crunch. Now Jobs, with Woz in tow, went to see Baum and his father, Elmer Baum, to ask for $5,000. It was one of those shameless experiences that test every new entrepreneur.

Once again with Steve Jobs, father and son agreed to make the loan over their own personal doubts about the borrower. Allen Baum said later, "I had no doubt it would be repaid. Steve Jobs had this silver tongue that could talk anyone into anything." Including Allen Baum. His father was even more skeptical and was in a worse position to invest. But he too went along, saying afterward, "I did it because he was Allen's friend. I was in pretty bad shape financially but Steve gave me a pitch. If I hadn't known him, I would have thought he was real good."

With the Baum money, Jobs had bought the survival of his little company into autumn. Now he turned, as always, to his ace in the hole: the Woz.

4.5 LOCAL COLOR

A visitor to the Jobs house at the end of the summer of 1976 would have been amazed at its transformation. What had been a sleepy suburban house, with the kids gone and an aging middle-aged couple heading toward retirement, was now a hive of business activity. Apple had become too much for the bedrooms of the Jobs house, so it moved to the garage.

Once again, Steve's parents were more than willing to sacrifice for their boy. Paul Jobs surrendered not only the garage but temporarily his car restoration—he was working on a Nash Metropolitan at the time, creating a nice symmetry between one of the least successful consumer designs and one of the most. Jobs *père* even set up the garage for ersatz clean-room production, lining the walls with plasterboard, installing lights and adding an extra telephone line.

Paul Jobs also built for his son a "burn-in box," a wooden case about the size of a coffin, and fitted it with heat lamps. In that box, a dozen boards could be placed at one time and heated for several days to simulate months of real-world use. It was a sophisticated idea in a fairly crude form; nevertheless, about this time a few miles away in Santa Clara, National Semiconductor Corp., which owned millions of dollars of burn-in equipment, was secretly *not* testing millions of chips destined for spacecraft and missile guidance systems. Thus, Apple was doing a better job at product testing than one of the Valley's biggest firms.

Still recovering from gallbladder surgery, having to pick her way around parts and worktables just to get to the washing machine, Clara Jobs nevertheless served as a receptionist for the company, answering phone calls and serving coffee to customers and suppliers. She even calmed a distressed Alice Wozniak whenever she called in search of her missing husband.

For a young man so dismissive of traditional values, and so alienated from his adoptive milieu, Steve Jobs enjoyed an incredibly supportive family. And it was from this secure base that he could launch his assaults on the marketplace. Meanwhile, back in the garage, he kept up morale and, most important, kept Wozniak focused upon improving the Apple I.

Like some geniuses (though probably not as many as the cliché would suggest), Woz had little personal ego. But he had infinite, easily bruised supplies of professional pride. That night when he showed off the Apple I schematics at Homebrew had been one of the defining moments of his life. Now the attention had turned elsewhere. Sure, the Homebrewers admired Woz's talent . . . but what had he done lately? And worse, to Woz, were the whispers that, despite all his cleverness, Woz had blown the Apple I by going with the second-rate 6502, a microprocessor deemed fit only for toys.

By midsummer the disdain—and, worse, the indifference—was beginning to get to Woz. Just as Jobs was facing humiliation every time he walked into a Byte Shop, so too did Woz feel increasingly out of the conversation at Homebrew. And each month the parade moved further and further away. The Altair was now coming up on its first anniversary. The IMSAI 8080 was now the darling of gearheads everywhere. The company was even giving away a book about microcomputers, written by a Brit named Adam Osborne, with every computer it sold. A new company, Cromemco, was designing boards to fit into the Altair and enhanced that computer's performance. Even on the other side of little Los Altos from Jobs's house a company called Microcomputer Associates had announced a kit called Jolt that, like the Apple I, featured a 6502 processor. And adding insult to injury, MITS had added to the Altair line a new low-budget hobby computer kit called the KIM-1—also using the 6502.

That was just what was already on the market, jostling the Apple I for retail shelf space. MITS was also working on a new computer featuring the Motorola 6800 chip. So was Southwest Technical Products (SWTP). The big electronic mail-order houses, like Heath and Ohio Scientific, were either offering their own kits or preparing to do so. And coming up on the horizon was yet another new firm, Processor Technology, that threatened to have the best computer yet.

Processor Technology had been started in a Berkeley garage in 1975 by Bob Marsh, a founding Homebrewer, with more than a little help from Lee Felsenstein, the spiritual leader of Homebrew and the man who had publicly doubted Woz's design. Pro Tech had begun selling replacement boards for the unreliable early Altairs, but by the summer of 1976 it had grown into a full-blown computer company. In the first year of its existence, Pro Tech had also matured into a professional outfit, with a superb product vision: a complete, stand-alone personal computer that could be purchased by anyone. And by the end of the summer that vision was to be embodied in the Sol Terminal Computer, named after Les Solomon, the author of that seminal *Popular Electronics* article that had set the whole revolution in motion.

All this frenzy of activity only made Woz more anxious to plant his own flag once again out ahead of the pack. And he did so in the usual manner: he told his fellow Homebrewers he was going to attempt the impossible, then he went out and did it.

This time it was a color display. Color was the latest fantasy of the home computer makers and the hobbyists who bought their products. In this era before word processing, spreadsheets and the decade-long dominance of symbolic displays, it was assumed that the next big use of PCs beyond running numeric programs was graphics. But black-and-white doilies on the screen were still pretty dull. But color! Color was the Grail. Color would put home computers right up there with the minicomputers coming out of DEC and

Data General. Cromemco had shown off at Homebrew a new computer prototype, called the Dazzler, that sprayed color across its display. Woz had been transfixed at the sight.

The only problem was that most designers figured that to put color on a home computer would require another board, equal in size to the motherboard, containing forty or more chips. That would at least double the price of the computer, not to mention create all sorts of new problems with reliability, power consumption, cooling, etc.

It was the perfect challenge for Woz. Nobody alive could look at a chip design and simplify it by a factor of two or five or ten the way Woz could. And now, having announced his intentions, he set out to do it. And, being Woz, he also had his own silly, eccentric reason for doing the impossible: he wanted to play the game he'd devised for Atari, Breakout, on his own computer and not just on an arcade player.

Building a low-cost, small-chip-set, color computer was a bigger challenge than Wozniak assumed when he started. It would turn out to be not just a paring down of chips for ever-greater efficiency, but a revolutionary rethinking of the very nature of the computer itself.

In studying his own design, Woz well understood that the Apple I, like every other home computer of the era, had three areas of memory. One, the external tape drive, was out of bounds for anything but large-scale downloading and storage because it was so slow. That left two others with which to experiment. One of these memories, the cache, composed in the Apple I of chips capable of storing 8,000 bits, served only the main processor. The other memory, composed of simple shift registers designed to quickly pass on their data, served only the display. Woz decided that if there was some way to get around the design constraints of the registers and the processor's memory, he would not only save a considerable number of chips but also obtain the power he needed to drive a color display.

To make such a breakthrough, Woz thought back to an article in the Homebrew newsletter a year before. That article had asked: given the extraordinary speed of the microprocessor, and the fact that it didn't use its own memory cache for sometimes thousands of computation cycles, couldn't there be a way to tap into that memory for other tasks?

The idea was an outgrowth of what was being called, in the world of big-iron computers, "virtual" computing—the first application of that now ubiquitous term. Until the late 1960s, computers had been largely "batch-oriented"—that is, you dumped a whole bunch of raw data in and walked away for a few hours while the computer crunched it and then spit out the processed results. "On-line" computing replaced much of this with a continuous interaction between user, typically at a terminal, and the computer. On-line computing inevitably led to "distributed computing," in which multiple users, sitting at terminals in diverse locations, all talked to the computer at the same time. And this was possible only because the newest computers were designed to take advantage of the extraordinary speeds of the central processor in dealing with a single user *in between* its interactions with scores of others. The result, when everything worked, was that each user had the sensation of having the computer all to himself.

Not surprisingly, in the world of personal computers, where every inch of real estate on the motherboard was literally worth its weight in gold, virtual computing had considerable appeal. But no one yet had figured out how to do it.

Woz did it, and he did so by a twist of perspective and a clever piece of observation. Instead of another operator tapping into the microprocessor between beats, Woz instead made the display itself the user. The clever observation was in noticing that in operation a color television's three-gun raster scan works like a typewriter—sweeping out one line after another from left to right, then hopping back to start the next line. The twist was that Woz made *the display control the computer.* In particular, every time the raster swept across the screen, it had control over the main processor's memory. But the moment it stopped for its equivalent of a carriage return, the microprocessor regained control, doing all of its work literally in the blink of an eye before the next line was displayed. In fact, Woz even had to slow the microprocessor down a little to make the combination work.

It was a brilliant piece of mental gymnastics, as good as anything Woz did before or since. Today, when nine-year-olds can talk about 300 MHz PCs (machines capable of 300 million operations per second) as if they are discussing baseball cards, visualizing such a stunt is not too much of a stretch. But in 1976, even though personal computers were a thousand times less powerful than today, it was an amazing cognitive leap.

But it was also more than that, because in turning the process inside out and integrating the display driver into the microprocessor, Woz made possible the mass-market personal computer. Now you could put almost every part of the personal computer on a single board with a minimum number of chips. And that meant low power consumption, high speed, a small box and a low price. And on top of that, you could work in color.

Woz understood all of this. What he didn't appreciate—nor did anyone else—at the time was that in developing this new design he had also carved out a strong and defensible competitive niche for the entire personal computer industry. From this moment on, PCs would be a distinct business with a trajectory all its own.

4.6 RISK AVERSION

Looking back from the perspective of a quarter century, it is hard, at first glance, to understand why no established companies roared into PCs and, with mass marketing, superior manufacturing and economies of scale, stole the business away from all these eccentric tyros.

They easily could have. But the story of the technology revolution (in fact, of all industrial revolutions) is that of misidentification, misunderstanding and misdirection.

Take Intel, for example. Owning the 8080, as well as being the world's leader in MOS memory chips, Intel could easily have added some circuitry and a box and owned the personal computing industry in a matter of months. In fact, Intel already had a PC, perhaps the very first one, in the form of an in-circuit emulator (a form of test equipment) for its chips. But Intel was still struggling to get the microprocessor established and was riven by an internal debate over whether to turn the company completely to microprocessors or abandon them and get back to memory. Moreover, it was still trying to get its new generation of microprocessor, the 8086, developed, and a whole host of competitors—including Zilog, Fairchild, National Semiconductor, Motorola and Texas Instruments—were challenging it for the business. Finally, Intel had just lost tens of millions in a failed attempt at digital watches so wrenching that for the next twenty years chairman Gordon Moore would wear an Intel/Microma watch to remind him to stay out of consumer products.

The same story was largely true for the other big chip companies. Those that had microprocessors, such as TI, HP, National Semiconductor and Motorola, were either so burned by or still so enmeshed in calculators, digital watches, video games or CB radio that they had no inclination to jump into yet another. Those that didn't build microprocessors weren't in computation, so they weren't even thinking about microcomputers.

Why weren't the little personal computers crushed from above by the big established computer companies? After all, certainly *they* could see the potential of microcomputers.

And they did. Sort of. But that didn't mean those companies did anything about it. At least not for a while. A mistake of hindsight is to assume that once microcomputers appeared on the scene it was self-evident that this would be a huge market. But nothing was further from the truth. The very first PCs, such as the Altair, required a hundred hours of soldering, chip stuffing, wiring and testing, just to get a box that really didn't do anything. You could program it to do some mathematics—but after a couple of hundred hours more work you basically ended up with a very, very large calculator. You could use it to do typewriting, but that was incredibly difficult because there were no word-processing programs yet. In fact, when you got right down to it, the first personal computers were essentially a fairly meaningless way for gearheads to show off their technical prowess. That's why so many Silicon Valley professionals walked into the Byte Shop, then walked right out again, unimpressed.

In 1976, the big computer companies were enjoying one of the great business booms tech had ever known. IBM, DEC, Data General, Wang, HP, Burroughs, Univac, Control Data—all were experiencing a period of both prosperity and great innovation. And much of this excitement was occurring at the minicomputer level. Small, powerful machines were opening brand-new markets in small businesses, academic institutions and the divisions of large companies.

Success is a great suppressor of risk. The computer companies were slamming away at their own established markets, using their exploding profits in new product development to try to race ahead and gain an edge on their competitors. Just about the last thing they needed was to launch off into a brand-new, unproven business. Better to spend the money on distribution channel development, more salespeople and software design and grow the current customer base rather than screw around with an unknown, and unproven, new one.

There was a cultural reason as well. Ever since ENIAC and the other pioneering mainframe computers of the late 1940s, computation had been the province of Computer Pharisees. You see it in the old photographs: giant computers, which were fragile and often required sophisticated air conditioning and water cooling, operated within special facilities, managed by a priesthood of electrical engineers, computer scientists and professional programmers, typically wearing lab coats.

By the 1960s, this postwar computing in universities, government agencies and military centers had largely given way to the payroll and management information computing of large corporations. The client changed, but not the culture. Amost every great company had its own data processing center, often in a modernist glass box and filled with the next generation of information mullahs, now in suits and skinny ties. The very nature of batch computing reinforced the exclusiveness of this caste. You sent in your reports or filled out punched cards (in No. 2 pencil only) and the wizards in DP performed their magic rites and, miraculously, back came your paycheck or printout. Nobody knew exactly what these people did, but it was obviously pretty damned important.

The appearance of both real-time processing and the minicomputer, which allowed that processing to be distributed, only slightly changed the status quo. Now there was not just one big computer center but also smaller ones located in each company division or factory—though they too were operated by the equivalent of parish priests. Despite the fact that some allowances were now made for the corporate hoi polloi—for example, an office might have a "dumb" terminal to send information directly to the mini—that access was carefully circumscribed, and unrestricted electronic contact with the big mainframe was never allowed to the nonclergy.

By 1976, the situation had become rather tense. The minicomputer companies, in their ferocious battle for the new market base, had found that there was a tremendous demand in the corporate world for distributed information systems that actually let different corporate operating units perform their own processing and run their own programs. In response, HP, DEC, Data General and the rest began to build new minicomputers that were smaller, cheaper and more accessible to everyday users. Looking ahead, these manufacturers could visualize a world (which they were happy to describe to customers) in which there might be a computer in every company building, perhaps on every floor, and each sprouting a profusion of terminals . . . perhaps someday so many that one could put a terminal on every desk!

The minicomputer people were so sold on the concept they even gave it a religious vision: the paperless office. And that extraordinarily seductive phantasm haunts the computer industry to this day.

It was all so perfect, so progressive, so democratic. But there was only one problem. It threatened the power, prestige and even the employment of the Data Templars. And since they were the folks who typically approved all computer purchases in the corporation, the DP directors typically did their best to veto or at least impede the adoption of distributed processing systems. The heresy had to be stopped at all costs.

The result was something of a war at many companies, with marketing and manufacturing arrayed for battle against data processing and accounting, with senior management caught in between. Luckily for most of these corporations, executive row despised the computer praetorians as much as every-body else and were happy to quash their growing power.

By the time Woz and Jobs were teaming up for the third time and starting Apple, this internecine war for control of corporate information was still far from over. But the end was in sight. The big-iron companies like Burroughs and Univac were essentially doomed, and the minicomputer firms on the road to triumph. Among the mainframers, only IBM, the biggest tech company of them all, was clever (and rich) enough to play both sides. Having introduced its own minicomputer line, while dissembling that it wasn't *really* in the minicomputer business, Big Blue managed to quickly become the leading supplier to this new world of data processing.

The new computing paradigm had won, the lesser nobles of minicomputing had brought King Mainframe to bay. But the minicomputer companies were exhausted. They had fought this battle during an economic depression, they had invested billions in product development and gained thousands of customers with great expectations who would need to be serviced. It was time now to focus on upgrading existing product designs, developing a library of software applications, building a service and support structure and starting to turn those investments into profits.

That was one reason why HP passed on Woz's prototype, a scenario re-peated at other computer companies throughout the world. There would be enough time after the mop-up of minicomputing to worry about the next field of battle, personal computing by end users, if such a market even existed. And, when the time came, how hard would it be? Moore's Law already suggested that within eight or ten years it would be possible to put minicom-puting power in a desktop box. Then it would be just a matter of scaling down the rest of the components. For now . . . well, you could tell it was too early just by looking at those half-baked, underpowered computers like IMSAI and Altair being sold to the (literally in Jobs's case) Great Unwashed.

It was here, on this critical question of scalability, that Stephen Wozniak, quietly and unseen, shut the door on the computer industry. With his design breakthrough of putting multiple functions on a single processor, he took the rule book away from its biggest players. From this point on, the game would be not, as the computer companies wanted it, how to dumb down big com-puters for the personal market, but instead how to add more power and performance to small, inexpensive PCs without changing their size or price.

It was not a game the big boys were philosophically or structurally pre-pared to play. They would eventually learn—but until they did, the minicom-puter companies, to their dismay, would find themselves at the losing end of a war almost identical to the one they waged and won against mainframes. The lesser nobles had defeated the King only to see the serfs revolt.

Though no one knew it, Woz had bought his partners at Apple, his buddies at Homebrew and peers like Bill Gates in Albuquerque, five years of freedom in which to live out their entrepreneurial fantasies. They would have to live them very fast. The few that did survived.

4.7 PRO TECH IN CHECK

By the end of the summer of 1976, as the Carter and Ford presidential campaigns kicked into high gear, and Americans sat in front of the television on hot August afternoons to watch Edwin Moses, Sugar Ray Leonard and Bruce Jenner win gold at the Montreal Olympics, Stephen Wozniak, working at home and in Steve Jobs's garage, was putting the final touches on his improved Apple I.

He was running out of time. On Labor Day weekend in an aging hotel in what was then the dying resort town of Atlantic City, there was to be a personal computer show, an imitation of the big computer shows like Wescon, and the prototype of what would become a multibillion-dollar personal computer industry show drawing hundreds of thousands of attendees to events like Comdex.

Needless to say, this show would be a lot more modest: two dozen exhibitors and a couple of hundred gearheads walking among the card tables looking for a good buy on memory boards. Nevertheless, it was the biggest thing the personal computer industry had yet seen, and everybody of importance was going to be there. Rumor was that Processor Technology was going to introduce the Sol at the show. If the Sol was everything it was reputed to be, it had a good chance of stealing away the entire industry. That's why Jobs not only had to be there but needed to be able to show Woz's new design.

Woz was still tweaking the prototype minutes before they left for the airport. But it was done. Armed with the computer, a suitcase full of Apple I boards and a sheaf of flyers, the two took off on the flight to Philadelphia, excited but filled with apprehension.

As has happened a thousand times since, the flight to the show was filled with competitors. And, as always, each of these little teams was smug in the knowledge that it had the edge over all the others—and at the same time nervously eavesdropping on those others to make sure it was true.

But one group on this flight was more smug than the rest. This was the team from Processor Technology. In fact, they were downright arrogant about it. Pro Tech was the worst nightmare of all the garage teams. First, with Lee Felsenstein on board, it had the pedigree. Next, it was like a real company: it had salespeople, and executives who wore suits and ties. But most of all, it had the Sol, and the Sol was beautiful. It had a keyboard, and motherboard and tape drive and display like (almost) everybody else, but *it had them all together in a sleek, magnificent sheet-metal case.* It not only ran like a computer but it even *looked* like one . . . well, at least like a real computer terminal. It certainly made all the other computers look like, well, what they really were: kluges soldered together by amateurs with no understanding of manufacturing, marketing or product design.

You had only to look at the slick Pro Tech boys and their even slicker computer and see the future of personal computing. This was a computer a corporate suit would be proud to walk into a Byte Shop and buy and not feel he was skulking into a porn shop to buy illicit goods (fittingly, the original Byte Shop building is now home to just such a business). You could put the Sol on your desk at the office and it would be all but indistinguishable from the Honeybee and HP terminals down the hall. The Pro Tech team had a winner and everybody on the plane knew it.

The absolute antithesis of that team sat, by coincidence, in the row of seats just in front of them. Scruffy and unprofessional, Jobs and Woz looked already like the ghost of Homebrew past. For Lee Felsenstein, sitting right behind the two, it was vindication. After all, he had dismissed the Apple I as a dead end. Now, as he peeked over Woz's seat, he could see the two young men poring over a crude mock-up mounted in an equally crude case typically used by amateur engineers. He would later say, "It was thoroughly unimpressive. These two guys just had a cigar box. What the hell did they know?"

He had in fact seen the future. And the end of his own company.

In Atlantic City, Woz and Jobs were joined by Dan Kottke, who'd since his couch days earlier in the summer had moved to New York City. They set up a card table and sold the older Apple boards and parts throughout the day to sparse crowds of young East Coast technophiles. At night they played with the new machine on the color TV screen in their room, dazzling select visitors with rainbows of arching color. Those who saw the demonstration, and then the little box it emanated from, came away convinced they'd seen the real winner at the show.

The pair came home from Atlantic City with a few dollars in their pockets, some promises for orders and, most of all, a sense that they could take this market within the year. They also needed some help. This time from grownups.

4.8 MIXED SIGNALS

For all the successes in the final weeks, the summer of 1976 had not been a happy one for Jobs and Woz.

Entrepreneurial start-ups are like submarines. Detached from the outside world, under continuous pressure and facing the perpetual risk of obliteration, start-up teams very quickly begin to crack. Resentments form, personalities clash, the idiosyncrasies of others become unbearable. The story of Silicon Valley is filled with broken friendships, fistfights in hallways and nervous breakdowns among the team members of the thousands of start-ups that built that community. Feuds still fester between Valley pioneers decades after the original blowup in some tiny storefront. And it is a standard rule that by the time a tech company becomes successful it will have lost at least one of its founders.

Apple had already lost that co-founder in Ron Wayne. But during the ramp-up to Atlantic City, the two principals themselves came shockingly close to a breakup. And the reason was, of all things, Woz's pride.

Those merely acquainted with Wozniak during that era would have been surprised to learn this slovenly figure was deeply proud. But those who spent time with him at Homebrew knew better. What else could have compelled him to risk marriage, career and health over the last year devising one technological miracle after another? Woz wanted his peers to recognize him as the best among them; later he would expect the same from history.

But now, for the first time, Steve Jobs was beginning to intrude on Woz's private obsession. It was Jobs who was out there representing the product, who was becoming synonymous with Apple I—and for all Woz knew (and he wasn't far from the mark), getting the credit for its invention. Even worse, as the summer progressed Jobs was even beginning to intrude upon Woz's designs. They had a blowup over how many slots to put into the back of the color computer. Woz, dreaming of all that he wanted the computer to do, wanted eight slots. Jobs, thinking about price and about market targeting, wanted only two.

After Atlantic City, the situation only got worse. Woz, having stared into the eye of the Sol, was ready to give up. The Processor Technology guys obviously knew what they were doing. They weren't amateurs like Steve Jobs. Woz began to harbor notions of jumping ship. In particular, he seriously considered selling the color computer to Pro Tech. *They* would know what to do with it. And Woz also knew he was within his rights to make such a sale: the original Apple agreement allowed him to retain all rights to his invention.

Wozniak's family backed him in the mutiny. His wife wanted him home.

And his parents and siblings at last voiced the concerns they'd always had about Steve's questionable choice of best friend. His sister Leslie would later say that Jobs had always been described as "this schlunky-looking guy with bare feet and dirty hair." Woz's parents had long wanted him to abandon this distracting pipe dream and get back to settling down in his marriage and career. So, as work continued at the Jobs house, at the Wozniak house and apartment the prayers were for the worst.

If Woz had caved at the sight of the Sol, Jobs was thrilled. He'd gone against the best the industry had and, technologically at least, defeated it. The Sol didn't frighten him now at all; rather, he saw a wealth of good ideas to steal. Jobs knew he could build a better Sol, but Pro Tech couldn't build a better Apple. Not as long as he had Woz.

Sure, Woz balked when Jobs pressed him, but hell, Woz always got upset when he actually had to deal with the real world. Left to his own devices, Woz would have turned the Apple I into yet another Homebrew Wonder of interest to nine guys with empty wallets. Jobs knew it was he, and he alone, who could keep Woz aimed in the right direction. And if Woz didn't understand that, too bad. He would someday. In the meantime, Jobs could handle him—or so he thought.

There were other, more important things to worry about. One was to get the Apple computer into some sort of Sol-like box. And to do that required more than just bending sheet metal; it involved completely rethinking the problem of power supply and cooling. Jobs had noticed that many of the new enclosed designs were noisy as hell thanks to cheap built-in cooling fans. The Zen meditator appreciated the value of silence.

There was no more complete silence in a computer than to have no fan at all. But getting rid of the fan meant you needed a great power supply, a transformer so small and so well designed that it could run nearly forever without external cooling while still not turning red-hot and melting the case and motherboard.

While the public has always understandably focused upon the digital processing side of electronics, within the profession success or failure has often been decided by the quality of the supporting analog circuitry. After all, as clever as the Cream Soda Computer had been, it had still been burned up by a bad power supply. Analog circuitry, especially in the form of linear chips like capacitors and resistors, had long been the most invisible, yet most rarefied, of all the semiconductor design professions.

Whereas microprocessors were designed by committees, analog circuits were typically created by lone geniuses, often eccentric wild men, who were living legends in the industry. The most famous of these, Bob Widlar, became renowned at Fairchild and National Semiconductor for picking drunken fights at industry conferences, chopping down company trees when frustrated and, once, bringing a sheep to National Semi in the trunk of his Mercedes to chew the grass on an unmown lawn. Yet Widlar, who spent the last twenty years of his life in Mexico like a character in a Malcolm Lowry novel, still regularly would fly up to Santa Clara to deliver some splendid new design to National Semi or, later, Linear Technologies.

Woz had already proven he was no analog guy, so Jobs set out to find someone else to do the job. With almost no Valley contacts, he was reduced to going back to Atari, where he was not exactly the most popular guy around. Yet, in typical Jobs fashion, he managed to get in with Al Alcorn and talk his old boss into recommending an Atari employee to work as a consultant. Even more amazing, Alcorn recommended the best he had, Rod Holt.

Even in the cranky world of analog design, Holt was one of a kind. A middle-aged chain smoker, he had a raw voice and a drawn face that looked as if he'd slept in it. He had been variously a radical activist, treasurer of the National Coalition Against the War in Vietnam, the author of a book on Marxism, a leader of the Revolutionary Socialist Party, a manufacturer of stereo systems and a builder of racing motorcycles. He talked endlessly about everything, much of it cast in terms of the struggle of the proletariat. And like most revolutionaries, he knew the value of the dollar. When he told Jobs his high consulting rate, Jobs merely replied, "No problem."

"He just conned me into working," Holt said later.

Holt's work would prove critical in the years ahead. For now, he unwittingly played an equally important role: He was a grown-up. A strange, rather unlikely one perhaps, but a grown-up nevertheless. Jobs had seen what grownups could do, first at Atari in the form of Al Alcorn, then at Sol, and now Holt. They might not have the inspired creativity or boundless energy of the young people with whom Jobs had surrounded himself until now, but they countered that with discipline, gravity and, most of all, experience. And Steve Jobs needed all the experience he could get. He was headed into a dangerous and mysterious country now, of large-scale manufacturing, corporate finance, law and marketing, and he knew that without experienced guides he'd never survive.

Jobs also needed grown-ups in Apple for another reason: to help control the children, whose numbers were growing by the day. At Homebrew, Woz had already gained two teenaged acolytes, Randy Wigginton and Chris Espinosa. One was a former juvenile delinquent, the other a budding political activist; both were now born-again computerphiles. They followed Woz everywhere, acting as his gofer, his cheering section and his protégés.

And their Pied Piper was himself becoming a handful. Woz's first attempted mutiny may have been quelled, but worse was to come—and it would come at a time when Jobs, over his head in business negotiations, was most vulnerable.

4.9 THE SCARIEST MAN ALIVE

If the big computer and semiconductor companies were too distracted to chase the personal computer market, there was still one mysterious and sinister company willing to take a shot: Commodore. And it was just down the road in Santa Clara.

Well, sort of. It was hard to know exactly where Commodore was. The company was registered in the Bahamas, incorporated in Canada, listed its headquarters as Santa Clara, but at times appeared to be run out of Norristown, Pennsylvania. And the company's pedigree was equally suspicious. Ten years before, its chairman, Powell Morgan, had died suspiciously as he was about to be investigated for defrauding investors of millions of dollars through an investment firm called Atlantic Acceptance. It was one of the biggest financial scandals in Canada to that time and the resulting Ontario Supreme Court report implicated Commodore.

A few years later, Commodore sprang up in Silicon Valley, a major player in adding machines, then calculators, backed with money from its new chairman, financier Irving Gould. But it was the company's CEO who drew the most attention. His name was Jack Tramiel, a bald, tough Holocaust survivor who was already becoming legendary for his aphorisms ("Business is war"), his risk taking and his willingness to kill off suppliers by holding back payment for his own cash-flow needs. Tramiel was something of a terrifying figure, a role he relished. In a room of intellectuals he would wait until the right moment to say, "Yes, I went to university too. I went to the University of *Auschwitz!*"

Needless to say, Tramiel played for keeps, and he had no patience with human shortcomings or delays, which made working for Commodore a pretty horrible experience. But Tramiel was a winner. He had come late to calculators, but with a line of brilliantly conceived, shoddily built, low-cost models, he carved out a sizable market share. Then the market crunch came in 1974 and he was forced to write off a worthless inventory of chips. Tramiel swore he'd never be put in such a position again, and two years later he went out and bought a failing semiconductor company at a budget price.

The firm he bought just happened to be MOS Technologies, the makers of the 6502. And with MOS came Chuck Peddle, the 6502's creator and the man who had sold one of those chips to Woz nearly a year before and set Apple in motion. Tramiel was never afraid of a new business opportunity, and Peddle gave him one: home computers. Even better, suggested Peddle, go out and find the best new start-up company building a 6502-based computer and buy it while it's still cheap. With a good design already established and Commodore's financial strength we can own the market before any other real potential competitor even notices it.

Peddle knew what company he wanted too. He'd been to the conferences and shows and seen in what kind of awe the industry held Steve Wozniak's design. Best of all, the outfit appeared to be little more than two guys in a garage with absolutely no business experience. They ought to jump at the sight of real greenbacks.

So it was that a few weeks after Woz and Jobs returned from Atlantic City, two suits arrived at the Jobs garage. One was Peddle, with gray wavy hair and aviator glasses, the other Andre Souson, Commodore's vice president of engineering. Peddle, in fact, had visited Apple once before, when MOS was still independent, to demonstrate a kind of microcomputer called an in-circuit emulator to help engineers develop products around the 6502.

This time the two men had come for the company. They explained their intentions and asked Jobs to come up with a price. The numbers Jobs returned with were reasonable: $100,000, plus some Commodore stock, for Apple, plus guaranteed $36,000-per-year jobs for him and Woz. Peddle and Souson agreed to take the offer to their boss.

If the numbers Jobs threw out were apppropriate for Apple, they were utterly outrageous for its two principals. Once again, this time faced with a giant potential competitor, Jobs had shown incredible cool. He and Woz were looking at a nearly $90,000 payoff in the first year, and that didn't even count the stock—more money than either of them (or their fathers) had ever seen in a single year. Yet when Jobs set his price, he barely blinked.

After the emissaries left, Jobs spent the next few days doing due diligence on his potential new employer. He called everyone he knew who had ever worked for Commodore, sold anything to the company or bought one of its calculators. And with each conversation, his optimism faded. Everybody hated Commodore. Their calculators were shit; clever functionality in a lousy package. You could park a car on an HP calculator and still use it; with a Commodore calculator you had to worry about punching the keys too hard. Working there was a nightmare, with everyone from the vice presidents to the janitors in terror of Jack Tramiel. And nobody worked *with* Commodore—instead you delivered according to the terms of the contract and then prayed you'd get paid someday. Finally, to a person, everybody who had ever dealt with Commodore warned Jobs about the pending negotiations.

"The more I looked into Commodore," Jobs would say later, "the sleazier they were. I couldn't find one person who had made a deal with them and was happy. Everyone felt they had been cheated."

In the end, Jobs withdrew his price. It was a brave call to walk away from a deal that would have put him on the Sunnyvale equivalent of Easy Street after just a summer of hard work. But as it happened, there never would have been a deal: when Peddle and Souson presented the proposal to Tramiel and chairman Gould they were quickly vetoed. Commodore didn't want to spend money for two freaks in some suburban garage. Rather, the company would design its own computer.

Faced with his first great business challenge, Jobs had made the right choice. But others thought differently. Woz in particular, saw the Commodore offer as the solution to all of his problems. He could bury his debts with the big cash-out, get out of the madness of this start-up company, see his baby turned into a real mass-market product sold by a major corporation *and* get a high-paying job in the process. He didn't want to hear Jobs's second thoughts about Tramiel and Commodore.

His father agreed. Until now, Jerry Wozniak had stayed on the sidelines, worried that his son was again mixed up with the ever-dangerous Steve Jobs, and at the same time proud of his son's brilliant new invention. For this Lockheed veteran, a Commodore deal would kill two birds with one stone: it would not only get Stephen out from under Jobs's controlling personality but also establish him in a corporate setting as an important engineering visionary.

There was more. Commodore's impending counteroffer also brought to a head the old issue of ownership. The original agreement had given Woz all rights to the technology. And what was Commodore buying, after all, but the design of the Apple I? They certainly weren't buying the Jobs garage or Apple's crude distribution system. So didn't that mean Woz deserved the lion's share of any payout?

Jerry Wozniak fretted over the threat posed by his son's new partner for weeks. By one of those strange coincidences that are a reminder that the Valley is a small town, his wife, increasingly involved in local politics, had offered their house for a neighborhood "meet the candidates" tea. The guests of honor were two candidates for the Sunnyvale city council. Both were members of the new city liberal splinter group, Orchards, and both lived in the neighborhood: Dianne McKenna and Dave Barram.

Regis came along to support his wife. Recognizing him, Jerry Wozniak took him aside and slowly began to pour out his heart. I'm worried about my boy, he told McKenna. He's gotten himself mixed up with this strange young man who seems to have some kind of power over him. Now he wants my boy to leave a great job at HP and join him in some crazy new company. What should I do?

Regis didn't know what to say.

It all came to a head one evening in September, as the Apple narrative shifted momentarily from the Jobs's house to the Wozniaks'. Jerry Wozniak confronted Steve Jobs. He had told his son Mark that he "was going to make the little son of a bitch cry and that'd be the end." And that was what he did. He told Jobs, as Mark overheard, "You don't deserve shit. You haven't produced anything. You haven't done anything." Jobs burst into tears. He told Jerry Wozniak that the veteran engineer didn't appreciate all that he, Steve Jobs, had done for the company. Then the tearful young man turned to his partner and said, "Woz, if we're not fifty-fifty you can have the whole thing."

Whether Steve Jobs cried out of betrayal, surprise or calculation is impossible to know. But even though he cried, as Jerry Wozniak had predicted, it was not the end. Through the tears, he had called the bluff of this rather unusual pairing of a middle-aged man fighting in the place of his grown-up son. And when it was over, Steve Jobs was still in charge, and he still killed the Commodore deal.

It had been the classic high-tech confrontation of engineering and marketing, writ small. As a lifelong engineer in a giant corporation, Jerry Wozniak was as naive about the true nature of business as his son. He was a good man and a good father, but a lousy businessman. R&D always believes that it makes the real contribution to a company's success, while management merely follows behind sweeping up the credit. Management knows better, but is forever embarrassed about not being clever enough to work on new inventions in the lab.

In that odd three-way argument in the Wozniak living room, it was Steven Jobs, with the least amount of work experience, who was right. His 50 percent share might be stretching things a bit after the first six months, but it would be low in light of things to come. He had, after all, built the company. In the ever-repeating story of high tech, engineering leads only for the first few months of a new revolution and thereafter marketing is king. Wozniak's design was brilliant, but it never would have happened without Jobs's prodding.

Moreover, if there hadn't been Wozniak, Jobs would have found someone else. Without Jobs, Wozniak would still be a low-grade engineer at Hewlett-Packard.

Jobs, his cheeks glistening with tears, had won the debate. But something had been torn in the friendship that would never again be fully mended. In another year, this friendship would be world-famous, in another decade it would be legend. But already, while Apple Computer was still known only to a few hundred computer hobbyists, Stephen Wozniak and Steven Jobs began to slowly drift apart. And though the tear would often be stitched together, usually for public occasions, the patch would never again be seamless or strong.

4.10 SEARCHING FOR DADDY

Steve Jobs now knew more than ever that he needed the help of grown-ups. But finding them was a different matter entirely.

Of the few he knew well, some, like Holt, were too odd. Others, like his workmates at Atari, hated him. Even his partner's father thought he was a conniver. And the businessman he most admired, Nolan Bushnell, was busy with his own company.

So Jobs decided to start cold. Leafing through electronics magazines, he'd been struck by Intel's advertisements. In an era when chip and instrument companies were still selling their wares through impenetrable tombstone ads or using women with big breasts, Intel's ads were stylish and abstract.

Intel has always been known as a great technical innovator; but in fact its technology has rarely been triumphant. The real key to Intel's success, in 1976 and now, has been its marketing. In the mid-1970s, before almost anyone in tech, Intel recognized that in the new world of electronics, the user experience would matter more than product specifications. The result was a celebrated series of ads that used race cars to symbolize speed, a hamburger for customization and a meat cleaver for cost cutting. This was followed by stylish ads composed of illustrations of elegant people. It was microprocessors as lifestyle; and the ads were a decade ahead of their time.

Jobs saw these ads and was entranced. Alone among the players in his industry, he saw the value of this type of advertising. And if chips could be sold as fashion, just think what you could do with a personal computer. And Jobs also knew that only such ads could top the expensive five-page color ads now being placed in computer magazines by his nemesis, Pro Tech.

Somewhere behind those Intel ads, Jobs decided, was the grown-up he needed. Jobs called Intel's marketing department—and Intel referred him to a public relations and advertising agency in Palo Alto called Regis McKenna Inc. A few years hence, after he became famous, Jobs would be notorious for not returning phone calls. But now, when the agency's director of new business development, Frank Burge, proved unresponsive, Jobs refused to accept the silence and simply hounded the man with calls until he got a reply. Worn down by the assault, Burge agreed to visit the Jobs household.

Almost from the moment he agreed, Burge had doubts. PR agencies in Silicon Valley were, and are, constantly approached by new start-up firms with big ambitions and little money. A few turn out to be industry giants; most turn out to be bankruptcies that pay their contractors pennies on the dollar, if anything. "As I was driving over to the garage," Burge would say later, "I was thinking: Holy Christ, this guy is going to be something else. What's the least amount of time I can spend with this clown without being rude and then get back to something more profitable?"

But Burge, like so many others, came away a changed man. Though he still wasn't convinced Apple was a viable company, he was impressed by Jobs's personality and the sophistication of the product. Just to make sure he wasn't crazy in his optimistic evaluation, he called Paul Terrell over at the Byte Shop. Terrell told him that Apple was both financially and organizationally over its head, and that Jobs wasn't a very comfortable marketing man, but that nevertheless Apple had something there.

That was enough to keep the ball rolling. There were other meetings. The agency finally proposed taking on Apple's entire marketing campaign in exchange for a percentage of the company's profits—an unusual arrangement, as agencies usually would bill for hours, set a monthly retainer or, with the most interesting companies, work for equity. The most likely reason for this deal was that RMI had serious doubts about the long-term viability of the company, not to mention its short-term ability to meet its bills, so decided to take its money right off the top.

A few years later, while writing *The Little Kingdom*, Michael Moritz would uncover an early agency memo that read, in part: "Though he moved a quantity into retail distribution, there is as yet no evidence that the retailer(s) are successful in finding customers." It went on to note that "Steve is young and inexperienced" but that "[Nolan] Bushnell was young when he started Atari. And he claims to be worth $10 million now."

Jobs had, for the moment, made the cut. And that meant a meeting with Regis McKenna Himself (as the man's business card famously said).

Regis was a small, delicate-looking man, with a soft voice and an air of fragility about him that was largely due to a lifetime of battling the diabetes that had already killed one of his six brothers. But appearances were illusory, because McKenna was tough as nails, with an Irish temper that would explode when ignited. Like almost every Silicon Valley success story—and McKenna's was one of the most unusual because of the tangential path he had chosen—Regis was arrogant, shockingly brilliant, and suffered fools not one bit.

Yet for all the hobnobbing he did with Valley executives, and despite the fact that his name would eventually be synonymous with theirs, McKenna was not like the rest of Silicon Valley's elite. Like them, he came from humble beginnings—in his case a working-class family in Pittsburgh—but unlike them he had never graduated from college, much less gone on to grad school. He was also a true-blue Democrat when much of the rest of the Valley's leadership was Republican—a fact which cost him some business in the early years (his vindication came twenty-five years later, when a now Democratic Valley watched in envy as President Clinton had dinner at the McKenna house). Moreover, while the rest of the Valley's winners typically used their first real money to move off the Valley floor and up into the hills of Los Altos, Saratoga or Woodside, McKenna stayed in his surburban house in Sunnyvale, just blocks from the Wozniak home, where Dianne could pursue the political career that ultimately made her a county supervisor.

But what most distinguished Regis McKenna from his peers was that he was an aesthete in a world of gearheads. He had begun his career at Fairchild during its golden age, then jumped to National Semiconductor, where he did an impossibly good job for a company composed largely of hard-nosed, unimaginative chip builders. McKenna then broke out on his own in 1970, just in time for the first big Fairchild explosion, the one that created the modern Silicon Valley. Having worked with all of these Fairchildren, he had a superb network of contacts when they all became entrepreneurs and started their own Valley chip companies.

Not surprisingly, the chip company McKenna took on as a client was the most gilt-edged of the bunch: Intel, founded by the man who ran Fairchild semiconductor, Robert Noyce; Fairchild's top scientist, Gordon Moore; and its chief applications specialist, Andrew Grove. Regis would ride Intel to glory—a glory, even Intel would admit, that was in large part due to Regis McKenna's efforts.

For a guy trained in mass advertising, Intel posed a difficult challenge: how do you make silicon memory chips exciting? The fact is, you couldn't. But within months, fortune dropped into Regis's lap the biggest opportunity in high-tech history. The microprocessor.

It is to Regis's eternal credit that he understood the value of the microprocessor to Intel even before its founders did. While Noyce, Moore and especially Grove were hemming and hawing about the dangers of spreading the company's already thin resources on a whole new product line, Regis lobbied for the microprocessor in every way he could think of. Recognizing that nobody at Intel could figure out what to use this new invention for, McKenna hurriedly prepared a white paper offering scores of potential microprocessor applications. While some of the ideas were wacky (airport marijuana-sniffing machines) and others well beyond the capabilities of the chips at the time (blood analyzers, automatic toilet flushers), the white paper did, more than any other study of the time, accurately predict the extraordinary breadth of applications that would eventually appear for the microprocessor as it became the signal invention of the postwar world. McKenna's efforts played a critical role in convincing a doubtful Intel to stick with its new invention.

That was only the beginning. By 1976, McKenna was beginning to formulate in his mind a radically new model for high-tech marketing. The off-center Intel ads were a clue. What Regis realized before anyone else was that digital electronics, as it moved outward from laboratories to offices to daily life, would increasingly be sold not from the top down in the form of performance specifications and hard technical detail, but from the bottom up in terms of applications, user experiences and the complete *system* of not only product but software, packaging, design tools and customer service.

This in turn would require a new kind of marketing communications that went beyond merely mailing press releases to trade magazines. Instead, the goal would be consumer publications such as *Time* and *Newsweek* and business magazines such as *Fortune* and *Business Week*. But to get to these publications and their readers would require the cultivation of key industry "opinion makers" whose learned judgment on new products would be taken as gospel by both mainstream reporters and consumers.

Needless to say, this would be pretty tough sledding with a product as arcane as a microprocessor. In 1976 there were still chip company executives who didn't understand how the damn things worked. It wouldn't be until 1980 that McKenna's ideas of a system approach to chips would be made manifest in Intel's Operation Crush. Crush would be the seminal event of modern high-tech marketing and the antecedent of "Intel Inside" a decade later, which would prove to be one of the most successful marketing programs in modern business history.

Now, serendipitously, this funny little computer company with the even funnier name had dropped into Regis's lap. It was the perfect test bed for his new ideas. After all, unlike chips, home computing was something the average consumer actually might be able to understand. Regis had already experimented with some of his ideas using the Byte Shop, which happened to be another of his clients. But retailing was a different game—this was now manufacturing, with its opportunity to create brand identification. And a cute name like Apple certainly wasn't a bad way to start.

However, before anything could get underway there was the matter of the founders themselves. And Regis's doubts about these two neophytes weren't eased by their first conversation. Regis prided himself on his professionalism, his erudition and his ability to be comfortable around business Brahmins. Now across the desk from him were these shaggy near-juveniles without an ounce of tact or gracefulness between them.

Even the small talk went to hell. Regis asked the pair about how they were promoting their product. Woz mentioned that he was working on a technical article about the Apple I for a trade magazine. "Oh really?" asked Regis, who had spent a decade using just such articles to make unknown engineers into industry gurus. "I'd like to see it." Then he offered some free (and very useful) advice to the Woz: keep the article relatively untechnical and you'll reach a larger audience of not only your peers but also potential customers.

Woz visibly bristled. "I don't want any PR man touching my copy." Regis, understandably proud of his achievements, was not going to take this from some long-haired troll.

"I think you both better get out," Regis said very slowly, trying to restrain himself. For once, Steve Jobs dropped his usual role as troublemaker and played peacemaker between his resident genius and the adult who was to guide them out into the big world. It only partially worked. The pair left Regis having apparently blown their first shot at professional help.

4.11 VALENTINE'S DAY

Apple still needed money, serious money, if it was ever going to ramp up to catch Pro Tech or MITS now or prepare itself for the inevitable arrival of the big players in the months to come.

The only guy he knew who had ever raised that kind of money was Nolan Bushnell, so Jobs went back to visit his old boss and mentor. They were an interesting sight in Bushnell's office: Nolan with a beard, permed hair and pin-striped suit and Jobs with his own beard, lank hair and jeans; one of them the most celebrated name in consumer electronics, the other preparing to supplant him.

Bushnell still had a soft spot for his young apprentice, and spent more than an hour giving Jobs a tutorial on how venture capital worked. In 1976 it was a relatively new profession, having made its first important appearance in Silicon Valley just seven years before when Art Rock had helped fund the creation of Intel. Now there were perhaps a dozen venture capitalists investing in Silicon Valley, a number of them congregating in an industrial park in Menlo Park on Sand Hill Road, just behind Stanford University.

As Bushnell explained it, venture capitalists managed funds of money formed from private and institutional investors willing to take a sizable risk on new start-up companies. The venture capitalists identified those firms with potential, and then invested some of the fund's money in a series of rounds— seed, second, third, mezzanine—in exchange for equity, at founders stock prices, in the company. Sometimes a round was covered entirely by one venture firm, though more often it was a consortium. The amount of equity they took varied with the round. Typically an early round investment would be small—say, $200,000—but since the value of the company was also low, that would buy 20 percent or more of the company's total stock. If the company was successful, later investment rounds might be higher, often in the millions of dollars. But since the company would also have a higher value by then, the actual percentage of ownership lost would be smaller than in earlier rounds.

Nevertheless, it was probable that by the time the company was fully invested, these venture capital firms would own a majority of the firm . . . and that ownership, combined with the usual demand by these investors for one or more seats on the board of directors, would mean that the founders, who started down the road to have control over their own lives, would end up not even in control of the company they built. But then again, they might also be multimillionaires. So would be the venture capitalists and their fund investors. The payoff would come when the company, now successful, had its initial public offering, "going public" with its first open sale of stock and a listing on a stock exchange.

That, of course, was if everything worked right. And it rarely did. A venture capitalist who managed to get one public company out of every five investments was something of a star, and the one winner would usually more than cover all the losses of the others. But it was precisely because of these low odds that venture capitalists were notorious for exercising their control during tough times and booting the very entrepreneurs who'd built the company in the first place, replacing them with more experienced hands and, sometimes, personal friends.

This, in so many words, is what Bushnell told Steve Jobs. It was both an invitation and a warning: come join the game of big-time entrepreneuring, but don't be surprised if you lose it all.

Jobs was undaunted. He asked Bushnell to recommend a venture capitalist. Bushnell—and it is hard to know whether he was trying to help or teach Jobs a lesson, or both—gave him the name of one of Atari's investors: Don Valentine. The name wasn't new to Jobs, despite his limited knowledge of Silicon Valley. In fact, Regis had given him the same name a few weeks before.

One of the longest-standing myths in Silicon Valley is that when you go in to see Don Valentine, you come out either a tycoon or with a new asshole— and either way, the experience is not pleasant. Valentine was, and remains, the man with the golden gut. From Atari to Cisco, his masterpiece, he has had an uncanny ability to spot a potential winner, build it into a hot company (even if he has to fire all of the founders) and then take it public at exactly the right moment.

But to be on the other end of the process, as an entrepreneur, is akin to a ride through a wood chipper.

A truck driver's son, Valentine was a founder of Silicon Valley. At Fairchild, where he first met McKenna, Valentine served brilliantly as marketing manager and sales manager, in both roles putting in place organizations that held the company together for years to come. An imposing figure, variously described as "the straightest guy in the world" and a "real taskmaster," Valentine had enormous intelligence and integrity. Fairchild was essentially a drunken, skirt-chasing brawl, but Valentine would have none of it. In one respect that was to his credit, but it also pointed to a weakness: Valentine lacked the ability to deal with clever (as opposed to brilliant) people—in the most celebrated case, treating a subordinate named Jerry Sanders so crudely that the two men maintained a thirty-year feud that lasted long after Valentine had become a famous venture capitalist and Sanders the even more famous CEO of Advanced Micro Devices.

From Fairchild, Valentine had gone to National, where his toughness was a match for Charlie Sporck, then moved on to create his own venture firm, Sequoia Capital (he also sat on the board of Regis McKenna Inc.). Hard as nails, a master business strategist, wary of cleverness, dressed like a banker, it was hard to imagine anyone less suited to deal with a trickster like Steve Jobs. Even when Valentine made friendly conversation there was something threatening in his words. And when he smelled a deal, Valentine could be as terrifying as God Almighty.

And yet, on a bright autumn morning in 1976, Valentine drove down to the Jobs garage. Being a business community, Silicon Valley has very few classic visual images. But this is one of them: Don Valentine, thick head of hair, rugged good looks, in a rep tie and dark suit, climbing out of his Mercedes and warily trudging up the walk into the Apple Fairyland and wondering just what in God's name he was doing there.

As one might expect, it did not go well. Valentine would later call McKenna and ask, "Why did you send me these renegades from the human race?" But Valentine could live, albeit uneasily, with that. What bothered him much more was that the duo had no business strategy. They basically demonstrated the product, told Valentine that the market was going to be big and suggested that Apple could do very well on just a fraction of that business. This was heresy to Don Valentine, and just about the stupidest thing you could possibly say. He would recall thinking, "Neither one knew anything about marketing. Neither one had any sense of the size of the potential market. They weren't thinking anywhere near big enough."

Valentine didn't invest in entrepreneurs and their companies to be in fourth place in a market; he invested in companies that would do anything to *own* that market, to set the standards, steal the biggest customers and crush the opposition. His companies did not take prisoners. Time has shown he was right. Every new tech industry quickly fills with players, then experiences a devastating shakeout that leaves one clear winner, a couple also-rans and a bunch of corporate corpses. The only strategy in such a world is to play to win everything; to aim for second place is a form of business suicide.

End of meeting. Yet Valentine's golden gut told him that these goofballs had a diamond in the rough. He gave them some advice: get an experienced marketing guy and I might think about investing.

Once again, Steve Jobs's native brashness led him to do the right thing at the right moment. Know anyone? he asked Valentine, when a more veteran entrepreneur might have merely gulped. Lemme think about it, Valentine replied. Even the mighty Don Valentine could be momentarily disoriented by the Reality Distortion Field.

Back at Sequoia, Valentine dug up three names of marketing guys he'd worked with in his chip days. He called around to see what they were up to. Only one was currently free: an old Fairchild subordinate named Armas Clifford Markkula, known to everybody as Mike. The latest word on Markkula was that he had gone to Intel, made a few million in founders stock when Intel went public, retired at age thirty-three when someone was promoted ahead of him and was now spending his days with his family at home in Cupertino, going swimming, playing guitar and polishing his gold Corvette. Valentine gave him a call and suggested he go visit a garage just a few blocks away.

4.12 MIKE MARKETING

Mike Markkula was an interesting combination of tight-ass and show-off rarely seen in Silicon Valley. Raised in Southern California, he had come to Fairchild from Hughes Aircraft. Jumping to Intel, he had made something of a name for himself in the company for his skill at the details of marketing: customer relationships, order processing, pricing. Even at hard-nosed Intel, Markkula was, in a word, boring. A tinkerer, secretive in his moves and notorious for being negative about every new idea he heard ("You wouldn't get three words out of your mouth before he'd say, 'No, that's not the way it is,' " recalled one workmate), Markkula was the kind of middle manager on whom great companies are built but who never see the inside of executive row except to make a presentation. He managed to reach the job of product marketing manager for memory chips, and though he dreamed of greater things, no one else was surprised when he was passed over (Jack Carsten was promoted instead) for the job of corporate marketing director.

Away from the office, Markkula was, to all appearances, pure of heart, a dedicated family man and a loyal employee. There were only three things he hated. One was jokes about his hair, which he combed straight forward in a bang (a decade after one reporter called it a "Dutch boy haircut," the reporter understood Markkula blackballed him from the Santa Clara University Ethics Center he'd funded). Another was the use of his real Christian names. And a third was conflict with the employees he managed. Otherwise, he was as plain vanilla as Silicon Valley gets.

But sometimes within such a corporate Bartleby there is wild man just waiting for the chance to kick out the jams. Markkula had that beast, and thanks to some judicious purchases of company stock, when Intel went public Markkula surprised everyone by checking out. He wasn't a tycoon, but he was rich enough never to have to work again. In the process, the drone became a peacock; now set free, the wild man took to living the high life, with expensive clothes and a fast car.

Real entrepreneurs are start-up junkies. No matter how much money they make, they can't keep away from the next deal, even if it costs them their fortune. Markkula, by comparison, showed little interest in getting back into the game. It is possible he never would have returned to corporate life were it not for Don Valentine's call.

So it was that Mike Markkula drove over to the Jobs house and became richer and more powerful than he'd ever dreamed.

What Markkula saw in the Jobs garage was not a bunch of long-haired amateurs, but a wonderful little toy, a personalized version of the big computers Markkula had worked with when developing Intel's order entry system. The Apple I, he would later say, "was what I had wanted since I left high school." It was better than a Corvette.

Markkula walked out in the daze of a teenage crush. He called Valentine, told him he was interested and asked for a meeting. The two met. Valentine expressed his concerns, but Markkula wasn't worried. He was convinced that a nice little company could be built around this product given a mature hand at the helm, an intelligent marketing strategy and a real organization. Valentine, knowing well that the enthusiasm of the CEO was half the game, agreed.

With Valentine's words of support still in his ears, Markkula went home and told his wife that he was going to jump into a new start-up. Mrs. Markkula, who, like many Valley wives of the era, had been down this road before, made Mike promise not to give the company more than four years of his life. Next Markkula called Regis, told him that he was investing in Apple and asked the PR guru to forgive the kids and come on board. McKenna, who was in the business of forgiving slights, agreed.

Then Markkula called the boys and made their dreams come true: he would join Apple and support the development of the company's next product by underwriting a bank loan of as much as $250,000.

Apple Computer finally had its own in-house grown-up.

4.13 ANNIVERSARY

As 1976 ended, Steven Jobs had done nearly the impossible. In less than a year, starting with little business and no management experience, he had assembled a new company team, prototyped and tested a first product, built it in volume, established a distribution channel, improved that product and, finally, located both professional management and a seed round investment. Nine out of every ten new start-up companies in Silicon Valley never get this far, even though many are composed of teams of industry veterans with a hundred times the combined work experience of Jobs and Wozniak.

Little Apple Computer wasn't out of the woods yet, but it was on the way. There were still much larger competitors already in the market, and even bigger ones now just weeks away from entering the market. But, thanks to Wozniak, Apple had the best product design. And thanks to Jobs it now had on board the best marketer in high tech in Regis McKenna and, in Mike Markkula, a man who could give the fledgling company the marketing infrastructure of a giant corporation. With this combination, Apple could hold its own against anyone—at least for a while. Soon it would need a follow-up product, a second winner even better than the Apple I. The good news was that Woz was already at work on it.

But Steve Jobs had done something else in that first year that was not as apparent. He had stamped the company forever with his personality. And that was good news and bad. Companies that bear their founder's personality must live with the strengths and weaknesses of that personality even after that founder is gone. Hewlett and Packard were great men, and they had built a great company. Nolan Bushnell was an exciting, but mercurial, man, and Atari would prove to be a thrilling place to work right up until the moment it disintegrated. Jack Tramiel was a brilliant, but controlling figure, whose companies could never grow beyond his reach.

Steve Jobs was as talented an entrepreneur as any of these celebrated figures. But he was also more deeply flawed. He was now embarked on creating a company that wasn't just a business, but a children's crusade. Apple was to be the Krupp of a social revolution. And for nearly a decade, Jobs's personality gave Apple enough momentum to live out that dream.

But even as he founded Apple, Jobs was embedding into its personality the flaws of his own character. He had a company, but it had been built with a technical genius who no longer quite trusted him, a marketing man who didn't want to work anymore and hated the rough-and-tumble of management and a staff held together not by management or leadership, but by charisma and manipulation. Most dangerous of all, the company philosophy was steeped in self-actualization. In the HP Way, the first rule, before all the nice stuff about community service and management by objective, was *profit*. In the unwritten Apple Code, the first rule was *self*, and all selves were subordinate to, and existed in the reflection of, the Supreme Self, Steve Jobs. The Jobs Reality Distortion Field now enveloped all of Apple Computer, and from there would encompass millions.

These other, disturbing character flaws, would be buried under the extraordinary success of Apple's first two decades. But they would never disappear. Rather, they would grow in the dark, eating away at the company's heart, biding their time and waiting for a moment of weakness to emerge.

But that moment was still many years and many billions of dollars away. At the moment, it was moving day at the Jobs garage.

5.0 BLOSSOMS

As the new year began, the duo had become a troika. Now each set about inventing their corner of the business.

For Wozniak, the task at hand was to create the new computer, to be called the Apple II. For Markkula, it was to create a real company out of the ragtag pieces at hand. And for Jobs, it was to re-create himself. Thus, each set about to do what he did best.

But before they could begin there was the matter of ownership. The first step was to incorporate. That officially occurred on January 3, 1977. In mid-March the company bought out the original partnership for $5,308.96. This second move accomplished two things at once: it reconfigured ownership to allow for the presence of Markkula and those key employees who would follow, and it finally got Ron Wayne out of the picture.

By all accounts, Wayne, who had spent months dreading the inevitable call from Apple's creditors, was thrilled to get a check for $1,700. Given that his stock would one day be worth tens of millions, Wayne might appear to be the greatest loser in the Apple story; but seen from another perspective, he was a winner, because that check put him in the select ranks of Valleyites who ever made money from a start-up.

Having killed off the old Apple, Markkula now had to construct a new one to take its place. And the first step was to redivvy up ownership. This is a painful moment in any new start-up. Typically, the founders have spent months, even years, devoting their life to building the firm. Then along comes some Daddy Warbucks, who has done nothing for the company except write a check, and he demands the lion's share of ownership—in the process diminishing the ownership of everyone else. And though the total value of those diminished shares may actually be greater, it is still a bitter pill; one that further stresses the already tense relationship between the players.

That was certainly the case at Apple, turning long-standing fissures into fractures. The restructuring meetings took place during succeeding evenings in the cabana by the pool at Markkula's house in Cupertino—showing that while he didn't like confrontation, he didn't mind controlling the setting to his advantage. There, in the setting of a rich man's backyard ("See?" it whispered. "You can have all this too."), Markkula dropped the bomb: he wanted one-third of the company. And that, in turn, meant that he wanted to be the largest shareholder.

The grown-up had spoken. The reaction of the two founders was as diverse as their personalities. Jobs accepted the proposal; he was beginning to understand that this was what it took to build a real company, and the fantasy of being a powerful, albeit progressive and benevolent, business tycoon was taking over his dreams.

Woz was agreeable too, but for entirely different reasons. He had frankly been amazed that anyone would put big money into Apple, and already predicted to his parents that Markkula would lose it all. But Markkula's folly wasn't really his concern, because Woz had no intention of staying with the company. His wife was dead set against the financial riskiness of a start-up and she was pressuring him to stay with HP and move to Corvallis. Woz's workmates tried to talk him into going as well.

Only Rod Holt appraised the offer with a hard eye. Markkula, he saw more clearly than the rest, "had a certain arrogant bearing and the subtle self-confidence of those people who have a lot of money and believe that somehow or other they have a birthright to it. I was suspicious." Nevertheless, like many revolutionaries when they encounter real money, Holt went for the gold: even a few percent ownership of a big successful company would make him a rich man.

But acceptance wasn't enough. Markkula was smart enough also to demand commitment. With Jobs that was easy: he was already in with both feet. As for Holt, Markkula was largely indifferent, except that he wanted to make sure the sardonic anarchist could be trusted. So he personally checked all of Holt's references for the last twenty years. There were to be no revolutions at Apple except those of Mike Markkula's choosing.

But the real commitment Markkula wanted was Wozniak's. Not part-time either. Woz had to quit HP and join Apple. No new tech company ever becomes great without a resident engineering guru. Though Markkula had great expectations for Jobs, he also believed the young man could be replaced. But Woz was a different matter. Without him, at least until an engineering department was created, Apple could not go on.

Moreover, the guileless Woz was completely transparent; Markkula knew he was hesitating about committing himself to such a risky venture. It was obvious in Woz's behavior. He griped about Jobs getting too much of the company, suggesting that his old partner would never make it in the real working world the way he, Steve Wozniak, had. He prevaricated every time the conversation turned to his future with Apple.

If Markkula had a sense that Woz was hesitating, Jobs knew his old friend well enough to realize that Wozniak, and thus the whole enterprise, were at great risk of being lost. He told that to Markkula and Holt at secret meetings. And he set out to do what he had done so well all these years: turn Woz's head and heart.

Getting people who *want* to be part of a start-up to stick around is hard enough; convincing someone to give up everything and stick around when they believe the enterprise is doomed, is almost impossible. But, of course, Jobs had faced those odds with Woz before. Only now his partner was an adult with a solid career, a wife and parents who no longer believed in the good intentions of Steven Jobs.

Faced with this, Jobs put on a full-court press the likes of which Woz had never before experienced. He cajoled Woz, he begged, he threatened. He had mutual friends call Woz and try to convince him. He even went to the amazing length of entering the lion's den—the home of Woz's parents—to solicit their help . . . bursting again into tears (hey, it worked the first time). Holt joined in too, telling Woz of the magnificent technical opportunity of creating his own product line.

But it was Markkula who proved decisive. Emotionally beaten down and exhausted, Wozniak was ready for a lifeline. Markkula threw it to him, telling the young man that only at Apple would he be able to take his genius and convert it to real wealth. For Woz, who had never been that concerned about money, the world suddenly became crystal clear. It was so simple now to say yes. "Once I decided I was doing it to make money," he said later, "it made the rest of the decision easy."

To the disbelief of his parents and his wife, Woz quit Hewlett-Packard and joined the fledgling, and to his mind doomed, company.

But if Markkula demanded enormous sacrifices of time and energy from his new partners, he was unwilling to make them himself. In what would become characteristic of his tenure at Apple, the longest of any employee, when the time came to step up, Markkula backed off. He told the others he had no intention of running Apple on a day-to-day basis. Rather, he would do it by remote control—or, as he said it more colorfully, he would put in the money, and find someone else to mind the pennies.

5.1 COMMANDER SCOTT

The man Markkula picked to be Apple's first CEO wasn't far away. A thirty-two-year-old bachelor, Mike Scott was obese (a situation he made worse by usually wearing a too tight T-shirt), wore aviator glasses and was perpetually tense. He burned off most of his nervousness by walking around with clenched fists and twisting his short hair around his finger. And when that wasn't sufficiently pacifying, he sometimes went ballistic.

Yet, on other occasions, Scott could be stunningly sentimental, delivering bouquets of flowers, taking staffers—usually the lowest-level employees—en masse to a movie or cruise.

On first glance, Scott would seem the very antithesis of the cool, debonair Mike Markkula, yet the two had an unusual bond. Both had been hired by Fairchild on the same day in September 1967. They had adjoining offices. For a few months Markkula had even worked for the younger Scott. But most amazing of all to the two men was the discovery that they had the same birthday, February 11. They made it an annual ritual, even after their careers took them in separate directions, to have their birthday lunch together.

During his tenure at Fairchild, Scott not only worked with Markkula but also reported to Gene Carter, Don Valentine and Charlie Sporck—all of whom would play a role during his tenure at Apple.

As Markkula's career took him deeper into marketing and eventually to Intel, Scott's talents led him to manufacturing and to National Semiconductor. And whereas Markkula's proved to be a mixed career success but a huge financial victory, Scott, though he never became rich, showed he could not only rise above the pressure cooker of life under Charlie Sporck but become a rising star at National. Starting in marketing, he in time moved over to manufacturing, becoming overall director of the company's hybrid circuit family.

But then his career hit a wall. As he recalls: "In 1976, after three years at the company, I turned down the chance to head National Semiconductor in Hong Kong. And that was not the thing to do if I wanted to keep advancing through the ranks." So, by the time his annual birthday lunch with Markkula rolled around a year later, Scott was looking for a way out. "That's when Mike told me about the two Steves and this intelligent terminal they had called an Apple I. He also told me they had a follow-up machine, the Apple II, in prototype.

"Mike also showed me the preliminary business plan. Apparently, the two Steves had not only never written such a plan, but when Valentine visited them and mentioned one, Jobs replied, 'What's a business plan?' We laughed about that."

Then Markkula made his pitch. Recalls Scott, "Mike said to me, 'I can sell more of these computers than you can make. Why not come over and run Apple? Right now it's run by a couple of inexperienced kids, but it's got a great product, and a market that's about to take off.' He wanted me on board to handle the details, which he never liked to do. Mike never liked to do the dirty work." Turn it into a real company, Markkula told Scott, and you may find yourself president of a company even bigger than Fairchild or National.

In the days that followed, Scott sat in his office at National and played out scenarios in his head. "It's like a chess game," he would say a few years later, "except the moves continue to happen. The challenge is to put together a system that works without being minded and has its own checks and balances. I wanted to see if I could build [such] a system from scratch."

He told Markkula he was in.

Adding the first new employee at the newly reorganized Apple, especially since this new arrival was also the CEO, was a potentially risky maneuver. But it all seemed to go swimmingly. Markkula, in his usual diplomatic/passive way, didn't force Scott on his partners, but merely suggested him as a possible candidate. Woz and Jobs agreed. And that was that.

But beneath the surface, things were much more complicated. Woz initially welcomed Scott, pleased that the company would finally have a pro who would get his next design built on time and in volume. But Woz would also soon learn that same professionalism also expected some discipline from the notoriously flighty chief technologist. And once Mike Scott put that pressure on Steve Wozniak, Woz would turn on him.

Jobs meanwhile, at late-night meetings with Woz and Holt at Bob's Big Boy in Cupertino, played Hamlet. Holt would recall, "Jobs didn't know whether he wanted to run the show or not." He had been intellectually mature enough to accept the idea of professional management, but emotionally unready to accept the reality of it. He saw the brief interval between Markkula's suggestion and the final vote on Scott as his last chance to decide to run the company himself. To others he couched his doubts in concern about how well Scott's meat-and-potatoes style would fit with Apple's antiestablishment philosophy—but it was really about power.

In the end, Jobs voted for Scott. He accepted that his apprenticeship as a business executive was not yet over and that Scott was the best man to lead Apple. For now. But Jobs also knew that one day his training would be complete and he would be ready. And when that day came, Mike Scott would be in Steve Jobs's crosshairs—and not even his birthday pal would fight to save him.

Mike Scott, thrilled at the challenge facing him, had a dim premonition: "I wondered whether I could really get anything done or whether we would argue all the time. My biggest concern was whether Jobs and I could get along. He was concerned that I wasn't doing consumer stuff. I was concerned that he didn't know what he was doing." But that was all. He failed to neutralize his greatest threat while he still had the chance.

Mike Scott joined Apple for some stock and a salary of $20,001, which was a fraction of what he had been making at National, but a dollar more than anyone else at Apple. But as everyone in Silicon Valley knows, it's the stock that matters—and here Scott was in a dangerous position. "I realized pretty quickly," he says, "that as president I was over the two Steves and Markkula—yet all three of them had far more ownership of the company, and thus more power, than I did."

Scott's first task as Apple president was to tell Jobs to bathe. Steve had only marginally improved his hygiene since his Atari days and it was now becoming a problem within the crowded confines of company headquarters. It was Scott's first test: could he stand up to the young founder?

Oh yeah. Twenty years later, Mike Scott laughs. "I think I'm *still* the only person who can stand up to Steve Jobs. I told him. And he did listen, but always, as I learned with Jobs, he had to get something back. In this case, I had to agree to read a book by some Indian guru that argued—obviously against the evidence at hand—that eating only fruits and nuts was so purifying that you never had to take another bath."

Scott came away from this encounter, and the many that followed, with considerable respect for the young founder. "The great thing about Jobs was that you always understood where you stood with him. He *never* said what he thought you wanted to hear. His positions were always well thought out, and he always told you where he was coming from. It could be very stressful, but the trick was not to take it personally."

Wozniak was a different matter. Like everyone else, Scott thought Woz a genius; but unlike the rest, he was less forgiving of the young man's eccentricities. "Woz was very, very creative, but it came in spurts. And he would cover himself during the in-between times. He'd never say he wasn't making progress on a project. Instead, he'd say everything was coming along just fine, and meanwhile he would be waiting for the little light in his brain to switch on and save him."

Scott's frustrations working with Wozniak were a warning of what was to come as Apple hired more and more computer whizzes. And to his credit, Scott heeded that warning, ultimately creating "a parallel management structure in engineering just to make sure the engineers got their annual reviews, their laundry done, etc." In the near term, it was clever strategy, freeing first Wozniak, then those who followed him, to devote themselves to innovation — and produce the great Apple products of the next seven years. But in the long run, well after Scott was gone, it created an environment at Apple that led to failed or misdirected projects that never rose above their own self-indulgence.

5.2 UNDRESSED FOR SUCCESS

The biggest challenge faced by Scott and his growing team immediately after its incorporation in early 1977 was getting the Apple II ready for introduction. Since his design breakthrough at the end of the summer, Woz had been perfecting his design. It was now nearly ready.

Holt too had come through as promised. He'd had his own design breakthrough, abandoning the traditional linear power supply used by the other personal computers for a more sophisticated switching power supply normally found in advanced instruments. The result, in what was historically the Achilles' heel of personal computers, was a major improvement in reliability, efficiency and, best of all, size.

Thanks to the efforts of these two, the finished Apple II would contain just 62 chips (other personal computers had more than 100) and weigh less than 12 pounds (compared to 20). In fact, the II was so light that the company even considered putting lead weights inside to give it a more "serious" heft.

Jobs, meanwhile, had gone back to Howard Cantin at Atari and hired him to design, as he had with the Apple I, the printed circuit board for the II. As was becoming his signature, Jobs wanted a world-class design. So when Cantin returned with a merely adequate first design, Jobs sent him back to the drawing board to produce a crisper (and thus more reliable) design. Cantin grumbled that he would never work for Jobs again, but Steve Jobs got his board.

But there was still something missing. A case. The personal computing world had changed radically in six months. Ever since the appearance of the Pro Tech machine, no computer company with any hope of survival dared to introduce a new model not encased in steel. On top of that, rumor had it that a Commodore machine, the Pet, was about to be introduced. Tandy was reported to have something in the works as well—and it was bound to produce a slick machine to sell to all its loyal customers at the thousands of Radio Shack stores.

So the Apple II needed a box. But not just any box. As was his gift, Jobs had visions of merchandising grandeur. The II, he decided, would not have a heavy, crimped metal enclosure like the Pro Tech machine, but instead a smoothly curved hard plastic case. Said Jobs, "I got a bug up my rear that I wanted the computer in a plastic case." His exemplar was the Hewlett-Packard calculator family, as well as the cool new European-derived appliances that were showing up each week in the Macy's advertising supplement in the local paper. Jobs visited the Macy's store in San Francisco just to hang out in the kitchen department and study the toasters and mixers.

As for what the actual design would look like, Jobs only knew what he didn't want: neither the concept designs he had solicited from a guy he knew at Atari nor those from the departed co-founder Ron Wayne. The Atari design was way too space age, full of complicated—and probably expensive—curves. Wayne's design was a clunker, with a Plexiglas cover and a tambour front that looked like a cross between a record turntable and a rolltop desk.

Jobs was at his wit's end when an old workmate of Wozniak's at Hewlett-Packard suggested a designer. Jerry Mannock had worked as a case designer at HP, grew bored with the endless stream of identical instrument boxes, left to design products for a company that made devices for the handicapped, felt unappreciated, quit, sold cars, traveled and finally set up his own struggling design firm in his house.

In January 1977, about the time the new Apple team was organizing itself, Jobs called Mannock and invited him to the next Homebrew meeting. Mannock arrived to find Jobs holding court, amazingly keeping up three conversations at one time. "I'd never run into anybody who did this," he later said. Mannock was impressed, especially when Jobs made him the fourth.

What I need, Jobs told him, are three plastic cases for my new computer. And I need them in twelve weeks. He offered Mannock $1,500 to complete the mechanical drawings of those cases, payable on acceptance. Mannock refused; he wanted his money up front. "These were flaky-looking customers and I didn't know if they were going to be around when the case was finished." Jobs, flush with the new deal with Markkula, assured him that money was not a problem.

Mannock took three weeks to come up with a design, but it was a beauty, one of the classic designs of the electronics age. Thanks to Mannock's brilliant amateurishness (he'd never designed a computer case before) and Holt's low-profile power supply, the Apple II case was smooth, simple and elegant—best of all, it made all the other computer designs of the next five years look like tractors beside a Duesenberg. Mannock even made a foam mock-up of the design. It wowed everyone who saw it. He got his $1,500; but Jobs refused to pay him the additional $300 for the mock-up.

Jobs brought a similar sense of quality to the company's new logo. Until now, the Apple logo had been a rather complicated ink illustration of Sir Isaac Newton sitting in a wide landscape reading a book, his back resting against a tree. Above him, hanging from a branch, was a glowing apple, presumably about to fall and impress the famous noggin. Wrapped around this image, which was in a crest shaped like a car radiator, was a windswept banner reading "Apple Computer Co."

It was not a bad logo for a head shop, but it was all wrong for a computer company that wanted to be the class of its field.

This time Jobs got what he wanted on the first try. At Regis McKenna's outfit there was a young art director named Rob Janov who had an intuitive feel for what Jobs was looking for: simple, graphic and knowing. "Steve always wanted a high-quality look," he recalled. "He wanted something that looked expensive and didn't look like some chunky model airplane." Janov drew the simplest and most iconic apple shape possible, then tried to identify it even more by having a leaf sprout from the top and cutting a deep cleft into the bottom.

Still, to Janov's mind the image still looked too much like a cherry tomato. So to give it scale, as well as to make a sly play on "bytes," he carved away a bite mark on the right side of the apple.

Now it needed color. Janov chose a rainbow effect in stripes from the top to the bottom of the apple. For the main body of stripes he chose a spectrum from yellow through red to violet. But the top stripe was to be different. In a brilliant stroke, he made it and the leaf the same brilliant apple green—a color so uncommon in industrial graphics, even in that postpsychedelic era, as to be unforgettable.

Being a professional, Janov realized that printing such a logo would be expensive because of the problem of bleeding between the colors. So he proposed that thin lines be drawn between the stripes to separate them. Jobs, who had been hovering over the project from the beginning, bugging Janov by day and Regis by night, wisely nixed the idea. Apple was going to go first class.

Mike Scott would later say, "That damned logo was an endless headache. Nonstandard colors, seven separate print runs and then varnish on top of everything to keep the colors from bleeding. God knows how much it cost Apple over the years."

5.3 HAPPY DAYS

Like a good field general, during this period Jobs seemed to be everywhere at once. For a short while yet, until Scott came on board and learned the company, Apple was still Jobs's playground, and he intended to make the best use of every second.

Meanwhile, Apple couldn't wait around for its new CEO. A signal event in the personal computer story was coming up fast. Steve Jobs, perhaps more than anyone in the industry, realized that this was a point of inflection, a dividing line between the players in this industry and the also-rans. And Steve Jobs was going to be a player, whatever it took.

The event was the first West Coast Computer Faire, slated for May in the underground Brooks Hall across from City Hall in downtown San Francisco. There had been several other personal computer shows in the preceding year, including that one Jobs, Woz and Kottke had attended in Atlantic City the previous summer. But most had been held in technology backwaters like Trenton, New Jersey. This time the Computer Faire would be in the Homebrew Heartland, and could be expected to draw not only every one of the 1,500 club members but thousands of influential Silicon Valleyites. After years of sandlot ball, this was the big leagues.

Jobs also assumed, correctly, that this would be the first show where the major players, such as Commodore, would roll out their new models. Jobs had seen what it was like to stand with the rest of the losers at a card table with a paper sign taped on the wall behind you and watch real professionals like Pro Tech in their flashy booths with smoked Plexiglas displays and carpeting and stacks of brochures. He was never going to let that happen again.

Yet, as he was doing all of this preparation, Jobs still had to run a real company. Apple needed to move out of the garage, ramp up for production of the Apple II and start hiring employees. Every day presented a new and seemingly insurmountable distraction to getting ready for the Faire.

The first step was to get the money. That is, establish Markkula's line of credit. Don Cviestusa, who was with Bank of America at the time, remembers seeing Jobs and Woz shambling into the B of A building in San Jose to meet the corporate loan officers. "To those professional bankers," he recalls, "Jobs and Wozniak couldn't have looked any stranger than if they'd just landed from Mars."

But with Markkula's collateral they got the credit line.

The next step was to find a new home for the company. They located an office suite on Stevens Creek Boulevard on the other side of Cupertino. Suite E-3 was just 2,000 square feet, neighbored by a weight-loss clinic and an employment agency, in a shingled building all but indistinguishable from the thousands of other Silicon Valley concrete tilt-ups. But to the young Apple team it was miraculous, especially after a year in the Jobs garage. And, like new start-up teams before and since, they reacted to their new home by behaving like six-year-olds. In the evening, Jobs, Woz, Espinosa and Wigginton would sit in different parts of the office and try to ring each other's phones first.

The suite itself was divided in two by a plaster wall. One side was administration (desks) and the other the laboratory and factory (lab tables). Several times each day, the entire crew would troop across the parking lot to the Good Earth restaurant and eat tofu and fruit smoothies and share their dreams. So important did the Good Earth become to the Apple gestalt that in the years to come all of the headquarters facilities it would either lease or build would be within a few blocks of the restaurant.

In the modern Silicon Valley, where high-tech parks stretch for fifty miles in every direction, populated by 5,000 companies and 750,000 workers, it can be hard to remember the isolation in which the early Apple operated. Most of the rest of the major Valley companies, such as Fairchild, Amdahl, Intel and National Semiconductor, were five miles away, on the other side of the Valley floor near the San Francisco Bay. HP and the Stanford Industrial Park were ten miles to the north. The closest tech enclaves were tiny clusters of three or four companies a mile away to the west on Bubb Road (Zilog, Measurex) or east (Four-Phase, Timeshare) on Sunnyvale-Saratoga Road. The businesses surrounding Apple's little office suite included a Chevrolet dealership, Cali Bros. grain and feed, Cupertino Nursery, the Old West Steakhouse (a popular breakfast place for bikers) and United Auto Parts (a favorite among street racers). In the modern Silicon Valley one can walk into any coffee bar, supermarket or restaurant and hear conversations about field programmable gate arrays and Internet search engines; but in this era Silicon Valley was still crowded into a few enclaves buried in the still regnant Santa Clara Valley— and none of those tech communities were anywhere near Apple.

Perhaps because of that, this was in many ways the happiest time in the Apple story. No fame, no glory, no bureaucracy, not even much money, just the little band working day and night against enormous odds. Everybody took on whatever job needed to be done. Every decision was meaningless, yet momentous. And at night, long, deeply felt discussions at the Good Earth, making plans that—incredibly—came true.

While Jobs and soon Scott were constructing the skeleton of the company, Woz and his team of hippies and teenagers were trying to get the Apple II built. Their deadline was even earlier than the Faire. An ad placed by Jobs in the Homebrew newsletter had set the II's introduction date as April 30. Given the Valley's history of product slippage, lags between introductions and actual shipments, that was awfully soon.

Moreover, Woz was running into the realities of working at the cutting edge of technology. For example, other companies were misrepresenting shipment dates and product specifications as well. Thus, Woz had planned to put in the II a hot new read-only memory chip from American Microsystems Inc., located just down the street. But when the time came to order, AMI just couldn't deliver and Woz had to settle for a lesser chip from Synertek. Similarly, a linear chip in the II's new keyboard proved to be hypersensitive to static electricity and crashed the keyboard every twenty minutes.

But these were technical problems and technical problems could be fixed—especially once the engineering team learned how to work with one another and around Woz's eccentricities. In particular, one of the traits that distinguished Woz from most technical (but not artistic) geniuses was his combination of lassitude and a need for acclaim. It was Holt, the only adult in the group, who made this discovery. Woz loved to come up with new ideas, but would then do the minimum required to prove it could be done. He was content to merely breadboard a working demonstration; after that, in his mind, the actual process of turning that design into a clean, reliable working prototype was scut work, mere window dressing, to be done by lesser mortals. Worse, Woz wouldn't even do that much if he didn't have someone to watch what he was doing and be impressed by his genius.

"I hardly ever trusted Woz's judgment," Holt said later.

The solution, Holt quickly realized, was to constantly stay on Woz's ass, demanding that he establish benchmarks, prepare diagrams and demonstrate results—and to keep the young genius constantly surrounded by acolytes before whom he could show off. For his part, Holt took on the quality-control job, using multimeters and oscilloscopes to test every part as it arrived and every computer as it was finished. The Apple II was not going to be another Altair.

Hardware was only half (well, three-quarters) of the story. Both Markkula and Scott, when he arrived, were convinced that the success of the next generation of personal computers would depend upon a systems approach. This was the Intel marketing model applied to consumer products. It wouldn't be enough, they agreed, to simply ship Apple II's in a box with a few instructions, leaving customers to figure it out by themselves—not if they were going to reach beyond the Homebrew types to mainstream markets.

Scott and Markkula had an idea of just who those new customers would be. Almost from the day he joined the company, Markkula had been working on a more sophisticated business plan. It was just the type of organized structural activity that was natural to him but alien to the two Steves. What slowly dawned on Markkula as he prepared this document was that, for the near term at least, personal computers had essentially three markets.

To date, only one of these markets had been developed: computer hobbyists, a group distinguished by deep, almost obsessive understanding of computers, a pride in the technology for its own sake and a near-messianism about particular hardware models and software programs. This was an ardent market, but a comparatively small one. And it was being fought over by what would soon be scores of competitors.

But Markkula also saw two other, infinitely larger markets that were still unprospected. One was professionals, especially doctors, who had a native curiosity about any new technical gizmo and the disposable income to purchase it. With this group, which would eventually merge with the hobbyists, Markkula first identified what would eventually be known as *early adopters*, a sizable and growing population that every tech company would depend upon to pay the high prices needed to cover the high development costs of emerging technologies. In the process, Markkula, who had always been known as more of a detail than a visionary marketing man, proved he could run with the best marketing seers.

The third market Markkula identified was even bigger—and more ambitious. This was the fata morgana of high tech in the 1970s: the home. The home consumer market tantalized with its millions of customers and billions in potential sales. But it only looked easy. One giant electronics company after another had been badly bruised (or dashed to pieces) trying to crash its way through the front door of suburban America. Still, the Apple II might be the product to do it. Markkula, the happy tinkerer, mused that maybe the computer could control operations around the house, like the sprinkler system.

For a guy who had made his reputation as a stickler for detail, this was a pretty wacky business strategy. There were no market figures for total size or estimated demand or just about anything else. It was mostly wishful thinking—*very* wishful, as it would turn out, given that doctors would prove to be among the last groups to buy personal computers, and the home controller would still not be a household feature twenty years later.

At least Markkula knew he was dreaming. John Hall, a group controller at the pharmaceutical outfit Syntex up the road in Palo Alto, didn't have that option. Markkula brought in Hall, a casual acquaintance, to turn those fantasies into hard numbers. It was work Hall had performed for many start-ups in the past. Scott was now on the scene, and he also enlisted Hall to help construct a bill of materials and project manufacturing costs for the II.

Markkula hoped to pull Hall in as Apple's vice president of finance, but after two weeks of vacation time constructing Apple's revenue predictions, Hall decided to steer wide of the little start-up. "I didn't believe the business plan and Mike Markkula didn't believe it. I felt it was a weak plan strategically." Nevertheless, because hope springs eternal, in exchange for his work Hall asked for some founders stock. Markkula turned him down, so Hall took $4,000 and went back to Syntex.

As a Valley veteran Markkula knew that, pipe dream or not, a written business plan was a crucial first step to building a company. Everybody knew most business plans were fantasies. But that didn't matter—what counted was the spirit of the company as conveyed in the plan: the moxie of the business strategy, the technical acumen of the staff and the chutzpah of the management. That was the key to raising money. It also helped in recruiting talent. And, what the hell, they could always rewrite it.

Amazingly enough, Apple never really had to. Probably the most famous business plan in Silicon Valley history (if you don't count the ones, like MIPS, so technically brilliant that they were funded from notes written on place mats) was that of James Treybig, who walked out of HP, sat down for six months at Mayfield Fund venture capital and produced a plan so prescient that the company it created, Tandem Computers, hit every one of Treybig's sales and profit predictions for the next five years.

Apple's plan, though much less celebrated, was nearly as remarkable. In the details Markkula was wrong, but in the larger predictions it was dead on. For more than a decade (critics would say even longer), Apple's three markets remained early adopters, professionals and home users. That was the good part. The bad was that, in being such an accurate prognosticator, Markkula also made his first big mistake. The fourth market, bigger than all the rest, the one he neglected to list, was corporate customers. Obviously, during this era of minicomputer hegemony, it was hard to imagine a PC ever sitting in an office. Yet that day came, and Apple, so identified with the other three markets, would spend the rest of its history trying and failing to reach this new market. Meanwhile, johnny-come-lately competitors, not tied to this installed base of consumers, grew fat and rich off the business market.

5.4 MAKING A SHOW

The Computer Faire was just days away and Apple still wasn't ready. There were the usual little things, such as the business cards not being back yet from the printers.

But there was also one very big thing; a deal breaker: no enclosure cases for the computers. Working with Mannock, Jobs had learned that there were basically two ways to mold a plastic enclosure for electronic equipment: reaction injection or structural foam. Reaction injection, which filled an epoxy mold with polyurethane via an expansive chemical reaction, was the cheaper method because of the lower setup costs. But its weakness was that the reaction didn't always produce enough pressure inside the mold to fill all the edges uniformly.

By comparison, structural foam used metal molds to hold hot, pressurized plastic as it was injected into the form. The result was more reliable and smoother, but much more expensive up front for the tooling.

For once, Jobs's inclination toward quality abandoned him. The rationale was that since the business plan predicted no more than 5,000 Apple II's would ever be built and sold there was no way to justify in volume the tooling costs of the better method. Since that had never stopped Jobs before, he either got a temporary case of the cheaps, didn't care or was overruled by Markkula.

Whatever the cause, it was a dumb decision. The first cases came back a disaster: bowed lids, pockmarked and uneven surfaces, incomplete edges flashing, filled voids—just about everything that could go wrong with molded plastic. But now there was no going back. The whole team spent the final days slicing off overpourings, sanding down lumps, puttying holes and, ultimately, spraying the crude cases with beige paint. They left for the Faire knowing that some of the machines had no air vents and, if left on too long, would burn themselves up.

The team spent the night in Union Square at the St. Francis Hotel—a big deal for guys who usually slept in dingy apartments or on the office floor— then got up early in the morning to head across town to Brooks Hall, where just eighteen months before Woz had purchased his first 6502.

In an age when a show like Comdex can draw 200,000 people to three giant halls in Las Vegas to see thousands of personal computer vendors, it is hard to capture the pocket-sized thrill of that first West Coast Computer Faire. Even with the spate of new personal computers on the market, as well as the rise of the first home computer retailers, to own a personal computer in 1977 was to still feel isolated, a pioneer, unsure if there really was anyone else out there.

But 13,000 people walked down the ramp into the underground hall that weekend. It was the gathering of a tribe that had little idea it even existed. Jobs had been right: this was a turning point, the galvanizing event that pushed personal computing from being a mere novelty into a real product with a real market. No computer company of any size could now look at those 13,000 souls and still dismiss home computing as a marginal business.

By the same token, those thousands of engineers, computer buffs, teenagers and the simply curious who entered the hall, past the messy stacks of mimeographed advertisements and flyers announcing show-only sales, had little trouble distinguishing the real companies from the fly-by-nighters. The Faire was set up as a central body of larger and more elaborate booths leased by the big companies like Commodore and Processor Technology, surrounded by a ring of smaller booths filled with people selling everything from manuals to T-shirts to loose chips. This was the slums of the personal computing industry, populated by quick-buck artists, one-shots, poor up-and-comers and folks who sold stuff on the periphery of every electronics show.

The amateurishness of these little outfits was evident in their pathetic little displays. Form followed dysfunction: long-haired guys in glasses and T-shirts with limited business experience talking to equally inexperienced business owners selling arcane, usually undocumented products ("You don't know what 8K ROM DIP packaging is?") and hawking their wares out of torn-open boxes and paper bags. Most didn't take checks, much less credit cards, could rarely make change and looked surly when you asked for a receipt. And that was only if you managed to get their attention as they talked to one another, old friends or their neighbors in unintelligible technogook. These were obviously people who still believed it was about technology, despite the evidence from the center of the hall. They were so utterly doomed that they didn't even know it.

And there, amid this detritus of the first personal computer revolution, Jobs and Wozniak, as they toured the Faire, could see the sorry booth of Computer Converser Corporation, with Alex Kamradt selling Woz's box and already fading into history.

Kamradt wasn't alone. Much of Homebrew lined that outside wall. Its day was almost over. From the instant you walked into the Faire you knew a sorting had already taken place between the early winners and the never-gonna-bes. The eye and mind gravitated to the center of the hall, where you could see the big booths, with their professional-looking displays and their even more professional signs: Cromemco, Altair, Processor Technology, Tandy. But, most of all, you saw Apple. It was right in front. By identifying the importance of the Faire early, Jobs had been able to sign up the best booth site in the show. And if the company's display was small compared to some of the others, the $5,000 that had been spent on location, professionally printed business cards, signage and flyers and black draping for the tables had a dramatic effect.

So did the team of Apple employees, all dressed in suits behind the tables. Markkula had wisely ordered everyone to dress up. So Regis took Jobs to the elegant Wilkes Bashford haberdashery in the city to buy him a suit. It was the beginning of Jobs's noted sartorial style. (Years later, when the pair were walking through San Francisco past that same store, Jobs turned to Regis and said, "Did I ever tell you about the first time I shopped here?" Regis, knowing Jobs too well, suppressed a smile and replied, "No, Steve, you didn't." Jobs then launched into a long, convoluted story featuring a blind man who gave him directions and a host of other phantasms. When he finished, Regis said, "Actually, Steve, I brought you here. Remember?" "Oh. Yeah," Jobs said, and walked on.)

When you walked up to the Apple booth that first day of the Faire, you sensed you were in the hands of pros. And you knew you were when you saw the sleek beige computer with the brown keys and the color image on its screen. Now *this* was what a personal computer should look like. It was an impressive enough of a presentation that Apple would field more than 300 orders in the next few days—more than 2 percent of the show's attendance, half again as many orders as the Apple I enjoyed in its year of existence. For weeks after, people would walk into Apple's offices off the street, having found the address on the show brochure, count out twelve $100 bills and walk away with a machine.

In later years, when Apple became a success, the first West Coast Computer Faire was presented not just as a turning point in the company's history but as an unalloyed triumph over the competition. This wasn't quite true. The show's organizer would later say that Apple wasn't the strongest exhibitor. The issue of *Byte* magazine covering the show never even mentioned Apple. And there was a host of anecdotal remembrances from attendees that other companies had better exhibits.

But that revisionism missed the point. Apple had no dreams of taking the Faire; there were simply too many big, experienced players in contention to ever accomplish that. For now, Apple only wanted to be seen as a real company, to make the cut, to leave the ranks of the losers in their crude booths on the periphery and be seen as a real player out in the middle of the floor. In that, Apple more than succeeded.

There was one other lesson to come out of the Computer Faire. In the midst of all the hard work, Woz decided to play a practical joke. Exactly where he found time to do it is anybody's guess, but Woz had always had found that extra little bit of energy for a joke. It was fun, it built morale and it made him feel superior to the straights. It was also Woz's little revenge on Markkula, Scott and, most of all, Steve Jobs for having stolen his pure little computer, forced him out of his dream job and made him against his will into a tainted entrepreneurial capitalist.

It was a simple joke. Woz spent $400 printing up (secretively, in Los Angeles) a bunch of lime-green broadsides announcing a new computer: the Zaltair, an Altair using the hot new Z-80 microprocessor and featuring "BAZIC" programming language. It was a pretty crude joke, but an effective one, because it separated the illuminati, who caught the joke instantly, from the unenlightened, who stood in slack-jawed acceptance of every bit of news from the industry, and most of all from the poseurs, who pretended they knew what they were talking about.

Woz and his techie confederates distributed the flyers around the show, then awaited the response. There wasn't much. The pros laughed and everyone else dutifully stuffed it into their plastic shopping bags with the scores of other promotional sheets, never to look at it again. Only MITS got angry, especially when it noticed that the flyer included a money-back guarantee on all Altairs. For a company suffering from quality problems this was not a joke. Soon an ad hoc Altair SWAT team was racing around the show floor stamping NOT REAL or FRAUD on every Zaltair flyer it found. As it turned out, they were in a race with Woz and his crew, who belatedly realized they might be liable for all those returned Altairs and were in a panicked search for the papers as well.

But the practical joke nevertheless managed to hook the biggest fish in the pond. Woz showed the flyer to Jobs, who bought the story completely, shouting, "Oh my God! This thing sounds great," and expressing relief that the performance chart on the back showed the Apple II a close third.

It was the first salvo in what would be an ongoing war at Apple, sometimes cold but more often hot, between the techies and the suits. The techs would always believe themselves intellectually (and thus morally) superior to management; and management would be forever convinced that the techies were brilliant children, forever plotting puerile games, and rarely to be trusted with responsibility.

Meanwhile, Wozniak had gotten his revenge. He had put into place the first brick of the countermyth that Steve Jobs was not really a technologist at all, but a brilliant fake, a parasite on real geniuses like Stephen Wozniak. This contrary image, regularly fed by just enough evidence to seem true, would haunt Jobs for twenty years.

But Jobs too got his revenge. Never again would Wozniak be trusted by Apple management. Never again would he be given decision-making power. And never again would he be allowed to run loose. The day would come when Woz would need that influence—and would find that he had long ago frittered it away.

5.5 SANDBOX'S END

The Apple Computer that came out of the West Coast Computer Faire was different from the one that went in.

It had a new product. It had orders. But, most of all, it had Mike Scott. As Scott saw it, his job was to turn Apple from a day-care center into a real company . . . fast. There was no time to delay. Scott knew well what happened to companies with fast growth. It took everything those firms had just to keep from blowing up under the stress of success. One tiny crack in the operations of one department could open up under pressure and split the company in two. That's what had happened at Fairchild, where too much talent and too little discipline had set off a devastating chain reaction. Markkula's former company, Intel, was emerging from just such a crisis.

Scott knew that he had to move fast. He had to staff up the administrative offices, construct a financial department, organize production in such a way that it could scale up to tens of thousands of units per month, build a marketing department, establish national distribution channels, stay on the engineering department for product upgrades and meanwhile find funding for the next round of company growth. And while he was doing all of this, he also had to control the founding children, who had little idea what it took to create a real company and who resented him for trying to do so.

Woz was the immediate problem. He refused to take anything but his own work seriously. And even on his own projects he was notoriously mercurial, working feverishly one moment, blocked the next, and forever at risk of going off on some technical tangent that momentarily appealed to him. Sometimes Scott couldn't move Woz at all, and then he had to bring in the big artillery of Markkula—who, for example, had to convince Woz to remove the word BULLSHIT from the Breakout game he was adapting for the Apple II.

Jobs was another matter altogether. Here Scott faced a dangerous, potentially fatal dilemma. In so many ways, Jobs *was* Apple. Rod Holt might say that "Scotty could fire anybody. But it was hard to imagine Apple without Steve Jobs." From the first confrontation, Mike Scott had prided himself on his ability to handle Jobs. But there was another side to the coin. Scott knew as much as anybody at Apple that Steve Jobs was too great a talent to lose (and, given his stockholdings, almost impossible to fire). The young man had extraordinary vision and an amazing capacity to make those visions real. But he was also a tyro, who believed he could do any job better than the person doing it, no matter how experienced. That included Mike Scott. Jobs also was indifferent to organization charts, ignored job boundaries and, depending upon the situation, treated employees, suppliers and customers like lovers or like dogshit.

He even disrupted board meetings. As an appalled Scott watched, at one such meeting, Jobs put his smelly sandaled feet up on the table. "Get your dirty stinking feet off the table!" bellowed Markkula. "Then put out your disgusting cigarette!" Jobs shouted back, demanding that the room be divided in half between smokers and nonsmokers.

Jobs was the most dangerous man in any organization: the irreplaceable destroyer. Scott had seen other characters like Jobs in his Silicon Valley career, but none so magnificent in this combination. Almost from the first day, Scott knew that "Jobs cannot run anything. He doesn't know how to manage people. After you get something started he causes lots of waves. He likes to fly around like a hummingbird at ninety miles per hour. He needs to be sat on."

A CEO can sit on the largest shareholder, but he cannot crush him. Jobs had to be given work and some responsibility. And every time he saw wiggle room, Jobs stirred up trouble. In setting up the company offices, Jobs got into a shouting match with Scott because he wanted the more expensive white desks for engineers while Scott wanted the cheaper gray models. They clashed over the layout of workflow. When Scott implemented a badge security system and gave Woz badge number 1 for having invented the computer, Jobs number 2 for creating the company and Markkula number 3 for being the first chairman (the rest were Fernandez #4, Holt #5, Wigginton #6, Scott #7 and Espinosa #8), only Jobs objected. He, in fact, threw a tantrum.

The exchange, as remembered by the other employees, went like this:
Jobs: "Am I number one?"
Scott: "No. Woz is number one. You're number two."
Jobs: "I want to be number one. Can I be number zero? Woz can be number one. I want to be number zero."

It was at such moments that Scott wondered why he'd ever left National.

And it only got worse. Put in charge of purchasing, Jobs created chaos. When IBM accidentally delivered blue typewriters instead of the beige ones he wanted, Jobs went crazy, demanding they be returned and replaced. The same thing happened with the phone company. Worst of all, Jobs mistreated key suppliers, driving down prices and high-handing salespeople as if Apple was a Fortune 500 company and not some little storefront operation that would be swiftly dropped if it got to be too much trouble. As Gary Martin, a new employee, observed: "We were all asking, 'How can you treat people like that?'"

Jobs could, and he did. And he got away with it.

The problems with the two founders aside, Scott was having the time of his life as the CEO of Apple. While history would record Woz and Jobs as great entrepreneurs, the one true, classic entrepreneur in the early days of Apple was Mike Scott.

"It was so exciting," he recalls. "For the first time in my life I got to build from scratch the complete organization of a company. Up until then, I'd always had a corporate umbrella over me, protecting me. This time, I was completely on my own."

In this hothouse entrepreneurial environment, Mike Scott thrived. Despite its outrageous numbers, Scott's Apple during its first five years met all the revenue figures in its business plan. When he wasn't putting information-reporting structures into place at the company, or managing Jobs and Woz, Scott was browbeating suppliers into better deals. He instituted a program to collect debts in fifteen days, but only paying bills every forty-five days, in the meantime putting the liquidity to use. "At least we *did* pay in forty-five days—most companies promised thirty days and delivered in ninety," he says.

When Finis Conor, the CEO of Santa Clara disk drive giant Shugart, suddenly jacked up the price of its drives—of which Apple represented half of all purchases—from $30 to $120, Scott was ready. Rod Holt merely had to ask, "Should I use the plane ticket?" Scott nodded and Holt was off to Japan and the disk drive maker Alps with a $20 million purchase order in his pocket. (Shugart's owner, Xerox, was so mortified that a few years later it bought a piece of Apple—which Apple sold in exchange for a look at that company's research. And that is what led Steve Jobs to Xerox PARC.)

When Digital Equipment was late delivering a second PDP-ll minicomputer that Apple needed for its internal information network—perhaps because, as DEC CEO Ken Olsen had told Scott during an earlier visit: "Personal computers will never be big"—Scott ordered a sixteen-foot white rose wreath sent to DEC's lobby bearing a note reading: "This is what I think about your delivery commitments." The computer was on an airplane that night.

In those early years, Mike Scott ricocheted around the company. Not trusting Woz's assurances about the environmental toughness of the Apple II, Scott had a Sunnyvale neighbor, a carpenter, build him a wooden test chamber. To impact-test the machine, Scott threw it off the roof of his house.

This eccentric, sometimes poignant, personal touch was also in evidence in the early days of Scott's management. He maintained a small slush fund just for wacky expenses, such as an Apple hot-air balloon and a mainsail emblazoned with the Apple logo for Holt's yacht. One Christmas, when things had settled to a dull roar, Scott put on a Santa Claus suit and walked around the office dispensing gifts. When Randy Wigginton wanted to quit to make more money for school, Mike Scott offered to have Apple pay for the young man's college education.

Scott drove a battered Pinto to work for months until Apple, fearful of losing its president to an exploding car, ordered him to stop. For fun ("I wanted to make the day memorable for Steve") he ordered a white rose wreath with the inscription "RIP" and a note reading: "From somebody watching over your shoulder," signed "Anonymous," delivered to Jobs's office on his birthday. Scott today laughs at the memory. "Jobs threatened everybody, trying to find out who did it. It was five years before he learned the truth."

Thanks to a Hollywood connection, Scott had read a script of *Raiders of the Lost Ark* long before the movie went into production. So, when the film hit the theaters, Scott booked San Jose's Century Theater for a preview showing and invited all five hundred Apple employees. They arrived through two arbors of white roses (by now a Scott trademark) and then, as they entered the theater, were handed a single white silk rose by Mike Scott.

5.6 A HOUSE DIVIDED

Like all new start-ups, Apple initially ramped up its employment by hiring friends and compatriots. Jobs, for example, hired Jim Martindale, an old workmate from Atari, to run production, Dan Kottke, home from college, and

Allen Baum. Woz hired his teenaged acolytes, Chris Espinosa and Randy Wigginton, the latter in turn hiring a high school pal, Don Breuner, as a part-time technician.

Mike Scott, as might be expected, hired pros. Gene Carter, who had worked with him at Fairchild (and, for a time, was his boss), signed on as head of sales and distribution. Sherry Livingston, from National Semiconductor, was hired as receptionist and secretary. She would gain Silicon Valley immortality as the secretary who made a million dollars when Apple went public — thus making her a model for staff workers everywhere. But, at the time, the only thing that convinced her to take a job at the unproven little company was Mike Markkula pulling open a desk drawer and showing her that it was filled with orders.

But the most important Scott hire, at least at the beginning, was Gary Martin, an accountant who had worked for Scott at National. Martin, on first seeing the Apple II, thought, "Who the hell is going to want this thing? I felt so sorry for Scott I tried to buy him lunch." But, no matter how dicey, new start-ups with their potential for founders stock, are the brass ring of Silicon Valley life. And since the Valley was and is one of the few places on earth that rewards rather than punishes entrepreneurial failure, there was every incentive for Martin to take the leap. The decision was made even easier by his current boss at National, who agreed not to let National know until Martin had given Apple a month's tryout.

Martin never went back.

Besides Woz's disciples, Jobs's contacts and Scott's workmates, there was a fourth type of new employee hired by Apple: the walk-ons. This group was exemplified by Wendell Sander, a Fairchilder who had been playing with an early Apple I for more than a year, designing his own memory boards and even programming a video game, based on *Star Trek*, for his kids. He walked out of a thirteen-year career at Fairchild to join Apple, later telling Michael Moritz, "If they had folded I could have gotten a job the next day. There wasn't much personal risk apart from the chance of getting a bruised ego. My career would not have vanished."

Sander's attitude was typical of many of Apple's professional hires. After 1974 and the worst recession the Valley had ever known, the local economy, driven by the rise of video games, minicomputers and consumer electronics, was on its way back. Experienced professionals were again becoming valuable, and well-paid, assets to local electronics companies.

With the arrival of these pros, the schism between the vets and the kids that had begun at Apple with the arrival of Scott now grew even more pronounced. Apple was now a company of both people who could get a job anywhere and people who probably couldn't get a job anywhere but Apple.

It was an impossible combination. But Apple did the impossible in 1977. The unlikely, and volatile, pairing of Steve Jobs and Mike Scott created a razor's edge of discipline mixed with creative license. The suits could for the first time take off their ties and be their weekend selves all week; while the freaks could at last function in a viable setting that channeled their talents. It worked so well—except for the occasional shouting matches—that soon the Apple corps began to believe it had created a whole new business philosophy.

5.7 CUTTING CORNERS

A fact that has gone unremarked about Apple Computer is that it was Silicon Valley's first native company. Jobs, Fernandez and Wozniak were all hometown boys.

They weren't alone. Gary Martin was also a local, though, unlike the others, his roots reached back into old Santa Clara Valley. His parents had come to the Valley before the war and for years had run Martin's Market & Bar in downtown Santa Clara and delivered bread for Wilson's Jewel Bakery, still a Valley landmark.

Gary had grown up in the grocery store, attended local Catholic schools and then gone on for an accounting degree at San Jose State. In the meantime, he had also become a world-class judo expert, twice winning the NCAA championship, and at one point was ranked second in the world.

Few old Valley types ever made the crossover to the new Silicon Valley. And Martin's career might have taken a typical path had not the air freight company he was working for gone bankrupt at the end of the 1960s. Desperate for work as the economy was sliding into a recession, Martin took the bold step of signing on with National Semiconductor, a $99 million manufacturer of products he didn't understand.

He was at National Semi for five years, and for much of that time he served as a controller under a brilliant product group manager named Mike Scott. National Semi, Martin would recall, was as wild a place as its legend suggests: "It was completely wide open. Whatever it took to ship, we did." But within that madhouse, Martin could see that Scott was something special: a cultured man, who not only could run the business side of the operation but also could contribute to the technology. "The design freaks loved Mike because he was one of them. He'd studied nuclear physics at Caltech. I remember at one point Mike came in on weekends and wrote elegant programs for one of our devices. Not many managers could do that."

Martin was there the day a stunned and red-faced Scott stormed out of his office shouting in disbelief, "Mike Markkula just retired from Intel!" And he was there in April 1977 when Scott announced he was leaving National to join Markkula's new company. But three months later, when Scott telephoned and suggested they meet for lunch, Martin still knew next to nothing about that company.

By the end of that lunch, he not only had a better idea but also a job offer. "I was thirty years old. I remember going home and talking to my wife about it. We finally decided that if this Apple thing didn't work out, I could always go back to National. Besides, it would be a good way to meet venture capitalists if I ever wanted to start my own company." Martin also took the job because, the founders aside, Apple by now had a "very credible team," with Markkula, Scott and Holt. Thus, in the summer of 1977, Martin found himself in the Good Earth facility. "They gave me a box of papers and told me to get the company's books together."

Martin had expected the usual problems putting a company like Apple on a strong financial foundation. He assumed it would be the standard three-part process: first, hand off bookkeeping and accounting to professionals; second, reconcile payables with receivables; a third, establish a financial measurement cycle that worked to the company's benefit. In this endeavor, he had the full support of Mike Scott.

The immediate task was to find the pros. Scott had already hired Bank of America (the standard quid pro quo for a line of credit) to implement a payroll and withholding program for Apple. It would be B of A that wrote Apple's payroll checks. Martin, looking down the road to the day when Apple might be a publicly traded company with extensive reporting requirements, got the bluest-beribboned accounting firm in town, Arthur Young, to run Apple's annual audit. It was a nice side benefit that Arthur Young, trying to woo new Silicon Valley start-ups, offered a discount on the first year's work to rookie customers.

Duplicating National Semi, Martin put Apple on a weekly, "Sporckian" calendar—which, with its 53-week year, gave Apple an extra week each year to stick in where it would do the most good. Meanwhile, studying the balance sheet, Martin also concluded that the company would cross the break-even point in late September—so, in order to take advantage of a loophole on estimated tax (it offered the equivalent of a fifteen-month loan by the government in the form of taxes not yet paid), Martin chose to set the fiscal year at September 30. "I had no idea I was setting the rhythm for the whole company for all the years to come," Martin said later. In fact, the timing was perfect, because henceforth money could then be reinvested in manufacturing each winter in what was proving to be the busiest time of the year for personal computer purchases.

But by setting such a near date for the fiscal year close, and then bringing in Arthur Young, Martin had also set Apple up for a legal nightmare.

Apple, it seemed, already had a skeleton in its closet. Several times each week, a station wagon driven by a Los Altos housewife Hildy Licht (wife of Woz's old Homebrew friend, Harry Licht) would pull up to Apple to deliver stacks of finished, stuffed printed circuit boards and power supplies, and pick up a new order. From there she would select the proper number of boards and components stored in her own home and drop them off at houses and apartments throughout Silicon Valley.

It was a nice deal for Apple, because it was cheap, delivery was prompt and orders could be quickly modified without complaint. There was only one problem: it was illegal. Inside many of those houses and apartments were rooms crowded with women, some of them newly arrived Southeast Asian immigrants, as well as a few Mexican illegals. These ladies would sit there all day, stuffing boards, gossiping and watching soaps. They were happy to be paid piece rates. No one ever mentioned minimum wage, or Social Security, or workplace safety laws. And thus, for more than a year, the Apple II, promoted as the machine to liberate people from the slavery of bureaucracies and office work, was in fact being partially assembled in sweatshops.

No one outside Apple knew of the arrangement. But with this first audit, Martin realized, the accountants were about to learn everything. He later recalled, "The auditor from Arthur Young was this little Jewish guy named Fred, and he was very diligent. He didn't just want reports, he wanted to tally *everything*. At the time, the motherboards were being stuffed by a legit outfit in town, but the power supplies were being built by Hildy Licht and her little band of housewives. He wanted to see it.

"So we piled into a little BMW—me, Fred and in the back seat a new hire at Apple, an ex-cop named Brian Fitzgerald [later vice president of Intuit]. As we're driving over, I introduce Brian by telling Fred that Brian was kicked out of the police department for killing too many suspects. Fred starts to sweat.

"We get to Hildy's, our second manufacturing center. It's a house in Los Altos, and all Hildy's got to show is a box of parts. Fred asks, 'Where's the rest?' and Hildy walks over to a closet, flings open the door and points at a blackboard listing apartments all over the Valley. 'There they are!' Hildy says.

"We passed the audit."

"Looking back, the whole place was hysterical," recalled Martin. "And by that I mean both fun and insane."

There were also numerous shouting matches. The biggest were between Scott and Jobs. Jobs had a habit of purchasing equipment and not deigning to fill out the purchase order. Says Martin, "We were always surprised when the stuff would show up and we didn't have it in our budget.

"Finally, Mike Scott couldn't take it anymore. Right there in the middle of this thirty-foot-square room he started screaming at Jobs: 'Goddamnit! I'm calling an emergency board meeting. Either you straighten up or I'm out of here!' Of course, between him, Jobs, Markkula and Woz, you could say that the board was meeting all the time."

Unlike some of the others, Martin wasn't bothered by the shouting matches. "Hey, I grew up in a family store working with relatives. This was nothing." But what Martin encountered in the other room at the Good Earth office was unlike anything he'd ever seen. There in the laboratory, he'd see Woz, in a kind of communion with the Apple II. "What most people don't realize is that in the earliest days of the II there was no way for it to store its own code. We also didn't have a paper tape machine to download onto every night. So each morning, when Woz started up the machine, he would have to reload the entire operating code. That was hundreds of lines of code, and as near as I can tell, he did it all from memory. He *thought* in code.

"And that wasn't the strangest part. I remember walking in more than once and seeing Wozniak *talking* to the II. He would say something to it, while he typed, and then the II would reply on its screen in hex[adecimal] code. Then Woz would talk and type some more. It was as if they were carrying on a conversation, like a patient father teaching a dutiful child."

5.7.1 BREAKING THE MOLD

When the numbers came in, it turned out that Apple had made $775,000 for the 1977 fiscal year. That was about Hewlett-Packard's annual budget for coffee and cinnamon rolls, but in the still tiny world of personal computing it was proof that Apple was now a serious competitor. Even better, orders were tripling by the month, with no sign of slowing for months, even years.

Meanwhile, Scott was scrambling. In one respect, he was the best kind of start-up company president because he had no sense of protocol when it came to getting things done. He would scrub the toilets, deliver boxes to UPS, pick up lunch for employees, whatever it took. In Wigginton's words: "Scott's motto was let's make some money. Let's get something out the door." It was a good philosophy, but it ran into resistance.

One was staffing. Given the pace of orders, there was no way the little company could ramp up manufacturing, especially board stuffing, fast enough to keep up with demand. Scott's solution, a not uncommon one, was to contract the work out. But outsourcing was expensive and Apple didn't have much money. So Scott cut corners by using Hildy Licht—in the process putting himself in some bad company. He later justified it by saying that he only hired Hildy, and how she chose to do the assembly work was her business—but that wasn't enough, especially not from a company that claimed to have cornered enlightenment.

The other obstacle, as usual, was Steven Jobs. With his usual sense of grandeur, Jobs wanted to create a professional-looking manual to be placed in the box with the Apple II. Such a manual was seen as a perfect project to keep Jobs out of the way. After all, how could he screw that up?

By being late, actually. Before long, deliveries of the company's computers were being held up waiting for Jobs's literary masterpiece. Finally, exasperated, Scott cut through the Jobsian knot and ordered the waiting II's to be sent out with simple data sheets (xeroxed in the shopping center across the street) showing the computer's features and describing how to set it up. Now it was Woz's turn to object. He argued that serious users would want information on subroutines, source codes, even a copy of Sander's *Star Trek* game. Fine, said Scott, just to end the conversation. If anybody asks, we'll send him the stuff you want. Henceforth, that collection of hard-core Apple II material would be known as the Wozpack.

Without knowing it, Scott had set a pattern for lousy manuals that would haunt Apple for years. Both Jobs and Woz had been right: users really did want extensive, professionally prepared documentation. Yet even the manual for the Apple III at the beginning of the 1980s would leave users dumbfounded with its kiss-off opening: We will assume you already know how to use a computer . . .

In the end, the only thing that saved Apple on the documentation front was that the manuals and user packets created by its competitors were even more awful.

But sweatshops and miserable manuals were minor compared to what came next. The punishment for Jobs's uncharacteristic decision to go with cheaper packaging wasn't over yet. In September, about the time the first audit was taking place at Apple, the tooling for the Apple II's enclosure broke down at the contractor. No plastic box, no computer. Scott was already running as lean as he could within the company's limited resources; this breakdown threatened to shut Apple down through the end of the year. That was enough to kill the company.

"It was life or death for us," Scott would remember. Unanswered orders backed up, as did the finished boards from the sweatshops. Meanwhile, new employees, crucial for the company's growth projections for 1978, were put on hold. Apple prayed they'd still be around when Apple could at last afford to hire them.

At a time when the slightest flicker in a struggling young computer company's reputation could scare off its entire market, word was out in the incestuous Homebrew world that Apple was in trouble and might not last out the year.

Steve Jobs was the person who got the company into this mess, and it fell upon him to get the company out. He was also the perfect man for the job. Fear turned the dials up high on his reality distorter. He jumped on a plane for Seattle to visit the same plastic molding company, Tempress, that made hundreds of thousands of HP calculator cases each year. It was a long shot that such a company would take a risk on such a small order from a financially desperate firm. Robert Reutimann, Tempress's vice president said later, "I thought to myself, 'Does he know what he's doing?' I was a little afraid of going ahead with the project. I thought, 'Here comes another guy with big ideas.' "

But Steve Jobs had talked his way past such skepticism before. He did it again. He talked Reutimann into taking the contract, then, in a new twist that showed he was already learning something about management, sweetened the deal with an incentive of $1,000 for every week that the new mold was delivered before the deadline. Apple was back in production in less than eight weeks—a nasty financial hit still, but not a crippling one. By December, orders were not only being filled but once more tripling by the month.

Jonathon Martin, the first Apple baby, was born in 1978 to Gary Martin and his wife. He was followed soon after by a child born to secretary Jean Richardson. The company was still so young and new that it had no medical coverage for pregnancies. So Martin and Richardson simply established a new employee program—a "baby bonus"—and awarded the first ones to themselves.

5.8 LOST BOY

As usual, the vagaries of daily business at Apple barely touched Woz. He already had most of his staffers, as well as a regular supply of walk-ons who had stopped by to see what was up and stayed to help.

Thus, at least on the job, Woz could happily hide in his hermetic world and play with his technology toys. He was content to work all hours of the night, drag himself home in the morning, work on the computer he kept there, then race back to work.

Unfortunately, try as he might, real life kept impinging on Stephen Wozniak. His wife, Alice, had long since grown tired of playing a distant second to silicon chips and cathode-ray tubes. And if she felt excluded from her husband and his friends during the garage days, the situation had only grown worse as Apple became a real company. Now Markkula and Scott, sensing what was coming, were keeping her at arm's length. "Steve was told not to bring me to Mike Markkula's house in case they discussed company business," she said later.

Finally, unable to take any more, she threw Woz out. He took to sleeping on a couch at the office, where he was happiest anyway. Meanwhile, as the trial separation moved inexorably toward divorce, Woz suddenly and suspiciously (one can hear the whispers of others) got interested in not giving Alice any stock as part of a possible settlement. In the end, Markkula intervened, at the request of Woz, and connected the young genius with a lawyer. Alice Wozniak, after seventeen lonely months of marriage, nevertheless managed to walk away with 15 percent of Woz's stock.

Meanwhile, for Woz it was like being free to live on the Island of Lost Boys. He could now spend all of his time at Apple playing with brilliant teenagers to his heart's content. Sure, there was always some grumpy grown-up like Holt or Scott to make them clean up the work they'd started, but that wasn't much of a sacrifice for all the fun in between.

The walk-ons saw all this fun and wanted to play too. And Woz, with his legendary lack of discrimination, let them stay. It was the perfect setting for disaster. And that disaster arrived in the eccentric form of Cap'n Crunch himself. John Draper was now out of Lompac prison, and looking for work. Contacting Woz, Draper proposed designing a new board for the Apple II that would turn the machine into a powerful automatic telephone dialer.

Only a fool would hire a convicted felon to go back into his old line of work. But Woz, in fact, was thrilled with the idea, dreaming of programming his computer to harass a friend by dialing his phone a thousand times. "It would have been one of the great products of all time," he said.

Others at Apple were terrified. And with good reason. Chris Espinosa looked at the card—called the Charlie Board—and instantly saw that it was in fact the ultimate blue box. With a little research he concluded that a dozen Apple II's equipped with Charlie Boards and networked together could pull down the entire U.S. telephone system. With other Apple engineers, and without Draper's knowledge, he secretly tried to modify the board to remove its hacking capabilities. Jobs too, when he found out about Draper, went nuts.

Luckily, relief came from a not wholly unexpected source. Draper, who had decided that Apple management, especially Jobs, "were chickenshit and paranoid about having me on the premises," pulled up stakes and disappeared. Not long after, he was arrested in Pennsylvania and charged with stealing $50,000 worth of telephone calls. Once again, Cap'n Crunch was thrown in jail. But he would be back.

Meanwhile, one of the items found in Draper's possession during his arrest was an Apple II with a Charlie Board mounted inside. Apple wasn't charged, but the police inquiry finally brought the news to Scott that his resident technical guru had been risking the company on an illegal project. Scott was understandably furious. He went to Markkula and the newly constituted Apple board of directors and asked that Woz be fired. Woz, who got wind of this, was worried. "Scotty is the only guy that would [dare] fire me. That guy could do anything," he later recalled with a shudder.

Somehow, the directors managed to calm Scott down. Woz was too important for Apple to lose . . . especially now that he had turned his attention to a bigger (and more legal) series of technology challenges.

5.9 OUTSIDERS

The Charlie Board may have been a fool's errand, but it pointed to where Woz's head was going: continuously adding new capabilities to the Apple II via add-in cards. And for the next eighteen months, Woz and his crew kept the attention of the home computer industry riveted with one new hardware enhancement announcement after another. There was a ROM card, which quickly added more core memory (16,000 bits!) to the computer. A communications card, which made possible limited networking. A serial interface card, which took advantage of the newly emerging industry (IEEE) standard for linking together instruments, computers and peripherals. And a printer card, to allow the II to output to the newly introduced, low-cost thermal dot matrix and typewriter-like daisy wheel printers.

But that was just a warm-up. Input and output interface cards were useful, even valuable, but they weren't revolutionary. Memory was. Already, just a couple of years into personal computing, PC owners were discovering to their chagrin one of the fundamental maxims of computing: no matter how much memory you have, it ain't enough. That was because every leap in information storage soon led to a commensurate jump in the size of the applications and files using that memory. Pretty soon you were full up on stored memory, with no place to put new files unless you wanted to start purging out important stuff to make room.

Moreover, in 1977 you didn't have to be a computer genius to appreciate that the days of cassette memory were numbered. Cassettes were designed for audio, where inherent weaknesses such as tape stretch and flutter were nearly invisible. If a note in "Stairway to Heaven" bent a little more than it used to, your ears couldn't tell the difference. But have that same tape stretch while downloading the millions of ones and zeros in BASIC or the *Star Wars* video game and the whole system crashed. The microprocessor inside a computer like the Apple II used that flow of binary digits not just for information to process, but also to synchronize the entire chip with the cycles of electricity flowing through it. Slip a millisecond-long half-beat and it was like having motion-picture film jump out of its sprocket holes or, more precisely, like skipping a line on the answer sheet of a very long multiple-choice test.

And that was only part of the problem with tape. The other was that it was just too slow. Downloading a big program, such as BASIC, took so long you could literally go out to lunch and come back just as it was finishing. Like personal computers, cassette drives were a descendant of much larger and more powerful machines. Unfortunately, in the case of cassettes a lot more had been lost in translation. The long banks of big-reeled tape drives that were providing much of the storage for mainframe computers had the benefit of wide (thus faster information transfer), high-density (again, plus more accuracy), and thick (no stretching) Mylar tape, as well as multiple drive wheels to adjust tape speed with precision. By comparison, the cassette players used with machines like the Apple II were indistinguishable from the ones teenaged girls used to play Carpenters tapes.

But a solution was already waiting in the wings. Disk-drive technology was nothing new in mainframes, having been around since the late 1950s—and, coincidentally, invented just down the road from Apple at IBM in San Jose— but its implementation was. The disk drives of 1976 were giant spinning metal platters covered by iron oxide with read/write heads flicking back and forth on cantilevered arms across the disk's surface reading millions of bits of data off thousands of tracks in a matter of seconds. They were a technological marvel, but also a tough technology to get into reliable, mass-producible form.

Yet, by the early 1970s, most of the world's mainframe computers had switched over to a combination of disk and tape memory (a third form, drum memory, was abandoned). The minicomputer revolution gave an added impetus to the creation of smaller, less costly versions. Once again, it was the IBM San Jose crew that came up with a solution. They used a new design for the read/write head and arm—code-named Winchester technology, after nearby Winchester Boulevard (and the mall where Woz and Jobs were at the time playing Alice in Wonderland), which in turn was named after the famous Winchester Mystery House. With Winchester technology, the IBM team had a semiconductor-based technique for building disk drives that let mass memory tap into the magic of Moore's Law.

Soon the platters got smaller, as did prices, while capacity held its own. Adventurous little companies, such as Shugart, sprang up to license this technology and experiment with new formats.

The most fruitful of these formats (discovered first by IBM in 1972) proved to be a revisit to Mylar tape—only this time not a ribbon, but a flexible disk the size of an LP record, etched with rings of magnetized dots. One had only to pick up one of these pizza-sized, razor-thin sheets out of its case to appreciate how it got the name "floppy disk."

The Homebrewers, as always keeping tabs on the big-iron boys, had watched disk memory coming for as long as the club had been in existence. Everyone in the industry knew that floppies were the future of personal computer memory. But as many of them well knew, it was a long way from a sexy dream to the real thing. Still, being computer freaks, they were not inclined to wait.

There were a number of private attempts to bolt a floppy drive onto an existing Altair, IMSAI or even Apple, but the resulting jury rig was usually a slow, unreliable kluge. These failures became particularly frustrating when companies like Shugart took the process to the next step and began offering drives for 5¼-inch disks. If ever there was a disk drive *made* for personal computing, this was it. The drive would even fit *in* the box!

But like every other big step in the personal computer story, it only looked easy. One of the first companies to try to put a floppy drive into its computer was—no surprise—Processor Technology. Pro Tech teamed up with another company, Diablo, to build a disk drive with the necessary accompanying controller. Before the whole mess was over, Diablo had tried to back out, the drives proved unreliable and Pro Tech, having promised a disk drive for the Sol, finally had to offer a more expensive version no one wanted. It was the beginning of the end for Processor Technology. Two years later, Apple's first great competitive threat was gone.

But if the failure to offer a reliable disk drive killed some of the early players, successful designs opened the door to the arrival of hot new companies, such as Morrow, Vector Graphics and NorthStar—the last in an especially good position as the leading Shugart licensee.

Obviously, if Apple was going to stay in the game, it would need its own disk drive. And just as obviously, the only person to do the job was Woz.

5.10 DISCOPOLIS

Wozniak officially first learned of this new company strategy at a company executive board meeting in early December 1977. But he must have known of it ex officio for several months, because Rod Holt, who was also at the meeting, was already pissed at Woz for being his usual procrastinating self.

"Woz," he later told Moritz, "would take a product right up to the crisis point and do it." It was almost as if he needed the adrenaline spike of approaching disaster in order to create. Holt apparently wasn't the only member of Apple's staff to appreciate this feature of Woz's, because at the meeting Markkula walked up to the board and listed Apple's product goals for the next couple of years and put "Disk drive" at the top. Then he turned and pointedly informed Woz that he was to have such a drive ready by the January Consumer Electronics Show . . . that is, in four weeks.

Woz knew about disk drives, of course. He had thumbed through a Shugart manual during his HP days. He'd even momentarily played in his mind with a circuit that could control such a drive. But other events had intervened. Now Woz realized he didn't have a clue how disk drives actually worked—and he was going to have to find out, fast.

Over the next two weeks he pored over every manual and reverse-engineered every drive he could get his hands on. IBM. Shugart. NorthStar. The deeper he dove, the more Woz realized he was back to the same problem he faced with the color display: synchronization, this time between the computer and the read/write head. More research showed him a second problem, standardization, which he came to realize might be turned into an opportunity.

The synchronicity problem initially seemed a deal breaker. Understanding why it was so complex requires a little background on computer operation. A computer's CPU, in this case its microprocessor, performs a series of operations as defined by the software program under which it is operating. Each step of that program typically has two components: the operation it is supposed to perform and the data upon which that operation is to work. That data is waiting in a temporary holding area on the chip called the cache. But to get it to the cache can be a convoluted process, because that data can be sitting on a memory chip on the motherboard or it may be sitting at some address out on the disk.

The problem is finding that data and getting it to the cache before the processor calls for it, and getting it there at the proper moment to match up with the right operation to work on it—and do it accurately a million (these days, 400 million) times per second.

To accomplish this, the engineers at IBM devised an elaborate disk-drive controller that essentially put the CPU and the disk drive on the same clock, a system comparable to having two traffic lights working together a thousand miles apart. It worked, but it was enormously complicated and expensive.

The more Woz studied the design of this controller, the more he recognized its sheer superfluousness. Once again, his genius lay in being a maverick, in throwing out the received view and having the hubris to start over from first principles.

He cast back to his old design for the Shugart drive. Back then, without really understanding how disk-drive controllers worked, he had nevertheless come up with an elegantly simple solution. All that it lacked was synchronicity.

And that's when Woz made yet another legendary cognitive leap. *What if you just ignored synchronicity?* After all, why did the disk drive have to operate in perfect tandem with the CPU? Let 'em go their own ways. Let the disk drive self-synch. When the microprocessor wants something, it merely has to call for it, the disk drive will send it in and the cache will hold it in queue until it's needed. The data would behave like cars reaching the tollgate on the Bay Bridge. The commuters didn't all have to leave their houses in Oakland and Berkeley at exactly the same moment; rather they merely had to wait their turn through the tollgate before entering the bridge. On the far end of the bridge, San Francisco saw only a continuous, even flow of traffic.

As for the problem of standardization, the good news was that there wasn't any. IBM, which made the earth shake every time it moved, had forced its disk interface standards on the industry at every step of the way. Thus, you either played by Armonk's rules or you didn't play at all.

Except in the 5¼-inch format. That market was so new that it hadn't fully consolidated yet, much less standardized. Woz therefore had a brief window of opportunity to come up with his own design and, with brilliance and luck, convince the rest of the industry to follow. He made the best of his chance.

IBM had spent millions of dollars and tied up scores of engineers for months designing its disk drive interface. Wozniak did the same thing alone—and better—in two weeks. And he knew what he had done. He had outwitted Big Blue. It made Cap'n Crunch's escapades look like petty vandalism . . . and on top of it all, it was legal. Woz knew he was about to wow his peers in ways he'd only dreamed of.

But first he had to build it. And he had two weeks to do it in, including Christmas and New Year's. But then again, he no longer had a wife or a home. What else was there to do but work day and night?

That's what he did. Even on Christmas Day, he left his parents' house after opening presents and went into the office to work for ten hours. Throughout this banzai run he kept young Randy Wigginton by his side, trusting the kid to take on any tasks he handed off to him with a minimum of explanation. Day after day they worked on the disk drive. Woz constructing the board, Wigginton writing the code for the disk formatter, Woz creating the read/write software.

Woz at these moments became both superhuman in his creativity and animal-like in his focus and endurance. Holt, whose job it was to ride herd on the pair and make sure they did not leave any loose ends, actually began to worry that Woz might go crazy staying so deeply immersed. Jean Richardson, who usually unlocked the office in the morning, would often let an exhausted and delirious Woz out the door as she came in. "He was a ghost who came and went at odd hours," she would recall. "He worked through the night . . . Eating and sleeping didn't seem to matter."

By New Year's, the pair were testing the controller by storing and downloading data to and from a Shugart disk drive. It worked faster and more accurately than any personal computer disk drive to date. It wasn't finished, but it was near enough to risk showing to the world. They had run out of time. With Apple's management team, the pair jumped on a plane for Las Vegas.

They arrived in the evening. The show was to open in the morning. Woz and Wigginton helped set up the booth, then went back to their room to finish the drive. They worked through the night, taking breaks to cruise the excitement of the casino floors below. For Wigginton, just seventeen, Vegas was a revelation. He even had the typical adolescent thrill of sneaking his way into various games of chance. So, while he was helping change the world upstairs, his real excitement that day came from winning thirty-five dollars at craps.

So excited was Wigginton that when he returned to work he managed to erase the entire disk. It took him and Woz most of the predawn hours to reconstruct the lost data. At 7:30 A.M., once again finished, they tried to crash for the couple of hours before the show started—but they were too wired to sleep.

That morning, the Consumer Electronics Show threw its doors open to nearly 100,000 attendees. Hot-air balloons, hookers waiting outside, car radios booming out hundred of watts of sound, CB radios, screaming video games, porn stars signing autographs, $10,000 stereo systems, electronic toys—the whole panoply of human entertainment and desire, all filtered through the wonderful world of electronics.

The decision to exhibit at CES was a canny one by Markkula, the marketing man. Showing at the West Coast Computer Faire was one thing. Everybody in personal computing did that. But to show at CES was a statement; it said that the personal computer was no longer just a toy for phreaks, but an important new *consumer* product, one that would soon be sold to everybody who now owned a Pioneer receiver or a Sony television set. And to be there first among its PC competitors was a way for Apple to say that it best understood this future and was already prepared for it.

In that respect, Woz's efforts on the disk drive controller were superfluous to the event. Most of the people wandering the floors of CES had little idea of how a computer worked, much less the radical innovation of a self-synchronizing disk-drive controller. But it *had* served the purpose of giving Woz the deadline he needed to focus his brain . . . and guaranteed that Apple would be ready to show off the controller to the group that really mattered three months later at the second Computer Faire.

Now the basic design was done. Thanks to Markkula's artificial deadline, Woz and Wigginton (with Holt, as always, riding herd) had time to perfect their creation. In particular, after Howard Cantin proved too busy (and too angry at Jobs) to lay out the circuit board for the controller, Woz took on the job himself. For two weeks, Woz worked until two o'clock each morning, teaching himself circuit board design as he went.

It seemed to go smoothly until near the end, when, just as he was completing the design, Woz noticed a problem. It was a crossover between a couple of the conductor lines on the board. That junction had the potential to create a "feedthrough" of signals between the two lines and wreck everything. In just twenty marathon hours, Woz redesigned the entire board around a relocated connector and fixed the problem.

He really didn't have to do so. Feedthrough was an unpleasant, though seemingly inevitable, part of electronic life, and finding a way to reroute the wires around such a crossover was usually a daunting, if not impossible, problem of topology. But Woz not only fixed that feedthrough but then found yet another and redesigned the board a second time.

The result was an engineering masterpiece, one of the last great works of solo electronic design in the century. Even Woz knew he had done something amazing, later saying, "It's something you can *only* do if you're [both] the engineer and the PC board person yourself. That was an artistic layout. The board has virtually no feedthroughs." In years to come he would call it "the favorite design of my life."

Woz liked an admiring audience, and this time he got it in spades. Word had already leaked out about Apple's disk-drive introduction at CES. At the West Coast Computer Faire, the company that had used every artifice the year before to be seen as a major competitor now had no trouble being the star. *Everyone* went by the Apple booth to see the new floppy drive for the II. The hard-core techies came away dumbstruck by the beauty and simplicity of Woz's design. Even Lee Felsenstein, who never had anything good to say about Apple, would remember seeing the Apple disk controller for the first time: "I nearly dropped my pants. It was so clever. I thought: We'd better keep out of the way of these guys."

In two years, in a series of extraordinary creative bursts, Stephen Wozniak had designed one of the world's first personal computers, then built the first practical home computer complete with color display; he had also written the programming language for those computers, and now he had brought mass memory to the average computer user. Hardware, software, display and storage: Woz had pulled off an engineering hat trick that has not been matched. He was already a legend.

Yet Woz was still just twenty-five. For the next decade, his face, with its beard, bangs and glasses, would become synonymous with the new generation of computing whizzes. *California* magazine would cement that image forever with a cover story declaring him "The King of the Nerds," in the process adding a new term to everyday language. Woz's odd little obsession had changed the world, and given its happy victim a kind of immortality.

So there was every reason to assume that he was not yet at his creative peak and that even greater inventions lay ahead. But the disk controller would prove to be Woz's last great contribution not only to Apple but to high technology.

5.11 PERSONA

While Woz was secreted away working on the disk drive, Jobs was making a nuisance of himself. But a good nuisance this time. At a moment when the organization was beginning to consolidate into a real company, complete with the endless compromising and corner cutting that comes with bureaucratization, Jobs still held out for the impossible, but thrilling combination of "insanely great" solutions and world-class style.

It didn't make him popular with Apple's growing army of employees, but Jobs, given his character, didn't much care. And in sticking to his principles, he assured that Apple didn't, like so many hot tech companies, take its success and fall into early middle-aged complacency.

On top of being the corporate conscience within Apple, Jobs also played an equally important role outside the company. The metamorphosis of Steven P. Jobs was now nearly complete. His hair cut, but still fashionably long, his beard trimmed, wearing his finely cut suits, Jobs was no longer the unkempt hippie with questionable hygiene. As the confused 1970s turned into the materialist 1980s, Jobs was becoming *cool*. His unique blend of Buddhist obscurantism, vegetarianism, cold calculation and handsome raptor looks was capturing the imagination of a whole generation. To the early baby boomers, he was the hippie who hadn't sold out, who could spout koans and talk revolution while hawking an electronic appliance. To the late boomers, he was a proto-yuppie, sleek and predatory, still a kid but able to run with the Brahmins of Corporate America.

Jobs could never supplant Wozniak in the hearts of technology buffs; they would always see Jobs as a usurper and poseur. But Woz could have that crowd; its days were already numbered. The real audience now was the millions of young business professionals: middle managers, doctors, government bureaucrats, advertising copywriters, lawyers, college professors. They were the future of the personal computer. And Steve Jobs had their number. When the time came to buy a computer, and that day was coming soon, they would look at the Commodore Pets, the NorthStars and the Tandys, see only faceless corporations, and turn away. But then they would see a smirking Steve Jobs, smooth and maybe a little vicious, and the Apple ads that bore his stamp, with their sly balance of cheekiness, warmth and boomer sensibility—Regis's first Apple II ad showed a couple in their kitchen, the wife preparing a meal and the husband pounding away at the computer—and they would know where they belonged.

Here, from 1984, is an early appraisal (by this author) of how the Jobs Reality Distortion Field began to emanate out over the entire consumer world:

> Jobs's youthful pluck and hipness obviously struck a responsive chord not just among hackers and long-haired computer engineers, but also among the millions of young business people who had grown up in the sixties and early seventies, the flower children, the Wood- stock Generation, the baby boomers who had sworn themselves to an alternative lifestyle, to the Amerikan revolution, good dope and com-

munity—but who instead cut their hair, put on business suits, grabbed their MBAs and dove into the capitalist world with more selfish greed than the forefathers they had once derided. No matter what they said to each other over quiche and white wine and lines of coke, they knew in their bones that they had sold out in a big way, and they hated themselves for it. As they drove home in their BMWs and Volvos to their singles apartments or single-parent kids, these [aging] children knew that they had become just like their parents—but without the family or the patriotism or religious faith or any of the other fascist institutions that made these sacrifices worthwhile.

Jobs reached these people better than anybody else because he seemed to be *one of them*. As they sat in their offices, with the dwindling mementos of their youth and their dreams, they would turn to an enormous photo of Jobs in his beard and wicked smirk and think, "That bastard did it. He stuck by his principles and still can tell the establishment to kiss his ass." Then they'd get a little thrill of excitement mixed with envy. The revolution hadn't been lost after all, their lives weren't a sham. The campus guerillas had merely evolved into corporate freedom fighters.

And in their hearts they wished they were Steve Jobs.

Regis McKenna understood better than anybody in high tech that while a good product can make a company successful, corporate immortality only comes when a client begins to personify an era. McKenna knew what he had in Jobs and played that card for all it was worth. Jobs, for his part, was clever enough not only to go along for the ride but to add his own odd, but shrewdly entertaining, twists.

By the time Apple moved to a new and much bigger facility a couple of blocks away on Bandley Drive, Jobs had nearly perfected his new persona. The new facility, hard by the Cupertino nursery and a few doors from the Donut Wheel, a longtime hangout for dating teenagers and swing-shift cannery workers, was fifteen times larger than its predecessor. In moving there Apple began the inevitable process of physically separating its operations.

Walking into the building, the first impression was one of considerable unused space. The second was one of anarchy. There were boxes and papers everywhere. Desks were piled with books or hardware parts or computer magazines. And nowhere was the mess greater than in Wozniak's cubicle, which, with its stacks of printed circuit boards, wiring harnesses and test equipment, looked like an unoccupied storage area for broken parts.

At the other end of the building, Steve Jobs was carefully constructing his own reality. The office itself wasn't as interesting as the ideas with which Jobs was perpetually filling the space. Almost from the moment he arrived—usually late, an insulting habit that grew longer with the years—Jobs would pepper the visitor with an overwhelming, and seemingly unconnected, array of questions, typically about whatever he had most recently learned about. "Have you read Kuhn's *The Structure of Scientific Revolutions*? No? I'll get you a copy." "What the Apple computer really is is a fractional horsepower motor. Or, rather, it's a bicycle." It was the conversation of a brilliant autodidact; wildly enthusiastic about today's intellectual discovery. Jobs never seemed to care if you understood what he was talking about—only that you understood that *he did*.

It was all crazy and narcissistic, the clever offense of an emotional bully who preferred that the people who faced him be on their heels. Long or short, the meeting would always end abruptly, as if what seemed like a budding relationship had suddenly, inexplicably, turned into a royal audience . . . and that audience had just ended. The visitor came away feeling intellectually and spiritually molested, thrilled that this already legendary figure should so appreciate the visitor's intelligence, not sure whether he had just been hustled, and mostly, just exhausted. But later, when you recovered and pondered what Jobs had said, you were struck that it was not only correct but sometimes even profound. It is the megalomaniacs who control the symbols and thus our imaginations. Jobs was, in fact, trying out new metaphors for the personal computer revolution, playing Pied Piper to anyone who came near, searching for the tune that would make them follow.

And once you the target had taken a first step in pursuit, Jobs had his answer and moved on. The Steven Jobs Reality Distortion Field—more accurately now a zone, as Apple itself began to manifest his personality—quickly became the most exciting, and terrifying, experience in Silicon Valley. You approached it at your peril.

But if Jobs was brilliantly transforming time and space at work, he wasn't so successful at home. About the time of the Second Faire, Jobs, his old high school girlfriend, and Dan Kottke had set up house in a suburban ranch home in Cupertino. They tried to be ironic about the process—nicknaming the style of the house they rented Rancho Suburbio Special, denigrating their square neighbors—but they were in fact playing out the same game as all of their other Homestead High counterparts, embracing the bourgeois lifestyle of their parents without admitting they were doing so.

It was all pretty conventional. Jobs and girlfriend played mom and dad, and Kottke was the man who came to dinner. He took to sleeping in the living room, while filling the spare bedroom with foam shards for the neighborhood kids to play in. Kottke was trying to be antic, but it was also a little creepy.

The relationship between Jobs and his girlfriend, for all the meditation and radical talk, was also conventional. Jobs went off to work at Apple each day, and his girlfriend stayed home and slowly went mad. She would later say, "I was really insecure and young men in their early twenties are not very good with women. They need to prove themselves. I was afraid to go out. I didn't have any money." Instead, she trashed the house, punching holes in the wall, knocking down shelves, writing obscenities on the wall with charcoal. And when she wasn't being destructive, she was pleading for help, calling Jobs at the office at all hours, demanding he come home to fix some small item like a broken light socket.

But there was one way to shatter Jobs's carefully constructed reality. His girlfriend became pregnant. Steve Jobs's reaction was predictable, but unconscionable: he refused to accept paternity. "Steve didn't care that I was pregnant," said the woman later. In a terrible expression of his own selfishness, the abandoned child had now abandoned his own.

But the woman didn't give up easily. Desperate, and increasingly without support, she took a job on the assembly line at Apple. Feeling sorry for her, Holt tried both to advise Jobs about his responsibilities and to get his girlfriend to take some training in drafting. Both efforts failed. Finally, the woman moved out—"I had to get away from Steve, Apple and people's opinions"—and, on Jobs's advice, headed to Oregon and the farm of that old drug-dealing con man from Reed, Robert Friedland.

There, in May 1978, about the time Woz was showing off the new disk drive in San Francisco, the child, a girl, was born. Jobs drove up a few days later and, in one of their last encounters for years, named the little girl Lisa. Then Jobs, unencumbered by such messy matters as fatherhood or marriage, returned to ever-growing fame at Apple. Lisa's mother, meanwhile, struggled to raise Lisa through odd jobs such as waitressing and housecleaning. Eventually she moved back to the Bay Area and the Peninsula.

During this period, Jobs exhibited some paternal responsibility by voluntarily paying a modicum of child support. Lisa's mother finally asked for a $20,000 settlement, and though Markkula suggested Steve should pay four times that amount, the young man balked at what he considered a shakedown. Soon the child-care payments became fewer and farther between. Increasingly desperate, little Lisa on government relief, her mother turned to the legal system for remedy. It worked. Whenever a payment was late, Lisa's mother, with the help of her family, would bring in a lawyer. And Jobs would pay.

Finally the mother played her trump card. Lisa was now a year old. Her mother asked Jobs to submit to a blood test to finally establish paternity. For some inexplicable reason—perhaps he believed he was now above the laws of organic chemistry—Jobs agreed.

The test, conducted by UCLA, established a 94.41 percent likelihood that Jobs was the father. Jobs still refused to accept the inevitable. By multiplying all the error margins, he was able to convince himself that the real likelihood was just 72 percent. And that is what he told the world: "Twenty-eight percent of the male population of the United States could be the father." It was exceptionally cruel phrasing. For having betrayed his vision of himself, Jobs wasn't content to merely deny the fatherhood of the child, he had to intimate that her mother was a whore as well.

It would be two more years before Jobs, now a famous public figure with a reputation to protect—and faced with the possibility of a $10 million lawsuit—agreed to a court-ordered settlement. It was a pitiful amount for this now multimillionaire: $385 per month and $5,856 to pay back the welfare administrators of San Mateo County for having helped raise his child. As with everything else to that point in his life, Jobs got off easy.

5.12 GROUND ZERO COOL

As noted, in September 1977, Apple had revenues of $775,000 for the fiscal year, with a dozen employees and enough profits to buy a few fried tofu meals at the Good Earth. The company was located in a single rented office. Three years later, Apple was a publicly traded corporation, valued at more than $1 billion, with sales of $118 million, profits of $11.7 million . . . and more than 1,000 employees. These employees were based in thirteen buildings, including eleven along Bandley Drive in Cupertino and others in locations as diverse as Texas, Holland, Ireland and Singapore. Apple was also the most famous new company in the world.

Covering that extraordinary distance in that extraordinary brief amount of time had less to do with Steve Jobs's vision or Stephen Wozniak's inventive genius than with the chaotic, but ultimately successful, infrastructure built by Mike Scott. It was a herculean task, and in the end it destroyed him.

It has been said that Silicon Valley's greatest contribution to modern business is its willingness to accept failure, and thus to celebrate entrepreneurial endeavors no matter how doomed. But its other great contribution is the endless résumé: the establishment of career paths that have nothing to do with longevity or seniority and everything to do with the perpetual hunt for a spot on the leading edge. The result is a gypsy workforce, hopping from job to job, sometimes staying less than six months, rarely sticking around for more than three years, before moving on to the next big opportunity.

Here is where the long-standing comparison to the Forty-niners of the Gold Rush really does hold true. When one claim begins to dry up, you abandon it and move on to the next diggings in hopes of striking a rich new vein. And in modern Silicon Valley that perpetual flow of talent is as diverse as assembly-line workers spending lunch breaks at recruitment fairs hoping for another dollar per hour, to top managers and engineers hopscotching from one hot new company to the next in search of fame and founders stock.

By the beginning of 1979 Apple had bubbled to the surface of the Valley's consciousness. The word was out that this strange little outfit, with its unlikely founders, was the biggest new deal in town. It wasn't long before talented people, most of them young, were converging on Bandley Drive, résumés in hand.

The only thing more difficult than failure for a new start-up is great success. And Apple was a supreme success. Within a couple of months after Apple had moved into the first Bandley building, it had to add two more. The newly hired employees moved in while structural modifications (without a city permit) were still being made. Soon those buildings too were filled.

In every way it was an exhilarating, terrifying mess. Every decision was made with the knowledge that it might prove fatal to the company—and yet those same decisions were often made on the fly, with little consideration or consultation, sometimes by people who had no responsibility for the result. Apple had no facilities manager, no legal officer, no corporate communications manager, some buildings didn't even have a receptionist. Security was a disaster, the organizational chart was only intermittently observed, and when all else failed, work was contracted out.

And yet, one of the miracles of entrepreneurial start-ups is that despite (some would say because of) this confusion they thrive. When employees don't have precise job responsibilities but only enthusiasm and loyalty, they often migrate to the work they do best. So, precisely because there are no rigid walls, employees in start-ups tend to self-sort by talent and desire.

Like Jobs, Apple was becoming cool. Because of that it increasingly attracted bright young people coming out of college. Apple was also beginning to dominate its market. While the other early contenders began, one after another, to stumble and disappear, Apple continued to gain market share. And that in turn made the company more interesting to other companies, big and small, who saw a market in designing software and aftermarket hardware for the Apple II. Soon there were scores of interesting new companies working to make Apple a success.

This external activity proved critical to Apple during this difficult period. First, it filled in the blanks—and there were a hell of a lot of them in the company's organization and catalog. But just as important, these outsiders could help grow Apple's market faster than the company, with limited capital and staff, could by itself.

Two examples illustrate what these other players could do.

Jef Raskin had been on the periphery of the home computer revolution from the beginning and with computers long before that. He had run a computer center at UC San Diego, working with the people who would later invent the Pascal computer language. He had been a visiting scholar at Stanford and worked with the crowd at Xerox PARC. He and his friends had also build Altairs and IMSAI.

Raskin had finally landed at *Dr. Dobb's Journal of Computer Calisthenics and Orthodontia* (Running Light without Overbyte), a hobbyist magazine that exists to this day as a technical journal. Raskin was an odd guy—he had resigned from UC San Diego by ascending in a hot-air balloon, playing his soprano recorder and proclaiming his departure—so when he was sent by the magazine to interview two guys building a computer in a Cupertino garage, he felt an instant bond with the company. He would recall, "I loved the name Apple instead of the techie names everybody else was using; it fit my iconoclastic spirit." He even helped the pair write a section of the Apple I manual.

Two years later, he was contracted by Apple to manage the company's documentation. Apple was in desperate need of help in that department, as a letter kept by Markkula from an angry customer of that era suggests:

> You fucking bastards. I bought an Apple with floppy and nobody, I mean nobody, in L.A. or San Diego knows how to use the sonuvabitch for random access files. I really feel "ripped off." Everybody talks about this great manual in the sky that is coming out soon??? Shit! Shit! Shit! I need this computer now in my business, not next year. Fuck you. I hope your dog dies.

This wasn't the only such customer "testimonial." In moving to the consumer market from the gearheads business, Apple had taken on the task of supporting these computer neophytes. It was failing badly. Obviously, Raskin had his work cut out for him. Unfortunately, as he quickly discovered, the one guy at the company who knew enough about the Apple II to write such a manual was leaving. Chris Espinosa, Woz's teenage acolyte, was off to Berkeley for his freshman year. Despite this, Raskin somehow talked Espinosa into writing a manual for the II that would once and for all explain to the neophyte how the computer really worked.

What happened next is a testament to the kind of loyalty Apple could instill in its employees, ex-employees and users. Espinosa worked on the manual all through the term, somehow managing to do his classwork as well. When the term ran out and his dorm room closed, Espinosa still wasn't finished with the manuscript. So, all his belongings stuffed into a backpack, he slept in computer labs on campus when he wasn't caught and in a nearby park when he was. Since he was also writing eighteen hours each day, the amount of time he actually slept was thankfully small. He typeset the finished manual on school equipment and delivered it to Apple just as the new term began. The finished "red book" proved a great success at soothing the customers.

Jef Raskin went on to give Apple's publications their celebrated look: clean, white, with splashes of color (Apple was the first of the home computer companies with color publications) and a witty style. By the end of the 1970s, Apple had hired Raskin to work inside the company. Three years later, he would lead the team that invented the Macintosh.

Dan Fylstra, by comparison, was an Apple enthusiast who never joined the company. Tall, with owlish glasses, and a long, blond premature comb-over, Fylstra had earned a Harvard MBA (at the same time Bill Gates was a freshman) while running a small personal computer software company called Personal Software.

Personal Software was, in its own way, a pioneer. It didn't design software, but licensed and marketed the creations of others. One of those creations was from a fellow MBA candidate, Dan Bricklin. Bricklin had an idea for a program to perform financial forecasting on a personal computer, and despite ridicule from one of his professors (*another* financial forecasting program, the professor said) Bricklin managed to get in touch with Fylstra, who'd been another of that professor's students.

Fylstra, who had researched the personal computer software market as part of his degree, recognized a good product idea when he saw one. He supported Bricklin's project, even lending him the one computer Personal Software had on hand, an Apple II. Bricklin in turn hooked up with a brilliant mathematician named Bob Frankston, and the two, creating their own company called Software Arts, worked long winter nights in a cold attic devising the program.

The result, marketed by Fylstra as VisiCalc, wasn't just a stunner, it was the first *fundamentally new* piece of software for the personal computer. Word processing programs, games, everything until then designed for the personal computer was essentially a watered-down version of a program already done, better, on mainframes or minis. But VisiCalc was sui generis; it was the world's first electronic spreadsheet. You could sit down and type in your indices and the computer would draw out a vast array, of which only a part appeared on your computer screen and the rest existed in virtual space. Then, when you typed in your data, the computer would automatically fill up the table. Then you could navigate around this giant matrix, checking out the results at the coefficient you desired—the motion itself providing a clue about personal computing to come.

But even more amazing, you could play 'What if?' with Visicalc. You could change an entry with the flick of a key and the *whole damn grid would recalculate itself.* Today, when spreadsheets are routinely bundled with word processing and other office productivity tools, it is hard to imagine the stunning effect of watching that recalculation occur for the first time. Calculations would take days to do by hand, so nobody ever did them. Even on big computers, processing time was far too expensive for everyday users to futz around with alternative scenarios. But VisiCalc was a reminder that the Apple II belonged to *you.* You could sit and play all night with different numbers. What happens if we raise prices by 4 percent? What if I hire the new controller for $4,000 a year less? What happens over the next eight years if I can cut the cost of goods sold by 3 percent per year and invest those savings?

For the very first time, the personal computer had an application that was all its own. Better yet, that application was the lifelong dream of every small business and new start-up company on the planet.

Not that Apple appreciated what Fylstra had. Moving his company to Sunnyvale, Fylstra showed up at Markkula's office with a prototype of Visi-Calc and offered to give a demonstration. Markkula watched, unimpressed, and then showed the visitor a checkbook-balancing program of his own devising. Fylstra left, stunned but undeterred.

One person at Apple who did appreciate Fylstra was Jef Raskin. He too tried to convince Markkula and Jobs to buy VisiCalc, but when he was also turned down, he managed at least to get a leave of absence from Apple to join the fledgling software company. There he played an important role writing the tutorial section of the VisiCalc's manual.

In October 1979, Fylstra formally introduced VisiCalc. It was initially priced at $100, but soon was raised to $150 when Fylstra saw the market would accept that price with nary a blink. Even at its new price, VisiCalc took off like a rocket, within two years selling more than 12,000 copies per month, making it the first great personal computer software best-seller.

More than that, because it was initially available only for the Apple II, VisiCalc also legitimized Apple Computer. Now, for the first time, the average user had a reason, besides novelty, to buy a personal computer; it was a productivity tool, an investment that might pay for itself many times over. In the end, despite being turned down by Markkula, VisiCalc, as much as the Apple II or Woz's disk-drive controller, made Apple Computer. Mike Scott estimated that VisiCalc alone sold more than 25,000 Apple II's by the end of fiscal 1980, almost 20 percent of Apple's total unit sales.

Fylstra, Raskin and Espinosa weren't the only outsiders helping to turn Apple into a business and social phenomenon. There were hundreds of other manufacturers and programmers throughout the world working on Apple II-related products. Most were newcomers to the playground, but others, like ghosts, reemerged from the shady past. One of these ghosts, remarkably, was John Draper, back out of prison. This time Cap'n Crunch played it straight, designing a simple, but popular, word-processing program called EasyWriter that sold through Information Unlimited Software in Berkeley. It too helped the sale of Apple II's, Draper at last in some way paying back the two boys for all the times he'd led them astray.

It was through the efforts of all of these people that the Apple II soon had the largest software library of any personal computer—more programs, in fact, than the Commodore Pet, the Morrow Designs Inc. Adam, Vector Graphics and all the others combined. All these programs represented millions of hours of work by thousands of individuals, far more than Apple could ever have mustered alone. Moreover, in hopes of their own big score, these designers took all the risk, while Apple sold the box. And that in turn was why, as early as mid-1978, Regis could run ads proclaiming that the Apple II "is the world's best-selling personal computer" without indulging in too much misrepresentation.

5.13 ANTIBODIES

Of course, you couldn't just wait for talented people to show up in the lobby with job applications. Knowing what slots needed to be filled and having no time to waste, Apple's veterans went out searching for talent. Not surprisingly, the places they chose to raid were also the ones they used to work for. Thus, Markkula chased employees at Intel, Scott at National Semiconductor and Jobs, still working out his lifelong obsession with Bill and Dave's company, went after Hewlett-Packard.

The good news was they were successful. The bad news was they were successful. Raiding top-notch companies for their best minds was a time-honored Valley tradition, and Apple went about it more honorably than, say, National Semiconductor had a decade before. But in raiding companies with strong corporate cultures, Apple also ran the risk of infecting itself with those same sensibilities.

That was what had happened to Intel just a few years before when a contingent from Texas Instruments had acted like a tumor within the body of its new employer. Eventually the group was either fired or absorbed into Intel's own special culture — but not before grinding the company to a near-halt and damaging employee morale.

Apple was now growing much faster than Intel ever had. Mike Scott, overburdened, had little time to extend his will over the organization, Jobs was too quixotic to do so and Markkula, ever retiring, would never have considered such a thing. So, lacking any structure imposed from above, these new employees fell back on what they knew: how things were done at their last job. The result was that by 1979 Apple was quickly dividing into fiefdoms, the largest of them ruled by the people hired by the troika. And each of these duchies had its own territory and culture.

There was a Hewlett-Packard contingent, characterized by endless, tiresome niceness and consensus building. Its strength was attention to details and quality. The HP crowd was exemplified by Tom Whitney, who came from HP's desktop calculator division (he was Woz's old boss) and took over Apple's engineering. Whitney, in typical HP fashion, quickly organized Apple's new product development under specific guidelines, each with its own forms and subcommittees. Project teams were created, each with its own leader. It was all so organized and enlightened and decent that it made everyone want to puke, but for the moment it worked.

The Intel crowd — and there were enough of them so that Andy Grove, a major Apple shareholder, even complained to Markkula about Apple's raiding — not surprisingly congregated in the technical operations, where it installed Intel's legendary engineering arrogance and "creative confrontation" (shouting). The best-known ex-Intel employee at Apple was Ann Bowers, the personnel director, who just happened to be Bob Noyce's wife. According to secretary Sherry Livingston: "Everything had to be done the Intel way. [Bowers] wouldn't go to the left or right." One of Bowers's first decisions was that everyone in the company would henceforth drink only decaffeinated coffee. The result was a general mutiny. "My biggest hiring mistake," Mike Scott would later say.

But the most outrageous enclave at Apple belonged to the recruits from National Semiconductor. Chip guys are notoriously savvy, crazy and mean, but National Semi employees were, as the company's promotion said, "The animals of Silicon Valley." They were the true spiritual descendants of Fairchild, without the sense of humor. Charlie Sporck, National's president, was the toughest of all. He ran National as if it was a billion-dollar factory floor and he was the world's greatest shop foreman. The assembly lines were dangerous, the administrative offices spartan when they weren't jammed with boxes and the sales force did whatever it took, from misrepresentation to borrowing a competitor's designs. And all of this took place under eerie, strobing sodium vapor lights that made daily life at National even more disorienting, strange and unhealthy than it already was. Years later it would turn out that during this period National was intentionally undertesting millions of chips destined to be used in military weapons systems and the space program. It was scary and depressing, but it worked: in the depth of the chip wars, only National Semi met the Japanese head-on and survived.

One might think that National would be the very antithesis of Apple Computer in the late 1980s. But, in fact, that's what made its people appealing to the new company, especially in the two departments where the hippie-gearhead mentality ran smack into the reality of running a serious business: sales and manufacturing. If the HP people were Scoutmasters and church deacons, the National Semi boys were thugs, who bullied suppliers, padded their expense accounts and lied to customers. Where the HP contingent said, "Why can't we all get along? Good products and good service are the best way to keep customers for life," the National Semi crowd's philosophy was "Fuck 'em. We can always find another customer."

As one Apple employee would later describe the contingent to Moritz: "There was a real sense that they were going to ship this shit one way or another and they were going to get the dealers to fix it. They more or less said, 'We're going to ship this sucker, to hell with the customer.' "

But there was another side to the National culture at Apple, and it was best represented by Roy Mollard, whose résumé included not only National but Fairchild before that. Mollard was from Liverpool, just like his old Fairchild boss Wilf Corrigan, after Tramiel the second-scariest man in Silicon Valley, and they both shared the same single-mindedness.

What Mollard brought to Apple, as its director of manufacturing, was a different facet of adulthood. Not the talent and maturity of Markkula, but the other side of being a grown-up, the hard-assed, no bullshit, "crack a few heads to make things happen" kind of adulthood. The adulthood of the guy who ran the graveyard shift at the cannery or led young recruits out of foxholes or who wore a title like "warden."

Mollard had no patience for the airy-fairy manufacturing line he inherited. Here was a company on the cutting edge of a new technology and it ran its manufacturing line as if it was building headlamps for Hupmobiles. Critical records, such as purchase orders and production rates, were kept by hand, division of labor appeared to be made up by the day and a single supervisor controlled twenty-eight assemblers. Other Apple employees felt free to wander in and out of manufacturing, asking questions, hanging out, getting their own orders taken care of first.

It was no wonder that Apple was barely able to build 150 computers and just fifteen disk drives per week. And senior management not only acquiesced in this mess but even contributed to it. Jobs, for example, had found a great deal on plastic, bought about two years' worth of inventory and had it stacked in the assembly area, where it took up nearly half the room.

This kind of undisciplined behavior was a drawing-and-quartering offense at National, and Mollard brought that attitude to Apple. In Mollard's memorable phrasing, his task, and that of his department, was "to hose out computers." In his mind, Apple's manufacturing department was the Augean stables, and he was there to clean it out, to get the computers on the loading dock and get them sold. And Mollard wasn't going to let anything stop him or his people.

One way he did this was to put the fear of God into his own staff. Out went the luncheon Ping-Pong games, in went hidden microphones and alarms. He hired security guards and fired anyone who wouldn't get with the program, including the quality-assurance manager. He reorganized the assembly floor into work teams, each with its own supervisor; and he removed every storage device, from drawers to cabinets, to make sure that no inventory could be hidden away.

And Mollard was just as tough on those outside his team. Jobs believed in an open company, in which employees could walk anywhere. Mollard, who had seen millions of dollars of National's inventory walk out in pockets, briefcases and salted scrap, quickly put the nix on that. Before long, the security guards were checking the names of every visitor for clearance. Steve Jobs complained, but ultimately deferred to Mollard. In the end, not surprisingly, Apple's manufacturing became a lot less fun and a lot more productive.

As incompatible as these three groups might seem, as long as Mike Scott (and the Apple dream) could hold them together they gave Apple extraordinary strength and resilience. The combination of Intel technology arrogance, HP's class and integrity and National's hardball attitude was every CEO's dream team. Better yet, Scott supplemented this triple play with individuals from across society, from academics like Raskin to outsiders like Wendell Sander.

It didn't always work. For example, in its rush to take some of the load off an increasingly overworked Holt, Apple managed to hire two people for the same senior position of running the engineering lab. One, as already noted, was HP's Tom Whitney. The other was Chuck Peddle, the man who had sold the 6502 chip to Woz and had once tried to buy Apple for Commodore; now he was just trying to join the company. Instead, he found himself redundant in the job for which he had been hired, and quit after a few weeks to return to Commodore and lead the attack against Apple. He should have stuck around, because Whitney's obsession with organization soon began to grind his operation to a halt in an HP-like blizzard of reports and reorganizations.

But despite such occasional snafus, Scott somehow managed to hold the whole snarling, infighting mob together long enough to tame most of its members into a coherent team. And those who couldn't give up their former allegiances either cracked or were driven out.

It was a virtuoso performance by a remarkable manager. Scott, because of what was to come, has never been given proper credit for his achievements at Apple. Successful Silicon Valley companies are like the old Soviet encyclopedias. Once you are purged, you become a nonperson, lost down the memory hole, and your entry in the company story is pasted over with a new, official history—in Apple's case, one that rewards the leadership of Steven Jobs . . . not the fact that much of the success of the early years occurred in spite of him.

The real credit is Scott's. Scott was neither as brilliant as Wozniak nor as charismatic as Jobs. Instead, to those foxes he played the role of hedgehog. The one thing this hedgehog knew was that if you didn't get products out the door, then you didn't have a company. And it was from this obsession to ship units that Scott's style arose.

Mike Scott could be a bully (he sometimes began memos with YOU ALL BETTER READ THIS), a Captain Queeg (one memo ordered employees not to talk in the hallways or while standing up) and a technocrat (he not only put into place a management information system that finally organized Apple's operations but also used it to run his own private spy system). But there was also that sweet side. Wigginton's tuition and the Santa Claus visit were just two examples. A year or two later, when the Star Wars trilogy first appeared, Scott rented the local Century Theater and took the entire company to see it, first sending them engraved invitations, then meeting them at the door with white roses. When some employees missed one of these movie outings because they were at a trade show, he called them to his office and escorted them to the theater in a bus tended by liveried waiters.

Scott was a CEO who could terrorize you one moment and at the next throw you a party. He would object to first-class travel for executives, then blow thousands on company entertainment at Christmas. He was alternately shy and in your face, cruel and embracing, a public man at the office and invisible in his private life. He was a man on a tightrope, and for three years he managed to keep from falling. He also made Apple into a real company; but in the process he divided the company into his enemies and his friends. Unfortunately for Mike Scott, his enemies were far more powerful.

5.14 MOOLAH

While Mike Scott was turning Apple into a real company, Mike Markkula was looking for money. And though he would remain at Apple longer than anyone else, it was his accomplishments in this search over the first three years of the company that would be his greatest achievement.

Markkula's first money search began in the fall of 1977, during the plastic case disaster. The company spent so much time patching bad cases, losing revenues during the shutdown and then ramping up to make up for lost time that it exhausted its cash reserves. That time, Markkula and Scott dipped into their own pockets for a one-time cash injection of nearly $200,000.

Neither, understandably, was willing to do that again. The next time Apple needed money it would have to come from pros. As it happened, even as he was writing the check Markkula already was talking to potential investors. He did so with trepidation. Even before 1977 a pattern had emerged with venture capital that had not been lost on entrepreneurs: the earlier you allowed in venture capital, the more you gave up control of your firm. Take their money early enough—say soon after the company's founding—and before they were done the venture capitalists would own your company. They might even throw you and the other founders out and put in their own guys to protect their investments.

So the strategy was to hold off accepting outside capital for as long as possible. Typically, in a successful start-up there were about four rounds of investment. The first, usually called the seed round, was the funding that set up the company and got the first product designed and built. Apple, with Markkula's money and Bank of America's line of credit (banks, by law, couldn't take a stock position), had made it through that round without outside investment. But ahead lay the second round, typically used to set up the company's manufacturing operations and distribution channels, a third round, often used to launch the follow-up product, and a final mezzanine round to prepare the company for the Big Payday: the initial public offering (IPO) of stock.

The Going Public Day of the IPO, if it ever occurred (and it did for only about 10 percent of all high-tech start-ups), was the reward to everyone—founders, employees and investors—who had helped make the company a success. Tens, even hundreds, of millions of dollars in stock wealth would be distributed that day to holders of founders stock.

Unfortunately, by then most of that stock would be in the hands of the venture capitalists and their funders, because in each of those rounds, in exchange for ever more money, the company would have given away 10 percent to 40 percent of its total value. Thus, it was not unusual for a company at the IPO to have given up 70 to 90 percent of its total worth to venture capital firms. One study, done in the early 1980s, found that in the typical start-up that went public, only the founder(s) and the first four employees realized more financial gain than they would have if they'd stayed at their old jobs.

By escaping the seed round, Apple had saved perhaps 30 percent of its stock for its employees—a fact that would be celebrated three years hence. But the plastic case debacle, a tiny Steve Jobs mistake that was now taking on enormous proportions, signaled the end of Apple's independence. The company would never be able to bootstrap its financing again.

For all the costs of venture capital, there were also some enormous advantages. Venture capitalists, because they had independent control of giant funds of $50 million or more, could provide a lot of fast cash. Moreover, they were not constrained by law from collusion, so it was not unusual for multiple venture capital firms to team up on an investment, especially the big-money later rounds. Most of the high-tech venture capitalists worked alongside one another in the 3000 Sand Hill Road industrial park on a hill above Stanford, and many joint investment deals were worked out over lunch at the Sun Deck restaurant there.

A second advantage of venture capitalists was their experience. Many of the best venture capitalists were former high-tech company executives, such as Don Valentine, who had already successfully been down the path their young charges were now facing. They knew what came next and how to get through it. These industry veteran venture capitalists, and their numbers grew by the year as each generation of talent got rich and then retired to play with their investments, combined with bright young things fresh out of Harvard and Stanford. This latter group offered endless reservoirs of energy to crunch financials and study industry reports. Together, old and experienced with young and energetic, venture capitalists represented an asset to a new start-up nearly as great as the money they proffered. For Apple, with its senior management ranks utterly lacking in anyone with CEO experience, this was a critical need.

The final, and least tangible, advantage offered by venture capitalists was the legitimacy they conferred. The right venture capitalist on your board of directors (and the big investors always took a board seat, sometimes the chairmanship) told the world that your company had been tapped as the Next Big Thing, that it was gilt-edged, that it was a place where winners wanted to work. Ultimately, it also signaled to the best underwriting firms that this was a company to keep track of, to one day represent in its IPO.

Mike Markkula understood all this very well. He also knew that the trick was to find the most respected and influential venture capitalists possible to invest in and advise Apple Computer—while at the same time not give them the whole store in compensation. An immediate obstacle was that, like most corporate types, Markkula didn't really know any venture capital firms. However, Silicon Valley being what it was—a very large and wealthy small town in which everybody at one time works for or against everybody else—this impediment was quickly vaulted.

As it turned out, Markkula had worked at Fairchild and Intel with a guy named Hank Smith. Smith had moved to New York and was now a general partner at Venrock. Venrock was a big deal, not just because it was the venture capital wing of the Rockefeller family but also because it had one of the best reputations in Silicon Valley for making smart investments (it would soon invest in VisiCalc as well). It would be good bait for other venture capitalists too. And the good news was that, unlike many of the other big names, Venrock hadn't yet invested in a personal computer company.

But one didn't just show up at Venrock's offices in Manhattan and ask for money. Getting venture money from a top-line firm, especially for an established company, is a very carefully choreographed process, with lots of mating dances, mutual sniffing and invasive procedures. So, though the initial contact between Markkula and Smith occurred in the spring of 1977, about the time of the Computer Faire, it wasn't until autumn, after Smith had visited the company several times, that Apple's executives were invited to New York to make a presentation.

Even then, Venrock exhibited some of the disdain for funky little start-ups that would cost it industry leadership in the years to come. As Smith would say later: "We probably would not have looked at Apple had I not known Mike Markkula."

Of course, Apple did nothing to help its image. Markkula, working with Gary Martin, put together an investor prospectus larded with wild speculations. Sherry Livingston, who watched the process, would tell Moritz, "It was a joke the way they came up with projections. There were so many projections they'd almost flip a coin." Bullshit financials were hardly uncommon in new start-ups, where the market is usually new and unknown, but by now Apple was an established company. To make up numbers at this point suggested that the company was almost flying blind.

But equally amateurish was the production of the document. While Markkula and Jobs flew on to Manhattan, Scott and most of his staff stayed up eating increasingly stale pizza and collated, stapled and bound the dozen prospectuses. Then Scott caught the red-eye flight out of San Francisco and joined his partners for the morning meeting at Venrock. The whole thing might have been a disaster, but plastic cases aside, this was the era when Apple could do no wrong. Venrock signed on.

Markkula knew enough not to hit up just one venture capitalist. The idea was to get multiple players in order to maximize the investment, dilute control and get as much prestige and experience on board as possible. The one guy Markkula wanted on board was Andy Grove, president of Intel. Bright, terrifyingly intense and a man who would battle failure to the death, Hungarian immigrant Grove was already on his way to becoming one of the great businessmen of the century. He was the dream corporate director, the man who not only could tell you how to run a billion-dollar company and set up the most sophisticated manufacturing plants ever known, but also just happened to be the world's leading supplier of microprocessors. But Andy's heart, as always, belonged to Intel. Still, having until recently worked for him, Markkula thought he might have a chance.

Grove's response was unvintage Andy: he bought 15,000 shares. That was the good part. The bad was that he refused a board position, saying that his time was devoted to Intel. That was a huge loss, because Andy Grove's money was much less important than his wisdom. One can only imagine that when the dark days came for Apple, what a difference it might have made to have the insights of the CEO of Intel Corp. Instead, Grove's role in this part of the Apple story was to telephone Mike Scott regularly over the next few months to ask to buy more stock and to bitterly complain about Apple stealing his employees.

But the Grove gambit did have one unexpected payoff. Markkula's demonstrations of the Apple II hadn't just occurred in front of Andy alone, but also before the Intel board of directors. And one of those directors just happened to be the Patriarch of Venture Capital: Arthur Rock.

Rock was a slim man who resembled, in his glasses and his piercing look, an IRS examiner. He was dignified, even courtly, but also often cold and reserved. And he had a mind as precise and as sharp as a laser beam. More even than Hewlett and Packard, it could be said of Rock that without him there would have been no Silicon Valley. It had been Rock who had taken the risk to invest in eight renegade scientists from Shockley Semiconductor when they'd decided to break out and form their own company, Fairchild. Then, a decade later, when three of those Fairchildren (including two of the original founders) had decided to break away again, it was Rock who put up their seed money for Intel. Along the way, he had put money into a company called Scientific Data Systems, which, when it sold to Xerox in 1969, netted him $60 million. Now with Intel humming away at the top of the microprocessor business—Rock had played a key role in getting the company to stay in that market—he was on his way to being worth ten times that.

Markkula hadn't gone to Rock because, well, you just didn't go to *Arthur Rock* on a whim. But there he was at the demonstration. And soon, something even more amazing occurred: he called Apple to inquire about an investment. It was if Zeus himself had reached down from the clouds and touched Apple, making it glow with a golden light.

Regis McKenna, Andy Grove, Art Rock. This wasn't just the hat trick of Silicon Valley, this was like owning the arena itself. And there was still one more name to go. Markkula, Jobs and Hank Smith were dining one night at the Villa Felice, an old Los Gatos restaurant catering to veteran Valleyites. They were discussing the Venrock investment when a bottle of wine appeared at the table with a note attached. It was from Don Valentine: "Don't lose sight of the fact that I'm planning on investing in Apple."

Valentine. Who just a year before had come away shocked after visiting the freaks in the garage. Now he wanted to play. And even though Apple's management assumed the man's motives were cynical, they too were cynical enough to take his money. As with the Patriarch of Venture Capital, nobody turns down the Man with the Golden Gut.

Ultimately, the investments, totaling $517,500 and formally completed in January 1978, included the following: Venrock $288,000, Valentine $150,000 and Rock $57,600. Apple was now valued at $3 million. Woz and Jobs were now, at least on paper, well on the way to becoming millionaires. Not bad for two kids who only wanted to sell a few computers over the summer.

That was just the beginning. As expected, the presence of this Investor

Murderers Row quickly caught the attention of the rest of the investment community. In June, while running a booth at the Consumer Electronics Show in Chicago, the Apple team was contacted by Continental Illinois Bank, located nearby. Continental wanted in, to the tune of $500,000. But in the intervening six months, Apple had become a much more valuable commodity. Woz had introduced the disk drive, the plastic problem was solved and orders were coming in fast. Apple was now valued at about $9 million — so Continental's half million bought only as many shares (about 5 percent) of the company as Valentine had purchased at the beginning of the year.

Meanwhile, another player, this time a friend of Rock's named Henry Singleton, also anted up a little more than $100,000. It wasn't huge money, but Singleton was also chairman of Teledyne Inc., the legendary conglomerate that had its fingers in everything from dental waterpicks to military tank motors. With his investment, Singleton accepted a board position — something he had never done — and thus further added to Apple's financial luster.

Treating this cluster of investments as the equivalent of another round, Markkula then went back to his original investors and gave them the opportunity to purchase more shares at the new price. Only Valentine refused, angrily complaining that at $9 per share Apple's stock was absurdly overpriced.

5.15 Game Plan

With the completion of the second round of investments, Apple had the funding to match its products and talent. Now it needed three other factors to make it into a major corporation.

The first was distribution. Apple already had a deal with the Byte Shops, but that chain was beginning to stumble. So the company began to look elsewhere. One growing phenomenon that was hard to miss was the rise of independent personal computer shops. Most of these were tiny, with limited inventories, and run by hobbyists who'd decided to make their obsession pay for itself. But there were also scores of these shops springing up just in Northern California, and hundreds more around the rest of the country. For now, at least until the big retail chains like Sears began to sell computers — and no one knew how far off that day might be — these little shops would be the point of entry for most first-time computer buyers.

And these little shops needed all the help they could get. An antisocial longhair who spoke in assembly code behind the counter and a bunch of shelves bearing complicated electronic boxes and old issues of *Dr. Dobb's* was no way to make computer neophytes feel secure in their first purchase. These shops needed sexy displays, appealing point-of-sale materials, colorful flyers and other collateral to hand out, and computers that didn't look like something left over from a Flash Gordon serial.

Jobs, who had wandered these aisles long before any of his peers at Apple or his competitors in the industry, understood this need better than anyone. So, while Commodore and the other major players played hardball with the stores, treating them like expendable serfs, Jobs and Apple romanced the shopkeepers. With Regis's help, Apple flooded the little stores with flashy sales support items. And, in the most inspired marketing move of the company's early years, Apple became the first personal computer company to enter into co-op advertising deals with its retailers.

Co-op in this case also meant co-opt. By agreeing to share the cost of advertising with the little stores, Apple not only helped to locally promote its products everywhere it had a store, but at the same time the resulting ads made it appear to all the world that the shop was dedicated to Apple. Commodore and Atari seethed, because their products were more properly targeted at consumers than Apple's more premium-priced machines, but Apple got all the attention.

Yet Apple could also be a demanding lover. It expected the shops to act more professionally, even to the point of changing their names. Ultimately, this was to the good, as the stores named after, and with clerks that looked like, Tolkien characters had little chance of survival. But not so heartwarming was Apple's treatment of those same stores when, like the Byte Shops, they were no longer up to snuff. Then Apple cut them off.

Inevitably, all of this petty entrepreneurship would toss up one figure of vision who would begin the process of consolidating the market. That turned out to be Ed Faber, founder of Computerland. And as Computerland began to open one store after another across the United States, Apple's spadework with small shops began to pay off big. Faber, faced with the huge cash-flow demands of opening a new store every few weeks, was more than happy to join Apple's co-op program. He would later say, "It frightened other manufacturers. They thought we were so closely allied with Apple that they wouldn't get any recognition in our stores."

By 1979 Apple had in place the best distribution system of any personal computer maker, one extensive enough to hold its own against Tandy's own string of Radio Shack stores. Just as important, it had, in Computerland, close ties to a retail chain that was as innovative and sophisticated in its style as Apple itself. Said Faber, "It was one of those mutually advantageous relationships. Apple had a product; we had the beginnings of a retail distribution system. The more success we had, the more success they had. The more success they had, the more success we had."

The second factor Apple needed to become a real corporation was public recognition. It was one thing to be respected in the world of personal computing and to be the coolest thing around to guys who wore plastic pocket protectors; it was another to be an object of interest and affirmation by the world's leading business executives, politicians and investors. The first group bought your products, but the second bought your stock. And if Apple was planning to go public, this second group would be even more important than the first.

This would be where Regis McKenna's theory of opinion makers faced its ultimate test. Could you take a comparatively small company in a still largely unknown business, a company still just a few years away from two hairy scofflaws in a garage, and capture the imagination first of institutional investors and underwriters, then of society itself?

Regis had done a little of this work at Intel. But despite his best efforts, microprocessors wouldn't really be sexy for another fifteen years. And at Apple, until now, his agency had done some clever work, but it still wasn't far removed from the same old high-tech PR scam of taking credit for articles that advertising-hungry trade press editors would have written anyway. The same was true for the company's advertising, which, though smart, essentially echoed the bloviating claims of the competition.

And there was more competition than ever. Now the field included not only Cromemco, Atari and Commodore but also Mattel, the idiotically named Kentucky Fried Computers (which changed its name, too late, to NorthStar), Ohio Scientific, Tandy and now the biggest gorilla of them all, Texas Instruments.

TI scared the bejesus out of everybody. And with good reason. Not only was it a billion-dollar company but it also made its own chips. On top of that, it had just spent five years conducting, in pocket calculators, one of the harshest scorched-earth marketing campaigns the electronics industry had ever seen. TI was at the time the leading proponent of "learning curve pricing," a theory propounded by the Boston Consulting Group (BCG), which argued that all new high-tech products followed a life cycle from high prices for early adopters at the beginning to heavy discounting and commoditization for the masses at the end of the product's career. Knowing this curve, BCG argued, meant that, as with Moore's Law, you could predict the future and leapfrog your competition to get there. Texas Instruments read that to mean you priced today at the lower future price, snatched up all the market share from your competitors and then held on with a near-monopoly for the big payoff.

TI had tried this strategy on pocket calculators and nearly destroyed the industry. Except for HP, which, though singed, still managed to cling to the premium market, almost everyone else was soon run out of calculators by TI's aggressive pricing. That TI crippled itself with losses in the process didn't matter; everyone assumed in 1979 that the company's payoff for owning the calculator market would soon come.

And now the behemoth of Richardson, Texas, was turning its sights on personal computers, and everyone expected it to once more leave a charred wasteland as it passed.

Now was the time for Regis to prove himself. Like many Valleyites, he usually worked best during the big moments and grew bored during the successful lulls that came afterward. With Intel cruising along, still a couple of years away from the collapse that would lead to Operation Crush, Regis was in just such a lull. But the arrival of TI, combined with the announcement by Apple's board that the company was preparing to ramp up for an IPO, set Regis's heart beating again. He knew what he had to do.

It was a four-pronged plan, much of it driven by public relations. Advertising would continue to play up Apple's strengths, especially vis-à-vis the competition. For example, the Commodore Pet was in many ways a technically better computer. But it was also shoddy, with a little calculator-quality keyboard, a bent metal case and a tiny black-and-white display. So Apple would play up the elegance of its computer. Atari's machine wasn't great, but it wasn't bad either. The company was equated with video games and thus not taken seriously. Apple played up its reputation, as one magazine called it, of being "the Cadillac of home computers." Tandy, with its massive distribution but questionable quality, was met with the co-op campaign and advertisements promoting the II's quality and reliability.

But TI was a different story. Its machines, the 99/4 and the soon to appear 99/6 were top-notch. They were also, as might be expected, competitively priced. But TI had one big weakness: Everybody *hated* those cutthroat bastards, especially the press. And the feeling was mutual.

That's where the PR side of Regis's plan came in. Advertising could help, especially by emphasizing the playful, friendly side of Apple (with its implicit comparison with the nasty, cold-blooded company in Texas). But the heart of the campaign against TI would have to be fought in the press. This would in turn have the long-term advantage of positioning Apple before the reader-ship—that is, potential Apple shareholders—of those publications.

Thus, the other three prongs of Regis's strategy were aimed at influencing different segments of the Fourth Estate. The first of these was the trade maga-zines, the verticals. This was a pretty malleable group, eager to please advertis-ers and thrilled to be noticed by industry leaders. Regis fed them with a continuous stream of "loaner" computers, press releases, exclusive interviews and visits. Embraced by Apple and thrown crumbs by TI, the magazines soon reflected their loyalties in their editorial pages.

The second PR target was key opinion makers. These were the folks whose judgment determined for thousands of customers, analysts and developers whether a product or a company was perceived as a winner (with the atten-dant success) or a loser (decline and death). In an industry as young as per-sonal computing there really weren't any such thought leaders—except per-haps Lee Felsenstein and he was tainted by his corporate connections.

But there was such an opinion maker in the world of microprocessors and Regis knew him well: Benjamin Rosen. Rosen was a small, almost elfin man, with delicate Southern manners. But he also had a powerful intellect, nerves of steel and, best of all, a beautiful style. In just a year he had turned his personal newsletter into the most influential voice in the microprocessor in-dustry. One word from him in the newsletter could make or break a com-pany's reputation, sending its stock value shooting up or down in increments of millions of dollars.

From microprocessors it was only a small jump to personal computers. And Regis set out to help Rosen across. It turned out to be easier than anyone imagined: Rosen, in fact, already owned and admired an Apple II. And he was already at work becoming a personal computer pundit.

But getting Rosen to write about computing was one thing, getting him to write positively about Apple was another. Unlike the craven trade press edi-tors, Rosen could not be bought. And his newsletter took no advertising. Moreover, since he was more clever than anyone he dealt with, he was almost impossible to charm. He had made his reputation (and growing wealth) by telling the truth, no matter whom it hurt, and he was not going to abandon that principle just because some little computer company in Cupertino winked at him.

But, like all pundits, Rosen had one weakness: he was only as good as his information. He needed that information both to render his considered judg-ment and to offer his subscribers inside stuff they couldn't get elsewhere. Being nearly as clever as Rosen, Regis understood this. The rest of the computer industry, suffering from either the technomumbles or paranoid gigantism, clearly did not. So Regis played this card for all it was worth.

Before long Rosen was being constantly fed the latest insider news about Apple. When he needed help with his computer, he had only to call Apple to get the best possible service. And Apple executives cleared their calendars whenever Ben was in town, devoting long hours to deep discussions about technology and markets.

The point man for much of this was Mike Markkula, who had first met Rosen years before at National Semiconductor, and in one of those sweet Silicon Valley ironies, had been taught by Rosen how to operate a programmable calculator. Now Markkula, the chairman of Apple, was always there at Rosen's beckoning, even taking phone calls at home to answer Ben's technical questions. Markkula became such a close friend of Rosen's that he nearly destroyed the whole campaign by offering Ben stock. Luckily, Rosen politely refused.

The strategy paid off in spades. Rosen never lost his objectivity, he still called them as he saw them, but that didn't matter. It was too early in the game for the major players to really screw up anyway. What mattered was the quality and quantity of copy. And in that game Apple won hands down. Rosen gave Apple so much attention that venture capitalist Hank Smith would later say that Ben was "one of Apple's best salesmen."

But it was even better than that, because Rosen was also Apple's entree into the fourth prong of Regis's strategy: the mainstream press. These were the guys Apple had to seduce if it was to have a successful IPO. And Ben Rosen opened the doors for Apple to that world.

Almost from the beginning, personal computer companies had been trying to break into the general press. They mailed out press releases, held events, toured product demonstrations, mailed out gifts—and all they had to show for it was a few brief mentions in the *San Jose Mercury News* and *Business Week*. Regis had done his share of this kind of low-rent flackery for Apple.

But the support of Ben Rosen changed everything. Based in New York, he was becoming the world's leading tech guru and a quote source for the nation's leading media. And when reporters read Rosen's newsletter, they couldn't help but notice the attention he paid to a wacky little computer company in California. And when they visited his office they couldn't miss the fact that he was working on an Apple II. Soon Apple's name was starting to appear in publications such as the *New York Times* and *Fortune*.

Then, remarkably, Rosen went one step further. He began to play matchmaker between Apple and the press. He organized luncheons to introduce the company to publications like *Time*. Apple was now on its way to becoming a business phenomenon. In Markkula's words: "We were carrying the corporate image far out in front of the size and reputation of the corporation."

Regis had proven his theory.

There was one more matter before Apple could go public. It needed a new product.

In the late 1970s, personal computers were still so new that no one was really sure how long a product generation ought to last. A new generation of mainframes, dragging along their ever-growing burden of software, might last nearly a decade. But pocket calculators were as evanescent as mayflies. In between, microprocessors and other semiconductor chips turned over every couple of years according to the dictates of Moore's Law.

It would seem, then, that personal computers, dependent as they were upon the latest generation of microprocessors, would also have a middling life expectancy—shorter if the model was a dog, longer if it had an active base of users, programmers and aftermarket hardware designers.

The Apple II certainly seemed to fit into this latter category. Not only was it a best-seller but it had a very popular software library with the likes of VisiCalc, EasyWriter and a superb new word-processing program, called AppleWriter, written by an Apple fan named Paul Lutus in a tiny log cabin in the wilds of Oregon. Programmers liked Apple for the same reason journalists did: it was approachable. You could show up at the Bandley Drive headquarters, ask for Steve Jobs, show him your new program and if he liked it he might very well count up your lines of code and pay you on the spot. A few weeks later you'd be in the catalog of the world's best-known personal computer. Who could pass by such an opportunity? Especially when almost everybody else treated you like a carpetbagger and an intruder.

As for hardware, it seemed as if every mechanical engineer who bought an Apple II ended up building some add-on for it. Already there were electrical surge protectors, screen filters, specialty keyboards, drawing tablets, high-speed bolt-on cooling fans, even furniture for the Apple II. One enthusiast even carved a *wooden* Apple II, as if it was some totemic object, and presented it to the company.

But even given all that activity, Apple had to assume that by 1980 the Apple II would simply be obsolete. After all, hadn't the Apple I been competitive for only a year? By the end of the decade, the II would be four years old, ancient in small computer terms.

There were two ways to deal with this problem, and Apple chose to pursue both. The least of the two was to simply let the increasingly insular and eccentric Woz play with II and see if he could find some wrinkle to give it extra life. Woz, in fact, did have a notion about improving the machine's performance with the use of custom chips.

Being the great Woz, he was funded and left alone to follow his muse. Unfortunately, that muse had grown increasingly mute. In the end, Woz, working with an assistant, mainly futzed around, never really completing a new design. It would be others who would take some of his ideas, add their own and build the Apple IIe almost five years later.

Apple's management, recognizing this was a dead end, tried desperately to find an activity that would reanimate the company's resident genius. So a second project was begun, this one to create a new type of personal computer that would use "bit-slice" technology to divide up processing between multiple microprocessors. But Woz lost interest in that as well. He complained about having to attend too many distracting meetings, so many that he "was lucky to have two hours a day to myself." That project, after many incarnations, would become Lisa.

The fact was that Woz was tanking. Whatever it was that had caught him in its grip fifteen years before was finally sated and had moved on. Woz still had the genius, but he no longer had the heart. He was much more excited about playing practical jokes, such as sneaking Alka-Seltzer tablets labeled "for your convenience" into the menus at Bob's Big Boy or dousing fellow employees with green slime or putting a live mouse (another bit of technological irony) in another programmer's machine. He also lost himself in mindless activities like computing transcendental numbers on his computer, and in gambling away his salary at the casino tables in Reno.

His fellow employees weren't sympathetic. One programmer would say, "Woz lost the challenge. People stopped telling him that what he was doing was bullshit. He acquired the status of being a wizard and after a while he believed it. He knew better in his heart, but he loved the role." Randy Wigginton, his onetime disciple, was even tougher: "He preferred being the Messiah."

With Woz disintegrating, Apple's other-product strategy moved front and center, soon consuming most of the company's precious time and resources. This was the creation of a radically new computer design, a replacement for the Apple II.

Apple was nothing if not ambitious: three distinct product designs, as well as a new disk drive, were to be pursued concurrently. Like Woz's project, each was given a code name: Lisa, Mac, Sara and Twiggy. Twiggy was a low-profile ("skinny") double disk drive, so named because, in the loutish world of computer engineers, the two mini-floppies made them think of the famous model. Lisa and Mac were further off into the future. In the near term, Apple's next big play would be Sara, a direct replacement for the II. Ultimately, and unimaginatively, it would be named the Apple III (Apple played with the actual logo using symbols from the keyboard: thus, the Apple II was presented as][, and the Apple III as ///).

The III was to be Apple's proof that it was not a one-hit wonder. It was also to be the company's first shot at the business market. And finally, it was to serve as a financial bridge to the more innovative Lisa and Mac, which weren't expected to appear until the mid-1980s.

In the end, the Apple III accomplished none of these. But at least its failure was well timed.

Tom Whitney, at that time the new head of engineering, gave the Apple III project to his old Iowa State classmate Wendell Sander. Sander seemed the perfect choice: he was a fine engineer, disciplined and widely respected within the company. He was also intensely loyal to Apple. It was just the kind of choice most established companies make when choosing a product manager, especially a company sick of nursing prima donnas. But there was one thing Sander was not: a person who would fight his superiors for the integrity of his product. And at this point in the company's history, this was the skill the Apple III manager needed more than any other.

Because Sander was a good soldier, he accepted almost without complaint the product requirements set for him by senior management. At first glance, they didn't seem onerous. The III, unlike the stock II, was to have a 80-character-wide screen and upper- and lowercase characters. It was to feature some basic graphics and offer an improved operating system. And it was to have an internal electronic clock.

So far so good. These were *engineering* enhancements, derived from the needs of the market, from the experience with the Apple II and from a recognition of the improved technologies now available. But then management tacked on two other requirements that had nothing to with engineering, but with the company's own *marketing* needs.

The first was that the III must run the Apple II software library—the logic being that the III would thus be introduced already possessing the largest body of software in the personal computer market. That would give Apple users a smooth upward migration path requiring only the expense of new hardware.

The second management requirement was that the first III prototype be ready in one year. The ostensible reason for this speeded-up development cycle was that the II was getting old and that newer, more competitive machines were coming onto the market. But, in fact, the II was doing better than ever. In the fiscal year ended September 30, 1979, Apple sold 35,100 of the machines, four times that of the year before. And in 1980 that number doubled again, passing the unit market leader, Radio Shack, and regaining its position as the best-selling personal computer in the world. The real reason to rush the III to market was to have a hot new model out just before the legal "quiet period" began for the Apple IPO.

The end result of these two extratechnical requirements, as Sander soon discovered, was that he was boxed in. One reason for the extraordinary success of the II was that Woz had begun with a blank slate, unconstrained by a corporate structure. Egged on by Jobs, he had built the best machine imaginable. Sander, by comparison, had to fight a bureaucracy all the way, while dragging the Apple II emulation requirement behind him like an anchor. He could not build the best machine imaginable, only the best machine possible under the circumstances.

Not that he didn't give it his best shot. With Dan Kottke as his assistant, Sander spent each day designing some new part of the motherboard, then handed the drawing over to Kottke, who would make a clean drawing, then work into the night, usually under headphones, wiring that design into a real board. It was a very effective partnership, and one that met its deadlines, but in the end it still couldn't overcome the underlying limitations of the design.

The biggest of those limitations was the II emulation. Sander knew it, Kottke knew it, the whole engineering staff knew it. But marketing wanted the feature, and marketing prevailed. The problem with emulation is that it requires a translation function in software. Pumping programs through this emulation mode feature slows everything down. And the problem becomes especially acute if the translation must bridge between two entirely different microprocessors.

No problem, said Apple management, we'll use the same processor in the III as we had in the II. But that was the 6502, the underpowered microprocessor that Woz had compromised on originally because it was all he could afford; a processor that was never designed for a task as complicated as running a personal computer. So now an obsolete chip was going to run Apple's new flagship computer as it entered the 1980s. Worse, it was going to have to run a computer with two or three times the 64K core memory of the II.

Sander knew this was a mistake and proposed adding a second processor.

That was nixed by management because a dual-processor machine would have to be priced above the company's target for the III.

Now Sander was in a box. But still he didn't complain. Instead he came up with a severely compromised design. The III would still have the larger memory, but it would be divided up into banks, each of them no larger in capacity than the memory of the II—that is, at the functional limits of the , 6502. In this new design, the computer would use some of its processing power to keep track of which bank a particular piece of data was in and shuttle back and forth to reach it. This meant the III could have internal memory as great as 256K or more, but would grow less efficient with each jump in capacity.

It was an ugly solution made even uglier by the fact that all this Apple II emulation ultimately precluded the III from offering any better graphics than its predecessor. Woz might have helped overcome this difficulty, or at least used his pull at the executive level to get a more practical set of product specifications. And, in fact, Sander sometimes went to Woz for advice. But Wozniak stayed away, played his practical jokes and repeated that Sander was the best man for the job. Later, however, he was one of the loudest critics of the III's emulator, saying, "Apple claims they've got it and they don't," and announcing that he would have found a better solution.

Still Sander soldiered on. Now the unrealistic time requirement took its toll. Sander hit his deadline, but at a cruel price: between the time the prototype was completed and manufacturing was to begin, National Semiconductor informed Apple that it would not be able to deliver the clock chip in the volumes needed. Those that did arrive usually failed after three hours. Jobs screamed at Sporck—a remarkably brave thing in itself, given that the six-foot-four Charlie could have broken the young man in two with his hands—but it had no effect. Apple was not going to get its chips.

One could think of this as Charlie Sporck's revenge for having Apple raid his people, and Sporck certainly played for keeps. But revenues meant more to Sporck than revenge, especially in 1980, when the regular-as-clockwork four-year business cycle was hitting the chip industry hard. In truth, late and unreliable chip deliveries were standard procedure for the U.S. chip industry during this era—and for this lassitude the American semiconductor companies would soon be taught a nasty lesson by their Japanese competitors.

Meanwhile, Apple was without a clock chip for its new computer—a capability already being promoted by the company's overanxious marketing department. Needless to say, engineering got the blame . . . and the resulting distrust by both sides set in motion a feud between the two camps that would haunt the rest of Apple's history. For now, however, with the IPO just six months away, and with the III already trumpeted in the company's prospectus, Apple decided to go ahead with the clockless computer and take any publicity hits that might result.

As Raskin later told Moritz: "It was the classic story of people at the bottom saying, 'Things aren't working here. We're in trouble.' Then the next level up would say, 'We're in some trouble with this,' and the level above would say, 'We're getting around the trouble,' and the people at the top would say, 'It will be okay. Let's ship.'"

And Sander wasn't the only person forced by the deadline to make compromises on the Apple III. The need to make the III fully compatible with the II, combined with the entirely different hardware layout of the III from keyboard to memory, meant that nearly every single operation on the new computer had to be modified. That in turn meant most of Apple's programming team spent every second it had just trying to make the III work, much less work well or feature any new functions. It would be a year after the III's introduction before Apple's programmers had a version of the Pascal language to run on it.

With software running this far behind, it was inevitable that Apple's outside developers would be even further behind. After all, with nothing available for them to design for, they could hardly begin. Even Fylstra at VisiCorp, the single most important outside developer for the III, didn't receive his first III prototype until two weeks before the computer's formal introduction.

But perhaps the most compromised group of all was Apple's publications group. Apple, after all, had pulled itself head and shoulders above its competitors largely by the quality of the support it gave its users. The Apple II manual, when it finally appeared, helped thousands of neophytes smoothly enter the world of personal computing. In creating such documentation for the II, Apple had set the bar higher for everyone, including itself. From now on, any new computer would have to come with a well-written, in-depth library of support documents.

But with the III so late, with its final lineup of features apparently changing by the day, the publications team was paralyzed. As a result, the final documents were rushed, and new Apple III owners, many of them first-time computer operators, found themselves with badly written and poorly organized manuals, some describing capabilities that weren't even in the computer.

Still, for all of its flaws, the Apple III was introduced on time, gathered some good initial reviews from the slack-jawed press and it accomplished what it was designed to do. It gave Apple a follow-up product to prove that the company was not a one-hit wonder, propped up the stock at the IPO and gave the company a bridge, albeit a creaky one, to the business market in preparation for the more interesting Apple machines to come.

5.16 THE LITTLE MAGIC KINGDOM

The Apple III was introduced at the May 1980 National Computer Conference in Anaheim. Apple stole the show. The company rented Disneyland for an evening and drove 20,000 attendees over to the Magic Kingdom in red double-decker buses.

The sheer brazenness of the act stoked the imagination of the computer industry. Babes in evening gowns and bathing suits, sure. Maybe a TV star to sign autographs or a pop band to cover their hits or even a cocktail party in the best restaurant in town, *but take over Disneyland!* That was righteous; that was flash!

It was an eerie experience to walk through Disneyland that evening just before the party began. Disneyland on a warm night at the edge of summer . . . empty. Just a few Apple employees scurrying about, some Disney employees waiting to operate the rides. The Magic Kingdom seemed strangely small and old. A light misty rain, rare in May in the Los Angeles basin, was an augury of what was to come if anyone had stopped to notice.

Then the London buses rolled up and spit out their riders, long-haired programmers, junior marketing execs in suits, salesmen eyeing both a good time and a clever close. The event was a huge success, lasting until the wee hours. It was a metaphor both for Apple and for the Apple generation. Grown men and women acting like children, in an amusement park built for children, on a night when real children weren't allowed. There were echoes of the past—Jobs and Woz working as the Mad Hatter and the White Rabbit; the Disney science documentaries that had captured the imaginations of a whole generation of future engineers; and the Tomorrowland of rockets and plastic houses that had managed to miss the biggest revolution of all in information. And there were glimpses of the future—of product introductions that were cultural events, of marketing style hiding failures of engineering substance and of a generation that would refuse to ever be adults. And at the very center of it all, the King of the Lost Boys, a Peter Pan who would soon be rich enough to never have to grow up, was Steve Jobs.

The Disneyland party was more than just a celebration of the Apple III; it would also prove to be the kickoff for the Apple IPO in December. And from that night, Apple never looked back.

Today, nearly two decades later, after hundreds of IPOs by high-tech start-ups, some of them of even greater financial magnitude, many of Apple's antics in the next six months would be cause for the SEC to suspend the stock sale. Just a decade later, MIPS Computer's IPO was nearly stopped at the eleventh hour because a harmless article about the company unexpectedly appeared in *USA Today*.

If the Securities and Exchange Commission, the cops of the stock market, eventually grew wary of hyperbole and price manipulation surrounding high-tech IPOs, it was because Apple had set the pattern that every company tried to follow. And if Apple got away with it, it was because there was no precedent for what happened in the weeks preceding the company's Going Public Day.

Some of the credit for this success went to Regis McKenna and his crew. Beginning with the early ads and press tours, Regis & Company had carefully built interest in Apple toward a crescendo. He had made for the company the right contacts in the press and the analyst community, he had trained Apple's management in how to be public figures and then controlled their accessibility to just the right people. And now, as the mainstream press finally began to notice Apple, he was ready. Soon stories about the growing excitement over the Apple IPO began appearing in newspapers and magazines such as *Time*. And for the first time ever, average people began take an interest in the first public sale of a company's stock.

But Regis's success also carried with it failure. Because just as the ramp-up to the IPO began, Apple went out and hired an internal PR director to help manage investor relations. And this wasn't just some flack out of the Fortune 500; this was Fred Hoar, the only publicist in the Valley considered Regis's equal. If Regis was Mr. Outside, the ultimate agency man, Hoar was Mr. Inside, the prince of corporate PR managers. Big, blond-haired and square-jawed, perpetually hail-fellow-well-met, his words littered with classical allusions, Hoar was a corporate spokesman out of central casting. Once again, Apple, for all its public posturing as a new kind of company, had, when the crunch came, gone out to Old Valley for help.

Hoar's arrival did not set well with Regis & Company. Before, Regis McKenna Inc. had essentially been Apple's marketing and marketing communications wing. Now Hoar controlled the latter, and with it access in one direction to the press and in the other to Apple's management. It was months before the edges of the respective territories were established.

But for all that tension, the double play of Hoar and McKenna worked beautifully. Both men were pros, and both knew that the most important task of the moment was to get Apple successfully public. Moreover, Hoar offered many talents Regis lacked. Regis was something of pharisee: serious, ironic, always slightly embarrassed by the sordidness of PR, he preferred to sit above the fray and develop strategy. Fred Hoar, by comparison, loved the sweat and funk and fraud of good old-fashioned flackery. He knew it was all bullshit, but he reveled in it. And he winked to let you know he knew that you knew it was bullshit too.

It was a great combination, the strategist and the tactician. Regis devised the big campaign and Hoar went out into the mud and the blood and executed it. Regis organized the receptions for newspaper editors and presidents of investment funds; Fred made sure the Apple executives got to the event on time, then went out and slapped the backs and pumped the hands of everyone in the room.

The decision to go public was not the usual result of careful corporation consideration. On the contrary, in typical Apple form, the company found itself in crisis, and rushed out to make the best of it. This time the catalyst was another naive blunder by Woz.

Recalls Mike Scott: "At the June board meeting I had to report that Mr. Steve Wozniak, even though he was not allowed to sell stock, was nevertheless giving away 1,000-share blocks to relatives, friends, acquaintances and just about anybody else he could think of.

"That wasn't all. The real problem was that with Woz doing this, Apple was rapidly heading toward the SEC threshold of having more than five hundred shareholders. And when that happened, we would have to begin filing a 10K report." In other words, Apple was about to be a public company whether it wanted to or not. "So," says Scott, "we elected to pull the trigger."

By late summer the Going Public Campaign was picking up speed. By autumn it had taken on a momentum of its own. A year before, the company had gone out for a final, "mezzanine" round of venture investment to reward its friends, to line up new blue-chip investors and to fund the final drive to the IPO. That round raised $7.3 million from shares priced at $10.50 apiece. Among the sixteen investors were some of the big venture capitalists, including LF Rothschild and Brentwood Capital; Xerox Corp., both a potential competitor and a source of new technologies; and a private investor named Fayez Sarofim, who was a friend of Art Rock's. Mezzanines are also times when founders get a last easy and nearly painless chance to sell some of their own holdings for cash. That's exactly what Markkula and Jobs did, selling about $1 million worth apiece. For Markkula it was no big deal, but for Jobs it was a stunning accomplishment: in five years he had gone from starving in a rented room to being a millionaire. He would be able to go into the IPO already looking like a success.

But not everything went smoothly. Don Valentine, claiming a financial restructuring created by the closeout of one of his partnerships, used the mezzanine to sell all of his Apple holdings. It was an unwelcome act. To lose a major investor, especially one of Valentine's stature, in the mezzanine round might be read by the market as a signal of impending disaster. Luckily, it went by almost unremarked—so much so that Valentine is still often miscredited with being Apple's key investor.

But the loss of Valentine created another problem: with his departure, Apple had lost the man with the golden gut about the perfect date to go public. Luckily, Art Rock was still around, and if he didn't have Valentine's clairvoyance at picking IPO dates, he still had as much experience at going public as anyone else in tech. It was Rock who helped Apple select the underwriters for the IPO—hometown boys Hambrecht & Quist for the action, gray-suited Morgan Stanley for the stability (Morgan Stanley screamed; it was the first time it had to share underwriting)—and then worked with them to ultimately set the date as December 12, 1980.

Now, more than a year after the mezzanine, with the press giving more coverage by the day to the upcoming Apple IPO, hysteria began to form both inside and outside the company.

Initial Public Offerings are times of paralysis for companies. "It was a three-month paperwork nightmare," Scott recalls. For one thing, management is divided in two; with half preparing the prospectus, meeting with underwriters, then racing about the world holding investor road shows. Meanwhile, the other half is trying to keep a dynamic, fast-moving company growing at the same pace without missing a step. And down in the bowels of the company those with stock daydream about what to do with their new riches, and those without stock spend their days scheming to find out who does have stock, how much they have, and then hating them for it.

Founders stock, equity, in a new start-up is never handed out equitably. Draw a cartoon for the company's first flyer when the firm is just three people and you may end up paid with more stock than the executive vice president who is hired ten years later when the company has a billion dollars in annual sales. Inevitably, on Going Public Day managers discover they have less stock than their subordinates, secretaries have more than their bosses, and, of two equally qualified people sitting side by side, one will become a tycoon and retire while the other can only look forward to another thirty years of mortgage payments.

Even in the most sobersided company the new start-up equity game is built on luck, timing and connections. In a company as chaotic and improvised as Apple, the situation was bound to be even more arbitrary and explosive. Once again, the presence of an arbitrary, punitive and mercurial Steve Jobs only made matters worse. One engineer would later say, "The amount of stock that people were given had nothing to do with their ability to work. It had everything to do with their ability to get stock." Rod Holt was philosophical: "The fact that a turkey who is worth a million and a half doesn't deserve to have an office in the building is a quirk of fate."

There were three ways to get Apple stock options. One was to be an investor—and that was a game for millionaires in search of more millions. Another was to make stock options part of your employment contract with Apple's management—but that only went to senior managers.

A third was to play on a major shareholder's conscience or soft heart. Needless to say, the softest of those hearts (and some would say heads when it came to money) belonged to Woz. Some stock Woz sold because he was asked—to Rock's friend Sarofim (that's where he got the stock in the mezzanine round), to one of Rock's partners and to personnel director Ann Bowers. Another buyer was Stephen Vidovich, the scion of a local orchard family grown rich leasing out most of the business districts of Cupertino. Vidovich happened to own the De Anza Racquet Club, where Apple had a corporate membership. He bought 25,000 shares.

Those who took advantage of Woz's sympathy included more than thirty Apple employees whom Woz felt had not been given a fair shake. They got it, 80,000 shares worth $7.50 apiece. As Jobs would say: "Woz couldn't say no. A lot of people took advantage of him."

Perhaps, but at least Woz was selling stock to make Apple more equitable to its people, not to mention giving his parents more than enough shares to buy financial independence. By comparison, Job was using his shares as a bludgeon. When it was learned that Dan Kottke, who had shared Jobs's house and helped him build the first Apple I's, was ineligible for stock because he was still merely a technician, Rod Holt went to Jobs and suggested they both chip in equal amounts for their old friend. "Great!" said Jobs. "I'll give him zero." When Kottke's supervisor approached the board of directors with a proposal to give him stock, Jobs shot the proposal down again.

Others were screwed too. Elmer Baum, who had lent the money to help found the company; Bill Fernandez, the childhood friend and first company employee; Chris Espinosa, who'd slept in the park while writing the Apple II manual—all were left out of the big payoff for Apple's success. Espinosa would tell Moritz, "We missed out on the American dream because we were too nice to grab part of it. Kottke was too nice. Fernandez was too Buddhist and I was too young . . . We all realized to some degree we weren't heavy enough. We weren't obnoxious enough to make ourselves millionaires."

At the same time, there were some unlikely beneficiaries, including Sherry Livingston, the mythmaking millionaire secretary. Other shareholding employees sold their stock to everybody from Caribbean investment funds to the HP pension fund to Charlie Finley, owner of the Oakland A's (who would later sue over the stock price).

As December approached, the hysteria seemed to grow by the day. Inside Apple, the company became increasingly paralyzed as rumors flew back and forth about who had stock and how much, and as those with holdings drifted off into reverie about how their lives were about to change. Even reports that the early shipments of Apple III's were DOA didn't seem to faze the company.

Meanwhile, Apple's various support entities, from Venrock to the underwriters to Regis McKenna Inc.—nearly all of them standing to make millions in the IPO—were scrambling to keep the whole process from derailing. Even in that permissive era of the SEC, there was still such a thing as too much publicity for an IPO. Apple likely passed that point by late October. McKenna and Hoar did their parts, honoring the prescribed "quiet period" and killing ads, publicity campaigns and interviews.

But there was no dampening the hysteria. By November, the Apple IPO was on its way to becoming the most famous, and popular, initial stock offering in American business history. By the first week of December, it had all gone completely nuts. It seemed as if everyone in America wanted a piece of Apple, and if they hadn't before, the nation's newspapers and newsmagazines convinced them they should. In the newsroom of the San Jose Mercury News, the technology reporter was besieged at his desk, in the cafeteria, even in the lavatory by other reporters, ignoring rules about conflict of interest, trying to find out how to get a few shares.

Big IPO fortunes sometimes go to those who are shameless enough to play on any connection to the company, no matter how tenuous, to beg for a few shares. If you ever delivered a pizza to Bandley Drive or lent Woz a soldering iron in high school or worked with Mike Scott for a week at Fairchild, you felt you were a key contributor to Apple's current success and deserved to be compensated for it. There was no penalty for being pushy or obnoxious or self-degrading—after all, Apple's own employees were doing the same thing.

For weeks before the big day, bags of pleading letters poured into the underwriters, Apple employees were accosted by relatives, neighbors, even strangers. Every public statement (not to mention private remarks) by Apple executives was deconstructed for clues about how to get stock.

It seemed as if everybody in the capitalist world (and probably many in the Communist world as well) wanted shares of Apple stock, believing that it would shoot sky high the instant it began trading on Nasdaq.

They were correct. In August, during a private placement with Hambrecht & Quist, Apple's stock was valued at $5.44 per share. When Apple published its prospectus on the sale on November 6, it formally predicted that the stock would be priced between $14 and $17 at the IPO. That, as everybody knew, was standard underwriter palaver. *Every* high-tech IPO seemed to be priced at $14 to $17. What counted was how high the stock would go in the hours immediately after the opening bell.

Just how high was anyone's guess, and everyone's fantasy. Certainly the signs were good: Genentech, the hottest biotech firm around, had gone out in October at an opening of $35, jumped to $89 by afternoon and settled back at $71 by the end of the first day. That was a different company in a different industry, but it hinted that the market for new tech issues was strong—as if the madness surrounding Apple didn't scream that already.

5.17 LOCUS

Finally, the day came. On the morning of December 12, 1980, Apple went public. There was so much pent-up demand for the stock (listed as AAPL, the letters picked by Hoar) that it opened at $22. That was already 50 percent above the expected opening price. But any early morning speculation that demand had already been sated evaporated as the stock price began to climb.

Every company freezes on the day it goes public. And Apple was no exception, especially since much of America froze with it. In the buildings along Bandley, employees were alternately giddy and sober, vocal and contemplative. There were spontaneous parties and speeches, hugs and tears. Meanwhile, through these various incarnations of a life-changing event, every eye was on the many computers around the company hooked up to the Dow Jones ticker.

When the market closed at 1 P.M. P.S.T., Apple's stock was selling for $29 per share, nearly double the original estimated opening price. It was one of the great Going Public Days, the biggest since Ford went public in 1956, and everyone and everything it touched was changed forever. Apple itself had raised $82.8 million—money it didn't really think it needed, but would soon want badly.

As for individual shareholders, the numbers were even more staggering. Even before the IPO one Apple clerk had quit because she couldn't emotionally deal with the kinds of numbers she was seeing processing stock options. And the real numbers were even bigger. Jobs came away with $256.4 million for his 15 percent ownership. Markkula made $239 million, Woz $135 million, Scott $95.5 million. Among the outside investors, Art Rock made $21.8 million, Venrock $129.3 million and Teledyne's Henry Singleton $40.8 million.

But even among lesser lights the sums were astonishing. Rod Holt was worth $67 million. John Couch, who'd demanded stock in exchange for joining the company and running the Lisa project, made $13.6 million. Jef Raskin and Sherry Livingston also became millionaires.

And, this being Apple, there were the oddball stories as well. Alice Robertson, Woz's ex, made $42.4 million on her settlement stock—then complained she'd not gotten enough. But driving around in a new gold Mercedes with a license that read 24 CARAT seemed to calm her down. And Tom Whitney, Woz's old boss, the guy who'd beaten out Chuck Peddle for a job at Apple, then proved a disaster, came away with $48.9 million.

It was sheer madness. Mike Scott calculated the number of new millionaires that day at 104. In a single day, people who'd been working for $40,000 per year, people just a half dozen years out of college, were suddenly worth tens of millions of dollars. Some were now among the richest people in the United States. It was so much money they couldn't imagine it; they couldn't even figure out how to spend it all.

The only proper thing to do was to celebrate. Some went to the Good Earth; others went home as soon as they could to try to understand what had just happened. The big winners were gathered for a celebration around a speaker phone hooked up to Morgan Stanley's offices in New York. Mike Scott, never one to miss an excuse for a party, brought in some champagne, but even he seemed dazed through all the toasts and handshakes.

Only one man appeared unaffected by all of this success: the husband of Ann Bowers, the human resources director. But then, he was Robert Noyce of Intel, who was still (barely) the richest person in the room. He was kind enough to keep his own counsel and not spoil the moment by warning the others of what was to come.

Jef Raskin, who was also in the room, said it suddenly struck him that "all the people in the room were millionaires. The forceful thing was the world had shifted. I hadn't seen that happen before."

The world had indeed shifted. Apple Computer, just five years before nothing more than two antisocial postadolescents and a pile of parts in a dingy suburban garage, was now a billion-dollar company, its founders on their way to becoming living legends, its products transforming the home, the school and the office. Apple was now the first great company of the new age in electronics, the first great enterprise created by children of the baby boom. As such it would forever be the benchmark for any accomplishment of that generation, and the paradigm for the thousands of companies to follow. The kid who once neglected to bathe had become the voice of a new high-tech generation.

That night, after the parties finally faded out, the children of Apple went home to their new lives. IPOs are convergences. In the run-up to Going Public Day, companies often enjoy the greatest morale and cohesiveness in their histories. For five years, Apple had been a great crusade—a Children's Crusade, with all the attendant grandiosity, immaturity, posturing, missteps, victories and boundless enthusiasms—all working toward the common goal of making this foundling company a success.

Now that success had come. All the career trajectories had finally intersected on a sunny December day. And from now on, they would diverge. There would be other convergences, including an even greater one four years hence. But that, with a few exceptions, would be for a new group of Apple employees, not for this one. Even as they finally fell asleep that night, the lives of Apple's first round of winners were already heading off on different tangents that would take many far from Bandley Drive.

For some, that departure would come much sooner than expected. Having reached such a lofty pinnacle of success, Apple was now about to fall into the abyss. But at least it would have a full wallet for the trip.

6.0 BEARING FRUIT

High-tech companies nowadays go to great lengths to control the impact of going public. They try to stop employees from burning up their new wealth on wasteful and ostentatious toys. They try to keep the celebrations down to a controlled riot. They sometimes bring in financial managers to teach the new tycoons how to deal with their overnight riches and to understand that stock (which many hold for the first time) is a volatile and temperamental instrument that can suffer wild swings in price. And they try, though it can be very difficult, to keep their senior executives from either walking away with their incredible wealth or staying and doing something selfish and stupid that pulls down the company.

They do these things because Silicon Valley has learned its lessons about IPOs. And two of the biggest of these lessons came in the early 1980s, during the Valley's first great going-public boom. One of these warnings came from Eagle Computer, a short-lived personal computer company that managed to go public at just the right moment in June 1983. On that day, the company's forty-year-old CEO, Dennis Barnhart, celebrated his new wealth—$9 million—by having lunch with a yacht salesman, getting drunk, then driving his new Ferrari off a cliff.

The moral wasn't lost on other CEOs who could easily imagine themselves in Barnhart's expensive shoes. To this day, IPO boardroom celebrations remain comparatively sober affairs.

The second lesson taught to the high-tech world about IPOs came from Apple Computer. No company had ever flown so high in such a short time, and no company ever screwed up in so many ways in the weeks and months thereafter. What actually happened to Apple after its IPO is largely forgotten by Valleyites, but to this day both employees and executives of newly public companies are obsessed with the fear that their company will now begin to fall apart. Yet, even armed with that knowledge, many still do.

When Apple went public, it had neither of these warnings. Nor, with the

arrogance and narcissism that had characterized the company from the beginning, would it likely have listened if it had. So instead, the company devoted
its days for the next few months tracking the roller-coaster ride of the company's stock. If the stock had a good day, so did Apple—employees were
happy and motivated, work got done, products were shipped. If the stock
faltered, dark clouds formed over Cupertino, the staff grew moody and sullen
and nothing got done.

Meanwhile, employees who owned company stock devoted a considerable
amount of the day to figuring out how to protect those shares from the government—and how to spend them on themselves. This was when local banks
around Silicon Valley first learned how to make loans by accepting stock
options as collateral. One group of employees even flew out of the country to
Vancouver, British Columbia, on April 15 in order to legally file for an extension on their 1980 taxes.

Even to the outsider, the transformation of Apple was obvious within a
week after the IPO. Where the parking lot had been Volkswagen vans, Volvos
and beat-up American clunkers, suddenly, almost overnight, the same slots
were filled with Mercedeses and Porsches.

Executive row was no more immune to this than any other department at
Apple. A conversation about business was likely to devolve into a discussion
about relative merits of private airplanes, the amount of time needed to get a
multiengine license and the relative difficulty of getting a good space at San
Jose Airport.

Bill Atkinson, at the time an Apple programmer, said with dismay, "Some
people spent half their waking hours counting their stock options." And it was
even worse than that, because once they finished counting, many of these
same employees realized that in a couple of years when the stock fully vested,
they could sell out, quit Apple and retire forever.

The loss of key employees after an IPO is a common problem. But Steve
Jobs only made matters worse at Apple. Before the IPO, he had used options
as a bludgeon against enemies and former friends; now he used it as a test of
loyalty. That Markkula had taken some of his money, bought a used Learjet
and paid two pilots to operate it, or that Woz, caught up in Markkula's flying
fever, had bought his own Beechcraft, didn't seem to bother Jobs—in fact,
it pleased him, because it increased his comparative ownership. But let a
lesser mortal at Apple try to sell his stock and Jobs saw it as a betrayal to the
cause.

Jef Raskin landed on Jobs's enemy list for just such a sale. This was especially ironic because Raskin sold his stock precisely because he didn't want to
have to worry about it anymore and because he wanted to focus again on his

work for Apple. Nevertheless, Jobs would never fully trust Raskin again, a change in attitude that would have enormous implications for the company.

To Jobs's credit, when it came to stock he lived his philosophy. His quality of clothes improved a little—he was already becoming a noted fashion plate—as did his lifestyle, which now included an expensive, but famously spartan, home, a Mercedes and a motorcycle. But in light of his fabulous new wealth, this was pocket change. He didn't need to touch his stockholdings. And Jobs expected no less from anybody else at Apple.

Admirable as this asceticism might be, it also signaled that Jobs was just as obsessed about his stock as everyone else at Apple. Nobody but resentful nonshareholding employees was minding the store.

That might have been okay for a little while, except for a growing high-tech tumor in the corpus of the company: the Apple III. It was still being shipped DOA or ready to blip off within hours of being turned on. And nobody knew why. While everyone was watching the stock ticker, Apple was sliding toward a PR disaster that could turn all those stock certificates into wallpaper.

It wasn't until January, luckily while the world was still in Apple IPO afterglow, that the cause of the III's electronic aneurism was finally isolated. One person had actually discovered the cause weeks before: Dan Kottke, the founder who'd been refused stock options by a vengeful Jobs. Kottke had been working with a III that would unexpectedly die. One day, furious, he picked the machine up a couple of inches and then slammed it down on his work-table. The III jumped back to life. A faulty connector, Kottke decided. But he told no one. Later he would say that, as a lowly engineer, he didn't feel in a position to bring his concerns to his superiors. "Lowly engineer," of course, was a phrase Jobs had used in explaining why he wouldn't give Kottke stock. It was Kottke's revenge.

Sander's boss, Tom Whitney, assuming that everything was fine with pro-duction, told Mike Scott that all was well and III's would soon be rolling off the manufacturing line. Then, despite Mike Scott's request that he stay in Cupertino in case of an emergency, he left on a business trip to Europe. Whitney returned to be fired. He left with his millions.

In the end, the bad connection proved to be the one to the Apple III's heart. Sander, trapped by the impossible performance and design demands made on the product, had been forced to build the III using two printed circuit boards full of chips: the motherboard and a smaller board containing all the memory chips stacked precariously atop one another. Even worse, that memory board had to be made out of the thinnest printed circuit material on the market.

It was a perfect recipe for disaster. Some machines actually ran until they were bolted into their enclosures, then the memory board flexed and shorted out. In other III's, the problem was on the motherboard. To protect the all-important microprocessor chip in this dense layout, it was mounted in a pit within a raised platform for the connector. Unfortunately, the pit itself wasn't much bigger than the chip, leaving no clearance for the assembler's fingers to line up the little lead wire "legs" of the chip to fit into the proper slots. In shades of Jobs's sister building the Apple I, Apple III assemblers were reduced to pushing down the chip with their thumb and hoping for the best.

Still other machines shorted out the moment they were turned on because the metal conductors plated on the surface of the printed circuit boards were so close that they exceeded the tolerances of the PC industry. And in still others, the wiring was so close to screw holes holding everything together that the act of assembly would drive the screws through the wiring insulation and either short the machine out or threaten to set it on fire.

The whole situation was so absurd that Kottke's "bounce" test temporarily became a recommended manufacturing step. Each III was to be picked up three inches and dropped to knock some sense into it. And even that wasn't easy, since the damn computer, thanks to a heavy metal case (used because of fears the FCC would soon rule against excessive RF—radio frequency—leakage), weighed about as much as a microwave oven. That weight, combined with the fact that the III was unbalanced by a heavy power supply against its rear wall, made it literally a backbreaker for assembly workers and owners performing the Kottke Bounce. So a visitor to the III manufacturing line in early 1981 would have met the astonishing sight of employees smacking the brand-new Apple III's with rubber mallets.

At any other time, Apple would simply have bitten the bullet and stopped production of the III until the design and manufacturing problems were worked out. But the company was stuck. It had announced the delivery date of the III in its stock prospectus and didn't dare back off. So now, the product that was to replace the aging Apple II, the killer computer that was to smash the existing competition, scare off potential new ones and forever position Apple in the corporate market, was proving for many buyers little more than a $5,000 paperweight. And even when it worked it lacked its most promoted, and anticipated, design feature.

For all that, the Apple III was not a bad computer. Just a benighted one. It had a sophisticated operating system (which was called just that: SOS), a full-sized 80-character screen, as much as 512K of memory, and a magnificent keyboard. In time it would be the first mass-market personal computer with an optional hard disk drive, the Profile. But none of that mattered, because the horrible launch of the III had already doomed it.

As bad as the hardware problem was for the III, it masked a deeper, and ultimately more far-reaching failure in the machine. Because of that, Apple never learned what should have been the real lesson of the III debacle. In an executive meeting several months before the III introduction, Jobs and Markkula got into a long conversation about the incredible number of new companies—board builders, software developers, hardware makers—that had sprung up surrounding the Apple II. According to an attendee at the meeting, the two executives then began to ask each other, "Why should we allow people to make money off of us? Off of our innovations?"

"It was a turning point," recalled that individual fifteen years later. "From that moment on, Apple fought all third-party development. All the way down the line. It even killed Radius, a $300-million monitor company that was doing a great job. Over time it got worse, and it became not just about money but ego. This attitude developed at Apple that nobody could do anything better than Apple could. That's why the company kept building its own keyboards and everything else—and why Apple computers became so much more expensive than everyone else."

6.1 III Be Gone

By the end of 1980, after all the attention over the IPO ended, the first in-depth reviews of the III appeared, and they were almost uniformly negative. The press had wanted to love the Apple III, and they had shown their ardor at Disneyland. But there was no mistaking that the machine was a beauty on the surface but a dog at heart. And a dog without a brain—two months after its introduction, the III had only three software programs available for it, one of them a mail management program written by Markkula himself . . . and few new ones expected for another six months. The III also had a terrible habit, especially for a journalist on deadline in the middle of writing a story about it, of simply crapping out, responding to a SAVE command with that most depressingly final of technology phrases: SYSTEM FAILURE.

So bad were the reviews that Apple finally accepted (but never publicly admitted) failure, and pulled the III. On Regis's advice, the company stopped all advertising and promotion of the III and went back to the drawing boards. The guts were redesigned for greater reliability, more memory (to a total of 512K) was added, the clock chip was finally put in, new manuals were prepared, and a complete software library was rushed to completion. Existing III owners with a dead or malfunctioning machine (sometimes the second or third one) were allowed, without cost, to swap it for the new, more powerful machine.

Finally, at the end of 1981, as if nothing had ever happened, the Apple III was formally relaunched.

It was a bit of chutzpah on Apple's part, but it wasn't unique for the industry. Throughout the 1970s, Hewlett-Packard had to reintroduce its 3000 minicomputer three times before it finally got the technology right. It went on to become one of the best-selling computers in industry history.

Apple, however, wasn't so fortunate. The fixed III was a fine computer, a fact recognized by hundreds of businesses, which bought them by the dozens each, and by thousands of individuals who, even after the misery they had been through, became rabid Apple III loyalists. But by 1983 only 65,000 Apple III's had been sold—a figure only a little higher than Apple had expected in sales the first year.

Still, some Apple marketers and engineers wanted to stick with the III. After all, its wrinkles had been smoothed out, it had penetrated the all-important business market and the company had some obligation to the III's user base. But one figure was adamant about burying the III like a dead cat: Regis McKenna. He saw the III as a living reminder of Apple's ability to screw up, and an enduring symbol of the company's arrogance. Regis wanted to clear the decks for the new computer families to come. He refused to promote the III and it quickly died.

It was a mistake. Until then, Apple, in its style, its carefully crafted image and its public pronouncements, had always presented itself as different from other companies. It was the people's computer company . . . as the ads would say in a few years, the maker of "computers for the rest of us." A company like that didn't abandon its loyal customers, it didn't summarily kill a computer line and make orphans of its users. Apple wasn't supposed to do things like that . . . but now it had, and those thousands of III owners (and many more thousands of II owners who were watching) would never completely trust Apple again. Even at Apple, it seemed, business was still just business.

Pissed off III owners were only part of Regis's mistake. The full implications of his error wouldn't be known for years. Unwittingly, by killing the III early, McKenna never allowed its real flaw—limited third-party hardware and software—to be fully felt. Had he let the Apple III limp on for another year, its internal problems fixed, but its software library still bare, Apple might have learned the one big lesson about open systems that would have later saved it. Instead, Regis killed the patient when it began to cough, before the cancer made itself known. Now, Apple could convince itself that the real problem had been a procedural problem, a bug, and not a systemic collapse.

6.2 Shattered Genius

One measure of just how interesting new wealth was at Apple right after the IPO—and, conversely, how boring the daily business of cranking out II's and fixing III's was by comparison—was to talk to Markkula or Wozniak during the early months of 1981.

Markkula, accustomed to wealth, was a little more discreet, but nevertheless was delighted to get off business and talk about skiing, vacation home and, most of all, flying his Learjet.

A conversation with Wozniak during this period was much more disconcerting. There in his office, surrounded by the detritus of the computing revolution he'd helped to spark, Woz too would drift off into discussions about flying, about how he'd bought a Beechcraft Bonanza back before Thanksgiving with some of the proceeds of his private stock sales, how he was finishing up his pilot's license and his dreams of getting a multiengine license and eventually working his way up to pilot his own jet.

It was wildly disorienting. Here was a young man just pushing thirty, who just a couple of years before had been so indifferent to the material world beyond his computer screen that he regularly forgot where he was. Now he was behaving like a spoiled prince. It was as if Woz, struggling to resurface in the world after all those years lost in the fun house of computer technology, had suddenly been shaken awake by all the excitement around the IPO. Now he found himself not only back in the world but richer than God. His father once discovered $250,000 in uncashed checks in his son's new Porsche and said mournfully, "A person like him shouldn't have that much money."

And with the emotional development of a teenager who had never grown up, Woz set out to indulge as many experiences and buy as many toys as he could. To hell with computers, now it was time to live.

That explained the gambling at Lake Tahoe and the fast car. And when his lawyers advised him to expand his portfolio, Woz went out and bought a movie theater in the Hispanic barrio of East Side San Jose. The theater soon showed the provocative gang film *The Warriors*, which provoked a small riot, and Woz soon found himself attending community meetings and apologizing to angry residents.

He also became engaged again. Candi Clark, the daughter of a contractor from the East Bay, was an Apple employee. According to her childhood friends, she had always wanted, from an early age, to find a wealthy husband. And one fine day she found him, a man so wealthy it would be hard to ever burn up his money and so innocent as to fall in love at first sight, on the other side of a water-gun fight. And in that little vignette—childish play, a shrewd companion and a naive Woz—could be seen the pattern for the next decade of Stephen Wozniak's life.

There was about Woz during this period and ever after the sense of an innocent fool, caught up in situations more complicated and more sinister than he could ever understand. He was the Candide of the computer age, doing everything wrong, but earnestly and with good intentions . . . then somehow managing to emerge, alive, from the resulting rubble.

Alive, but not always intact. In the future it would be his bank account that would take a beating. But not now. On February 7, 1981, Woz, Clark and two friends drove up into the nearby Santa Cruz mountains to the airport at Scotts Valley and climbed into Woz's Beechcraft.

It was a strange time for Woz. Personally, his life couldn't be better. He was rich, engaged and a living legend. But professionally, his life had not been happy. His workmates, many of them his greatest fans and former apostles, were getting sick of his unproductiveness. And nobody was more annoyed at Woz's apparent goldbricking than Mike Scott.

Angry that Fylstra and Personal Software had begun to design VisiCalc for Apple's competitors, Scott decided to get even by rendering the software company irrelevent. His strategy was to have Apple design its own spreadsheet program and have it bundled in with every II or III. But Scott also knew that pushing such a project through Apple's growing bureaucracy would take forever. Atypically, he circumvented his own organization chart and assigned the project to Randy Wigginton, Woz's erstwhile acolyte. Scott reasoned that Wigginton would undoubtedly enlist Woz, and that might in turn get the resident genius off his butt and back to creating.

But it didn't quite work out as planned. Wigginton did convince Woz to help work out some math routines. But then Woz wandered off, figuring he had lots of time to get to it. Meanwhile, Wigginton tore through the code writing and suddenly found himself ready for Woz's routines and Woz hadn't even begun.

Wigginton was pissed, but not nearly as much as Mike Scott. From the beginning Scott's job had been that of not only running a high-profile, fast-growing corporate superstar but also babysitting the two founders. That meant controlling Jobs and motivating Woz. Jobs, perpetually wandering off the reservation to make pronouncements outside the company and interfering with the work of departments within, had initially been the greater challenge. But Woz's deepening inertia in the months leading up the IPO had been increasingly worrisome.

Now it was threatening Mike Scott's own authority within the company. Before it was too late, he set out to make an example to other slugs coasting along at the newly rich company. He decided to put the screws to Woz.

Throughout January 1981 Scott made Wozniak's life a living hell, hectoring him, buffaloing him, ragging his ass almost every day. In response, Woz seemed to return to his old form. He worked day and night constructing the routines. As always, once he set his mind to it, he made amazing progress.

Through it all, Woz did manage to retain his sense of humor. He even managed the classic Wozniak revenge of pulling a practical joke on Scott. Knowing Mike was a George Lucas fanatic—Scott had mentioned his dream of inviting the movie director onto the Apple board—Woz talked a friend into calling Scott's office when he knew Mike wasn't in. Impersonating Lucas, the caller left a message saying he'd call back. Scott nearly swooned when he heard the message, and became so obsessed with being on hand for the call that he stayed off Wozniak's back for nearly a week.

By the first week of February an exhausted Woz had the routines completed except for a final check. He decided to celebrate by getting away and doing some flying. And that's what found him with his fiancée and two other friends at the Scotts Valley airport. He likely had the routines with him in the plane when it took off, planning on putting on the finishing touches later that day.

Even before takeoff, Woz had been nervous and jumpy, complaining about headphone interference. At takeoff, the plane had climbed just fifty feet in the air, bounced down again off the tarmac, then careened off at an angle through two fences and into an embankment.

Exactly what happened is a matter of speculation. The first reports had it that Woz and company were practicing touch-and-go landings as part of Woz's training for his next-level pilot's license. If so, it was an incredibly stupid and reckless act on Woz's part: an unskilled pilot performing high-risk maneuvers with a plane full of people. Later the story was that the group was actually leaving for Southern California to pick up Woz and Candi's wedding rings. It may even have been both.

The National Transportation Safety Board never found a mechanical cause for the crash. But, pilot error or not, the result was nearly catastrophic—

the plane came to rest just two hundred feet from a roller-skating rink jammed with teenagers.

If the skaters were spared, the passengers in the plane were not. Candi Clark suffered severe enough cuts on her face to need plastic surgery. The back-seat passengers were battered and bruised.

But it was Woz, slammed into the controls and dashboard, who took the worst of it. He bit through his upper lip, fractured the socket of his right eye and took a bump on the head sufficient to cause double vision. But he was conscious and, all things considered, seemed normal on the trip to El Camino Hospital in Mountain View, the facility nearest his home and his parents.

But he wasn't all right. The blow had caused amnesia. He retained his long-term memory, remembering events up to a day before the accident, but could not recall the day of the crash itself. Nor, it seemed, could he form any new short-term memories. The near-present seemed perpetually lost. He was a computer with a disk drive but no internal memory.

Then, most frightening of all, as he lay in his hospital room waves of paranoia swept over Woz. He refused to eat, acting as if it might be poisoned. He announced in conspiritorial tones that the government was plotting to take his money and, presumably with him in it, blow up the hospital.

The paranoia was obvious to his friends and family, but the deeper neural injuries were not. After a few days, Woz seemed on the mend. He awoke one night to tell Candi that he dreamed he'd been in a plane crash, and was stunned to find it had actually happened. He began to regain the present. Finally, after a week in the hospital, he was released. If he seemed any different from the experience, it was, some noticed, that he seemed slower, as if his mind had to wind itself up before it could render a judgment.

At Apple, paralyzed and in shock over its beloved founder, resident genius and mascot being nearly killed, there was a sigh of relief that Woz was okay. And when he left the hospital, it was generally agreed that after a brief rest he would soon be back to work at Apple.

But Woz wouldn't come back for five years. Sitting at home, he was as lost and confused as he'd ever been in his life.

6.3 BLACK WEDNESDAY

It was to be a season of losses and betrayals. The failure of the III demanded its pound of employee flesh. Mike Scott, displaying the hard side of his personality that was always there with his sweetness, set out to do the butchering.

In the months leading up to and just after the IPO, Scott had grown convinced that Apple had become too bloated with employees who were either superfluous or not up to their jobs. In most companies growing as fast as Apple, this temporary excess could easily have been remedied by some transfers, a few pointed suggestions about finding work elsewhere and a temporary hiring slowdown.

But Scott, an offspring of Fairchild and National Semiconductor, decided instead to do all in one swift, brutal stroke. The result, known forever after at Apple as Black Wednesday, came in late February less than three months after the IPO. As with the day of the introduction of the Apple III, it was rainy; but this time it was miserably dark and cold as well. It was a good day for slaughter.

Companies almost never have layoffs so soon after an initial public stock offering. For one thing, they are usually too rich and growing too fast to worry about a little deadwood. The natural attrition of people wealthy enough not to have to work anymore also helps solve the problem. And finally, management is usually too obsessed with its newest challenge—keeping tens of thousands of new stockholders happy—to risk bad publicity for a while.

But Mike Scott didn't care about any of these things. He believed the III mess called for extreme measures if Apple was ever going to get back into fighting trim. "Apple had been doubling its employment almost every quarter," he recalls. "We had grown from 500 to 1,500 in just the previous year. What started it was one guy we had running peripherals who was a real turkey, and I made up my mind to fire him. I starting wondering how many others at the company were out of their depth.

"So I brought it up at a staff meeting. I said, 'Maybe we've made some mistakes. Go back and look over your list of new hires and determine who should be laid off.' "

He had his supporters in this move. Gary Martin for one: "I was in the meeting with Scott and Don Bryson of the III group before the III's introduction. I said, 'Hey, are we ready to go with the product?' He said, 'Yes.'

"Then Scott asked, 'Would you bet the company on it?'

" 'Yes.'

" 'Would you bet your job on it?'

" 'Yes,' Bryson said.

"But they weren't ready. They screwed it up, and they deserved to be fired."

It was to be a ritual purging to purify Apple for the battles to come. At least that was Scott's plan. Just three weeks after Woz's accident, while the company was still in shock, Scott circulated to the department heads a list of eighty people to be canned and asked if any should be kept around. The shocked managers acted like managers everywhere when faced with such an edict: they protected their friends by marking them off the list or transferring them to other departments, and got rid of their enemies, including not only incompetents but goldbricks, malcontents and contenders for their jobs. As a result, some good people, many who'd recently been awarded raises or good performance reviews, or who were accidentally in the wrong place on the organization chart were hauled into Scott's office with all the rest, given a month's severance and summarily fired. The final tally was forty employees laid off. Scott, setting a pattern for future Apple CEOs, filled Whitney's slot by naming himself director of engineering.

The newly laid-off employees were also forced to endure another humiliation before they left. After the ugly mass layoffs in Silicon Valley of a few years before, many local firms had abandoned the old policy of mass firing and out the door the same day that had ruled at places like Fairchild during the previous two decades. The new procedure was to announce the layoff as much as a month in advance, bring in employee placement experts and handle the transition as delicately as possible. Mike Scott neither understood nor adopted this new policy. "I did it my way. The Charlie Sporck way. No pre-notice. We handed out the checks and escorted the employees out the door. I've always thought that was the most humane way, instead of paralyzing the company for weeks and leaving people worrying if they were on the list. I know a lot of people don't agree."

Forty employees. A small number, but it had a devastating impact. Mike Scott had expected the company to react to the layoffs by bearing down and becoming more disciplined, and for the market to applaud the move. Instead, both recoiled with horror. This wasn't the Apple each group thought it knew. Apple was *family*, it was caring, it was the antithesis of mean old capitalism. Apple didn't just throw people out on the street. That's why you came to work at Apple, that's why you invested in the company—because it was *special*. Besides, wasn't it the most successful new company in the world? Hadn't its employees done superhuman things to make it so? And this was their payoff?

Scott, of course, saw it differently. He had weeded out the incompetents— *after* many of them had been amply rewarded by the IPO. He had done it swiftly and precisely. "And I even tried to soften the blow by calling it a layoff," he says. "I didn't realize how loaded that word had become. If I had known that, I would have just called it what it was: forty individual firings."

From the beginning, Steve Jobs had said that he wanted to build Apple on the same principles as Hewlett-Packard's philosophy, the famous HP Way— but without being as staid and boring. But in more than forty years, through wars and recessions, good times and bad, Bill Hewlett and David Packard, retrograde and old-fashioned as they seemed to Steve Jobs, had never laid off a single employee. Now, after just five years in business Apple had already shattered its avowed philosophy.

Steve Jobs, powerless as a manager, but with veto power as the leading shareholder, had done nothing. A furious Chris Espinosa found him and hissed, "This is no way to run a company." A disconsolate Jobs (who, with Markkula, had approved the layoffs) gave only the Pontius Pilate reply, "How do you run a company?"

Apple couldn't, and wouldn't, be quite the same again. From this point on, employees knew that management not only carried a meat ax but was willing to use it. A decade later, when the first of the giant layoffs came, thousands of fired Apple people would again howl, but they couldn't honestly claim they'd been betrayed. After all, they'd been warned by Black Wednesday.

But perhaps the worst of it was that Black Wednesday had exactly the opposite effect anticipated. The market price of the stock didn't appreciably change. Customers weren't left more trusting of Apple's business acumen, but wondering why the company had so many incompetents that it had to resort to such extreme measures. And most devastating, at a time when the company itself needed to recoup from the failure of the III, hold on to its now wealthy best employees and get to work on new products to consolidate its control of the market, Apple collapsed into a dispirited, paranoid funk. Woz was hurt and perhaps gone forever, Jobs was sullen and depressed and the once bright company, the hope of a generation, now seemed in the hands of a heartless slavemaster.

"All of a sudden," said Fred Hoar, "Apple values were tanked and in its place we had ruthlessness." Another employee, Phil Roybal, told Mike Moritz, "A lot of people always assumed that sort of thing couldn't happen at Apple. Th[is] was the first sign of grim reality. People didn't know what the world was coming to. Their values had been turned upside down. Suddenly we were a company just like any other." Added Bruce Tognazzini, "It was the end of a lot of things. It was the end of innocence. It was the end of loyalty. It ushered in an era of incredible fear."

All of that from the layoff of just forty people; departures that could have easily been handled one at a time over a period of several months.

Mike Scott had blown it.

There had been about Scott in the year leading up to Black Wednesday a growing sense that he was beginning to crack under the pressure of running Apple. His behavior, always erratic, had grown even more unpredictable and even, contrary to his nature, cruel. He stomped on those around him, as even one of his admirers later admitted, "in the way a gorilla enjoys raw, unabated power." He left requisitions hanging, awaiting his signature, just to remind underlings who had the power. He cut off subordinates both in person and in memos. And at times he seemed completely out of control, marching around the company aisles, looking in over the tops of cubicles and demanding, "Are you working your ass off?"

By the beginning of 1981 Scott was acting paranoid, muttering dark threats about setting things straight, saying, "I'm not going to put up with things I don't like." Even his body began to succumb to the stress. Years of overwork, combined with his weight problem, had already given him diabetes. Now he developed a viral eye infection so severe that it threatened his sight. Eyeless in Cupertino, he bluffed his way through the day and then at night secretly had all of his communications read aloud to him by his secretary.

To his credit, Mike Scott knew as much as anyone that he was beginning to succumb to the stress. He had worn himself out over the previous two years building the company and taking it public. And looking ahead, he saw no break: the Mac, the impending attack by IBM, the problems with the Apple III, a second major stock offering in May 1981. His one relief, and great love, was opera, and he had long planned to attend the Wagner *Ring* cycle at the Seattle opera. But when he looked at his schedule, "I suddenly realized that I had every day booked for the next year. I was trapped."

Scott approached Markkula and asked him to help run half the company. It was both a strategic decision and a cry for help. Apple's engineering group was in disarray and in desperate need of close management attention. Scott had already moved his desk to the center of the III group building in Sunnyvale. The proposed plan was for Scott to take over engineering and straighten it out, while Markkula, as CEO, would run the rest of the company.

It was a solid plan, and Scott assumed that Markkula, both as a good businessman and as one of his closest friends, would readily accept.

But Markkula, with one foot already out the door in happy anticipation of a second retirement, refused. As Gary Martin recalled: "Markkula was always retired. He was always saying, 'I'm retired. I'm just doing this for fun. Scott's in charge.'"

"It was all on me now," recalled Scott. "I asked Mike for help and he turned me down. That's what hurt the most." They would never again be good friends.

By Black Wednesday, Scott was both a frightening and a sad figure. That afternoon he called a company meeting in hopes of getting the company past the layoffs and focused on a bright new beginning. But with the gloom over the company as dark as the leaden skies outside, the meeting, appropriately held in a company basement, didn't have the least chance of succeeding. The employees desultorily drank a little beer and sneaked disgusted or fearful looks at one another. Finally, Scott got up and gave a little speech designed to restore morale and regain the old Apple spirit. It was disjointed, uninspired and terribly inappropriate. Every figure in the room, even the Mike Scott fans, even the people who agreed that Apple needed a little downsizing, at that moment resented the man who had built their company.

In the grim weeks that followed, it was obvious that only another sacrifice could expiate Apple's sin. There were even anonymous memos passed around calling for concerted action. One such memo, signed by the Computer Professionals Union, read in part: "The thing they fear most is concerted employee action; the tactics they use are divide and conquer, and threats of economic reprisal. They can't get away with it if we unite! Apple was once a good place to work; management preaches to us about the 'Apple Spirit'; let's show them what a little bit of real spirit is like and ram it down their throats."

This was unionization—the bottommost circle of hell in the Silicon Valley theology. There would have to be blood for blood. And everyone knew whose blood it should be. But even then top management hesitated. It was only when Scott began to mutter darkly about Black Wednesday being only the first of several rounds of layoffs that he sealed his fate. He had to go. "I got scapegoated," says Scott. "Every v.p. in the company had contributed to the layoff list. Now it was all my fault."

Since the president is the highest-ranking line officer of a company, the only way he can be fired is by a vote of the board. In this case, that really meant a decision by the chairman, Mike Markkula, both because of his massive stockholdings and because of his daily involvement with the firm. And Markkula did it in the characteristic Markkula manner: he waited until Scott was out of town.

Scott, his eye problems now matched by a nasty and unresponsive case of sinusitis, planned to recover his health with a long weekend in Hawaii. While he was gone, Markkula convened a meeting of senior Apple managers—although some of Scott's strongest supporters were intentionally left out—to discuss what to do about the company's president, the man who had taken them, in one of the most extraordinary business trajectories, from a garage to international fame and $300 million in annual sales. In a single voice vote, the managers ruthlessly ended Scott's Apple career.

Scott returned to a message from Markkula asking to see him. Their conversation began with a little forced chitchat, and then Markkula cut it off by saying, "Scotty, the executive staff has voted to ask for your resignation." He added that he wanted that resignation, in writing, by morning.

Traditionally, a company's first era, its corporate adolescence, ends with the first public offering of stock. But Apple's adolescence, appropriately, was attenuated. It ended the next morning with Mike Scott's resignation. Officially, he was promoted to vice-chairman, Jobs to chairman, and Markkula assumed Scott's old role as president. In doing that, Apple set yet another pattern—the ritual purging of CEOs by management mutiny—that would haunt the company for years to come.

The transition could have been handled more smoothly, after a search for a new and experienced CEO. Certainly there was no shortage of talented veteran executives with Fortune 500 experience who would have killed to take the wheel of Apple Computer. Instead, the reins would now go to a marketing man who only dreamed of ski slopes and his second retirement and to an immature global celebrity whose managerial experience, because no one trusted him as a boss, was still essentially zero.

Scott's departure was cheered by many of the troops. To them, the ogre was gone at last. And the transition occurred so quietly, the subsequent rewriting of history so complete, that Mike Scott essentially fell down the memory hole. The public barely noticed his departure then, and barely remembers him now at all. It was all done so smoothly that Art Rock, who knew from experience what good and bad executive executions were like, complimented Apple on its handling of the whole affair. In fact, in the press, Scott's firing was treated as comparable to the regular and benign job rotation Intel performed every few years among Noyce, Moore and Grove.

But Mike Scott's resignation was anything but benign. Against almost impossible odds he had performed a business miracle. Under his command, Apple had grown into a $300 million company growing at nearly 200 percent per year, with a market capitalization of more than $1 billion and an astonishing productivity rate of $200,000 in revenues per employee. At the end of his tenure, Apple employed hundreds of people based not only in Cupertino but at manufacturing plants in San Jose, Dallas, Los Angeles and Cork, Ireland, sold its products through 3,000 dealers and dominated the profitable corner of the fastest-growing new industry in the world.

Mike Scott had taken a manufacturing operation that consisted of a handful of people in a garage backed by a few dozen immigrants doing illegal piecework and converted it into a state-of-the-art assembly plant supported by one of the best computerized corporate information systems of any company its size. And finally, of course, Scott had managed the company through the most difficult of all challenges to a young business, an IPO, and pulled off one of the greatest stock sales ever recorded. Don Valentine, no mean judge of executive talent, would call it one of the best executive performances he'd ever seen.

Against all that, from twenty years' perspective, Scott's occasional cruelties, his arbitrariness and his increasingly erratic behavior seem minor. If the Apple Corps wanted to see what tough looked like, they merely had to drive down the street to National Semiconductor or Commodore. And if they wanted a close-up look at executive capriciousness, they merely had to spend a day visiting Atari . . . or the Apple that was about to be created by the newly unleashed Steve Jobs.

But the deed was now done. Scott was out. Meanwhile, Apple, as it scapegoated Scott, turned Black Wednesday into a far bleaker event than it had ever been. Now, inculcated into its culture would be the vow to never allow such a terrible layoff to ever happen again. And for the next decade, the company would keep that promise—as it grew bloated, unmanageable and top-heavy with employees and managers who had no reason for being there. And Apple would hold to its vow right up to the moment, too late, when it would spectacularly shatter it.

From the perspective of two decades, Regis McKenna would conclude that Scott's firing, as welcome as it seemed at the time, was in fact a horrible mistake. "Intel was just a few years older than Apple, yet by this point it had already developed a body of distinct management processes. Decisions were no longer made by someone's flip idea of the moment.

"Mike Scott was a tough and demanding boss. But he was also intent on putting some sort of systematic decision-making process into place at Apple. And Apple got rid of him. Looking back, he was Apple's last chance to institute some kind of order. After that, the culture became so overwhelming that even the toughest manager would come in to shake things up—and instead find himself two months later lounging on a beanbag chair."

There has always been something suspicious about the official story of Mike Scott's firing. Why would a public company, so soon after its IPO, toss out the CEO who had done such an extraordinary job getting it there? For being stressed out and mercurial? That's why leaves of absences were invented. HP and Intel already had established programs for exhausted executives. Three months on a beach and a diet and Mike Scott would have been renewed and back at the helm of Apple Computer.

For Black Wednesday? Against the recession of a few years before, in which electronics companies had laid off thousands, or the aerospace crash of 1970, in which Lockheed had fired 10 percent of the Valley's adult males, the Apple layoff wasn't even a blip. Sure it was traumatic to the utopians at Apple, but they would have gotten over it, just as they had rationalized their other ethical lapses.

In fact, there was one other, decisive, reason why Mike Scott was driven out: he was homosexual. It was hardly a secret, and Scott, though discreet, had never tried to hide the fact—certainly not from his old friend Mike Markkula. But what had been a matter of indifference when Apple was a small private company suddenly loomed large in many minds when Apple was a publicly traded giant. It didn't fit with the profile of a Fortune 500 CEO; and especially not the tough cowboy world of Silicon Valley.

But Mike Scott today is forgiving: "Great people sometimes make thoughtless mistakes. Great companies do too. I like to think this was one of those times."

At first, Mike Scott seemed to take his impeachment well. As a consolation prize he was asked to manage the expansion of his beloved management information system. He lasted a month, long enough to make one presentation to his former lieutenants. Then he cracked. He wrote a bitter and sad memo, saying (in an ironic echo of the Computer Professionals Union memo) that he was through forever with the "hypocrisy, yes-men, foolhardy plans, a 'cover your ass' attitude and empire builders." In defense of his own autocratic style, he added: "A company's quality of life is not and cannot be set by a committee."

Then he was gone. Now rich enough to never work again, Scott began his retirement by flying off to the Seattle Wagner Festival.

But life without Apple wasn't as easy as he had imagined. "It was like a death in the family," he says. He returned to become a lonely hermit, hiding in his suburban house for days at a time, listening to Wagner, sleeping during the day, sitting alone with his cats and watching TV or playing the organ. When he went out, it was often to the city dump to fire off model rockets. He rarely had visitors, but when he did, they usually found him heartbroken, living over and over his fall from grace. One visitor reported that Scott's spirits only lifted once: when he found he could still remember the model numbers for all the parts in the Apple II.

He had loved Apple Computer—"my baby" he called it—and assumed that his love would be requited. Unfortunately, as he should have known from the beginning, he didn't have enough stock for that.

As the weeks turned into months and Scott showed no signs of recovering, and did not respond to entreaties for him to get reinvolved in the company, many of his old compatriots began to worry. Even Steve Jobs was haunted by Scott's plight. Four years later Jobs would admit, "I was always afraid that I'd get a call to say that Scotty had committed suicide."

But Mike Scott never did away with himself. In time, he pulled himself together and went on with his life. He started a rocket company, visited Africa numerous times, rented a square rigger and took many of his old Apple associates on a weeklong cruise. He turned his house into a garden spot atop its Los Altos Hills ridge. And be became a leading expert on color gems and minerals, eventually assembling one of the world's great private collections.

Mike Scott was happy again. And, on special occasions, he still sent white roses to secretaries and receptionists at Apple.

6.4 BLOODSHED

With the Apple III back on the drawing board, the Apple II somehow managed not just to hold its own but to leap even higher in sales. As a result, Apple believed it could breathe easy. The months after an IPO are almost always a letdown, but at Apple they had been the very nadir. It was as if after flying so high the company had to find a balance by hitting rock bottom. But now, with sales still holding strong, it seemed as if Apple had truly dodged a bullet.

TI and Radio Shack, though their PC sales were strong, had never caught the market's imagination. TI's TRS-80 had been nicknamed the "Trash 80" because it was so crudely built. And Radio Shack, because it sold its computers through its own stores, was limited to selling only to the kind of people who shopped at Radio Shack.

Commodore was also selling a lot of computers—it would be the first, in 1983, to reach a billion dollars in sales, Apple's claims to the contrary—but its Pet computer and its successor, the VIC, ultimately reflected the personality of Jack Tramiel. That is, they were made to reach the widest possible audience at the lowest possible production cost. Thus, they were simultaneously brilliant in conception and cheesy in execution, innovative in technology and out of date in design. It was the kind of computer bought by people who didn't know anything about computers, worried that they needed one, didn't want to spend much money and were willing to admit all that to anyone. Commodore played on this by running a brilliant ad showing a child returning from school, apparently having flunked out for not having a computer.

If Commodore's market was at the low end of the business, it wasn't alone. Everybody was there. And as expected, as the smaller players faded away, the big boys arrived. Most of them came in through the back door, via video games, their goal to profit off cheap game players, then ratchet their customers up through more and more functions and add-ons. It was a sound strategy: after all, then as today, the microprocessors in game players were as powerful as those in low-end personal computers.

Thus, by the early 1980s Commodore was running into Mattel and Atari, both of them offering proprietary game machines and inching their way upward. Mattel never quite got there, but Atari made it, and in a big way, with a line of attractive, graphics/game-oriented computers that were as impressive as anything on the market.

This was a different Atari than Jobs had left four years before. Nolan Bushnell was now long gone, having made himself rich selling Atari to Warner Communications. Now he was building a new start-up, the Chuck E. Cheese robotic Pizza Time Theaters. The new Atari was a much different company. Indeed it was different from any other company in Silicon Valley. Whereas the old Atari was like an endless dorm party at San Jose State, the new Atari was like a lawn party in the Hamptons. The president, Ray Kassar, a former rug merchant who kept a copy of a recent *National Geographic* issue about Silicon Valley in his desk so he could understand what was going on, ate in an executive dining room (a Valley first) and lived in a penthouse in San Francisco with beautiful furnishings. He was chauffeured each day to Sunnyvale in a Rolls-Royce. When Warner chairman Steve Ross visited Atari from his skyscraper in New York City, Ross wouldn't even stay in the Valley, the local inns being too déclassé, but would helicopter down from San Francisco to the company parking lot, where he would be met by a limousine to drive him the three hundred feet to the door.

Meanwhile, slaving in the kitchen at this big Atari party were the programmers themselves. Under Bushnell, they'd been the revelers. Now they were considered a necessary, if annoying, evil. Kassar even called them glorified towel designers and emotional prima donnas. But in high tech, only a fool pisses on his programmers. By the early 1980s, Atari was bleeding its best game designers to a new company, Activision, which not only gave them credit for their work but treated them as superstars.

The impact from all that lost talent wouldn't be felt for a couple more years, especially after Atari had the foresight to acquire the home rights to the phenomenal Pac-Man game from the Japanese company Taito Ltd. In the meantime, the company had money to burn. And what better place to burn it than on computers? They were, after all, the logical future of game machines.

Atari had a resident guru to tell it where computers were going. Alan Kay was a brilliant young man who played classical piano as he formulated the most compelling vision of the personal computer era: the Dynabook, the book-sized work slate with enough computer power to configure itself to any application the user desired. So compelling was the Dynabook's siren call that any computer executive who heard it, from Ray Kassar to John Sculley, was instantly seduced and driven onto the nearest set of rocks.

Kay had first made his name at Xerox's research laboratory, where he had invented an intuitive, graphics-oriented user interface for computers called Smalltalk. Smalltalk pointed the way to future products such as Macintosh and, in theory, the Dynabook. As a result, Atari snapped Kay up. Though it never did anything with his ideas, Atari seemed content to just have Kay around.

For now, Atari's strategy was to build a personal computer that would run the usual crude word-processing programs, along with VisiCalc and, most importantly, Atari games. The resulting model 2600, did just that, but little more. It sold a lot of computers, largely because of the game function, but it could have done much more had not the company been completely distracted by the home video game boom. Three years hence, when the video game business collapsed into a five-year bust, more powerful computers might have saved Atari. But it was too late.

In early 1981, as Apple surveyed the competitive landscape, the Atari debacle was still years away. But even against the formidable Atari of the era, Apple could only be pleased. Each of the major players, Radio Shack, TI, Atari and Commodore, had deep structural flaws, either in products, management, distribution or orientation. Moreover, the high-end machines, the ones that should be its competitors, were either junk (TI) or hard to get (Tandy), while the good machines (Commodore and Atari) were targeted at the low end of the market, far from the Apple II and III.

Thus, despite all the problems facing the III, Apple still held the high, profitable ground all to itself. In his memoirs of his years as Jack Tramiel's assistant, Michael S. Tomczyk would write of the envy he felt for Apple's position: "Apple had chosen not to enter the low-priced computer market, wisely deciding to stay upscale and make more money per unit. Apple sold fewer physical units than Commodore, but for several years had higher dollar sales." Apple, he added, never had to slug it out against bargain basement competitors at places like the Consumer Electronics Show, but could do classy things like show at Wescon and rent Disneyland.

As the 1980s began, more and more companies dove into the personal computer market. But all went either the budget route (Sinclair) or toward video game players (Coleco). The only radically new products were the first "portable" computers—which were still heavy enough to induce sciatica in owners trying to lug them through airports. The first of these, from Osborne Computer, created a small sensation, but it was the next competitor in that market, Compaq, that would last.

With all these competitors squabbling over the low-end market, Apple could float above the fray, with the computers everybody wanted but only the serious could afford. The company seemed invulnerable, with a clear pathway ahead to dominate quality personal computing for at least the rest of the decade.

But it was all an illusion. In losing two years to the debacle of the III, Apple had missed its one and only opportunity to close the door on the upper half of the personal computer market. Had the III been the killer machine it was meant to be—had Woz been more involved, or Jobs not dumped on his old colleagues, or had the IPO been held off for another six months—Apple might have had time to both drive a defensible beachhead into the corporate market and set the standard for quality consumer machines.

But it had failed on both fronts. And now, the biggest, scariest computer company of them all was preparing to hit Apple head-on.

IBM.

6.5 CRUSH

In the story of Apple, it is hard to keep from tripping over all the ironies. One of the biggest had to do with Regis McKenna and his legendary work with his other big client. In late 1979, while Apple was buried in the latter stages of developing the III and plotting the Disneyland party, Intel Corp. was in trouble.

Intel, the Valley's newest giant, had known hard times before. Its heavy investment in new product research sometimes left its coffers empty when the chip industry went through one of its quadrennial busts. But these were comparatively minor stumbles; in the mongrel world of semiconductors, Intel was the one true thoroughbred. It had the finest management, the top engineers and, always, the best technology. Intel had been the first to make a mark in

MOS circuit electronics, in memory chips and, most important, in microprocessors. Everybody else paddled in its wake.

Now Intel was in trouble in the one area no one would have imagined possible: technology. Just eighteen months before, in June 1978, Intel had introduced its fourth-generation microprocessor. Called the 8086 it was created in just two years and was destined to be the ancestor of every Intel microprocessor to this day. Its announcement advertisement, "The Birth of a New Era," was not an exaggeration. Intel soon ran over the market.

But one competitor was not willing to admit defeat. Motorola had long given Intel a run for its money and it had its own new microprocessor waiting in the wings. The 68000, like the 8086 a 16-bit device, was introduced in mid-1979. It was a beautiful piece of work, with an elegant architecture that displayed the extra year Motorola had to study the weaknesses of the Intel chip and improve upon it.

Even the executives at Intel had to admit that Moto now had the better chip. In fact, as Intel's director of microprocessor marketing at the time, William Davidow, later admitted, it was becoming obvious that not only was Motorola now the first-place company in the market, but that Zilog's Z80 was second and Intel was third and fading. The market recognized this too, and by autumn 1979 Intel was experiencing for the first time in nearly a decade the regular loss of new design wins to a competitor.

By December, the situation had become critical. A meeting was hastily called by Andy Grove on December 4. Davidow was there, as were several other Intel managers. So was Regis McKenna.

What came out of that meeting and those that followed was the realization that not only was Intel at risk of becoming an also-ran with the 8086 but there was no new product in the pipeline to come to the rescue. Instead, the company would have to use its wits and work with the inferior product it had.

The product of this desperation was Operation Crush, the seminal marketing program of modern electronics. What the Crush team did was invent a brand-new product entirely from what it already had. The 8086 alone might not be as good a chip as the 68000, but if you thought of it as only the most important component of a total package that included design tools, peripheral chips such as math co-processors, in-circuit emulators, documentation, software and Intel's service and support operations . . . in other words, if you looked beyond mere performance stats to what it actually took to *use* one of these microprocessors, the 8086 compared mighty well indeed with the Motorola and Zilog offerings.

It took just three intense days for the Crush team to come up with this new marketing strategy. Yet it changed electronics forever. Henceforth, all successful tech products would have to be sold not as stand-alone products, but as complete *systems*. And once the systems approach was in place, it was a mere step to giving this system an identity—"branding" in marketing parlance—of its own, even if it was merely a component of an even larger system. Thus, Crush begat "Intel Inside," one of the most successful and influential product branding campaigns in any industry in modern times.

Having identified what it believed to be a truly competitive product, the Crush team then had to sell it, first to Andy Grove and then to the sales force. Andy, willing to try anything at this point, signed off just two days later. Convincing field sales was a little more complicated. The team set about preparing, under Regis's leadership, a collection of sales materials emphasizing Intel's new, integrated systems approach. There were new advertisements and new data sheets. Even customers were invited to write glowing articles about their experiences with Intel chips. Within months, Davidow's team put on more than fifty technical seminars throughout the world.

Goals were set too (though with Grove's signature on the mission statement, it was more of a command): one new customer design win per salesperson per month in 1980—2,000 new users.

Operation Crush was brilliant. It was also largely a sleight of hand, asking customers to ignore what they saw with their own eyes and accept instead a new point of view. But it worked, brilliantly, partly because the biggest convert to this new worldview was a panicked Motorola. As Davidow would later say: "Had Motorola chosen to remain aloof from our challenge, I think Intel would have been in deep trouble." Instead, Motorola, caught off guard, tried to hurriedly construct its own systems-oriented sales program. In doing so, Motorola validated Intel's concept; in doing a half-assed job of it, Moto gave the game away to its biggest competitor. In the end, Intel landed 2,500 design wins for the year, made the 8086 the de facto 16-bit standard for microprocessors and gained a near-monopoly on the microprocessor business it has never relinquished.

But that wasn't the end of the story. One of those Intel salespeople, Earl Whetstone, under the gun one month to land a sales win and having no obvious prospects, took a crazy chance and called Big Blue. It was an impossibly long shot because IBM made all of its own chips, including microprocessors. But Whetstone was desperate . . . and, as it turned out, the luckiest man alive.

IBM was ready. It had played with personal computing now longer than anybody, with some projects dating back to the 1960s. But every one had failed, mostly because Big Blue couldn't get out of its own way. It couldn't help but approach this new market as if it was merely an extension of its existing mainframe and minicomputer businesses. Every new idea, every design, every marketing strategy had to be vetted over and over by corporate bureaucrats to make sure that it met the IBM style, that it didn't overlap other products or that it didn't interfere with the sales force's primary focus of selling computer mainframes.

It was no wonder that IBM couldn't make a start in the chaotic, improvisational world of personal computing. What was a wonder, though, was that Big Blue actually understood what it was doing wrong. It had watched Apple closely almost from the beginning, and had come to appreciate that if it was ever going to compete with such an agile, quick-witted company, it would have to cultivate some of those characteristics in itself.

Since that was never going to happen in a company that still wore white shirts, IBM took the unprecedented step of creating a separate, independent division in Boca Raton, Florida—as far from Armonk, New York, as you could get without going to California. This division was not only given the charter to produce the first true IBM personal computer, Project Chess, but, most remarkably, given the unprecedented freedom to purchase components *anywhere*.

And it was at this moment, to this division, that Earl Whetstone made his telephone call. Instead of getting the door slammed in his face, Whetstone was all but dragged across the threshold like a traveling salesman by a lonely housewife. Why yessss, purred IBM, we would be interested in a demonstration of your hardware.

If Whetstone's experiences started out like a stag film, they ended up a Hitchcock movie. The Manhattan Project had less secrecy than Project Chess. When Whetstone and his people were called in to give technical support, they often found themselves in a room on one side of a black curtain, while IBM's technical people hid on the other side with a prototype of their new machine. Said Whetstone, ". . . they'd tell us what was happening and we'd have to try to solve the problem literally in the dark. If we were lucky, they'd let us reach a hand through the curtain and grope around a bit to try to figure out what the problem was."

It may have been weird, but if that's what the world's largest manufacturing company wanted, Intel was more than happy to oblige. In the end, IBM chose to buy not the cutting edge 8086, but the safer Intel 8088. The 8088 was an entry-level, budget chip created by Intel to help current 8-bit users make the transition to 16-bit. It had many of the features of the 8086, but instead of being a true 16-bit processor, the 8088 had a 16-bit central processor unit, but only an 8-bit bus. This compromise in performance would make IBM PC users gnash their teeth for years.

But that didn't matter to Intel. Big Blue was now committed to the Intel architecture. It would mean, Whetstone would exult, that in a business where 10,000 units was major victory, Intel had landed a contract for tens of *millions* of units annually.

With the IBM contract, Intel won the microprocessor wars. And the victory was due to Operation Crush. Intel had been lucky, but it had made that luck. Regis McKenna, the PR man who dreamed of being a great marketer, had now earned his wings. He was deservedly now high tech's most famous marketing guru. But he had achieved his greatest victory at the cost of his most famous client. He had hooked up Apple's newest and biggest competitor with the best chip company on earth. He would now spend the next decade trying to help Apple survive the onslaughts from the partnership he'd just helped to create.

6.6 CHESS GAMES

For Apple, an Intel and IBM partnership was scary enough. But Boca Raton still needed one more piece to the puzzle of building its new PC: software, especially programming languages and an operating system.

Boca knew where to go for the former: a little software company in Redmond, Washington, called Microsoft. Big Blue had contacted Microsoft once before about buying a product, but nothing had come of it. Now, the unleashed Personal Computer group was ready to play ball.

In comparison with Apple, Microsoft had not come very far from its hobbyist roots. Bill Gates and Paul Allen had made enough money in both hardware design (notably an interface card for the Apple II to run software for Intel 8080-based and Zilog Z80-based computers) and software (BASIC language) to employ a dozen people. The pair made a strong, if combustible, team. Gates was a driven and fearless competitor willing to take on any assignment, no matter how unprepared his company was for the job, in order to build sales and beat the competition. But he was also an abrasive, unpleasant individual, whose personality (intellectual arrogance, spitefulness and contempt for others), mannerisms (a strange autistic-like rocking) and personal hygiene (he appeared to never brush his teeth) often got in the way of his talent as a businessman.

Allen, by comparison, was bearish, professorial and kindhearted. More than once he calmed the business waters roiled by Gates's behavior. Thanks to Allen, you wanted to do business with Microsoft; thanks to Gates, you had to.

In mid-1980 Microsoft, though far from the leading player in personal computer software, set out to claim that leadership by making its various software products universally compatible with all personal computers, no matter the microprocessor. It was a massive undertaking for such a tiny company. But strategically it was a brilliant stroke, because it would give Microsoft economies of budget from having to develop only a single program for all platforms and economies of scale by enabling it to market to all PC users. And that, in turn, would position Microsoft software as the first industry-wide standard—a novel idea in such an anarchic business.

It wasn't easy to pull off. The Microsoft team had to first perform the equivalent of translating all of its programs into Latin, then retranslating that into the different Romance languages and dialects. This was accomplished by rewriting all the company's programs (more than a quarter million lines of code) in a "neural" language that could run on a DEC mainframe. Once in there, it could then be translated out in microprocessor-specific versions.

The task would consume the company for many months. In the meantime, Microsoft still had to make money. So Allen set to work improving the company's BASIC for the 8086, and Gates took a contract from Atari to convert that same language to Atari machines.

They were buried in these projects when, in July, a call came from a representative of IBM Corp. Would Gates be willing to meet with some representatives from Big Blue to talk about a project?

A year before, another rep from Big Blue had contacted Microsoft about possibly buying a product. The deal had fallen through, but not before raising expectations throughout the little company, then dashing them. But Gates was always game. Sure, he said. "How about next week?"

"We'll be on a plane in two hours," said the IBMer, adding that he was bringing some researchers from Boca Raton.

As it happened, Gates had an appointment the next day with Atari's chairman, Ray Kassar. It came down to a deal in the hand with a billion-dollar company or one still in the air with a thirty-billion-dollar company. Gates blew Kassar off.

Bill knew enough about himself to appreciate that it might not be in Microsoft's best interests to face IBM alone. So he turned to his other partner, Steve Ballmer, an old friend from Harvard who'd done a spell at Procter & Gamble before joining Microsoft a year before. Ballmer was the practical side to Gates's vision, the orthodox, friendly businessman to Allen's absentminded professor and Gates's smart-ass kid. Gates asked Ballmer to sit in on the meeting.

The IBM team arrived to find Ballmer and a cleaned-up Gates in suit and tie. In the hours before the meeting, the normally cool Gates had been un-usually excited. Though he had no real evidence, Bill sensed something big was in the works. He hoped that IBM, like Atari before it, had come to buy Microsoft BASIC.

The meeting proved to be more tantalizing than decisive. Before it began, the IBMers asked Gates and Ballmer to sign a nondisclosure agreement. No problem, they said, without giving it a second thought. Then, as Gates would recall, the IBM reps asked "a lot of crazy questions" about what Microsoft was up to, and, curiously, what Gates thought were the crucial features in a competitive home computer. That was it. Gates and Ballmer told Allen what had happened; everybody shrugged and went back to work.

Then, a month later, another call from Big Blue. "What you said was real interesting," the IBMer told Gates. How about another meeting? This time we'd like to send five people, including one of our lawyers. Cool, Gates and Ballmer said and, as before, set out to counter the IBM team with equivalent firepower. The IBM team was met by Gates, Ballmer, two Microsoft employ-ees and the company's own hired attorney. The IBM crew, which included such hitters as the chief of corporate public relations, were impressed: these were people they could deal with.

Another, even more restrictive release to be signed by one and all. Before IBM began, the PR chief gave a nervous little prologue, "This is the most unusual thing the corporation has ever done." And then the Big Blue team set about describing Project Chess. Bill Gates saw for the first time the technol-ogy that would make him a billionaire.

He was not particularly impressed. He began to grill the IBMers about the computer, especially its processor. It appeared to be an 8-bit device. That wouldn't do Microsoft, or IBM, any good. So Gates argued vehemently for a 16-bit chip. Big Blue, to his amazement, listened. By the end of the meeting, Microsoft had a consulting agreement with IBM, with the goal of producing a report advising IBM on not only software but hardware.

Before they left, the IBM team had one more question for Gates. They had heard about a terrific new operating system software for personal com-puters called CP/M. Did Microsoft own that too? Would they be willing to sell it?

Well, *no*, Gates told them. CP/M belonged to a little software company called Digital Research Inc., located down in a California beach town near Monterey. But, Gates added quickly, he knew the founder, Gary Kildall, quite well and would be happy to get him on the phone.

At this point, history becomes shrouded in a fog of claims and counter-claims. Gates says that when he reached Kildall he impressed upon his counterpart that "important customers" were coming down to visit Digital Research and that Kildall should "treat them right."

But that obviously was not the message that Kildall received. When the IBM team arrived in Pacific Grove at Digital Research headquarters, Kildall wasn't even there. Instead the team was met by Dorothy McEwen, who was in charge of DRI's hardware accounts. The IBMers frowned at not meeting the founder, but decided to proceed anyway.

Where was Kildall? Gates, who liked to believe that all those he defeated suffered from the moral handicap of insufficient seriousness, would later say dismissively, "Gary went flying," as if Kildall was out joyriding in his plane instead of meeting with IBM. For the rest of his life (he would die in 1994 in a drunken fall in a saloon), Kildall would protest that he was flying to a business appointment and that Gates had not fully explained the importance of the meeting.

Meanwhile, back at DRI it only got worse. The IBM team pulled out the same disclosure release they'd used with Microsoft. McEwen balked, fearing she was putting her company in a vulnerable position. She called in the company lawyer, Jerry Davis. He read the release and agreed: Digital Research would not sign. The meeting ended before it began; and the IBM team flew back to Redmond to see if Gates would help them with an operating system. Digital Research was doomed.

Gates and Microsoft now had a shot at the brass ring of personal computing software. And unlike Kildall, Gates showed up at the next meeting ready to give Big Blue anything it wanted.

Unfortunately, what IBM wanted Microsoft didn't have: an operating system. But Microsoft had a neighbor in Seattle, Seattle Computer Products, that had an operating system for the Intel 8086 called SCP-DOS, designed by Tim Paterson, a friend of Paul Allen. So Gates met the disgruntled IBM team, expressed shock at their ill treatment by Kildall, then soothed their concern by noting that IBM didn't really need the 8-bit CP/M anyway. And as long as the business was up for grabs, why not look elsewhere? Say, at Microsoft?

In making such an offer, Gates for the first time displayed a part of his personality that would come to dominate the Microsoft legend. As software pioneer Gordon Eubanks, then at DRI, would say later to Robert Cringely: "The unstated rule around Digital Research was that Microsoft did languages, while we did operating systems. It was never stated emphatically, but I always thought that Gary assumed he had an agreement with Bill Gates about this separation and that as long as we didn't compete with Microsoft, they wouldn't compete with us." Digital Research was the first in a long line of companies to learn to its regret that there are no unstated rules with Bill Gates.

The IBMers were agreeable to Microsoft's proposal, but the final decision would have to be made at the top. And that meant the upcoming report by the team to IBM senior management had top priority.

It was finished in September, and Gates, Ballmer and another Microsoft employee (again, not Allen) caught the red-eye to Boca Raton. The daylong meeting was an almost continuous interrogation by the Chess team. IBM had set a one-year target for the entire project, an almost unprecedented pace for Big Blue, and the team was making sure it wouldn't be derailed by one of its suppliers. Intel had run the same gauntlet.

Gates would later say that by noon he figured he had the contract. He also admitted that the critical factor may have been that IBM's chairman, John Opel, recognized his name, having served with Bill's mother, Mary Gates, on the board of the United Way.

Whatever the deciding factor, Gates's noontime hunch was correct. Microsoft got the contract, signing the papers in November.

By then Gates & Company were already underway, establishing—to meet IBM's paranoid security requirements—a skunk works within the hot, windowless heart of the ancient National Bank building in downtown Seattle. The two companies even set up a pioneering private e-mail system to swap information . . . a lesson for the future not lost on Bill Gates.

Despite being told that "we were three months behind schedule before we started," Gates promised Big Blue that he would have both the new operating system and the translated BASIC ready by March 1981, just five months off. He was prepared to put the screws on both himself and his employees to get there.

Gates himself, along with Allen, took on the BASIC conversion. But the operating system was a different story. For this Microsoft had to depend upon the outsider Paterson and his Seattle Computer Products. That created considerable vulnerability: since Microsoft's languages were going to have to run with that operating system, if Seattle Computer Products screwed up or was incomplete on the specs, Microsoft would be stuck.

So Gates simply hired Paterson—and the operating system, SCP-DOS (for Seattle Computer Products—Digital Operating System), became Microsoft's: MS-DOS.

6.7 Apprentice Antichrist

In the midst of all of those proto-e-mails flying back and forth from Seattle to Boca Raton, Gates began to broach with his IBM handlers the possibility that the new computer might feature an open architecture. That is, unlike the thirty years of proprietary, closed IBM computers before it, the Chess personal computer would allow independent hardware and software developers to design products for it.

After all, Gates argued, the new computer was already a precedent setter at Big Blue, as it featured off-the-shelf chips from the likes of Intel, as well as MS-DOS, Fylstra's VisiCalc and the EasyWriter word-processing software designed by, of all people, Cap'n Crunch himself, John Draper. The message was: If IBM's greatest fear about open systems was letting every riffraff garage inventor offer add-on products and programs, well then, was there anybody out there scruffier and more menacing than the ex-felon they were already working with?

But the clincher to Gates's argument was, in yet another painful irony, the example of Apple Computer itself. After all, hadn't Apple outrun its competitors precisely because the Apple II was open? Hadn't that very openness given Apple the equivalent of a worldwide design army that no competitor—not even IBM—could match with an in-house R&D lab? And hadn't this army of designers also given Apple a global sales and marketing team as well?

Gates's Apple argument proved the clincher because the head of the Chess project, Don Estridge, happened to be an enthusiastic Apple II owner. IBM went for the open architecture, and the history of personal computing was changed forever.

Thus, thanks to chance, serendipity, guile and ambition, IBM found itself completely out of character with a new personal computer made out of off-the-shelf parts and featuring an open architecture. In other words, the perfect machine for the moment. But, what was even more important—and dangerous—Big Blue had also linked itself to Andy Grove and Bill Gates, perhaps the two best businessmen of the age. Had it made any other choice, had only one of these figures entered the narrative at this point, the story of personal computing likely would have been completely different.

But just like Apple two years before, IBM's Boca Raton division was blessed with uncommon luck during this period. It made all the best choices—at least for the near term. In the long term, those same choices would carry a sting. It didn't know it yet, but for all its size and strength, IBM was the least of the three partners. By both opening its architecture for

Microsoft and tying itself to the Intel 8086 chip family, Big Blue had already unwittingly preordained its own fate.

But if IBM was in a vulnerable position, at least it was at the table. Apple's position was much worse. It wasn't even in the room. The honeymoon, in which it had owned a billion-dollar market by itself, was over. Now it was facing the world's biggest computer company, the world's largest microprocessor company and the world's most competitive software company. A single misstep would be fatal. And coming off the Woz crash, the Scott purge and the Apple III failure, a sudden return of Apple's surefootedness was pretty damn unlikely.

And yet the unlikely, even the impossible, was exactly what Apple did for the next two years. It was a business miracle not seen by the electronics industry before or since. Good companies produce one brilliant, industry-transforming product; great companies invent two. Apple became immortal because it not only invented that second product but did so at the moment it needed most to do so.

Tim Bajarin, director of Creative Strategies Inc. and the most veteran of Apple watchers (he began in 1977) and consultants, also had the unique opportunity to be invited to consult the Estridge group at IBM Boca Raton at the time of the PC introduction.

"I was struck by two things at Boca," he later recalled. "The first was how limited the group's expectations were. The business plan only called for IBM to sell only 240,000 units in the entire lifetime of the PC. They ended up doing that in a matter of a few months.

"The second was the utter disregard with which they held Apple. They saw Apple as little more than a toy—an opinion that didn't change until 1988. One IBM executive there had a daughter who was married to an early employee and so had a chance to buy Apple stock. He passed on the opportunity. That's how little they thought of their new competitor."

IBM introduced the Chess computer on August 12, 1981. Big Blue may have changed its rules for product creation but it hadn't forgotten its old arrogance. The new computer was called, simply, the IBM Personal Computer, as if it was the only one of its kind in the world, having sprung from the void. Henceforth it would be called the PC, creating endless confusion between the product name and the general term for all the industry's products.

Against the monolith of IBM marketing, even Bill Gates couldn't win every argument. Thus, MS-DOS became PC-MOS—though it did remain the PC's primary operating system, consigning Kildall's CP/M to the ash heap of history.

But the zenith of IBM's arrogance regarding the PC was its advertising campaign. It featured an actor playing Charlie Chaplin as the Little Tramp. It was designed to be charming and cute and help potential customers overcome their fear of computers: after all, if the childlike man in the derby and baggy pants could run a PC, why couldn't you? Thus, the biggest capitalist company on the planet had co-opted the image of the world's most popular Marxist, whose most famous movie image (from *Modern Times*) was of being crushed between the giant gears of industry, in order to sell expensive boxes to the proletariat.

Of course, it worked. By December, IBM had shipped 13,000 PCs, and for years thereafter, the demand curve ramped up almost hyperbolically. By the end of 1993, more than a half million machines had been sold.

Needless to say, Apple had known for months, even years, that IBM was coming—according to Mike Scott, it was even predicted in the company's original business plan. And in the weeks before the August 12 introduction, the greatest fear among Big Blue's future competitors was that the PC would contain some extraordinary new technology that would make every other computer on the market look like a paperweight.

But that fear aside—and many in personal computing were skeptical that IBM could even be that innovative—it was generally assumed that Chess would be, in typical IBM style, a solid but uninteresting box priced too high that would sell to the legions of IBM lovers. That, the industry decided, would be good news: the very presence of IBM would validate the personal computer market for the first time. Big Blue would make personal computing something more than the perceived land of geeks, hippies and nerds, turning it into a legitimate and growing sector of the computer industry. Armonk might take a big slice of that pie, but it would make the pie so big that everyone would win.

This was cockiness crossed with whistling through the graveyard. It had its purest expression in the famous Apple ad that appeared in *The Wall Street Journal* the day of the PC introduction:

Welcome IBM
seriously.

Welcome to the most exciting and important marketplace since
the computer revolution began 35 years ago . . . We look forward
to responsible competition in the massive effort to distribute this
American technology to the world.

It was a classic bit of cheekiness, almost unique in U.S. business history—
actually welcoming your biggest, scariest competitor, a firm forty times your
size, into your market.

But the confusion and dismay that day at Apple didn't match the self-
confidence of the ad. Jobs and company were relieved that the IBM PC didn't
contain any great technological breakthroughs. In fact, it contained no breakthroughs at all. Its sheer prosaicness was disconcerting: off-the-shelf parts, a
competitive price. What the hell was going on here? This wasn't the Big Blue
everybody knew. Should they be relieved or terrified that this new computer
was so uninteresting?

They got their answer as the world's attention suddenly shifted away from
Apple, which had grown accustomed to the limelight, and toward Big Blue.
Apple, its management having grown up either in the world of semiconductors or hacking, had never really experienced the true force of IBM. This was
a company that had more cash on hand than Apple had sales. It had an
advertising budget bigger than the rest of the computer industry, from mainframes to micros, combined. Whereas most personal computers had dozens of
salespeople, IBM had thousands.

But it was more than that. Since the late 1950s IBM had owned three-
quarters of the world's computer business. It was the sun and all the other
companies mere planets. Most companies, large and small, banks or broker-
ages, car makers or fast-food suppliers, didn't just have computer departments,
the had *IBM* computer departments. IBM established industry standards
around its products and architectures by the sheer mass of its presence in the
marketplace.

This had been the case for twenty years and several generations of computer center directors. You used IBM equipment because your company's first
computer purchase had been from IBM—and so had every purchase since.
To even considering buying, in their day, a Burroughs mainframe or a DEC
mini or an Apple II was heresy. And everyone knew what happened to here-
tics. As the phrase went in corporate offices throughout the world: "No one
ever got fired for buying from IBM."

This was the behemoth that Apple and the other personal computer companies now faced. Within months it became apparent that Big Blue was almost effortlessly penetrating the corporate market, slipping across the barrier that Apple and the others had banged up against for years. Worse, IBM was also, for the first time ever, successfully reaching out to the small business and consumer markets as well. After all, if you were buying your first computer, wouldn't you feel better ordering from the World's Greatest Computer Company? The one that put the mainframe in your company's computer center and the mini down the hall and the Selectric on your desk?

Like a mob elbowing its way backward after suddenly looking down the barrel of a cannon, the low-end computer and video game companies began scurrying down the price-performance chart to get out of IBM's way. Crushed together at the bottom of the market, Commodore, Texas Instruments, Atari and Coleco were reduced to scrabbling for a dwindling market share. An explosion was inevitable.

And who better to light the match than Jack Tramiel? "I guess we started the price wars when we introduced the VIC for under $300 when everyone else was selling computers for $600," wrote Mike Tomczyk. By August 1982, just one year after the IBM announcement, the low-end computer companies, particularly Commodore and TI, were in a battle to the death. That month TI announced a $50 rebate on its budget machine, the 99/4, bringing its retail price down to just $200. Commodore responded in kind. It even stopped publishing suggested retail prices to let them float. "Capitalism in its purest form," according to Tomczyk. Pure suicide too.

By December 1982 Atari had slashed the price of its budget machine, the 400, to under $200. Meanwhile, the model 800 was cut to $500. That was a 20 percent price drop, yet it was still not enough to keep it in the game. Meanwhile, Atari had much bigger problems to worry about. At the beginning of the year, the company had celebrated passing the $1 billion sales mark, and there was every reason to expect 1982's sales to double that. Waiting in the wings for the prime Christmas retail season was a new video game of E.T., the all-time movie moneymaker still showing in theaters around the country. Sure, the game was derivative, but how could it fail?

But fail it did. Before Atari could blame the game's design, suddenly the entire video game industry began to stall. After a thrilling, decade-long run, a period in which Atari became one of the most successful companies of all time, it seemed that a generation of children had finally grown tired of playing video games. Nobody was buying the product that Christmas, nor would they again until a new generation arrived at the beginning of the 1990s. Atari, which had undersupported its fine computers in lieu of much more profitable video games, now found itself burying millions of unsold game cartridges in the Arizona desert and looking to those computers to bail out the company . . . only to find that a price war was squeezing all the margins out of that business as well.

So Atari disintegrated. As early as September, the company secretly began planning layoffs. In December, Ray Kassar and executive vice president David Groth sold some of their stockholdings not long after hyping the company's earnings predictions (the SEC would get Kassar for this later). Then, in January, the bomb was dropped. The response was so ugly that Atari stock was temporarily suspended on the New York Stock Exchange.

Then, on a Friday afternoon in February, without any warning or support, Atari summarily laid off 1,700 people. It would prove to be one of the biggest quarterly losses in modern business history—and the biggest layoff Silicon Valley had ever seen, and would not see again until . . . Apple Computer. By June, a total of 3,000 employees were gone and Atari was on its way to losing $500 million for the year. By December 1993, the once great company of Nolan Bushnell, Steve Jobs's old employer, was little more than an empty shell.

It was one of the biggest business meltdowns of all time. It was also a harbinger of things to come. In the rest of the low-end personal computer business, the price war was only growing hotter. In January 1983, even as Atari was dying, Commodore cut the retail price of its top-end Commodore 64 to $400 and started selling it in Kmarts. TI responded a month later by cutting the 99/4 to $150. There were almost no profits left. *Home Furnishings Daily* ran a cartoon of Tramiel dressed as a real Commodore, using his cutlass to slash through price tags.

In February, TI announced that there was a problem with the power packs in their computers—they could set the machine on fire—and froze production for a month to fix both new and old machines. Commodore used that opportunity to announce that it would give a $100 rebate on any computer turned in to purchase a Commodore 64—which led to a run on little $50 Timex computers in department stores around the country.

Terrified, TI preannounced its own price cut, saying it would make the announcement in June, then panicked again and announced it in May.

It was almost over. At the June 1983 Consumer Electronics Show, Commodore finally killed the industry. It cut the price of the Commodore 64, its flagship, to $200—a machine that nine months before had retailed for three times that much. On top of that, Commodore cut the price of its software library in half.

Within a few weeks, TI announced a $100 million loss, the president of its computer operations resigned and TI left the personal computer business forever. Commodore, with its superior manufacturing economies and ruthless style, had won the war for the low end of the computer market. But what had it won? Sales, certainly. As the last survivor, Commodore finished 1983 as the first company with personal computer sales of more than $1 billion. That represented 3 million computers and 600,000 related books. The company held a press conference to celebrate.

Then, one week later, after a falling-out with the chairman, Jack Tramiel resigned. He had been too harsh, his health was at risk, the company now needed to move past the warrior stage and be run by sober, professional managers—there were many explanations. But the bottom line was that the toughest son of a bitch the market had ever seen was gone, having taken most of the rest of the industry down with him. And without Jack Tramiel, Commodore was soon gone as well.

6.8 GRUDGE MATCH

Thus ended the second generation of personal computer companies. The first generation, the hobbyists, had been annihilated by the arrival of the professionals. Now the pros had been taken out by an industry consolidation driven by the arrival of the first of the behemoths. It was the archetypical story of a high-tech industry.

All that was left now was Apple, IBM and debris. The victor of the first era was now about to meet the second in a grudge match. Jobs had already predicted this: "When you have nothing to lose you can shoot for the moon. So we shot for the moon, and we knew that if we were successful it would come down to Apple and IBM. And that's exactly what's going to happen."

The personal computer industry was now eight years along from the first Homebrew meeting. Perhaps fifty computer companies had now come and gone, 10 million personal computers had been sold, more than $10 billion had been made, *Time* magazine had named the personal computer its "Man of the Year" for 1983 (it would have been Jobs, but the IBM PC introduction ruined it) and the little hobby machine made out of wood and hand-soldered boards was now the heart of a new zeitgeist sweeping the classrooms, offices and dens of the industrial world.

Technology industries rarely learn from success, but always learn from failure. The runaway success of personal computing in the mid-1980s was entirely due to the lessons learned from all the individual and corporate disasters that had preceded it. From the disasters, the industry had learned a number of important lessons:

• *The right processor is everything.* Those companies that had built their computers around the wrong microprocessor doomed themselves from the start. Apple alone had hooked up with the wrong chip and survived, thanks to a superior design. Henceforth, any company that attempted to build around anything but an Intel or Motorola microprocessor had no chance.

• *It takes brawn, brains and balls.* The best personal computer and software companies had a combination of a market visionary, an experienced businessman and a technical guru. Those firms that were run only by technologists (IMSAI, Cromemco and most of the first generation of companies) could not compete once the market matured and customers demanded quality, service, competitive pricing and documentation.

By comparison, the companies that were run by good businessmen typically fulfilled those tasks, but eventually zigged when they should have zagged in adopting a new technology. By the mid-1980s, as demand reached millions of units, the game increasingly went to the company that could best get a new model out of prototype and into full production, then down the best distribution channels. Tandy had solid machines, but sold them only through Radio Shacks. Atari killed TI by being so much more efficient a manufacturer that it could price its biggest competitor out of business.

Still, even these advantages weren't enough. For a personal computer company to survive over the long run it also needed a vision of where the industry was going and the influence to turn the company in that direction. Atari lacked that vision, so did Mattel and TI. Commodore had it fitfully, but Tramiel lost the support of his board.

By comparison, Apple had managed to cover all the bases with its team of Markkula, Wozniak, Scott and Jobs. But now half that team was gone, and the company would have to move fast to replace them. IBM had the combination too, but its makeup was even more unusual: while its in-house manufacturing and business management were unequaled, its visionary and software guru, Bill Gates, worked for another company, as did its hardware expert, Andrew Grove. Thus, whereas Apple had to reconstitute its damaged team, IBM had the best team in the land—but one with divided loyalties.

• *The less control the more command.* Apple had taught this lesson to the rest of the computer industry. By not only allowing but actively supporting third-party software developers to design applications for its machines, Apple effectively multiplied its corporate manpower and collective intelligence without having to spend a dime. Personal computers were only as good as their use, and no single company—not even IBM—could dream up all the possible uses for personal computing. But several thousand computer buffs, coming from all walks of life, could. Dan Fylstra and Cap'n Crunch had been as important to Apple as any of its employees. And if VisiCalc made millions in the process for somebody else, so what? It also sold thousands of Apple II's . . . and that meant not only revenues for Apple, but ever-precious market share.

Hewlett-Packard, for all of its technical prowess, missed that lesson. But thanks to Gates, who had learned from Apple, IBM got it. Now it would be Gates's turn to teach Apple a final lesson about the power of open systems and standardization.

• *It ain't just hardware and software.* For sheer performance for the price, the Commodore VIC was probably the best personal computer in the world in its day. Had the market judged the new machines solely on their performance, Commodore would have won. But it didn't, because Commodore never captured the imaginations of more than a fraction of the total market— mostly third-generation hobbyists and techie eccentrics without much money. It wasn't cool to own a VIC, even less so to own an Atari 2600. You weren't serious; you weren't part of a movement. Not like you were when you bought an Apple II and proudly put the rainbow apple decal in the rear window of your car.

Regis McKenna understood this and geared Apple's marketing campaign toward precisely that image. Members of the Apple Corps were rebels, they were hip and sardonic and sly, they were contemptuous of suits. And most of all, they were out to make the world a better, freer place through personal computing. Apple was a style, an attitude, a *movement.* And all those traits were personified in a single figure, Steve Jobs.

Jobs understood this too and, at least publicly, he played the role brilliantly. And why not? The world now saw him as he always saw himself: special, golden, selected for some higher calling. Regis's ads and Steve Jobs's personality; it was a perfect combination.

IBM, by comparison, perfectly filled a niche antithetical to Apple. It represented security, predictability and strength in a market until now characterized by insecurity, mercurial figures and fly-by-night storefront companies. It even took the industry's nomenclature as its own branding—as if nothing in this industry had been real until Big Blue arrived. IBM induced the kind of fear that could best be assuaged by submitting to it. Jump on board before you are run over. When you joined IBM you too became part of the juggernaut. And if Apple positioned itself against IBM, IBM merely ignored Apple as superfluous.

It was to be the establishment versus the counterculture. The social wars of the 1960s were now about to play themselves out in the computer wars of the 1980s.

The only trouble was that it looked as if the war would be over almost before it began. IBM had a hot new computer notching up ever more market share by the month. It had already crushed a half dozen of the most successful companies in the personal computer business, and it had both invaded and occupied an enormous market of its own in personal office computers. Apple, meanwhile, had fired its president and replaced him with a guy who only wanted to retire, made a postadolescent its chairman, lost its technical genius to a plane crash, introduced a botched product that nobody wanted and was living off another aging computer design.

Yet, within a year, Apple would recapture the world's imagination, and then hold it with almost religious fervor for a dozen more years thereafter in one of the great corporate Second Acts. And it would accomplish this with a product it did everything to kill.

6.9 THE GREAT MYTH

The personal computer industry has many stories, anecdotes and tales. But it has only one legend:

> As part of its agreement to let Xerox Corp. invest in it before the IPO, Apple demanded and got the right to visit Xerox's famous Palo Alto Research Center, where, rumor had it, Xerox was developing some of the most interesting new computers around.
>
> Steve Jobs, relentless in his quest for innovative new ideas, took advantage of the deal as soon as possible and in late 1979 or early 1980 (the stories vary) took a tour of Xerox PARC with some other Apple technical types, including Bill Atkinson. What he saw there changed the course of computing.
>
> Like Paul on the road to Damascus, Jobs saw his own brilliant burst of light—in this case, a demonstration of the Xerox Star, Alto and several other prototype personal computer models. Each model featured one or more of the most creative new ideas about personal com-

puting. For example, the Star not only had a detached keyboard but also used a small external device—a "mouse," the descendant of the original devised by Douglas Engelbart more than a decade before—to control the motion of the cursor on the screen. The Star and Alto also had a unique and intuitive way of presenting information in the form of "windows" that could be arrayed across the screen and accessed by pointing the mouse. Integrated with these windows was a collection of "icons," representational images for common commands. Finally, though sadly Jobs didn't notice, the computers were also able to talk to each other through a new networking scheme.

Jobs and his group were so impressed by what they saw that they began to press their tour guide, PARC director Larry Tesler, with one question after another. Tesler would later tell Jobs biographer Jeffrey Young, "What impressed me was that their questions were better than any I had heard in the seven years I had been at Xerox . . . Their questions showed that they understood the implications and the subtleties . . ." Tesler was so impressed that he quit PARC and joined Apple.

Jobs returned to Apple literally with Stars in his eyes. He had seen the future and it computed. Better yet, he knew Xerox would never get the product to market. So he made it his crusade to do so, even if he had to steal Xerox's ideas.

The first Apple project to incorporate all of these new ideas was the Lisa, a project directed by John Couch, but really driven by Jobs's enthusiasm. When completed, the Lisa was a remarkable computer, one that proved the appeal of the new Apple interface, but at $10,000 was just too expensive. What the world really needed, as only Jobs fully understood, was a computer that incorporated all of these new features but carried a price affordable to Everyman. A Volkswagen of personal computing.

The result was a second, complementary development project called Macintosh. It was originally run by Apple veteran Jef Raskin, but when he proved unable to bring the project to completion, Jobs stepped in and, using all of his skills at threatening, cajoling and seducing, drove the Mac team to a heroic effort.

The finished Macintosh was introduced in 1984 and quickly became the most famous personal computer ever, turning Apple's fortunes around and proving forever that Steve Jobs was both a great visionary and, putting old doubts finally to rest, a true technologist.

This legend, promulgated for years by Apple's PR department (one of the most successful PR campaigns ever in high tech, not just because it succeeded, but because no one knew any better), has been picked up and repeated in almost every history ever written about Steve Jobs or Apple. In the uplifting versions, say Steven Levy's *Insanely Great*, Jobs is presented as the one person who could see what Xerox PARC had and then make it real for the masses. The cynical versions, such as Cringely's *Accidental Empires*, suggest that Jobs essentially stole the ideas from Xerox, ramrodded them through Apple, drove the Lisa team until he saw that it wasn't going to be a winner and then hijacked the Mac project, elbowing Raskin out of the way.

But whatever the approach, all of them have missed one fundamental fact about the legend: *it isn't true*. It endures because we want it to be true. And we want it to be true because it fits the form of a good legend: it is simple, and it involves a superhuman individual, a latter-day Prometheus, heroically stealing a magical secret from the gods and delivering it to mankind.

Real life is much more random and tawdry. This need for myth explains, but it certainly doesn't forgive, Cringely's written reply when told the real story by Jef Raskin: "As for all the business of what project started when, whether the Lisa started before or after Steve visited PARC, whether the Mac had already begun or not, well I don't think that matters very much. My attempt was to EXPLAIN (I say that at the front of my book), not to be a historian."

So much for facts.

The evidence has always been there. Had any journalist, author or historian actually *used* a Xerox Star or Alto, he or she would have quickly discovered that the look and feel of their primitive interfaces, while certainly pointing the way to the Mac Operating System, were far from it. That would have been obvious the first time they grabbed the three-button mouse and tried to drag an unmovable window across the screen.

There is also the evidence of Xerox's belated lawsuit against Apple. Xerox had read the same books and convinced itself that the Mac violated PARC's intellectual property protections. So, the case should have been a slam dunk. Instead, Xerox lost.

Meanwhile, in the intervening years, no one ever publicly asked exactly when, in those years after the Apple II, Jobs suddenly became a technology savant. A brilliant young man, certainly. Probably a genius at product packaging, positioning and branding. But a guy capable of walking into one of the leading research institutions in the world, seeing a collection of radically new technologies whose implications weren't even fully understood by their inventors and then, like the young Jesus before the rabbis, extemporaneously peppering the director of that institution with questions so penetrating and knowing that even the experts were taken aback? Please.

And finally, the most obvious clue that something wasn't right with the story had always been available in the Apple archives: a chronology that showed that both the Macintosh and Lisa projects were proposed in the spring of 1979 and were approved and begun in September—*at least three months before Job's visit to PARC.*

Jobs, it seems, had only managed to discover the obvious. He had been set up.

But he would have his revenge in the history books.

6.10 MACINTOSH

If Jobs didn't "discover" the Macintosh, who did?

Here again, neither Apple nor the people who rewrote its press releases are much help. Apple did hint that it knew a deeper truth in later years, after Jobs had not only left the company but become a competitor. Then the official story was rewritten to give credit to Bill Atkinson and Andy Hertzfeld, two Mac development team members. This Soviet encyclopedia-style revisionism was not particularly original, especially in a town where a company's value is often judged by the quality of its in-house creative talent. Intel had set the pattern in the 1970s by giving Ted Hoff complete credit for inventing the microprocessor, and all but erasing the equally important role of Federico Faggin, who had inconveniently gone off to Zilog. Jobs too might have gone down the memory hole, had he not been already too big to stuff through.

It was not until mid-1996, in an obscure journal called *The Analytical Engine*, the journal of the Computer History Association of California, that another version of the Macintosh story appeared. It was the memoirs of Jef Raskin, the Apple pioneer who had led the Mac team until purged by Jobs. Raskin was no more humble than Jobs, but he was a real technologist. And once one filtered out Raskin's own self-promotion, the story that remained had the ring of truth. It was messy, ugly, tossed about by greed, ambition and mutual loathing, and best of all, it explained all those obvious contradictions in the official legend.

Most companies, when flush with a successful IPO, come down with a bad case of grandiosity and embark on the killer product about which it has always dreamed but could never before afford. This is the fantasy product that incorporates every feature of every fantasy and is designed to conquer the market once and forever.

Many companies wisely abandon this pipe dream early on. Those that continue to pursue it usually end up compromising it so much that what finally is introduced to the world is either a mess (the Intel iAPX 432, the HP-01 digital watch) or just another incremental and disappointing improvement over what came before (the Apple Newton). A few tragic companies (Triad, Dynabook) pursue their vision all the way into oblivion.

Apple's story is almost unique because its pipe-dream product not only came true but really did all that was claimed for it. It revolutionized computing. And, though this seemed the least likely of possibilities at the beginning, it also saved the company.

In 1979, Apple was rich with Apple II profits and looking at even greater riches from the impending IPO. And so great was the company's imagination (and hubris) that within a matter of months it set out to create not one, but *three* new killer machines.

One of these, the Apple III, was to be a safe, incremental product. But it ended up so compromised and crippled that it suffered through a few miserable years and was mercifully destroyed.

The second, the Lisa, was to be Apple's golden machine. A premium computer that would be so awe-inspiring that it would not only give Apple the high ground in personal computing but also begin carving up the underside of the minicomputer market. John Couch was given control of that project.

The third product was the most fantastic and unlikely of them all. Aimed directly at the newly emerging low-end game/computer market, it was to be so user-friendly as to be irresistible; more a home appliance than a data processing machine. This was to position Apple as the industry's leading consumer mass marketer.

A brainchild of Markkula, this third product, which he designated Annie, was to cost $500 and be primarily used for games. In other words, a player much like those being offered by Atari, Coleco, Commodore and TI. In March 1979, he called Raskin in, asked him to study the Annie project and consider running the team.

But Raskin wasn't interested in something as pedestrian as a game machine. "So I counterproposed a general-purpose, low-cost computer based on my own ideas—and dreams—for an interface."

Raskin had been dreaming for a long time. As far back as 1965, when he was still a grad student at Penn State, Raskin found himself frustrated with the needless complexities of working with computers. His thesis two years later even made the then radical proposal of developing computer displays based on graphics, rather than characters. The thesis itself was written in a multiple-font format that presaged desktop publishing twenty years later. At one point, frustrated by the problem of getting all this graphic data into a computer, Raskin tried to build a device to do the job—a failed early attempt at a mouse.

Tired of Pennsylvania and Penn State, Raskin turned in his thesis, jumped into a car with his wife, Karen, and lit out for the territories. He ended up at the University of California at San Diego, where Karen took a job at the Institute of Geophysics and Planetary Physics and he got a job at the University Computer Center.

Within a couple of years, frustrated with both the bureaucracy of the main computer center and its allegiance to big mainframes, Raskin had opened his own minicomputer-based computer center elsewhere on campus. Raskin would later say that a visitor to the center in 1972 would have seen the purcursor to the Mac in the "low tables with small rectangular monitors and detached keyboards," all linked to a pair of Data General Nova minis.

Summers, Raskin would take one of the Novas home and use it as his own personal computer, even once carrying it into a restaurant to compute the bill and tip. "These experiences with a 'portable' computer system gave me a foretaste of what it would be like to own a personal computer," wrote Raskin. "Like the crocodile in Peter Pan, I would never forget that taste, and craved it for years."

Wozniak, of course, was coming to personal computers at the same time. But as much respect as the two computer geniuses had for the other, it is important to note that they arrived at this new world from different directions. Woz came from below; his goal was to figure out a way to own a minicomputer, even if he had to build it. Raskin came from above. He had begun with mainframes, then moved to minicomputers the moment he got a chance— and by the mid-1970s he was trying to get away from the constraints of minis as well. This difference in perspective would be made manifest in their inventions.

Summer wasn't only a time for Raskin to play with his computer at home. It was also a time to travel, especially north, to Stanford University. In the summer of 1973, Raskin visited SAIL, the Stanford Artificial Intelligence Laboratory—and while there was given a tour of Xerox PARC a mile down the road. He was mightily impressed. The next summer, when he was invited back to SAIL as a visiting scholar, "I found myself gravitating more and more toward the beanbag chairs at PARC."

It was there, more than five years before Jobs's fateful visit, that Raskin learned for the first time about the work of people like Doug Englebart. He saw the beginning stages of the finished work Apple would ultimately draw upon. And if that wasn't enough, back at SAIL, Raskin learned to send proto-e-mails on the ARPAnet, the precursor of the Internet. He was standing at a crossroads in the history of technology, watching the two great movements of the rest of the century as they formed and converged.

Raskin never forgot what he had seen at Xerox PARC. And when, a couple of years later, he visited the garage to interview the two Steves for *Dr. Dobb's* he knew he was seeing the future. He joined Apple as its thirty-first employee on the day it incorporated in early 1977.

So, by 1979, when Markkula approached him about building the $500 game machine, Raskin knew exactly what he wanted to do instead. He duly mulled over Markkula's proposal, then came back with his radical counterproposal.

The choice of Markkula, then chairman and not considered a hard-core technologist, as champion might seem odd. But Raskin knew what he was doing. After two years of working with Apple, first as a contractor, then as an employee, Raskin had come to some unsettling conclusions about Woz and Jobs, whom he characterized as "a strange mix of the radical and the conservative. They wanted to create personal computers, but expected them to work much like the hard-to-use minicomputers from DEC, HP and Data General. Dragging the two Steves into the interface future was like preaching in an unknown tongue . . ."

But Markkula was a marketer, a consumer guy and a tinkerer. He might just understand. Besides, as chairman he could also trump the two Steves. So Raskin made his pitch: How about instead of a game player I build you an easy-to-use consumer computer for the same price? I've got some ideas for a new interface . . .

Markkula was enthusiastic. He agreed to present the plan with his backing to the executive board. In the meantime, Raskin wrote down his ideas in a paper presciently entitled "Computers by the Millions" and distributed it around the company. The paper, which proved to be the philosophical foundation of the Mac (and, by extension, the future of personal computing) dealt not only with the design and manufacture of a new generation of computers but also with the potential effect of those computers on society itself. Apple management found it so insightful that it refused to allow Raskin to disseminate it outside the company until 1982.

But he could pass it around inside Apple—and in doing so, Raskin unknowingly set the stage for his own demise at Apple three years hence. That's because one of the readers was Steve Jobs. Raskin: "Jobs, unaccountably, did not at all agree with my views of the future, nor with my distributing them internally at Apple, even though I was doing so at Markkula's request. By proposing new strategic ideas and products independently of Jobs, I began to get on his 'wrong' side."

While waiting for company approval, Raskin joined the Lisa team. The Lisa had actually been proposed after, but approved before, the Macintosh. In his short tenure there, Raskin managed his usual combination of making important contributions while simultaneously stirring up trouble. His biggest contribution was to recruit one of his former UCSD students named Bill Atkinson, who ultimately would prove to be the central and enduring figure in the Mac story.

But the trouble came when Raskin managed to convince the first Lisa team leader, an ex-HPer named Ken Rothmuller, to adopt the distinctive bit-mapped display for the Lisa, thus making the computer more graphics-friendly and establishing the stunning print-on-paper look of the next generation of Apple (and all other) machines. Raskin had tried the same argument with Woz and Jobs three years before and had been brushed off. Now Raskin had a victory—a short-lived one, at least for Rothmuller, who was soon fired by Jobs for being too difficult to work with.

In September, just before the Annie project was finally approved, Raskin talked the Lisa team—now managed by another, more politically astute former HPer, John Couch—to join him on a tour of PARC. There, the Lisa team, watching the demonstration of the Alto, the Star, the mouse and the Crosstalk network, had its own epiphany. For Raskin, who had seen it all before and who had long ago determined exactly where the Xerox technology could be improved or revised, the trip held no revelations. He even told Tesler as he left, "We don't need this, but I'm glad they saw it."

But in fact, the Lisa team decided this was exactly what they needed and embarked on a program to build the most powerful personal computer yet. Raskin, with his Everyman philosophy, was soon left on the sidelines. But it didn't matter, because literally within days Markkula finally gave Raskin the Annie project, and let him take it in the new direction.

Jobs was not happy. He told anyone who asked (and many who didn't) that the new project was the "dumbest idea" he'd ever heard of. Raskin remembered, "He would often recite a list of imagined advantages that the Lisa project had over the Mac and put obstacles in the way of my obtaining staff or supplies." Jobs would, in fact, despise the Mac project almost until the day he took it over, when he would declare it so great that it "would make a dent in the universe."

Still, Apple's third, and least, new-product program was finally underway. But with the company's most powerful figure its sworn enemy, few gave it any hope.

With its three new products in the works, Apple was heading toward a defining moment. The only problem was that the company didn't know that it was.

With the Apple I and II, the strategy had been straightforward. The personal computer industry was then still largely monolithic, so the task was narrow: build the best machine possible and then market the hell out of it. But by 1982 the PC business had sufficiently matured to begin segmenting into distinct submarkets with identifiable customers and product specifications. Apple, by embarking upon its three-pronged new-product strategy, seemed to be targeting these different markets. But that was mostly an illusion. The real market divisions emerging were between consumer (including home computers and games), professional (including professional offices and small businesses) and corporate products.

Conceivably, at this early point in the game, a company could produce two types of products—consumer and business—and have sufficient product breadth to still cover the industry. That was what IBM was rumored to be doing.

Apple too seemed to be moving in that direction. The company had a consumer machine, the II. It also had, largely by default, an extensive business software library and corporate customer base. Now Apple was developing two new computers, the III and the Lisa, both aimed essentially at the business market, where the Lisa would hit the corporate market, while the III would be appealing to professionals and small businesses. Finally, there was Raskin's Macintosh, the volkscomputer, which would target the personal and home markets.

It all might have worked if Apple had maintained this segmentation, worked on intercompatibility among the different product lines and moved the four product lines forward in a combined front. But that required corporate discipline: four different product groups operating in coordination toward a common purpose, giving up common markets for the common good. Needless to say, that wasn't Apple Computer.

In fact, even at the most elemental level, the company seemed organically incapable of sticking to a single business model. It didn't help that, with only a couple exceptions, there wasn't a single business veteran in the whole management team. And those who were, such as Floyd Kvamme, came out of chips, not corporate or consumer marketing. Regis McKenna once sat in a senior staff meeting at Apple, and was stunned to realize that he had more big-business experience than anyone in the room. And he wasn't even an employee. How, he asked himself, do these people even *presume* to know what the corporate world wants, much less sell to it? The veterans consistently tried to tell the youngsters that Apple had to decide upon an overall business strategy; that if it wanted to sell to the corporate world it had to bring in experienced marketers who understood it; that, whether it decided upon the consumer or corporate market, it *had* to link up with a giant company that knew how to market, sell and distribute there.

As early as 1983, Regis put together a white paper for Apple that was prescient in its understanding of the distinct personalities of the two markets. It clearly showed that the corporate market would increasingly move toward networking, large central computers, electronic communications, sophisticated information management software and a demand for strong service and support. Conversely, consumer computers would be open systems linked to hundreds of third-party developers, sold retail and via mail order and be highly price-sensitive.

"I kept saying, 'There's a split here. You need to make a decision. Whether you want to be a Sony or an IBM. You can't be both,'" recalls Regis. "I gave that presentation for years. I wrote papers; I drew diagrams. 'You have to decide what company you want to be. This path [corporate] goes toward systems, and systems are different things than stand-alone computers. They need heavy support, infrastructure. You can't just sell *things*. If you want to sell things, then go the other way. Be like Sony. There's certainly nothing wrong with Sony. *But you've got to decide!'"

But Apple didn't want to decide. It wanted both markets, products and systems, consumer and corporate, Sony and IBM. It thought that it could cut through these divisions by sheer technological brilliance. And Apple believed this because most of the people making those marketing decisions had very little sense of how great the gulf was between these two markets—*no* single computer would ever again be able to vault it.

So, with no division in its strategy, Apple embarked on its second generation with fragile firewalls between its products. The result was that whenever one of the products hit a snag in one market, it simply crashed sideways through the wall into the Apple product already there. The Lisa, which was to be a corporate product, was also marketed as a consumer product, and later as an enterprise server. The Mac, the people's computer, became a premium office product. Apple's new computers were soon being marketed as all things to all people.

And the poor Apple II got hit from every direction.

6.11 Dreams Team

The first thing Raskin did when given approval for the new project was to change its name. He hated the code word "Annie" because "I felt that the trend in the company to give new products feminine names was sexist—and if you had spoken to the namers you would agree." Instead, keeping with the Apple motif, he chose "Macintosh" because it was his favorite variety of the fruit. He intentionally misspelled it, instead of McIntosh, in hopes of avoiding legal problems with the well-established stereo component company. (He failed: Apple eventually had to reach a settlement not only with McIntosh Ltd. but also with a British raincoat company.)

The second thing Raskin did was to embark on a journal, *The Book of Macintosh*, which contained not only all the documents from the project but also regular updates by team members and even Raskin's own musings. It would eventually reach 400 pages.

Years later, Steven Levy would get a chance to peruse *The Book*. In an entry from January 1980, he found a note from Raskin that read: "The purpose of this design is to create a low-cost portable computer so useful that its owner misses it when it is not around . . ." A month later, Raskin wrote: "The personal computer will come of age when it goes the way of the calculator or the telephone, or probably both . . . it will become a nearly indispensable companion." It was probably the earliest statement of a mature philosophy for the personal computer.

Raskin's words are uncannily like those Steve Jobs would use a few years later in his public flights of hyperbole about the finished Macintosh. By then, of course, he'd read *The Book of Macintosh*. For now, though, he hated the very idea of the Mac. The Lisa was his baby, and with it he intended to rule the computer world forever. Toward that end, he made of himself a general nuisance around the Lisa group, dropping surprise visits on poor programmers and designers to alternately tell them their work was shit or pure gold in his patented motivational technique. He made life a living hell for John Couch, second-guessing the latter's every decision despite having only a limited understanding of what was going on.

Meanwhile, the Mac team continued to grow. It now included programmers Bud Tribble, a former medical student, and Brian Howard, an old friend of Raskin; hardware designer Burrell Smith, a brilliant programmer plucked out of Apple's repair department, and UC computer department dropout Andy Hertzfeld. Raskin also hired an ex-PARC tester named Bruce Horn; Steve Clark, one of Raskin's old UCSD students (and brother of Woz's future bride); technical writer Donald Reed; and, in marketing, Joanna Hoffman, an MIT anthropology student. Chosen as much for their musical skills (Raskin was an ardent musician) as their programming were two old SAIL colleagues, Gareth Loy and Bill Schottstaedt; and, most unlikely, Bana Witt, a poet and former music student of Raskin who would go on to marry yet another team member, Bruce Tognazzini. As a licensed minister, Raskin performed the ceremony.

There was one other, secret, member of the Mac team, who would later prove to be vital: Bill Atkinson. Despite being a member of the Lisa team, Atkinson had fallen in love with the idea of the Macintosh. So when Jobs forbade him to join Raskin's group, he secretly worked under the table.

Even by personal computer industry standards, it was a remarkably eclectic group. Insular too. Before long Jobs had become so obnoxious and interfering that Mike Scott, then still CEO, moved the Mac group to an office building behind a Texaco station, next to an old Catholic social hall, and across the road from the rest of Apple. Jobs would later claim the move was his idea to protect the brilliant team from industrial spies and interference by Apple itself.

During this period, Jobs's greatest contribution to Apple was to make himself into a shared problem for the two product teams, thus forcing natural opponents to make common cause against a shared enemy. According to Raskin: "By the end of 1979 it was clear to many people that unless Jobs had a better understanding of what was being attempted on both the Lisa and the Mac, he would continue to inadvertently sabotage the former and be antagonistic to the latter."

So they set him up.

A year earlier, Raskin had tried to talk both Woz and Jobs into visiting Xerox PARC, but neither was interested. Jobs told Raskin that it wasn't possible for a giant company like Xerox to create anything innovative and exciting. For his part, Woz saw his own turndown at the hands of HP as proof of just such corporate myopia. Raskin also knew that anything he recommended to Jobs would be dismissed out of hand. So the trick was to find two messengers Jobs trusted who could encourage him to go. It fell to Atkinson, the double agent, and Raskin and Couch's boss, Tom Whitney.

Jobs bought it—and the rest, one might say, was rewritten history. When one knows the truth, the events of that visit to PARC become a lot clearer: The fact that Raskin was pointedly not invited. The brilliant questions with which Jobs's group peppered Tesler (of course, they'd been working on the same stuff for seven months). And why, on the way out of PARC, when Jobs famously turned to Atkinson and asked, "How long will it take to duplicate all of this?" Atkinson calmly replied, "About six months." Only a fool or a man who thought he was already halfway done would give such an answer.

6.12 WINDOWS ON THE PAST

The 1970s ended with Apple on top of the world. A year later, the company was gloriously wealthy, thanks to the IPO, and also in serious trouble, thanks to the Apple III, the Woz crash and the Scott coup d'état.

Atkinson's prediction had proven to be wildly optimistic. The Lisa team's love affair with the Alto and Smalltalk hadn't faded after the team left PARC that first day, but had grown into an obsession. Almost from the hour they returned to Apple, Jobs sat down with one of his top people, Trip Hawkins (who would later have his five minutes of fame as founder of Electronic Arts), and they defined all the new parameters of the Lisa, including windows, mouse and an icon-driven interface. Soon, Larry Tesler quit PARC and joined the Lisa team. Later, inevitably, Alan Kay joined Apple as well, as an in-house guru and founding Apple Fellow.

But all this resident talent didn't accelerate the Lisa's development, but rather slowed it down. Not just duplicating, but actually improving upon, all those features of the Alto (which was, after all, a multimillion-dollar proto-type) proved not only more time-consuming but more expensive than anyone had imagined. And an ambitious operating system wasn't the only problem. The initial design also called for the ill-advised use of the company's own proprietary Twiggy 5¼-inch disk drives, whose software-controlled automatic ejection and micro-stepping head technology were too advanced for the era and led to endless quality problems. Working out the bugs in these new drives further ate up precious time.

One group within the Lisa team that never fully bought into the PARC philosophy were the old HPers, including Couch. But if this group didn't have the Xerox obsession, it had the next-worse thing: the Hewlett-Packard disease. This was HP's worst era; Hewlett and Packard had pulled away from the daily activities of the firm, and their company, now in the hands of John Young, was growing richer but more bloated, somehow producing overpriced, overengineered and overdue products in between seemingly endless meet-ings. The HPers, who should have brought a measure of discipline to the Lisa project, instead contributed their own portfolio of failings.

Finally, there was the ever-present Jobs. Jobs's perpetual yo-yoing of em-ployees between seduction and humiliation often produced great results, but it was hugely stressful and horrifically time-consuming. Months of work would be lost in a single morning when Steve would suddenly and capriciously change his mind. Trapped in their secure team area, never knowing what to expect from their mercurial and arbitrary captor, many Lisa team members, like other Apple employees before them, exhibited something like the Stockholm Effect in relation to Jobs. They feared him, despised him, protected him and worshipped him all at the same time. The real lesson of the PARC visit, team members quickly learned, was to first present the new idea to Jobs, have him reject it, then wait a week for him to convince himself that it had been his idea all along and announce it as the team's new strategy. It usually worked, but it wasted time and emotional energy to regularly enact such a charade.

Jobs knew the effect he had on subordinates and played it to the hilt. Raskin had his own ax to grind with Jobs, but his description is accurate to anyone who ever worked with Steve Jobs: "By this time Jobs had begun to have people who were 'in' and those who were 'out'; if you were 'in,' everything you did was golden; if you were 'out,' everything you did was rotten. . . . Most people worked around him or sucked up to him or were in awe of him. In fact, he was no genius; he resembled a planet shining by reflecting the light of others. Yet he thought of himself as the Sun King. He could not abide someone who was unimpressed by Steve Jobs."

Cringely has provided one of the most memorable descriptions of Jobs in action:

> Coming up to an Apple employee, he'd say, "I think Jim [another employee] is shit. What do you think?"
>
> If the employee agrees that Jim is shit, Jobs went to the next person and said, "Bob and I think Jim is shit. What do you think?"
>
> If the first employee disagreed and said that Jim is not shit, Jobs would move on to the next person, saying, "Bob and I think that Jim is great. What do you think?"

The Jobs Reality Distortion Field was now complete and running at full wattage. He might, on a given day, make the lives of Lisa team members a living hell. But to outsiders—especially members of the increasingly beleaguered Apple II group—it looked like paradise, especially after Black Wednesday left the Lisa team untouched.

All successful breakthrough products have a technical genius behind them somewhere. And if that genius is lucky, he can overcome almost every other problem associated with the product. The Lisa, it turned out, had its own

Woz in Bill Atkinson. Having shot his mouth off with Jobs and set the whole PARC play going, he now performed a miracle by making the fantasy real.

Atkinson had come out of the University of Washington's neurobio-chemistry department and had joined Apple in 1978 after falling in love with Woz's Apple II design (as he would a few years later with the Mac). Atkinson went on the PARC tour having a pretty good idea what the Alto, Star and Smalltalk were all about, and was well on his way to developing his own version of each of their novel functions.

But in his visit to PARC, Atkinson had experienced a dangerous misapprehension. Watching a brief demonstration of Smalltalk, Atkinson was struck by what seemed to him a working version of an operation called clipping. This was the effect, when windows overlap on the computer screen, of not actually constructing the entire screen(s) peeking out underneath the top one. This saved considerable processing power by the computer, but it also required some unprecedented software. In seeing Smalltalk do just that, Atkinson came away convinced that it could be done and dedicated himself to the task.

The trouble was, Atkinson only *thought* he saw clipping. What he actually saw was much closer to a side-by-side tiling of windows of predetermined size, with some slow simulation of overlap. In other words, the clipping technology Atkinson assumed had already been developed had in fact not yet been proven.

Atkinson began to realize his mistake just about the time he went nuts trying to figure out how Xerox did it. He spent months trying to duplicate the process—even getting up in the middle of the night to jot down notes from his dreams. And little by little, Atkinson began to solve the puzzle, developing algebraic equations to quickly describe the cutout pieces as a window "disappeared" behind another.

So focused did Atkinson become on the project that, nearing completion, while driving his little Mazda RX-7 to work, he failed to notice that the semitrailer truck he was preparing to cross behind was in fact *parked*. He drove right under it, tearing the roof completely off his car and nearly decapitating himself. In the end, he was only knocked unconscious, awakening in the hospital to see a worried Steve Jobs looking down at him, fearful of a Woz II. "Don't worry, Steve," he told him, "I still know how to do regions."

Atkinson knew how to do other things as well. He took the iconography that he saw at PARC and combined it with Raskin's one-button mouse technique, which he'd seen on his secret forays to the Mac building, and came up with a method of using the mouse to drag both icons and windows around the computer screen. This, along with the clipping technology, enabled Atkinson to create a revolutionary user interface that brought together the familiar experience of moving papers around a desktop with every messy person's fantasy of being able to instantly uncover that crucial buried item.

The Lisa was on its way. But before it could go much further, one last bottleneck had to be removed. With some very careful diplomacy that landed the support of Mike Markkula, Jobs was tossed—gingerly—out of the Lisa project. The rationale, which he eventually accepted, was that the chairmanship was in itself sufficient responsibility, even for a man of his caliber. The Lisa team took a collective sigh of relief and went back to work.

But it would still take longer than anyone imagined. Even after the hardware configuration and packaging were established, the Lisa's wildly ambitious software proved endlessly troublesome. One unexpected problem popped up after another.

It became like a burlesque routine. The software engineers would see a problem and present an innovative solution. The marketers (especially the HPers) would argue that it would take too long to complete. The software engineers, often Atkinson, would pull all-nighters to prove them wrong. Then Tesler would take the solution and try it out on new, inexperienced Apple employees. He would find that it worked, but that the process had identified a whole new problem—and the cycle would begin again.

There was also the matter of the name. Lisa just wasn't a proper name for a computer, especially with its rumored connection to Jobs's daughter. Here once again the underlying tension between the suits and the freaks at Apple reared its head. The marketing and business types, looking to the corporate market, wanted to call the new computer something sober and formal, like the Apple IV or the TI-like Apple 400. The hackers screamed *no, no,* the whole point of the Lisa was to be different from all the others. It was supposed to be a friendly, approachable computer, a tool to enhance your lifestyle, not just crank out spreadsheets. Their candidates included Esprit (already taken) and Applause. The result was the type of deadlock that in a few years would characterize all of Apple.

In the end, the company just swallowed hard and went with the status quo, praying that the Jobs paternity connection wouldn't come out. It did, in *Time,* of course. So much for secrecy.

By now 1980 had turned into 1981, then 1982. Finally, in mid-1982, the Lisa at last approached completion. Physically, it was as impressive a machine as the computer industry had yet seen. An elegant, beige box whose rectangular face contained on one side a twelve-inch black-and-white screen and on the other the stacked slots for two Twiggy disk drives. But that wasn't the first thing you noticed. Rather, your eyes instantly went to the keyboard. It wasn't built in! Instead, it was connected to the central processor box by a looped, telephone-like electrical wire. And then, next to the keyboard was another, tinier satellite, also connected by a wire to the computer. With its single giant button, it was like a kid's toy . . . a mouse.

But there was still something wrong. The hardware was fine, as were the special functions. But something was unsettling about the user interface. When you first fired up the Lisa, on-screen there appeared a Filer program that welcomed you and asked you what you wanted to do. The problem was this questioning process was akin to an interrogation. Some Lisa group members jokingly called it the "20 Questions Program." Others inflated that to "100." It is always a bad sign when the inventors begin making black jokes about their own creation.

Yet as late as mid-1982 the Filer was still slated to be the standard front-end interface for the Lisa. Luckily, that potential disaster was averted by the Wife Test. Doing a little field testing of his own, Dan Smith, the designer of the Filer, took it home and asked his wife to use it. Try as she might, Mrs. Smith couldn't figure the Filer out.

That did it. Smith was brave enough to admit he had made a mistake. He went to Atkinson and told him the problem, convinced that Apple would never allow such an expensive revision so near introduction. But Atkinson, who by now was getting accustomed to stealth, had a better idea. He proposed that he, Smith and a third engineer named Frank Ludoloph meet in an extended secret cram session at Atkinson's house and come up with an alternative. Atkinson even tried to tell his plan to his boss, Wayne Rosing, director of engineering for the Lisa project. Rosing replied, "Don't tell me what you're working on, but good luck."

Weeks later, the trio reemerged with a new Filer interface, now called the Desktop Manager. And of all the amazing new features on the Lisa, this one would prove the most memorable, and the one most associated with Apple Computer.

Now, instead of being bombarded with questions, the owner was met with a simulated desktop, complete with folders bearing labels. These folders merely had to be tapped by the mouse to open and display an array of files, each designated by both a name and an icon of its type (application program, word processing file, etc.). The file was then opened by tapping the single button on the mouse twice. When you were done with that file you merely tapped once on a square in the upper corner. You could put the file back into its folder, create a new one or, coolest of all, drag the file's icon down to the lower right-hand corner of the screen and throw it into a trash-can icon—an act so cute and so lifelike that it was usually the first thing most new Apple users tried.

6.13 FLACKING, FLOGGING AND FLOUNDERING

The Lisa was slated for a January 1983 introduction. Apple's publicity machine kicked into overdrive. Both Regis McKenna and Fred Hoar were intent upon making this the biggest product introduction in electronics history.

They succeeded. The Lisa was the high water mark for Silicon Valley flackery. The national press had all but ignored the introduction of the Valley's other great products, the HP-35, the Intel 8080 microprocessor, the Amdahl and Tandem computers, even Pong. Now it seemed to be atoning for this past indifference by treating the Lisa introduction as if it were the Salk vaccine. The result was the most successful new-product introduction since the Boeing 707, the Ford Mustang or pull tabs for beer cans. Hoar, having done his job with the IPO and the Lisa, left soon after. Fifteen years later, as Apple stumbled, he would still be a Valley heavyweight, and would tell Apple jokes as part of his famous introductions at industry gatherings.

Jobs, the man who had to be thrown out of the Lisa project for it to go forward, finally got his *Time* cover (complete with halo) in the yearlong ramp-up to the introduction. Meanwhile, the Brahmins of high-tech business reporting (Andy Pollack of the *New York Times*, Dick Shaffer of *The Wall Street Journal*, Ben Rosen) were given an early glimpse of the machine and dubbed it more than worthy. They lauded its packaging, its interface, the company's decision to go with the new Motorola 68000 processor, its megabyte of memory and its remarkable Lisa Office System suite of seven powerful software programs (LisaWrite, LisaDraw, LisaCalc, LisaGraph, LisaProject, LisaList and LisaTerminal). And when the Lisa finally appeared for public viewing and coverage by the lesser lights of the press, it was hailed as Apple's Great Comeback, its answering shot to IBM.

But it wasn't. Even as Apple geared up for the Lisa introduction, there was a gnawing sense that something was wrong. For all of its revolutionary attributes, the Lisa was also so freighted with features and overwritten new programs that it had become painfully slow in operation and, at a typical price of $12,000 (almost ten times the price of a basic Apple II), was shockingly expensive. It had to be to recoup the $50 million invested in creating it, $20 million of that in software alone. The Apple II, by comparison, had cost just 1 percent of that, $500,000.

For the early reviewers, folks who would never have to buy one of these computers for themselves (or hundreds of them for their companies), the price was easily rationalized away by noting that the only computers currently available with the Lisa's power were $40,000 minicomputers. That was true, but consumers and small businesses weren't buying minis.

What the Lisa team had invented was the first computer workstation. Unfortunately, that market wouldn't appear for another six years. And when it did, in the hands of Sun Microsystems, Silicon Graphics and Hewlett-Packard, these new workstations would shrewdly be designed for engineering applications, where all that computing firepower could immediately be put to use—not for business, where all this power needed sophisticated (and as yet unwritten) software to prove its worth.

In the end, the Lisa was a great product without a market. It was one of those rare products that manage to do everything right, while also doing everything wrong. It couldn't help but fire the first shot of a new era, and then be the first casualty of the resulting revolution. Even as it sat in the lobby of the new Apple headquarters building, its smooth sides dully reflecting the neon decorative elements of the surrounding lobby, the exotic bit-mapped images bursting on its screen, you couldn't help but admire the Lisa for its brilliance and yet secretly sense that it was the Edsel of computers.

But if Lisa was an Edsel, Apple at least still had the Volkswagen. By the end of 1982, the company had sold 600,000 Apple II's, by far the largest installed base in the personal computer industry. Even the fast-growing PC had sold only a third as many machines. Moreover, the II had the best software library in the industry, with Apple and third-party developers coming up with dozens of new titles each month. Woz's little boxes were now the driving share of Apple's $583 million in revenues. And they showed little signs of fading.

That was good news. But IBM was still coming on fast. By mistakenly, but serendipitously, losing control over its architecture and operating system, Big Blue had left a very big door open. Copycat manufacturers were free to jump into the market with "clone" machines that imitated the PC's performance and ran its software. By the end of 1983, more than a hundred such clone companies were in the market, many with only a fraction of the PC's functionality, but some so close to perfect compatibility that it made no difference to the average user. Using off-the-shelf parts, manufacturing that was sometimes superior even to IBM's and prices that were often half that of the PC, these third-wave clone makers very quickly became a market force in themselves. Ultimately, they played as great a role as Big Blue in destroying Atari and the second wave of personal computer makers.

In all the hoopla about the Lisa, less noticed was the simultaneous introduction of a new, more powerful Apple II, called the IIe. The annual meeting/press conference, when the two products were rolled out, was entitled "evolution/revolution." But it was obvious to everyone present that the one person whose views counted, Steve Jobs, didn't give half a damn about the IIe. Revolutionaries don't like incremental change.

Ironically, both on the Apple balance sheet and in the hearts of millions of schoolkids, the IIe was by far the more important product. It was a gutsy little machine that Apple, thanks to the increasing power and miniaturization of chips, would eventually build for under $100 and sell for more than ten times that amount. The IIe would not only prop up Apple's market share and give it the capital it needed to launch the Mac, but would also create a generation of Apple fanatics that would buoy the company for the next decade. Most important, it gave Apple an enduring share of the market's heart long after it lost most of its share of the market. Unheralded, but beloved, the Apple IIe may well have been the greatest personal computer ever built. And it didn't even get top billing at its own introduction.

Still, in one respect, Jobs was right: without a new breakout product, Apple was destined to slowly fade away. The Apple II, no matter what its form, would never be the future. Though he had already turned against it, Jobs had no choice for now but to put heart and soul behind the Lisa. That the world considered it his baby was only added motivation.

Apple predicted sales of 10,000 Lisas in the second half of 1983 (when deliveries would begin in volume) and 40,000 in 1984. In the end, the company sold 80,000 of the machines, or 13,000 per each quarter of its short life—a figure not far from the company's projections, and one that was ramping up toward the end. But almost from the beginning, it was obvious that the Lisa, while not a disaster like the III, was also not going to save Apple.

Now it was up to the Macintosh. Lisa's ill-treated and disreputable baby brother had now become Apple's last hope.

6.14 HEADLESS HUNTING

Even as the Lisa was being introduced, Steve Jobs was in negotiations for a new company CEO. Markkula was ready again for one of his regular retirements. Jobs, both because he was chairman and because, having been booted from the Lisa project, he needed something important to do, made it his project to find someone to run the new, more mature Apple.

Using headhunters to help in the search, Jobs began looking in October 1982. By Christmas he had narrowed the list to two individuals: One was Don Estridge, the guy from Boca Raton who had given IBM the PC. The other was John Sculley of Pepsi-Cola, reputedly the best marketing guy of his generation, the man who'd done for Pepsi's market share what generations of his predecessors had failed to accomplish. The guy who invented "The Pepsi Generation."

Estridge would have been a great choice. He was Apple's kind of maverick executive (and he'd done it inside the most conformist corporation of them all). As a former software engineer he knew more about computers than Jobs and Markkula combined. And, as icing on the cake, his departure would rob Apple's biggest competitor of its leadership.

But if Estridge seemed made for Apple, there was one problem: he wasn't made for Steve Jobs. Author Frank Rose would write about Estridge that "like Jobs, he was full of energy and intelligence and charisma," but, unlike Jobs, "he also had a remarkable generosity of spirit. He could give you an idea and make you think it was your own, and he could put so much trust in you that you'd break down walls to get your job done."

It is said that a con job works only on people with a little larceny already in their hearts. One of the interesting features rarely remarked about Steve Jobs's Reality Distortion Field is that it too worked most effectively on people whose personalities shared some of its attributes. Not being a natural self-mythologizer, Estridge not only resisted Jobs's blandishments but was actually repelled by them. When Jobs tried to seduce him with conspiratorial stories about his felonious activities of old, Estridge was disgusted: I'm going to work for a kid who is *proud* of being a criminal?

But there was more than that. Estridge believed in traditional notions long in disrepute in Silicon Valley. Like loyalty. Estridge was proud he worked for IBM; and he was even more proud of his team at Boca. Going to work for Apple would betray them both.

So in the end, despite being offered millions in salary, bonus and stock—more money than he would ever make at IBM—Estridge turned Steve Jobs down. When an IBM vice president later asked him why, Estridge explained simply that when he was talking to a stranger on a plane and was asked where he worked, he wanted to say, "IBM."

Now Steve Jobs had two choices. Either go with the number two choice or start over. He chose the former. It was, after his little larceny with Woz, Jobs's second big mistake. Until that point, Jobs had done the right things in his recruitment program. He had not only accepted that he wasn't yet ready to run a corporation (not an easy thing for him to admit) but had consciously gone out in search of a grown-up, for someone who combined corporate experience with a maverick style, a technology background mixed with proven marketing skill, and, most importantly, someone who was smart enough and secure enough to see through Steven P. Jobs.

Unfortunately, Jobs had found somebody better than himself, only to run him off. If he had been brave enough or patient enough, Jobs would have started over. He should have repeated what he did so brilliantly with Apple's computers by refusing to settle for anything but the very best. In time he would have found that perfect individual, because Apple was the biggest lure in American business.

Instead he settled for John Sculley. Why? Perhaps because he felt he was running out of time. Or maybe he really did believe that Sculley was the best man for the job and that any additional searching would find no better candidate. Maybe it was just because in Sculley he found a talented man he could still intellectually seduce. Once again, with Steve Jobs it may have been all three. But whatever the reason, Jobs had made his second great mistake. It wasn't as venal as the petty theft from Woz, but it was nearly as devastating. Steve had understood the need for an experienced CEO, but when he went looking he settled only on variations of himself: Estridge the entrepreneur, Sculley the marketing legend. But Apple already had those positions filled— by Steve Jobs. What the company needed now was a more experienced and emotionally stable Mike Scott, an executive who could keep the company's books in order, negotiate strategic partnerships and get products out on budget and on time. Jobs never liked such people, and didn't hire one.

6.15 MOLES

The Mac group had taken good advantage of its years of isolation. Raskin had assembled his team quickly and thoughtfully. He could be insufferably arrogant, but he also recognized and supported talent when he saw it. Never was this more the case than with Burrell Smith, the kid from the repair department. Atkinson had found Smith, took him to Raskin's house one evening and announced, "Here's the guy who's going to design your machine for you."

Raskin was dubious, but he quickly came to respect the little man's talents. And it didn't hurt that Smith quickly became a true believer in Raskin's vision of the Mac as Everyman's companion, the Swiss Army knife of computers. Still, it took an extraordinary leap of faith that December for Raskin to turn over the assignment of building the first prototype to the kid.

Smith didn't let him down. For the next month, Burrell hunkered down in the Mac area, working day and night through Christmas, scrounging parts whenever he needed them (an advantage of being a former repairman was knowing where to look) and constantly keeping in mind Raskin's seemingly impossible goal of a $1,000 machine that nevertheless featured bit-mapping and built-in keyboard, display and mass memory. This stringent price goal led to some distressing compromises—for example, the prototype had to settle for the lame little Motorola 6809, a microprocessor hardly more powerful than the II's now obsolete 6502, as well as a rotten cassette player instead of the current industry-standard floppy disk—but Smith soldiered on.

He finished right after New Year's, putting the motherboard and other subsystems into an Apple II box. That last night, as he finished, Smith sent a note to Andy Hertzfeld, apprising him of what he'd accomplished and challenging Hertzfeld to come make it work.

Hertzfeld took the challenge, working most of the night. In the morning, Smith arrived to see the computer's display glowing, appropriately, with an image of Scrooge McDuck and the words "Hi, Burrell!"

Smith got his display, Atkinson got a real role at last in the Mac group and, most important, Raskin got his prototype. And all of them would soon be working for the 1980s version of McDuck, a figure rich enough to even buy history.

6.16 THE PRINCE OF THIEVES

Nineteen eighty was Macintosh's year in the wilderness.

Three times in the course of the year, the project teetered on the brink of cancellation. The third time, in October, it was officially canceled—only to be saved at the last moment by Raskin successfully begging Mike Scott for a three-month extension. The team somehow struggled on. But the writing was on the wall: come the first of the year, if the Mac didn't show something spectacular it was gone.

Then a miracle, the last miracle in the Apple story. And like the other Apple miracles, it managed also to be a little tawdry. Steve Jobs, tossed out of the Lisa project and wandering about looking for something to do, came upon Raskin's *Book of Macintosh*. Jobs was enough of an ersatz technical visionary to recognize the real thing when he saw it. There it was, the insanely great idea Jobs always talked about. In his characteristic way, Jobs adopted the vision as his own—and since it was he, not Raskin, in the public eye, fielding press interviews and giving industry speeches, the Macintosh soon became synonymous with Steven Jobs. Henceforth it would be his idea.

But co-opting Jef Raskin's ideas was only the beginning. The ideas were, after all, being made manifest in a real product. The Mac group had by now moved to its little rented office behind the Texaco station. The team members named its hole-in-the-wall the Texaco Towers, set up a Ping-Pong table and styled themselves rebels—pirates—from the rest of Apple.

And it wasn't long before Steve Jobs started hanging around, talking to the team behind Raskin's back. It was hard to resist his charms. Apple was public now, and Jobs was the richest young entrepreneur in the world. He was more famous than most rock stars. The public considered him a business genius. And he could talk the talk. He'd read *The Book of Mac*; he could spout the liturgy almost as well as Raskin. But, unlike Raskin, Jobs could also make things happen at Apple. Pirates they might be, but not by choice. With Steve Jobs in the building, all of Apple—hell, the entire world—would be looking their way.

Meanwhile, at the II and Lisa groups (and, rumor had it, on executive row) everyone was glad to have Jobs distracted and buried off in some dead-end corner of the company where he couldn't do much damage.

But to focus solely on the deceits and petty cruelties of Steve Jobs during this period would be a mistake. Because if his methods were often improper, even on occasion despicable, there is no denying that Steve was still the preeminent market visionary and product positioner of his generation. And for all the damage he was about to do to the lives of everyone connected with the Mac project, he also gave them a little share of immortality. He would take a little, dreamy, probably doomed new-product idea and turn it into, as Steven Levy would later claim, the commercial product of the century.

Despite his later protestations, Jef Raskin could never have done that. He may have been the father of the Mac, but he was a difficult parent. He was not a martinet like Jobs (he was in fact a very supportive manager), but Raskin had a character weakness nearly as damaging as Jobs's: he was a dogmatist. The Mac of his dreams had little memory, a cassette drive, no mouse and none of the Xerox software innovations. In a first prototype, these weren't huge flaws; rather they proved the concept of a $1,000 computer at a time when most machines cost three times that much.

But Raskin was unyielding. Left to him, future Macs would likely have perpetuated those flaws. Jobs was different; he was attached to an idea only as long as it worked, then would compromise it or abandon it (and pretend he'd never been part of it) if it failed. And it certainly didn't hurt to be chairman, rather than merely a product manager, when it came to making such unilateral decisions.

Raskin was well liked as a manager, but his ideological narrow-mindedness was wearing thin. The team would build his machine, with its puny microprocessor, but they craved a chance to blow out the spit valves. So when Steve Jobs began to lurk around making suggestions, plying his charms, offering the team members a chance to prove what they could do, they met his mutiny halfway.

Jobs's first move was to work on the team's version of Woz, Burrell Smith. It was a technique he knew well. He dared Smith to build a Mac with the hottest chip then on the market, the Motorola 68000. Smith couldn't help himself—and there went another Christmas vacation spent on all-nighters and a new prototype.

The result was a dragster among PCs. It hadn't been easy to build. Putting the 68000 in the econobox of the Mac was the digital equivalent of stuffing a big-block Chevy engine into the back of a Volkswagen: if you didn't find a way to control and channel all that horsepower it would simply twist the transmission into a pretzel and tear the wheels off the car. Smith's comparable problem was that the 68000 was processing information so fast, blasting off bursts of data, that it would simply overwhelm the keyboard, display and every other peripheral device. Smith's solution, an elegant way of queuing and managing the transmission of data off the processor called "bus multiplexing," would be a hallmark of all PCs in the years to come.

Smith's 68000 Mac was the death knell not just for Raskin but, as time would show, for the Lisa as well. The new Mac did everything the Lisa did at a tenth the retail price, and a twentieth the development cost. In this new prototype Jobs saw the future of computing, and Apple. Now if the new Mac could just run some of those Xerox programs he'd seen that day at PARC . . .

By the end of January, Jobs had attached himself fully to the Mac team. As Joanna Hoffman would tell Levy: "When Steve started coming over, Jef's dream was shattered on the spot. It was difficult on everybody and there was an air of allegiance to Jef, but Steve had his own competing aura. He immediately started talking about what it would look like, feel like, how we would sell it . . ."

It wasn't long before Jobs started complaining that Raskin was a poor manager, and worse, that he was too slow. The Mac was never going to get to market in another year as Raskin claimed, Jobs said, so the project needed a firmer hand at the tiller. (Needless to say, it would in fact take Jobs three years.)

The confrontation peaked on February 17, when Raskin was scheduled to give an informal lunchtime "brown bag" seminar on his vision of the personal computer. Other Apple employees were anxious to know about the topic, and Raskin had agreed not to give out any trade secrets about the Macintosh. Jobs

257 / INFINITE LOOP

had already canceled one such event by Raskin in January. Now, just two hours before the talk, he called Raskin and told him the seminar was canceled once again.

But Jobs, perhaps because he had forgotten or perhaps because he wanted to injure Raskin's reputation by making him look unreliable, never told the seminar's organizer. As a result, when in a spur-of-the-moment decision just after noon, Raskin decided to stroll over to the seminar site, he found a hundred Apple employees waiting for his talk. So, not above a little deviousness himself, Raskin got up, announced the cancellation, then launched into a different talk on his current work at Apple. He didn't mention Macintosh by name, but everyone in the room knew what he was describing.

Jobs was furious. He called Raskin into his office the next morning and fired him. Raskin knew better; he told Jobs he'd come back later in the day. When he did, Jobs had changed his mind: Raskin wasn't fired, but he was put on an extended paid leave.

Jef Raskin was many things, but he was not a fool. He knew what was coming. But he had no intention of giving up easily the most important creation of his life. So, even as he was being purged by Jobs, Raskin fired off a memo to Markkula. He would later claim that the rest of the Mac team was going to sign the letter with him, but chickened out.

For whatever reason—exhaustion, a recognition of his own limitations, or, as he presented it, the need to focus on the technical side of the project— Raskin had already spoken of the possibility of getting a professional manager to run the business side of the project. It was a big mistake, as he now realized to his horror, because by admitting weakness he had allowed his biggest enemy in through the front door.

In his memo to Markkula, currently the CEO, Raskin made a last-ditch attempt to ward off the specter of Jobs. As Raskin described it later:

> I didn't want Steve to be in charge. The memo specified, in detail and in my judgment, Jobs's many and egregious failings as a manager . . .
>
> The memo reflected the running joke that the way to get Jobs to agree to something was to tell him about it, let him reject it and wait a week; when he came running to tell you about "his new" idea, you'd exclaim, "Great, Steve, we'll do it right away!" In the memo, I also made the prediction that was to prove exact: "Jobs was wrong on his Apple III schedule, wrong on the Lisa schedule, wrong on the cost and price estimates, and he will be wrong on Macintosh. He is a prime

example of a manager who takes the credit for his optimistic schedules and then blames the workers when deadlines are not met.

That wasn't all:

> While Mr. Jobs's stated positions on management techniques are all quite noble and worthy, in practice he is a dreadful manager. . . . He was late for appointments, he attacked other people's work without understanding it, he sowed divisiveness and discontent, he played favorites, he had no idea of realistic scheduling . . .

Raskin asked that the memo be kept secret. But somehow Jobs got a copy. Markkula would later suggest that, Apple being an open company, it had been taken off his desk. Just as likely, he showed it to Jobs. Either way, Raskin would never touch the Mac project again. While on leave, he bought a plot of land in the Santa Cruz mountains and restored the old house on it. When he returned, Apple offered him the job of head of the company's research division, a job he'd taken once before, only to see his staff slowly bled away to other projects. "In those days, Apple didn't know what research meant, and looked at the talented people I hired as resources wasted if they weren't working on current products. Besides, there was the matter of personal integrity. Steve Jobs had become impossible for me to work with . . . [and] the only alternatives left for me were to leave or learn to toady to Steve Jobs."

So Raskin quit Apple. Later, Canon of Japan would hire him to build the computer of his dreams. The result, the Cat, combined Raskin's strength in design (it was perhaps the easiest-to-use computer ever built) with his weaknesses in corporate politics (it was marketed as a secretarial tool and never allowed to operate at full performance). It failed miserably.

Looking back at his Apple experiences, Raskin would write:

> Steve had chutzpah in the extreme . . . And you can explain Jobs with another Yiddish word, mensch. It is high praise to say of a person that he (or in these enlightened days, she) is a mensch or "a real mensch." A mensch is cultivated without losing the common touch, upholds high principles while remaining practical, is kind and generous without shortchanging himself, and is attentive to his responsibilities to himself, his family, his business, his associates, his community and the world. If you understand the qualities that make a man a mensch, then you understand a lot about Steve Jobs. Everything a mensch is, he isn't.

Perhaps, but Steve Jobs had also won. He now had his hands on the greatest product of the age.

6.17 WE LUCKY FEW

Steve Jobs once bet John Couch $5,000 the Macintosh would beat the Lisa to market.

It was a bet he was lucky to lose. The success of the Lisa as an invention, and its failure as a product, proved invaluable lessons for Jobs and the Mac team. It suggested the right path for the product: a combination of Raskin's budget computer for the masses, the Xerox/Lisa interface, and Jobs's own flair for packaging and design.

That mix alone would take time; but added to it was Jobs's own mercurial style, his endless flip-flops about one feature or another that ran the Mac team ragged. On top of this was Jobs's own paranoid style in a volatile mix with his thirst for revenge against all those who drove him out of the Lisa group or who suggested that he was little more than a con man who'd hooked on to Woz.

All this came together in a symbolic event: Jobs had a pirate flag (with Apple logo eyes) raised above the Mac team's building, where it could be seen by the rest of Apple. The message wasn't lost. Jobs was symbolically giving the finger to the rest of the company. But what has been little remarked about this little Peter Pan moment is that Jobs was at this time also *chairman of the board* of Apple. It was as if the founder and governor of a colony had suddenly rowed out to command a pirate ship to attack his own home. It is hardly surprising that Jobs wanted it both ways, rebel and pillar of the corporate establishment, but what is amazing is that he pulled it off. "Chutzpah" almost isn't a strong enough term.

Jobs's arrival also meant some radical changes to the work environment of the Mac team. No more scrimping and praying the project wouldn't be canceled. The Dauphin was now in charge, and nothing was too good for the team. Before long, the Mac group was ensconced in Bandley 3, right smack in the middle of the Apple campus. Now, besides the old Ping-Pong table, the lobby featured a Bösendorfer grand piano, Jobs's BMW racing motorcycle and a Defender video arcade game. Rock and classical music boomed day and night from giant studio-quality speakers. There was even a masseuse on staff to rub and Rolf bodies back into celestial harmony.

It was a building you entered with both trepidation and delight. Trepidation because everything screamed at you that here were special people performing special tasks to which you were not privy; but thrilling, because it looked like the coolest place to work in America. Bandley 3 would prove to be the prototype of every product design shop in Silicon Valley and Seattle for the next quarter century. And, like those that followed, Bandley 3 was in fact a very well-appointed sweatshop, whose inhabitants worked days that would have been illegal had they been paid by the hour.

Thanks to Burrell Smith, Jobs had his hardware prototype, a supercharged version of Raskin's box. Now he needed the Lisa interface. That task fell to Andy Hertzfeld, and he knew just what to do. Unconstrained by the bureaucracy and the compromise of working on a large, expensive team, Hertzfeld simply raided the Lisa interface for the pieces he liked best. And, having little respect for most of the Lisa team, Hertzfeld took almost exclusively from a single source, Bill Atkinson. As he told Levy: "Anything Bill Atkinson did, I took, and nothing else."

Hertzfeld didn't work in a vacuum. From the beginning, partly because of Raskin's loose management style, the Mac team worked democratically. New features were often put to a vote by the entire team, and typically those that won were selected because they were interesting or fun. Jobs's arrival didn't change that. Rather it amplified it. Now added to the mix was Jobs's goal of an "insanely great" product. That was a license to pursue the cool.

Meanwhile, the team slowly learned to deal with the mercurial Jobs, playing the game Raskin described of waiting out his goofier ideas, allowing the young chairman to take credit for ideas that weren't his and, most important, letting him run cover for the team in the rest of Apple. With Jobs in the Mac group, the rest of the company might pray he would fall on his face, but no one would dare take him on.

Jobs was more than just a champion and a nuisance. What he brought to the group was what he had provided Apple from the beginning: an aesthetic. Cringely would later say that Jobs was the most dangerous man in Silicon Valley because he didn't care about money. Others would say that Jobs was dangerous because he didn't care about any other living thing. But whatever the truth of those statements, they missed an essential fact about Steve Jobs: he was dangerous because he was important. And he was important because he was essential. And he was essential because he was the only person in the entire personal computer industry who operated at the nexus between the digital revolution and the artistic one that preceded it. If he was a monster, he was a monster like Picasso, not like Rockefeller. He had stolen the Macintosh from its creator, but now he made it his canvas, adding new ideas, then painting them over and trying something else until he got it right.

One thing he got right the first time was the box. Jobs wanted the Mac to be a memorable object in itself and the only person he knew up to that standard was the man who'd designed the Apple II, Jerry Mannock. Jobs told Mannock (who, one will remember, had said he'd never work for Jobs again) that he wanted a design that would get into the Museum of Modern Art. That swashbuckling ambition was a hallmark of Steve Jobs in this era. He also said that he wanted Tom Wolfe to write his biography. And he would, in time, hire I. M. Pei to design his New York apartment (so much for his austerity).

But it was more than name-dropping, or affiliating himself with famous names. Jobs simply wanted the best, and those were the people he was most likely to get it from, artists who were the greatest living masters of their craft. As Jobs once explained: "When you're a carpenter making a beautiful chest of drawers, you're not going to use a piece of plywood on the back, even though it faces the wall and nobody will ever see it. *You'll* know it's there, so you're going to use a beautiful piece of wood on the back. For you to sleep well at night, the aesthetic, the quality, has to be carried all the way through."

This comment (though betraying a lack of experience with real antique furniture) nevertheless showed Jobs's deep, Zen-like sense of purity when it came to the design of his products. Sometimes this obsession would lead him astray; for example, he spent a couple of weeks hanging around Macy's appliance department convinced that the Mac should resemble a Cuisinart. But throughout his career, from the Apple II to the NeXT computer to *Toy Story*, when the moment of truth came Jobs had an almost perfect eye for the right look.

Thus, when he saw Mannock's design for a friendly little upright box with a facelike display, a floppy-disk slot like an off-kilter mouth, a detachable keyboard and a footprint no bigger than a piece of stationery, Jobs knew he had the design of his dreams. It was Raskin's Swiss Army knife computer crossed with the cool elegance Jobs dreamed for himself and his machines. Even more important, the Mac's design was *friendly*. Its anthropomorphic shape, similar to the little robots seen padding around the background of *Star Wars*, made it appear like one of the Seven Dwarfs, or Sancho Panza. It was the companion that Raskin had written about four years before.

Jobs's perfect eye came through for him one more time during the Mac project. Chiat/Day of Los Angeles had the reputation as the hottest and most innovative television advertising agency of the day. Needless to say, Jobs was drawn to it and was instrumental in hiring the agency to represent Apple. But the partnership had not begun well. The agency's first ad for the Lisa was entitled "Alone Again." It was a lifestyle ad, rich in texture (music by Wyndham Hill, a dreamlike floating room featuring a young man at work on his Lisa)—but also unintentionally funny. In view of the few Lisas being sold, if you did buy one you certainly would be alone.

But what Chiat/Day did have going for it was the director Ridley Scott, a Brit who was making himself famous in feature films directing *Blade Runner* and *Alien*. Scott had begun in advertising and had escaped the stigma of his roots so well that he was able to return to them without fear. He would direct a series of Apple ads, "Apple People," featuring slice-of-life images (the lunchtime basketball game, etc.) that were well received less because of their clichéd content than for the filmlike quality of their production.

Now, with the prospect of a revolutionary new product like Macintosh, Scott wanted to cut loose and make an equally revolutionary commercial of the likes American television had never seen. If the Mac was to be introduced in 1984, then by God, let's give the audience a vision of Orwell's *1984*. IBM would be Big Brother and Apple a Winston Smith who really does defeat the regime. Scott wanted the look to be a cross between the gray Eastern Europe at the time of the Hungarian uprising, the worn-out machinery of his own *Alien* and the Deco cities of *Metropolis* and *Things to Come*. The only soundtrack would be Stalinist gibberish emanating from Big Brother on a giant screen.

The original plan was to have a beautiful woman enter the scene and, in a play on old Stalinist socialist realist filmmaking, throw a sledgehammer that shatters Big Brother's image and frees the workers. However, during an audition in Hyde Park, the model trying out for the part lost control of the heavy implement, threw it the wrong way and nearly brained a little old lady walking by. So Scott and company switched to an athletic young woman, her brilliant red running shorts the only saturated color in the entire commercial.

When Jobs saw the storyboards, he wasn't impressed. But he also knew that Scott was the best, and when the director announced that he would do the other planned Apple commercials only if he could do "1984," Jobs quickly agreed. Later, when Jobs saw the rough cut, he knew he had one of the most amazing commercials ever shot.

It was all there: the philosophy, the hardware, the software, the look and now the promotional campaign. Every part of the Mac was a breakthrough over what had come before. Jobs could now sleep at night knowing that "the aesthetic, the quality, had been carried all the way through" and that even the back was beautiful.

6.18 DR. JEKYLL AND MR. JOBS

With Steve Jobs, the brilliant always came with the beastly. And because the Mac project was in many ways the highest point of his extraordinary career, this was also the period when his behavior was often at its most destructive, cruel and just plain difficult even for the people he supported.

For all the perquisites that came with it, being on Jobs's side during these years was not a particularly enviable place to be. There might be a grand piano in the lobby at Bandley, but that didn't mean the centimillionaire who ran the Mac group was willing to pay his team a decent salary. Some of the Mac team members made little more than $30,000 per year. In view of the hundred-hour workweeks, they would have made more money picking cherries at one of the few remaining Valley orchards.

Moreover, just as Jobs was perfectly willing to send the team off for weeks on some tangential project, then change his mind, recall the troops and then send them off in a different direction on his latest brainstorm, so too did he sometimes get so fixated on an idea that no amount of reason or evidence could move him. The preeminent example of this was the Mac's core memory. Raskin, trapped in his own ideology, had decreed that the Macintosh would be shipped with 64K, the same as the seriously underpowered (and ungraphic) IBM PC.

Jobs had his own biases. He held to the 64K memory size until long after it was obvious that the Mac would never work as planned without a lot more memory. And even then, Jobs grudgingly only let the capacity double to 128K, despite the fact that, thanks to Moore's Law, the new doubled capacity was actually *less* expensive than the original. The Mac team nodded agreement with Jobs's decision and then, in secret, designed the computer for the inevitable 512K the market would demand.

That one could be fixed. Other Jobs decisions could not. When Jobs had visited Xerox PARC he had seen not only the graphical user interface but also computer networking and even a primitive version of the Internet. He ignored them. In the hermetic world of Steven Jobs one didn't share information with others, so why would one need to wire computers together? Thus, the Mac would be designed as a stand-alone system, solitary and self-contained in its operation and its philosophy. It couldn't even multi-task—that is, perform multiple operations at the same time—because the solitary user rarely needed that kind of performance. As a result, a decade later, when the world linked itself up in one gigantic networked daisy chain, as users wanted to simultaneously receive e-mail, work spreadsheets and print out a word processing file, the Mac would find itself almost paralyzed and mute before such overwhelming demands.

Jobs could be nasty and demeaning with his teammates in order to motivate them. But when they succeeded, he would shower them with praise that was both absurd and irresistible. Meanwhile, Jobs saved his real cruelty for his enemies, both inside and outside the company. There was one story, likely apocryphal, that went around the computer industry during this era that Jobs, while on a trip to Massachusetts, had taken the time to visit Ken Olsen, the formidable CEO of Digital Equipment. DEC, still a minicomputer giant, had been struggling trying to acquire a beachhead in PCs.

As the story went, Jobs strolled into Olsen's office, put his feet up on the man's desk and informed him that Apple was going to kick DEC's ass in personal computers. True or not, the story was accepted by the industry, cheered by those (usually young newcomers) who admired Jobs for his cockiness and guts, decried by others (usually veterans) who thought only a damned fool would antagonize the lion in his lair.

But Jobs could be just as cruel to his own people, even though he was chairman of the board, if they were not, like the Mac team, part of his praetorian guard. And he was not above the nastiest sort of revenge. After the Lisa introduction, that product's design team and development group closed shop and readied themselves for the next project. Some of these three hundred employees even harbored fantasies of joining the Mac team as it now raced toward its own product introduction.

Standing before the assembled throng, Jobs looked down with contempt. "I see only B and C players here. All the A players work for me in the Macintosh division. I might be interested in hiring two or three of you. Don't you wish you knew which ones I'll choose?"

This was the most despicable type of bullying, the schoolyard behavior of a spoiled nine-year-old. Jobs had been kicked off the Lisa team and now he was going to get even, the company be damned. Those employees he had just spat upon had given years (and sometimes their families, their youth and their good health) to realize what had been Steve Jobs's onetime dream. They had done all he had asked of them and more. If the Lisa had proven to be only a moderate success, it wasn't their fault, but that of the men who had first visualized the Lisa, including Jobs himself. Now he dumped his own culpability on them.

Until that moment, many of those Apple employees had admired, even loved, Steve Jobs. Now he had created a cohort of enemies. Within months he would need their help. And they would return the favor.

Jobs knew that his reputation at Apple and increasingly in the computer industry was tanking. Once, over a sushi dinner, he leaned across the table and asked a writer, "People think I'm an asshole, don't they?"—using precisely the vulgarity most commonly associated with him. There was no hurt in the question, or embarrassment or dismay. It was simply asked out of curiosity.

It was not a problem he saw as needing remedy. On the contrary, he got even worse.

By 1983, even getting to see Jobs was a crapshoot. He was notorious for leaving subordinates, reporters, investors—everyone but celebrities—waiting for an hour or more in the reception area. Then at last he would arrive without apology. Depending upon his mood, Jobs could be vicious and belittling ("Your magazine/newspaper/work/report is shit") or, alternately, charming, inviting you for a ride in his new Mercedes, playing tracks from a tape of the new and unreleased album by his girlfriend at the time, Joan Baez, discussing great metaphysical topics with you and all in all making you feel that the most famous young man of his generation had at last found in you a soul mate. Most disorientingly, sometimes he would be both characters at once.

But if Jobs's personal stock was falling in the computer industry, it continued to rise in the outside world. On recruiting tours to major universities, he was treated like a rock star (just as among rock stars he was treated as an intellectual genius). The national press and its readers couldn't get enough of his enigmatic remarks and the anecdotes about his wealth and lifestyle. Readers especially liked the stories about the empty home and Jobs's gruesome habit of massaging his feet at the office by putting one foot, then the other in a flushing toilet (relaxed toes apparently being more important than E. coli) and the rumors about the ultracool new computer he was creating in a not very well-hidden secret project. And Jobs never let them down. He charmed the college kids ("How many here are still virgins?"), he seduced the press and, if now as much through fear and hatred as love and admiration, he kept the cult of his personality alive at Apple.

Yet, even as his fame approached a peak, Steve Jobs was already becoming an anachronism. A late baby boomer, he had nevertheless adopted the philosophy of his near-elders. He was one of the last creations of the 1960s. But now it was the 1980s, a less romantic but more pragmatic age. And not many months after his own appearance on the cover of *Time*, the face of another young computer tycoon appeared in the same spot. A few years before, at a dinner at Arnaud's in New Orleans at the Ben Rosen Conference, the assembled industry leaders had feted, and roasted, Steve Jobs. Sitting at a table in the back, the youngest person in the room by far, this future cover boy had been all but ignored. He had watched the entertainment with a tiny smile, his arms folded. Now Bill Gates was the heir apparent to Jobs's throne. And Gates was a 1980s character through and through.

Still, for the moment, Jobs had the spotlight to himself and he was prepared to put on a show. It was an extraordinary juggling act, and a glimpse into the sheer complexity of Steve Jobs's soul. And it was in the midst of this madness that the darkest corner of that soul suddenly was illuminated. Thanks to his new fame, Steve learned the answer to the question he had asked all of his life: Who am I?

 Through a process that has never been publicly disclosed, at age twenty-seven Steve Jobs finally contacted his natural parents. His father, it turned out, was a respected political science professor, his mother a speech therapist. They had married and settled in Green Bay, Wisconsin, not long after Steve was born and put up for adoption. The marriage had produced a daughter two years later, Steve's sister, Mona Simpson, who grew up to become a successful novelist (*Anywhere But Here, The Lost Father*).

Nothing is known of a reunion with his parents, but Jobs did become close to his natural sister, visiting her often in Manhattan. "We're family," he would later say. "She's one of my best friends in the world." Simpson for her part published a novel in 1996, *A Regular Guy*, about a Silicon Valley entrepreneur. The first public acknowledgment of the relationship came at a book party for Simpson, put on by George Plimpton and *The Paris Review*, at which Jobs arrived with his birth sister and birth mother.

The adoptive parents of many children born before 1960 were told by the adoption agency or foundling home that their child's birth parents were successful professionals. "College professors" was a common story. And a generation of adopted children, like Steve Jobs, grew up believing that story, dreaming that they had been denied a richer, more fulfilling life than the one in which they had found themselves. But only Steve Jobs would grow up to find the story to be true. He *was* special; everything he had dreamed on those lonely days in a tract home in Mountain View had come true.

The realization that he had indeed been blessed in this life, that he had been lucky in both heredity and circumstance, might have induced in Jobs a certain humility, a thankfulness for all his blessings. But instead, it had no discernible effect on his behavior. It was too late. The news was no longer big enough to fill the hole.

Ken Krugler was one of those few "B and C players" on the Lisa who made the cut to the Mac group. He had just earned a degree in computer science from MIT and while still in school had worked for both IBM and Data General. "I decided I didn't want to work in cubes all my life. So I talked with my adviser and she suggested some West Coast companies that had a more relaxed atmosphere." He found Apple, joining the firm in July 1983, as employee number 4788.

It wasn't quite the relaxed atmosphere he expected — in fact, within a year he would be diagnosed with high blood pressure ("I thought it was strange since I had always had low pressure before") and told by his doctor to take a leave of absence.

After finishing his work on the Lisa project, Krugler was assigned by the Mac team to several projects, including preparing the now dying Lisa to run Mac software, then on development tools and an operating system code for future Mac models.

One of the first things that struck Krugler as different at his new employer, compared with Data General and especially IBM, was its size. "I was amazed at how small Apple was at the time. When I got there, there were just ten people in the Macintosh system software group." And that in turn meant considerable freedom: "If you had a good idea and pitched it to the right person, you could do it. You could find someone who agreed with your concept and they'd give you the go-ahead.

"That was both a blessing and a curse for Apple. It allowed people to be creative and develop innovative new technology, but it also created an environment where no one had a clear concept of all the different technologies being developed and how they worked together."

Lurking about in all this chaos was Jobs himself. "Jobs was around a lot. He always approached developers with a challenging demeanor. He'd come up to you and say something like 'Have you done anything great for the company today? Have you made a difference for Apple today?'

"Jobs used to see things in black and white. You were either really great or you were a complete bozo. Then, as the project progressed, he changed a little. Now he had four stages of evaluation: bozo, okay, good, great. We used to joke that it was a big improvement."

Returning after his leave of absence, Ken Krugler took an offer from Apple Japan and left the country for three years. There was chaos at the Japanese office as well, but at least it was far from headquarters and it had a solid new boss named Michael Spindler.

6.19 ROYAL AUDIENCE

The final run-up to the Macintosh, originally planned to take a few months, instead took two years. Even the compromise introduction date of March

1983 slipped ten months. The sheer complexity of the project grew by the week. The interface had to be perfected, including the title bar, the icons and the many built-in typefaces that would give the Mac an unprecedented "print-shop" capability. So too the handful of programs that the team planned to bundle into each computer—MacPaint, MacWrite—had to be created.

Most important for the long-term sales of the Mac, armies of outside software developers had to be enlisted and cultivated to provide the Macintosh with a large and growing library of applications.

Jobs and the Mac team had learned their lesson. They may have held the Lisa group in contempt, but they had enormous respect for the Apple II—and not just because it paid the bills. Woz's brilliant design had only carried that computer a couple of years; the II's miraculous six-year reign at the top of personal computing had been almost entirely due to the legions of independent programmers still busily cranking out scores of new programs for the II each month. Technically almost obsolete, the II survived now on sheer momentum, on the triumph of its usefulness.

The goal for the Mac, then, would be to introduce not just an amazing new piece of hardware but a platform for a plethora of programs. It wouldn't be just Apple up there onstage, but Microsoft and VisiCorp and all the other big names in personal computer software.

But there was a problem. Jobs was pissed off at VisiCorp—with some reason, as that company was busily developing its own (ultimately doomed) Xerox-like operating system. And, of course, Gates was happily making himself and IBM a lot of money with MS-DOS.

Jobs wasn't ready to make nice with VisiCorp, but Microsoft was too big a force to be ignored. So Jobs flew to Redmond to try to work some of his magic on his old friend.

Gates, as might be expected, was immune to Jobs's blandishments—he found his elder's behavior boorish when it wasn't annoying—but he *was* interested in the Mac. In later years, when wealth and the complexities of running a multibillion-dollar corporation would distract him, Gates would become sluggish identifying hot new trends, most famously the Internet. But in 1982 he was not only the smartest man in the computer industry but also the quickest. He looked right past Jobs's blather and saw the computer of his own dreams. *This* was the computer the world had been waiting to experience, this was the synthesis of hardware and interface and ergonomics that he had tried to describe to others for years.

When Steven Levy went to visit him a few months later, Gates first described how irritating and hyperbolic Jobs had been on that visit, but then stopped and said, "People concentrate on finding the guy's flaws. Why? He's in the center of things. They ask, 'Does he know the instruction set of the 68000?' I don't think that's super-important. There's no way there would be anything like that Macintosh without Jobs."

It was the sympathetic appraisal of one giant for another. And, like the great corporate field general he was, once Gates recognized the potential for the Macintosh, he threw every available soldier he had at it—until by the time of the Mac's introduction, Microsoft was fielding a larger Mac team than Apple itself. And the presence of Microsoft Word for the Mac would prove a key factor in the computer's success.

Meanwhile, of course, Gates made other plans. He had not yet gained his reputation as the High-Tech Python, whose embrace was always fatal. The world still saw him as a lesser Jobs. But, in fact, the two young men were almost perfect opposites. Steve Jobs, the last child of the 1960s, really did want to save the world—but only if he could be the Savior. Gates, was far more pragmatic: he didn't want to save the world, only to own it. It was an equally impossible goal, but it had the advantage of being realistic in the short term.

Gates had now seen the Mac interface close up and knew he wanted it. Even as his people were at work on applications for this new operating system, Gates was also setting others to work to destroy it. This new, graphical operating system, to be called Windows, was too late to beat the Mac to market, but Gates figured it could at least meet head-on a more immediate concern, VisiCorp's new software. With that threat out of the way, he could then devote months and millions to undermining his old acquaintance and new partner, Steve Jobs.

6.20 LUST OBJECT

With the industry leader now in the stable, Apple set out to scoop up the rest of the software industry. To do so, it embarked on a unique program that, in its own way, was as innovative and far-reaching in its influence as the Mac itself. The Mac group had hired a new marketing manager, Mike Murray, with a charter to use any trick he knew to round up third-party developers. The best gimmick he came up with was to hire people for the sole purpose of being true believers in the Macintosh and in Apple. They would be "evangelists," and the most famous was the third one Murray hired (and who devised the name): Guy Kawasaki.

Kawasaki would not only prove to be a brilliant evangelist for the Mac; he would take those skills (he had a unique talent at being both supremely sincere and ironic at the same time—"I know this is bullshit and so do you, but it's also the truth"—that was like St. Paul giving you a knowing wink as he ushered you through the Pearly Gates) and turn them into a philosophy of marketing. He wrote a best-selling book on the subject, *The Macintosh Way*, and went on to become one of the most popular business speakers of the 1990s. The *San Jose Mercury News* would write that Kawasaki had achieved the final breakthrough in high-tech business: from selling almost nothing (semiconductors) to nothing (software) and now less than nothing—enthusiasm!

But in 1983 software evangelism was an unknown profession trying to sell an unknown product to a skeptical market. That the evangelists succeeded, and brilliantly, is a testament to both their skills and the Mac itself. The patter of the evangelists almost always fell on deaf ears until the developers finally sat down in front of a Mac prototype . . . at which point all the extravagant claims almost seemed too humble. As the first evangelist would say after a few months of successful pitching, "People were uniformly blown away. I remember one guy who had just designed what he thought was a good accounting program. After seeing the Mac, he felt like he had just designed the best propeller in the world, then saw a jet fly by."

Even Apple competitors, such as software companies committed to the PC world, tipped their hats at what they saw. Mitch Kapor, the founder of Lotus Development Corp. in Cambridge, Massachusetts, whose spreadsheet product, Lotus 1-2-3, would soon wipe out VisiCalc and dominate the PC world, met the Apple representatives with "I'd sell my mother to get a Mac." A few weeks later he would give Levy the definitive epigram of the era:

"The IBM is a machine you can respect. The Macintosh is a machine you can love."

Lotus immediately set to work designing a spreadsheet program, to be called Jazz, for the Mac.

Kapor wasn't alone. Scores of other software developers fell in love with the Mac the moment they saw it. It was a glimpse of what would come when the first Macs hit retail stores. Two of those developers were independently pursuing their own visions of what the computer of the future should be. One, legendary programmer John Warnock, had founded in Silicon Valley a collegelike company called Adobe to develop fonts and typefaces that would give computer output a more professional, printshop-like appearance.

The other, Paul Brainerd, driven and difficult where Warnock was professorial and avuncular, was chasing a complementary idea: software that would allow the user to mix text and graphics on the personal computer in a format that would look the same on the printed page as it did on the display. This "what you see is what you get" (WYSIWYG) technology was dependent upon the advent of low-cost laser printers—and Brainerd was betting his company, Aldus, that Moore's Law would deliver those printers to him in time.

Like the many others, Warnock and Brainerd saw in the Mac the launch pad for their dreams. They would be too late for the Mac introduction. But within a year, the pair would return the gift of the Mac by being the answer to Steve Jobs's prayers. Together, they gave the Mac its desperately needed Killer Application, *desktop publishing*. And that in turn would forever change the relationship between owners and their computers.

6.21 CHICLETS

After endless delays, the Macintosh introduction was formally set for Tuesday, January 24, 1984. The Ridley Scott commercial, which alone had cost $500,000, was to be placed, for another $1 million, in the third quarter of the broadcast of the Los Angeles Raiders–Washington Redskins Super Bowl.

There was no going back now. For three years, Jobs had driven the team on using every gambit he knew. He had even been reduced to that cliché of every second-rate manager: the slogan. These slogans would appear, sometimes unannounced, sometimes part of a pep talk, on an easel in the Mac offices. The first, *"It's better to be a pirate than join the Navy,"* was his final co-option of the Raskin philosophy. Another, *"The journey is the reward,"* was Jobs's old Buddhism at work (and the title of his biography). Another, written a year before the introduction, was a reminder that the time for innovation was over and the time for completing the project had begun: *"Real artists ship."*

Of course it was pure hokum. Jobs knew it and so did the Mac team members. They might joke that it was hard to be a pirate when you worked for the Admiral of the Navy; that it was easy to say the journey was the reward when your net worth was $300 million, not $30,000; and that the real artists would have shipped a year ago if Jobs hadn't changed his mind so many times—but even as they joked, they also believed the truths behind those slogans. One of Steve Jobs's greatest traits was that he was willing to be absurd, and he never used that skill better than now.

The final three months leading up to the introduction were madness. First there was the Finder program. That solved, Apple itself suddenly became an impediment. The company had smugly predicted $1 billion in sales for the Lisa and had geared up its corporate infrastructure accordingly. Manufacturing capacity was increased with a new factory, 3,000 new employees were hired and millions were spent on point-of-sale materials, advertising and sales support. So convinced was the group that the Lisa would run over both the business market and the rest of Apple that it even held meetings at nearby De Anza Junior College to discuss whether Apple should change its name to something "a little more corporate."

In the first few months after the Lisa's introduction, as the orders poured in and exceeded the company's backlog, it seemed as if all the predictions for the product's success were coming true. There seemed no need to rein in.

But by June 1983, disaster appeared on the horizon as quickly as a summer storm. Lisa orders slumped. The new factory, now with overcapacity, was forced to sit idle. New hirings were frozen and a few employees with bad performance reviews were fired. For the fourth quarter ended September 30, Apple's profits plunged 80 percent, from $25 million to $5 million, and the company's stock went with it, falling from $31.50 (reflecting a two-for-one split) per share in June to $23 in October.

IBM, for once with perfect timing, dropped a bomb that summer: the introduction of the IBM PC XT, a more powerful second-generation machine. The PC XT was ideally suited to run Lotus 1-2-3, the now preeminent business spreadsheet program. Small and large businesses flocked to IBM. By autumn the company had passed Apple in total personal computer market share, 28 percent to 23 percent. The Intel-Microsoft architecture had now taken the industry leadership from Apple . . . and would never give it back.

Apple responded as best it could with an old beloved computer and a young unwanted one. It redoubled its marketing of the II and hurried development of a new generation, the IIc. It also expanded the dealer base, unbundled the software and slashed the price of the Lisa. It only helped a little. The company went into the critical Christmas season praying that its old workhorse, the Apple II, still had enough momentum to keep the company profitable. If it failed, the big Macintosh introductory splash would have to be canceled. And no one wanted to say it but that might be the beginning of the end of the company.

There was no shortage of skeptics. Soon after the PC XT introduction, several trade magazines (presaging the flood to come) called upon Apple to admit the jig was up, abandon its new operating system and join the growing army of IBM clone makers. The company could still win, they said, on marketing, software and design.

Though Apple never seriously accepted that possibility (not with the Mac waiting in the wings), even the more thoughtful minds in the company had to agree with the industry observers that a turning point had occurred with

IBM's rise to industry leadership. And everyone in the industry waited for what was generally agreed would be the final, decisive battle in October. Then, it was rumored, Big Blue would introduce a new budget consumer computer that would do to the low end of the market what the PC XT was now doing to the high end. With that victory, IBM would enjoy complete industry hegemony.

As autumn rolled around, everyone held their breath. Was the game already over?

No. The new computer, the IBM PCjr, was . . . a turd. It was so awful, the press actually ridiculed it, something that never before happened with an IBM product. Underpowered, with a mediocre screen, not enough software and a horrifyingly inept keyboard full of cheap and barely functional keys—"chiclets" one industry wag described them (and, to IBM's horror, the nickname stuck).

But Big Blue wasn't used to failure. It was used to power. So the company spent $50 million promoting its new machine, complete with ads featuring the now tiresome Little Tramp. The campaign and the product failed miserably. The PCjr became synonymous with condescending product design.

The game was still on.

It was, for Apple, the first good news in a long time. The PCjr had not stolen the Mac's thunder or the II's market—instead, it had created a void, a hunger, for truly *personal* computers that were both powerful and easy to use.

Just as important, the cratering of the PCjr also gave Regis McKenna one last lesson. Operation Crush had taught him the value of selling a complete experience, as opposed to merely a product. The II and the Lisa had shown him the new power of key industry opinion leaders. Now, with the PCjr he was given a demonstration that, unlike, say, selling Pepsi-Cola, in PCs no amount of company prestige or money spent on mass promotion could counter the power of those opinion leaders. Dick Shaffer and Ben Rosen, as well as a new generation of cocky trade press reporters like John Dvorak, were now more powerful than all the advertising in the world. Regis would remember that as the Mac introduction approached.

But even as the auguries pointed toward a major Mac introduction, the company hesitated. Would there be enough money? Had the failure of the PCjr sufficiently sullied IBM to make the mainstream market take a second look at the II? Or had it simply scared everyone off?

Then a second roadblock. The executive team showed the new Macintosh "1984" commercial to the Apple board of directors. The opinion was unanimous: they hated it. Worse, several of the outside directors thought that it was the single worst television commercial they had ever seen.

The response was probably not surprising. Dr. Henry Singleton, the legendary founder of the conglomerate Teledyne; venture capital giant Arthur Rock; Peter O. Crisp, managing partner of Venrock Associates venture capital; and Philip S. Schlein, CEO of Macy's California were not exactly young men weaned in the Age of Television. What was amazing was the extraordinary vehemence with which this notoriously passive board expressed itself. (The following conversation was recorded by John Sculley.)

"Steve," one board member asked, "you're not really going to run that thing, are you?"

"We haven't made a final decision on it yet, but we had planned to run it on the Super Bowl."

"How much does that cost?"

"About a million dollars," said Mike Murray, the Mac's new marketing manager."

"Oh my God!"

Apple's management finally agreed to tell Chiat/Day to try to sell the Super Bowl spot. And that if it couldn't be sold *and* if the II had a good Christmas season, *then* Apple would go ahead and run the ad.

In the end the company could only sell the spot for half price and the II, perhaps benefiting from the combination of the incredible amount of promotion for the PCjr and the bad reviews for the product itself, had a terrific Christmas—110,000 computers sold for a total of $160 million. The Mac commercial and the big kickoff event were given the green light. The Macintosh era of Apple would get the roaring start it deserved.

6.22 IGNORANCE IS STRENGTH

The "1984" commercial ran as scheduled for the one and only time to a wide audience (it was actually shown to a small midwestern audience in December to make it eligible for awards) during the third quarter of the Super Bowl.

Wozniak, with characteristic naiveté, nearly wrecked the plan. Invited to appear on *Good Morning America* a few days before the Super Bowl, he decided to take a copy of the commercial with him to show on the air. Luckily, he was caught in time.

Apple had wanted to make a splash with "1984." What it got was Eniwetok. The biggest single splash in the history of television advertising. Only one other commercial had ever had such an impact from a single showing, and that was the infamous Johnson political attack ad against Barry

Goldwater showing a little girl pulling petals off a daisy as the voice-over began the countdown to a nuclear explosion.

On this Sunday afternoon in the winter of 1984, 43 million Americans saw the corporate analog of that infamous commercial. The bleak, gulag-like world. Big Brother on the screen intoning:

> "My friends, each of you is a single cell in the great body of the State. And today, that great body has purged itself of parasites. We have triumphed over the unprincipled dissemination of fact. The thugs and wreckers have been cast out. And the poisonous weeds of disinformation have been consigned to the dustbin of history. Let each and every cell rejoice! For today we celebrate the first, glorious anniversary of the Information Purification Directive. We have created, for the first time in all history, a garden of pure ideology, where each worker may bloom secure from the pests of contradictory and confusing truths. Our Unification of Thought is a more powerful weapon than any fleet or army on earth. We are one people. With one will. One resolve. One cause. Our enemies shall talk themselves to death. And we will bury them with their own confusion . . ."

If it was gibberish, it was also just coherent enough for the audience to understand. Never before had a major U.S. corporation been described in such a way: evil, brainwashing, antidemocratic, totalitarian. Hundreds of thousands of jaws across America dropped in unison.

And then the Avenging Angel ran on-screen in her tank top and gym shorts. She flung her hammer, shattering the projected visage of Big Brother, unleashing a windstorm of shattered glass—stunning and awakening the sleepwalking prisoners like a shaft of sunlight bursting into Plato's Cave.

Then the final voice-over: "On January 24, Apple Computer will introduce Macintosh. 1984 won't be like 1984."

In ten million households from coast to coast there was a collective gasp, then, echoing the on-air words of one of the sports announcers, "Wow, what was *that?*"

6.23 THE MOST FAMOUS COMPANY IN THE WORLD

The next day, the world was still talking about it. It was on the evening news. Millions of unfortunate people who had been in the kitchen or bathroom at the moment still claimed they saw it, so as not to be left out. In one minute's time, Apple, still a cult company to much of the consuming world, had become the coolest place on earth.

It was, indeed, insanely great. The commercial, which would never be broadcast again, thus adding to its legend, would go on to be the first American commercial to win a Grand Prix award at Cannes.

Now Apple needed a closer: the formal introduction on Tuesday. The commercial had primed the marketplace. It had done everything Jobs had wanted for it. Now he had the chance to capture the culture itself.

With the help of Regis McKenna, a willing press and a perfect historical window, he did it. The Mcintosh introduction was the great set piece of the digital age. All others that aspire to the title are in some way deeply flawed. The Windows 95 introduction eleven years later drew thousands to all-night vigils in computer store parking lots around the world. But it was an act of submission: desperate users awaiting the largesse of a monopoly. The Intel Pentium Bug debacle certainly shook the electronics world and beyond, reminding the semiconductor industry that it was now a global consumer force, with all the responsibilities that flowed from that role — but it was also essentially a boneheaded screwup.

The Macintosh introduction, by comparison, was uplifting, transcendent. Sitting there in the Flint Center auditorium on the De Anza College campus, just a block from Apple's first office, there was the sense of being part of history, of being present at a thrilling discontinuity in the story of computing. *This* was what a computer was supposed to be. Plucky little Apple, already being written off by industry cynics, had somehow managed to jump to its feet and throw a fast one right into the chin of the biggest, baddest corporate goliath of all. You couldn't help but laugh, it was so outrageous. And then the computer itself turned out to be so goddamned *cute*.

It really was a turning point. Before the Macintosh, electronics companies were institutions that aspired to the stature and gravity of their manufacturing counterparts. When they introduced products, it was almost always at a staid press conference before an audience of tech insiders who looked at the spec sheet before they looked at the product itself. After Macintosh, every tech company, to prove that its product was important, was forced to create some sort of extravaganza, develop a unique logo and motif and try to link its product to the train of history.

But they would never pull it off. They couldn't, because no matter how great the product or how elaborate the promotion, those later companies could never recapture the delirious shock of experiencing such a moment for the first time. Even Apple would fail in the years to come to conjure up the old magic, until near the end its big events became only sad, forced parodies of the past.

Flint Center could hold two thousand people, but the event drew only about half that—less than attended a travelogue a few days before. But the empty balcony was nearly invisible, so the room seemed full. Of the crowd, fully half were Apple employees serving as shills. But that was still more people than any comparable event before, and those non-Appleites who were there were the cream of high-tech investment, analysis and reporting. Regis had seen to that, and he had made sure that each had received a packet containing not only a press kit but other freebies, notably a T-shirt with a cleverly simplified (and groundbreaking) graphic of the Mac.

The day before, during rehearsals, the dark side of Steve Jobs had emerged. He belittled the hardworking stagehands, yelling at their every mistake while flubbing his own lines over and over. He changed his speech, tossed out and reinserted slides and generally cast a pall over the proceedings. More than one Apple employee left Flint that night praying the next day wouldn't be a complete disaster.

But it was the other Steve who stood behind the curtains the next day. He privately confessed, "This is the most important moment of my entire life. I can't tell you how I feel. It's the most incredible thing I've ever had to go through and I'm really nervous."

Then he walked out from behind the curtains, apparently calm, with the smirk so tiny that it seemed less contemptuous than ironic at the sheer unlikeliness of it all. This was the new Steve Jobs, only a decade but a million years from the smelly ascetic, now sleek and chic, wearing a double-breasted, European-cut charcoal-gray suit and a bright red bow tie that managed to look at once intellectual, revolutionary and arch. He cut a striking figure, one that was nearly as significant to the audience as the product he was about to introduce: *Jobs is going for it!*

There was a murmur of expectation. Then Jobs, the last child of the 1960s, began to recite Bob Dylan's famous lines about "the times they are a-changing" for the last famous time.

It was a tocsin to the Woodstock generation: *Don't sell out! Don't forget the dream! Stay free!* And in that hall filled with boomers, both from Apple and from the press, most of them now with babies and first mortgage payments, receding hairlines and business suits, a thrill shot through a thousand hearts. *Yes! We've been sleepwalking. Wake us up!* There was a hush of expectation. Where will the Pied Piper lead us?

But Jobs had already slipped backstage. The audience, ready to rise up and rush the stage, instead had to sit impatiently through the company's annual meeting. Quarterly earnings and announcements of new facilities and joint ventures. Yeah yeah yeah blah blah blah. Even the reporters put down their notebooks. They could get all this financial garbage off the press release. *Where's Steve?*

Then, as suddenly as he had disappeared, he was back, gleaming in the white spotlight. He spoke with the disarming, confiding earnestness he used for his biggest seductions. His head was cocked just slightly, his body rigid, but his arms and hands punctuated every sentence. He began almost lightly, but, feeding off the embrace of the audience, seemed to grow more confident and powerful with each paragraph. He was twenty-nine years old and this was the greatest moment of his life:

"It is 1958. IBM passes up the chance to buy a young, fledgling company that has just invented a new technology called xerography. Two years later, Xerox is born, and IBM has been kicking itself ever since.

"It is ten years later, the late 1960s. Digital Equipment Corporation and others invent the minicomputer. IBM dismisses the minicomputer as too small to do serious computing and, therefore, unimportant to its business. DEC grows to become a multi-hundred-million dollar corporation before IBM finally enters the minicomputer market.

"It is now ten years later, the late 1970s. In 1977, Apple, a young fledgling company on the West Coast, invents the Apple II, the first personal computer as we know it today. IBM dismisses the personal computer as too small to do serious computing and therefore unimportant to its business.

"The early 1980s—1981. Apple II has become the world's most popular computer, and Apple has grown to a $300 million corporation, becoming the fastest-growing company in American business history. With over fifty companies vying for a share, IBM enters the personal computer market in November of 1981 with the IBM PC.

"1983. Apple and IBM emerge as the industry's strongest competitors, each selling approximately $1 billion worth of personal computers in 1983.

". . . The shakeout is in full swing. The first major firm goes bankrupt, with others teetering on the brink. Total industry losses for 1983 overshadow even the combined profits of Apple and IBM for personal computers.

"It is now 1984. It appears IBM wants it all. Apple is perceived to be the only hope to offer IBM a run for its money. Dealers, initially welcoming IBM with open arms, now fear an IBM-dominated and -controlled future. They are increasingly turning back to Apple as the only force that can ensure their future freedom . . ."

Jobs paused, as if steeling himself for the enormity of the task ahead. He looked out at the audience, as if asking them to join him at the battlements of computing freedom. Then his voice dropped a half octave, as if at the sheer magnitude of corporate evil. Oh the humanity . . .

"IBM wants it all and is aiming its guns on its last obstacle to industry control, Apple. Will Big Blue dominate the entire computer industry, the entire information age? Was George Orwell right?"

"No!" shouted the audience. "No!" shouted the first five rows, filled with the Apple team. "No!" shouted the other Apple employees and the analysts and the distributors and dealers and retailers and shareholders. No! said the assembled journalists secretly to themselves.

Steve Jobs smiled. Enough with that Zen bullshit about the "journey being the reward." *This* was the reward.

He walked over to a table bearing an ominous-looking bag. With a flourish, Jobs unzipped it . . . and there, the color of brown stone, like a little primitive totem, a friendly phallus, was the Macintosh. An appreciative murmur went up from the crowd. It was instantly drowned out by the amplified theme from the movie *Chariots of Fire*. It was corny, but nevertheless spine-tingling.

"Today," intoned Steve Jobs, "for the first time ever, I'd like to let Macintosh speak for itself." That couldn't be true: Apple had never actually tested speech synthesis on the Mac until this moment. But what the hell, go with the flow. It was all too exciting to quibble.

Jobs touched a key, and in a quivering little voice—its very crudeness perfect in its antithesis to Big Brother—the Mac announced:

"Hello, I am Macintosh. It sure is great to get out of that bag. Unaccustomed as I am to public speaking, I'd like to share with you a thought that occurred to me the first time I met an IBM mainframe. Never trust a computer you can't lift. But right now I'd like to sit back and listen. So it is with considerable pride that I introduce a man who has been like a father to me, Steve Jobs."

"Like a father" was the appropriate phrase, as Mac's real father was at that moment living in the Santa Cruz mountains. And it was a bit cheesy to even steal Jef Raskin's line about not trusting computers you can't lift. But it didn't matter. The crowd laughed and cheered—even those in the front row who knew better.

It went on like this for another twenty minutes, losing momentum by the minute. After all, how could you top the introduction of one of the greatest products of the century? Still, those final depleted minutes did manage to establish a second turning point in the history of personal computing: this was the day the press, especially the computer trade press, formally and publicly, sold out.

It was hard to resist. After all, Apple was now the underdog, and the press loves underdogs. And the Macintosh represented such an unbelievable comeback. And IBM was a tight-assed pain to deal with, with its PR department keeping a database on every reporter and firing off angry notes every time you suggested the company was bigger than the corner drugstore—while Apple was young and brash and answered the phone and was always good for a quote. And almost everybody in the press owned an Apple at home even though they had to use IBMs in the newsroom. And, not least, Apple bought a lot of advertising pages, especially in the last month.

It was just so easy to succumb. And never more so than at this moment of triumph for Apple. Onstage, the company introduced the publisher of a new, purportedly independent magazine called *MacWorld*, dedicated entirely to the Macintosh. It was an amazing moment in modern journalism, and nobody seemed to notice. On the contrary, the reporters reminded themselves to get subscriptions.

If the electronics trade magazines, dependent upon Apple advertising revenues, finally revealed themselves as lickspittles at the Mac introduction, the general press was only slightly more reserved. Esther Dyson, who had taken over Ben Rosen's newsletter and was on her way to becoming the preeminent opinion maker in personal computing, actually sat through the event wearing her free Mac T-shirt. The story passed around that she had changed into it while driving down from the San Francisco Airport—to the entertainment of men in nearby cars. Other writers were discreet enough to wait until they got home before putting on, literally and journalistically, Mac shirts of their own.

Then it was over. Jobs, drained and tearfully happy, made his way back behind the curtain. "It's really happened," he said. "Mac is a real product now."

The press rushed the stage, where Apple representatives, from publicists to Art Rock, held forth in little clusters of reporters. When will the Mac be available? What different configurations are available? How much market share do you think you can take back from IBM?

In one of the largest of these clusters, Regis McKenna held forth. "Where are the cursor keys?" asked a reporter. "It doesn't have any cursor keys." "I know," said Regis, reliving an argument he'd had a few months before. "I tried to talk them into it. But they wanted a mouse and a mouse alone." He shrugged and smiled, as if to say: I know it's nuts, but what are you going to do? It's Apple.

By now, the January afternoon had turned gray. The reporters rushed off to file their stories. The Apple staffers wandered back down the street to their offices. And no one had the slightest doubt that a new era had begun.

7.0 EARLY HARVEST

7.1 ENIGMA

There was one other figure onstage at the Macintosh launch. A protean figure so elusive that everyone in the computer industry had already invested him with their hopes and fears for Apple Computer. And they were right to do so, because unbeknownst to them (and to himself) he had already made a series of decisions that would guide Apple's future and seal its fate.

John Sculley had been with Apple now for nine months—nearly a year if you included his rounds of job interviews. He had even been with Jobs at the Chiat/Day premiere of the 1984 commercial. Yet he still remained largely an enigma both inside and outside of the company.

It was Sculley who shook Jobs's hand just before he stepped out from behind the curtain, and it was Sculley, Apple's new CEO, who took over the middle of the presentation to talk to the assembled shareholders about the company's financials. And it was John Sculley, now in the cockpit of, for the moment, the most exciting corporation in the world, who broke from his prepared text to say, "The most important thing that has happened to me in these nine months has been the chance to develop a friendship with Steve Jobs. The two of us have had tremendous challenges together in leading this company, and the rapport and friendship that have developed between us mean an awful lot."

At the time, the comment was a minor note in the major chord of the Mac introduction. Most people assembled weren't really listening. Rather, for many it was a first public glimpse of the East Coast businessman Jobs had lured to run Apple. They noted his thin runner's form, so skinny that his clothes seemed to hang from his skeleton, and his face—hawkish like Jobs's, but less bland, pale and Yankee. A chicken hawk to Jobs's falcon.

Yet, in retrospect, those first, ostensibly impromptu remarks were vintage John Sculley. Sensitive and personal to the brink of tears, unexpectedly passive for a corporate executive and, behind it all, calculating. The hidden message of the remark, unexpected even to the people running the cue cards, was: *I am now Steve Jobs's equal in this company. I am his new friend. I may be new, but I have more power than anyone here.* And to Jobs, standing behind the screen, who amazingly said to Sculley at the rehearsal the night before, "I think of you just like Woz and Markkula. You're like one of the founders of the company. They founded the company, but you and I are founding the future," the comment carried a personal message: *"See, I think so highly of our new friendship that I'm willing to tell the world about it."*

The greatest corporate politician in American business had just given a brilliant lesson in his craft, and the audience, being largely Silicon Valleyites, was too inexperienced and naive to notice.

7.2 CHALLENGE

It was the day before Thanksgiving 1982 when John Sculley received a call from a headhunter.

Sculley had gotten these calls many times before and rarely returned them. But this one was from the best in the business, Gerry Roche, chairman of Heidrick & Struggles. Roche had called before, each time with an intriguing offer: the presidency of Norton Simon cosmetics, chairmanship of NBC, CEO of Warner-Amex. But Sculley had always passed. "Pepsi," he would later write in his memoirs, "was my life . . . I made the company my extended family. The mere thought of entertaining another job would have provoked the angst of a personal separation or divorce." And he wasn't kidding: Sculley had once even been married to the chairman's daughter.

John Sculley's life to that point had been one of great success, but also of competing, and opposing, forces. His father was a stern and demanding Wall Street lawyer, his mother a free-spirited native Bermudan with an artistic bent. Each contributed to their son's character. As a toddler, Sculley had enjoyed the tropical freedom of trips to Bermuda, but as a boy he had been sent first to the prestigious Buckley School in Manhattan, then as a teenager to board at St. Mark's in Southboro, Massachusetts.

The struggle of countervailing forces in John Sculley's life, and increasingly in his personality, probably made its first appearance in a painful stammer the young man developed as a child. He was cured as a teenager by hypnosis. But without a doubt the tension was still there when the time came for young John to choose a college. When he told his father he wanted to attend an art school, the old man was furious. "I sent you to one of the finest preparatory schools in the country. I sacrificed everything. You've had every advantage in life and you don't even want to go to college. You want to study design. I can't believe it."

If Steve Jobs's father had given him almost infinite latitude, John Sculley's old man brought down the whole weight of family tradition and parental guilt to constrain his son. And young John, having long since learned to defuse a challenge by diplomacy and compromise, agreed to go to Brown University, but only if he could attend the nearby Rhode Island School of Design at night. Then he did it again by earning an MBA from Wharton, but afterward going into advertising.

Alongside the battle between good son and renegade aesthete, there was a second one taking place in John Sculley's soul between business and science. Although this other part of his youth was considerably exaggerated once Apple's PR department got its hands on the story, it was a fact that as a boy John had been a bit of an electronics bug. He apparently got it from his maternal grandfather, a wild inventor and adventurer. Sculley would later claim, Woz-like, that as a boy he would wake up early in the morning to read *The Radio Amateur's Handbook* until it became dog-eared. If that seems dubious, there is the fact that by ten he was rewiring radios, by eleven was a ham radio operator and by fourteen (in 1954) had designed a single-gun television tube not unlike what would become the Sony Trinitron. His father helped him apply for a patent, but the boy was beaten out by only a few weeks by Ernest Lawrence, of Lawrence Livermore Laboratories fame.

But by the time he departed for Brown and RISD, John Sculley had left electronics far behind. Like his two brothers (who would later make their names as president of H. J. Heinz USA and senior vice president of Morgan Guaranty), John abandoned the passions of his youth to make his way in the business world. While still at Brown he met and married the stepdaughter of Don Kendall, soon to be Pepsi's CEO. It was Kendall who convinced Sculley to abandon his dream of a graduate degree from the Penn School of Architecture and go to Wharton.

After a four-year stint at an advertising agency doing competitive research for Coca-Cola (he neglected to tell anyone that he was the son-in-law of the head of Pepsi) and a divorce (which didn't seem to dent his relationship with Kendall), John finally went to work for his ex-father-in-law's company.

He thrived, soon gaining a reputation as the company's hottest new star — and also one of its most devious corporate politicians and hatchet men. At thirty, he was the youngest vice president in the company's history. He was not well liked, and as he would himself admit, was lousy at handling people.

But even those at Pepsi who disliked him had to admit that John Sculley was some kind of demon marketing man. Over the next few years he would prove himself one of the best American industry had ever seen.

No battle in American business history has been as protracted or vicious as that between Coca-Cola and Pepsi. For nearly a century, the two companies have beaten up each other in the marketplace, cheering a percentage point shift in market share as either a magnificent victory or a crushing defeat.

In this competitive marketplace, Pepsi had always been the also-ran. And it didn't look like the status quo would change for another century—not when Pepsi's current ad slogan, "The taste that beats the others cold," was up against Coke's landmark "The Real Thing."

But Sculley had his own ideas. For a start, he committed the ultimate marketing sin of revivifying a marginally successful marketing campaign the company had abandoned a few years before—"The Pepsi Generation." Next, he added the incoherent, but catchy tag line "You've got a lot to live and Pepsi's got a lot to give."

This was lifestyle marketing just at the moment baby boomers became independent consumers. Coke, still playing off its history and tradition, was caught with its pants down. And Sculley didn't stop. He spent millions on advertising filled with vignettes of the youth culture. And he backed up this fluff with some hard reengineering of point-of-sale presentations, a reorganization of the company's reporting structure and a redirected emphasis on important new retail channels, such as drugstore chains. The result, beginning in 1970, was a record three and half years of continuous gains in market share.

It was a remarkable achievement, though in the process Sculley had become notorious in the company for tearing through one subordinate after another. So, for this combination of ruthlessness and creative brilliance, Sculley was "rewarded" (many in the company thought it a demotion) with the job of running Pepsi's screwed-up and unprofitable international foods division.

He then spent nearly four years traveling the world, putting out fires everywhere he went. He shut down some operations and rebuilt others. In some countries, he focused on manufacturing, in others on marketing and brand awareness. It was exciting stuff. And in the process, Sculley built a kind of SWAT team of talented people who traveled with him, ready to deal with anything they encountered. Over the months this team became very tight-knit, and Sculley, for the first time submerging his personality into a team, was enthralled.

Once again he succeeded brilliantly, turning an $83 million business with annual losses of $16 million into a $300 million business turning an annual pretax profit of $40 million. Sculley himself was so happy where he was that he repeatedly turned down entreaties from headquarters to come home.

Finally he relented. "The thought of having to be confined in the United States was terribly demoralizing. It just wasn't what I wanted to do with my life." But he was a company man, so he came home. He politely endured a comment from Kendall about getting his hair cut. He married again (for the third time), to Leezy Hersh, the divorced wife of a senior Pepsi marketing executive.

It was not a happy time for John Sculley. He missed the globe-trotting, the independence of making his own decisions. He missed being part of a close-knit group. His new wife was the target of a hissing campaign by other company wives, who saw her as trading her way up from a vice president to a company president. And worst of all, he was trapped in the backstabbing political life of corporate headquarters—a world in which he was a master, but now found distasteful.

So, the answer was to go back to his first love: marketing.

Before he left for International, Sculley had commissioned some studies comparing the responses to Pepsi and Coca-Cola in a taste test. The results were stunning: Pepsi not only won the majority of these tests, it came close to winning them all. Time would show this had as much to do with a momentary reaction to the greater sweetness of Pepsi, but as raw data this was dynamite. Unfortunately, the company only saw it as a firecracker. While Sculley was overseas, the company used this data to construct a last-ditch marketing campaign for Pepsi in its weakest domestic market, Texas, where Pepsi had just a 7 percent market share. Even then, the campaign was a largely renegade effort, driven by the company's executive vice president for bottling and his own vice president of marketing, the future Mrs. Sculley's ex-husband. They even hired a local advertising agency.

The result was the Pepsi Challenge, in which local residents, seemingly live on television, were invited to blind-test the two major colas. Pepsi, as expected, nearly always won. That much wasn't particularly new—competitors in different industries had advertised similar tests for decades. The real innovation was that the Pepsi Texas team then took the Challenge out to the streets, inviting anyone and everyone to taste tests at local fairs, supermarkets and other public locations.

It was a smashing success. Pepsi gained market share wherever the Challenge was held. So pleased was the company that it expanded the Challenge to several other southern states where Pepsi had nothing to lose. But there it stopped. After all, the reasoning went, it was one thing to use the Pepsi

Challenge in markets where the company had nothing to lose, but why would you risk the company's market share on the vox populi in regions where Pepsi was the leader? What if you held the Challenge in, say, Illinois and everybody picked Coke?

That likely would have been the end of it, except that John Sculley had come home from the world to PepsiCo headquarters in Purchase, New York, as Pepsi's youngest president. He saw in the Challenge a way not just to build sales in losing markets but to expand them in winning ones.

It was a dangerous strategy. Wiser heads at headquarters objected. Bottlers, fearing kicking off a price war that would undermine with falling profits whatever was gained in market share, complained angrily. But Sculley had a sense that America had changed. Watergate, Vietnam and the 1960s were behind it; now the consuming public wanted wide-open, honest competition. He pushed ahead, forming SWAT teams that raced around the country (usually followed by camera crews) holding Challenges. Only once did Sculley make a mistake—he took the Challenge himself at the Daytona 500 and picked Coke—but luckily no camera crews were present that day.

The Pepsi Challenge was one of the great marketing successes. For months, it was a hot topic throughout the country, a fad that was also a marketing program. One reason for its success, Sculley would admit later, was that it blurred the line between news and public relations. "Event publicity" it was called, a technique that Steve Jobs, working with Regis McKenna, would discover on his own a few years later. There was another factor as well: although, thanks to the Challenge, Pepsi enjoyed a remarkable market-share jump in an industry that was considered all but frozen in the status quo, most of those gains came not from Coca-Cola but from lesser brands. Against mighty Coke, a situation comparable to Apple against IBM, Pepsi could still barely make a dent. Coke drinkers were unshakable in their loyalty.

But what the Challenge did accomplish against Coke was to throw the venerable giant off its game. Coke's public reaction to the Challenge was almost hysterical. It accused Pepsi of trying to destroy the industry; it tried to distract the market with various forms of advertising chaff; it called for a moratorium on taste tests. Basically, Coke went nuts—and just how nuts would not be known for several years. That's because Coke executives, obsessed with the Challenge, ordered a newer, sweeter Coca-Cola that could win the challenge. The result was New Coke, easily the worst new-product marketing debacle of modern times, greater even than the PCjr. Thus, the Pepsi Challenge almost, but not quite, destroyed one of the world's most successful consumer companies. It was a near-victory not lost on the rest of the world, even on the young chairman of a computer company in Silicon

Valley facing the same competitive scenario. Jobs thought that if IBM could similarly be knocked off balance, there still might be a chance to reorder the industry.

7.3 ODYSSEY

In 1978, after decades of ferocious competition and pitched battles around the world, Pepsi for the first time passed Coca-Cola as the market leader. It was an extraordinary moment, and much of the success could be credited to the Pepsi-Cola's young president John Sculley. He was now a celebrated figure on the business scene. A marketing legend in his own time. A cover story in *Business Week*. An object of awe within his company. He was even on good terms with his ex-father-in-law, PepsiCo CEO Don Kendall, considered one of the toughest bosses anywhere.

He had it all. And for the next four years he stayed at the top of his game: extending the Challenge, beating Coke to market with a caffeine-free product, carving into Coca-Cola's ownership of beverage sales to fast-food chains. His third marriage also appeared to be going well.

But, like the clichéd plot of some midlife-crisis novel of the era, beneath it all John Sculley was restless and unhappy. Entering his forties, he found the old conflict was still there. He was a thinker, an artist, a creator, not just a businessman. Sure, he could devise amazing marketing campaigns, but was that all he was put on this earth to do?

It was an existential crisis faced by many middle-aged business executives at the peak of their careers. Some cure it with new mansions, new wives or new hobbies that scare the bejesus out of insurance underwriters. But in the end, most get over it. John Sculley would have likely done the same by, say, underwriting a PBS series on technology, and gone on to a distinguished career at the company that had been his life. Instead, at his most vulnerable moment, when he himself didn't yet know what was wrong, the young piper appeared at the gates of Pepsi and lured him away.

Sculley paid his first visit to Apple in December, a week before Christmas, not realizing that was always an important time for the company. This was, in fact, the same period when Burrell Smith was preparing to squirrel himself away on the new Macintosh design.

In *Odyssey*, his earnest and opportunistically self-effacing autobiography (now even more risible in light of subsequent events), Sculley describes that first visit with the Sturm und Drang of a man meeting his fate—an event even more symbolic than he would know:

With a map and a Hertz car, I navigated my way south on Route 280 to Silicon Valley in a downpour so heavy it caused mudslides in the landscape. The strong winds pushed my rented Datsun around the freeway. It was a thirty-mile drive through fog and rain to Apple Computer in Cupertino. . . .

As I came off the freeway exit onto De Anza Boulevard in Cupertino, the first building I saw with the Apple logo in front was the three-story glass-and-concrete Mariani Building. I thought this must be Apple's headquarters building because it was the only large building around. It wasn't.

Instead, the company was headquartered in a much smaller, more modest building on Bandley Drive, which cut through the middle of Apple's hodgepodge campus. At one end of Bandley was the Any Mountain Ski Shop, at the other end a supermarket. In between were a spate of flat, one-story huts from the Taco Bell school of architecture. At each entrance was a redwood sign carved with the company's rainbow-striped Apple emblem.

I was taken aback when I found that Jobs and Markkula were ensconced in a two-story wood-frame building with a shingled roof. It seemed more appropriate as a branch office of an insurance company than the executive office of a fast-rising corporation. Outside the building hung a small employment sign. As I parked the car, I noticed a surprising number of Mercedeses and Porsches in the adjacent parking lot. One sported a license plate with the letters THX APPL . . .

With that storm as a warning, Sculley began his own odyssey. But in his case there would be no return to Ithaca. He was about to fall under the spell of Steve Jobs, the Circe of Computing.

It was a typical Apple day of that era. Everyone was nearly too busy to talk. The Lisa announcement was only a month away, and the place was boiling with nervous anticipation. Sculley had a brief meeting with Markkula, then was taken in to see the *enfant terrible*. Jobs played his role to perfection. He was dressed like a college student, his manner alternately distracted, curt and messianic. At lunch, he was apparently bored by much of what Sculley had to say, then suddenly would focus like a laser beam on his tablemate and launch into a monologue about how Apple would change the world.

It was disorienting stuff, but thrilling to a man who was the ultimate corporate infighter, yet styled himself as a rebel. A cynic might say that even at that first meeting Sculley had seen enough of the flaws in Steve Jobs's character to know how to handle him. But that is probably not true. A more likely explanation was that Jobs, with his amazing intuition, unwittingly and more by what he didn't say, struck John Sculley's most vulnerable point.

Here was a middle-aged man, a great success in his field, who was looking ahead at his career and seeing only more years of the same old thing, trying not to screw up and waiting for the CEO's job to be handed to him like an award for perfect attendance. He was the colonel growing tired of long road to a brigadier's star.

Just as bad, John Sculley had Marketing Man's disease, a syndrome common among marketing professionals, who come to believe that (a) marketing is the key to a corporation's success and (b) therefore no one but the top marketing guy is worthy of becoming CEO. Generations of marketing CEOs screwing up companies because they didn't understand manufacturing, personnel or R&D, had done nothing to cure this illness. And John Sculley had a serious case. Sure, he was president of Pepsi-Cola, but Kendall and PepsiCo still hung over him like an unyielding father. He had come to Apple that December day already with his own notions about how Apple should be run—that is, how it should improve its marketing. A visit to a computer store during the stopover in Los Angeles had convinced him that neither Apple nor any of its competitors really knew how to present computers at the point of sale. And his own frustrating experiences as an Apple II+ owner—"At Pepsi, I found the Apple to be more work to us than it was worth"—further convinced him that he understood the needs of the company's new corporate market better than anyone at Apple did. In fact, so pumped was Sculley when he left the luncheon that on the flight home he drafted an eight-page letter to Jobs outlining just how traditional corporate hierarchies worked and how they presented obstacles to the adoption of personal computers.

A third and final reason Jobs struck home with Sculley had to do with the technology itself. In Jobs's youthful success Sculley saw a chance to rev up his old excitement about his career. And in Jobs's callowness about corporate life Sculley saw a chance to put his awesome marketing skills to work in an exciting new field. But it was in Jobs's enthusiasm about the Lisa (ironically, the project he was no longer part of) that Sculley saw the chance to reignite his own childhood love affair with technology. In the end, Apple was the antithesis of Pepsi, and to his own surprise, that was exactly what John Sculley discovered he wanted.

But wanting and taking are two different matters. And a great corporation politician like John Sculley doesn't make it to the near-summit of corporate life by instantly chasing every dream that catches his fancy. Like a married man in love with a younger woman, Sculley at first denied his obsession even as his days turned increasingly to thoughts of Apple. More and more in his mind Apple came to represent lost youth, the thrill of starting out again, a return to the team spirit of Pepsi International.

It was also fame. Sculley thought he knew what business fame looked like. But Apple was something else. Before his first visit to the company, he had told his stepdaughter that he was meeting with Steve Jobs. She reacted as if he was visiting a rock star. This too was something Pepsi could never provide.

Still, he resisted. On January 12 he agreed to meet with Jobs again, this time in New York City, where Jobs was conducting the Lisa preview tour for the press. Sculley met with Jobs and two other Apple executives for an evening meeting at the Carlyle Hotel. By making Sculley feel like an insider to a secret project, and even more important to Sculley, part of a high-spirited team again, Jobs further set the hook. At the same time, Sculley was sufficiently acute to recognize the simmering tension between John Couch and Jobs, though he as yet didn't know their history. He also noticed that Paul Dali, one of the general managers of the Apple II group and the man on the tour charged with demonstrating the new Apple II+, was all but ignored. Thus, in a matter of a half hour, being the politician he was, Sculley deduced most of the underlying dynamics of Apple Computer.

From the Carlyle, the group made its way to the Four Seasons for dinner. Now it was Sculley's turn to seduce. For more than three hours he conducted a near-monologue on the marketing lessons of Pepsi and how they might apply to high technology. He talked about the positive message of the Pepsi Generation and how it had endured one of the most turbulent eras of American history by conveying a comforting message of optimism. He talked about the Pepsi Challenge and how it complemented that long-standing campaign by adding a personal, empirical dimension. He talked about how the Challenge also represented a new hybrid of advertising, PR and news. That's exactly what we're trying to do with the Lisa, said Jobs and Couch in rare agreement.

Finally, in the crowning moment, Sculley suggested that, if there could be a Pepsi Generation, why couldn't there now be an *Apple Generation?* A silent shock wave rolled around the table.

It was nearly midnight, the restaurant closed and the bored waiters pacing around, when the little group finished and strolled out into the cold night. On the walk back to the hotel, Jobs suddenly turned to Sculley and announced, "This has been one of the most exciting evenings in my whole life. I just can't tell you how much fun I've had tonight." It was a perfect Steve Jobs moment. What made it remarkable was that he wasn't the only one who felt that way. John Sculley too was in a near-swoon. For a few hours he was back in Mexico and Brazil and Sweden with the Pepsi International team. "In some queer way, I felt more kinship with these young renegades from Apple than I did with many of the people I had been working with at Pepsi-Cola for years."

He went back to Pepsi, but now he was a changed man. As he would later write, in an extraordinary admission: "I was one of Kendall's most competitive soldiers, yet after sixteen years of being constantly tested, I was discovering that I didn't enjoy competing, I enjoyed building."

Had Steve Jobs known at the time that these were John Sculley's real feelings, the subsequent history of Apple, Pepsi, Sculley and Jobs might have been entirely different. Sculley, it seems, had a completely misguided view of the personal computer industry—because beneath the teamwork and the innovation and the youthful energy lay one of the most competitive business landscapes of all. The cola battles only *seemed* more competitive; yet so established was the marketplace that even the biggest executive screwup in that business might mean the loss of a point or two of market share. In personal computing, by comparison, you could appear to make all the right decisions and be dead tomorrow. What John Sculley saw as a youthful adventure, a creative experience, was in fact a bloody life-or-death struggle.

Thus, at the very moment when they seemed most simpatico, Jobs and Sculley were actually a world apart. And this mutual lack of understanding foretold disaster.

For now, though, Sculley played hard to get. This wasn't college anymore. He couldn't cut it down the middle, being a buttoned-down Pepsi man during the day and play at Apple at night. He had to choose. And each day that choice got more painful, yet easier to make.

Apple, needless to say, nudged him along. The day after the dinner, headhunter Gerry Roche called to say how thrilled Jobs was about the evening before. Then, every few days thereafter, Roche, Jobs or Markkula, tag-teaming, would call to check in, ask for advice, plumb his feelings about joining Apple—anything to capture Sculley's frame of mind.

After a few weeks, Markkula jumped in his jet and paid a visit to Sculley's imperial offices in an effort to get him to sign on. It was a precipitous moment: the Lisa had just been introduced to acclaim, the computer was *Time*'s Man of the Year and Jobs was on the cover of *Fortune*. Apple, it seemed, had caught the tide of history. Markkula's visit all but screamed: What better time to join the company?

But again Sculley put him off. He would love to advise Apple, be a friend of the company, but he just couldn't imagine ever leaving Pepsi.

Then it was Jobs's turn again. He visited New York a couple of weeks later, on the pretext of getting Sculley's advice on buying an apartment. It was a Sunday afternoon, so the visit began at Sculley's exquisite modern home in

Greenwich. Jobs toured the grounds, met Leezy Sculley, then the pair retired to the library to talk. "Why are you talking to me?" Sculley asked. "Why don't you go talk to somebody at IBM or Hewlett-Packard? Why do you want somebody out of the soft-drink industry? I don't know anything about computers."

A lot of people would ask the same question in the years to come. In reply, Jobs said, "What we're doing has never been done before. We're trying to build a totally different kind of company, and we need really great people. . . . My dream is that every person in the world will have their own Apple computer. To do that, we've got to be a great marketing company."

It was a magnificent answer. A Steve Jobs answer: full of sweeping gestures, flattery, perfectionism and bravado. But it was also a silly, flip answer to a very serious question, the answer of a young man in love with his own romantic poses. Sculley was right to ask: in the history of the electronics industry, no nontechnie had ever successfully taken over the reins of a major company. Hewlett and Packard were technologists, as were Charlie Sporck, Bill Gates, Robert Noyce, Gordon Moore, Ken Olsen, Andy Grove, Jerry Sanders, even Regis McKenna, Nolan Bushnell and Jack Tramiel. The sole exception was Irwin Federman, who successfully ran the midsized Valley chip company Monolithic Memories—but though a finance guy, Federman had spent years at MMI before being given the top spot. Why indeed wasn't Jobs looking for the new Apple CEO at IBM, DEC, HP or one of the hundreds of other computer-oriented technology companies? But if Sculley, to his credit, recognized the flaw in Jobs's approach, it was to his discredit that chose to ignore it and be flattered instead.

The rest of the afternoon took on all the characteristics of teen love. The pair jumped in Sculley's car and raced out to look at PepsiCo's magnificent headquarters building. Jobs acted like a wide-eyed first date as Sculley toured him through the building with its world-class sculptures, fountains and sprawling office suites. Young Steve charmed the older man by being both in awe of and contemptuous of all this corporate ostentatiousness. Then they jumped in the car again and raced over to look at IBM's headquarters, much more anonymous than PepsiCo, but chilling in its excruciating perfection. Sculley explained to Jobs that IBM even sterilized the surrounding trees so that they would blossom but not bear fruit that might rot on the ground. "Rotten fruit are forbidden fruit at world headquarters." The too obvious metaphor was not lost on his young charge, who jokingly suggested that Apple ought to rent a jet to fly in the whole Macintosh division to look at this corporate monstrosity (as if the group had not already seen a corporate monster up close).

Then it was back to Sculley's house, where a limousine was waiting to take Jobs back to Manhattan. Once again, Sculley suggested that Apple ought to make a more focused search in electronics for its new CEO. Once again Jobs ignored him. Back in the house, Sculley asked his wife what she thought of Steve Jobs. "I just don't know," said Leezy Sculley. A thrice-married man should have heard warning signals coming from such a noncommittal answer. But John Sculley's mind was already in the clouds.

7.4 AERIE

A week later, Sculley was in Hawaii to give the keynote speech at the annual convention of several thousand Pepsi bottlers. He had done such a speech many times before at similar events. But this time would be different. As a test, he decided to devote the speech to the computer revolution and its impact on the future of the soft-drink business.

The ostensible subject was how personal computers could improve the productivity of independent bottlers. But the real purpose was for Sculley to see if he really could stand up in front of an audience—as he would every week as Apple CEO—and talk both compellingly and knowledgeably about PCs. The speech was a success. Afterward, the producer of the event found Sculley standing in the wings, crying.

On the way back East, Sculley stopped again in Cupertino. This time Jobs took him to Bandley 3, and there gave Sculley his first look at the Macintosh and the group that had built it. This was the team within the team—Atkinson, Hertzfeld, all the others—a group so eccentric that it left Sculley disoriented. This was beyond anything he had ever known at Pepsi. That too should have been a warning.

Before he left, Sculley stopped by Markkula's office. There, the current CEO made his potential replacement a formal offer: $300,000 in salary and options for 500,000 shares of stock. It was a classic Silicon Valley offer—take a salary cut, but bet on the success you'll help create. Even at the current market price of $36 per share those options (assuming Sculley stayed around long enough for vestment) were worth $18 million.

But for an East Coaster, Markkula's offer came as a rude shock. Almost an insult. Pepsi was currently paying Sculley a $500,000 per year salary. What kind of fool would take a 40 *percent* pay cut? And that wasn't half of it: all the assorted pensions and bonuses at Pepsi came close to doubling that salary figure. Apple didn't give bonuses *and it didn't have a pension plan!* Why

should it? This was Silicon Valley; this was a children's game. Nobody expected to be around long enough to get a ten-year pin from the company,
much less a gold watch. Markkula tried to explain the facts of Valley life, that
if Apple continued to grow as it had the stock would be worth $100 million or
more. But Sculley wasn't listening. Only an idiot would choose to speculate
on the prospect of future wealth rather than nail down a firm salary commitment.

Sculley went home deeply disappointed. He called Gerry Roche and told
him there was no way he was going to work for Apple at such a salary,
especially as part of a contract that contained no long-term deferred compensation. And, he added, he would never take Leezy to California unless they
could move into a home equal to the one they enjoyed in Greenwich. Roche
said he'd tell Markkula.

Not surprisingly, Steve Jobs soon called and requested another meeting
with Sculley. They met on another Sunday, March 20, this time at the Carlyle. They had lunch, then went for a walk in Central Park. Sculley would
later remember how chagrined he was by all the people recognizing Jobs—it
was hardly the anonymous meeting Sculley had hoped for.

"I want you to come and work with me," said Jobs. "I can learn so much
from you."

They walked through the Metropolitan Museum of Art. Sculley explained
to the young man the differences between Archaic and Periclean Greek
sculpture. "Apple wants to stand for great design," said Steve Jobs. "Anything
that Apple does, we want to be the best. It has to be the best."

As they walked, Sculley began to imagine himself as the teacher of a
brilliant student, an Aristotle, say, to Alexander—or perhaps just John Sculley
to his younger self. Sculley told Jobs how he vacationed in Paris, drawing in
his sketchbook and visiting the Louvre. He confessed that if he hadn't been a
businessman he probably would have become an artist. Jobs, in a remarkable
coincidence, said that if he hadn't become a technologist, he would have
been a poet in Paris. The birds twittered in the trees.

They walked up the West side, stopping to look at jazz records, then on to
the twin-spired San Remo apartment building. As it turned out, Jobs was
considering buying the two-story penthouse apartment in one of those spires,
an apartment fomerly owned by Jacob Rothschild.

The younger man led the older man out onto the terrace of the penthouse, thirty stories above the great city. Sculley, who suffered from vertigo,
hugged the wall as Jobs pointed out the extraordinary view. Sculley's head
swam. He would later write, "It seemed as if the two of us were standing out

there above the world, above the world of New York that I knew and that Steve was now trying to discover, and above the world he was going to change."

It was a scene out of an Ayn Rand novel. The young superman, fearlessly looking out over the landscape from his skyscraper aerie, challenging the older, less immortal man to join him. Now it needed a climax. Jobs asked Sculley if he intended to join Apple. Sculley recapitulated his concerns about salary, home and deferred compensation. It was oh so prosaic. Jobs waved it away. "Even if I have to pay for it out of my own pocket, I want you to come to Apple. We'll have to solve those problems because you're the best person I've ever met. I know you're perfect for Apple, and Apple deserves the best."

Scully protested weakly one last time. Couldn't he just be an adviser to Apple?

Jobs dropped his head until his chin rested on his chest, as if the burden of his thoughts were too great. He stared down at the distant sidewalk and street. Then he said in measured words, "Do you want to spend the rest of your life selling sugared water or do you want a chance to change the world?"

It was the single most famous moment in Steve Jobs's life. Just twenty-eight years old, he had fully learned not only the part of business tycoon but also the mythology. The scene, the words, the style, all had their effect. Jobs's question tore right through John Sculley's guts. As he stumbled off into the early evening, "I realized for the first time in four months that I couldn't say no."

7.5 PREMATURE MATURITY

It was a magnificent seduction, orchestrated by a master. Steve Jobs had proven that he could work his charm and will not only on lesser mortals under his command but even on the cream of American business Brahmins. On that rooftop high over Metropolis, Jobs had reduced John Sculley from a figure who easily commanded the destiny of thousands, and who controlled the flow of billions of dollars, to a befuddled, fawning disciple.

But like many seducers, Jobs was more in love with the chase than the object. He had accomplished something extraordinary in luring John Sculley from Pepsi to Apple. But did Apple really need John Sculley?

Certainly the company needed a CEO. Markkula, in his usual manner, had never wanted the job in the first place, and now was anxious to get off the hot seat. Jobs too, to his great credit, recognized that he was still too young and inexperienced to become the chief executive officer of a billion-dollar corporation.

With the usual arrogance, Jobs also concluded that no one beneath him in the company was sufficiently qualified for the job. Yet, in fact, there was a new arrival to the firm who was so qualified that everyone else at Apple assumed he had joined as the heir apparent. This was Floyd Kvamme. As one of the youngest Fairchildren, Kvamme had been the junior member of the group that left with Charlie Sporck to take over National Semiconductor. Handsome, brilliant, multilingual, Kvamme was like a swan amidst the tough, ugly ducklings at National Semi. He was not only the nice face Sporck liked to put on the company for public events but also the company's best marketing man.

In a departure from its usual chip business, National had been a major supplier of IBM-compatible mainframe computers to the giant leasing company Itel Corp. When Itel began to totter, instead of renegotiating the contract, Sporck simply pulled the plug, leaving Itel to crash in one of the biggest financial meltdowns of the era (it almost took Lloyd's of London with it), and took over Itel's computer-leasing operation. Renamed National Advanced Systems, the subsidiary was given to Kvamme to run. If NAS's greatest success was a perverse one—IBM used it for the big FBI sting that nearly drove its two biggest Japanese competitors, Hitachi and Fujitsu, out of the computer business—the subsidiary still was well run and proved a neat little business for National for more than a decade.

Kvamme himself came out of the deal with his reputation stronger than ever. Now he knew not only chips but computers—and IBM. He also showed he could run a company. So when he decamped for Apple it was generally assumed that he would spend a few months learning the business, then step into Markkula's shoes.

But it never happened. Jobs already had decided that what the company needed now in a CEO was a veteran of large corporations who had the skills to take a still raw and volatile Apple Computer and turn it into a smooth-running, competent, *stable* enterprise. He was looking beyond Apple now, and never seemed to glance in Kvamme's direction.

Jobs's moves were entirely justifiable in strategic terms. Yet they were also profoundly wrongheaded. They were based on two assumptions on Jobs's part—assumptions about which, as an industry founder, he should have known better.

The least dangerous of these was that Apple needed to grow up. Certainly, as a major industry player, the company needed to refine its processes, ramp up manufacturing while still improving both quality and service. It also needed to grow up in other ways; notably the ad hoc nature of the company's organization. A company with several thousand employees could no longer behave like a frat house. On the hand, those problems were largely of Jobs's own doing. In fact, in the Apple II area, in marketing communications and in sales, the company was becoming quite professional. It was Jobs himself who was jumping around the firm, interfering with operations, setting up skunk works such as the Mac team, overruling standard procedures. He'd also helped drive off Mike Scott, who'd made the first real attempt to give the company structure.

The more dangerous assumption that Jobs made was that the industry was about to grow up as well. This was no doubt a reaction—after all, executive search began not long after the Apple III introduction—to IBM's arrival. Faced with this juggernaut of a corporation, the largest manufacturer in the world, the embodiment of corporate maturity and hierarchy, Jobs tried to be clever by trying to beat Big Blue at its own game. If the personal computer industry was about to settle down into a premature middle age, then why not beat the competition to the punch? Why not turn Apple into an HP with spark? And the only way to do that was to find a guy who knew his way around a Fortune 500 boardroom, a big-time CEO who knew how to sell to his own kind.

But in thinking this way, Steve Jobs betrayed his own inexperience—and the dangers of being too clever by half. In fact, the personal computer had not settled into a comfortable maturity. The shakeout it had just seen was only the first round, taking out the incompetent pioneers. Even with IBM in the market, there was still extraordinary room to maneuver—as the growing number of IBM cloners proved. Moreover, Moore's Law said that the next generation of microprocessors was due any day, and that would start the game all over again. And if none of these facts convinced Jobs that the personal computer industry was still young, then he needed to look only as far as his own Lisa and Macintosh design teams. Wasn't it Steve Jobs himself who went around proclaiming that these two computers were going to change the world? If he really believed that, why wasn't he looking for a feisty CEO/technologist prepared to deal with, and triumph over, change?

But Jobs was playing from his own rule book. A big-time corporation needed a big-time CEO. He and Markkula approached a local headhunter, Ed Winters, who'd proven an effective recruiter for Apple in the past, and gave him orders to look for the best CEO candidate in the country. It was Winters who led them to Don Estridge of IBM.

When Estridge turned down the offer, Jobs in his usual manner set out to find the best headhunter in the business. He ended up at the doorstep of Heidrick & Struggles and Gerry Roche. Roche, as was his standard procedure, asked Jobs and Markkula to come up with a list of attributes they wanted to see in the new CEO. The list they provided was telling: the new CEO needed to have consumer marketing experience, be interested in high tech, serve as a mentor to Jobs, adjust quickly to the unusual Apple culture and act as a visionary in the industry. It was not your typical set of CEO job requirements, especially the part about mentoring the corporate dauphin.

This need for a CEO with consumer marketing experience betrayed a dangerous shift in Jobs's thinking, encouraged by Markkula, the marketing man. They had decided that the future of personal computing was not as a technology business (hence that amazing second requirement of only an *interest* in technology), but as a consumer business—and that the key to managing that transition would be brilliant marketing. It was an extraordinary philosophical shift by the leadership of Apple and it occurred at the worst possible moment. There was no evidence that personal computers were becoming consumer products—quite the contrary, the game computer business was a wreck, while the successful companies like IBM and Apple were selling to schools, professionals and corporations.

And why marketing? Apple already had a marketing expert in Markkula, a legend in marketing communications in Regis McKenna and a budding marketing genius in Steve Jobs. If anything, Apple had too much marketing for its own good. What it needed was a firm and experienced hand in manufacturing or sales and distribution or administration.

Taking his orders, Roche set about creating a list of potential Apple CEOs. At one point it ran to almost 150 names, including most of the leading lights in American industry, such as Charles Brown, chairman of AT&T; Buck Rodgers, IBM's senior marketing vice president; and, of course, John Sculley. But as the search went to the contact phase, nearly all of the blue-chip names turned Apple down. Increasingly the list came down to John Sculley as the last major figure who fit the criteria yet had not peremptorily dismissed the Apple job.

This was the critical moment in Apple's middle years. The search for a CEO had stalled. The one remaining solid candidate not only was reluctant to take the job but had no computer, even electronics, industry experience. This was the moment when a wise executive would have stopped to take stock. A billion-dollar company was on the line. Jobs needed to ask himself, in a variant, the same question he would pose to Sculley: Am I willing to turn my computer company over to a man who has spent his entire career selling sugared water? Can I trust Apple to a man who has operated in a largely static market; and who has never really had to bring a new product through design and into large-scale manufacturing in a matter of months?

But Jobs never asked himself any of these questions in a systematic way. Once he had John Sculley in his sights he went after him with the relentlessness of a stalker. If anything, the prospect of landing a CEO from another world appealed to Jobs's romantic sense of himself. He would do something so daring no one else in the industry would dare try it. And when Sculley succeeded, Jobs's genius would again be acclaimed.

That was only part of it. The criterion about mentoring Jobs was a clue: Steve didn't want someone who would triumph in this new job and become synonymous with the company; rather, Jobs wanted someone to run Apple competently *until he could succeed him.* That may have been one reason why Kvamme, who far better fit Jobs's requirements, was passed over. By comparison, one of the things that made Sculley so appealing as time went on was that he was apparently in complete thrall to Jobs. Sculley was a great businessman whom he could handle, and Jobs liked that.

Jobs got what he wanted. But his luck, so remarkable until now, had finally turned. Because in John Sculley what Jobs got was a new Apple CEO who would run him out of the firm, lose the company's image as the industry thought leader, wasn't fully grounded in the underlying technology and would be unable to introduce a successful new product line for the next decade. John Sculley—in Steve Jobs's words that day in the Manhattan penthouse, "the best person I ever met"—would do the one thing worse than killing Apple Computer: he would make it boring.

7.6 BLIND DATE

John Sculley's acceptance of the chief executive's post stunned the rest of Apple, not least the senior management team. Only a couple of executives even knew of Jobs's recruitment efforts. The rest assumed that Kvamme was the man and were too busy with the III and the Lisa to give it much more attention.

Then on the morning of Friday, April 8, 1983, Mike Markkula called a meeting of the executive staff in the Bandley 6 boardroom. There he announced the hiring of John Sculley. It was a classic Apple moment. Markkula gave a quick biography of the new CEO: forty-four years old, president of Pepsi-Cola Company, senior vice president of PepsiCo Inc., MBA from

Wharton, third wife Leezy, etc. Then, attempting to prepare the team for Sculley's atypical personality, and perhaps for the only time to show his own doubts, Markkula added that the new CEO was an outstanding individual, if somewhat uncharismatic.

At that point, Steve Jobs jumped up to say that he thought Sculley was very charismatic. The others in the room were left to their own opinions, most deciding to wait until they met the man. But it was hardly a propitious beginning. After all this searching for the perfect CEO, the current CEO and the chairman couldn't even agree what he was like?

Pepsi made the announcement later that day. Kendall had accepted Sculley's resignation well, albeit with considerable amazement. It was too late for the dailies and for television news to carry more than the headline. But by Monday, the first of the "Who is John Sculley?" articles began to appear, notably in *The Wall Street Journal.* That's when the real industry talk began. The appointment itself had been a shocker—nobody in tech had ever tried something this outré. But then as the industry learned more about this buttoned-down Yankee corporate type who'd been married to the boss's daughter, the shock was replaced by stunned disbelief: Was this genius, or had Apple finally gone nuts?

The nature of the deal got out as well. Sculley had been hired for a salary of $1 million per year, *plus* another $1 million first-year bonus, *plus* a $1 million severance package, *plus* options on 350,000 shares of stock, *plus* a $2 million loan to buy a house·(what they didn't know was that John and Leezy had gone to real estate people in the wealthy enclaves of Atherton and Woodside and told them to look for a house priced at *exactly* $2 million—no less, they wanted the best they could get, but no more, because they had no intention of putting up their own cash).

It was an amazing employment contract—the kind of deal that impresses outsiders and pisses off insiders. The last time anybody in Silicon Valley had cut such a deal was when Dr. Les Hogan was recruited from archrival Motorola to take over Fairchild after Noyce's departure. Hogan's salary was henceforth derisively used as a standard Valley salary measure (one Hogan, two and half Hogans, etc.) and brought up every time Fairchild stumbled thereafter. By cutting a comparable deal, Sculley guaranteed that henceforth he would be a target.

In the meantime, it was obvious that Kvamme was the odd man out. He would be gone in a year, off to a long and respectable career as a venture capitalist at Kleiner Perkins. A decade later his son would get a measure of family revenge by buying a crippled Apple's television studios and using them as the centerpiece of his very successful multimedia production company, CKS Inc. CKS would go public in a wildly successful IPO at the same time that Apple was losing hundreds of millions of dollars.

Yet the management team had still not met their new boss. That encounter occurred on Wednesday, April 13, when Sculley held his first executive staff meeting.

If Apple's management had been confused about the situation before, they weren't left much better off by meeting's end. On the one hand, Sculley was reassuring. He told them he wanted to preserve Apple's unique entrepreneurial style, not allow it to sink into the bureaucratic inertia he'd seen at the big eastern corporations. He even used a Steve Jobs phrase, "leveraging Apple's critical mass," a nebulous, but meaningful phrase that meant that Apple, while it still had the most popular personal computer (the II), the largest installed base and the market's imagination, must combine all of these advantages into a single, monolithic marketing strategy.

There were other things Sculley said that day that also gave the executive team reason to be both surprised and optimistic. One was that he wanted Apple to shift from a single-product to a multi-product company. On the surface that was not a startling remark, given that Apple now had the II family, the III, the Lisa and the impending Macintosh. But on reflection, it was a powerful statement, especially as Steve Jobs seemed to be doing everything he could to kill the II, ignore the III and humiliate the Lisa team. *Hey, maybe this guy isn't Jobs's patsy after all!*

And that was just the beginning. Later in the meeting, which lasted hours, Sculley bowled over the room by announcing that if Apple was to succeed in selling to the business world—one of his goals—then it would have to move away from selling individual computers and begin selling a "total systems environment." In other words, the company would have to move into networks: PCs that acted like terminals, data communications systems, large central computers, the whole shebang. This was amazing stuff; Sculley was actually proposing that Apple start acting like IBM.

It was a gutsy call for Sculley, to take the war back into IBM's territory. But just as gutsy was his proclaiming this strategy in the presence of Steve Jobs, the young man who had built Apple on the old Homebrew antiestablishment policy of "one person, one computer." Even as Sculley was saying these words, Jobs had the Mac team hard at work on a computer that would be the very embodiment of solitary use, that would be specifically designed *not* to network with other computers.

As Sculley's words sank in, there were surreptitious glances at Jobs, expecting a blowup at any moment. But instead, in the words of author Frank Rose, who was covering Apple at the time, "Steve sat through all of this like the proud owner of an ingenious new toy. It was the first clue to the executive staff that the relationship between the new CEO and the young tycoon was going to be different from anything they'd ever seen with Steve Jobs."

But if Sculley's words assuaged the team's worries (*Hey, he understands this stuff more than you'd think*), his manner did not. Later observers would make much of the fact that John Sculley wore a suit and tie in a world of jeans and (sometimes) sport coats. But that is reversing the cliché a little too much. Silicon Valleyites were not that alienated by business clothes; after all, the Valley's founders had all looked like IBM refugees. Some of the veterans at the meeting, such as Kvamme, still wore ties. At places like Apple, it was more of a game than anything else for the more casual baby boomers to get their elders to shed their business uniforms

No, what made Sculley seem so out of place was his manner. He seemed perpetually nervous, even frightened, and when he spoke (perhaps as a residue of his old stutter) he often sputtered as though he was fighting to get the words out. First-time encounters were the strangest: in the years to come, at Valley social events, more than one person walked away from meeting John Sculley saying, as a woman was overheard muttering at a fund-raiser in Menlo Park, "*That* is the president of a billion-dollar company?" She, like many others, had been met with averted eyes, a limp and cold handshake and a whispered greeting.

The Apple executives, seeing this, first said to themselves, *Jesus, Markkula was right about this guy. He has no charisma at all. What was Jobs thinking?* Then they asked themselves how this nervous, shrinking figure before them was going to represent Apple Computer on the world stage. Could he face down top-flight journalists, giant investors and sly competitors? Could he go on television and convince you to buy an Apple computer because he was a great technological visionary or because he was more clever than his counterparts in the industry or, most important, because he was a tough, take-no-prisoners businessman? Could John Sculley really present himself to the world as a *winner*?

There was something else as well, an undertone that only the most subtle in the room could detect. It lay beneath the phrases Sculley used, such as "power curve" and "vision." Everybody at Apple, in emulation of Jobs, threw terms like that around. Hyperbole and imprecision were the very air you breathed at Apple. Even the veterans who really ran the place occasionally tossed out these stock phrases in their conversations to prove they were fellow travelers. But they also knew it was bullshit, that what really counted was moving iron. Talk all you want about a cosmic revolution in consciousness, but first you've got to build and sell the goddamn boxes.

Now here was Sculley using some of these same airy phrases. He was supposed to be from the hard-knuckle soda-pop business; where did he learn the lingo so fast? Was he always like this? Was he just sandbagging Jobs or, God forbid, did he actually believe it?

As they would discover, the answer to the last was: a little of both.

7.7 Babel

To the outsider, the first few months of the Sculley era at Apple were largely indistinguishable from what had come before it. Nevertheless, for someone coming from a giant corporation he moved with amazing alacrity. What was even more impressive was the subtlety with which he did so. To those he met, Sculley professed to be in a "learning-curve mode," which meant that he followed Steve Jobs around the company or wandered about on his own, asking questions and writing notes in notebooks. He said he had a lot to learn—not just about Apple but about computers and the industry. And by the end of the year he would fill up twenty notebooks.

But, in fact, Sculley was using his naiveté as a cover for some very serious analysis of the business, the organization and the culture of Apple. From the beginning, he knew enough to take Jobs's point of view about Apple and its competitors with skepticism. Sculley noticed immediately that under the Jobs regime the Apple II group was being screwed. Here was the heart of the company's balance sheet and the chairman referred to its members as bozos. The II group had been exiled to a rented triangular building overlooking the freeway four miles away in Santa Clara. Jobs had also publicly suggested that the Lisa team, the people behind the most important new company product in a decade, were a collection of second-raters and losers. Meanwhile, Jobs's pets, the Macintosh team members, were treated like pampered rock stars, right down to their own masseuse.

Having identified this early, Sculley was more dismayed than surprised to find that Apple had become a collection of opposing camps, each with its own culture, style and business strategy. The II, III and Lisa lines all had their own advertising and promotional campaigns—and as Sculley found out when he visited Chiat/Day with Jobs, the Mac group was about to embark on yet another. They also had redundant marketing teams, R&D operations, manu-facturing groups and staff positions.

Having come from such a world, Sculley knew well the dangers of a company divided against itself. But for now he kept his counsel—so well that his lieutenants assumed that he had bought Jobs's point of view hook, line and sinker. John Couch shuddered one day to hear Sculley describe Jobs as "my boy genius," figuring it meant the apotheosis of his worst enemy.

Sculley identified troubling features about Apple's products as well. For example, the Lisa and the Macintosh, though they had overlapping markets, were utterly incompatible—and as long as the two product groups despised each other, they would remain so forever. The Lisa itself had already been introduced by the time of Sculley's arrival at Apple, so he had no control over its design or packaging. But he could still revamp its market and certainly could change the direction of follow-up products. He chose to do both.

As for organization, even Apple veterans recognized the company was turning into Babel. New operating divisions had proliferated under Mike Scott, but exploded under Markkula. There were now *thirteen* autonomous divisions at Apple, most of them with redundant staffs. And it was precisely this autonomy that allowed the II, III, Lisa and Mac groups to remain at each other's throats. Sculley, who had enjoyed the pleasures of autonomy during his overseas sojourn, also knew well its dangers. He also knew that to pull the diverse groups together would require the glue of a common management and of shared information systems.

Finally, Sculley was deeply disturbed by Apple's (that is, Jobs's) attitude toward its competitors and its target customers. As he would later write in his autobiography:

> [In] October, a *Business Week* cover story declared IBM the "winner" in the microcomputer race. I was furious, but no one at Apple seemed to notice. If it had appeared in *Computer Currents*, a freebie street paper in the Valley, the story probably would have had more impact. Apple people didn't really read business magazines. So absorbed in what they were doing at the company, many had no touch with the outside business world.

In other words, Apple was planning to take on the business computing market without understanding either the customer or the largest manufacturer in that industry. To Sculley, this was flabbergasting. You might despise Coca-Cola, even deride it, but never for a moment did you forget that it was the largest and most venerable company in your industry. The same was even more true for IBM. Big Blue's share of the business PC market in 1984 would be more than 36 percent, compared with less than 13 percent for Apple. And while

Apple had screwed up the III and taken forever on the Lisa and the Mac, big, slow IBM had shown itself to be surprisingly nimble: now in the summer of 1983 it was preparing to introduce a brilliant new machine, the PC XT, aimed right at the heart of the office workplace.

The buzz was everywhere, already burying the coverage of the Lisa. It seemed that the old minicomputer line about never getting fired for buying IBM, so derided by the personal computing crowd, was proving true after all. Corporate directors of management information systems, who for years had refused purchase requests for computers with that funny name from those hippies in California, were now at last caving before the inevitability of the PC revolution and allowing purchases—as long as they were from IBM. Average office workers, though surveys found the majority preferred Apple, bowed too before the inevitable. Why fight the power (and pay out of one's own pocket for an Apple) when the company would pick up the tab for a PC? Even before the Lisa, Apple's sales team had discovered that most of its "corporate" sales were in fact small orders from renegade offices.

As Sculley knew all too well, corporate sales was Lisa's target market. And Apple understood that market so little that it was going after it with *lifestyle* ads—precisely the thing to reach those office renegades, while confirming to corporate officers that this was an artsy-fartsy outsider company too flaky to deal with.

Along with a handful of chip-industry veterans like Markkula and Kvamme, Sculley did understand the corporate marketplace, with its intense desire for predictability, security and the need for everyone involved with a decision at every level to be able to cover his or her ass if anything went wrong. That's why *Business Week*'s prediction of IBM's victory over Apple was so terrifying: no corporate purchasing officer in his right mind would ever buy from a company that didn't appear to have a future.

It went deeper than that. The corporate world, especially the world of giant Fortune 500 companies, had very distinct structural requirements. Like the military, it bought in giant volumes—a purchase order for PCs might run to the hundreds, even thousands of machines, the order totaling millions of dollars. Reaching that decision point could be a long and arduous process. But given the sheer size of the order, anything less would be irresponsible. Moreover, in making that decision, dozens of signatories up and down the organization chart might be required. That was the dark side of corporate bureaucracies, and what ultimately killed many big firms. Finally, before making the deal, the large corporate buyer exerted due diligence to confirm that the supplier was viable, trustworthy and able to provide service and support effectively for years to come.

That was the bad part. The good part was that once the order was made, the supplier didn't simply fulfill that order but entered into an enduring relationship with the company. The initial checkout complete, dealing could now be made more quickly—sometimes even automatically—and might continue for decades. Thus, the enormous front-end expenditure in time and money to land one of these big corporate whales was often paid back many times over in generations of sales.

IBM knew this process well. It had cut its teeth selling computers to big companies back in the 1950s, and was even now enjoying the payoff with the PC. HP had learned the lesson too, as had DEC. Sculley had learned it at Pepsi. But now he was running a company that not only did not understand this fact but had a culture consciously designed to be the antithesis of that corporate world. How were you going to sell to General Mills or General Motors or General Electric when your own founder proudly discussed his days as a drug-abusing felon and the company currently flew a pirate flag over one of its buildings?

Within Apple, the conviction, even among those who despised Steve Jobs, was that if you created a product that was truly insanely great, then everything else would follow. It was a classic Silicon Valley point of view, one which explained not only why so many great technical innovations had come out of this small community but (though no one at Apple seemed to notice) why the Valley was littered with the wreckage of so many dead companies.

Nevertheless, a small amount of reality had managed to penetrate Apple's fantasyland. Having projected the Lisa to become a $1 billion business by itself, the company had scrambled to put in place enough infrastructure to handle that kind of load. New salespeople were added, bringing the total Lisa sales force to 100; new dealers were also signed up. Apple itself was hiring at the rate of 250 people per month. But was this enough to drive a young company, and a disreputable one at that, into the loving arms of corporate America? Was it enough to supplant IBM, which had more salespeople than Apple had employees? And most of all, was Apple stable enough and organized enough to maintain the consistent marketing and sales contacts the Fortune 500 expected of its suppliers?

So, in the end, Sculley saw empirically what Steve Jobs already sensed: Apple could never hope to maintain its current growth or its industry leadership, or successfully penetrate its new target markets unless it streamlined its operations, formed linkages between its competing product lines, developed a coherent and relevant message and committed itself completely not just to designing great products but also to getting them sold. In other words, Apple had to grow up and get its act together. It had to become a real company.

7.8 ON THE BEACH

How John Sculley reacted to his analysis of Apple Computer is a glimpse of both his character and his understanding (or lack thereof) of the new industry in which he found himself. Whether he knew it yet or not, the exciting, successful company he had jumped ship to join turned out to be in very great danger of hitting the rocks. This wasn't the soda-pop industry, where success or failure might be a century-long process. In Silicon Valley even the most robust-appearing companies could die overnight. He had only to look at Atari, the toast of American industry three years before, now in straitened circumstances and facing oblivion.

In retrospect, the decisions John Sculley made in the first six months after his arrival at Apple, during his so-called honeymoon, helped to determine the story of Apple ever after. Though the effects of those decisions in some cases might not be known for a decade, by the time Sculley stood onstage at the Macintosh introduction and introduced his own self to the world, the die had already been cast. The fate of the most exciting company in the world had been placed in the hands of a man who understood neither company nor its world.

Nevertheless, if one can fault Sculley for taking the job, one can hardly accuse him of being indecisive during those first few months. All of that walking around and all of those filled notebooks had given him a plan and he didn't waste any time putting it into motion. One reason for this decisiveness was Sculley's recognition that he had only a brief window of market opportunity to position Apple for the future before IBM shut it. But just as important, Sculley shrewdly appreciated that any moves he might make against Jobs had to occur now while the young founder was still doting upon, and forgiving the mischievous behavior of, his new protégé.

The immediate concern was the Lisa, and if there was little Sculley could do now about the machine itself—beguiling in its interface, but too slow in its performance and way too expensive for its market—he could at least do something about its marketing. As Jobs had reminded him that day on the rooftop, computers weren't soda pop. Lifestyle advertising worked best with undifferentiated products, like sugared water, precisely because they were a minor part of an overall pattern of living.

Personal computers, by comparison, were highly differentiated, complex and a major part of the life of anyone who used them. They didn't reflect a current lifestyle, they helped *define a new lifestyle*. With only one out of every twenty people in the United States actually using a computer, and most of the rest wary of the complexity and cost of these new machines, potential customers still had to be taught to like personal computing. Nowhere was this more true than at the executive level in corporations. It was about this time that a new magazine, *Personal Computing,* actually spiked a cover story on how CEOs were using personal computers because it discovered that most of them *weren't.* Word processing was something their secretaries did; spreadsheets were for accountants.

This world of hard-nosed businessmen was precisely the target market for Lisa. Yet the Lisa ads—themed "Alone Again" and featuring images such as a solitary man playing a flute—were almost a parody of the worst kind of insufferably cute lifestyle advertising. Sculley, the man who had virtually invented lifestyle advertising at Pepsi, positively hated the ads. They were in fact his worst nightmare of how not to sell to executive row. One Apple dealer had it right when he described the ads as "nice foreign movies."

So Sculley killed them. It was a smart tactical stroke, but Sculley flinched from the much more difficult strategic campaign his action implied. If Apple really was determined to drive the Lisa into the world's corporate offices, then it would have to make the necessary commitment in time and resources. Sculley hedged, perhaps wisely given the Lisa's flaws, and the product built to save Apple was doomed.

Sculley quickly moved to streamline Apple's operations, forcing out three redundant vice presidents and cutting thirteen autonomous divisions into three. He pulled the Lisa and the Macintosh together into what he called Apple's thirty-two-bit family—an optimistic call to say the least, given that the Lisa and the Mac were utterly incompatible and the two product groups despised each other. Still, it was a gutsy move, one at odds with Sculley's already growing reputation for being Jobs's patsy. So was his next move, of forcing Jobs to make the Mac compatible, if not with the Lisa, then with its planned follow-up, the Lisa 2. By gutting out the center of Apple's management with these moves, Sculley effectively flattened the organization a decade before downsizing became a national trend. In doing so, he cut overhead, streamlined operations and, most important for Apple, forced the unfriendly parties to work with one another.

But all of this flattening had unanticipated results. By removing the intermediaries, Sculley knew that he was increasing the number of people reporting directly to him. He welcomed that, in the belief that it would speed decision making and provide him with a superb vantage point on the company's day-to-day operations. It also appealed to his paranoia that somehow the techies were pulling a fast one on him. But in time it all but buried him in raw information and the entreaties of corporate courtiers.

In the years to come Sculley would try to overcome the first by instituting sophisticated management information systems (MIS), some of them quite innovative, to reduce the mountains of raw data to manageable summaries — in the process putting into place computer networks that ironically undermined Apple's (especially Jobs's) own argument for the role of unlinked personal computers in corporate life. Yet even with all of this MIS firepower, Sculley never did get fully on top of the data flood. Moreover, none of these systems overcame the lack of an official decision-making process in the company — in fact, they worked against its creation.

This endless parade of Apple employees trying to catch John Sculley's ear only grew worse with the years. Ultimately, John Sculley would discover to his rue that by radically expanding his span of control without countering it with firm rules of access, he had not reduced factionalism at Apple but increased it. Apple stopped being a body of warring camps and, over the next decade, became an anarchy of everyone for themselves.

Sculley's other organizational move during this period was equally ambiguous in its results: he named himself head of the Apple II group. Little noticed at the time, this was a telling move in several ways. For one thing, despite his image both inside and outside of Apple of being joined to Jobs at the hip, Sculley almost from the first day began positioning himself *against* Jobs. He had forced the Mac group to integrate with the rest of the company and then he had taken over the product group that formed the greatest impediment to Jobs's strategy for the company. Sculley would later present these moves as the inevitable outgrowth of events at the time — but they show that Sculley hadn't left his political gifts at Pepsi. Certainly it was good for the morale of the II group in its exile down the freeway in the triangular building: *At least the new CEO appreciates us!*

But if his clever maneuvering at the start of his tenure, moving fast while Jobs still had stars in his eyes, showed Sculley at his best, his decision to take over the II group was the new boss at his worst. Just as, during his final days at Apple, he would take over as the company's chief technology officer, Sculley showed that when he couldn't trust anyone else to do the job he would do it himself, even when he was manifestly unqualified for the job.

This flurry of executive activity on Sculley's part culminated at the beginning of May in a weeklong Apple executive team retreat at Pajaro Dunes, a gated community on the beach near Monterey that in years to come would become best known as the site of Tom Peters's Skunk Works seminars. Though the attendees didn't realize it at the time, it would prove to be one of the most important events in Apple history.

Pajaro, a collection of homes embedded in the sand, by its very nature supported small, informal gatherings, campfires and long, meditative walks.

But that same detachment from everyday life can also lead to disassociation from reality. More than one group has left Pajaro Dunes over the years armed with disastrous strategies that seemed just brilliant at a 2 A.M. bull session.

The week began with a presentation by Chiat/Day of the new Apple commercials for each of the company's product lines. It culminated in plans for the Macintosh. The agency was understandably concerned that everything the Mac claimed to be—friendly, easy to use, affordable, etc.—had already been co-opted by competitors for machines that were manifestly unfriendly, hard to use, expensive, etc. So what Apple needed to do, creative director Lee Clow proposed, was to come up with a kickoff ad as groundbreaking and unforgettable as the Mac itself. He offered two storyboards. The first played off the scene in *King Kong* in which the giant ape bursts through the two-hundred-foot-tall iron gates that protect the tribal village. In this version, the gates would open only a crack to let a few little people through—the same tiny opening the Apple II had made in the monolithic world of computing. Then the gates would burst open, freeing nine thousand people—all thanks to the Mac, the "computer for the rest of us."

It was a terrific story line, but an expensive one, given the legions of extras. The second ad idea was expensive too, but at least it was manageable. This was "1984," stepchild of a year-old essay by a Chiat/Day copywriter named Steve Hayden entitled "Why 1984 Won't Be Like *1984*," which had been planned to run in *The Wall Street Journal* as part of a series of institutional ads. The ad was spiked, but the idea was reborn on Clow's storyboard. Sculley and Jobs loved this second theme, and Chiat/Day was sent off to create it.

Among the other topics addressed that fateful week in the dunes was products. Here, once again, the main topics were the Lisa and the Mac. The III was forgotten and the II all but ignored. The news on the Lisa was mixed. First shipments had originally been targeted for April, but like most new tech products, had slipped—in the Lisa's case until June, three weeks hence. That wasn't so bad, and it might have given Sculley the opportunity to redouble his support of the product's drive into the business market. But back orders were now approaching 20,000 units and the projections were still holding steady at nearly 60,000 Lisas to be sold in the next year. That represented more than a half billion dollars in revenues, tracking right along with the $1 billion targeted sales for Lisa during its two-year life span . . . and better yet, enough to push Apple to fiscal 1984 revenues of as great as $3 billion.

The Macintosh news was just as encouraging. The commitment to the 1984 campaign meant that the Mac had to be ready for introduction by no later than January, when George Orwell would be on everyone's mind. After that, Big Brother would be old, and overworked, news. But the Mac, which had already slipped from August, was still no gimme for January. The big problem was the floppy-disk drive. Jobs had originally wanted the Macintosh to contain the Twiggy drive. Twiggy was a godchild of Woz's classic design of a disk controller, created during his great marathon effort in 1977. So clever had been Woz's design, reducing seventy chips on multiple boards to just eight on a single board, that Apple began to get ideas of becoming a disk drive maker.

The original plan, after Scott's showdown with Shugart, had been to buy the new 5¼-inch floppy drives from Shugart—or, better yet, just use Shugart's design—add Woz's controller and have Alps Electric Co. in Japan put it all together. It was the incredible profit potential that turned Apple's head: the whole package would cost less than a hundred bucks, yet could be sold to Apple II owners for $500—and still be more than competitive with the kluges being sold at the time by Shugart and the rest.

The result, officially designated the Disk II, proved to be a great success not just for Apple, which made a lot of money, but for the Apple II computer. The added mass memory made the Apple II a true computer in the traditional sense. Arguably, the Disk II did as much to set off the personal computer revolution as did the computer to which it was attached.

But now Apple, swellheaded from having pulled a fast one on the disk memory industry, made the dangerous mistake of believing that it was a disk drive *designer*. Vice president of engineering Rod Holt, the guy who had made the slick move with the Disk II, decided to embark on a wholly new disk drive project, capable of even greater feats of storage, speed and reliability than the Disk II. This project, called Twiggy, proved to be a disaster almost from the start, not least because nobody at Apple actually knew how to design a disk drive.

As Frank Rose would write in *West of Eden*, his book about this era at Apple:

> [An official] Apple Value might have been "We work here, so we must be brilliant." Twiggy was the most visible result of this hubris, but the attitude itself was pervasive. Everybody at Apple seemed to think he was Woz. And the result was Twiggy, an engineering project that had turned into a nightmare.

Four years later, the result—expensive and unreliable—appeared on the Lisa, and played a major role in compromising that already compromised machine. John Vennard, who now ran the mass storage division (he was an old National Semi buddy of Mike Scott) after having run off Holt, continued to promise that Twiggy's problems would be cured in time for the Mac's first shipments.

Luckily, just as happened in the early days of the Mac project, members of the Lisa and Macintosh teams were quietly (that is, without Jobs knowing about it) talking. In particular, in February, Wayne Rosing, the Lisa engineering manager, dropped a few ugly facts on Bob Belleville, his Mac counterpart.

What Rosing said left Belleville in shock: Twiggy was proving to be a disaster. Apple's disk manufacturing plant in San Jose could not produce the drives anywhere fast enough to meet demand, primarily because most of the finished drives were defective and had to be rebuilt. And of those few that did trickle out to the Lisa manufacturing plant, many later blew up anyway. If you depend upon Twiggy, Rosing warned Belleville, you won't get the Mac out on time—maybe never. "Wayne," Belleville yelped, "there's no possible way!"

Needless to say, Belleville immediately ran to Jobs. Jobs, in fact, had been partly responsible for the problems with Twiggy: his rule, laid down for aesthetic reasons, that Apple computers not have noisy cooling fans had made the creation of Twiggy nearly impossible from the outset. Disk drives, with their electric motors, spinning platters and moving armatures, produce a lot of heat. In the uncooled heart of an Apple computer, a high-speed, advanced drive like Twiggy simply cooked, burning out its own chips and melting or distorting the Mylar diskette.

Jobs dashed off an angry letter to Markkula saying he'd lost faith in the mass storage division, then grabbed Belleville and took off for the San Jose plant. There, a furious Jobs interviewed the workers. The factory, a potential bottleneck for all Apple manufacturing, was a disaster. Most of the workers not only were temps but had never built disk drives before. The workers further admitted that it was a rare event—sometimes it didn't occur for scores of machines—when a Twiggy drive came off the assembly line for the first time and actually worked. And even many of those had to be sent back for minor repair. In other words, the initial yield of usable Twiggy drives, the guts of the Lisa, and soon the Mac, was *zero*.

At that news, Jobs nearly became unhinged. He threatened to fire everyone in the place. Belleville all but had to drag him out of the building to the parking lot, reminding him over and over that these were just foot soldiers, that the man he wanted was Vennard.

That showdown occurred at a Valentine's Day party. It was cinematic. The event was the announcement by the company of its newest Apple Fellows, Rich Page and Bill Atkinson of the Lisa group. Under a huge white tent, the Stanford marching band played, the company executives made speeches, employees drank from champagne glasses etched with Apple logos . . . and out at the far end of the parking lot, Steve Jobs verbally reamed out John Vennard.

But deep-sixing Twiggy only created the added challenge of coming up with a new disk drive system on the shortest possible notice. Mac team members flew in every direction, searching for a solution. The search centered on Japan; and it wasn't long before an anxious Jobs joined them.

The first stop was Alps. There, Jobs, Belleville, Holt and Dave Vaughan, head of Mac manufacturing, were given a presentation by company executives desperate to keep Apple's business. The Disk II had gotten Alps into the mass memory business and had made this second-tier company into a major player. So the company had gone all out in preparation for the meeting. The pièce de résistance was a mock-up, in milled aluminum, of the drive. It was gorgeous. Jobs and Holt were sold.

Belleville wasn't. He had a reputation for pessimism, but in a fairyland like Apple that was an important trait to have. Where Jobs saw a sleek new design and Holt saw the continuance of a happy business relationship with a strategic partner, Belleville rightly identified an unproven new design that might take years to perfect. Needless to say, he was pleased the group decided to continue its tour of Japanese manufacturers, even though Jobs thought it would be all but pro forma.

The rest of the trip was pure Jobs. Here's how Rose described it:

> For the next three days they visited other companies and looked at other drives. They weren't impressed by anything. They'd be ushered into a room and rafts of engineers would come out to show them their drives and Steve would pick one up and examine it for a minute with a look of extreme distaste and cry, "What are you showing me *this* for? This is a piece of crap! *Anybody* could build a better drive than this." . . . It was Steve's first trip to Japan, and he was indifferent to the niceties of doing business there. He'd show up wearing blue jeans at formal meetings with the heads of major corporations. The underlings were flabbergasted, but the corporate chieftains loved it. They'd all heard about this brash young California millionaire industrialist who'd started in a garage, and to meet him in person was—well, it was almost as good as going to Disneyland. And then, when he explained that the only reason he was holding their products up to ridicule was because he admired their company and he wanted their products to be the best

in the world—when he did that, with that riveting intensity that turned his eyes into magnets, they nearly swooned.

The team's final visit was to the venerable Sony Corp. Sony was building its drives by hand a few hundred units at a time and selling them to Hewlett-Packard. In other words, the drive was still essentially in the beta stage, still being checked out by customers, and so Sony had it located in a slummy skunk works outside Tokyo in the industrial town of Atsugi. Visiting the Gary, Indiana, of Japan was already guaranteed to put Jobs in a foul mood. Then, actually seeing the product, a messy kluge that looked half assembled, only made things worse. Jobs, and Holt with him, left Japan having decided to go with Alps. The lone dissenting vote was cast by Vaughan; as a manufacturing man, he could look past the clutter and see the quality of the Sony design. He was voted down.

Belleville, knowing better than to confront Jobs directly, kept his own counsel. He waited until the time was right and then went to Markkula. Markkula told Belleville to do what he had to do to get the Macintosh out in time. (It is interesting to note that this time Markkula didn't tell Jobs, which suggests a change in the relationship between the two.) And from that moment on, Belleville played double agent. He secretly met with a representative from Sony America, apprised him of the situation, and within days Hidetoshi Komoto, the Purdue-trained engineer who'd invented the drive, was flown over from Japan and sneaked into Apple. For the next week, Bandley 6 resembled a French farce, with Komoto whisked away into a far cubicle whenever Jobs appeared, then dragged out for hurried meetings whenever Jobs was gone. Komoto for his part never seemed to have understood why he was regularly yanked into corners.

Indeed, this farce even had a climax, which occurred when Jobs stopped off at a local drugstore to check out the magazine rack and ran into Komoto doing the same thing. Back at the office, Jobs wondered aloud what Komoto from Sony was doing in town. He was met with shrugs and blank stares.

In the end it was just as Belleville had feared. Alps couldn't get the drive right. Weeks slipped into months. The planned August introduction for Mac evaporated and now everyone at Pajaro knew that January was at risk. And if Apple missed January, especially with the still unknown PCjr, waiting in the wings, it could be disastrous.

The magnitude of that disaster was underscored by Floyd Kvamme. In one of his last contributions to the company, he ran the assembled executives through a thought problem—"target analysis process" was the formal gobbledygook—he'd often used at National Semiconductor. He drew a bull's-eye on a blackboard and solicited nearly forty answers to the question: What is the most important thing Apple has to accomplish in the next year? Then, with the group, he spent the next hour culling out the least important goals. In the end there was only one goal left in the center: "Successfully introduce the Macintosh."

There it was. Even the II and Lisa people agreed: everything depended now upon the Mac. And the Mac wasn't ready. This opened the gates. The assembled group turned on Jobs, who could only retreat. He offered them projected sales figures, but the group dismissed them. Everyone knew that all that mattered now was whether the Mac would be ready in January. Would the drives be ready?

Jobs, taken aback, could only prevaricate. In sixty to ninety days, he said, we'll know. That would be September, and everyone knew that left no margin for even the slightest slip. Moreover, they no longer trusted Jobs's pronouncements. They turned now to Belleville, the man immediately in charge of the drive problem. "Well, Bob?" asked Sculley.

Belleville was the only man in the room who knew that Komoto would be in town the next week with a working prototype designed exclusively for the Mac. He had betrayed his boss, but likely saved the company. Now he was about to be exposed. "In thirty days," he said, "we'll know for sure."

Jobs stared at him. How? In thirty days you could only test a finished . . . Then it hit him. He laughed. "You son of a bitch!" Once again, he had been saved from himself.

7.9 COPYCAT FIGHT

There were other events at that pivotal Pajaro meeting. Some were silly: for example, like two kids at Scout camp who can't get along, Jobs and Couch were sent out one evening on a walk along the beach to work out their differences. The walk was predictably futile. In a few months, buried under the Lisa collapse, Couch would be gone.

Another meeting proved much more fruitful. Apple's vice president of sales, Gene Carter, wanted full software compatibility between the Lisa and the Mac. That was understandable if the sales force was going to really offer the corporate world a full family of products. Jobs was adamant in his refusal: to make the Mac compatible with the Lisa would result in a much more expensive machine. They compromised on a special window on the Lisa screen where a user could run Mac software.

But it was another small gathering, one of such little moment at the time that Sculley didn't even mention it in his autobiography, that would ultimately determine the fate of Apple Computer. Sculley himself served up the notion that if Apple really wanted to succeed in the corporate world, then it should make its computers compatible not just with one another but with IBM too. This was, of course, heresy of the highest order. It was also the right thing to do. Sculley's instincts, trained in the Cola wars, were telling him the right thing. Just as Pepsi had copied Coke, ridden its coattails to riches, then used its superior innovation to pull ahead, so too might Apple, instead of trying to slow the IBM juggernaut in the workplace, join it, use its muscle to penetrate the market, then pull ahead with better products.

But having gone that far, Sculley stumbled. Apple was paying now for hiring a man without technical expertise. His proposal was quickly attacked by everyone. They pointed out the incompatibility between the Intel 8086 microprocessor and the II's 6502 and the Lisa/Mac's 68000. They argued that MS-DOS was optimized for the 8086, that it simply couldn't be carried over to the Apple machines.

But Sculley asked, now less forcibly, can't we add an Intel chip to our machines via one of the card slots? No, was the unanimous reply. Well, actually, yeah, except on the Mac, which had no card slots. But why do that? the group asked. If we play IBM's game they'll price-bomb us into dust. And besides—and this Jobs argued most vehemently—the whole meaning of Apple is to be the alternative to IBM, not its copycat. We've gone this far, succeeded this well, by setting our own standards. Why should we now imitate our own imitator?

At that, Sculley caved. He had his chance, but he had neither the will nor the knowledge to force it. The Apple management team, caught up in their own world, insular in their illusions about the business market, convinced of their own brilliance by the early success of the Lisa, closed their minds. The pirates, proud of their risk-taking bravery, had cowered from taking the biggest chance of all. There was only one person in the room who alone could have changed Apple's history by siding with Sculley: Steve Jobs. He wasn't afraid of risking everything. Moreover, he'd seen the Mac user interface and knew that nothing in the IBM arsenal could match it.

It would have been the visionary's greatest vision. And looking back over the intervening years and the rise of giant IBM clone companies that would dwarf even Big Blue in PCs, the mind swims. Imagine Apple in 1984 as a combination of Dell, Compaq and Gateway 2000, all with the Mac operating system. A world without the hegemony of Bill Gates and Microsoft.

But beating IBM at its own game wasn't an aesthetic that suited Steve

Jobs. He preferred to go his own way. And for now John Sculley couldn't stop him.

7.10 Stumble

The Pajaro meeting ended on a happy note. The distant storm clouds were obscured by the glow of the immediate good news. Lisa orders were strong, the Mac's problems seemed to be resolved, compatibility issues had been addressed and the new Apple II, the IIe, would be ready for the January launch event. Sculley even got caught up in the excitement. He boldly announced that he hadn't come to Apple to take it from a $1 billion to a $2 billion company. He was here to make it a $10 billion company. Everybody cheered. It was like the last day of summer camp.

The team returned to Cupertino energized and ready to tackle the hard but exciting months ahead. But by August, all hell had broken loose in the Lisa group as the 15,000 orders slumped to 12,000, and falling. Worse, the latest forecasts showed demand and production converging. Then they crossed. By September, estimated demand was 6,400 Lisas per month. Instead of the anticipated overdemand, there was overcapacity. Apple had invested in infrastructure for a demand of 11,000 Lisas per month. Now it was approaching the point where it would lose money on every computer it sold.

There were a number of reasons for this change of fortune, none of them good. The initial burst of demand had come from a new class of customers, still only barely understood, called *early adopters*. This group would buy anything new in technology, merely for the sake of being there first. This was not a large group, especially for $10,000 computers, but it temporarily inflated sales. Lisa went through that crowd in just three months. Now it was facing the real market of cold-blooded corporate MIS directors who looked askance at expensive, non-IBM computers from offbeat companies.

On top of that, even mainstream consumers quickly divided into two camps: those who wanted the Lisa but couldn't afford one, and those who were initially excited by the machine in concept but were disappointed by its reality.

Other factors were at work as well. The personal computing bubble had indeed burst, and the same shakeout that killed the game machine makers was now spreading up the ranks. More than a billion dollars would be collectively lost by the computer industry. Consumers, already overwhelmed by the Babel of different computers and operating systems, were now, having seen some major players fold, frightened to buy anything. Many decided to hold their purchases until the shakeout was over—when they would not only know who the winners were but could get a better deal. Those who *had* to buy now typically went to the safest vendor: IBM. Even the Apple II, the Iron Horse of personal computing, suddenly experienced a slump in sales.

The wreck of the PCjr didn't help anything but Apple's morale. In the company's eyes, there was now nothing in the path of the Mac. But in reality, IBM had not really been wounded: it actually gained a little market share. And, worse for Apple, consumers were now even more wary (even IBM can't be trusted!) of buying radically new computer designs.

This industry-wide recession was not the triumph John Sculley had in mind. Instead he was reduced to damage control. Apple's rapid hiring was stopped, its employment frozen at 5,500. Sculley slashed the price of the Lisa, while at the same time expanding its dealer network from a controlled collection of 150 top-notch stores to just about anyone who wanted it (the final number was about 350 dealers). But still he couldn't stanch the bleeding. For the fourth quarter ended September 30, 1983, Apple's profits fell 80 percent from $25 million to $5 million. The stock tumbled too. Sculley had been justifiably proud that, under his brief tenure, Apple's stock had hit a historic high of $63 per share. That was in June; by October it had collapsed to just $23, a bottom it wouldn't reach again until the crisis of 1997.

It got so bad that Don Kendall called from Pepsi and joked that at a recent board meeting someone had calculated that Sculley had already made and lost $9 million in personal wealth in little more than a half year at Apple. That was a little reminder of Sculley's treason to the Old Guard by going out West for stock options. Then to rub it in, Kendall, laughing the whole time, asked his ex-son-in-law if he'd like his old job back.

Sculley would later write:

> How could we introduce a revolutionary new product like Macintosh from a failing company? Momentum and timing are everything in marketing. Few people would want to buy a computer from a company that isn't doing well. We had to get the momentum back.

7.11 RESCUE

In the end, of course, it was the Apple II, the Little Computer That Could, that pulled a sidetracked Apple over the mountain. Treated with contempt by the spiritual leader of its own company, perpetually reduced at Apple family gatherings to the role of maiden aunt who refuses to die, Woz's creation nevertheless had become a cult object to millions of computer owners. Like the Model T, it could be adapted for a hundred different tasks and do all of them, if not brilliantly, then with predictable pluck.

After a half decade, the II was no longer merely an Apple product. It was instead an industry, an extended family, and a religion. It was also a money machine that had financed the III, the Lisa and the Mac. Apple sold it to dealers at three times the manufacturing cost, then the dealers themselves added their own sizable markup—and customers *still* saw it as a bargain. Scores of little companies had sprung up to offer special internal boards and external support machines for the II. Hundreds of others, from large companies like Microsoft to solitary programmers with a clever idea, had designed a well-stocked library of application programs for the II—the first such library of its kind for a personal computer and the model for every important computer that came after. And Apple II's, new and old, stock or so stuffed with custom Input/Output boards they nearly ignited, could be found in professional offices, household dens and, perhaps most of all, classrooms throughout the world. More than any other machine, the Apple II had created the personal computer revolution dreamed of by the idealists at Homebrew. It had also brought computers to education. And, though unacknowledged and often sneaked in through the back door, the II had also cut the path for Apple into the corporate world.

But Steve Jobs no longer cared about the II. He publicly derided it, saying the II group was the dull and boring division, that it had "shitty" ideas, and calling its engineers "Clydesdales" because they were little more than dull draft horses. Even worse, Jobs undermined sales by broadly hinting to the world that once the Mac arrived on the scene the II would be obsolete.

Sculley's assumption of the leadership of the II group, so celebrated at the time, did nothing to help. When he asked his question at Pajaro about IBM compatibility, not even he mentioned the II as a possible vehicle. And while the executives were living it up at the beach, the II group (with the III team) were meeting in the cramped quarters of Rickey's Hyatt House in Palo Alto in one of the tiny rooms stuck in the parking lot behind the hotel. The III team didn't even know its presence was superfluous: at Pajaro the top brass had decided to kill their product. The new-product manager, Dave Fradin, readying a follow-up machine, the Apple III+, found out his fate through a roundabout series of calls even as the meeting was taking place.

But if the II group was starved for love within Apple, it drew strength from its loyal customers. Every time the II seemed to fade the team managed to perform another miracle. The original II had been supplanted by the II+, then most recently by the brilliant IIe, the last in many ways the apotheosis of the first generation of personal computing.

Now there was a new II in the works, the IIb, which would ultimately see life as the IIc. But its introduction was still a long way off—it wouldn't help Apple in the desperate months to come. To get the Mac introduced right, Apple would have to depend upon the III it despised and the current II it ignored.

Both came through. Even as it was being discontinued, the III was still selling 2,000 machines per month. Moreover, thanks to an automatic order system in the accounting department, the previous December Apple accidentally ordered the equivalent of a year's worth of new III parts. That meant Apple had enough machines still in inventory (about 6,000) and enough parts (the equivalent of about 12,000 machines) to keep selling III's into the spring of 1994. Even at the current rate, that meant $30 million or more in unexpected revenues that otherwise would have to be written off. It was perhaps the last time Apple would successfully screw up.

Dave Fradin, having seen the plugs pulled on his project just weeks before, now was thrilled to find the patient still breathing. In a heroic bit of planning and hard work—the kind of thing Apple project managers and team members were becoming famous for—Fraden and his III team put together in two weeks a complete plan for the future of the III, including a rollout of the III+ as a niche-oriented product for legal, medical and real estate professionals complete with specialty software. The plan succeeded so well that in the end Apple sold off most of its inventory of III's. After that, the III's user base of 120,000 owners proved so loyal to their machines that they continued to buy III's and develop software among themselves into the early 1990s . . . long after Apple had effectively erased the III from its official history.

The Apple II, on the other hand, was very much alive, even if its sales had taken a momentary stumble in the face of the PCjr. Sculley became a true believer—and in the autumn of 1983 he at last shone as a II lover. It may have been, less than one year into his ten-year tenure, Sculley's finest hour at Apple. The II slump played to his strengths: it was a marketing problem, the public was confused and resistant and the biggest competitor was preparing to unveil a new killer campaign. Sculley had been down this road many times. He immediately boosted the ad money for the II, and at the same time slashed prices, offered dealer incentives and rebates to buyers—all in the face of the expected PCjr onslaught.

It was a slick play, a lesson from a master of consumer marketing.

Christmas now approached. Consumers, still wary after the PCjr, took a second look at the II, with its great reputation and new low price . . . and decided to buy.

As noted, in December 1983, the last month for Apple to turn around its fortunes, Apple sold 110,000 Apple II's, for total company revenues of $160 million. It was the biggest single month's sales in the II's history. The Apple II had pulled it off one last time. Even the Lisa's sales temporarily improved. Apple was now positioned to charge into the Mac introduction with flags flying.

7.12 WOZ REDUX

One of the most satisfying aspects of the II's last great hurrah was that its creator was on hand to see it. One morning in June, a few weeks after the Pajaro gathering, the greatest inventor of the PC era quietly strolled into the Triangle Building, walked up to the receptionist and inquired about a job.

In anybody else, this might have been a clever bit of role playing, the "humble genius." But with Steve Wozniak, it was genuine. He had no appointment. He didn't really know who was running the Apple II division now. The stunned receptionist sent him to Dave Paterson, one of the general managers of the division. There, Woz announced that he wanted to work on the II project.

He got the job.

It had been a long, strange two-year trip for Steve Wozniak since the plane crash. He had officially remained an Apple employee at a minimal salary, but in fact he had been far away. Coming out of the semi-coma had been like flipping a reset switch in Woz's brain. It was as if in his thirty-year old body he had regained the mind he'd had at eighteen before all the computer madness had begun. And when that happened, Woz found he had little interest in engineering or design. Rather, in an odd sort of way, he wanted to start over fresh.

But, of course, that was impossible. He was famous, rich, twice married and a public figure. Yet, in a poignant way, Woz still tried. He went back to Berkeley, this time attending under an assumed name, "Rocky Clark" (derived from his dog's and wife's names) and took classes in subjects like economics and psychology, with a little computer science thrown in. No one was fooled. His classmates and teachers humored him, but almost from the first day the word was out that he was the Great Woz.

Even playing poor student, Woz couldn't escape the charms of his own great wealth, the legions of hangers-on willing to turn whims to reality. One of those whims hit Woz while he was driving from class to his home in Scotts Valley. He was listening to music on the car radio when it suddenly struck him: Why not put on a concert? And not just any concert, but a Woodstock for the 1980s! With computers and bands and New Age ideas and all the rest!

A lot of other people were probably musing on the same idea at the same time, this having been the proper interval from the 1960s to call for a regathering of the tribes. But none of the others were as rich as Steve Wozniak. It wasn't long before Woz, via the conduit of a Santa Cruz nightclub owner (of course) was connected with Peter Ellis, a Santa Cruz businessman, est graduate and promoter (of course) and they hooked up in turn with the San Francisco rock impresario Bill Graham (of course, of course).

The result was the US festival, a production of UNUSON (unite us in song), an organization founded and financed by Woz. The event itself, which took place in a hot desert valley in the San Bernardino Mountains east of Los Angeles, drew 200,000 people and featured such acts as Tom Petty, the Police and Fleetwood Mac. If the music wasn't particularly memorable, the activities surrounding the show were. There were laser shows, a giant video screen showing the performers, an inflated "Sensonics Theater" dome featuring videos and high-quality sound, a hot-air balloon with the Apple logo and air-conditioned booths exhibiting the latest computers and other equipment. Woz sat in his headquarters, an old house on the hilltop above the madness, listening to the music and occasionally venturing down into the throng.

Ever loyal to its favorite founder, Apple was there too, with a booth showing off its wares. The company had been involved with the event from the beginning—though not without reservations. UNUSON's management was filled with unusual characters—sharp-eyed figures who talked the New Age talk but walked like used-car salesmen. The Apple folks, many of them est graduates themselves in the 1970s, recognized the look and silently prayed for Woz. They were secretly relieved when the festival went off without a major hitch.

Woz himself was out $12.5 million for his little vanity Woodstock, an amount more than offset by the $18 million he made that summer on his Apple stock. In fact, he was so happy about the event that, despite the warnings of friends and acquaintances, he announced he was going to do it again the next year. Once was eccentric; twice was stupid. This time, Apple bowed out, as did most of the other honorable people involved with the project, leaving USII in the hands of every con artist, sleazeball and sharpie who could figure out a way to get their hands on the multimillionaire's wallet. The Candide of computers had now become the patsy of the pop world.

USII, held on Memorial Day weekend in 1983, just days after Sculley and crew were meeting at Pajaro, drew an equally enormous crowd, but of a wholly different demographic. This mob came to party. The result was a disaster: 145 people in jail, 120 hurt, one dead from an overdose, another beaten to death with a tire iron.

The dead, the hospitalized, the jailed, the feuding bands, the trashed site—all were merely prelude to Ellis and the other organizers rewarding themselves with hundreds of thousands of dollars for a job well done. Everyone, from the est devotees to the musicians to the promoters, took Steve Wozniak's money and went home. Woz, having burned up $25 million in just two weekends, ignored the world's laughter, pronounced the two US Festivals a great success ("I think the fans got their money's worth. I know I got mine") and within a month was standing in the reception area of the Triangle Building. In October 1998, co-hosting a Bay Area rock radio station, Woz would make the extraordinary remark that he had fully anticipated that the US Festivals would be profitable, "because, after all, profitability is the real test of whether an idea is good or not."

Woz arrived at Apple in time for a late summer meeting of Apple III engineers, convened by Sculley to tell them that their product was dead. Woz came away impressed that Sculley was a real businessman. Sculley didn't even recognize Woz.

As summer turned into fall, and as Apple started to ramp up for the Macintosh introduction, Woz devoted his time to making a mouse work on the Apple II. He succeeded, but not without the endless distractions that came with fame. Once the world heard he was back at a desk at Apple, the phone perpetually rang with requests for interviews, advice, speeches and connections. Woz's very presence improved the II group's morale in this dispiriting period, but any hopes the group had that Woz would become its champion on executive row were soon dashed. Woz wanted nothing to do with headquarters or managing; he wanted to once again hide in his cubicle and design.

7.13 EPIPHANY

The great revenue figures in December brightened the first days of January 1984. Apple owned the buzz again. By the first week of January, as rumors about not only the Mac but the 1984 ad began to swarm, Apple became the focus of every eye in high tech.

There were many doubters. After all, Apple had promised the moon a year before and all it delivered was the Lisa, which everyone now knew was a failure. Add to that the fiasco of the PCjr and there was some question not just whether Apple could come out with a fundamentally new computer but if anyone could at this point in the industry's history.

The day after the Macintosh introduction even the hardest skeptics had to admit that Apple had pulled off an unprecedented coup in personal computing. On first glance, Apple seemed to have done *everything* right. The Mac had all the innovations of the Lisa (and more), the sturdiness and low price of the II and a charm all its own. Jobs got his wish: the Mac design was simple, yet elegant—a true classic. Even the graphics in the ads and documents supporting the Mac were superb: the vast white spaces, the lean and elegant typeface so reminiscent of Jobs himself, the simple slashes of color that effortlessly captured the form of the Mac box and screen. If the IBM PC was your lawn mower, and the Apple II was the nice kid down the street, the Mac was your pet, even your child. The bond was instant and visceral. Thousands of people loved the Macintosh the first time they saw it, and more than a decade later were still deep in that affair.

Everyone interested in personal computers—and by 1984 that numbered in the tens of millions in the United States alone—was anxious to see a real Macintosh in person, to put their fingers on the keyboard and slide the mouse around (still a very new sensation) and see if the image on the little screen was as precise as it appeared in the big *Newsweek* advertising supplement. And when the first Macs started showing up in local computer shops—and they arrived quickly, thanks to a magnificent new $20 million automated Mac factory across the Bay from Cupertino in Fremont—people lined up for the chance to see it. Even the most cynical IBM PC loyalist took a moment to sneak over and play with the little Mac.

The experience was electrifying. From the first-time computer user to Bill Gates, everyone who walked into a computer store and experienced the Macintosh knew that it was touched by magic. The experienced programmers dismissively tapped a few keys, then, blown away by the sharpness of the bit-mapped display and by the versatility of the windowed interface, sat down for an hour of intense experimentation. The graphic artist who neither liked nor used computers, played with the mouse—then suddenly drew a bouquet of flowers. The middle-aged couple stepped in from the sidewalk out of curiosity, took their first look at the New Digital World and concluded that these computers were easier than they thought. The boomers listened knowingly to the Wyndham Hill background music on the instructional cassette and concluded that computers were no longer just the province of freaks, but *cool*.

Steve Jobs had done what he set to do when he hijacked the Mac project. He had created the first true *personal* computer, a masterpiece of form and function.

7.14 THE PEOPLELESS COMPUTER

And nobody bought it.

Before the Mac was introduced, Jobs had confidently predicted two million would be sold the first year. Even the realists within the company were wildly optimistic. An early estimate predicted monthly sales of the Mac at 80,000 per month, or one million units per year. Kvamme had managed to cool that ardor somewhat by pointing out that a million Macs represented $2.5 billion in revenues, a mark reached in the first year by only one product in history, the Boeing 727, a product with a wholly different market and pricing structure. So the figure was lowered to 425,000 units in 1984—still a billion dollars, and equal to Apple's total sales in 1983. But the Mac launch was so strong, the product so well received by both the public and the press, the Mac marketers saw no reason to doubt their predictions.

But even as Jobs and the gang were setting off on the road show to pitch the product, the Mac's weaknesses were beginning to show. One of those mistakes was Sculley's, and it was evident the first time you saw the Mac: its price tag. Raskin's $995 People's Computer had become, under Jobs, a computer with a target price of $1,995. Given all the added features, that was still a tremendous bargain. To sit down at the Mac for the first time, give it a test drive, then look up and see it was all available for under two grand . . . that would have been exhilarating. Jobs knew it better than anyone; by now he had an intuitive sense of how the market valued new computers.

But the decision wasn't his. And John Sculley, coming out of the soda-pop world, operated under a more rigorous and traditional pricing model. You priced high up front to cover development and initial marketing costs, then systematically cut prices to gain market share. It was a good model for video games, calculators and even minicomputers. But it was wrong for a still immature business like personal computing. There, the game was still to maximize market share in order to control the industry standard. The big profits would then be made on the back end in software and future generations of hardware. That's why, a decade later, Microsoft, running late behind Netscape and trying to capture the standard for Internet browsers, gave away its first generation of products. Sculley didn't understand any of this yet. He looked at the multimillion-dollar ad campaign (including twenty-page ad inserts in *News-*

week, *Time, Forbes, Fortune* and *Business Week*), the $20 million factory and the tens of millions spent on developing the Mac, and—after neatly juking Jobs into believing the $1,995 price would hold—announced that the Macintosh would sell for $2,495.

The announcement did more than break the Mac team's heart. It also forever removed the Mac from being the People's Computer. At $1,995 it was a no-brainer; but at $2,495 it became a premium product you thought twice about before buying. Some began to have doubts. For example, on the matter of software application programs, there was a word processing program—but you couldn't write more than eight pages at a time. There was a slick little spreadsheet program—but it was slow. Macpaint, a graphics program, was thrilling—but it quickly raised expectations beyond what the Apple could give. And Apple was willing to sell you a modem to put the Mac on a network—but it didn't have a telecommunications program to run that modem. What other software was available for the Mac was usually buggy and slow, the former due to the rush to market, the latter to the huge memory requirements for that nifty screen.

But these were minor problems compared to the Big Mistake. If the price was Sculley's error, the Mac's tiny memory was Jobs's. Jef Raskin had originally wanted to put on 64K of memory in the Mac, a tribute to his own dogmatism (people don't need more than that) and the era (memory was expensive in 1980). But Moore's Law and rising consumer expectations had done their part, and even from the most conservative perspective the 64K of 1980 should have been 256K by 1984. A progressive view would have realized not only that memory was becoming essentially free but that demand for it (thanks to ever-larger files and programs) was becoming insatiable. From that perspective, any new computer should have had a 1Meg of core memory at the time of the Mac introduction.

But Jobs saw things differently. Half of him was still stuck with the vision for the Mac he'd co-opted from Raskin. The other half, like the senior citizen who still secretly believes that houses should cost $25,000 and cars $1,000, was still trapped in the Homebrew world, where 4K of memory was not only horribly expensive but more than enough to do anything you could imagine. Being also incredibly facile, Jobs managed to rationalize all this—and convince those around him—by wrapping his prejudices in contemporary philosophy: in this case, Joseph Schumpeter's "Small is Beautiful." Anyone who disagreed with him, as Mac marketer Joanna Hoffman did in 1982 when she proposed a hard disk for the Mac, got verbally abused and accused of being a Xerox bigot or a minicomputer lover.

As a result, the Macintosh hit the streets in 1984 with only 128K of memory (the same as the PCjr), a single floppy and no hard disk drive. By then even Jobs should have known better: that legendary verbal greeting from the Mac at the product's introduction had been possible only because the machine on display was a fake—it had been custom-built with beefed-up memory to do the job.

A 128K memory wouldn't have been too bad if the Mac had been an ordinary machine. Thousands of PCs with that much memory were still being sold every month. But the fancy bit-mapped display on the Mac was a giant memory black hole. Once you turned on the display there wasn't much memory space left to do anything. The nightmare really began when you attempted to engage in some memory-intensive activity on the Mac, such as copying a disk. Then, because the machine could hold only small chunks of data at a time, you were forced to pull out the original diskette, put in the copy, then pull it out and put in the original . . . over and over again endlessly. One test put the number of diskette reinsertions at fifty times per copy. It was enough to kill an afternoon, tear apart your elbow and drive you insane.

Yet, for many, even that limitation wasn't enough to keep them from achieving congress with the Mac. Author Douglas Adams (as quoted by Steven Levy) explained it this way:

> I can remember when . . . a group of people [were] crowded around a small beige-colored box that looked like a toy . . . I watched, at first with mild curiosity, then gradually I began to feel that kind of roaring, floating sensation which meant I had my first experience with MacPaint. But what I (and I think everybody else who bought the machine in the early days) fell in love with was not the machine itself, which was ridiculously slow and underpowered, but a romantic idea of the machine. And that romantic idea had to sustain me through the realities of actually working on the 128K Mac.

But for every romantic like Adams, there were a dozen others who loved the Mac, wished they owned one, but decided against making a purchase. For them, the Mac became the perfect computer to play with at your friend's house.

And "play" was the operative term. Underpowered and overpriced, with a tiny software library and with an arrogance that manifested itself in everything from the single diskette drive to the missing cursor keys to the lack of add-in board slots, the Mac, which seemed at first to announce a new consumer revolution, now seemed little more than a clever novelty, a toy for the techno-obsessed. Certainly that was the angle many tech writers now took, their message pushed along behind the scenes by an IBM that feared the Mac much more than it let on. Sales began to plummet. By late summer, there were months when Apple sold only 5,000 Macs, a tenth of its goal and no better than the Lisa. Apple was very close to having a second disaster in two years.

But there was one crucial difference. This time, the world wanted the Mac to succeed. Part of this (nonbuying) support came from the charms of the computer itself, but much also derived from the growing fear of IBM hegemony. With the shakeout now over and most of the other corporate players dead or crippled, Apple was now seen as the last best hope for a personal computer industry free from Big Blue's control. The media pressed Jobs for a solution: Was there a more powerful "Fat Mac" in the offing? Sure, said Jobs, vamping, and we'll have it ready by early 1985.

Once again, Steve Jobs was unexpectedly saved from himself by one of his subordinates. This time it was Burrell Smith. From the beginning, Smith had disapproved of Jobs's decision to put only 128K of memory in the Mac. Smith simply went around Jobs and secretly designed the machine to hold four times that much memory without any major redesign. As a result, the 512K Fat Mac proved ready to ship by September 1984. It cost the early adopters a thousand bucks to upgrade to the new memory size; but grumble as they might, they had no choice. Not if they wanted to run any of the tardy applications programs that were just now coming out for the Mac. Throw in another $400 and you could add a second disk drive that plugged into the back of the computer. In other words, for just under $4,000 (not including software) you could now own the Mac that should have been.

7.15 FOLLIES

The upgrades silenced the detractors, but did little for sales. Meanwhile, a kind of collective madness seemed to descend upon Apple Computer, beginning at the very top, then spreading first to the Mac group and then to the entire company.

Jobs's behavior, always quixotic, had become bizarre in the year before the Mac introduction. In February 1983 he put on an appropriately late Christmas party for the Mac team. It was a formal dinner-dance at San Francisco's St. Francis Hotel; black tie with music provided by two orchestras. That nobody else on the team even owned a tuxedo (or wanted to), that few were familiar with ballroom dancing and that most had little experience with an evening in a grand hotel seemed to have no impact on Steve Jobs. This was the kind of event a world-class team like the Mac group should have, and by God, they were going to have it.

Jobs's date that night was Joan Baez, whom he had been seeing lately. Baez had been a hero of Jobs's in high school, and this burgeoning relationship had caused considerable talk. Anyone who rode in Jobs's big new Mercedes was treated to a hearing of Baez's unreleased new album. That Baez, almost old enough to be Jobs's mother, knew nothing about computers and was as much out of place with the Mac crowd as they were with her, didn't seem to matter to Jobs either. In his black tux, he was Jay Gatsby putting on a swank party and dancing with the Daisy of his teenage dreams.

The weirdness only increased as the months passed. One rich source of it was the relationship between Jobs and Sculley. They seemed almost inseparable, the bonds greater than mere mutual respect. Sometimes they even seemed to finish each other's sentences. They spent weekends together, and there were even shots of the pair in the woods, shirtless, looking part father and son and part lovers. And to sit through a meeting in the boardroom with the two, as they carried on a private dialogue with each other, reinforcing each other's views, ending each other's thoughts, smiling knowingly at each other's code words and refusing to allow disagreements to stick, was to realize that no lovers or family members were ever *this* simpatico. Then you understood that what you were really seeing was two boys, two best pals, so deeply involved in a game and each other that they had lost track of the rest of the world. They were deaf to their mothers calling them home for dinner.

As Sculley would later recall: "He was the only person I ever met whom I could speak with on multiple levels. We felt we were living life on several different planes at all times. We spoke, thought and worked in synchronization."

Jobs, now playing FDR facing the Depression, publicly announced that the Mac would be made or broken in the first Hundred Days. Soon that became the rallying cry for the entire company—and the benchmark set for Apple by both industry analysts and the press. Meanwhile, exactly what constituted true success was unclear: Jobs was quoted at saying he expected to sell a half million Macs the first year; Sculley publicly cut that number in half. Meanwhile, the internal memos predicting a million units sold by the end of 1985 had also been made public.

Jobs responded to this challenge by hitting the road armed with Macs to give away to every faddish artist, image maker and trendsetter he could find. It was a jetted-up version of his old days riding the bus around Silicon Valley trying to line up computer shops. And the group he took with him was remarkably similar: Wozniak, his old friend Dan Kottke, Andy Hertzfeld and Burrell Smith. Hard-core freaks and techies, pulled together again as if they were good-luck charms, on the road once more selling Bibles to believers.

They crossed the country visiting computer clubs to give demonstrations, and, when they could find them, celebrities on whom to bestow free Macs. It should have been a great time, a celebration of Apple's first decade by the geniuses who'd built its great products. But it was the opposite. Smith and Hertzfeld, coming off their herculean labors on the Mac, were exhausted and showing the first signs of battle fatigue and depression.

But Wozniak was far worse. Hertzfeld had taken along on the trip a copy of a new book about Atari. Finishing it, he handed the book to Woz. And there, on the plane, in perhaps the most poignant moment in the Apple story, Woz finally read the real story of the computer game Breakout: how Jobs had taken advantage of him, suckered him into doing the design work, and worst of all, then cheated him out of nearly all the money he had earned. As he sat there, stunned, rereading the words, the truth of what had happened rolled over Woz like a wave. All those years of trusting his friends, the company they'd built together, *everything* was based on a lie.

He cried. No one on the plane knew what to say.

It was a miserable time for Steve Wozniak. He had wasted a fortune on a boondoggle, learned of the betrayal of his best friend and in a few months would be publicly humiliated around the world when his wife was arrested in Los Angeles trying to scalp the free tickets to the Summer Olympics she'd been given by Apple. Within a year, increasingly embittered, unable to focus on the design of a new Apple II, Wozniak again walked out of Apple Computer. "Poor Woz," said Steve Jobs.

Meanwhile, Jobs was in his element. The program to hand out Macs to the famous, a more cynical version of Apple's 1982 "Kid's Can't Wait" program to get corporations to donate Apple II's—for a tax write-off—to elementary school classrooms, had been mischievously dubbed "Stars Can't Wait." Jobs took to it with abandon. He was in his element. He flew across America to deliver a Mac to Mick Jagger (whose daughter proved more interested than he was). He sat on the floor of Yoko Ono's apartment at Julian Lennon's birthday party and demonstrated the Mac to Andy Warhol, who shouted with uncharacteristic excitement, "My God! I drew a circle!" (and a year later did ads for the Commodore Amiga).

Meanwhile, Jobs's personal life was taking on a similar celebrity sheen. He had become an overnight sex symbol among the chattering classes, and his social calendar was filled with high-profile partnerings. Some of these relationships, like that with architect Maya Lin, of Vietnam memorial fame, appeared to be serious, then quickly cooled. He was a global figure now, one of the most famous people in the world, a torch carrier of his generation.

And when he wasn't out chasing stars or being one himself, Jobs was back at Apple obsessing over his own latest fantasies.

The most emblematic of these was the Apple 1984 annual report. Annual reports are among the greatest paradoxes of modern business. All public companies are required by the SEC to make an annual report to shareholders of their earnings or losses and of their assets and liabilities. Theoretically, this could be done in about five pages of an earnings statement, balance sheet and footnotes. But companies almost never settle for that. Instead, they produce a slick booklet that typically contains a collection of vanity photos of the company's executives, a few thousand words about the company's operations that are so vetted by lawyers as to be meaningless, color photos of company operations that show exactly nothing and a letter to shareholders from the CEO that is a small miracle of euphemism, cliché and evasion. The company proudly hands the reports out by the thousands to people who never read them. And every twelve months the cycle begins again.

It was just this fragile and worthless vehicle upon which Steve Jobs chose to waste his precious time and energy. The 1984 Apple annual report, he decided, would be not just any annual report, but the greatest annual report of all time, a document for the ages, a masterpiece of design and content that would be a touchstone for anyone in years to come curious about the wellsprings of Apple's greatness. It was as if Jobs had decided to create the finest owner's warranty in business history, the greatest and most beautiful power cord. In choosing the annual report, Jobs was making a devastating statement about himself as a manager: unable to distinguish between things of importance and mere trifles, he was a young man without perspective.

It was a magnificent folly. Three succeeding teams of professional writers prepared drafts of the body copy. None of them met Jobs's approval—though all received handsome checks. In the end the copy was written in-house by the same person who'd written the more pedestrian (and more realistic) 1983 annual report. For the photos in the annual report, Jobs hired, at $50,000 per day, the team that had shot the classic black-and-white photos for Fleetwood Mac albums. The assignment was to record the members of all of Apple's product teams (with emphasis on the Mac). When the first round of shots didn't meet Jobs's standards, the camera crew was brought back—to the tune of $100,000. Finally, the capper of the report was to be a photo-essay showing all those famous stars Jobs had contacted proudly using their free Macs to change the Course of History. But it didn't quite work out that way. Sure, there were famous folks—the photo of Jim Henson was particularly striking, but more for his puppeteer's fingers than anything to do with computers). But with the exception of Kurt Vonnegut, who'd written the first two pages of his new novel *Galapagos* on his Mac, most of the applications were impressive only in how pedestrian they were. Dianne Feinstein, for example, wrote business letters on her Mac, a task she could have performed a lot better at that moment on an IBM PC.

This was Jobs as Ozymandias. The thousands who received their 1984 Apple annual report looked at it, were impressed, then threw it away. The shrewder shareholders asked how much this little vanity project had cost and wondered what kind of company would be this needlessly extravagant with its profits. In fact, the annual report had cost between $5 million and $10 million, according to inside reports. In the end, the editor on the project, who'd slept on his office floor for most of two months and who had bowed before Jobs's every changing whim, was scapegoated and fired.

But before that happened, one writer got an unexpected glimpse of the turmoil roaring at the heart of the company. Late one night, sitting with a company vice president in a conference room at Apple headquarters, struggling with the fourth draft of the second iteration of the copy, this writer was stunned to watch the vice president (later a key figure in the Sculley era) suddenly lose it. Frustrated and tired, the executive suddenly began to rant about everything that was wrong with Apple: the prima donnas, the little fiefdoms, but most of all, the unpredictability of Steve Jobs. Then the executive leaped to his feet, marched over to a poster on the wall—it showed a still from the "1984" commercial—and punched it to the floor. "You want to know where Big Brother really is?" he shouted. "It's not at IBM. It's right here!"

At the end of 1984, Joanna Hoffman, back marketing the Mac in the United States after international duty, was asked to prepare a forecast of Mac sales for a meeting with Jobs. As she studied the numbers covering Macintosh sales to date, she realized to her shock that these weren't real sales numbers, but estimates dating back to the weeks just after the Mac introduction back in January. The entire company was operating off fake numbers. As she told Steven Levy: "Nobody had the guts to tell Steve that his original forecasts were stupid." Instead, Jobs, tucked deep in his psychic bunker, heard only good news from the front.

As the real sales numbers began to leak out to insiders, they could no longer ignore the depressing truth: They had built the greatest computer in history, an invention that was supposed to change the world, and nobody wanted it. One by one the team began to drift away. Bruce Horn, who had been part of the heroic last-minute fix of the Filer program, felt he hadn't gotten enough credit or money for his contribution and quit. His partner on the Filer project, Steve Capps, moved to Paris and tried to write music-related third-party software for the Mac. Randy Wigginton, who kept himself distracted for months working on a cleanup version of MacWrite, collapsed and spent much of the next year in bed watching television. He later said, "Everyone who worked there identified totally with their work—we all believed we were on a mission from God. When people didn't buy it, we were majorly depressed."

In the autumn of 1984, frustrated by the inertia in the Mac design program and tired of waiting for orders from above, Burrell Smith set out on his own initiative to restart the lab. Gathering together other Mac veterans, he created his own skunk works, "Turbotown," to build a new, more powerful Turbo Macintosh. This new Mac would feature a pair of new custom chips that would make the machine not only more powerful but less expensive, a crisp, photographic-quality black-and-white screen and, most important, a built-in hard disk drive. It was an engineer's dream computer, and Turbotown would be an engineer's dream work environment, free from all the suits and rules and memos, just as the Mac operation had been in its early days.

But that was the problem. The new Apple, the one being built by Sculley with the tacit approval of Jobs, didn't want unruly Turbotowns anymore. It also didn't want the Turbo Mac either, at least as it was configured. And as Smith bogged down in chip design, the ever-skeptical Bob Belleville made his move. At yet another off-site meeting at Pajaro, Belleville made his case: Apple could not afford two new Mac projects: the Turbo Mac and the one he believed more salable, a modular Mac with a full-sized screen and an optional disk drive. In the meeting, Jobs held out for the Turbo Mac, but afterward in the hallway he changed his mind. And by the time he returned to Cupertino on Monday, he had decided to kill the Turbo Mac and with it Turbotown. He informed Smith, in the ultimate insult to a man who hated bureaucracies, that the design of the new Mac would have to be left to a committee.

In retrospect, Belleville and Jobs were probably right for that time. They got their modular, big-screen Mac—though it would soon also hold a hard disk. But their heavy-handedness, Jobs's inexplicable failure to use his wiles, cost them Burrell Smith. Smith went on to co-found Mac display maker Radius Inc. with Mike Boich, the first Macintosh evangelist. But he was so bitter that for years he refused even to drive by Apple's headquarters.

That left one last founding figure on the Mac team, Andy Hertzfeld, who had been there from the Texaco Tower era. These days, Hertzfeld seemed an anachronism, the last designer with the old Homebrew sensibility in a company that was trying every day to be more like IBM. Hertzfeld had a running feud with Belleville, whom he believed personified everything wrong with the new Apple. When he heard that Smith was leaving, Hertzfeld snapped. Hertzfeld's dream was even more ambitious than Smith's: he saw Turbotown as the core of a new design team that would set out to create the next insanely great Apple project, the true successor to the Mac. And Smith was crucial to the plan.

Now that dream was dying fast. In desperation, Hertzfeld took his case to Sculley. As Sculley listened, he dumped out all of his frustrations with Belleville, with the new Apple, with the death of the dream. Receiving no response, Hertzfeld grew desperate. The situation is so bad, Hertzfeld told Sculley, that Apple is now about to lose the man who created the Macintosh: Burrell Smith himself! The name hardly seemed to register with Sculley. Lab guys were lab guys. Sculley thanked Hertzfeld for stopping by.

Andy Hertzfeld walked out of the meeting and out of Apple. He kept up a good front, but later admitted that for a month thereafter he cried himself to sleep every night.

7.16 BLUE BUST

By early 1985, there was no denying that sales of the Macintosh were nowhere near predictions and that the company was in serious trouble.

Apple had managed to keep up a good front through the previous year. By the summer of 1984, it could still proclaim terrific sales figures, but a sizable chunk of that (50,000 machines) came from a single group, the Apple University Consortium, a group of twenty-four schools, including Stanford and Harvard, which offered the Macs to students at discount prices. Thanks to that order, Apple could announce on Day 101 that it had shipped 70,000 Macs. That was a little less than the internal projection, but a lot more than the public one. As a result, Apple could claim the Mac was a huge success, profitable in its very first quarter.

Unfortunately, the company began to believe its own press releases. Now it predicted 80,000 units for the month of September alone. August saw only 15,000 Macs shipped. In desperation, the Mac sales force, realizing that the business market wasn't panning out fast enough, began trying to sell the machine to schools—thus poaching on the II's territory and further aggravating the hatred between the two groups.

In October, the company had its second annual sales meeting in Hawaii. The 1983 meeting had been a wild success and Apple, now addicted to Big

Events, decided to make this year's even more spectacular. It would prove to be Apple's biggest party ever, complete with laser shows, Don Ho, banquets, lei-making seminars and endless quantities of booze and sun.

Given the location, the incongruous theme of the meeting was "Bluebusters," a play on the previous summer's hit movie *Ghostbusters*, with a touch of *The Blues Brothers*. It seemed that everywhere you looked there was a figure in blue suit, fedora, sunglasses, briefcase and ceramic mask cakewalking to the Bluebusters' theme song:

> *When the big machine*
> *Wants to take control*
> *Who ya gonna call?*
> *Bluebusters!*

Zaniness is, of course, the rule at sales meetings, but usually it is in direct proportion to the success of the preceding fiscal year. With the Lisa and the III dead or dying, and the Mac not hitting projections, this was not exactly the time for this kind of party.

In fact, the Big Blue that Apple was pretending to bust was growing stronger by the month. In May, IBM dropped a bomb by announcing that it would soon be possible to link up all of its computers, from mainframes to PCs, in vast, company-wide networks. This announcement, which shocked everyone in the computer business, proved to be more vaporware than anything else. But a few weeks later, IBM made a second announcement, and this one wasn't smoke: a new "PC Cluster" networking scheme that would enable users to link as many as five machines (four PCs and one PC XT with hard disk) into a self-contained network capable of carrying electronic mail, swapping files and storing common documents. At $2,500, PC Cluster was no bargain—customers were already buying cheaper networks with comparable performance from the likes of 3Com—but it was a reminder to the corporate world of IBM's commitment to the workplace.

Given all this, one might have presumed that the Hawaiian sales meeting would have emphasized the real reason for such gatherings: to prepare the field sales force for the challenges of the next year, provide them with sales tools for fighting the competition and preintroducing them to the new products they would sell. The Apple sales staff especially needed this kind of help because the company had added more than 200 new salespeople just to the Mac. Instead, the sales force, new and old, got piña coladas and dancing Bluebusters. Jobs and Sculley, meanwhile, made the cover of *Business Week* together ("The Dynamic Duo") wearing luau shirts.

Soon after the hungover salespeople returned, Apple kicked off a new, $12 million promotional campaign, "Test Drive a Macintosh," which appeared as a forty-page special supplement in the election issue of *Newsweek*. Test Drive was the brainchild of Mike Murray and his Mac marketing group. Once one got past the overblown and alarming *(How much did Apple pay for this?)* supplement, the idea of the campaign was rather clever: everyone was invited to walk into any computer store of their choice that sold Macs, plunk down a credit card for deposit and take a Macintosh home for the night to play with. The Test Drive was meant to be the solution to the growing opinion inside Apple (confirmed by watching customers in stores) that if people would just sit down and try the Mac for a few minutes, they'd be sold forever.

There was only one problem with the idea: Apple apparently did not hear the grumbles of the dealers who were forced to sign on to the idea. It didn't seem to notice that the Test Drive, guaranteed to create chaos even in a slow month, was being dropped right into the middle of the Christmas rush, the year's biggest selling period for personal computers. Thus the dealers responded to the Test Drive in a predictable way: they sabotaged it through neglect . . . *Sorry, our loaner's out. Come back after the first of the year.*

7.17 APPLE II FOREVER

By the end of 1984, Apple had sold 250,000 Macintoshes. It was not, in fact, a bad figure by any measure, except Apple's own expectations. And those expectations continued to grow.

In a most extraordinary move, Apple's senior management decided in October—against all evidence to the contrary—to adopt a business plan that called for Apple to sell 80,000 Macs per month for the next fiscal year. A million Macs, just as Sculley and Jobs had dreamed ten months before. Combined with the Apple II's revenue predictions, this gave Apple predicted revenues in fiscal 1985 of $3 billion. That meant a doubling of Apple's size in the next twelve months. It was sheer madness, partly brought on by Jobs's emotional need for the Mac's business to be the equal of the II's.

Obviously these numbers couldn't stand, but because Jobs wouldn't budge unless the II group backed off as well, company planners raced back and forth between the two groups to pound out a compromise. They finally reached it at $2 billion in revenues, with equal contributions from each group.

For revenues to be that big, Apple would need to have a $1 billion Christmas season. Not only was that unprecedented; it was probably impossible. And if Apple was going to have a billion-dollar quarter, then its factories and suppliers were going to have to gear up for full-scale production. And so, to mollify one man, an entire corporation put itself on the line, risking its fiscal health and the livelihoods of all the people who worked for it and their families.

Of course it failed. Though, thankfully, not horribly. It proved to be a $700 million quarter, enough to keep Apple afloat but also awash in unsold inventory. The company now had 250,000 Sony disk drives on hand, a year's supply, just as Sony was about to introduce a new model. When Apple begged the company to stop production, Sony refused.

Now looming ahead was January, traditionally the month when Apple displayed itself to the world. Two years ago it had been the Lisa, last year the Mac. Now the world had come to expect miracles from Apple at Super Bowl time. But this year Apple had little to show. The II group had been given its own moment in the sun the previous April when it had introduced the IIb (for "book"), almost renamed the Pippin in response to the Macintosh, and finally called the IIc (for "compact"). The IIc was designed to be an entry-level machine, a small miracle of redesign that put the IIe into a box the size of a large book. The IIc had been targeted for $995 (without monitor), a price point perfect for housewives, students and other first-time users.

Unfortunately, at introduction the machine was priced at $1,295 retail, with another $200 bucks for an Apple display. Even worse, the company announced at the same time that the IIe, with one disk drive and no display, would now be priced at just $995. Thus, in one stroke, Apple undermined its own new product. The introduction itself didn't help.

Planned to be the latest in Apple's new "event" publicity style, the II's introduction took place at San Francisco's Moscone Center. It was an early glimpse of all that would go wrong with Apple events in the years to come. First, it was ridiculously overblown, from the hagiographics of replicating the Jobs garage to the bombast of giant television screens to the silliness of II engineers arriving in tuxedos. There was a sense of desperation, obvious in the theme "Apple II Forever." Then the event was momentarily hijacked by Jobs, who came onstage to discuss the status of the Mac Hundred Days (60,000 shipped!) program. Finally, and most pathetically, Steve Wozniak came out onstage and played stand-up comedian. It was embarrassing: "I ran into Ronald Reagan downstairs [the Democratic convention was to be held at Moscone in a few months] and I asked him what he thought of the PCjr. He told me he was against abortions!" Behind Woz, Jobs covered his face with his hands.

It ended, mercifully, with Sculley. His words would be recalled later with some irony:

Apple is going to become a great marketing company. McDonald's and Burger King are great marketing companies in their industries, just as Pepsi and Coke are in theirs. The Apple challenge is built on great foundations—that product innovation and marketing innovation can play the major role in shaping this dynamic growth industry. If we are right—and we believe we are—Silicon Valley will never be the same again.

There was yet another II in the works, the IIx. It might have been the greatest Apple II of all. Certainly it had the right pedigree: its microprocessor was to be a new and more powerful second generation of the original 6502 chip, this time to be developed by the Western Design Center in Phoenix; and its design leader was to be Wozniak himself. The IIx was to be the Super II, and its most interesting feature was to be a second processor slot in which the user could plug in everything from the Intel 8088 (to make the IIx fully IBM-compatible) to the Motorola 68000 (to make it a pseudo-Mac). But the IIx ran into a host of problems. A few of those problems were technical—the first chips from WDC arrived four months late and DOA. But most were political. The IIx had no champions. Woz, the erstwhile design leader, was growing more erratic and distracted by the week. By early 1984 he seemed to lose interest in the project altogether. Meanwhile, the Macintosh group, especially Jobs, hated the very idea of the IIx, which threatened to out-Mac the Mac to an audience of millions of loyal II users.

With the September introduction date lost, the product design still incomplete, the support for the product within the company fading, the coup de grace to the IIx came in March. That's when the IIx's own product manager, Ida Cole, circulated to management her prediction that the machine would sell only 25,000 units per month. Nine months later, Apple would have killed for a product with those sales figures, but in early spring the company was still dreaming of 80,000-unit months for the Mac and 100,000 for the IIc. Thus, even before the Moscone event, the computer that might have bridged the gap between the II and the Mac, as well as taken Apple into the IBM clone world, was quietly killed.

So the II group was out of the picture for the big January 1985 extravaganza. That left only the Mac team. But the 512K Mac had already been introduced. The only new product left on the horizon was something called the Mac XL, which was basically a Lisa with a hard disk drive. It was something, but hardly earthshaking. In response to the IBM network threat, the team had also been working on a new idea called the Macintosh Office.

In developing the Office, Apple knew it had no chance of competing technologically against the enterprise-wide networking scheme being proposed by IBM. It could not even compete directly against the new PC Cluster. But Apple knew it might succeed with an alternative tack: a very low-cost ($50 per node) network that would tie together up to six Macs with a common printer and a disk drive-based FileServer to create a kind of computing "work team."

With no little irony, Apple even knew where to go for the networking model: back to the old days of Xerox PARC and the Ethernet networking system developed there. A lot of Valley companies were experimenting with Ethernet at this time, so it wasn't an outrageous notion that Apple could create a slow-speed networking scheme that might handle the transfer of files and other data.

Laser printers too, though horribly expensive ($10,000 was a typical entry-level price), were becoming common. So it was not too difficult a task for Apple to establish a repackaging agreement with the leading laser printer engine manufacturer, Canon, and then build its own custom box around it.

But convincing Apple to make such a commitment was another matter.

"Desktop publishing totally saved Apple," said Tim Bajarin, "and the laser printer made desktop publishing possible. So even though Steve Jobs didn't think up the Mac, he certainly deserves credit for standing behind laser printing. Everybody else wanted to forget it. But Steve—coached by John Warnock—stuck with it. Even Apple's board wanted no part of it. Steve nearly had to stage a hissy-fit to keep it. I think it was Jobs's biggest decision at Apple."

Office automation software was equally problematic, but that obstacle was breached when Lotus agreed to create Jazz, a Mac-oriented version of the wildly popular Lotus 1-2-3 suite of programs.

The FileServer was yet another problem. Apple was not a hard disk drive designer. And it soon found itself at sea just coming to an agreement on what such a server should do. The marketing department, of course, wanted it to do everything, from electronic mail to full work team collaboration. The designers, by comparison, weren't even sure where to start. No one had been down this path before. There was no e-mail software yet. And how did you deal with two people working on the same file at the same time? How did you protect private files, while leaving others wide open? And how did you link up with other networks in the organization, including those with IBM computers? The answers might eventually be found, but not before the January announcement.

7.18 LEMMINGS

And so Apple went into the January gauntlet with a new product missing its critical component.

As in the year before, the extravaganza kicked off at the Super Bowl. The good news was that the game was being held at Stanford Stadium just up the road and that one of the contending teams was the San Francisco 49ers. This was seen as a good omen: the first Silicon Valley Super Bowl featuring Silicon Valley's home team.

The promotion had two parts. First, nearly 85,000 seat cushions bearing the Apple logo were placed in the stands. It made an impressive sight, one noted by the announcers and seen by millions of viewers when they were waved by fans. Second, in the final time slot of the game, Apple was to premiere its new commercial—a fact it heralded in newspaper ads across the country warning people not to go to the bathroom during the fourth quarter.

The moment finally came. Thanks to an exciting game, America was glued to the TV. The commercial was entitled "Lemmings" and featured a line of blindfolded businessmen in suits marching across a blasted landscape singing, like middle management dwarfs, a weary and heartless "Heigh-ho, heigh-ho." Then, as the camera pulled back, the viewer saw that each man in turn was stepping off a cliff. Only the last businessman in line stopped at the brink, pulled up his blindfold and thus, illuminated, saved himself from certain death.

The commercial was a complete disaster. Dreary, obvious and unpleasant, it not only lacked the sense of freedom and liberation that had made the "1984" ad so thrilling, but, in its death-filled way, managed to insult the very businesspeople Apple was trying to reach. It was unbelievably misguided and inappropriate. Like the "1984" ad, but for entirely different reasons, it was never shown again.

"Lemmings" was an augury of things to come. The annual meeting/new product extravaganza proved an equal disaster. It was again held at Flint Center, and this time the place was overflowing. In a metaphor for the year before, the Mac group was warned to be there early, so they filled all the best seats, while the II group was told nothing at all—so many had to watch the event from across the street at the movie theater in the Oaks Shopping Center. Their place, out of sight and mind, may explain why someone called in a death threat against Jobs. Some Mac group members responded by painting bull's-eyes on the backs of their T-shirts and calling themselves "bullet blockers." Whatever the source of the threat, prank or real, the place swarmed with security men.

The event kicked off with "Lemmings." Jobs tried to riff off the ad by coming out onstage wearing a blindfold. It went over great with the Apple folks, like a lead balloon with everyone else. Having essentially accused IBM and all of its customers of being blind and suicidal, Jobs then held out what he called "a hand of peace":

When we spoke of a two-horse race in personal computers in 1984 it might have seemed like we were on a collision course with IBM. But in 1985, as the smoke clears from the '84 shakeout, many of those large corporations are telling us that they're going to use both Apple and IBM workstations, or that they want to use Macintoshes to talk with their IBM mainframes. It's imperative that we talk with the IBM part of the world, that we exchange information and have frequent discourse. So, for 1985, Apple proposes détente with IBM.

As he said this, a mock-up image of the front page of *The Wall Street Journal* was beamed overhead. The unlikely headline read: "Apple Declares Détente with IBM."

In just a few words, Steve Jobs voided the entire previous year's marketing campaign, beginning with "1984." Moreover, his ex cathedra declaration ignored one important question: Was IBM willing to declare détente with Apple? The entire event reeked of desperation and confusion—meaning that it did an excellent job of portraying Apple at this very moment. This, of course, was not what the company had in mind: it preferred the press to come away with the story Jobs told of a letter from a six-year-old boy who was doing a crossword puzzle and substituted "computer" for "pie" in the phrase "As American as Apple . . ." That Steve Jobs, of all people, was resorting to the last refuge, patriotism, was a hint of how bad things really were.

With all the fanfare the company could muster, the components of the Mac Office were introduced: the Mac XL, the LaserWriter printer, Lotus Jazz, and the AppleTalk network. They each were applauded, but everyone in the house couldn't help but think of the missing guest of honor, the FileServer. It was promised for autumn, along with e-mail software and the plug-in cards for linking up PCs. Members of the press muttered to one another: Apple has just introduced a nonproduct.

Afterward, as Jobs came out to meet the Mac team, Bob Belleville burst into tears. "We've got so much to do!" he sobbed. "And it's all such a mess!"

The board of directors meeting that afternoon was worse. Markkula and the others had been hearing a lot of complaints, on the record and off, about what was going on at the company. They took both Sculley and Jobs to task.

Sculley was told to start taking charge and acting like a CEO. That's what he was being paid for. Jobs, conversely, was told to *stop* acting like a CEO, leave the II group alone, stop playing petty monarch and start focusing on running the Mac group properly. Sculley took the criticism like a professional. Jobs, pouting, went back to his office and began typing on the computer like a schoolboy kept after school, "I will not criticize the rest of the organization. I will not criticize the rest of the organization. . . ."

The meeting with stock analysts was held the following morning. Underscoring the fact that this was not an Apple-controlled production, the meeting took place in San Jose, in the more dour confines of the big, anonymous Red Lion Inn next to the Bayshore Freeway. These weren't shareholders, but the people who made the market on Apple stock, and as such they demanded much more inside financial information.

In particular, they had some tough questions to ask about the apparently contradictory nature of the recently released quarterly results. Even if Apple had not met its own internal projections, it had more than met those of these analysts. It had indeed been a killer quarter: just short of $700 million, and almost a 100 percent jump from the previous Christmas. Coming at the end of a tough year for the Lisa, an industry-wide shakeout and the depredations of IBM, this was impressive stuff.

That was the good news. The bad news was that Sculley, having been informed that orders for both the Mac and the IIc had collapsed right after New Year's and that thousands of unsold machines were piling up at dealers, distributors and Apple's own warehouses, was obliged to add in the release a warning that the next few quarters' revenues would be much lower. Those words alone dropped the stock by two points. Now the analysts wanted to know more. They asked Sculley and Jobs to break out the revenues by product group, something Apple had not been required to do in its public filing. This was the moment of truth. For a year, Apple had been covering up the reality of the Mac's disappointing sales not only from the world but from itself. Now it had to fess up.

The Mac, Jobs admitted to the group, had been "left out in the cold" over the Christmas season. Sales were just $200 million—meaning that the II, the forgotten Apple, had contributed nearly $500 million. And, Jobs added, he didn't expect the Mac's sales to pick up anytime soon.

There it was: the truth at last. Eyebrows lifted around the room. But the analysts weren't done. Now they peppered the pair about the Mac Office. Why wasn't it complete? Where was the FileServer?

Then an extraordinary thing happened, something few of the analysts had ever seen: in response to a whispered message from an Apple staffer, Sculley got up and left the room, leaving the meeting in the hands of Steve Jobs. The analysts glanced at each other inquisitively: what would pull Sculley out of an analyst meeting?

The "third-largest shareholder in the company." That was how Steve Wozniak introduced himself when Sculley picked up the telephone. Woz had taken this moment of all moments to lodge a bitter complaint. Sculley, recognizing the legal and voting power behind that self-introduction, listened politely.

Woz was furious, a rare emotion for him even in those difficult days. He was calling from the Triangle Building representing, he said, the entire Apple II group. Sculley, Wozniak continued, had presented a fraudulent view of the company the day before at the shareholders' meeting. If the stock remark hadn't already set off alarms in Sculley's ear, Woz's words certainly did. *Lawsuit!*

How so? Sculley politely asked. Well, said Woz bitterly, you failed to give adequate time to the successes of the Apple II. In particular, we had a demonstration showing that not only the Mac but the II worked with the new Laser-Writer. But that demonstration was pulled at the last moment. Woz was on a roll now. I'm used to this kind of treatment, he continued, I've watched as the II has taken a back seat to every new company computer, from the III to the Lisa and now to the Mac. But the new people in my group aren't and it makes me angry to see them hurt and demoralized like this. Now they're talking about writing a mass protest letter to you. I decided to call you first.

Sculley relaxed. *Is that all?* He would just calm Woz down and get back to the meeting. Listen, Steve, Sculley told Woz, the II got its own event back in April; besides, the Mac Office was the only new product available in time for the annual meeting.

But we didn't get the April event, Woz replied. Jobs hijacked it to give a presentation on the status of the Mac. Why wasn't the II given the same courtesy yesterday? We weren't even allowed to make a presentation at the business session.

Well, Sculley replied, you're getting your moment right now. When you called I was presenting the II's financials to the . . .

But Woz had already hung up on him. A few days later, Wozniak quit Apple Computer, slamming the company as he left: "Apple's direction has been horrendously wrong for five years," he told the press. Woz, seething in anger and resentment, had timed the moment perfectly to stick a knife in the company and Steve Jobs.

With Wozniak's departure the technical disintegration of Apple Computer was now complete. In just one year's time, the company had managed to drive off the last of its first generation of technical geniuses. To Jef Raskin's name could now be added Burrell Smith, Bill Atkinson and now the greatest of all, Steve Wozniak. There was now only one founding visionary left.

7.19 SUGAR DADDIES

Where was John Sculley during all of this? Obviously not running the company with an iron fist. Even the board recognized that. Nor was he fighting to make peace among the company's feuding factions. That had been the message of Woz's angry telephone call.

Sculley was, in fact, having a helluva good time living out a dream of empire building. With the Mac successfully launched and the numbers apparently terrific, he embarked on a grand strategic campaign of transforming Apple from a clever upstart into a corporate titan—and if not that, then finishing the Apple story with a glorious climax. After all, what would be a better capstone to his career than either to grow Apple through mergers and acquisitions into an IBM-like giant or, better yet, to walk away to the cheers of shareholders and his peers after having sold the company to the highest corporate bidder?

Sculley's plan was not entirely selfish. Unlike many of his lieutenants, he had a very good idea of what it would take to compete against a corporation as huge and well established as IBM. For all of its successes to date, Apple was still just a Tokyo citizen trying to survive against Godzilla. The success of the Mac and the failure of the PCjr had merely stubbed the monster's toes. IBM would recover—then sooner or later Apple would be squished underfoot. The only solutions were:

- *Get out of IBM's way.* Almost impossible unless the home or other as yet unknown computer market suddenly took off.
- *Grow Apple big enough to hold its own against Big Blue.* Nearly impossible through internal growth (especially in a slow market), but conceivable using the more than $100 million in cash on hand to make intelligent acquisitions.
- *Hook up with another corporate Godzilla.* The most likely scenario: Sell Apple now, while it was America's darling and about to have its best quarter ever, at a premium price to a big company wanting to expand into consumer electronics. Short of that, sell off a minority of the firm to one of these companies for enough money to fund a massive expansion.

This buyout scenario had the added advantage of enabling Sculley to walk away a corporate hero, cheered by Apple shareholders and his peers (if not by employees) before he had to deal with the hard work of coming up with new products, building existing machines and dealing with a mutinous rank and file. So why should he worry too much about the nasty details of daily corporate life? After all, soon they would be somebody else's problem.

Besides, it was fun. Throughout 1984, during their evenings and weekends together, Sculley and Jobs happily tossed business scenarios at one another. Nothing was too crazy to imagine—especially not in that era of corporate excess, leveraged buyouts and junk bonds.

Author Frank Rose, inside Apple during this period, describes it best:

> During the day they might quarrel and snap at each other, but alone together in the boardroom, late at night, they sensed no limit to the things they could do together. They could get a billion-dollar loan from GM or GE or AT&T and float enough junk bonds to take over Xerox and dominate the office automation market. They could run for president together and take turns being vice president and run the country between them for sixteen years.

In fact, GE, AT&T and Xerox were just the companies Sculley was looking at, along with Ford and, through its newly acquired computer services company EDS, General Motors. As Sculley saw it, each had a reason to be interested in Apple, from computer phones for AT&T to computerized factories for Ford and GM, to desktop office automation for Xerox. And each had billions of dollars on hand to burn.

So, throughout the summer and fall of 1984, often unbeknownst even to other top executives at Apple, the company was visited by delegations representing each of these corporate giants. Apple was on the block.

Roger Smith of General Motors stopped by to tour the Macintosh plant. EDS head H. Ross Perot came out to Cupertino too, representing GM. The little Napoleon, now thanks to the GM buyout "the third-craziest billionaire in Texas" (Molly Ivins's phrase), showed perhaps just how crazy he was by coming away from the visit powerfully impressed by not only Apple but Steve Jobs. In fact, he recommended that GM consider Apple only if Jobs agreed to stay.

AT&T sniffed around Apple too, as did some smaller players, such as workstation maker Wang, then at the height of its success. But the most serious discussions took place between Apple and General Electric. Jack Welch, whom many considered the best (and scariest) businessman of his generation, had restored GE from a declining dinosaur back to a vital business powerhouse. He'd done so through scores of mergers and acquisitions, followed by ruthless reorganizations. Neutron Jack was the one top businessman in America who not only could understand what Apple was about but could also knock some sense back into it. And GE's computer-leasing company already had a contract with Apple. Pretty soon, visitors from GE corporate were regularly flying out to Cupertino, and Sculley and Jobs were returning the favor by flying back to Fairfield, Connecticut.

With all of this activity and interest, it seemed inevitable that Apple would find a Sugar Daddy. But in the end, it all proved to be sound and fury, signifying nothing more than the fact that Apple was Corporate America's Playmate of the Month.

In the midst of all this, one other business opportunity also presented itself. Once again the uncelebrated Floyd Kvamme played a key role as facilitator. The proposal was brought in by Apple's old friend Ben Rosen. Rosen, the shrewdest of high-tech journalists, had shown just how clever he was by selling off his newsletter to Esther Dyson and going into the venture capital business. In time, his investments would make him nearly as rich as Steve Jobs, but for now, Sevin-Rosen Partners was struggling. Its biggest investment had been in a new IBM computer clone company based in Texas called Compaq.

Compaq had just enjoyed one of the most amazing first years in business history—$111 million in revenues—but it was cash-poor and, thanks to IBM price bombing, short on profits. Would Apple be interested, Rosen asked, in acquiring Compaq? The deal would cost just $100 million, well within Apple's budget. This was Sculley's first scenario—growth by acquisition—but Sculley was far more distracted by the third. Why waste time on acquiring a little Texas computer company when General Electric was knocking on the door? As for Jobs: Compaq was in the IBM business. Enough said.

And so a golden opportunity to beat IBM at its own game was ignored. In a few years, Compaq would be bigger than IBM in personal computers. It would also be bigger than Apple. By 1998, having bought Tandem and Digital Equipment, it would be the third-largest computer company on earth.

7.20 COUP D'ETAT

Apple had bet everything and lost. It had wagered that it would have a huge Christmas, that the Mac would take off and that a White Knight would arrive to save it from the Armonk dragon.

Now it was adrift, demasted and rudderless. In a year's time the company had gone from the most celebrated new-product introduction in high-tech history, a historic collection of talent, a charismatic leader of worldwide celebrity and the prospect of huge financial success—to a disorganized and squabbling collection of fiefdoms, its technical heroes scattered to the winds, one founder gone and the other under assault and warehouses filled with unsold products. Everyone working within the company and watching it from without knew that some sort of terrible reckoning was due. And most had a good idea on whose neck the ax would, and should, fall.

The 1985 Steve Jobs was even more eccentric and infuriating than ever. Before the board had warned him off interfering with other company operations, he had tried to destroy Apple's distribution system by suggesting (on the basis of a casual conversation with the founder of Federal Express) that Apple should entirely replace its current infrastructure with, say, FedEx jets landing on a private runway next to the Milpitas plant. That guaranteed that one more department in the company hated him. He also talked about moving the entire company to a campus site in the hills south of San Jose—as if the company wasn't already isolated and introverted enough. Now Jobs wanted to make it Super Turbotown, the Anaconda Copper of Computing. That terrified just about everybody. Even members of the Mac group were now growing tired of Jobs's mercurial and high-handed style.

They weren't alone. One local reporter took an informal poll of everyone he knew—reporters, Apple employees, suppliers, customers, etc.—who had dealt with Steve Jobs. They were asked to use one word to describe Jobs. The vote was almost unanimous: "asshole." The same word was whispered by a few attendees at Jobs's thirtieth birthday party in late February (the St. Francis again, this time with Ella Fitzgerald) after he walked away leaving their carefully chosen gifts behind.

Other outsiders noticed too, especially the analysts and industry observers who established the market for Apple products and stock. Said Doug Cayne with the Gartner Group, "Jobs tends to decide where he thinks the personal computer ought to go, which isn't always where the market thinks it wants to go." Said Joan McKay of Kidder, Peabody, "People either think Jobs is a brainchild or they hate him. He's not a personality you're neutral on." Most influential, though, was Esther Dyson, who would announce as a postscript to the episode, "Clearly something had to be done, and it seems Jobs was in the way of things happening."

In the midst of all this, *Time* reporter Michael Moritz published *The Little Kingdom*, the first (and best) book about Apple. It was devastating, because for once a reporter had looked past the well-polished myths about the company and its beginnings and simply told the truth about Steve Jobs.

Suddenly, unexpectedly for many people still, it became possible to imagine an Apple Computer without Jobs, or at least one without him in a position of authority. After all, Woz had gone and come and gone again without the sky falling. And once that taboo thought became imaginable, it slowly became practical.

Steve Jobs, who had lived by his unique personality, now began to die by it. As Jobs himself, with his love of philosophy, would appreciate, his subordinates, minions, acolytes and admirers underwent a gestalt shift. Now, his endless reversals of opinion were no longer seen as symptomatic of his brilliance, but of his inconstancy. His charm was no longer soulful, but manipulative. And his eccentricities, like his disgusting foot massages, were no longer the mark of a rebel, but a crank. And when Jobs, the day after the party, sent around a memo, "Rough Sailing Ahead," suggesting the Apple employees give up their free juice, first-class tickets and off-site retreats, most employees just laughed. They had seen Jobs pull his scapegoat routine before, and they knew who really was to blame.

By March, Jobs was prone to explosive outbursts. The worst came when he visited frogdesign, the brilliant designers of the Mac box, and discovered the team there was also designing a product for Wozniak's new company, CL9. Jobs lost it. He warned the designers they would have to choose between him and Woz—then for good measure called Woz and threatened to destroy his company.

All that was left to destroy was the perfect partnership. For a couple of months after the annual meeting fiasco, Sculley and Jobs had been staying pretty much apart. But Sculley never fully escaped the shock waves Jobs was creating. At one seminar, he found himself confronted by several middle managers, one of whom asked him bluntly, "Who's running this company anyway? If you're running the company, why is Steve Jobs going around telling us what to do?" Now as the Macintosh problem deepened, as Sculley learned that no one was even working on a second-generation machine—and as he began to hear reports of Jobs bad-mouthing him on the sly—Sculley decided it was time for a confrontation. He feared it was too late. "I had given Steve greater power than he had ever had and I had created a monster." Jobs's little group had now swollen to more than 1,000 employees.

The meeting took place on a rainy evening in Jobs's crowded office. They were joined by Jay Elliot, Apple's human resources director, who during this period often seemed to be the only person holding the company together.

Elliot had long been pushing for this meeting, rightly believing that only Sculley could handle Jobs. But Sculley, for his part, wasn't even sure of that— he still remembered the seduction in the Manhattan aerie. Sculley began the conversation by saying that no one admired Jobs's "brilliance and vision more than I do." Nevertheless, he continued, "I have lost confidence in your ability to run the Macintosh division."

Jobs was stunned, but still clever enough to take an unexpected tack. As he had done when recruiting Sculley, he became the student at the foot of the master. "Well," he said, "you've got to spend more time with me."

That, as intended, confused Sculley, but he pressed on. "I want you to know that I'm going to bring this up with the board and I'm going to recommend that you step down from your operating job of running the Macintosh division. And I want you to know that ahead of time."

Jobs said he didn't believe it. But Sculley held firm. At that point, Jobs leaped to his feet, paced the room and began a tirade against Sculley. "If you do that, you're going to destroy this company! I'm the only one who understands enough around here about manufacturing and operations, and I don't think you understand these things yet. You're too far removed from the actual day in, day out operations, and if I'm not overseeing this, we're not going to get any new products out and we're not going to succeed!"

That was only the start of the argument. Before it was over, Sculley was more convinced than ever of the need to remove Jobs from line responsibility. Jobs, for his part, appeared to believe that Sculley wouldn't have the guts to follow through on his threat.

But Jobs was wrong. At the April 10 board of directors meeting, Sculley announced that he was asking Steve Jobs to step down from running the Mac group. He also informed the directors that if they weren't willing to back him on this, they could find a new CEO.

The board meeting ran the entire evening, and all of the next day. Separately, the directors called in Sculley and Jobs to grill them. At three-thirty, the board unanimously voted to back Sculley.

Outside, waiting in the hallway, it was at last Steve Jobs's turn to cry.

7.21 ABDICATION

In the weeks that followed, Jobs tried to play the good son. He worked on Sculley, promising to behave himself if only he could get his old job back. But Sculley refused to cave. So Jobs took a different tack and assaulted his ego. "I think you really lost your stride," he told Sculley. "You really were great the first year and everything went wonderful. I can't pin it down, but it was sometime during the end of 1984 . . ."

It was all very petty, but behind the scenes Jobs was playing a bigger, more dangerous game. After the board meeting, Jobs hid out for a few days away from Apple, then took off on a scheduled trip to Japan. There, with Bob Belleville, he hatched a coup plot. The plan (along with a nasty late night call he made to Sculley) so thrilled Jobs that he seemed to come out of his depression. In fact, he felt so good that when he ran into Wayne Rosing, engineering director of the Apple II division, Jobs so belittled him that Rosing decided that Jobs was back in charge of Apple . . . and quit the company.

On May 23, on the eve of his executive staff meeting, Sculley and his executive team were having dinner at the home of Apple vice president Al Eisenstat. During the evening, Sculley was pulled aside by Jean-Louis Gassée for a private word. Gassée, who had been a sensation running Apple France, where he had defeated even IBM, had been brought over to be Jobs's replacement in the Mac group. For the moment, he was the group's marketing manager, having replaced Mike Murray, whose days had been numbered ever since the Test Drive.

It was, for the first time in a long month, a happy evening. Sculley had been invited to China for a celebration of a big order for Apple computers. There was to be a major ceremony in the Great Hall in Beijing, and after months of misery, Sculley was excited about going. Besides, it might mean billions in future sales.

But Gassée had a dangerous message to convey. Don't go to China, he told Sculley. "John, you should be aware that there are real forces going on to try to throw you out of the company." It seemed that Jobs had decided to spring the coup while Sculley was halfway around the world. But in his typically impatient way, Jobs had done almost everything wrong. He just wasn't subtle enough to be devious. For example, he didn't even try to regain the trust of the board—which meant that even if the coup had succeeded it wouldn't have been ratified. Then, unwilling to wait, he began rounding up confederates for the coup even before Sculley's departure. That's how Gassée heard. And knowing that Jobs hated him for taking his job, Gassée, no minor corporate politician himself, had gone to Sculley.

Sculley canceled the trip.

At the Friday morning meeting, which was ostensibly about developing a new action plan for the company, Sculley waited until Jobs arrived, then dispensed with formalities. "Steve . . . it has come to my attention that you'd like to throw me out of the company, and I'd like to ask if that's true."

The room froze. Jobs's knew this was his one chance. "I think you're bad for Apple and I think you're the wrong person to run this company. You really should leave this company. I'm more worried about Apple than I have ever been. I'm afraid of you. You don't know how to operate and never have.

"John, you manage by monologue! You have no understanding of the product development process. You don't know how manufacturing works. You're not close to the company. The middle managers don't respect you. . . ."

The worst of it was that everything Jobs said was true. Jobs may have been incapable of truthfully judging himself, but he had nailed Sculley perfectly. Sculley, for his part, was so disturbed by the words that he reverted to his childhood stutter. The other executives sat around the table in stricken silence. They had all been party to Jobs's conspiracy, but now they weren't sure whom they'd pick if forced to choose between someone they didn't respect but admired and someone they respected but didn't admire.

Then Sculley threw down the gauntlet, "If I left, who would run the company?"

"I think I could run the company," Jobs replied.

It was a galvanizing moment. Suddenly the executives around the table could see in sharp relief what they had almost done. Sculley knew it too. He called for a vote, asking each man and woman in turn to state their views. Most told Jobs that they loved him, but they all voted for Sculley. Perhaps the most devastating vote came from Regis McKenna, who was sitting in on the meeting. Regis, who'd been there with Jobs before everyone else, who had seen him grow this company from a garage, told him straight: You shouldn't run this company.

Jobs rose wobbily to his feet. "I guess I know where things stand," he said, and ran from the room.

No one followed.

8.0 BLIGHT

8.1 Pastoral

One of the problems facing any history of Apple Computer is how to deal with the Sculley era. Apple's first decade is a straightforward and exciting tale of genius, heroism, ego and venality. It is the epic of Steve Jobs; an updated, funkified tale out of Dreiser in which the ambitious young man makes it to the top and is then destroyed. It is an adventure yarn, a mystery and a cautionary tale all in one—with a few touches out of Dostoyevsky and Kafka.

But the Sculley era, especially after the cleanup of the corporate wreck in 1985, is a different kind of story altogether. Suddenly the headlong rush of the Jobs era comes to a screeching halt and the narrative suddenly goes nonlinear and expansive. In the Sculley era at Apple, time seems to stop. New products are regularly introduced, some marvelous, some rotten, but none ever again has the impact of the original II or Mac. There are big promotions and events, but none fix in the mind years later.

Instead, we are left with a different type of story, the kind that fills up shelves of endless, boring authorized corporate biographies. A sequence of minor events that seem to start nowhere, meander around and end up nowhere. If there are none of the deep horrifying troughs of the Jobs era, neither are there the dizzying, exalting peaks. The screaming roller-coaster ride becomes a Sunday afternoon drive: mildly interesting, sleepy and largely eventless. The narrative is now a novel of manners, Trollope with a shot of *Buddenbrooks,* in which apparently minor decisions made in distraction take on a life of their own, and eventually lead to the downfall of what seemed impregnable. It is a pastoral, where, though nothing ever seems to happen, great forces are forming just over the horizon that will one day blow this peaceful Little Kingdom to bits.

8.2 DEAD ZONE

Pax Apple didn't begin calmly. By the time of the vote that forced Jobs to step down from the Mac group, Apple was a company in serious trouble. The Great Bet of 1984—run at full capacity, break all sales records over the Christmas quarter to cover past mistakes, then sell off the tarted-up company to the highest bidder—had failed. Now Apple, its distributors and its retailers were awash in unsold Macs and IIc's. The company had too many employees on the payroll, had spent too much on advertising and had no new products in the pipeline. There was no hiding from the truth now: Apple was going to have to take its punishment—and nothing less than a huge hit would do the job.

Meanwhile, Jobs had only been demoted, not fired. And his intuition told him that he still had a chance, if he moved fast, at wrenching the controls back away from Sculley. He was, after all, just thirty years old and he owned 11.3 percent of all Apple stock—a voting block worth nearly $120 million. He had youth and equity on his side.

The next four days were as crazy as any in Apple's crazy history. Immediately after the vote, both Sculley and Jobs had to attend a meeting downstairs for representatives from all company departments to discuss what to do about the impending business crisis. Nothing was said about what had just happened, but everyone in the room knew something was wrong. Jobs came into the room like a wraith, unexpectedly took a chair in the back and sat with his arms folded and head down. Sculley, who had called the meeting, looked equally worn and exhausted. The crowd had come expecting marching orders; what it got was platitudes, calls for reducing expenses and the creation of "study teams" to report on the problem. As they watched, Sculley seemed to evaporate before their eyes. He began by standing in the middle of the room, then, as he started to crumple, he leaned against a nearby pillar. By the end of the meeting, as he took the final questions, Sculley slumped against the *back* of the pillar, almost hidden from the room.

Both men stumbled out of Apple that day in shock. Sculley told Al Eisenstat he was ready to quit, and even put in a call to Gerry Roche, the headhunter who'd brought him there. Leezy Sculley, who had disliked Jobs from the very first day, was so pissed off when she heard the news she drove down to Cupertino in search of Steve. She caught him in front of the Sun & Soil natural foods restaurant a block from Apple. She had been waiting for him in her Mercedes, and when he walked up with a group of Macolytes she jumped out and called him over. For a moment Leezy thought about slugging Jobs, but she chose to yell instead. She hadn't planned her words, but once she started they came roaring out.

"Do you have any idea what a privilege it has been even to know someone as fine as John Sculley? He has been a real friend to you, but you'll never know it until the day you're on your deathbed."

Jobs hung his head.

"Steve," she yelled, "can't you even look me in the eyes when I'm talking to you?"

"You don't understand," said Jobs. "You don't understand."

"Look at me when I talk to you," Leezy demanded. Jobs finally looked up.

"No," said Leezy, "Never mind. Don't look at me. When I look into most people's eyes, I see a soul. When I look into your eyes, I see a bottomless pit, an empty hole, a dead zone."

"You don't understand."

"I think I understand everything there is to understand, Steve. I feel sorry for you." Then she turned on her heel and marched off. Leezy Sculley had proven she had more guts facing Steve Jobs than her husband did. And in the annals of Silicon Valley, in which there is no shortage of strange and bizarre anecdotes, this is the only time a CEO's wife ever kicked the ass of a company founder in a public parking lot.

Meanwhile, back at Apple, everything was confusion along executive row. Just that morning, the company's executives had sworn fealty to Sculley—and now the word was out that he was thinking about quitting. Jesus! Did that mean Jobs would take over now—and have their heads for betraying him? Loyalists to both Sculley and Jobs began to crack under the stress. Bob Belleville, who'd played his hand with Jobs, scribbled out a resignation note, packed his stuff and marched out. Jay Elliot, the human resources director who'd sided with Sculley, stormed out as well, saying, "Fuck this."

Eventually, with nothing better to do, the management of Apple finally drifted off into the night and the three-day Memorial weekend. Most were exhausted and depressed. Only Jobs, recognizing that his time was short, managed to pull himself into action the next day. He called around, polled his supporters, then called Sculley to arrange a walk in the mountains the next day, and called Markkula to set up a meeting after that down at Markkula's spread near Big Sur. Then, to pump himself up, he set out to watch the movie *Patton* with Mike Murray, but failing to find his own copy or one at the video store, watched a Hitchcock film instead. It was the perfect choice.

The Sunday walk was up Dish Hill behind Stanford University. At the top Sculley and Jobs could look down the back slope to the west and see the stretch of Interstate 280 where Jobs and Woz had first come up with the name of their little company. That was the beginning. And this was to be the end.

Jobs gave it his best shot. He proposed running the new combined R&D operation that Sculley was planning to create out of the II and Mac groups. Or he could be Sculley's coequal and run product development while Sculley directed corporate sales and marketing. Neither received a response. So Jobs pulled out the big one: what if Sculley were to move up to chairman and let him become the new CEO.

It was completely nuts and completely Jobs. Booted out of one job, he took a shot at landing an even better one. Once again, high above the landscape, Jobs tried to seduce and overwhelm John Sculley. And the mere fact that Sculley had foolishly agreed to such a rendezvous suggested to Jobs he had a chance. But it was too late. As Sculley would later write: "When I joined Apple, I had come to terms with what I was going to be in life. I believed that the blithe spirit in fading jeans and Velcro sneakers was one of the important figures in our country during this century. I was going to help him succeed. I never imagined that I would run the company by myself someday. Now that was the reality and our friendship was over." The selflessness of the first part of that remark is a little hard to believe, but certainly the final words were accurate.

Jobs's visit to Markkula fared no better. Markkula was key to the board. Only he could smooth over the feathers Jobs had ruffled in the preceding months. But Markkula wasn't listening—at least to Jobs. As soon as Jobs and the others arrived, Markkula announced that everyone but Jobs would be allowed to talk and make the case for keeping him. It was over before it began.

Sculley went back to the office on Monday, while Apple was largely deserted, and had a series of private meetings with his lieutenants on what role they thought Jobs should have at Apple in the months and years to come. He was amazed to find that most of them were aghast at the very question. Most wanted Jobs out of all positions of responsibility at Apple *forever*. Better yet: out of the company. Sure, it would hurt the company's image to lose the face most people attached to Apple, but it sure beat the alternative.

So on May 31, exactly one week after receiving the warning from Gassée, John Sculley signed the papers that officially booted Steve Jobs out of any line responsibilities at Apple. The founder was now a man without a job in his own company. Sculley met Jobs for breakfast to tell him that the chances of him having line authority at Apple were now thin, then drove up to Markkula's house in Woodside to learn his own fate.

Mike Markkula had every reason to be furious. Since the beginning of the year, his net worth had dropped by $200 million. After five years of hard work he had at last pulled away from the day-to-day operations of the company, believing he had left the running of Apple Computer—and the care and feeding of Steve Jobs—in the hands of a pro. Now it was obvious that through incompetence, distraction and a failure of will, John Sculley had brought the company to the brink of chaos, had allowed the feuds between the different product groups turn into all-out war and had allowed Steve Jobs to run amok while giving him more and more power. "There was a lack of respect for Sculley because he wasn't managing Jobs," said one Apple manager who quit during this period. ". . . It was a very destructive environment."

In April, the board had given Sculley the green light to deal with Jobs— and in response he had done worse than nothing. Now, at the worst possible moment in terms of vulnerability, Apple was about to have its second founder, one of the most famous people in the world, also make an angry and noisy exit. Though Apple had consistently grown during Sculley's tenure, at no time had it ever met any of the revenue targets he had set for it. Employees were demoralized, business partners angry and customers confused and concerned. And IBM was still gaining market share and now owned the corporate market for personal computers.

Markkula told most of these things to John Sculley, and those he didn't Sculley announced against himself. In fact, for much of the four-hour meeting, Markkula didn't say a word. Instead it turned into a monologue by Sculley, soaked in sweat, struggling to save his career and reputation. He took the blame upon himself, promised (uncannily like Jobs a few days before) to do better and offered a strategy for getting Apple out of its current mess. It was a courageous play by Sculley, though that courage would have been better used in the months before.

Markkula listened, and then in the end did an extraordinary thing: he kept Sculley on as the pilot of Apple Computer. "You've got my support," he told Sculley, "but I'm very disappointed Apple is in this position." Incredibly forgiving words from a man who held ultimate responsibility for the livelihoods of 6,000 employees and for the investments of hundreds of thousands more.

It was Mike Markkula's biggest mistake. But he was only the most powerful figure at Apple to make this decision. The same conclusion had been reached by those senior managers around the table the previous Friday. No one at Apple still believed that John Sculley was either a great businessman or a great leader of men. Rather, the consensus was that he was a superb marketing man who'd been Peter Principled to the top. Yet, bizarrely, there was also an agreement that Sculley remained the best choice for the helm. During this time of crisis it would be too much for Apple to take off on yet another CEO search and risk finding a replacement who knew even less about computers than Sculley. Sculley wasn't much, it was quietly agreed, but he was their guy.

But was this really the case? Was there really no one out there in electronics suited to take charge of Apple, clean out the rot at headquarters and rev up product development? Nobody checked. Instead, Markkula in the lead, Apple stayed with a man almost everyone agreed was not up to the job, and who, just the day before, had proved his loyalty by threatening to quit. Steve Jobs's crimes were legion, but one thing he had never done in his tenure at Apple was to settle for anything but the best. With his departure, Apple seemed to revert to what it would have been without him: a company that was content with the merely adequate.

Resurrected and revivified, Sculley left Markkula's house that evening and went back to the office. There he polled his managers, then called Steve Jobs to tell him his fate: He was out. They couldn't fire the company's second-largest shareholder, but he had been stripped of not only the Mac division but every other possible operational role in the company. Steve Jobs was now merely a figurehead, with no power within the company.

Jobs did not take the news well. Instead he spent the rest of the evening calling everyone he knew, from Mac team members to family members and sobbed into the phone. He cried, rambled, at times became nearly incoherent in his grief. As even a company spokesperson admitted to the press, Steve "lives and eats and breathes Apple. It's very difficult for him to admit that somebody else runs it."

Steve Jobs had created himself through Apple Computer; it had been the centerpiece of his entire adult life. But his creation had turned on him, declared him worthless, made him for the second time an orphan. Now he was calling everyone he cared about to tell them goodbye.

One of the calls was to Mike Murray. In a shattered voice, Jobs thanked him for the best years of his life, told him goodbye and hung up. Murray was sufficiently frightened by what he heard that he jumped in his car and raced over to Jobs's house. Murray worried that he would find Jobs dead on the bare floor of the bare house. The giant front door was open—an awful sign. Murray raced through the house, finding nothing. Then he spotted a tiny light in Jobs's bedroom. He burst in, expecting the worst.

Instead he found Jobs, his face swollen from crying, wrapped in a blanket on the mattress on the floor. "Oh, hi," said Jobs distractedly, as if from far away. Mike joined him on the mattress, held his former boss in his arms, and the two cried together.

"This is not a power play," Regis McKenna told the newspapers the next day.

8.3 AFTERMATH

The future of Apple Computer was now officially in the hands of John Sculley.

Jobs was now not only out of the organization chart but out of sight. When he was in Cupertino he had the only office in a nearly empty building, the Little Napoleon on St. Helena. But most of the time he was on the road. *What do we do with Steve?* stopped being a question asked in desperation and instead became a subject for after-hours bullshit sessions. One rumor, quickly quashed, was that Jobs was considering a run for the U.S. Senate.

Another possibility, that of being one of the first of the new civilian astronauts on the Space Shuttle, did appeal to Jobs for its manifold glories, but he dropped it after learning of the months of training involved. It is interesting to speculate what would have happened to the Jobs myth if he had stayed with the program and become, instead of schoolteacher Christa McAuliffe, the civilian astronaut on *Challenger.* Would he have become the Elvis Presley or Princess Diana of high tech?

Finally, there were even rumors that Jobs was plotting yet another coup, this time by accumulating other shareholders to create a powerful voting block. But that seemed an unlikely bet, as, in the words of Valley veteran Jan Lewis of InfoCorp.: "Most of the finance community, by and large, [sees] Jobs as a negative to the community and Sculley a positive. Under those conditions, it will be hard to get financing." A counter-rumor was that Jobs was preparing to sell off his Apple shareholdings. That one would prove to be the most accurate.

Meanwhile, the career plans of Steven Jobs were of little consequence to John Sculley and his team. They had much bigger problems to worry about. Sculley had somehow caught a break with Markkula and the board. But it would not happen again: everyone on executive row knew that if Apple wasn't turned around in six months, Sculley would be only the first to go.

There were huge problems facing the company. It had to get itself organized, revive morale in the II group and restore the momentum to the Mac team. It had to regain control over its finances. And most of all, Apple had to reaffix itself to the Myth now that the Great Mythmaker was gone. Said Anton Bruehl, an analyst and onetime competitor as head of Atari International,

"Apple employees need to get behind the company again. It will take a lot of work to bring it back. With the combination of old and new employees, some loyal to Jobs, it's not going to be an easy task for Sculley [when] the market isn't helping him."

The market, in fact, was nearly in free fall. After the Christmas boom at the end of 1984, sales of computers for homes—including the IIe and IIc—fell 58 percent in the first quarter of 1985. Business computer sales did better—a drop of just 8 percent—but it was IBM PCs that made up most of that market, not Macintoshes. With nothing new to offer, Apple could only fall back on slogans. Having already described the Mac as an "appliance" and "the computer for the rest of us," the company now tried feebly to court industry professionals with "power tool for the mind." It didn't work.

On June 5, 1985, Bill Gates sent a special three-page memo to John Sculley and Jean-Louis Gassée entitled "Apple Licensing of Mac Technology." It would remain hidden from the public eye until 1996, when Jim Carlton, writing a book about the Sculley era at Apple discovered it.

The ideas within the memo were not originally Gates's, but belonged to a twenty-seven-year-old marketing manager at Microsoft named Jeff Raikes. Raikes had worked at Apple for a year after graduating from Stanford, then left to join Microsoft in 1981 ("Microsoft will go out of business," Jobs reportedly warned him when he quit). Thus, this early in the game, Raikes was one of the few people in personal computing with experience on both sides of the hardware-software fence.

Because of this, Raikes had come to realize early what the rest of the world would only come to five years hence: in personal computing, software (and processors) drove hardware, not the other way around. From the perspective of fifteen years on, when Windows and Pentium own the world, that might seem obvious. Even at the time there was already considerable evidence of this truth: witness how VisiCalc and the Mac operating system (OS) had saved the Apple II and Mac. But in that world, where tangible, physical assets ruled the day, the idea that lines of code could triumph over steel, copper and plastic was completely counterintuitive.

Whether Gates fully understood Raikes's vision or was merely indulging in some self-aggrandizing wishful thinking is a matter of speculation. But the memo was amazingly prescient.

The memo began with a brief overview of Apple's current situation:

. . . Apple must make Macintosh a standard. But no personal computer company, not even IBM, can create a standard without independent support. Even though Apple realized this, they have not been able to gain the independent support required to be perceived as a standard. . . . IBM architecture continues to receive huge investment and gains additional momentum. . . . Any deficiencies in the IBM architecture are quickly eliminated by independent support. . . . The closed architecture prevents similar independent investment in the Macintosh. The IBM architecture, when compared to the Macintosh, probably has more than 100 times the engineering resources applied to it when investment of compatible manufacturers is included.

For all of these reasons, Gates concluded, "the industry has reached the point where it is now impossible for Apple to create a standard out of their innovative technology without support from, and the resulting credibility of, other personal computer manufacturers. Thus, Apple must open the Macintosh architecture to have the independent support required to gain momentum and establish a standard."

Gates then went on to list six reasons why the Mac had not become a standard, including that customers weren't secure buying from a sole source, Apple had a rep for being slow to market, recent bad publicity and a small sales force. He then went on to list a score of companies, both domestic and international, from TI and HP to Kodak, Xerox, Siemens and Sony, that would significantly enhance the Mac OS's reputation and distribution. Finally, Gates concluded with a half dozen reasons why these companies would be good strategic partners, ending with:

"Licensing Mac compatibles will enhance Apple's image as a technological innovator. Ironically, IBM is viewed as being a technological innovator. This is because compatible manufacturers are afraid to innovate too much and stray from the standard."

Gates and Microsoft pledged "to help Apple implement this strategy."

Jim Carlton would declare this "one of the most important documents in Silicon Valley history," and certainly if Apple had followed Bill's advice it would have become a much different—and perhaps more successful—company. But the subsequent fate of Gates and of Apple puts a little more of a luster on this memo than it probably deserves.

In fact, during this era Apple was getting advice from every quarter about what to do with the Mac OS, much of it having to do with licensing. Regis, for one, had been arguing the case since 1983. Even at the time Gates was drafting his letter, one could read calls in the trade press for Apple to license the Mac OS. Dealers, recognizing the need for multiple vendors, were calling for it too. In the midst of all of this, Bill Gates, still a comparatively small player and erstwhile competitor, was just one voice (albeit particularly perceptive) out of many—all of them doomed to be ignored.

Regis McKenna made the same case over and over again for the rest of the decade, begging, pleading and even demanding that Apple choose between being a consumer products company and being a manufacturer of information tools for corporations. But Apple Computer was of no mind to make a choice—not when it meant abandoning one market or the other. Instead it tried to finesse a path in between, never giving either market quite what it wanted.

As for Gates and the growing chorus calling for licensing the OS, Apple's top management, especially after the recent purge of Jobs, was simply too unstable and too unsure of itself to make a move with such enormous implications. On top of that, there was the long-standing attitude, shared by Jobs and Sculley, that any money made by anyone else off an Apple idea was essentially *stolen*. It was like giving away the formula to Coca-Cola.

And if all that wasn't enough to scare Apple away from licensing, watching IBM's troubles over the next few years with cloners sealed it. Regis's memos, Bill Gates's letter and the dozens of other documents with similar conclusions generated within Apple itself were merely filed away, awaiting future postmortems.

In the meantime, technology—and entrepreneurship—moved on. In 1988, Roger Pelton, a market development expert, was sitting in a meeting at a new Valley company, called Sun Microsystems, that had been founded to prospect a new kind of low-cost, graphics-oriented minicomputer called an engineering workstation. Sun had chosen to go with Unix as its operating system, and there was considerable concern within the company about competition from above (mainframe computers) and below ("super" PCs) squeezing out the market even before it formed. An even greater threat, the group agreed, was from another operating system setting a standard different from Unix.

"We finally concluded," Pelton recalls, "that the biggest danger we faced would come from Apple if it decided to license the Mac OS. That would *really* hurt us.

"Then we all looked at each other and said, 'Naah. Apple will never do it.'"

Little noticed in the larger world at the time was the impact the Apple binge and purge had on John Sculley's reputation in Silicon Valley. His arrival at Apple in 1983 had been seen by Valley veterans as an enormous risk. Could a nontechie really run a tech company? His initial success, culminating in the Macintosh introduction, had made the Valley safe for CEOs without EE degrees. Headhunters were now told to cast wider nets beyond electronics, to search for John Sculley-like figures.

All that changed in June 1985. Old-timers began to nod that they had been right in the first place, that the Valley was no place for amateurs. Hungry executives from the automotive, retailing and consumer goods industries, anxious to get into the Silicon Valley gold rush, suddenly found doors slammed in their faces. "That's because the John Sculley model has become suspect," said employment psychologist Richard Hagberg. It would remain so ever after.

Amid all this misery, the good news was that Sculley had gathered around him a team that not only was supremely talented but, in such a young business, could be classified as seasoned veterans. Some, like Del Yocam and Debi Coleman, were survivors of the Jobs era. Others, like Jean-Louis Gassée, had made a name at Apple far away from Cupertino. And still others, like Dave Barram, had just come to Apple after years elsewhere in high tech. This was John Sculley's team, and for good or ill they would define the company for the rest of his tenure.

It was a team as bright and talented—if not necessarily as capable—as any Silicon Valley had ever seen. The same, in fact, might be said for the entire company. Because of the big hiring rush the company conducted throughout 1984 and into 1985, much of the best young talent around found its way into the company, where its effects would be felt for years to come.

The operations side of the company was run by Del Yocam. But for the beard, he was a kind of Dickensian figure—pudgy, congenial, a devoted family man, the very embodiment of organization and attention to details. Sculley, noting how Yocam kept meticulous notes in a maroon notebook he always carried under his arm, was even reminded of Bob Cratchit. Yocam even walked carefully, as if making sure each fastidious step was properly placed. If Yocam had any enemies it was only among those who found him too agreeable, too willing to accept out of politeness whatever was being said to him, then ignoring it later. If Yocam lacked anything, it was a burning fire in his guts. After Jobs, that missing component in Yocam was welcomed.

Yocam joined Apple in 1979, another member of the Fairchild diaspora. His initial job was as director of materials. But he proved so competent that he was soon put in charge of the Apple II group. There he had kept the group alive and its morale as strong as possible through the endless push-pull of being either ignored by the rest of the company or assaulted by Steve Jobs.

It was a measure of Yocam's personality, being the absolute antithesis of Jobs, that he was always able to get along with Apple's *enfant terrible.* Coming out of that April board meeting where he had just been eviscerated by Apple's directors, Jobs had cried on Del's shoulder. Even as he was nursing Jobs, Yocam was also supporting Sculley, showing him the ropes at Apple, making decisions Sculley was too distracted to make himself. He was the perfect lieutenant, and in the end Sculley rewarded Yocam for that trait by giving him the perfect lieutenant's job: director of operations, in charge of R&D, the factories and distribution.

Needless to say, Yocam's promotion was welcomed by the II group, which saw at last a hope for true appreciation by top brass. And Yocam certainly cheered them by publicly announcing that "the pendulum swung too far on Macintosh."

The cheering quickly stopped. With Sculley's approval, one of Yocam's first moves was to finally end the internal feud that had torn Apple in two for three years—he merged the Macintosh and II divisions into a single product group organized by functions (such as manufacturing and product development) instead of products. "We are switching from being product-driven to being market-driven," said Yocam the day after Jobs was booted from daily management. It sounded easy, but behind the words was the touchy task of melding together one strong but humiliated team with another, arrogant one in disarray. As one insider complained at the time: "It's not clear who works where. Exactly where the line is is not a hundred percent clear."

Immediately under Yocam, the two most important figures were Debi Coleman and Jean-Louis Gassée. Both were more talented than Yocam, but neither had the experience yet for his job. And both were unusual even by Valley standards.

Gassée's nickname was "the King of France." Coming from Exxon Office Systems, Data General and Hewlett-Packard, he had made a name for himself within Apple by running Apple France so brilliantly that it even led IBM in market share. Back home he'd been a model for Yves Saint Laurent clothes (in *Vogue*), spokesperson for Vittel mineral water, talk-show regular and a poet (but not an engineer), and even was once listed as one of France's ten best-dressed men. In Frank Rose's memorable words, "he was the technocrat as café revolutionary, spouting existential mumbo jumbo about personal computers and the future." In France, wearing black leather, Gassée looked like a character out of an early Godard film. In California, wearing jeans, he looked like a Gallic Carl Sagan.

Gassée's sophistication (he once famously described IBM using the old Nazi phrase *"ein Volk, ein Bund, ein Führer"*) buffaloed the press and instilled a cultlike worship by many of his subordinates. But there were others who listened closely to Gasséeisms, like the one that the Apple II "smelled like infinity," and concluded he was full of shit. Gassée only abetted this suspicion with brazen public remarks . . . like the one to the audience at a product introduction when he announced that Apple's slogan at the time, "The Power to Be Your Best," should really be "The Power to Beat Your Chest."

More than one person came away from dealing with Gassée struck by how much he was like Steve Jobs, if not in ruthlessness then certainly in grandiosity. But whereas Jobs fixated on a single project to the point of madness, Gassée was scattered, pursuing a score of different projects at the same time, making hundreds of decisions every day. Apple thanked him by paying him $800,000, more than the salary of most Valley CEOs.

Debi Coleman, by comparison, cultivated no such flourishes, yet she was a far more unusual and eccentric individual. She may have been the most versatile businessperson Silicon Valley has ever known. Overweight to the point of obesity, and childlike in her lack of any social graces, she also had a devastating intellect and a natural ability to attract a small army of powerful protectors and people as awkward as she. This made Coleman both formidable and unthreatening. She could be tough one moment and delicate the next. Watching her gnaw on candy bars while holding a staff meeting that was like a support group, it was at first hard to imagine what this individual was doing inside a billion-dollar corporation. But if you listened closely, you realized that this was a kind of genius all its own, and that Coleman might be as great a visionary as Jobs himself.

Debi had begun her career at Apple as a Macolyte and Jobs functionary. She was his secret weapon. The daughter of a Rhode Island machine-tool shop owner, Coleman had gone to Brown and dreamed of a career in manufacturing—even one day running General Electric. Instead she got an MBA at Stanford and found herself in Silicon Valley working at HP improving production. By a fluke, she ran into an old business school classmate at the Good Earth one lunchtime in September 1981 and soon found herself applying for a controller's job at Apple. Given the choice between taking that job in the established Lisa group and working for the Bandley Pirates of the Mac group, Coleman took the latter.

She did the job brilliantly, though it was a long leap from production to finance. But most important, she learned how to handle Steve Jobs. Her gift for comforting tortured souls had found its perfect recipient. In return, Jobs adored her, and shrewdly gave her his most difficult assignments. To Debi's delight, the biggest of these proved to be manufacturing. Jobs had shown that when he had almost gone berserk that day in the Fremont plant. Not long after that, in May 1984, with Apple still predicting skyrocketing Mac sales, he made his move. At the Pajaro retreat, he took a walk on the beach with Debi and offered her the manufacturing manager position.

Coleman, who had prayed for just such a chance, took it and ran. She even had a replacement ready for the controller's job, Susan Barnes. Then, with a decisiveness usually associated at Apple only with Jobs, she made the gutsy call of shutting the plant down for a month. During the interval she tore the place apart. She threw out nearly $10 million worth of obsolete equipment, fired every deadbeat she could find, scrubbed the place out and re-painted the walls and then hired people who knew what they were doing. When the factory reopened in July it was a showpiece of modern American manufacturing. Even GM's Roger Smith stopped by for a look. At 43,000 units, the plant produced more than double May's figure — meaning that by the old standard not a single production day had been lost.

Coleman had remained a Jobs loyalist right up to the end. She had even been with him that day when Leezy Sculley reamed him out. But she had never turned on Sculley — Debi was too awkward and obvious to be a good corporate politician. She had simply gone about her work within her self-contained world. Sculley admired her for that. But nobody appreciated Debi more than Del Yocam, who put her by his side (as he would do again a decade later at Tektronix).

So operations was in good shape. Next, Sculley bolted together sales and marketing — always a dangerous move — and put it in the hands of Bill Campbell, the first person Sculley had recruited to Apple and at the time the head of the company's U.S. sales. Campbell was also an interesting character. Tall, robust, with a powerful voice, he appeared every inch the jock he'd once been. In fact, before working at Eastman Kodak (where Sculley found him), Campbell had been the football coach at Columbia University. Campbell had never lost his take-charge style, and it had served him well trying to rebuild the workforce he'd inherited from Gene Carter, getting 300 new salesmen in position to relieve the existing army of manufacturer's representatives, then dealing with the roller-coaster experience of the Mac launch, the summer doldrums, the Test Drive, the resurgent II and now the prospect of layoffs. Among Apple's dealers, Campbell's arrival was welcomed with cheers. Said one, "He's the kind of guy who gets things done."

Reporting to Campbell as director of marketing was Michael Lorelli, promoted from marketing manager of the II group. Like Sculley, Lorelli had come from consumer products, in his case from Playtex, where he'd promoted tampons and Clairol shampoo. Apple's image was now in the hands of two men with almost no experience marketing computers.

In human resources, Jay Elliot, the bearded surfer, had returned from his march-out and was back in position. Overseas, a taciturn, hard-driving German named Michael Spindler, who'd done good work as European marketing manager, was put in charge of international operations. Al Eisenstat, chief counsel and secretary to the board, also stayed in position and was promoted to a company directorship. He had been a Sculley loyalist, and now, in thanks for that loyalty, he was given the most dangerous task of all: playing chaperone to Jobs. Eisenstat had been Apple's point man on international deals, especially those involving embargoed countries, such as China. Now he explored the possibility of sales to the Soviet Union. Sculley, meanwhile, needed to get Jobs out of the company for a few weeks to conduct this reorganization without internal interference or snide remarks to the press. Take Jobs with you to Russia, he told Eisenstat. Keep him busy, keep him out of sight, and make sure he doesn't do anything crazy that hurts the company.

On the finance side, with the departure of Joe Graziano, who'd resigned earlier in the year when Sculley expressed a lack of confidence in his work, the newest team member was Dave Barram. Barram had spent a long career at Hewlett-Packard, eventually working his way up to corporate controller, then followed that with a brief stint at Silicon Graphics. As such, he carried the cachet of doing the books for the most financially respected company in high tech. Sculley made him chief financial officer and gave him the added responsibility of inventory control. Barram himself was an interesting character. The son of a Baptist minister, he talked in a low, sardonic voice that always sounded on the brink of a knowing chuckle. Though he was a competent finance man, Barram's real love was Democratic Party politics. Five years before he had run for the Sunnyvale city council on a shared ticket with Regis McKenna's wife, Dianne. She won, in time becoming a Santa Clara County supervisor. He lost, despite having walked to every home in the city. But he still managed to stay in politics through his wife, Joan, who was elected a few years later to the school board.

Barram, the McKennas and Sunnyvale mayor Larry Stone (later county assessor) composed a tight little coterie of yellow dog Democrats in a community where most of the corporate executives were Republican and even the local Dems often voted for GOP candidates out of fiscal prudence. The little group created something of a machine that ran Sunnyvale politics for nearly two decades. Through this connection and that of his wife, Barram found his way into various national education groups, as well as the Democratic Leadership Council. There he became fast friends with an up-and-coming young Arkansas governor and his attorney wife.

That was Sculley's crew. As even he admitted, it wasn't yet a team: "Trust and respect establish the basis of any good working team. Yet there wasn't much trust in the beginning. We didn't know one another very well; we hadn't worked together as a team before, partly because Steve and I called all the shots."

Still, Sculley was thrilled by the group. Its diversity appealed to him: this was what a real California high-tech company team should look like! As he crowed later in his autobiography:

> What a group to lead Apple out of its quagmire: a soda-pop executive from the East; a solid, though untested, Apple II manager; an Ivy League football coach; a French intellectual; a German conceptual thinker; an English literature major; a seasoned attorney; a Baptist philosopher; and a laid-back surfer!

It sounded nice, but there were two types of people missing from this walking diversity cliché.

The first missing party, to use Guy Kawasaki's term, was a *high priest* of technology. Not just a tech intellectual, like Gassée, but that elusive combination of visionary and evangelist, who could make everyone share his dream, then pull them along into it. Just about all who'd held that role, from cardinals like Woz, Jobs and Raskin to archbishops like Burrell Smith, were gone. And it was a dangerous glimpse into the holes in Sculley's knowledge of high tech that he didn't seem to know he needed such a figure. In time he would understand, but then he would make a disastrous choice.

The second empty chair at the executive table belonged to an even more unnoticed type: the industry veteran. Despite all the brilliance of Coleman and Gassée, and the business experience of Sculley and Campbell, there was nobody in the room who could be called a veteran of the computer industry. Here was a company that presumed to establish a wide line of computer products, from educational computers up to the brink of minicomputers; that planned, in large part, to sell its computers to the corporate world; and that knew eventually it would have to link its products in networks to the large and small systems of other computer companies . . . and yet, there was nobody at the very top of Apple Computer who had *any* experience selling computers to industry.

This was indicative of Sculley's ignorance and arrogance; his attitude from the start that selling personal computers wasn't really fundamentally different than selling soda pop, once you understood the nomenclature. It was a devastating position to hold, because ultimately selling PCs really *was* different, especially to the corporate world, and especially as part of larger enterprise solutions with other computer companies.

A few others saw it as well. One consultant, after a staff meeting at a Santa Clara Hotel, caught up with Sculley in the parking lot. Gassée had just been appointed director of engineering. Please, pleaded the consultant, don't turn Gassée into another Jobs (that is, the sole technologist who buffaloes all the amateurs, especially Sculley himself). You'll only be re-creating the same problem you just solved.

"How can I avoid that?" Sculley asked.

For one thing, said the consultant, by naming more technical people to the executive staff and to the board of directors as a balance. He even offered some names.

Sculley nodded, but in the end did nothing. Before long, Apple was in the thrall of the musings of the King of France. And when the time came—and it came within months—when Apple had to decide in which direction to go, there was no one at the table to offer the wisdom of experience.

8.4 Madness

There were many different explanations as to why Apple suddenly found itself in deep financial trouble, with products stacked up in warehouses, the founder impeached and a new executive team in command. At the time, most observers put the blame at the feet of Steve Jobs. Later, when the outlines of the Sculley era became clear, Jobs underwent a rehabilitation of sorts (*yeah, he was nuts, but he had the right idea*) and Sculley became the goat.

A valid case could in fact be made for either view. Jobs did go on a rampage. He behaved not like an executive but like a bully taking revenge on everyone who had slighted him. He'd also held hostage the careers of thousands of employees to live out, despite mounting evidence to the contrary, his little fantasy of success.

On the other hand, Jobs was *supposed* to be out of control. He was the corporate shaman, the cheerleader, the charismatic. He made the impossible real. Sculley, by comparison, was hired to be the mature grown-up. He was supposed to control Jobs and command the company. But he had done neither. Instead, he had bet the company on a foolish risk, then had covered his failure by first blaming Jobs, then giving him the boot.

There was also a third explanation for Apple's troubles: the company simply went mad. It was all just too much, too heady an experience for any company, much less such a new one filled with young and inexperienced people. This was how Guy Kawasaki saw it when he sat down in 1990 to write *The Macintosh Way*. Kawasaki was, of course, a paid Apple cheerleader, yet it was precisely that enthusiasm for Apple, its people and, most of all, its products that enabled him to put the positive parts of the story in proper perspective to the negative:

> This is what actually happened:
> Steve, the Macintosh division, and Apple blew a hole in the side of the invincible IBM ship. Along the way, we suffered through calamities, infighting, and strife.
> After the introduction, we were physically and emotionally exhausted. Bringing Macintosh to market was an impossible act to follow, and this, combined with our physical and emotional fragility, caused us to stumble and fall. Nevertheless, a core of true believers— Apple employees, developers, and early Macintosh owners—sustained Macintosh, and made it successful.

To Kawasaki, the real lesson to be learned from the episode was that

> [a] small team of bright, fearless and ambitious punks led by a charismatic high priest trying to do the right thing can defeat mediocrity and the status quo. The battle can cost a lot (even the life of the high priest), but it is so magnificent that the toll almost doesn't matter.

Well, perhaps. But the hole in IBM wasn't big enough to sink that dreadnought. And if Sculley or Jobs had kept their eye on the ball—and on the declining spirits of the Mac team—that talent need never have been lost. Finally, Apple would never have stumbled and fallen had the high priest just for a moment stopped deluding himself or bullying those around him into a silent co-conspiracy to deny the reality of the situation.

Kawasaki is right to see Apple's disaster in mid-1985 as the by-product of its huge success the year before, but he is wrong to assume it was inevitable.

And it *was* a disaster. Kawasaki was there; he saw it up close:

We brought our org charts to a large conference room in De Anza 2, the Apple building that housed most of the Apple executive staff, and wrote names on a white board. The people whose names weren't on the board at the end of two days of meetings were laid off. It was like being a master of ceremonies at a massive funeral, and I never want to go through an experience like that again.

The same scenario occurred in Apple offices and factories throughout the world. When it was over, and the layoffs were formally announced on Friday, June 14, just twenty days after the final Jobs-Sculley confrontation, fully one-fifth of Apple's total workforce—1,200 employees—had been laid off. As is almost always the case, the blow fell hardest not upon headquarters among the managers and executives who had been party to Apple's mistakes, but upon the factory workers. "The mood is very down," said one employee. "Even among people who kept their jobs, there's no rejoicing here today." A factory near Los Angeles, one in Dallas and one in Ireland were shut down. The IIc's assembly was moved to Fremont, the IIe's to Singapore.

"What happened to Atari can happen [at Apple]," Woz told reporters from his outsider's perch. "It's a time of desperation."

Back in Cupertino, 250 people were laid off at headquarters. In many ways, their shock was even greater. These were professional people who'd signed on to a skyrocketing company. They weren't accustomed to failure in either their careers or their employers. Worse, because of the unique nature of Apple, many had moved to Silicon Valley, bought homes or condos near Apple headquarters in what had become de facto company villages and socialized almost exclusively with Apple people. For them, being laid off meant losing not only their careers but their personal lives. They worked with Apple people, played with Apple people and slept with Apple people. Now they were pariahs, stripped of friends and lovers, marooned in the most expensive real estate market in America and facing a depressed job market.

8.5 REGROUP

The company swallowed its bad medicine all at once. On the same day as the layoffs, Apple also announced the first quarterly loss in its history. It would prove to be $17 million. The company had actually shown a profit on sales, but decided to take the negative news all at once by factoring in an anticipated cost of reorganization of $40 million.

It didn't help much. The stock quickly went into free fall with the news, bottoming out at $14.75 within the week—and even after the analysts made their reappraisal of the company's comeback efforts, it still managed only a feeble climb back to $16. The question all the analysts were asking was: Can Apple find sales for the Macintosh?

Sculley and his team were asking the same thing. They were in a crisis mode, meeting every day, determining the next move, then rushing off to implement it. Meanwhile, the shock waves from the purge were still rolling across the company, setting off new explosions at unexpected locations. Two of these were near the top. Bob Belleville had resigned during the excitement, but had been talked into staying by Markkula. Now, a few weeks later, he found himself squeezed out by Gassée.

Mike Murray was next. In the reorganization, the II and Macintosh marketing teams had been pulled together under Campbell's aegis. Given their bitter history, there was bound to be a clash. Then into this mix was added a new marketing director, Mike Lorelli, who had recently joined Apple from Playtex. Campbell and Murray had fought in the past; Lorelli's marketing style, right out of consumer products, was antithetical to that which had grown up around the Mac group; Murray was given a space-filler job reporting to both of them. It wasn't long before he too packed up his stuff and moved over into the empty building. Steve Jobs now had his first team member for the new era.

On Tuesday, July 23, 1985, at a black-tie-optional event for 2,200 reporters and dignitaries at Lincoln Center in New York City, Commodore International announced its new computer, the $1,295 Amiga. Industry analyst Tim Bajarin, usually known as an Apple fan, pronounced the event "the most impressive demonstration I've seen in microcomputers. Amiga sets a standard, not just in its price range, but in personal computers."

In many important ways, the Amiga was the rest of Raskin's volkscomputer. It had superb stereo sound and bright graphics. Andy Warhol, betraying the Mac in a heartbeat, showed up to use the machine to draw a portrait of rocker Deborah Harry—having just learned how to use the machine the day before. "It's everything the Mac should be," said Richard Matlack of Info-Corp.

The Amiga was multimedia, and it was cheap. That was the best. On the downside, it had little software, its user interface paled next to the Mac OS and there was always Commodore's lousy reputation for quality. But still, at the lowest moment in Apple's story, the Amiga suddenly now presented the first real challenge to the Mac on its own turf. And this attack had come from below, right there at Jobs's original price point. Now Apple could no longer even take its own market base for granted.

Almost the same day as the Amiga introduction, Andy Hertzfeld was a featured guest on a panel put on by the new subscription on-line service Compuserve.

Having left Apple several months before, Hertzfeld felt unconstrained by any confidentiality rules. In unprecedented detail, he told the audience about the projects Apple had in the works—and the problems the company was having with those projects.

One was the urgent matter of getting the Finder program of the operating system, the traffic cop of the Mac interface, off the disk and into the Mac's core memory. Until that happened, Hertzfeld said, the interface would continue to be frustratingly slow. The trouble, said Hertzfeld, was that the Finder program was too big for the Mac's current complement of read-only core memory. It would be 1986, he warned, before the Mac had enough ROM capacity to move the Finder to where it belonged.

Responding to the threat of the Amiga, Hertzfeld warned that Apple wouldn't have a color Mac ready until late 1986, and a portable Mac, Apple's response to the success of a now surging Compaq in the PC world, wouldn't be available until long after that.

But it was to numerous questions about an "open" Mac architecture—a greater capacity for hooking up to third-party printers, disk drives and monitors—that Andy Hertzfeld made his most devastating appraisal. "It's certain," he said, "that the next Mac will be more open hardware-wise, but I'm not sure how much." What about software? The operating system itself? These questions were so far out of the realm of possibility that Hertzfeld didn't even address them. The underlying message was: no IBM compatibility, not even any Mac clones, for the rest of the 1980s. Apple was going to go it alone.

Six months later, John Sculley underscored the point. At the next analysts meeting, he agreed that IBM "will be the major force in defining most systems standards," but still argued that Apple "can be the leader in bringing together a superior human interface with real functionality in an IBM-defined systems world." It was Apple's first public admission that Big Blue had won that standards war.

And Apple's solution? It had none, only the counterargument that as long as Apple computers could be hooked up to IBM networks it didn't matter anyway. "We've always done everything ourselves," said Sculley. "Compatibility is no longer a barrier to entry."

He was utterly wrong.

Throughout the summer of 1985, Apple was haunted by the specter of Steve Jobs. He was the crazy aunt in the attic, the one nobody talked about, but no one ever forgot was there. And as long as he was there, the hermit of Apple, glimpsed as he entered and left the building, Jobs's very presence tore Apple in two. Half the company, including the Apple II group and most of senior management, was pleased to have him out of power and wished there was a way to get him out of the company without killing morale and gutting the stock. The other half of the company, mostly the Mac group and all the people in the far reaches of the company who saw him only as a distant star, ached at his loss from the firmament and prayed for his return. Some put on T-shirts with barely disguised double entendres like "We Want Our Jobs Back" (subtlety never being a company strong point). Others, less brave, silently prayed for the return of their champion. Sure, they'd heard the stories about him, but they also knew this: when Jobs had been in charge, Apple had been an exciting, successful, *vital* place. The only thing of importance that had occurred on Sculley's watch was the Macintosh . . . and whose idea was that?

Jobs, for his part, remained elusive. Intentional or not, it was an effective strategy. Everyone, from Sculley on down, was thinking about the peripatetic founder. Where is he now? What's he doing? What is he plotting?

After Russia, Jobs went to Italy with his girlfriend. Then Paris. While there, he called Susan Barnes to apologize for forgetting a dinner they'd planned. As an aside he mentioned that he was having such a good time in Europe he might stay there permanently. Barnes, beside herself in frustration at what was going on at Apple, began to cry. She told Jobs that if he was planning any new venture, she wanted to be part of it . . . and thus Apple got a new rumor and Jobs yet another mutineer.

Then, in late August, he returned. Once again, his timing was perfect. While Sculley and his team had spent the summer cleaning up the mess with moves that had left the company bitter and fearful, Jobs had been off taking the high-profile Grand Tour. Now he returned, unsullied by all that had happened. *He* hadn't announced the loss. *He* hadn't laid off all those wonderful Apple people. In fact, the rumors were that he felt terrible about it, that *he* would never have done such a thing were *he* still in charge.

It was a perfect play. Jobs may have made the mess, but Sculley had to clean it up. Jobs was still fun, which was more than you could say for the increasingly sullen and defensive John Sculley. Sculley knew it, and the realization that Jobs not only had left him holding the bag but now was winning the PR battle merely by doing nothing seemed to drive him to distraction.

Scariest of all, Jobs still owned 11 percent of the company. Sculley may have declawed the lion, but he still had teeth. With these holdings, Jobs as chairman could raise hell with Apple at annual meetings and directors gatherings and on proxy votes. And the presence of that sword, wielded by his jilted former pal, took its toll on Sculley. At the dreary analysts meeting, following the bombshells of the previous weeks, including the Commodore Amiga announcement the night before, Sculley, the man who hadn't blinked in the face of mighty Coca-Cola, finally lost his vaunted self-control. During the questions at the end of his presentation, Sculley was asked what operational role Jobs would now have at Apple. None, said Sculley testily. "There is no role for Steve Jobs in the operations of this company either now or in the future."

That was it. Sculley had finally been goaded into saying his real feelings. If Jobs wanted to stay at Apple, his role would be strictly ceremonial. He would be just like Woz had been in the latter days: a figurehead carted out for public appearances, well supervised so as not to say anything controversial, and kept far away from doing anything of substance within the company.

Even Jobs, back from Russia, could not romanticize or willfully misconstrue the message. "That was about as black-and-white as you need to make things," Jobs would later say.

But where to go? Jobs toyed for a while with the idea of running for the Senate, that perpetual fantasy of wealthy men who imagine themselves both wise and beloved. There were other ideas as well. An encounter with Stanford biochemist and Nobel laureate Paul Berg had left Jobs enamored with biology. And, like a good autodidact, Jobs quickly turned that curiosity into a small obsession. He read everything he could on the subject and even, like Woz, contemplated going back to school to study it. And, like computer scientists everywhere, Jobs also began developing elaborate theories about the relationship between electronics and living organisms.

Biochemistry wasn't the only topic that captured Jobs's wide-ranging imagination. He contemplated the creation of educational charities, outgrowths of Apple's existing programs to put computers in schools.

He was also being pulled in the direction of entrepreneurship. The massive reorganizations and the rampant confusion at Apple had left many of the old Mac team despondent and ready to resign. Just a short time before they had been heroes of the company, celebrities in the world of personal computing. Now they were being blamed for the company's financial straits. But the last straw was the arrival of the arrogant Gassée, who treated them as if they were incompetent, when, after all, they had designed the greatest computer of all time. Gassée lectured them as if they were children, and, in the ultimate apostasy, seemed to be planning to make the Mac into a high-end computer, almost a workstation, instead of sticking with Raskin's (compromised) People's Computer.

This wasn't what they signed on to Apple to do. And it didn't help that they weren't being spoiled and pampered anymore under the new regime. They wanted out. They came to Jobs individually and in groups: George Crow, an experienced analog engineer from the Mac group. Rich Page, an Apple Fellow in charge of the next-generation Mac. Bud Tribble, back from medical school and now running the Mac's software engineering department. Susan Barnes, senior controller for U.S. sales and marketing. Daniel Lewin, marketing manager for higher education. Andy Hertzfeld. Bob Belleville. Each had his own ax to grind. Whatever their motives, each had the same message for Jobs: Start another company and let us join you. We'll re-create the thrill and success of the Mac project.

Jobs, tucked away in his empty building, bitter at the mutiny of his staff, listened closely. And with his unique skill at synthesizing multiple and diverse notions into a single idea, it slowly came to him: What if he, not Apple, built the Big Mac? That is, a powerful, graphics-based workstation targeted primarily at higher education and capable of performing such tasks as Berg's complex biochemical equations? And what if he didn't compromise on any part of the machine, but simply made it into the most elegant computer in the world? It would be the Mac Redux, without the Mac's flaws—and better, it would be the true successor to the Apple II in the education market. The idea hit all of Jobs's hot buttons—not least of which was revenge.

In one respect, and perhaps only in that respect, was Steve Jobs like Steve Wozniak: once a big idea captured his imagination he was incapable of letting it go. It took over his life, and he pursued it ardently and obsessively, caring only fleetingly about the consequences. That was Jobs with this new project, as it had been with the Mac and before it the Apple I. It was what made him one of the greatest figures of his time, as well as one of its most flawed.

But if Jobs's strength was his ruthless single-mindedness, his weakness was his transparency. As with the coup attempt, he seemed incapable of not telegraphing his next pitch. He signaled his plan beginning on July 22 by filing, with the Securities and Exchange Commission, his intention to sell 100,000 shares valued at $1.7 million. The next day, he filed again, this time for 250,000 shares, worth $4.2 million. Two days after that, he filed for another 500,000 shares worth $8.1 million. The total came to 850,000 shares worth $14 million—14.2 percent of his Apple holdings of 6 million shares.

In the end, he would sell 782,000 of those shares, for a total of $11.2 million. Then, in late August, he again filed with the SEC, for 500,000 more shares, worth $7.4 million. After this, he would be down to 5.5 million shares, 8.9 percent of the company. He would still be the company's largest shareholder, but the sale was hardly a show of faith.

Needless to say, there was considerable speculation about the play. Apple officially declared it a "private transaction," but others, notably securities analyst John Dean, had other ideas. "I have a feeling he is out there putting a company together," perhaps obtaining the liquidity from the sale to "buy out someone who is distressed. If he has cash available, he can do some tough deals."

John Sculley, with his sixth sense for corporate politics, tried to contact Jobs. He wrote him a note suggesting the two get together on the morning of Friday, September 13. Jobs didn't deign to reply. Instead, to everyone's great curiosity, he added to the agenda of the September 12 board meeting a final entry, "Chairman's Report." As the board filed into the boardroom, the expectation—especially by Sculley—was that Jobs would use his soapbox to harangue the assembled about the reorganization, the state of the company, the loss of key employees and everything else about the Sculley regime—the subtext being that things would be different were Steven Jobs in charge. Sculley wasn't worried: the board had made its decision, the die was cast, the reorganization was underway; there was no way the directors would rescind their decision now.

This time Jobs didn't telegraph his next surprise. Instead, he calmly got up and said dispassionately, "I've been thinking a lot and it's time for me to get on with my life. It's obvious to me that I've got to do something. I'm thirty years old."

He's quitting! Jobs went on as calmly as before, reading from a prepared script. He had, he said, done a lot of thinking over the summer about what he wanted to do with his life. Politics. School. Entrepreneurship. In the end he had looked back on his career and realized that the most satisfying experience had been his work getting computers into schools. For that reason he had decided to start a new venture aimed at the high end of the education market.

There were murmurs. Jobs quickly added that this new venture would not compete in any way with Apple, but would be complementary. And though a few Apple employees would be leaving with him, they would not be critical to

Apple's future plans. Jobs went on to suggest that ultimately Apple might be interested in becoming a distributor to whatever product was to be built by this company. And, on top of that, Jobs & Co. might want to license Macintosh software—an unusual twist from the guy most viscerally against any Apple clones.

If Jobs expected the Apple board to react in the same low-key manner in which he had made the announcement, he was mistaken. These were old pros, and red lights were going off everywhere. Quitting? New venture? Complementary? *Taking employees?! What the hell is going on here?*

No one was more agitated than Mike Markkula. He had taken this aggressive, brilliant, difficult kid and built a billion-dollar corporation around him. He had retreated to the shadows, pushing Jobs forward into the limelight until the young man had become synonymous not only with Apple Computer but with his entire generation. He had defended Jobs during the hard times and coddled him during the good; he had spent thousands of hours calming down the angry employees and putting out the wildfires that Jobs left in his wake. Now he was not only walking out in a snit but starting another computer company—and taking Apple employees with him.

It was the last that especially annoyed Markkula. "Why would you take anyone at all?" he demanded of the young man.

"Don't get upset," said Jobs, defensively, to his old mentor. "These are very low-level people that you wouldn't miss. And they will be leaving anyway. Don't look at this as a big issue."

If anyone in the room thought he was lying, they didn't say so until a few moments later after Jobs was asked to leave the room. Instead, the discussion revolved around the new company Jobs planned to build. As always with Steve Jobs, there was that contradictory feeling that he was utterly incapable of running a company, yet that he was clever enough to figure out how to do it anyway. And if so, what would that company be like? With the II covering the low end of the education market and Gassée already talking about making the next-generation Mac a more sophisticated and powerful machine, how could any product be *complementary* to Apple? Where would you go in that market without competing directly with an Apple product? But would Steve Jobs really compete with the company he had built, that he professed to love, in which he was a leading shareholder?

It was suggested, and agreed upon by the board, that Apple should take a position in Jobs's new company—as much as 10 percent. That would maintain the link with Jobs while retaining a defensive position in any decisions by the company that might go against Apple. And, if the new company really was complementary, and if it was successful, Apple would be in a perfect position to buy it out and bring Jobs & Co. back into the fold.

Sculley, of all people, was given the task of telling Jobs the news: "All of us have appreciated what you have done for Apple and we recognize you want to get on with your life. On the assumption that your business is complementary and not competitive, and that you're not taking key people from Apple, we want you to reconsider your decision to resign from the board." Sculley then offered the investment deal.

Jobs replied that he would like to consider both offers. They agreed to meet again in a week.

It never happened. The next morning, Friday the 13th, Jobs dropped his bomb. Knowing that Sculley had a regular staff meeting at 7:30 A.M., Jobs called at 7:10 and asked if he could come right over. When he arrived, he handed Sculley ("sheepishly," Sculley would later claim) an envelope containing a typewritten note. It said:

> Dear John,
> Today these five employees of Apple Computer will be resigning to join me in my new venture.

Then the names: Page, Lewin, Tribble, Barnes and Crow. It was the ultimate corporate Dear John (literally) letter. Jobs was not only leaving; he was taking with him the guts of the Mac team in education. As Sculley would later write:

> Together, they knew our internal schedules, our costs, the focus of Apple's next products, the schedule of when we would introduce them, how they would be used, and which individuals and universities we would work with to ensure their success. Their accumulated knowledge would give Steve a decided advantage to compete directly with Apple in terms of marketing opportunities and technical and product know-how.

"Steve, these aren't low-level people," a stunned Sculley told Jobs.

"Well," Jobs replied, "these people were going to resign anyway. They are going to be handing in their resignations by nine this morning, so I wanted to give you and the executive staff the courtesy of knowing that beforehand because I know you have your meeting this morning."

Silicon Valley had been built on teams of talented employees (though rarely by a founder/chairman) walking out to start new companies. And some degree of subterfuge had been involved in all of them—secret meetings at Denny's, coordinated resignations, etc. But this was ugly. Less than twenty-four hours earlier Jobs had blithely treated his new company as if it was just a notion still being developed and mentioned that he might be taking some minor Apple foot soldiers with him. He had lied about almost everything but the fact that he was leaving.

Furious, Sculley pressed him on his words before the board. *All* of this had happened since yesterday? Yes, said Jobs, we all met last night and agreed to resign together this morning.

It was bullshit. Sculley knew it. Every executive at Apple would soon know it. And if Steve would lie about that, what about the rest?

A few minutes later, an ashen Sculley marched in to his staff meeting. He gave the note to Eisenstat, then turned and told the others. There was an uproar. Bill Campbell reportedly announced, "We should expose him for the fraud that he is so that people here stop regarding him as the Messiah."

But, with consequences unimaginable at the time, Apple did nothing of the sort. The news of Jobs's resignation broke on September 17. In keeping with the sordidness of the entire affair, the press got a copy of Jobs's resignation letter to Markkula even before Markkula and Apple did. It was classic Steve Jobs: arrogant, self-pitying, and with one eye cocked on the publicity angle.

"Dear Mike," the letter began. "This morning's papers carried suggestions that Apple is considering removing me as Chairman. I don't know the source of these reports but they are both misleading to the public and unfair to me." Jobs went on to recount his version of the events of the previous week, portraying himself as sincerely presenting his plans to the board and encountering only "a hostile posture towards me and my new venture."

Then came the self-pity: "I find myself saddened and perplexed by the management's conduct in this matter, which seems to me contrary to Apple's best interests. . . . I continue to hope that calmer voices within the Company may yet be heard. . . . I am but thirty and want still to contribute and achieve. . . . I would wish our parting to be both amicable and dignified."

The result was a predictable media storm. If Apple had any plans for a concerted demolition of Jobs's reputation, they were quickly abandoned in the panic to maintain some sort of PR control on the frenzy. Apple could only react, and by the time it had a chance to recoup, the story was already stale. On the critical day after, a furious, frustrated Mike Markkula was reduced to releasing a terse formal statement saying that Jobs had implied that "he would not recruit any key Apple personnel."

At least in his exit, Jobs had checkmated Apple. And he had done so on the day the company planned to introduce several new products for the Mac and the II. Said one Apple executive, "He always gets even. That's the way he is." Said a former Apple manager, "This is one of the best soap operas in America."

But if Steve had hoped to wound his old company on the way out, he failed. His reputation now preceded him, at least among business leaders and technologists. Apple's stock actually went up a dollar per share with his departure. Still, there were thousands of Apple employees and millions of consumers around the world who still saw him, in Campbell's words, as the Messiah. That guaranteed him a willing audience whenever his new company decided to make an announcement—and scores of talented Appleites who secretly watched with envy and made plans to follow him.

John Sculley, in his autobiography, would claim that when Jobs's office was cleaned out, a worker found a framed photo of Jobs and Sculley, huddled together in one of their endless private conversations, taken just seven months before. On the back Sculley had written, "Here's to Great Ideas, Great Experiences and a Great Friendship." The glass on the picture was shattered, as if it had been smashed against a wall.

For his part, Jobs, reached at his home soon after the news of his resignation broke, would only say about his relationship with John Sculley that "it is surprising to me that John Sculley doesn't say anything" and "I'm more worried about Apple than I am about him."

In fact, Sculley called Jobs the next day, saying later only that the two had "agreed to set aside our friendship." He added, "I'm disappointed someone so big a contributor to the industry and such a shaper to Apple's success would get himself into this predicament." A few days later, he would add defensively, "I didn't come to Apple to take it away from Steve Jobs."

In its first decade, Apple Computer had slowly learned that it couldn't live with Steve Jobs; now it would spend the next decade coming to the realization that it couldn't live without him either. Other executives, and Sculley more than anyone, would make terrible business mistakes. But in the end, it was Steve Jobs who had placed Apple in this terrible dilemma.

Jobs, of course, didn't see it this way. It was he who had been betrayed. It was he who was the victim. He likened his experiences at Apple to "the first woman you've fallen in love with. . . . This has been such an awful thing." He said it felt as if someone had "punched you in the stomach and it knocks the wind out of you and you can't breathe."

Now he would go off and try to make himself famous and important once again. He would continue to raid Apple for talent, and he would find in

Canon and Ross Perot investors still bedazzled by his image. The result would be NeXT Computer, the most dysfunctional company family in Silicon Valley. NeXT was a glimpse of what Apple would have been under Jobs alone. It produced a magnificent, stylish computer—the most beautiful machine in industry history—out of equally stylish offices in Menlo Park. The press lauded the machine after its big showcase launch in 1988, but no one bought it. Instead, as Apple was about to enter the most successful and profitable era in its history, Steve Jobs sat in his glass box, a high-tech Heathcliff, terrorizing everyone around him from employees to caterers, watching lesser mortals like Bill Gates and Larry Ellison become even richer and more famous than he, and praying for his moment of redemption to come.

Looking back from the perspective of nearly fifteen years, Regis McKenna would say, "The biggest mistake we ever made was letting Steve leave the company. There had to have been some way to keep him; there must have been *some* role he could have played. Because after he left, the company was never again the same."

8.6 ANGELS IN THE PRINTSHOP

Apple remained a deeply troubled company. For the year ended September 27 the company's net income fell 4 percent to $61.2 million, much of that drop due to the fourth quarter. Sales had picked up—27 percent to $1.9 billion—but the company was still losing market share and still was not penetrating the corporate market in anywhere near the manner it needed. The II was getting older by the day and without a major redesign would be obsolete soon. Any new Mac was still in the distant future, the lost year of the Mac team now starting to tell.

The capper, one guaranteed to damage the company's already fragile morale, came on Halloween, when *Electronic Business* magazine announced that John Sculley, despite Apple's dreary year, the layoffs and the ousting of Jobs, was the highest-paid executive in electronics: $2.1 million in salary and bonuses.

In the midst of all this, there was one piece of bright news. Somewhere beneath all the dross, there hid a sterling company. Years of fame had brought to Apple an enormous number of talented people, and most had survived the layoffs. In fact, firing 20 percent of the workforce not only had not slowed Apple down but seemed to make it more efficient, if not more innovative. Also, despite the losses, the company's financial reserves had increased to

$254.6 million in cash with no debt—enough to finance several new product ventures. And, just as vital, there remained a loyal, even rabid, customer base. And there were superb products, from the IIe to the Turbo Mac to the Apple LaserWriter printer.

By the end of 1985, it was dawning on Sculley and the leadership team that merely by maintaining and growing the current product catalog and cutting out the gross inefficiencies, Apple could return to its former levels of profitability *without* any great new product breakthroughs or improved Mac unit sales. For a guy like Sculley, who always kept one eye on the stock price, this was wonderful news.

For the medium term, perhaps as much as three years, it also meant that Apple didn't have to run around and try to change the world yet again. The new team could take some time to get it right, rather than race against a declining bank account. But in the long term, the old problem had not changed: Apple was running out of room to maneuver. IBM and the army of clone makers following in its wake were slowly, inexorably gobbling up market share. Each percentage point gain increased the likelihood that the IBM-Intel-Microsoft architecture would become the universal (it was already the dominant) standard in personal computing, while reducing the interest by software developers in creating products for Apple machines.

The last year had shown that, despite exhausting efforts by the sales and marketing staffs, Apple was never going to dislodge IBM from the office market. Apple would always be a renegade, an outsider, in that world. So what did that leave? The home market might someday be vast, but prognosticators had been predicting that market to take off ever since Apple had been founded. Many good companies had died waiting for consumers to come around. Education? The II had that market sewn up. But how long could Apple depend upon that old workhorse? And though schools might covet the Macintosh, it was way too expensive. That presented the dangerous possibility that one day in the near future the II would suddenly become obsolete and the educational community, if it didn't find a low-cost Mac waiting in the wings, would turn forever to the far-cheaper IBM clones.

So it seemed at that moment, in late 1985, that Apple was trapped. Having lived on its image, it had now lost its chief image maker. Having created the mass market for personal computers, it now found itself either squeezed out of every submarket within that world or holding on to one of those submarkets with a geriatric machine. Unless some new market came along—which seemed utterly unlikely—the best Apple could do would be to run a tighter ship, introduce occasional product upgrades and try to slow as much as possible a long, inevitable decline to oblivion. That was a hard reality for the management of Apple to take: after all, despite the recent problems, the company was still the toast of the computing world.

So who was buying Macintoshes, besides early adopters, nonconformist corporate types and the wealthy curious? It turned out to be an interesting group, composed mostly of people in graphics-oriented fields: advertising agencies, designers, publishers, owners of newsletters. These were people for whom the computer culture had until recently seemed as remote as Siberia. But the Mac was something entirely different, a graphics-based computer, and the visual world understood it immediately. In this motley collection of customers, Apple might have gotten a clue to its future success. But nobody besides the sales force really noticed this group, or the interesting fact that many were also buying the Apple LaserWriter.

The LaserWriter, Apple's laser printer, had enjoyed a typically checkered history at Apple. Jobs had initially been against it, though by the time it was ready to appear he had turned into its greatest proponent. The goal of the LaserWriter team had been to create the functional equivalent of the wonderful new $30,000 laser printers, now being used with mainframes, in a $7,000 box that would work with the Macintosh. The team achieved its goal, using the combination of a Canon printer engine and a powerful motherboard (designed by Burrell Smith himself) that featured a new microprocessor, the Motorola 68020, that was actually more powerful than the one in the Macintosh. Thus, those in the know realized that the LaserWriter was in fact a computer in which the display and keyboard had been replaced by a printer mechanism.

It was a masterpiece of design, yet another in Apple's growing list, but within the company doubts were loudly expressed right up to the day of the LaserWriter's introduction. I don't care how good the printout looks, said the doubters, who the hell is going to pay for a printer that costs twice as much as the computer it serves?

And yet, month by month, the number of LaserWriters Apple sold increased. So solid was this business that during the dark months of mid-1985 one could have made a strong case for Apple being not a computer, but a printer company. And that was only the beginning. Because what happened next may be the best confirmation of the notion, held by some Apple fanatics even now, that Apple is a blessed place where lifesaving miracles regularly occur.

This miracle, for once, came not from inside, but from outside the company. Two young companies converged, seemingly out of the blue, at the moment of Apple's greatest need. And, like angels, these two companies helped Apple back on its feet and then off into the most prosperous period of its history.

One of these companies was the creation of an eccentric, bespectacled and unemployed engineer named Paul Brainerd, who, coincidentally, hailed from the Seattle area in Microsoft's backyard. Brainerd had a unique résumé for someone in high tech: he actually had real-life experience in a different field—in Brainerd's case, publishing. He had once been a newspaper editor. In January 1984, at the time of the Macintosh introduction, Brainerd was working for Atex, a company familiar to journalists everywhere as a purveyor of terminals to newsrooms. These were expensive and sophisticated systems, but they still offered Brainerd invaluable training in the relationship between computer technology and the physical process of composing, layout and printing newspapers and magazines.

When Atex was bought by Kodak, Brainerd, golden parachute in hand, hired four of his old engineers and set about building a new company.

Brainerd had a vision that computing technology had passed a threshold in price and performance that made it possible to stand an established industry on its head, revolutionize it and then dominate it. For Brainerd, this sleeping industry ripe for attack was printing—not just books, magazines and newspapers, but brochures, newsletters, flyers; all the various projects currently handled by printing shops and small presses. These industries were only now being touched by technology in the form of very expensive, computerized composing machines. Brainerd was convinced he could duplicate all but the most sophisticated forms of this work on low-cost personal computers, especially those equipped with the new laser printers. He called his idea "desktop publishing" and his company, Aldus, after the Renaissance printer Aldus Manutius, creator of the first low-cost pocket books.

Brainerd and the team spent the winter and spring of 1984 perfecting their product, which they called Pagemaker. And as soon as a crude prototype was ready on a stack of disks, Brainerd grabbed them and hit the road in search of investors, customers and, most of all, the right machine on which to run the product. So improvised was this tour that Brainerd actually showed up unannounced at Apple's sales office in Beaverton, Oregon, and asked to see one of the new Macintoshes he'd heard about. Luckily, the local rep was a shrewd judge of software—even though it was still so buggy that it rarely ran all the way through—and he not only promised to show Brainerd a Mac as soon as he had one available, but actually drove up to Seattle with the machine in his trunk and left it at Aldus for more than a month.

Needless to say, Brainerd and the boys were entranced. This was just the computer interface they needed to draw out the full measure of Pagemaker.

They decided to go with the Mac. Imagine, then, their thrill when a couple of months later, now being received at Apple as true business partners, they were given an early glimpse of the LaserWriter.

There it was. Everything Paul Brainerd had dreamed of: a composing room, a printshop, all in a personal computer and an accompanying printer with a total price of only $10,000. He was ready now to conquer an industry.

Brainerd not only had a great product but also had perfect timing. He had come to Apple just at the moment that Sculley and his team had reached the terrifying conclusion that the Mac had no markets it could call its own; and, just as bad, that in those markets where it needed most to be taken seriously—the office, the laboratory—it was still seen as a clever toy. It didn't help that the killer app software that was supposed to legitimize the Mac in the workplace, Lotus's Jazz, turned out to be not only a dud but an insult. Jazz was so elementary that it *confirmed* the shallowness of the Mac.

But Brainerd had the answer. With the help of a champion inside Apple, a young Harvard MBA with the bad luck to be named John Scull, the Aldus story was taken right to the top. Scull had asked Brainerd to prepare a document describing Pagemaker and its philosophy, and when Brainerd delivered a twenty-page white paper, Scull took it directly to Sculley. As Brainerd later told Steven Levy: "Apple was desperate to differentiate Macintosh from the IBM PC. Desktop publishing was the only option."

Sculley proved willing to throw some of the company's tight resources behind Aldus. It was Apple, not Aldus, that took out ads for Pagemaker in major magazines—and that subsidized Brainerd on a national press tour timed with Pagemaker's July 15, 1985, introduction.

There was a third player in this nexus. Adobe had been founded by a group of former Xerox PARC researchers led by John Warnock, who just happened to be one of the few people in the world Steve Jobs looked up to. Cringely would even claim that Warnock, with his programming genius, intellectual arrogance and personal dignity was "the father that Steve Jobs always wished for."

Warnock had his own vision of how personal computer technology could be put to use to create compelling graphics. He began this work at the University of Utah, then moved on to Xerox PARC. There he created a graphics programming language with fellow researcher Martin Jewell. Called JaM (for "John and Martin"), this language was further refined into a Xerox laser printer-compatible language called Interpress in the hopes that the mother company would adopt it as its own. But Xerox, keeping its streak perfect for stupid decisions in personal computing, spent two years hemming and hawing. Meanwhile, Warnock and his PARC boss, Chuck Geschke, who was Interpress's biggest supporter, finally said to hell with it and quit to start their own company.

Even more than Aldus, Adobe—named after a creek in Warnock's backyard in Los Altos—had a rocky start. The new start-up first contemplated building high-end printers, then computer workstations, then finally settled on what it knew best, software. In software, Adobe's initial business thrust was to use Warnock's understanding of graphics to generate typefaces on computer screens—type ultimately being just another form of graphics. The result was Postscript, perhaps the most influential software program in personal computing history.

Postscript enabled computer users to at last escape from a world of a single typeface in only a single point size that could only be capitalized and underlined for emphasis. By encoding fonts and typefaces into mathematical equations, Postscript allowed computer owners to pick from scores of typefaces, adjust character size as needed and switch to italic or bold or shadow at the press of a key. It all happened effortlessly, instantaneously and without any degradation of the image. You could even add graphics generated by the computer or inputted through a scanner.

In its own way, Postscript was as exciting as Pagemaker, and it had many times the potential user base. And, like Pagemaker, Postscript needed a crisp, bit-mapped display and a precise laser printer to really show its stuff. Postscript made the Mac special, not just clever, and that would prove the critical difference. Apple, recognizing a good thing, bought 15 percent of Adobe, for $2.5 million. It was Jobs's last great act of his first tenure at Apple, and it was a reminder of just how valuable to the company he could be.

The marvelous thing about Pagemaker and Postscript was that they dovetailed together beautifully—and, in turn, they could only work well on the Macintosh. It was a three-way synergy of a kind rarely seen in business. And the combination of desktop publishing and a graphical user interface sent waves of delight and terror, respectively, through the market and the competition.

Customers adored desktop publishing. Here, at last, was the first great new application for computers since spreadsheets. And better yet, it could be used by anybody. Graphic artists and printers loved the technology because it drastically simplified their work (working so well, in fact, that it put many out of business). In short order, even the magazines that had predicted the imminent demise of Apple were laying out their issues on Mac systems. Moreover, AppleTalk, that nearly forgotten linchpin of the Mac Office, now suddenly made sense. At seven grand, a LaserWriter was a lot of bucks for use with a single computer, but not with a dozen or more Macs scattered around a company.

For consumers professionals and small businesspeople, Mac desktop publishing was just as exciting. Ten thousand dollars might be a hunk of change, but it was justified for a machine that could not only maintain mailing lists and do payroll but also create mailers, newsletters, posters and invitations. It quickly became a status symbol to send out an invoice or flyer that was a riot of fonts and faces. By mid-1986, in a measure of how quickly desktop publishing was adopted as a standard in the corporate world, it was a rare day when you didn't pass a bulletin board or kiosk or receive an interoffice memo or a piece of mail that didn't look like an explosion in a type factory.

Almost overnight, Apple once again commanded the awe of the computer industry. It had the new killer app, and the penumbra from desktop publishing seemed to wrap the Mac in its warm light. Apple salesmen and evangelists found themselves welcomed into the halls of giant corporations. The same MIS managers who had looked upon the Mac as an expensive novelty now clamored to know all about desktop publishing.

And not just desktop publishing. The glow also extended to the Mac's graphical user interface and to any third-party software that took advantage of it. "Graphics" was the new buzzword and everybody wanted it. And for good reason. After sitting down at a Macintosh and constructing a cover page for a newsletter, complete with masthead, illustrations and multiple typefaces—all in a WYSIWYG ("what you see is what you get") format that looked just like the finished result—using an IBM/DOS computer ("C:load file") was like switching off half of your brain.

Desktop publishing made manifest what had always been Steve Jobs's dream. It made the Macintosh so cool that to own anything else was humiliating. The company for the first time had the attention and respect of creative types, small business owners, educators *and* the Fortune 500. This was the moment for Steve Jobs to shine; to bring his charisma, enthusiasm and risk taking to bear on this brief moment of opportunity and blow it open with new products, new promotions and a new attitude. But Jobs was gone, and there was no one at Apple now capable of assuming his mantle.

Just a few days after his resignation Jobs had a confrontation with Mike Markkula. Feeling it proper, for old times' sake, to formally put his letter of resignation in Markkula's hands (even though he already leaked it to the press), Jobs had driven with Tribble and Barnes over to Mike's house. He entered the home alone, with the condition that the other two retrieve him if he hadn't returned in fifteen minutes. What he encountered inside was not just Markkula but Eisenstat and Mike Brown, the attorney Apple had just hired to sue Jobs's new company. Before Susan Barnes ran in and dragged him off, Jobs found himself in a shouting match with Markkula. And in the midst of this, Markkula at last let his true feelings be known: If you had only waited, he told Jobs, if you'd only been willing to stand in the corner for a year, everything might have been worked out.

And it wouldn't even have been a year. It would have been only a few months before Jobs would likely have been given desktop publishing. Sculley & Co. would have grinned and bore it, because Jobs was the only person up to the task. It would have been the perfect vindication, not just of the Mac but of Steve Jobs's judgment. Instead he chose to pout and betray Apple. Apple in turn would make billions off desktop publishing, but it would take Sculley years to fully appreciate its importance—and by then it was too late, the opportunity to regain dominance of the market had been lost.

8.7 SILICON SYMPHONY

One person who did understand the import of desktop publishing was Bill Gates, and it scared him every way but witless. As with his arm's-length partner at Intel, Andy Grove, one of Gates's greatest skills was that he responded to every real or imagined attack with an instant, all-out counteroffensive. He never allowed his more inventive competitors to consolidate their gains. And he never showed this skill more brilliantly than in response to the threat from Mac desktop publishing. Gates had been smart enough to get a forewarning of what was to come thanks to the November 1983 introduction by VisiCorp of a new graphical user interface (GUI) for IBM PCs called VisiOn.

VisiOn proved to be a disaster, partly for design problems and partly because VisiCorp did just about everything to alienate applications developers, but its impending arrival had lit a fire under Gates. DOS, after all, was the franchise at Microsoft, and there was no way Bill Gates was ever going to allow a usurper to even get on the field. So he flogged the company to build its own GUI, called the Interface Manager, to be ready for introduction by the time of the VisiOn announcement. It wasn't, but Gates simply announced it anyway, preempting VisiCorp.

It would take him two years to fulfill that product announcement, and when the new operating system arrived, now called Windows, it proved to be a kluge—slow, unwieldy, ugly and counterintuitive where the Mac OS was elegant and self-evident. Having been built on top of the DOS core, it was compromised from the start—a weakness that would haunt Windows upgrades right to the present. But none of that mattered. What counted was that when the Macintosh finally took off, abashed IBM PC owners had a graphical operating system of their own, albeit profoundly flawed, that they could turn to instead of switching to Macintosh.

Of course, Gates didn't stop there. Once he saw the Mac, and then watched it break out with desktop publishing, he knew his franchise would only be secure when he could match Apple step by step on the IBM PC. To that end, he held the Windows development group to the fire, while at the same time began developing applications programs for the Mac (Microsoft would eventually be the Mac's largest software developer) and even licensed those parts of the Mac interface that Apple made available. In other words, he helped Apple (and made a tidy profit in the process) while learning enough to crush it. And John Sculley's Apple was happy for the help. Faced with the very last opportunity it would have to regain market leadership, Apple instead chose to embrace its most dangerous competitor.

And what was the company doing during this critical period? Redoubling its effort to consolidate its new market gains? No, celebrating its restored profitability at the annual sales meeting. On the last night, which happened to fall on Halloween, the Apple assembled threw a costume party. John Sculley showed up in long underwear, his face painted silver with multicolored stars for eyes, dressed as the "Spirit of Apple." But the real spirit of Apple was running a company called NeXT. Sculley only looked like a fool.

Now in the driver's seat at Apple, and despite being warned once by the board, Sculley was quickly reverting to his passive-aggressive ways. Not long after Jobs's departure, Sculley flew to San Diego to address Bill Campbell's sales team, ostensibly to thank the group for having kept its act together in the face of apparent chaos back at headquarters. Instead, Sculley reamed out the room. He told the sales force—the same people who had just brought in Apple's biggest new business partners—that they weren't even the best sales organization in their corner of the industry. That they paled against their counterparts at IBM and Compaq. He further warned them against cruising on their recent successes and slacking off in the months ahead.

The reaction was predictable. The staff was furious. Campbell was so hurt and humiliated that he was ready to quit. In the end, though there was a core of hard truth in what he said, Sculley backed off. Writing about that experience later, Sculley would say that, unlike Pepsi, where "toughness counted," such behavior by a CEO at Apple was "a terrible mistake" because it "created tremendous anxiety." In response, Sculley sentenced himself to reeducation and sensitivity training:

The image of the chief executive as a tough, aloof, nearly macho hero is an anachronism in today's world. The New Age leaders will lead not with toughness but powerful ideas. My natural instincts were to be authoritative, cool and distant. I was too consumed with solving a problem instead of the building for the future.

The New Age leader, he went on to write, "has to show his fallibility. Making mistakes is a very real and important part of succeeding."

Apple Computer was in the hands of a chief executive undergoing a midlife spiritual crisis, and the timing couldn't be worse. Thousands of lives were to be held hostage to the on-the-job self-actualization training of the CEO. Even worse, a company unequaled for its tiny fiefdoms, internecine battles, unmanageable prima donnas and runaway new-product development programs was now to be managed by a man who no longer believed in interfering or banging heads. John Sculley, the tough marketing genius who had been brought in to bring some rigor and maturity to Apple, had instead become, indeed, the Spirit of Apple in silver lamé tights. In his person, he embodied almost everything wrong with the company, while lacking most things right.

It was all there in that eyes-averted, limp handshake. But it also could be found in almost every action, every day, at Apple with John Sculley. And here too Steve Jobs had left his mark. When you heard an Apple vice president say to Sculley, "What's the matter, John? You seem sad. Have you meditated yet today?" you couldn't be sure, after Jobs, whether you were seeing a company careening toward disaster or were getting a lucky first glimpse of the enlightened CEO of the twenty-first century. After all, Jobs was crazy and he'd built Apple into a billion-dollar corporation, so if Sculley sometimes acted like he should be turning pottery and pouring candles instead of running a computer company, who was to say he was wrong? The press—and even analysts—gave him the benefit of the doubt.

Had John Sculley sold off Apple right after the Macintosh introduction, he might have been a hero. He had a second chance after the financial turnaround in 1985. Now he could take credit for fixing Apple *without* Jobs. He could have walked away an industry legend, his mysterious persona still intact, his reputation untarnished.

Instead, he stayed. Apple, like every other company in the personal computer industry, lived in a state of perpetual crisis and desperation. But behind this steady hiss of near-term problems and opportunities, there were larger market forces at work, sensed only as a deep, almost inaudible rumble under the chatter of today's news. The great industry leaders and innovators—from Hewlett and Packard to Gates—had always been attuned to that hidden sound. Other successful entrepreneurs and executives, such as Nolan Bushnell, Gene Amdahl and Tandem's Jimmy Treybig, had heard it once and built giant companies, but never heard it again. Woz had heard it too, in 1975, but as the failure of his new universal remote control company, CL9, proved, he now had a tin ear. Woz even ran off to Hawaii in search of isolation and inspiration—only to discover after four weeks that, according to *Wired* magazine, "He couldn't recapture that loneliness and the idealism that had once been the source of his prodigious concentration. He came back and hired other engineers to finish the job." Jobs, by comparison, heard the sound all the time, but in his arrogance thought that he was making it, and could control it, even change it.

Sculley never heard it. Perhaps it was impossible for him to do so. Perhaps you need to *live* the high-tech revolution, and fight in its trenches, not join up as a brigadier general. That was why the number of successful nontechnical business executives in electronics could almost be counted on one hand— and on close inspection every one of them was a special case. Sure, Irwin Federman, a finance guy, had largely succeeded at MMI, but he was a strong-willed boss of legendary personal integrity running a chip business in a mature industry. And in time, even MMI would get caught flat-footed during a technological shift and wind up selling out to a technologist with almost perfect pitch: Jerry Sanders of Advanced Micro Devices.

A similar story could be told about most of the other nontech businessmen running high-tech companies. Either they were in older industries in which most of the innovation had already been wrung out or they had at their right hand a genius chief technologist. Or they were living on borrowed time.

If John Sculley had ever heard the deep waves of technological change, it was only for a moment as a child. But twenty years at Pepsi had left him utterly tone deaf. So his only choice was to depend upon the talents of others. But he was too out of touch to choose the right mentors. Jean-Louis Gassée, with good Cartesian logic, could postulate those deep waves, even turn them into poetry, but he couldn't hear them . . . and he was Apple's chief technologist.

Instinctively, Sculley turned elsewhere in the company. But many of the most creative souls in the company had moved on during the failure of the III and the Lisa, or the collapse of the Mac, or the abandonment of the II. They had been replaced by the kind of people always attracted to highly visible, public corporations: risk-averse, highly competent professionals, typically from the very best schools. These were bright, talented people who, when faced with the choice of risking everything on a big stock payoff or merely taking a good salary in a secure job, would always choose the latter. Most swaggered like entrepreneurs, but in the end they were merely bureaucrats in mufti. Their mission—to the relief of many, because life in a start-up is brutal and exhausting—was to kill the entrepreneurial spirit and replace it with an organization built to last.

By the end of the 1980s, Apple's executive row looked more like Savile Row. The pirate days were gone, surviving only in company histories and advertisements. The more dangerous elements in Apple's past—the hacking, the sweatshops, the rip-offs—were now either buried or gelded into a nice, safe mischievousness that gave a little shiver of rakish frisson to the new legions of well-scrubbed, double-breasted young professionals who now roamed the company's halls.

The January 1986 Apple annual shareholders meeting was special, precisely because it was not.

For years, especially in 1984, Apple had used the occasion as the proscenium for its biggest product announcements. It was the moment when Steve Jobs would stride out onstage and announce Apple's newest insanely great creation, whether it lived up to that title or not.

But Jobs was history—and as if to remind the world of that fact—Apple decided *not* to use the event again as anything but a meeting of folks holding company stock. "We're going to be more discreet and less predictable in product announcement and not march to the dates we have had before. Our January shareholders meetings will be just that—a shareholders meeting."

The subtext was: *This is no longer a juvenile company run by Steve Jobs. We are now a mature corporation led by grown-ups.* But the fact was that Apple would never again have a new product introduction that riveted the world's attention.

The Apple being built by the new executive team was infinitely more efficient than the one it replaced. New products now mostly came out on time, neatly packaged and stocked with the right software and the crisply designed manuals. The company's advertisements and commercials were now cute and housebroken, as reinforcing of the values of yuppie boomers as those produced by Honda and, of course, Pepsi. Apple Computer was now sold in computer stores, department stores and even stereo stores using the most sophisticated point-of-sale tools, demos and promotions. And when new products were introduced, the company still held media events, now much more sophisticated and choreographed than the original Lisa and Mac announcements—and instead of taking place in the theater of a community college, these events now were put on at Apple's own trade show, MacWorld Expo, held each year in Boston and San Francisco, before tens of thousands of true believers.

Apple under John Sculley quickly became a satisfying (if not wonderful) place to work. The company that had no retirement plan because nobody figured to stay that long, got one. It got a day-care center too. And an employee store. And a real, honest-to-God working budget. Unlike in the Steve Jobs era, you could arrive in the morning and know that today would be much like yesterday. It was like a college campus with older, but better-dressed students. PhDs were everywhere: they filled the offices of the Mac educational group, of Apple University and the labs. As a boomer facing middle age, you could go to work at Apple and feel good about helping teach kids and fighting the totalitarian Intel-Microsoft monolith and sitting in meetings where important people talked about the philosophical challenge of making the world a better place. Then that night, at the Little League game, you could feel the countercultural, superior thrill of saying you worked for Apple Computer.

Boring as it was, the new Apple business model seemed to work. For the first quarter ended December 27, 1985, Apple announced record earnings far above even Wall Street's estimates. They were, in fact, the best quarterly numbers in the company's history. That morning the stock jumped two points to 22⅝.

It seemed a validation of everything Apple had done over the previous year: Jobs's ouster, the arrival of the new team, the layoffs, the reorganization, even the decision to remain PC-incompatible. Most of all, it was a testament to the wisdom of John Sculley. He had taken a troubled company run by a troubled founder and turned it into a lean, mean moneymaking machine. "Apple Computer is healthy and strong," he crowed in the announcement. The long corporate nightmare was over. Let the era of normalcy begin.

The company was feeling so cocky that Sculley felt safe to sell off 125,000 shares of his own without anyone reading anything into it but a CEO's justly earned reward.

Apple used its new public platform, the AppleWorld Conference in San Francisco, to introduce the $2,599 Macintosh Plus and LaserWriter Plus to 2,000 product developers and dealers. At the event, John Sculley announced that it would use some of its $441.5 million in cash on hand to create a $25 million venture capital fund to help found new Apple-oriented start-up companies. This was the classic move of a company that believes it now owns its market and is setting out to consolidate it. It compounded this image of business maturation by announcing it was embarking on strategic partnerships with, among others, Northern Telecom and 3Com.

At that moment, coming off a miserable year, Apple looked more than ever on top of its game. The theme song of the conference was Patti LaBelle's "New Attitude" and the title seemed to fit. Apple's Golden Age had begun.

Buried in all this good news, though, there were eerie signs of things to come. For all the glowing pronouncements about the Apple Computer to come, details were vague. Campbell, for example, once again mentioned a portable Mac, but declined to give a delivery date.

Meanwhile, copies of Sculley's speech announcing the new Mac Plus/LaserWriter Plus combination, the heart of Apple's desktop publishing strategy, were so freighted with typographical and spelling errors as to be a parody of the perils of word processing.

Sculley used the occasion to publicly pitch Apple's board for the company to buy a $15 million Cray computer, ostensibly for advanced modeling of future company hardware and software products. It sounded impressive, but as Regis McKenna and others who lobbied against it well knew, the Cray was little more than a vanity project, a fancy gift to R&D that had little to contribute to the company's creativity beyond helping to design plastic enclosures for the computers. In the end, Sculley wanted the Cray because he wanted the biggest, most powerful computer on earth. It was a warning of things to come.

But strangest of all were the "exhibits" lining the walk journalists and analysts took between the convention center and the speech in the ballroom of a nearby building. These were Plexiglas display cases containing real human beings in frozen poses using Apple computer products. Meant to be compelling, these tableaus were instead disturbing, partly because the cases were so narrow that the performers seemed in danger of suffocation. Thus, instead of the planned image of liberation through Apple computers, the result was the unforgettable metaphor of people trapped by a technology and in desperate need of liberation.

Apple culminated this celebration with the deification of its new leader. On January 29, John Sculley was named chairman of Apple Computer, officially replacing Steve Jobs. At age forty-six, three years out of "selling sugar water," he was now the most famous—and one of the most powerful—figures in high technology.

On March 15, almost five years to the day after the firing of Mike Scott, Steve Jobs officially sold the last of his Apple stock . . . all except for one symbolic share. That solitary remaining share, the last of his 6.5 million ($120 million) shares, was more than a mere memento of his former life: it also gave Jobs a ticket to all future Apple shareholder meetings.

The second quarter ended March 28, 1986, only brought more good news. Sales were down 6 percent, but they were off 11 percent for the industry as a whole. At the same time, profits had *tripled*; gross margins were 56.6 percent, the highest in the company's history. Three months later, the numbers were even better: compared to the $17 million loss the year before, Apple saw a profit of $32 million. And sales for the quarter had jumped 20 percent to $448 million.

The company was now feeling so upbeat that it fired its advertising agency, Chiat/Day, creator of the magnificent but dour "1984" ad, and replaced it with BBDO, Sculley's old agency at Pepsi, and famous for its upbeat campaigns.

"I'm having a ball," said Sculley. "I can't think of anything I'd rather do in the world." He had now traded in his suits for chinos, plaid shirts and deck shoes. Now, padding around Apple's offices, he looked more like the company psychologist than the CEO.

Apple employees, wary at first because of Sculley's lack of technical credentials and his history of snuggling with Jobs, slowly began to warm up to their boss as well. Not surprisingly, the first to come around was the beleaguered II group. As one of its members told the *San Jose Mercury News*, "Things have gotten better. No one has to hide anything anymore from other Apple engineers. When Jobs was around, if the II group had done a project he hadn't okayed, he'd just cancel it." Said another, "More people are happier at Apple than they were before."

Sculley himself would proudly say, with considerable justification, "Apple is a more disciplined, grown-up company today. People have grown to recognize that discipline is not a threat to innovation. . . . I know what it takes to be a success."

One of those ways, Sculley decided, was to promote Del Yocam to the post of chief operating officer. Henceforth, Bill Campbell and Mike Spindler would report to Yocam, not Sculley, the chairman/president/CEO. In one respect, this was standard operating procedure. Sculley, like any person running a multibillion-dollar publicly traded corporation, was being pulled in many ways, from captain of the corporate ship, to public advocate on industry issues, to liaison to Apple's millions of shareholders, to company figurehead. In the face of all this, now that the immediate crisis threatening the company appeared past, John Sculley needed a first lieutenant to take over the daily operations of Apple Computer.

He said as much in the news release announcing the appointment: "With Apple now set on a clear and positive course for the future, this was the right time to create this position."

Yet, as proper as the move sounded, it rested on a flawed assumption: that Apple's crises were now behind it; that having righted itself and enjoyed a few quarters of good news, the company now could look forward to years of smooth sailing.

But this was not the soda-pop industry. Changes didn't arrive slowly, with considerable advance warning that gave you time to prepare your response. In computers, just the opposite was true. Radical, life-threatening change more often than not arrived overnight, seemingly from nowhere. Sculley might have learned that lesson from the almost instantaneous appearance of desktop publishing—but then, he was the beneficiary of that revolution, not, like thousands of printing companies, its victim.

To run a high-tech company you had to be *engaged* at all times. Even while you were taking on all the other ancillary tasks. That's why Apple was paying John Sculley millions of bucks each year. The company was decidedly *not* on a "clear and positive course for the future," but only for the moment. And by stepping away like some East Coast corporate Brahmin, John Sculley not only abrogated his duties as much as Jobs had six months before but placed himself in the position of being perpetually disappointed by lieutenants who found it impossible to maintain the company on the sunny upward trajectory Sculley believed he'd set for it.

8.8 MESSIAHS

Now that success—the company saw profits rise another 47 percent in the fourth quarter—had freed Sculley to think higher thoughts, those thoughts turned to the task of restoring Apple's lost market mojo. In time he became convinced that he could resurrect the Old Spirit of Apple by finding a new visionary and a new figurehead to replace Steve Jobs. And for that task he found a most unlikely (and more manageable) pair: Steve Wozniak and Alan Kay.

Sculley was working on Woz's return even before Jobs left. Wozniak's huffy departure had been a minor distraction in the madness that was Apple in 1984. He had never actually quit Apple, but merely gone off with the company's modest blessings to start Cloud Nine (CL9), a maker of universal remote controls. There, he proved that as a CEO he was a good lab technician. He even reverted to his old ways: his secretary, echoing his mother, had to pull him away from his soldering gun and clean him up to attend company board meetings. The company was doomed from the start.

Woz was unruffled. In truth, he seemed happier up at his big home in the Santa Cruz mountains, putting on elaborate birthday parties and building cave mazes under the house for his kids. He continued to indulge the child-like side of his own personality—to often magnificent results. The greatest of these was as the lead benefactor of the Children's Discovery Museum in San Jose. Like all such projects, it had gotten off to a slow start in fund-raising. Then, like a bolt from the blue, Woz put up $2 million, nearly 10 percent of the funding goal. He posed for photographers putting handprints on a wall while kneeling with a group of kids. When asked by reporters why he had made such a remarkable gift, Woz harked back to his childhood, to reading Scrooge McDuck comic books and deciding that if he ever got that rich he would use his money to help people. It was charming, fixing forever the image of Steve Wozniak as a childlike saint/genius. And when the museum was finished, the name of the road leading to it was rechristened Woz Way.

But it was not all happy news. His second marriage broke up, with Candi Wozniak claiming that, in a heated argument, he had thrown her down the stairs at CL9. There was never any proof. Still, all was obviously not perfect with Woz. And so, when Sculley invited him back to replace Jobs as the face of Apple, Woz was happy to oblige. He told Sculley he had some great new ideas for the Apple II.

Wozniak turned out to be a terrific public speaker, and his eccentricities, like buying dollar bills by the sheet and simply cutting off whatever he needed for payment, were ingratiating. But with the decision not to clone IBM, the rise of desktop publishing on the Mac and the Internet still four years away, the II was nothing more than a winning antique, a holding pen for future Mac converts. Sculley didn't want it because it wasn't part of his regime, and he couldn't imagine a future for it. Gassée didn't want the II either, because it didn't fit his strategy of high-end, elegant machines. And Del Yocam, the II's last great champion, had been promoted away.

The only people who still wanted the Apple II were the folks who bought a billion dollars' worth of them every year, as well as twice that amount or more in software.

For them, the first generation of true Apple loyalists, the Apple II line was allowed a swan song. And it was a doozy: the 1986 Apple IIGS (for "graphics and sound"), perhaps the high-water mark of the computer maker's art and, in terms of quality, price and performance, the best computer Apple ever built. It featured an elegant box filled with the simplest componentry imaginable—all superfluity having been winnowed out over the previous nine years—a color display and stereo sound. It was a computer designed from the start to appeal to schools, which needed a reliable computer of considerable power at a reasonable price . . . yet so inexpensive to build that it was like a license for Apple to print money. Moreover, the IIGS actually outperformed the Macintosh on the Mac's own turf. It was the II group's last hurrah.

Hundreds of thousands of IIGS's were sold, used by a generation of kids right up to the mid-1990s, when they were finally junked—most of them still working as well as the day they were bought.

But as Apple support dried up, as the new products disappeared and third-party developers moved on, the customer base gradually eroded. It was a testament to the Apple myth that most bought Macs.

And as the II slowly faded away, so once more did Steve Wozniak.

But Sculley had a second guru waiting in the wings. Besides his tenure at Atari, Alan Kay had one of the finest minds and most distinguished résumés in personal computing. He arrived in the world of computing armed with degrees in math, computer science and biology. He was also a disciple of MIT's Marvin Minsky, the computers-in-education pioneer. This alone should have been a red flag to everyone thereafter: MIT is notorious—witness the Media Lab there—for coming up with brilliant, seductive ideas about the future of computing that never find practical application. Kay would be MIT's Typhoid Mary, bringing the pox of impracticality to Silicon Valley.

From MIT, Kay's career took him to the Utah operations of ARPA, that great government seeding ground of U.S. technology, most notably the Internet. There, Kay had his vision that would haunt personal computing forever. Watching a demonstration of a flat panel display, Kay suddenly realized that, with Moore's Law at work, this expensive form of output would within a decade be affordable to everybody. So too would the big mainframe computers he was working with. Put the two together you had something amazing: an affordable, book-sized computer with a thin display and the ability to be configured to any user.

When ARPA fell into disarray, Kay fortuitously landed at Xerox PARC, where he perfected his vision of this new portable computer, which he called the Dynabook: it would have the power of a minicomputer, with vast amounts of memory, yet be so simple and self-evident in its operation that a young child could play with it.

It was the single most compelling vision of the future that the personal computing world had ever seen. And it sucked into the crusade everyone who ever heard about it. Even among the arrogant engineers at PARC it proved irresistible. Soon the entire computer lab was dreaming of Dynabooks. Kay's vision had everything going for it: it was coherent, imaginable and years away from being practical. And that just spurred the scientists on.

The effect, at least at PARC, was both galvanizing and salutary. The group not only had a goal but had a template with which to select which new inventions were useful and which were not. Thus, the mouse was good because it reduced the need for punching keys. By the same token, graphic interfaces were superior to textual ones because they required less typing, less memorization of commands, and were more universal in application. The use of icons, such as garbage cans, helped simplify matters even further. And bit-mapped displays were good because they made the computer's operations transparent.

Kay had his own team at PARC, and just when the rest of the computer group would catch up with his current research, Kay would launch off in a new product direction. The best of these inventions was Smalltalk (named after the simplicity of conversations at cocktail parties), a programming language designed to be so simple that even children with their limited vocabularies could use it. Kay actually brought in a group of kids to test it.

It was largely Kay's work (combined with Douglas Engelbart's mouse) that Jef Raskin had studied before going to Apple, and that Jobs saw on his fateful tour. And it was Kay's vision of the Dynabook that underscored the Mac project—the idea that someday it too would be a handheld machine. In fact, along with Jobs's other mottoes that he put up in the Mac offices, one was dedicated to the Dynabook: "Mac in a book by 1986."

By 1983 Kay found his way to Apple. There, he was named a company Fellow, able to live elsewhere, play Bach on his grand piano and send ex cathedra missives full of his brilliance to company headquarters. His most irritating habit was dismissing almost every new idea he heard of as being little more than an outgrowth of his work at PARC. This was not guaranteed to make him many friends at Apple. But by constantly holding back his approval, and by suggesting that even the greatest breakthroughs were merely baby steps toward a greater goal, Kay managed to gain considerable influence among those in the company who knew the least about technology.

The most famous Kay memo even managed to piss off Jobs, his greatest champion, and the man who recruited him to Apple. The memo, sent to his other great champion, John Sculley (who thought him a genius) was entitled "Have I Got a Deal for You: A Honda with a One-Quart Gas Tank." In the memo, Kay argued that having such limited memory and a single disk drive in the Mac was a terrible mistake. It was classic Kay: arrogant, supercilious and painfully accurate. Kay reacted to the resulting outcry by professing surprise: after all, he had only criticized the Macintosh because it was the first personal computer worthy of criticism.

That remark didn't make him any friends either. But it did capture John Sculley's attention. And a few years later, when Sculley was casting about for a new tech guru, it was Kay who came to mind. Soon they were nearly as inseparable as Sculley and Jobs had been. Sculley would write, ominously, in 1987:

> After my breakup with Steve Jobs in the summer of 1986, I found a new teacher. Apple Fellow Alan Kay. He led me on an extraordinary journey by sharing with me many of his unique and inventive ideas. It was Alan, perhaps more than anybody else, who expanded my range of viewpoints. We have regularly held weekly discussions which are usually accompanied by his suggestion of a new book or two for me to read. When I trace the origins of the most exciting and outrageous ideas behind the personal computer revolution, most paths lead directly to Alan. He has been both a friend and mentor on this journey.

There was nothing wrong with Kay's ideas; on the contrary, they are vindicated every day now with the rise of "thin clients" and "software agents." But the Dynabook was a concept too dangerous for anyone without the industry experience to put it into perspective, who didn't appreciate that it was not a computer generation, but a *human* generation away; and that there were a thousand technological problems, none of them trivial, in between. And that to try to jump one of those steps was a recipe for disaster.

There were no philosophers of soda pop at Pepsi, so Sculley had no resistance to their charms. People like Don Valentine or Mike Markkula or even Steven Jobs, who had listened to a new theory of organization, technology or management every week for the last twenty years, were largely indifferent to their blandishments. They had seen hundreds of brilliant new theories come and go, and the most exciting ones were always the ones most likely to fail. Like every successful Valley veteran, they knew better than to jump on board the latest fad theory, but instead to steal what was immediately applicable and remain skeptical of the rest.

Even Jobs fell for Kay's theory—at least for a time. He even made some moves to co-opt the Dynabook. But eventually, recognizing the enormity of the task, he moved on.

But Sculley didn't just adopt Kay's Dynabook; he wanted to make it his own. He'd almost invented the Trinitron television, hadn't he? Why couldn't he be the inventor of the second-generation Dynabook as well? It was the perfect combination of glossy high theory and dim technological underpinnings to appeal to an amateur technologist.

The result was the Knowledge Navigator. And it stole John Sculley's heart like nothing since Steve Jobs. The KN was Kay's Dynabook with enough added wrinkles for Sculley to make it his own. It was to be, in Sculley's New Age hyperbole:

> . . . a discoverer of worlds, a tool as galvanizing as the printing press. Individuals could use it to drive through libraries, museums, databases, or institutional archives. This tool wouldn't just take you to the doorstep of these great resources as sophisticated computers do now; it would invite you deep inside its secrets, interpreting and explaining— converting vast quantities of information into personalized and understandable knowledge.

As Sculley described it, the actual product would be Kay's Dynabook (portable, flat screen, networked, full motion video, adaptive keyboard or perhaps just speech recognition) with the addition of a pair of joysticks on either side so that the user could "fly" like the Wilbur Wright of cyberspace through empyreans of knowledge.

8.9 FELLOW

This last idea was courtesy of a recent invention by Bill Atkinson, the creator of the Lisa user interface, inventor of the single-button mouse and, unlike the more publicized Kay, Apple's true technological guru and the one worthy successor to Woz.

Atkinson, thirty-five, an Apple Fellow now and struggling to keep from succumbing to the post-Mac depression facing most of his peers, was a typical Apple techno-eccentric. For example, he was convinced that mankind would one day soon be replaced by silicon-based entities descended from the work being done right now on computers. In other words, he was God—not a unique attitude among programmers. And Atkinson was one hell of a programmer, one of the two or three best in the history of personal computers.

It was his gift for programming, combined with his unmatched understanding of how mere humans dealt with the complexities of information, that enabled him to develop Apple's last truly great contribution to the computer revolution.

Atkinson had spent the months after Mac trapped in Kay's fantasy too. Atkinson's version of the Dynabook was to be called the Magic Slate, and it was to feature many of the traits ultimately found in Newton: flat display, touch screen and handwriting recognition. It was also to be so cheap as to be nearly disposable.

That Atkinson thought he could pull off the Magic Slate at that moment in history was a testament to how deeply he had internalized the old Jobs bravado. But it was also a reminder that even great programmers and designers must be supported by enlightened management. Apple no longer had that type of leadership. The project was killed. The irony was that just as John Sculley was dreaming about the Knowledge Navigator he was denying support to his best programmer for the intermediate step to his goal.

Atkinson was heartbroken, but he still hadn't given up. Amazingly, he had another, equally brilliant invention up his sleeve. It was called Wildcard, and it was a new way of linking information in a manner never possible before the computer. Wildcard was the first step in the realization of computer visionary Ted Nelson's dream, called Xanadu, of a worldwide interlinkage of the world's knowledge into a single metanarrative—a "hypertext," as Nelson called it. Atkinson's Wildcard literally represented a new way of thinking—an achievement that can be claimed by only a handful of people in history.

At the heart of Wildcard was Atkinson's realization that, unlike the world of printed pages and libraries, computer information was largely unconstrained by time or space. In the world of print, both the author and the reader are limited by the linear nature of narrative. Try to stuff too much information into that narrative and the meaning is lost and the text becomes impenetrable. In four thousand years of printed books, only a handful of ways around this intrinsic obstacle had been developed—footnotes, indexes, bibliographies, etc. But each of those had their own weaknesses, notably the lost time and energy spent flipping through pages or running to the library, and the resulting lost connection with the core text.

Until Atkinson, text on computers was still trapped in this old print paradigm. The biggest breakthrough until now had been the "search" function. What Atkinson recognized was that in the digital realm, text size wasn't important. If you chose, you could have a thousand pages of footnotes appended to a single paragraph. In fact, thanks to Moore's Law, you could soon make that one million or one billion pages. And you could append those thousand pages and then simply call them up from anywhere in the world with the push of a button.

This was powerful enough, but Atkinson, with his remarkable three-dimensional mind, took it even further. If you could append a thousand pages behind that single paragraph, why not link a thousand separate documents, all of them related to the topic at hand? And to those documents, why not be able to append a thousand more documents—some just sentences, others lengthy tomes—and on and on. One of these underlying documents, a dozen layers down, might even in fact be the original document—thus closing the loop, and tying together in a vast web all the relevant information on a topic. This was the medieval memory theater in binary form, but evanescent, created in real time according to the immediate desires of the user. You could state your interest and be led down and down deeper into that topic, until you finally got the bends, or, if you were sufficiently patient, broke through the bottom and found yourself back on the surface.

Atkinson's creation, renamed Hypercard, was so amazing that, almost uniquely in the world of high tech, everyone who saw it instantly knew it was great. Meanwhile, computer theorists talked about how, as computers became more powerful and communications faster and broader, it might be possible to hyperstack not only text but sounds, images, even moving pictures.

But Hypercard had one serious weakness: It was a networked product in a world of stand-alone machines. Nelson's Xanadu was still far off. Hypertexts were clever in a Mac or a PC, but profoundly limited. So what if you could link a half dozen of your different files together? You could count the uses for that—unless perhaps you were a teacher—on one hand. But what if a bunch of computers were linked together? What if thousands were, or millions? Personal computers and mainframes, giant databases and high-speed communications lines?

Just such a network was already in place: the ARPAnet, the linkup of thousands of computers at universities and defense contractors, all under the aegis of the Department of Defense. By the time Atkinson invented Hypercard, the ARPAnet was already fifteen years old, with nearly a million users, and already developing its own culture. Within another four years, the ARPAnet would be privatized into the Internet, and a vast organizing grid, the

World Wide Web, would be overlaid atop it. A year after that, Marc Andreeson and some fellow students at the University of Illinois would develop Mosaic, the first search engine for the Web, and the spark that would turn the Internet into the greatest global phenomenon of its time.

Ten years after Atkinson first began handing out test copies of Hypercard to his friends at Apple, one hundred million people each day would call up Web pages, then dive into the mountains of data stacked behind them, or tap on hot (hyper) links and zip around the world, surfing other sites—an entire world built upon Atkinson's new way of thinking.

It was all there in 1986 in Hypercard. Atkinson had given Apple an unequaled glimpse into the future. And with the Macintosh and its graphical operating system, Apple had the unmatched machine for exploring this new world. But to do that, Apple first had to proliferate the use of personal computers to millions of people through easy-to-use, low-cost machines—Raskin Revisited. It had to develop computers that performed more than one function at a time—multitasking. And most of all, it had to reorient the company away from stand-alone, isolated personal computers and toward machines designed for maximum utility in networked settings.

John Sculley's Apple did none of these things. Atkinson had hesitated to even show Hypercard to Apple, figuring the company would screw him. Instead, he considered quitting. But Alan Kay heard of his plans and went to Sculley to tell him to give Atkinson a hearing. Sculley did as he was told and even he was thrilled by what he saw. He wanted Hypercard. Atkinson, shrewdly, cut a deal: Hypercard would henceforth be bundled into every Apple computer sold—and if it wasn't, the rights to the invention would revert to Atkinson. Sculley agreed. Meanwhile, he also incorporated its implications into his growing model of the Knowledge Navigator.

With Kay's Dynabook and Atkinson's Hypercard, Sculley had nearly a turnkey vision of the future he could call his own. The final step was to bolt on the potentialities of the ARPAnet and a brand-new theory called software agency, in which "agents" created by software would interact on the screen with the user and do that user's bidding.

8.10 SURROGATES

The whole package made Sculley dizzy with excitement. Here was his Trinitron; his own personal Unified Field Theory of computing, the idea that would place him among not only the great executives but the great *thinkers* of computing. And it wasn't enough to merely give speeches about it or dwell on it in endless, breathless depth over the final third of his autobiography. Sculley wanted to make the Knowledge Navigator *real*. And since that was impossible—almost everything about the KN, from its color flat panel display to speech recognition, full motion video and high-speed broadband data links were at least a decade away—Sculley decided to simply *pretend* it was real.

He hired Lucasfilm, fresh from its *Star Wars* trilogy triumph, to create a series of expensive, Hollywood-quality videos, each five minutes long, of futuristic scenarios involving the Knowledge Navigator. The most famous of these was the first, which Apple showed to the world on every occasion it could think of for the next two years.

It was a homey, beautifully filmed, yet oddly sterile little infomercial that featured a Berkeley professor preparing a lecture for a class he is to teach later that day on the destruction of the rain forest. The tool he uses for this work is an intriguing little laptop/notebook computer that appears to be no more than an inch thick with an elegant Art Deco design: the Knowledge Navigator. The professor opens the Navigator and up on the screen pops the image of a young man wearing a bow tie. For viewers in 1989, it took a moment to realize that this young man was not real, but a creation of the computer—an anthropomorphized software agent who can understand what the professor says to him, reply and serve as the professor's surrogate by going out into the electronic world and gathering information from databases. The agent also attends to other matters in the professor's life, such as keeping his appointments (about which he gently hectors his boss), his phone list and personal records.

In the course of this interaction between biological master and software servant, the professor has the agent search the world's databases for movies and animations that vividly show the damage being done to the world's rain forests. These are quickly displayed on the screen, then melded together into a complete multimedia presentation with charts and graphics and video windows. The professor then orders the servant to get hold of Jill, another professor, who has recently written a paper on the same subject. The agent has already anticipated (!) this request, and already placed the call. Jill appears on the screen, she and the professor have a conversation and they sign off. The professor and the servant have a few more words, then he shuts off the Navigator and departs, no doubt to change the lives of his students forever and in the process save Mother Earth.

An impressive production, with tonalities as much High Spielberg as Lucas. And the video had the desired effect, especially upon first-time viewers with little computer experience. With this group, the typical response was "Wow! When can we get something like that?"

But upon multiple viewings, an uneasiness developed, especially if you knew something about personal computing and about Apple. Then the video became a banquet of subtexts, a picnic for deconstructionists. For one thing, the professor was something of a pompous jerk—apparently John Sculley's image of enlightenment. Then there was the matter of the servant. Prissy, impeccable and wearing a bow tie, the software agent became even more irritating with each viewing. Was the bow tie some kind of clue? Was this digital eunuch a stand-in for a castrated Steve Jobs? And, to take the allegory further, was this master-servant relationship, which Steven Levy accurately compared to slavery—"If for some reason he got out of line, his owner could drag him to the trash can and replace him with a more obsequious icon"— also a kind of wish fulfillment for Sculley?

Finally, there was Jill, the professional associate. Again, Levy, normally a staunch defender of Apple during this era, sounding the proper alarm: Was Jill a real person? After all, she didn't seem any more substantial than the eunuch. Or perhaps she was Jill's servant, in this case designed to look just like its master. And if the latter was true, what kind of hall of mirrors was the Knowledge Navigator getting us into? What would it mean if we couldn't tell the difference between what was real and what was a digital representation?

Luckily for Apple, most people didn't ask themselves these larger ontological questions. Instead, the video worked its magic all too well. After watching it, your own personal computer, even a Mac, seemed like an archaic piece of junk. Newcomers watched the video and wondered why they couldn't find anything like it at the electronics store. Veterans asked if this constituted a commitment by Apple to embark on a long-term project to build the Knowledge Navigator, and what that meant for company products between now and then.

But beyond promoting the idea of the Knowledge Navigator, Apple had nothing much to say. Even Sculley stopped talking about it after a couple of years, suggesting that it was little more than a vanity project, something to earn him his tech spurs. But in unexpected ways, the Knowledge Navigator campaign cost Apple enormously. When, in 1989, Apple finally introduced its first laptop, the Macintosh Portable, underpowered, oversized, heavy and with a short battery life, the outcry was in no small part due to the market's disappointment over the gap between these products and the ones they'd been trained to expect from the Knowledge Navigator.

But the real damage came a couple of years later with the introduction in 1992 of the Newton.

8.11 ABDICATION II

The Dynabook wasn't the only thing that rushed in to fill the void in John Sculley's attention as he pulled away from the daily running of Apple Computer.

The other was the game of moving executives about on the organization chart. For the rest of the decade after the 1985 shake-up, senior managers came and went under Sculley's rule, rising up through the ranks until they approached the throne itself, only to be ritually beheaded and their corpse cast out of the company.

As befit a corporate monarch, Sculley kept his court in constant turmoil. In his creepy passive-aggressive style, with its spooky combination of thoughtful altruism and scheming pragmatism, he regularly promoted managers into positions of unprecedented (and often undeserved) authority, at the same time pulling the rug out from under those veterans who got too close to the throne.

The game began with a flurry of hirings and appointments. Larry Tesler, the old Xerox PARC leader, was promoted from the directorship of advanced technology development to the new position of first vice president of advanced technology and membership on Sculley's seven-person executive staff. Kevin Sullivan arrived from DEC to become vice president of human resources. Allan Loren came from the Philadelphia insurance company Cigna to help Apple set up a management information system, a field in which he was an acknowledged expert. Then, inexplicably, he was moved sideways and put in charge of Apple's sales and marketing. Fred Forsythe, who'd done a fine job of running manufacturing at Apple, was made head of engineering.

Nearly every one of these moves would prove misguided.

But if unlikely promotion was the order of the outer rings of John Sculley's empire, being a long-standing member of his inner circle was akin to belonging to the Politburo in 1937. Sooner or later, almost everyone was purged.

The first to go was a surprise. Jean-Louis Gassée.

The fall came fast. In May 1987, Gassée, who was heading Apple's research and development team, was given management of the company's advanced technology research group. In June 1988, product marketing was placed under his control. By August, he had also been handed Apple's worldwide marketing operations. He was now Sculley's heir apparent. "It's clear Gassée's star is still rising," said Bruce Lupatkin, analyst at Hambrecht & Quist. Industry watcher Stewart Alsop was even more enthusiastic: "They've essentially handed Gassée the company." But then he added the foreboding words: "He and Sculley are clearly identifying with each other. It's one of those situations where one guy is finishing the other guy's sentence."

As Steve Jobs had proven, this was the kiss of death. By early 1990, stung by accusations that he wasn't getting enough hot new products out the door, Gassée resigned. The announcement stunned the Apple rank and file, especially in Gassée's own group. In what would soon be a standard response to any unpopular move at the company, a small contingent of a hundred employees staged a protest outside a company building a mile from Apple headquarters (it was chosen because it had a lawn). They sang "Louie, Louie, oh baby, THEY gotta go," waved signs and wore black berets out of solidarity with Gassée. They tried to chant the letters of Jean-Louis's name, but forgot how to spell it. After a half hour, they gave up and went back to work. "We're too old for real protesting," one of the employees said.

Rory O'Connor, the computing editor of the *San Jose Mercury News*, responded to the news with one of the first blistering public attacks on Sculley's presidency:

> In a dozen years, Apple has managed to take the ideas of a couple eccentric kids working in their garage and parlay them into a $5 billion company.
>
> Yet, despite all that has come before, the company that brought computers to individuals is now in danger of losing every semblance of influence and innovation in computing. For that, I blame Chairman, President and chief executive John Sculley, from whom the company derives little real leadership. . . . Charisma may not be vital to the chief executive of every company, but it is the coin of the realm at Apple, the stuff needed to motivate a company that resembles a religion more than a business.
>
> Even ignoring that unique aspect of Apple, Sculley also has failed in another aspect of leadership: clearly articulating a strategy for the company's future. I've seen Apple's endless stream of videotapes of what computers will be like in 20 years. What I can't fathom is what Apple computers will be like in two.
>
> The products Sculley's company has brought to market in the last year or two have been less than innovative. They seem designed simply to offer current customers faster, more expensive computers, not to broaden the appeal of the product line. As a result, Apple's growth rate is declining—now below both Wall Street's and Apple's own estimates—and its market share relative to the IBM world is shrinking.

> Without . . . leadership, without a clear plan for the future . . . Apple's star will surely plummet as fast as the fortunes of its top executives.

Debi Coleman, the most brilliant of Sculley's lieutenants, actually left Apple twice. Obese, manic to the point of hysteria, so driven by work that she barely had time for a social life, emotionally involved in the lives of everyone who worked for her, Debi was a time bomb waiting to explode. Having brilliantly run Apple's manufacturing; having learned to deal with both Steve Jobs and John Sculley; and most of all having played a crucial role in getting Apple through the tough times after the Mac introduction, Coleman was promoted to chief financial officer at Apple in August 1987.

She was only thirty-four years old and now one of the hottest stars in Apple. But already the pressures of her lifestyle had pushed Coleman to a state of near-collapse and, medically, at risk for her life.

At Apple, admitting weakness, especially in the form of a few tears, was acceptable, even admirable, among male executives. But taking a leave of absence due to stress was not acceptable in a fat woman executive—especially when that story was splattered all over the front page of *The Wall Street Journal* and a subject for discussion in boardrooms across America.

Debi took her five-month leave in February 1988 and lost thirty pounds. She returned that summer to find a different Apple—at least different in its attitude toward her. She took a post running the administrative side of Apple's headquarters—MIS, the television studio, etc.—and once again became a kind of star, with her own coterie of supporters inside the company. That was getting too close to the throne. Within a couple of years, she was gone for good, joining another former Sculley lieutenant, Del Yocam, in Oregon.

In terms of power the closest employee to Sculley, Del Yocam was also the most experienced senior manager in the company, especially when it came to personal computers. The combination of this experience and his conciliatory personality would seem to make Yocam the perfect Apple COO.

He lasted only two years in the job. In the same reorganization that made Gassée heir apparent, Yocam found himself stripped of the COO duties to become head of the education and Pacific divisions. At that point, said one analyst, "it became very apparent Yocam was not going to run the company some day. . . . Yocam is the last bastion of the old regime."

By early 1989, he too was gone. Yocam took over the CEO job at the venerable, and fading, Beaverton, Oregon, instrument company Tektronix, and immediately set about stripping down the company, divesting it of all the peripheral operations Tek had created over the previous half century. When

Debi arrived, he told her to take her pick of one of Tek's divisions, spin it off as an independent company, and the parent company would help out as a minority investor.

Coleman chose the most unlikely operation of all: Merix, a manufacturer of printed circuit boards. The PC board business was easily the dreariest and most retrograde industry in all of high technology, and Debi's choice, combined with her move to Oregon, signaled to Silicon Valley veterans a final admission of defeat.

In fact, it was just the opposite. Coleman had found the weakest and most vulnerable link on the electronics food chain, one filled with boring old companies content with their little corner of the market. Now she set out to turn it upside down. Within a year, she had taken Merix public, experimented with innovative new relationships with suppliers and was stealing market share from everybody. Meanwhile, Yocam eventually left Tek to tackle the turnaround of Borland, a software company in the Santa Cruz mountains that had flown high and then crashed under the spell of Philippe Kahn.

The saddest, and most costly, of Sculley's Peter Principled protégés was Michael Spindler. As head of Apple Europe, he'd done a superb job of holding on to Apple's market leadership. Taciturn, earnest and infinitely careful, he was a brilliant defensive businessman and probably Sculley's best lieutenant. But, because of his success, and perhaps because he posed the least threat to the throne, Sculley appointed Spindler president of Apple Computer, with Sculley himself remaining as chief executive. It was a cynical and ultimately cruel move disguised as a thoughtful gesture. A poor politician, a man with little flash and artifice and a businessman unaccustomed to going on the attack, Spindler, with his broken English, was a fish out of water in Cupertino. But, ever loyal, he gave it everything he had.

There were several other lesser-known figures hired, fired or shifted in John Sculley's great management shake-up of 1987.

Dave Barram, Regis McKenna's pal, had proven not to be a true CFO (ironic, since he would one day be the director of the U.S. Office of Management and Budget), so when he was replaced by Coleman, Barram was transferred to a new job, director of government affairs, which more accurately fit his abilities.

Ralph Russo, director of international operations, was moved over into Coleman's old manufacturing job. Chuck Boesenberg was named vice president of sales, then quickly joined MIPS Computer Systems in one of the celebrated Silicon Valley IPOs of the late 1980s. Bud Colligan, director of higher educational marketing and sales, resigned to join Authorware Inc. John Scull, in charge of Apple's desktop publishing business, quit to become president of Macromind Inc. Joe Schoendorf, marketing vice president, quit to pursue personal interests.

After executing or exiling most of his first team, and then promoting congenial second-tier players into the wrong positions, Sculley had no choice but to recruit real executive talent from outside. The best-known of these was Joe Graziano himself, who had quit Apple during the Jobs purge and gone to work at Sun Microsystems as chief financial officer. Sculley lured him back as CFO of Apple with a big salary and an even bigger signing bonus: $1.5 million, enough for Graziano to buy a couple of the vintage Ferraris (he'd graduated from Corvettes) that he collected, as well as the profits on another $1.35 million in stock options. The bonus package quickly became known inside Apple as "one Graz," a common measure by which all future bonuses would be measured. And there were a lot of Graz's and half Graz's flying around: Sculley needed management people badly, and talent was no longer flocking to Apple. Meanwhile, a few years later Graziano thanked Apple for this kind gesture by attempting to hijack the company.

The biggest winner in this management rondelle appeared to be Allan Loren, the new marketing and sales chief. About the shake-up, Loren would say smugly, "Our growth means we have to make some changes. Sometimes guys like it, sometimes they don't. Sometimes guys get promoted, sometimes they don't."

Within months, and much more deservedly than the others, Loren's head would be on the chopping block too.

Meanwhile, on April 22, 1987, Apple split its stock and announced a dividend. In May, Sculley was again named Silicon Valley's top-paid executive ($2.2 million). In July, company profits were up 66 percent. In December, the company announced that it would put up astronaut Sally Ride for a company directorship. In January 1988, company profits again doubled, as Apple raced to finish the year as a $4 billion company.

Meanwhile, after five years on the job, and tired from his herculean labors, John Sculley rested. He spent the summer on a nine-week leave of absence. The next winter, he bought a legendary mansion and estate in Woodside.

8.12 SEQUEL

Beyond these flights of fancy, both good and bad, Apple Computer mostly spent the end of the 1980s and the beginning of the 1990s in the business of settling down and designing and building products.

From now on, just as Jobs had wanted, Apple would be a Macintosh company. And now it was time for that company to take all that it had painfully learned from the first generation of Macs and apply it to a second generation.

It wasn't easy. The preliminary work on a new Mac had been started by Wayne Rosing and his team back in 1985. But Rosing had quit when he thought Jobs might win the feud with Sculley, leaving, with much of his team, for Sun Microsystems. Gassée and his team then took up the project, which by now was two:

- an upgrade to the 512K Mac, to be called the Mac SE ("system extended") featuring considerably more power and memory, as well as a circuit board slot for added functions;
- and the new-generation Mac II, with a larger display, more core memory, some added networking capabilities and a built-in hard disk drive.

The SE was designed to be a bridge product, bringing first-generation Mac users up to the brink of the II. It would also give them enough computing power to run the hottest software around, Microsoft's Excel for Mac, a Macintosh-compatible version of the best-selling bookkeeping software.

The Mac II, on the other hand, was something altogether new. It was to be the basic design of all Macintosh models well into the new decade.

The Mac II was Gassée's baby, and like so many products in Apple's history, it deeply reflected the personality of its creator. Despite the deep reservations of many inside Apple and out about Gassée's character and technical acumen—doubts reinforced by the man's affected style and woolly pronouncements—everyone agreed that the man was not afraid to follow his own opinions wherever they took him. Even if they collided with Apple's shibboleths. And, even though he ran his team like a pompous seminar instructor at the Sorbonne, Gassée still managed to retain the allegiance, even the respect, of notoriously freewheeling individualists like Guy Kawasaki.

Given his ego, his equating of computers with the infinite and, well, his Frenchness, Gassée managed to both worship the Mac and dislike almost everything about it. He didn't want to destroy the Mac, only help it find its destiny, to become its inner Platonic ideal: a high-powered business computer that would wow the corporate computer czars and stomp the PC and its clones into dust. That this lofty goal was also congruent with Gassée's own desire for respect as a hard-ass computer gunsel by these same MIS managers was, of course, only a coincidence.

The actual creation of the Mac II was yet another of those numerous recurring stories that make up Apple—in this case, the renegade that flies under the corporate radar screen, then surfaces at just the right moment to save the company. The hero on this occasion was a veteran of the Macintosh Office project named Mike Dhuey.

After the Macintosh introduction and the product's subsequent collapse, those Mac team members who still remained with the firm slowly shook off their depression and began to rouse themselves for what would come next. First came Burrell Smith's machine and Rich Page's Big Mac. To this was added a third project that never really got off the ground, code-named Jonathan.

But there was also a fourth Mac project, a solo venture undertaken by Dhuey simply because he believed his vision was correct and wanted to prove that fact to the world. That vision was for a modular computer, with a color display and, most important, slots for added function boards offered by both Apple and third-party suppliers. But this was still the Jobs era, and Dhuey well knew that to even suggest slots in the Mac constituted heresy and was grounds for excommunication. The Mac, in Jobs's eyes, was to always be a sealed, "closed" box.

So Dhuey kept his ideas to himself, working secretly with a hardware designer named Brian Berkeley. So fearful were they of Jobs's wrath that in their memos to one another they didn't even use the word "slot."

Then a series of events thrust Dhuey into the limelight. First, Jobs quit; then Gassée took over the group. And Gassée was not only open to openness, he was a fanatic about it—even his 240Z had vanity license plates that read OPEN MAC. Then all the other Mac projects began to fade out one at a time. Smith quit. Page joined NeXT Computer. And the Jonathan was stillborn. That left Dhuey's project, dubbed the Little Big Mac.

Needless to say, Gassée loved it, not least because it was the last interesting new Mac design left standing with its original creator. He had heard about it not long after taking over and had allowed it to continue with his tacit support. Dhuey thanked him by ultimately code-naming the project Paris, replacing its earlier names: Milwaukee (where Dhuey hailed from), Reno (slots, of course—good engineering humor) and Uzi (bad engineering humor).

Underground through the first phases of the project, Dhuey had been free from toeing the company design line. And that in turn left him open to the best solutions for the task at hand. Adding slots was only one example. Another was his choice of the Motorola 68020, a new high-performance 16-bit microprocessor, as Little Big Mac's brains, instead of the older 68000 used in earlier Macs.

In the end, Gassée selected the Little Big Mac as the Mac II not just because it was the only machine left (after all, he could have gone on upgrading the Mac I), or because it fit his own strategic model, but because it was a beautifully designed machine. To his credit, Gassée rewarded Dhuey for his efforts by promoting the young man into a leadership role on the project. Then Gassée gutted all the other Mac II projects and shifted their staffs to the Little Big Mac.

The Macintosh II was introduced in March 1987 and was an immediate sensation, in its various incarnations selling billions of dollars' worth of computers—and at last giving the Mac sales to match its reputation. But if the Mac II validated the Mac architecture, it undermined it as well. The Mac philosophy, promulgated by Raskin and elucidated by Jobs, was to produce the computer for Everyman: cheap, comparatively low-powered and turnkey. But the Mac II was almost the exact opposite. It was expensive, high-powered and configurable. All it really had in common with the original Mac was the user interface—no minor thing, of course—while its real counterpart was, ironically, the IBM PC. In that respect, the Mac II was Apple's first great surrender to the "Wintel" (Windows & Intel) world: it accepted the IBM paradigm for personal computer architecture, then set out to distinguish itself from the IBM clones (and demand a 50 percent higher price) through the uniqueness of its operating system.

The press loved it. It resolved much of the schizoid nature of the reporting that had always afflicted the industry. From the beginning there had always been the problem of having to report on a single industry that was divided into two self-contained worlds. You had to report on IBM and Apple not only separately but differently. It was as if the two companies appealed to opposite sides of the reader's brain. But now that Apple was building IBM-type boxes, you could at last compare Apples and oranges. And in such comparisons, Apple's ineffable edge in style and user experience played less well than IBM's tangible advantages in price, in libraries of applications and in the most obvious measures of performance. The Mac's sheer strangeness had been an important distinguishing feature, and now Gassée had taken that advantage away.

Once the Mac began playing the same game as the PC, the race suddenly came down to five very distinct factors: price, applications, third-party support, processor and operating system.

Price was a field of competition that Apple seemed almost determined to lose. The first-time buyer walked into a Fry's or Computerland or some other electronics chain store and tried out the various machines. Overwhelmingly, that person was drawn to the Mac. It was infinitely easier to learn to use. Then that person looked at the price tag—and decided it made better sense to spend a lot less money and devote a few extra hours to learning Windows.

Despite this lesson in price elasticity taking place a thousand times each day at stores around the world, Sculley and his team exhibited no inclination to compete with the PC world on price. For Sculley, showing his East Coast roots, high prices meant high profit margins, and high profit margins meant a good balance sheet—and that meant a strong stock price on Wall Street.

Filled with self-doubt, Sculley had submitted to years of training in technology by the best minds at Apple. He even grudgingly admitted, after the financial disaster of 1985, that he also had much to learn about the cyclical nature of the personal computer industry. But one thing he never would believe was that he also didn't understand the basic rules of business—after all, wasn't that what he'd been hired for?—in the digital realm. In personal computers (as well as software, semiconductors and just about everything else) the name of the game was, if necessary, to sacrifice short-term profits for market share. If you could dominate the market and set the standard you could make your fortune on volume and higher-priced upgrades. Bill Gates understood this, as did the clone makers. But Sculley and Gassée did not. Pressed by the media, they even grew surly. Steven Levy, attending one Apple press conference, heard Gassée reply to a question about high prices: "We don't want to castrate our computers to make them inexpensive. We make Hondas, we don't make Yugos."

Thanks to this pricing policy, the war in **applications software** was over before it began. With millions of IBM PC and clones now out in the marketplace, with the Wintel architecture the dominant industry standard, and with hundreds of software developers racing to develop new programs to tap into the wealth of this market, Apple didn't stand a chance. Increasingly, it had to wait in line while the biggest developers produced DOS and Windows versions first, then, sometimes a year or more later, a Macintosh-compatible version. The smaller developers didn't write Mac versions at all; they were able to sustain lively businesses on the giant PC world alone.

Thus, inexorably, the slower-growing Apple applications library became but a tiny fraction of its gigantic, and faster-growing, PC counterpart. This wasn't lost on customers. It became even harder to justify a Mac: not only was it more expensive but sometimes it didn't even run the one program you were buying a computer for. The modest Apple applications software collection was increasingly buried by the seemingly endless applications library for the PC. And that growing gap was as obvious at the computer store: the single wall of Mac programs and the aisles of DOS and Windows offerings.

Ironically, the one company that consistently (albeit tardily) produced Mac versions of all of its major products was Microsoft. Gates & Co. sold billions of dollars' worth of Word and Excel for Macintosh, the profits from which Microsoft used to develop new products that would ultimately undermine the Mac.

Responding to this situation, in 1987 Apple founded an "independent" (it retained 85 percent control) software company called Claris. Claris was initially created to help Apple overcome a problem that plagued much of the computer industry: every time you created a new piece of software and bundled it into your computer, you inevitably pissed off a score of developers working on or selling competitive products. So Apple initially decided to sell these programs as stand-alone products, and, in order to disguise their source, parked them under the Claris label. Nobody was fooled, especially since, as Guy Kawasaki would later point out, Microsoft salespeople ran around reminding developers of the cozy Apple-Claris connection.

But in its second role, that of creating major new software products to keep Apple in the game, Claris fared much better. In particular, Claris Works, a suite of office productivity programs (word processing, spreadsheet, desktop publishing), proved to be an effective argument for many professionals and small business owners to go with the Mac. But whatever its victories, Claris was just one company, part of a small cohort of Apple software designers, up against an army of PC developers. There was no way it could ever keep up.

Software developers were only one group of **third-party developers** upon which Apple depended. Just as important was a second constituency, Apple licensees. Unfortunately, they didn't exist. Repeatedly through the last years of the 1980s, the call went out, from developers, the trade press, analysts and even employees, for Apple to license its operating system. But Sculley refused every time. A decade later he would justify his decision by saying that such licensing would have damaged Apple's profit margins, turning the company at best into just one of a host of price-bombing clone makers and at worst into a software-only developer. In Sculley's reasoning, diminished margins meant diminished stock prices, and in the John Sculley cosmology, that was the worst of all fates. He simply could not imagine how Apple could be helped by low-cost products from competitors.

But the fact was, they could. Clones might give the Mac architecture a bigger market share (attracting more third-party developers) while at the same time forcing Apple to build better products. But Sculley wasn't hearing it.

Margins and stock price were the Gog and Magog of his business faith. Coke and Pepsi didn't sell their secret recipes, did they? And if that argument wasn't decisive, Sculley had only to point at IBM and its sudden shocking business collapse to show the dangers of allowing clones at the company picnic.

But Sculley missed the point. IBM had lost control over its own PC architecture to the likes of Dell, Compaq, Hitachi and HP not because it had allowed the licensing of its operating system, but because it never owned it in the first place—Microsoft did. Apple, in comparison, owned its OS. It would make money on every Mac clone sold. But more than that, IBM got into trouble because it fell down on the job—its new computers were ugly, overpriced and mediocre in performance. Clones kept you on your toes, and the big dinosaur of Armonk proved to be flat-footed.

So there would be no licensing of the Mac OS, at least not during John Sculley's tenure. Apple would have to go it alone against an ever-growing number of PC clone makers, some of them huge with vast distribution networks (such as HP), others with enormous manufacturing skills and low labor costs (Leading Edge, Acer, Fujitsu, NEC), and still others that were young, hungry and brilliantly managed (like Dell, Compaq and Gateway 2000).

As for the **processor,** Sculley would also later privately admit that one of his worst mistakes running Apple was not to switch from the Motorola 68000 family to the far more popular Intel 80×86 family, which by the end of the 1980s already owned nearly seven-eighths of the microprocessor business. On first glance, like so much about Apple, this judgment seems reasonable. But it really isn't. Apple's problem was not that it wasn't more like the PC world, but that it wasn't impressively *different* from it. The world had gone with the Intel-based machines not because of "Intel Inside" but because they liked the computer outside. All that counted was that the processor ran the DOS and Windows applications library. And that only mattered because Apple had let the PC become the industry standard. Andy Grove was a great businessman, but had IBM originally gone with Motorola, it would have been the same story with a different chip. The fact was that during this period, Motorola's microprocessors were consistently better designed and better performing than their Intel counterparts. Motorola didn't let Apple down; if anything, the reverse was true. A dominant Apple might not have made the Motorola microprocessor dominant, but it certainly would have kept Intel from becoming a near-monopoly.

That left only the **operating system** as the one competitive factor where Apple had a distinct advantage over the competition. The Mac OS was so clearly superior to DOS and even Windows 1.0 that its presence alone, in the minds of millions, completely trumped every other consideration. But by

1990, the Mac OS was as old as the Apple II had been when the Lisa and Mac projects had set out to replace it. Six years had passed, and though still magnificent, the Mac OS had not appreciably changed. There were some new projects in the works to come up with a replacement, but they might take years. In essence, Apple decided it had a great hand and chose to stand pat.

But across the table was a player extraordinaire, Bill Gates. The most relentless competitor in high tech, Gates had seen the future with the introduction of the Mac and had unceasingly chased this threat ever since. Windows 1.0 was a crude botch, but Gates, as always, learned from his mistakes and redoubled his efforts. In his peculiar and dangerous manner, Gates didn't look upon the Mac OS as competition, but as an intruder into a world that was rightfully his. As Gates saw it, the graphical user interface of the later Windows products wasn't a copy of the Mac, but his all along. Monomania combined with megalomania is a powerful thing.

Apple should have gotten a clue to Gates's attitude when, not long after the Macintosh introduction, the company sued Microsoft for copyright infringement. According to one of his biographers, when Gates was accused by Jobs of ripping off the Mac interface, Gates angrily replied, "No, Steve, I think it's more like we both have this rich neighbor named Xerox, and you broke in to steal the TV set, found I'd been there first, and said, 'No fair, I wanted to steal the TV set!' "

Leaving aside the fact that the Mac OS (unlike the Lisa) wasn't really a Xerox copy, what is breathtaking about Gates's comment is that it rewrites history to suggest that not only did Microsoft chance upon graphical user interfaces first but it had been so successful that there had been nothing left for Apple to use. Given the brilliance of the Mac OS and the ineptness of Windows 1.0, this is a glimpse into a mind more subtle, but no less solipsistic than Jobs's own.

The difference was that Bill Gates didn't alienate his own staff, behave inconsistently from day to day or refuse to understand the basic rules of commerce. While Apple fluttered about, Microsoft moved relentlessly forward in a straight line. And by 1990 it had its answer to the Mac OS ready, Windows 3.0. It was still inelegant, and, being built on top of the old DOS core, rather crude, but it looked a little like the Mac OS—and that was good enough. The tens of millions of Wintel computer users would never again have to hang their heads in embarrassment when comparing their machines with the Mac . . . and Apple zealots could never again be fully comfortable claiming uniqueness for their products. By 1993, Microsoft had sold 25 million copies of 3.0, more than the Mac OS and DOS combined.

And it didn't stop there. Windows 3.0 was just a way station for Bill Gates.

His other awesome trait was that once he took the war to an enemy he never stopped attacking until he'd won. Bill Gates was the Ulysses S. Grant of high tech; he was relentless in his assaults. Even before 3.0 was announced, Microsoft was hard at work on its follow-up, code-named Chicago and targeted on paper to eventually become Windows 93.

Apple, finally awakening from its five-year slumber, at last geared up to respond. But in a manner typical of the company in that era, it set off in several different directions, meandered about and frittered away all of its precious time. The most straightforward of these projects was an upgrade of the existing OS. It alone would actually see the light of day, appearing as Mac OS 7.0 in 1991. It was an adequate piece of work, but no earthshaker. Moreover, its solutions to many of the growing problems with the Mac OS in the new world of computing—for example, the graphical metaphor of files in folders was becoming obsolete when users now had hundreds of such files— were so jury-rigged (in this case the use of a system of aliases to let one file be filed multiple ways) that they not only didn't really solve the problems but made them more obvious. Windows 3.0 screamed for a powerful response from Apple, one that pulled the Mac as far ahead as the original Mac OS had been from DOS. Instead, 7.0 was a move *toward* Microsoft. It seemed that they were converging on some common middle—and on that killing ground, the victor was predestined.

Sitting behind the 7.0 was another project, this one Apple's real response to Windows. This one wasn't an imitation of anything from the past; a balls-out project to build a brand-new operating system as innovative as the Mac OS had been. Code-named Copland, it picked up speed at the beginning of the 1990s and slowly began to gobble up company resources from almost everything else. By the mid-1990s, as Apple's troubles grew deadly, Copland would become the symbol of Apple's deliverance, the next magical product that would pull the company out of its doldrums and put Apple back on top. In the end, it *did* become a symbol, but of a different kind.

8.13 PREDICTABILITY

What Apple did manage to do well during the late 1980s was build new products. Those new products in turn masked a greater loss. With the exception of Atkinson's Hypercard, Apple seemed to lose its ability to innovate. The company could still do a damn good job at improvement—the new Macs demonstrated that—but the days of radical, earthshaking creation were now suddenly, inexplicably behind it. Month after month, year after year, the world awaited the next great invention from Apple, but it never came.

Partly this was the environment created by John Sculley, which looked upon the discontinuities forced by major inventions (except, of course, Sculley's own Newton) as a threat to the orderly business of the company. But even more, this loss of imagination at Apple was a validation of the 80–20 rule of high tech: All the really interesting stuff in electronics is accomplished by 20 (some would say 2) percent of the people. All the other people—some brilliantly, some poorly, most adequately—perform the task of elucidating upon, upgrading, packaging, marketing, promoting and selling those good ideas.

That's why Silicon Valley's best journalists, investors and analysts identify the few important players in each market and track their movements. If those players suddenly converge on one company, as they did upon Apple in 1981, you can assume that company will soon be hot and a major innovator. If then you see those same players leaving the company in dribs and drabs—no matter how reasonable their explanations (I want to spend more time with my family, I want to pursue other interests, it's a time in my life when I'm ready for a major change)—the bottom line is that the company has lost its edge. It may look financially strong, have a good product portfolio and be hailed by the rest of the world—but without those key innovators, it is a hollow shell, a dead company walking.

And that is exactly what happened to Apple in the decade after the Mac introduction. One by one the 20 percenters had quit, abandoned or been driven out of the company. Del Yocam had recognized this loss as early as the layoff of 1985, saying, "This is very difficult for us. We are losing people who are great performers and are part of this family." But there was nothing he could do to stanch the flow.

The places where these special employees eventually settled—General Magic, Sun, Silicon Graphics—became the hot new companies. Sun and SGI were especially interesting because they pioneered a whole new computer field, graphics workstations, that essentially put a ceiling on Apple's business. These workstations, priced about as much as the original Lisa, but with hundreds of times the power and the ability to construct special-effects imagery, were the darlings of high tech in the early 1990s. The world's attention turned to these companies as they grew even faster than their personal computing predecessors. Because their machines could do everything from model weather to create computer animation to develop three-dimensional MRI scan images, they soon became the investment focus of everyone from Hollywood studios to stock market analysts. They drew the best talent too. The migration of expensive new cars that once headed west toward Cupertino now headed east toward Mountain View and Palo Alto, where Sun and SGI made their headquarters.

Sun and SGI now had the spark and the talent and everybody knew it. Steve Jobs certainly did. Presiding over NeXT, he had, as part of a larger strategy of buying content producers for his computers, acquired Pixar from George Lucas. Pixar, based across the Bay from San Francisco in Pt. Richmond, succeeded far better in its field, computer-generated animation for the motion-picture industry, than NeXT did in academic computing. One reason was that it managed to capture the best talent in the field and keep it. Another was that Jobs, distracted by NeXT, had only enough time at Pixar to be inspiring, not interfering. Having made several award-winning shorts, Pixar found itself in the early 1990s with a deal to make a feature-length film, *Toy Story*, for Disney. It set to work not with Apples or Windows or even NeXT computers, but with banks of the latest workstations from SGI, Hewlett-Packard and Sun.

Yet if Apple had lost its premier talent, (or, even worse, made them into Apple Fellows) it still had thousands of other employees, the cream of the previous decade of college grads and young industry up-and-comers. If these multitudes couldn't come up with revolutionary new products, they could reconfigure and enhance the hell out of the ones they had.

The result was an explosion of new products coming out of Apple that continued well into the new decade. Below is a list of Mac models introduced during Sculley's tenure:

Model	Date of Introduction	Date of Retirement
128K	1/84	4/86
512K	9/84	4/86
Plus	1/86	10/90
512E	4/86	8/86
SE	3/87	10/90
II	3/87	10/90
IIx	10/88	10/90
SE/80	1/89	10/91
IIcx	3/89	3/91
IIci	9/89	3/91
Portable	9/89	10/91
IIfx	3/90	4/92
Classic	10/90	9/92

IIsi	10/90	3/95
LC	11/90	3/92
Classic II	10/91	9/95
Quadra 700	10/91	3/95
Quadra 900	10/91	5/92
PowerBook 100	10/91	8/92
PowerBook 140	10/91	8/92
PowerBook 170	10/91	10/92
LC II	3/92	3/93
Quadra 950	5/92	present
PowerBook 145	8/92	6/95

With a few exceptions (the horrible Portable was kept around until a replacement, the superb PowerBook, could be found) the life span of each of these models is a clue to their quality. And on this list were a few beauties, including the Mac Classic, the IIsi and the first three PowerBooks.

After the embarrassment of the Portable, and a long frustrating wait by customers, Apple finally introduced its PowerBook series in October 1991. Sleek, solidly built, though a bit underpowered for their price (as was almost everything else at Apple) and with a miserable battery life, the PowerBooks—models 100, 140 and 170—were a revelation, if not a revolution. In those intervening years, Apple had taken the time to figure out what the experience of using a laptop computer should be like, and how it differed from working on a desktop. The result was a keyboard that didn't fill the whole lower wing of the computer, but only the top half of it. The lower half consisted of a place to rest your hands and, when the user's thumbs landed, a trackball mouse. Laptops were never the same again. So many people rushed to buy this first generation of PowerBooks that they were perpetually out of stock.

In fact, a lot of Apple computers were out of stock. As noted earlier, Allan Loren had been promoted from Apple's MIS department and put in charge of Apple's sales and marketing. One reason for the move was that Loren thought just like Sculley, especially about the primacy of profit margins over every other business consideration. Apple's profits had been slipping, partly because of the competitive pressure from the PC world that forced Apple to discount with retailers and partly because Apple had not been introducing new products innovative enough to keep up with Moore's Law. So Loren raised prices.

Robert Cringely, with his usual hyperbole, would call the move Apple's single greatest disaster and compare it to "asking the earth to reverse its direction of rotation." But one thing was for sure. Apple's extraordinary ramp-up over the last four years was now suddenly, jarringly over. Sales of high-end machines, now wildly (instead of merely) overpriced, slid. The low end was far worse: thanks to Gassée, Apple's budget machines had long been neglected. Now obsolete *and* overpriced, their sales plummeted. During the all-important Christmas season of 1988, sales of the Macintosh Plus and SE barely moved. And the market for the Apple II "almost disappeared," one shop owner told the *New York Times*. It was the end of the II; what Jobs couldn't do intentionally, Allan Loren accomplished through incompetence.

All told, Apple's market share fell. But the margins increased. Wrote Cringely, "Any momentum that Apple had was gone, maybe for years."

Well, two years. After hamstringing the company, Loren suddenly discovered he was no longer completing John Sculley's sentences. He was replaced by David Hancock, whom everybody at Apple but Sculley thought was a jerk. He in turn reorganized the department so many times (nine reorganizations in two years) that he threw the place into chaos, drove off the best talent and left the company in the crucial years of 1989 and 1990 effectively without a marketing operation.

8.14 AMATEURS

Having driven off Yocam, Coleman and Gassée, John Sculley now found himself with an executive team almost completely devoid of anyone with computer industry experience.

Sculley responded in a predictable manner. He hired Australian Ian Diery to replace Yocam as head of Apple Pacific. Diery came from minicomputer maker Wang, where he had been caught up in (and took some of the blame for) one of the biggest corporate craterings in computer history.

Next, Sculley recalled Michael Spindler from Europe and named him chief operating officer.

Finally, Sculley put himself in Gassée's job, in charge of all new-product development in the company. It was reminiscent of Mike Markkula's regular returns in the early years of the company to take over the reins of the company and straighten things out.

But this situation was entirely different, and one fraught with perils John Sculley seemed incapable of noticing.

For one thing, with the exception of Spindler, who would be distracted by having to adapt to life at headquarters, there were no longer any real personal computer technologists at the top of Apple. That created a dangerous power vacuum waiting to be filled by anyone with ambition.

Unfortunately for Apple, the three most ambitious men on the executive team were not technologists, but staff executives: CFO Joe Graziano, human resources director Kevin Sullivan and chief counsel Al Eisenstat. Before long, they had assembled their power blocs and taken de facto control of Apple's decision making. Recalled one individual who was in those meetings: "It was incredible. I'd never seen anything like it: here was a computer company that now was mostly being run by legal, personnel and finance. There was nobody there to say, 'Shut the fuck up and get out of here. Let real businesspeople and technologists run this company.'"

What power these three camps could not obtain proactively, they held through veto. None used that power more than Graziano, who could quash almost any new idea by announcing that it would hurt Apple's bottom line.

The lone voice of experience, the only person out in the field seeing what was *really* going on in the computer industry was Bill Campbell. But Campbell was running Claris now, so he wasn't *really* Apple anymore, and besides, Claris at the moment was taking shots for not having gotten more products to market sooner. So his comments were largely ignored.

Thus, at the moment when Apple was about to announce its best collection of new products ever, when its biggest competitor, IBM, was rumored to be in deep trouble and the head of the largest software company on earth was giving it thoughtful advice, Apple was not only lost but convinced that it knew where it was going. In fact, it was plunging deeper into the woods.

And into all this was dropped Apple's last true believer, Mike Spindler, the last line guy standing.

Unlike the rest of the executive team, Spindler really did understand the technology, manufacture and marketing of personal computers. Recalls one observer, "I remember when Spindler took over. There was this meeting at Apple with all the senior people. Mike stood up at the board and outlined Microsoft's strategy. Then he outlined all the clone companies and what they were doing. Then operating systems and their kernels. Then all the microprocessor strategies. Then he compared all of that with what Apple was doing. It was an incredible performance. It seemed almost to be incoherent when he started—and then as he went along it all came together. It was breathtaking.

"Then, when he'd filled the entire board up, Mike turned around and looked at the audience: forty blank faces. All Apple senior people, and none of them had a clue. Finally, after a few moments of silence, one British guy, a marketing vice president from Procter & Gamble, said, 'Brilliant, Mike,' and they went on with the meeting."

But Spindler plunged on. If he couldn't find internally the resources that he needed to turn Apple around, he'd look outside the company for strategic partners. And what better place than the biggest resource warehouse of them all?

IBM. It was a crazy idea, but what better time to do it than when Big Blue was wounded and desperate? Just imagine: the Mac OS on IBM PCs, sold by the best sales force in the industry.

He ran the idea past Regis McKenna. McKenna happened to know Jack Kuehler, IBM's president: the two had served together on a board at Santa Clara University. "So I literally jumped on a plane and flew back and proposed the alliance to Jack. He just smiled and said, 'That's a really great idea, but I don't think so right now.'

"But three months later he called Mike and said, 'I think now is the time to talk.'"

But now Spindler had a dilemma. He hadn't told Sculley anything about the IBM contact, because, as he told others, "he wants in on everything." Spindler had learned what other top managers at headquarters had known for years: Sculley, perpetually paranoid about threats to his position as well as deeply sensitive about his lack of technology credentials, didn't want any high-level meetings taking place inside or outside Apple without his involvement. Most of all, he didn't want his senior execs doing anything without him, Sculley, present.

Now Spindler had to tell him. Sculley took the news well . . . so well, in fact, that while Mike was off on a sabbatical, Sculley announced the new joint venture with IBM and took credit for creating it.

The joint venture between the two historic enemies was called Taligent, and it was chartered, as a test of the mutual chemistry of the relationship, to write a new kind of operating system based on the influential new theory of object-oriented programming. The appeal of object-oriented programming was that it enabled the programmer to skip the endless task of writing thousands of lines of code, and instead string together blocks of existing applications and then write only the connecting tissue of code. It was faster, more flexible and easier to upgrade. If 7.0 was a move toward Microsoft, and Copland was the big swing for the fences, Taligent was a challenge to Steve Jobs's NeXT computer. NeXT may have built a computer that nobody wanted, but in that computer was an object-oriented operating system, NeXTStep, that everybody admired.

But if NeXT was all cleverness and not much business sense, Taligent combined two companies that were all business and that had left their cleverness behind. It also smacked of desperation: two multibillion-dollar companies, one of them left behind by the market, the other squeezed into a corner by superior competition, now teaming up in an effort to get back into the game. Apple had, in fact, been working on object-oriented software for years with little to show for it.

It fell to Bill Gates to point out that the emperor had no clothes. "If the software is so important," he asked, "why did Apple give away half of it?" A poll of industry leaders found that most believed Microsoft, the deal's biggest competitor, would end up the winner.

It was a victory by default. Taligent was a bust. And the world assumed that the fault was entirely IBM's. After all, how could a slow dinosaur like Big Blue *ever* work with a jackrabbit like Apple? But the truth was just the opposite. Throughout the Taligent story, IBM executives involved with the project regularly complained that it was Apple that was impeding progress. Recalled one Valley executive, "IBM was saying to Apple, 'What's wrong? We want to work with you and now you don't want to work with us? What's going on here? You came to us. We're supposed to be the company that's hard to work with.'

"What it came down to was that old latent attitude of Apple emerging again. You know: 'It's IBM. The enemy. And nothing IBM does is right.' It wrecked the venture."

8.15 MASKS

John Sculley's need to participate in everything his lieutenants were doing betrayed a deeper desperation. Seven years at the top of the most famous technology company in the world had done little to resolve the schism within this divided man.

The passive-aggressiveness, the New Age/old guard and all the other obvious contradictions were merely symptoms of something much more elemental in the man. As early as 1984 the men and women in his inner circle had already noticed it. One confided privately at the time, "I often wonder who John Sculley is when he goes home and takes off the mask. And I have this terrible feeling that when he takes off that mask, all there is underneath is another mask."

Many people who worked with Sculley on a daily basis never felt they knew the man; he so rarely let down his guard. Even going out to dinner was usually a public event, complete with entourage. Said one Apple employee later, "Only once, at a sales meeting, did I ever see him relaxed and happy. I never saw him that way again."

Much of his dualism derived from Sculley's fear: Though the world increasingly saw him as a high-tech visionary, Sculley himself was forever afraid of being exposed as a nontechnologist. And no amount of tutoring by the likes of Alan Kay or covers of *Fortune* and *Business Week* could allay that fear.

That explained why, inside Apple, John Sculley was comfortable with an executive team of nontechnologists and among those scientists so brilliant and arrogant that they treated *everyone* like idiots. It also helped explain why Sculley was so obsessed with new inventions and fresh ideas—not just because they represented new opportunities for Apple but because they did so for *him*. With new markets and products, nobody was yet an expert.

Meanwhile, within the quotidian world of Apple, Sculley, perpetually afraid of being left behind, or made a fool, or simply exposed as an outsider, demanded to know everything going on around him. It wasn't, as some thought, a lack of trust in others, but a lack of trust in himself.

Outside Apple, the schism was even deeper. In a prepared setting, where he was presenting a new idea to a known audience, John Sculley was often magnificent. Those who went expecting the nervous Nellie with the halting voice were usually amazed. "When he was rested and armed with a good script," recalled one Apple employee, "Sculley could bring an audience to its feet. He could be extraordinary." But force him to improvise, say on television, before an audience he didn't know, and all the fears and flaws would come rushing in and John Sculley would splutter and stumble and look like a trapped animal.

Odd as they were in the CEO of a multibillion-dollar corporation, none of these personality tics were especially damaging as long as Apple was a successful company sailing alone in the economic sea. Apple's PR staff was more than adept at creating controlled settings in which John Sculley could shine, and protect him from those occasions when he would not.

But as the 1980s turned into the 1990s, the business climate changed. The age of the stand-alone personal computer was nearly over. Now, most of the world's business computers were being linked up into vast corporate networks centered on powerful mainframe servers. Tiny, unknown companies that supplied this new market—Cisco, 3Com, Sybase, Oracle—were now becoming giants. Meanwhile, in the home computer market, users were beginning to buy millions of modems in order to link up with the new information services, such as Compuserv and America Online, or visit chat rooms in the new "cyberspace" sites such as the Well. And waiting in the wings was the promise of a technology revolution as great as PCs—the Internet.

That was only part of it. In the personal computer industry itself, the once monolithic world of personal computer builders and software designers had now exploded into thousands of submarkets, each with hundreds of competitors. And all were racing to build better, faster, more powerful and cheaper products. This proliferation was so vast and all-encompassing, penetrating every niche business imaginable, that the ambitious user didn't even need to buy a finished computer anymore—rather, you could just order exactly the components you wanted and build a customized machine of your own. And soon even that market was filled with giant competitors, notably Dell and Gateway 2000, offering customized computers you could order over the phone and receive in three days.

Against this efflorescence in the PC world, Apple's strategy of verticalization, of owning every component possible, and of selling stand-alone machines, was increasingly untenable. The days of going it alone were over; and Apple, once the most progressive of companies, was now looking anachronistic. By the beginning of the 1990s, most people at Apple knew the company would have to enter into joint ventures with some of its erstwhile enemies, license its technology or get bought.

But there was the rub. The company was simply unprepared to do any of those things. Taligent was a microcosm of everything that was wrong: the glory-hogging CEO who is yet too full of self-doubt to give a project the freedom it needs to succeed and a contingent of inflexible true believers determined to make it fail.

And so it went with other such deals. A few (with DEC, IBM) actually became real enterprises, only to shuffle along weakened, unsupported and underpowered, then finally fade away. Many others never even made it that far. Once, Apple had the opportunity to discuss a joint effort with its Cupertino neighbor Tandem Computers. Tandem was also a billion-dollar company, its super-reliable "fail-safe" computers were the heart of thousands of sensitive data processing operations (banks, stock exchanges, newspapers, hospitals) throughout the world.

But Tandem was now being challenged by the new generation of client-server companies such as Sun. So a joint venture, even a merger, between Apple and Tandem made great sense: Tandem would give Apple the hub of the network, and Apple would give Tandem the nodes. And Tandem's CEO, Jimmy Treybig, a brilliant good old boy whose hobby was setting up ham radio stations on remote atolls, was known to be honest, fair and an enlightened executive of the HP school.

It seemed perfect. Contact with Tandem was made: they were interested. But at the last moment, Sculley balked. He was overheard bewailing to an adviser, "Does Treybig know *I'm not a technologist?*"

8.16 BONUS BABIES

Spindler's arrival at Cupertino and Gassée's departure in early February 1990 signaled the end of Gassée's strategy, which had dominated Apple for five years, of chasing the high end of the computer market. No more "I want to build ze perfect machines." No more pedantic lectures about how the world was composed of "passengers" (most people) and "sailors" (people who bought Macintoshes). That strategy would only have worked with a company that could still regularly create great product breakthroughs and owned a market—namely, corporations—that could afford them.

Since Apple could do neither, it now found itself with overpriced products that were perceived by most computer owners as not being worth their much publicized advantages. From this point forward, Apple would be pulled in two directions: trying to support its current customers (and high margins) at the high end, while chasing the low-end market with computers that usually were never quite cheap or distinctive enough. The damage was done. Thanks to overpriced products and a marketing operation that had been demoralized and disemboweled by company politics and Allan Loren, Apple was already boxed in. The Christmas season had been a nightmare. Instead of the usual jump in sales, Apple had seen revenues rise by only 6 percent. Meanwhile, profits slumped 11 percent.

The stock market, which had already seen this coming, sent Apple's stock into crash dive. From a fifty-two-week high in 1989 of $50 per share, the stock price dropped nearly 40 percent to $30. The only thing that kept it from falling further was the safety cushion of the company's $900 million in cash reserves.

On February 21, Apple announced the layoff of 400 employees, 280 of them in Cupertino. From the Night of the Long Knives, as it became known, to Gil Amelio's great purges in 1996, Apple would suffer more layoffs in a shorter time than any other successful company of its size. All were bitter, but none more than this one.

The heart of this bitterness was resentment over the growing inequality in a company that had once symbolized equality. It was no secret that Apple executives were paid well above the industry average. That was accepted: after all, Apple was a hot company filled with the fastest-trackers in high tech, and you paid top dollar for top talent. But the burst of outside executive recruitment over the last couple years had distorted those salary figures even more— 40 percent higher than warranted by the company's performance, one shareholders' rights group had determined.

The newly laid-off employees, rightly, saw all this as a betrayal. They had done their jobs, they had built beautiful new products, orders were going through the roof—and they still found themselves on the street. Those who were fired and those who remained would never forgive John Sculley.

Overpriced executives were still forgivable if those bonus babies did their job. But what the Apple rank and file saw was an environment in which the hardworking employees had produced one fine new product after another, month after month, and in the process had restored the company's old glory—and the revolving door of senior management ("An Apple vice president has the life expectancy of an armadillo on a Texas highway," wrote one Apple middle manager) had managed to screw it all up with long-term strategies that seemed to be revised weekly, idiotic pricing programs, endless reorganizations and misdirected marketing.

At the same time, Apple decided to cancel the expensive parties that employees had assumed were part of the company's culture, revised (that is, all but killed) the profit-sharing program that had enabled employees to take home thousands of dollars more each year and promised not to use security guards to escort newly terminated employees from their offices (thanks!). The company also said it would realign *all* salaries to bring them more in line with industry averages—a move certain to materially impact workers more than executives. This last claim was undermined by the word leaking out that Apple had given new hires William B. Coldrick (senior vice president for sales) and Donald P. Case (vice president for networking and communications) $2.1 million and $1.2 million, respectively, in future severance golden parachutes . . . and may have given Allan Loren several times that.

There had always been the sneaking suspicion among employees—aggravated by the man's manner and his big-business background—that Sculley never really cared about them. This was just the opposite of the truth, say former Sculley insiders. But this layoff, so close on the heels of a three-year boom in which Apple had grown as fast as any large company in history, seemed to confirm cold-bloodedness at the top. Killing profit sharing—"Looks to me like we all just took a ten to fifteen percent pay cut," one employee told the *Mercury News*—just underscored that belief.

It wasn't long before the company's electronic bulletin boards were awash with angry employee comments. "I've been at this company seven and a half years," wrote one employee. "Never have I seen the discord that is now running rampant." About the profit sharing, another employee wrote, "How about tying executive bonuses into the exact same formula?"

Apple's climate of shared values "may be beginning to break down," intoned Berkeley organizational behaviorist Charles O'Reilly with a scholar's gift for the obvious.

8.17 INCONSOLATION

On June 28, 1990, John Sculley announced that Claris, Apple's software subsidiary, would be folded back into the parent company.

"Claris has exceeded our expectations in establishing an independent brand identity and a competitive presence in the applications software business," he said. "While its spin-off market value would certainly be considerable, Claris has greater strategic value for Apple shareholders by remaining part of Apple."

He added, "Apple's goal is to significantly increase our unit growth. Developers should view our decision on Claris as a key indicator that Apple is very serious about this goal."

If Sculley had hoped to kick-start Apple's slumping stock, he failed. Company shares fell 25 cents to $42.75.

But the real loss was much greater than that. In folding the energetic and thriving Claris back into Apple Computer, Sculley cost the company two of its biggest assets: Claris itself and Bill Campbell.

In its three years of independent existence, Claris had become one of the shiniest jewels in Apple's diadem. After a rough start it had gone on to do exactly what Sculley had wanted of it: become a successful satellite that enhanced the value of Apple itself. Recalled Bill Joos, Claris's vice president of sales, "We all went there to become an independent company, on the belief that when it was spun off we'd have some skin in the game. Campbell created an aggressive culture. We were a group of rebels. The attitude was: Let's kick ass. Let's go out there and do things."

By June 1990, Claris was second only to Microsoft as the leading supplier of Apple software. Claris Works, its suite of office productivity tools, had pulled tens of thousands of new customers into Apple's orbit.

Much of the success of Claris was due to Bill Campbell. The old coach had proven himself to be one of the best business executives, and one of the best leaders, in the company's history. Now he was on the brink of fulfilling the dream with which he had started Claris: to take it public.

But he had made a terrible miscalculation. Campbell had strayed too far away. He threatened to become an even more successful and dynamic company than the one he was supporting. Moreover, says Joos, "Apple was scared that if Claris went independent it would have to start developing for Windows and Apple would lose control over its biggest software developer." So Sculley reeled Campbell in.

When Bill Campbell got the news that Claris was not only not going public but being folded back into Apple, he did something common among Apple believers, but uncharacteristic for him: he cried.

A few months later, he was gone . . . to found the software company Intuit, and to teach the world a lesson about how to tackle Bill Gates.

8.18 A BIG BLUE CRATER

Despite all these shuffles and reshuffles of management, employee layoffs and roller-coaster financials, Apple continued to design and build new products.

Every few months there was a new product announcement, or two, or three. And that meant that if you didn't like what you saw in the company catalog right now, wait a few minutes and you might find something new you liked. That in turn did a nice job of winnowing out the product line. New products that didn't get good reviews or a strong response from the market were allowed to die, while those that met with a positive response were kept around until interest faded. And there were always new candidates in the wings awaiting their audition.

But most important, newspaper headlines aside, all of this activity gave Apple the image of a glowing, healthy, prospering, lively company—an image that belied the gloomy predictions and the falling market share reports. The resulting cognitive dissonance was only to Apple's advantage. You might occasionally hear reports that the company was in a dangerous, vulnerable position—that was the perceived view in Silicon Valley by 1990—but a trip to the computer store or a glance at retail ads or an upbeat thirty-second spot on television seemed to contradict that image. How could Apple be a troubled company? Look at all their new products!

But Apple *was* a troubled company. It had missed one great chance after another to recapture its early market leadership. And now it was running out of chances. The introduction of Windows 3.0 effectively closed off the operating system software market forever. Copland, still a glowing possibility in 1991, would now, no matter how terrific, be little more than a stopgap in Apple's plunge.

There might still be an opportunity for some landmark new application program on the order of VisiCalc, Postscript or Hypercard, but it seemed unlikely that Apple would be the one to create it. And, of course, when those NeXT killer apps did appear, in the form of Lotus Notes and Netscape Navigator, they were, in fact, Windows-compatible. Claris might have come up with something extraordinary, but now it too was embedded in Apple bureaucracy.

That left only hardware. And here, remarkably, a window of opportunity opened up early in Sculley's tenure and only grew wider by the year. Somehow, IBM, generally considered at the time to be the best-run company in the world, managed to come down with a serious case of stupidity. In March 1982, Intel announced its newest-generation microprocessor, the 80286. It was the first of the "modern" 80×86 architecture processors that continue to define personal computing to this day. The 286 was a superb processor—and that presented Big Blue with a problem: the PCs that would be built with the 286 would be powerful enough to rival IBM's larger and more expensive family of minicomputers.

The rest of IBM had been jealous of Boca Raton for a long time. It was the renegade division in the buttoned-down company and it had to be stopped.

And it was. The division was stripped of its independence and assimilated back into mainstream Big Blue.

IBM then tried to hold back its clone makers by making proprietary the one part of the computer it hadn't given away to Intel or Microsoft: the wiring ("bus") that carried data around the computer's motherboard. By controlling the bus, Lowe believed, he could control the cloners, crush them when he wanted to and make them pay fealty until then.

Instead, it was IBM that was crushed. Big Blue could not order back the waves. Compaq Computer simply designed its own busing scheme and did an end run around IBM. The rest of the cloners soon followed. Two years later, Moore's Law (as well as Moore himself) did its work, and Intel introduced the 80386, the defining chip of the Windows 3.0 era. IBM was left behind. Within a few years it would suffer one of the most crushing business collapses ever. And even after it recovered, it would never again dominate personal computers.

For the rest of the 1980s, the personal computer market had been essentially leaderless as scores of companies, including Compaq, Dell, HP and the Japanese (NEC, Fujitsu, Hitachi) and Taiwanese (Acer, Leading Edge) scrambled to fill the IBM void. Apple alone had the name and the reputation. Had it produced an IBM-compatible computer—say, a new Apple II—or introduced a brand-new product family as innovative as the Mac, it might have owned the world. But, of course, it did nothing of the sort.

Only as the decade ended, as the clone industry began to firm up not around a particular box but around the Intel and Microsoft standards, did Apple finally begin to do something on the hardware front besides selling upgraded machines to its current customers. There were, in fact, two programs, one for a new product family capable of running both Mac and DOS-based programs; the other for a new kind of handheld consumer device.

The new computer family was to be the product of a consortium of three companies: Apple, IBM and Motorola. Like Taligent, this too smacked of desperation. The good news was the presence of Motorola, the one company of the three that still seemed capable of getting interesting things done. Thanks in no small part to Apple, Moto had never been a serious threat to Intel in processors. But it had always been an innovator. Meanwhile, in its other businesses, from microcontrollers (lower-powered processors used to manage automobile engines, streetlights and literally a million other applications) to cell phones, Motorola had become one of the most successful and respected companies in high tech. Now it proposed to take one last big shot at the computer processor business: the PowerPC, a family of high-powered, very fast processors that would use an alternative architecture called RISC (reduced instruction set computing)—Intel's chips were CISC (complex instruction set computing)—and be capable of running both Mac OS and DOS/Windows programs.

The idea was that Motorola would finally get a chip that could compete directly with Intel, Apple could build a new generation of computers, and IBM would once again be able to distinguish itself from the pack of clones. It was a great idea, and Motorola more than held up its end of the bargain. The first PowerPC chip, the 301, introduced in late 1992, was a beauty. In its *slowest* version, it was still as fast as the fastest new Intel chip, the Pentium. And within a year, the company introduced three even more powerful and faster models. It was as fast a creation of a new processor family as the semiconductor industry had ever seen.

But there was only one problem: the PowerPC was five years too late. By the time Apple introduced its first PowerPC-based PowerMac computers in 1994, they were no more than a welcome offering to Apple's own market base. By then, there were nearly one billion microprocessors in use in the world—and of those, nearly 900 million were Intel chips. It was just too great a market dominance for even Motorola to overcome. And Apple didn't help the cause: the Mac OS actually slowed the PowerPC chips to lower speeds in real-life use than the Pentium. Meanwhile, stumble-footed IBM announced that its PowerPC-based computers would be at least a year late. Through all this, Intel, kept running at ramming speed by Andy Grove, continued cranking out a new and more splendid ×86 chip (286, 386, 486, Pentium, Pentium Pro) every couple of years to make sure that Motorola would never catch up.

The second Apple hardware project, a consumer product, was the Newton, an electronic tablet, the size of a paperback book, designed to read handwriting on its screen, store sizable quantities of data and communicate with personal computers—all at a price that could be afforded by the average professional.

Pen-based computing, with a computer capable of using sophisticated algorithms to interpret handwriting, was the hottest new computer market idea of the early 1990s. Some of the best venture capitalists in the business, such as John Doerr of Kleiner Perkins, invested millions of fund dollars into new pen computing start-ups. In every way it appeared to be the Next Big Thing. And Newton, a handheld pen computer with an Apple logo in front and Apple's giant distribution network behind, looked like a surefire winner.

Apple certainly treated it that way. Compared to the skunk works of the early Apple team, whose members were shunned as corporate lepers, the Newton project was granted instant stardom. Its progress was treated like a royal caravan moving through the countryside.

Newton was an extraordinarily self-conscious production. The team even allowed itself to be photographed through the project in preparation for a celebratory book to be published with the Newton's introduction. In so many ways, Newton was not a new-product development project, but a simulation of one, an acting out of the process with one eye cocked backward at famous projects of the past.

But if the history of the personal computer industry teaches anything, it is that ritual re-creations of the past don't guarantee an equally glorious present. The Newton was the most anxiously awaited new Apple product since the Mac. But when it was finally introduced in 1993, it proved to be a bitter disappointment. Not that it was a bad little machine, but it fell vastly below expectations. And this was John Sculley's fault. He had spent years promoting the idea of his Dynabook, the Knowledge Navigator. He even had the temerity to claim that the Newton would be the centerpiece of a $3.5 *trillion* new market in personal information tools.

To paraphrase the absent Jean-Louis Gassée, that smelled a little like infinity.

Not surprisingly, when people first heard of the Newton, they thought it would be the KN dream incarnate. Instead, in the plastic, it turned out to be a little device of limited application that didn't even read handwriting that well. It quickly tanked, and Apple, showing the same loyalty to its products as it did to its employees, couldn't back far enough away from it. Ironically, later improvements on the Newton proved it to be a useful device. But the damage was already done. Descendants of the Newton, such as 3Com's Palm Pilot, inferior in technology (at least at first) but superior in meeting market expectations, captured the now booming field. The Palm Pilot in fact sold one million units in a single year. The Newton, which was to be the next Macintosh, became only a tragic footnote to the Apple story.

8.19 PROFITLESS ENDEAVORS

In late 1990 Apple announced yet another new plan: to bombard the market with a portfolio of brand-new desktop and portable computer models, slash prices across the board and sacrifice profits (current margins were 54 percent) for added volume and market share. "This plan has no sacred cows," Sculley told the press.

Publicly, Sculley talked about Apple becoming a $10 billion company in the early 1990s, but in the executive offices at Apple, the discussions were a lot more pessimistic. This new announcement was the first public admission (though few noticed at the time) that Apple was losing market share so fast that it was in danger of losing control of its destiny. Somewhere up ahead—a 5 percent market share, a 3 percent market share, perhaps even less—was a point of no return, beyond which Apple and its operating system would become superfluous, where developers would no longer be interested in building for it, stores would stop selling it and even the most loyal users would begin to fade away. And to keep from reaching that point Apple was now willing to sacrifice its profits—and, inevitably, the value of its stock.

The announced goal was a market share jump of three percentage points in 1991—an amazingly ambitious target for a company with only a 10.7 percent market share the year before. Apple threw everything it had into the campaign. "We're pulling out all the stops," announced Spindler.

It was the best multiple-new-product introduction in company history. First, and most celebrated, was the $999 Mac Classic. It was at long last the realization of Jef Raskin's now generation-old dream of the Everyman computer: a full-blown Mac I costing less than $1,000. With the even better Classic II that followed a year later, the Mac Classic finally set Apple on a path to build affordable full-power machines.

The second product, the Mac LC was even more impressive. At $2,499, it was the lowest-priced color Macintosh to date, evidence that Apple could compete even with the clone makers on price. It also offered, as an option, a $199 add-in board, that enabled the LC to run old Apple II software. Targeted at schools, this option was the last lifeline to be thrown out to the old Apple II fanatics.

Finally, at the Mac II level, Apple introduced the third machine, the midrange IIsi. It wasn't as interesting as the other two, but time would prove it to be one of the company's most enduring and reliable products.

It was an impressive collection. It had to be. As industry analyst and long-time Apple adviser Tim Bajarin said: "Apple is going back to its roots. It has to get the lowest-cost Macintosh into the hands of as many people as possible. It has to get more people addicted to the Mac." Then, ominously: "If they don't have this one right, they're in trouble."

The strategy worked almost as well as planned. It also produced as many bad consequences as good ones.

Almost from the beginning, Apple's new market share strategy provoked an outcry. Apple's 1,700 dealers read (correctly) into the news a hidden plan by Apple to expand its distribution network to superstores and other retailers. They went nuts. Said one Valley dealer pointedly, "Apple's problems have not been due to a lack of distribution."

The shareholders weren't any happier. The company's stock dropped $2.75 to $25 on the news—and the expectation that the company was about to suffer another bad quarter. But John Sculley wasn't deterred. He trumpeted the news that the three new computers had received more initial orders than any computers in the company's history.

He wasn't kidding. By January and the end of the next quarter, Apple's revenues had jumped 12 percent (to $1.68 billion) and profits leaped 21 percent (to $150.5 million, or $1.28 per share). And there was more good news: Apple had forestalled the expected drop in margins through greater manufacturing efficiencies: it had fallen only 0.6 percentage point from the year before, to 51.4 percent.

Some of that good news had already leaked out during the intervening months—so that by the January 18 announcement, Apple's stock was back up to more than $51.

It seemed as if Apple had once again turned itself around. Once again, acting as if he'd finally put the company on the right track, John Sculley announced that he was pulling away from the daily activities of Apple to focus on "breakthrough projects"—in this case, the Newton. And, once again, his assessment of the company's competitive condition was completely wrong. Meanwhile, with $16.7 million in salary and stock in 1990, John Sculley was the second-highest-paid chief executive in the United States.

8.20 OVERLAP

Meanwhile, the new-product announcements continued unabated. In May, Apple finally introduced System 7.0, the long-awaited upgrade to the Mac OS. System 7.0 was powerful and graphic, an adequate answer to Windows 3.0. Yet it was also obviously merely a step up for the Mac OS, not a quantum leap. The product also proved to be buggy, which scared off many users, already nervous about messing around with operating system upgrades. Others were put off by the $99 price Apple put on the product, the company in the past having given away software upgrades for free. The result was that Apple had to devote considerable time and resources on getting its user base to adopt a product that should have been met with a stampede. Meanwhile, the marketplace, fed on Copland rumors for years, waited for the big announcement.

Then, in October, there was another mass hardware introduction. And once again, some home runs.

The biggest of these was a new family of laptops: the PowerBooks. After the embarrassment of the Portable, and the long, frustrating wait by customers (some of whom finally gave up and crossed over to the numerous Wintel laptops), Apple finally had in the PowerBook a great laptop computer.

On the same day, Apple introduced the first pair (Models 500 and 700) of a new family of consumer Macs, called the Performa. Marketwise, these were the descendants of the Apple II, the Mac Classic, the Classic II and the LC. The Performas were nice, only slightly overpriced computers featuring a strong library of bundled software and a number of built-ins such as a CD-ROM drive.

All in all, an appealing package. But the Performa line, which grew like ivy, in many places overlapped the Mac II line. This was an inevitable result of crossing an entrenched bureaucracy with a program that yields good performance reviews for everyone involved. The good news was that such a proliferation of Apple models countered the growing skepticism in the press and among analysts that Apple could still compete against the Windows world. It made customers feel better about buying Apple products, it made developers more comfortable designing Mac-compatible products and it made analysts more willing to suggest the purchase of Apple stock.

But the bad news came when those same people actually decided to purchase an Apple. Now all that abundance looked more like chaos. Should I buy a high-end Performa or a II, or, starting the next year, a low-end Quadra? They're both the same price, so which is better? Apple didn't help matters by regularly yanking one product off the shelf and quickly replacing it with the other. Should I buy this óne or wait a year? Didn't Apple just announce a replacement?

It wasn't long before this shell-game affliction also infected PowerBooks. Just as the first generation of PowerBooks were reaching excited customers, Apple proceeded to declare them obsolete and announced a second generation. Even the model numbers were confusing. Then a couple of years later, before the market had fully recovered, Apple announced a third generation with a whole new numbering scheme. And this third generation of Power-Books was so shoddily built and, occasionally, so dangerous as to make users pine for the simpler days of the early PowerBooks.

It was as if Apple, having lost its way in new-product development in the late 1980s, had suddenly decided to make up for lost time in the first half of the 1990s. It had become a binge developer. The problem with all these new products was not their design, or even their price, but their orientation. Apple was now selling only to Apple people. By now, five years after IBM's stumble, PC owners had learned to live without an industry standard setter in hardware. Now they merely looked to Intel and Microsoft for validation of their purchases of Gateway 2000, Dell or Compaq computers. Apple, meanwhile, could look back on the previous five years and see an incredible profusion of new products for its existing customers—and a series of blown chances to do anything more. The company was again growing in revenues but it was also still shrinking in market share. The 1991 cost-cutting campaign managed to gain a couple of points of market share, but after that it began to fall once more—this time even faster.

Apple's fate was now set. From this point on Apple would be selling only within its 3.5 million-member family: schoolkids, art directors, graphic artists, writers. The young and the old and the computer-illiterate. Apple's only hope now would be that it could keep these groups constantly turning over and upgrading their equipment and that all those schoolkids learning now on Macs would grow up to become a new army of Apple fanatics.

In other words, Apple could only pray for a miracle—and that miracle was not a computer, but a human, generation away. In the meantime, it would have to pay for its latest strategy du jour.

8.21 MIDDLE-AGE SPREAD

As it passed its fifteenth anniversary, Apple, with its 12,000 employees and 3,000 contractors, spilled out of Bandley Drive to sites all over Silicon Valley and the world. Its very presence had transformed both the economy and the society of Cupertino. Employees still ate at the Good Earth and Bob's Big Boy and occasionally transgressed from correct dietary behavior by sneaking doughnuts at the ancient Donut Wheel. But now at the corner of Stevens Creek and Homestead, great changes were afoot. On one side, the Wagon Wheel restaurant, a 1940s remnant that catered to both bikers and programmers, was replaced by a red-brick building that housed Apple's educational group. Much more obvious, though, were the events taking place on the diagonal corner. There for forty years had stood R. Cali Bros. Feed Co., an anachronistic collection of dusty buildings and storage silos out of a 1930s precisionist painting. Now it had been bulldozed and was busily being replaced by the green lawns and tall glass towers of Apple's new corporate headquarters.

There is an old law in Silicon Valley that when a company builds a new corporate headquarters the shrewd investor shorts the stock. It is an investment strategy that has held for companies as diverse as Apple, Silicon Graphics and even Hewlett-Packard (though not Intel, which wisely continues to shrink from the very idea of a headquarters), and it comes from an understanding of entrepreneurship and human behavior. When a company grows big enough and wealthy enough to finally move out of the warren of rented buildings it has grown up in, it has also usually grown so staid and self-obsessed that it will soon lose track of its customers, its products and its markets. Moreover, once such a facility is announced, everyone with any authority in the company quickly becomes obsessed with getting the right office on the right floor with the best parking place, while minor matters like running the company are put on the back burner.

This, of course, is precisely what happened at Apple, though the company was moving toward that attitude long before the cardboard boxes full of office supplies were shipped over to the new building. But what made the Apple headquarters move not just the latest example of a dispiriting trend but also a classic tragedy was that, with the exception perhaps of Oracle's glass tubes, no office buildings in Silicon Valley more resembled those IBM and PepsiCo buildings Jobs had ridiculed that night seven years before.

In the ten-year reign of John Sculley, Apple's ersatz philosopher king, Apple had aged from the Little Kingdom to the Middle Kingdom. It shared many traits with dynastic China: isolation and insularity, contempt for outsiders, an elegant but decadent culture at the top, endless palace intrigue and indifference to the fate of average citizens. As the Khans looked upon Westerners, Apple looked upon Wintel users as either dupes or idiots, and certainly blind. And at the top of this cultish society was the Emperor himself, coolly detached from harsh reality. Fittingly, his glass-walled office in the new headquarters faced not outward at the big, ugly world, but inward, toward the not so little Kingdom.

Gary Martin, leaving Apple in 1992, was "amazed just how big the IBM-compatible world was. Inside Apple, we were so completely insulated from the vast non-Apple computing world outside."

In the Apple cosmology, Mac users were the true illuminati. They sported Apple logo stickers in their car windows and crowded into MacExpo to look at the newest products and read *MacWorld* or *MacUser* magazines for the latest dope. It was a beautifully self-contained world. And when everyone was talking to one another at the same time, it was almost loud enough to drown out the roar of Wintel barbarians just outside the walls, pounding on the gates.

At the center of it all was John Sculley himself. He had come to Cupertino to escape the politics and bureaucracies of Pepsi and the East Coast establishment corporations. He wanted to be an agent for change at Apple, and God was cruel enough to give him his wish: he managed to change everything for the worse.

Apple was also opening a giant new R&D facility a half mile down De Anza Boulevard, overlooking the freeway. The huge complex of buildings had once been the headquarters of Four-Phase Inc., a benighted computer terminal and network company that had been bought out years before. Now Apple turned it into a glass-and-steel metaphor of itself. The renovated facility had green lawns for employees to play Frisbee upon and a cafeteria that served everything from cappuccino to sushi. And all the buildings faced inward.

Even more telling was the name of the driveway leading into the complex. As a joke, the company had named it Infinite Loop, after the mistake in programming code that causes a program to repeat the same mistake over and over. Nobody seemed to notice that the name also was a devastating comment on the New Apple itself. Fittingly, this new facility along Infinite Loop was the home of the Copland team.

Narcissism had always been at the heart of the Apple way. It had once enabled the company to overcome enormous obstacles to success. It was also why the company could be so insufferably smug. But now, as they looked in the mirror, many Apple employees didn't like what they saw. Cringely, writing at the time, caught it perfectly:

> Today, the sense of anomie—alienation, disconnectedness—at Apple is major. The difference between the old Apple, which was crazy, and the new Apple is anomie. People are alienated. Apple still gets the bright young people. They come into Apple, and instead of getting all fired up about something, they go through one or two reorgs and get

disoriented. I don't hear people who are really happy to be at Apple anymore. They wonder why they are there, because they've had two bosses in six months, and their job has changed twice.

What Cringely didn't have to say was that the difference between the Old Apple and the New Apple was John Sculley. The pirate flag could now be found in the Apple museum, alongside stills from the "1984" ad and all the other crazy, thrilling, psycho things the young Apple had done. Now, at the Hapsburg Apple, wearing jeans to the executive offices was the height of bohemianism. Just about everything that had made Apple special had been driven off, gelded or packed away. Apple's republican days were now long gone, replaced by its Augustan age. Sculley had traded everything for maximum profits and stock price. Apple was now literally trapped on Infinite Loop.

There were stories of a kind of imperial arrogance taking over Apple's executive offices. Worried by what he was seeing, Regis brought in a series of consultants and speakers to try to teach Sculley & Co. how a corporation can both grow and endure, yet still remain vital and dynamic. "They would listen attentively to the speaker," Regis recalled with dismay. "Then when he was done they would walk out and go right back to what they were doing before." It wasn't long before McKenna, not without a little mourning for the company he'd helped create, began to back away from Apple.

Apple next decided it wanted a corporate jet. Despite the area's wealth, there were few such aircraft in the Valley. HP had a couple, but any employee could hop a ride to get to an outlying division. But at Apple, this would not be the Aircraft for the Rest of Us. Management only. But when the jet finally arrived, the executives were aghast to see that the Apple logo on the tail did not have the exact tonality in its colors. So, at a cost of tens of thousands of dollars, they had it scraped off and repainted.

But the last straw came when John Sculley had declared himself, in March 1990, Apple's new chief technology officer. The little inventor was at long last going to be a real engineer—even if he had to award the title himself. Outside Apple, the news was met with laughter and endless jokes. Whenever Sculley's name came up in conversation, the other person was bound to raise an eyebrow and ask solemnly, "You mean, Apple's *chief technology officer?*" followed by general laughter.

Inside Apple, it wasn't so funny. Down in the ranks of *real* engineers, nobody was laughing. They hadn't worked eighty-hour weeks for years to have to take this kind of insult. As Apple graphics engineer Konstantin Othmer told Jim Carlton of *The Wall Street Journal:* "Every engineer should have walked out when he did that. You're taking an executive from the soda industry and making him CTO of one of the best technology companies in the world."

From that moment, the technical ranks of Apple, the heart of the company, turned its back on John Sculley forever. They would cheer his departure and, even then, hold a grudge against him for years. Sculley, meanwhile, thought the decision one of the best he ever made at Apple.

8.22 SLAUGHTER

On May 20, 1991, via a morning voice mail message to Apple employees, John Sculley announced the layoff of 1,600 (it would eventually be 1,500) employees.

Rumors had been swirling for days. Experts had predicted anywhere from 500 to 2,000 layoffs. So it wasn't as bad as it might have been, although close. The number represented 10 percent of Apple's total workforce, including temps and contractors.

The layoff was described as the inevitable consequence of Apple's new strategy. The first quarter's strong sustained profits had been an illusion; now the arithmetic was taking its revenge. Reduced margins had to be matched with reduced overhead. For the quarter ended March 31, revenues had jumped 19 percent, driven by the new low-cost Macs. But earnings hadn't budged from the year before.

"Obviously, we don't like having to do this," said Sculley. "It will be hard for all of us to see some wonderful and talented employees leave the company." But, he added, "our industry has gone through a tremendous change very rapidly and these changes are affecting all major competitors, not just Apple."

Yet most of the cuts came in the distribution change and through a reorganization of the field sales force into fewer offices. This was bizarre . . . and illuminating. As observers noted at the time, Apple was one of the most productive companies per capita in its industry. Its $440,000 in annual sales per employee was the best in the industry, twice that of most of its competitors. Profits per employee—$37,400—were second only to Compaq.

In other words, the line operations of Apple were more than paying for its keep. On the other hand, Apple's management and administrative costs were also at the top of the industry—31.7 percent. Maintaining the palace and court were a real bloated cost on Apple's balance sheet.

It was Apple's biggest layoff to date. The pink slips arrived on June 20. Once again, there was a small lunch-hour protest. One hundred twenty employees showed up for the rally. They waved copies of Sculley's biography and called for Sculley to live up to his own enlightened management advice. One employee read a selection from the book:

> Let's say we stop judging business and planning in the future by the balance sheet. Every way we currently look at business has been financially focused. Instead, let's look at the creative value of a corporation.

Some wanted to burn the books in a bonfire. But in the end the group decided to mail the copies back to its author. The sole protest sign, carried by newly laid-off networking engineer Suzy Brown, read: "I used to have the spirit and passion for Apple. Now I'm just 'collateral damage.'"

But it was all meaningless. The protesters were just some of the last true believers. As they put on their pathetic show, the rest of Apple watched quietly from the company cafeteria. These hundreds understood now that Apple was no longer a dream or a family. Now it was just a business—and what mattered now was holding on to your job.

8.23 DIVINE INTERVENTION

Incredibly, even as hope was fading, Apple was given one last chance to get out of its Catch-22.

By now it was apparent to almost everyone that Apple's major operating system efforts, first envisioned at an off-site conference in March 1988, and now having sucked up hundreds of millions of dollars of Apple R&D money, were in trouble.

The three original projects had been code-named Pink, Red (being pinker than pink) and Blue. Pink was to be the revolutionary new object-oriented operating system. It would dead-end in Taligent. Red, which was to be even more outré than Pink, passed through a second phase, called Raptor, then mutated into the hydra of Copland and took on a life of its own. It would never be completed. Only Blue, the Mac OS upgrade, and thus the least ambitious of the three, ever made it to market.

Now, in February 1992, the new OS upgrade, System 7, completed, its project manager, Gifford Calenda, walked into the office of his boss, vice president for software development Roger Heinen, with a proposal. "Bill Gates is going to kill us because we are sitting at maybe eight percent market share," he told Heinen. It was only going to get worse unless Apple got the

Mac OS to work on another platform. Calenda asked for permission to give it a shot.

His timing was perfect. A week later, Heinen was contacted by a vice president of Novell Inc., the Utah computer network software giant. The representative, Darrell Miller, was speaking for Novell CEO Ray Noorda, Bill Gates's most single-minded antagonist. Noorda, looking for yet another end run around Microsoft, wanted to know if Apple would like to team up with Novell to create an Intel-compatible version of the Mac OS? And if not, would Apple sue if Novell went ahead without it?

Apple didn't need to do the calculations. Novell had twelve *million* customers. Heinen called Calenda back and told him to assemble a team and go for it. The project, in perfect techie style, was code-named Star Trek, because its charter was to "boldly go where no one has gone before."

But Apple and Novell still needed one more player: Intel, the guys who owned the microprocessor standard. And this was when it got interesting—because Intel was not only interested but got involved at the very top. So did Apple. In late 1991, John Sculley was interviewed by David Yoffie, a Harvard Business School professor and Intel director, when Yoffie was preparing a case study on Apple. Like most interviews, the conversation took off on its own, in this case about the Apple/Intel-Microsoft-PC war. "I don't think you have a prayer," Yoffie told Sculley. Why? Sculley asked. Yoffie explained that the growing power and performance of Windows atop Intel chips was rapidly closing the gap with the Mac and its OS and demolishing Apple's sole marketing advantage.

Sculley didn't buy the argument. So Yoffie offered to bring to Apple someone who could make the case far better than he. And so, in early 1992, a small, trim Hungarian emigrant with a look of infinite authority walked through the lobby of De Anza 7 for a meeting with John Sculley.

Apple's flacks had spent years molding the image of Sculley as a great manager, business titan and technology visionary. But Andrew S. Grove was the real thing. Unlike Apple in personal computers, Intel had started in the middle of the pack in a far rougher business and not only emerged as the leader but demolished the competition. It owned 90 percent of the market for microprocessors, the most important product in the world. And that made Andy Grove the most powerful business executive in high technology.

Grove was fearless, tough and brilliant. In five years, Intel would be worth more than the entire U.S. auto industry. On one occasion, its good quarterly earnings report would pull the world's stock markets back from the brink of a crash.

But Intel had an Achilles' heel: for all of its power, wealth and influence, it was married to Gates's Microsoft. And in this marriage, Intel did all the heavy lifting. It was no secret that Windows, built in layers atop the now ancient DOS core, was a kluge that depended for much of its performance upon Intel coming out with a new, more powerful chip every couple of years. Grove well knew he was being forced to put a race-car engine in a Buick, but he had little choice unless he could find another OS.

And that was why he was here at Apple Computer. The message Grove delivered in Sculley's fourth-floor office was a simple one. He presented Sculley with Intel's forecast for microprocessor shipments to PC companies in the year to come. It was far above anything Apple had imagined. Then Grove leaned forward with the look that drained the blood out of the faces of lesser mortals, and said, "John, you are going to get killed by Microsoft. You have to put your technology on Intel."

John Sculley, dazed, nodded. "I guess you're right."

Star Trek was given a bright green light.

One by one, Apple had been visited by the three Magi of PCs. Gates, IBM and now Grove. All offered salvation. Apple had blown the first two chances, dismissing Gates's advice and wrecking the IBM joint venture even before it began. Grove had come calling with one last chance.

This time, Apple seemed determined to follow. Calenda quickly pulled together a team of seven engineers, four marketers and two administrative assistants from Apple, along with four representatives from Novell. The project was so sensitive (being a greater apostasy inside Apple than outside) that the team moved out of Apple and set up shop at Novell in Santa Clara—ironically, just across the way from Grove's office at Intel.

It was like the old pirate days on the Mac team. The refrigerator was filled with Sierra Nevada beer, courtesy of the company. When someone joked about needing an arcade video game, it was delivered. The team even put on the door a joke company name: WE ARE ARROGANT BASTARDS & ASSOCIATES— which mortified Novell's largely Mormon staff and was eventually removed. Instead the team put up a new fake business title every week.

It was a wonderful experience, the last of its kind in the Apple story. The Star Trek team got a brief glimpse of what their predecessors had known a decade before. No company politics, no suits from headquarters looking over their shoulders. Just long days and nights, sitting at a pair of computers—one a Mac, the other a PC—writing code for one, then translating it for the other. When they didn't understand something about the chip (in this case the Intel 80486), a technician was always waiting at Intel to take their call.

Five years before, when Dan Eilers had suggested just such a translation project, Jean-Louis Gassée had declared it impossible. Gassée was partly right: the existing Mac OS code, some of it dating back to 1983, resisted conversion. But that didn't stop this team; they just rewrote the old code so it would work. And even that wasn't enough. The team was only chartered to translate the critical Finder program of the OS, but the members went on and converted the hot new graphics feature, QuickDraw, to DOS as well. Then, for fun, they even made the DOS version boot up with the same sound and the same happy face icon as the Mac. If you didn't look down from the screen, it would be impossible to tell whether you were working on a Macintosh or a Compaq computer.

It was not only an incredible achievement but an extraordinarily prodigious one. By November 1992, less than six months after they'd begun, the team held a demonstration of Star Trek for some Apple and Novell brass.

The demonstration was simple—the Mac OS tool bar, spinning dice, bouncing balls, the letters A-P-P-L-E floating in space, finishing with a Quick-Time video of a rocket taking off as the audio announced, "Liftoff. We have liftoff"—but it was historic. The first-ever bridge between the two worlds of personal computing. One Novell executive began giggling with joy.

On December 4, in De Anza 7, the Star Trek team was asked to give a demonstration of their achievement to the Apple executive team. They were all there, including Sculley, Graziano, Spindler, Sullivan and Eisenstat. As the presentation progressed, the team grew more and more optimistic. *Maybe they won't kill us like they did all the others.* Sculley was grinning. Graziano was so excited he couldn't stay in his seat.

When the demonstration finished, the execs began to pepper the team with questions, interrupting each other, repeating each other's questions. It was so chaotic that one Star Trek team member asked himself if these were really the men who ran Apple Computer. But it didn't matter. What was important was the enthusiasm. They were going for it! Star Trek was going to happen.

Then Fred Forsythe, head of Apple's engineering, said quietly, "This will mean a whole new business model."

Forsythe was concerned that Apple was already committed to the PowerPC joint venture and that any distraction might upset the partners and confuse the marketplace. That was the end of Star Trek. In the end, Apple chose the safer path. Though the executive team voted to continue funding and ramping up Star Trek, it was already over. A few weeks later, during the Christmas break, Heinen quit Apple to join, in the ultimate insult, Microsoft.

And so ended Apple's last chance to avert disaster.

8.24 DISTRACTIONS

"Ironically, the times when I had the most power [were] when Apple was in trouble," Sculley told reporter Jim Carlton. By end of the summer of 1991, the layoffs completed, the company having eaten a horrific $224 million to cover its restructuring—giving it its first quarterly loss, $53.1 million, since 1985—John Sculley found himself without an immediate crisis and hungry for a new crusade.

In November, the world got its first clue that Sculley's mind was wandering when he filed with the SEC to sell up to 100,000 of his 165,000 shares in hand (he had options on almost 600,000 more).

On top of that, Silicon Valley and the rest of high tech were finally, begrudgingly, beginning to accept the outsider who had now run one of its biggest companies through thick and thin for nearly a decade. The occasion for this reappraisal was the introduction of the Newton at the Consumer Electronics Show in Chicago at the end of May 1992. Its future as yet unknown, and apparently shining, the Newton was seen as a kind of culmination to Sculley's tenure after Jobs. "[Newton] represents perhaps the first tangible glimpse of a vision of technology's future," wrote the Mercury News, "a vision now shared by many of the world's biggest high-technology companies. Many people now credit Sculley with shaping that vision." Industry researcher Dataquest was even more ebullient; wrote one of its analysts, "Sculley is the leading visionary in the computer industry today."

It was true. His ideas might be derived from others, the Newton might not succeed as a product, but there was no denying that John Sculley had singlemindedly driven a new technology from a mere daydream into a real product that would soon set into motion a real industry. He had proven that he could duplicate what Steve Jobs had done—and do it in the much more demanding environment of a multibillion-dollar company with thousands of employees. Whatever happened from this point, no one could ever take that away from John Sculley.

Sculley's reputation, like that of so many business leaders, only increased the further away you went from company headquarters. He was disrespected by his own engineers, but lionized on the East Coast. After all, here was one of them, a clubby Brahmin, who had gone out West with the savages and who, like Kurtz, managed to become their ruler. For a while, Sculley was even short-listed to become the new chief executive of IBM. But there were even bigger ponds for John Sculley now to swim in.

In Silicon Valley, once you reach the top, the only place to go is inside the Beltway. As with so many things, David Packard had cut the path in the late

1960s, when he had accepted a job as Deputy Secretary of Defense. By the 1980s there was a continuous stream of Valley CEOs making the trip to lobby, testify and dole out contributions in the name of the American Electronics Association, the Semiconductor Industry Association and various legislative campaigns.

It was also great fun to go inside the Beltway, because unlike among one's peers back in San Jose, Valley executives were treated like visiting royalty in Washington—after all, electronics was now America's largest manufacturing employer, the key to its balance of trade and, the politicos hoped, a source for millions in campaign contributions. The nexus of Silicon Valley's curiosity about Washington, and Washington's lust for Silicon Valley, reached its peak in the 1992 presidential election campaign.

Despite their liberal credentials, the players in Silicon Valley, being bootstrap entrepreneurs and fiscal conservatives, had almost universally voted for the GOP for thirty years. But 1992 was going to be different. Most of the Valley's leaders were frustrated with George Bush's Rust Belt orientation and intrigued (and secretly thrilled) by Bill Clinton's apparent understanding of tech. Suddenly, it was okay to be a liberal in Silicon Valley, and closet Democrats started popping up everywhere. John Sculley teamed up with Ed Mc-Cracken, CEO of Silicon Graphics, and a number of other local Valley execs and venture capitalists to draft Clinton's technology white paper. The Clinton campaign thanked Sculley by leaking word that, until the selection of Senator Al Gore, Sculley had been a contender for Clinton's vice presidential running mate.

When Clinton finally made his way out to Silicon Valley, it was Sculley and the other execs who met him, wrote him sizable checks and then set up what was likely the most important single event of the entire campaign: a press conference in which a dozen of the Valley's top CEOs came out onstage to give their support to candidate Clinton. Cameras rolled, sending the image around the world. Later, one CEO would say he had been duped into the appearance: Gil Amelio of National Semiconductor.

The Valley press conference was a galvanizing moment for the Clinton campaign. The top executives of America's most important industry, guys who really knew the future and how America could best get there, born leaders who had single-handedly changed the modern world . . . and they had dubbed Bill Clinton their choice. It was no wonder that Clinton returned to the Valley again and again, not just during the campaign but throughout his first term as President. And as the election results rolled in that November night, hands were rubbed together in boardrooms all over the Valley—not least in Cupertino. Now the Valley had its own pipeline right into the Oval Office.

But at Apple, the connection went even deeper, thanks to Dave Barram, whose enduring friendship with that Arkansas governor and his wife had turned into a career Lotto jackpot. There was growing talk of Barram coming to Washington. Barram, being a loyal lieutenant, put in a good word for his boss. Soon John Sculley was being talked about as well for a job in Washington, or perhaps an ambassadorship. Sculley, it was rumored, had begun quietly campaigning for the job of Secretary of Education as early as the Bush Administration.

It was a perfect moment for Sculley to make such a move. As he saw it, he was at his very peak in power and prestige at Apple. Moreover, he knew the future looked bleak. Company stock had fallen 3¼ to $45.25 on news that the quarter ended July 31 had seen flat earnings from the quarter before—and it was only going to get worse as product prices fell and R&D rose to get Copland out to meet the newest Windows. Now was the time to get the hell out—*après moi le déluge*—while his reputation was still intact and, at age fifty-three, step up to an even greater role on the world stage. Meanwhile, to position Apple neatly, Sculley entered into conversations with Ray Noorda of Novell about a possible merger to take on Microsoft directly.

So, in every way, the fix seemed to be in. Barram was called back to D.C. for an appointment as Deputy Secretary of Commerce. Though he denied it, Sculley looked to be next. Certainly Washington insiders thought so: even conservative William Schneider of the American Enterprise Institute said that the Clinton White House considered Sculley to be "the very model of the modern business person." *Financial World* magazine named him CEO of the Year. And then came the appearance during the State of the Union address. John Sculley seemed poised on the brink of greatness . . .

Then months passed. Whether it was because the Clinton administration, notoriously slow in making appointments, never got around to him; or because it wanted him to stay where he was in Silicon Valley; or whether it didn't want him at all, the call never came for John Sculley. Once again, as had happened during the attempted sell-off of Apple after the Mac introduction, Sculley had devised the perfect exit strategy only to see it fade away. The Novell deal collapsed as well.

Meanwhile, the Sculleys had purchased a home in Connecticut and Leezy was spending much of her time there. Sculley himself, who had never hidden his preference for the East, began to talk increasingly about going back, maybe even opening an office in New York City and running Apple from there. More than one board member grumbled that the CEO seemed distracted and out of touch.

Then on June 9, 1993, Apple publicly projected a sizable drop in earnings for the rest of the year. Gross margins, well over 50 percent when Apple had embarked on its new strategy the year before, were now in the high 30s—and falling. Worse, analysts determined that in order to pump up volume enough to sustain its current earnings, Apple would have to cut prices. But that would slash margins. The new strategy had put Apple Computer into a dangerous downward spiral; yet another infinite loop. Another massive layoff was now inevitable.

At last, the board of directors, somehow rediscovering the spine it had been missing for a decade, decided that Sculley had been too attentive to his own career back East to mind the store at home. It asked for his resignation as CEO and as chief technology officer. He would be left with the chairmanship.

John Sculley was shocked by the news, both because he assumed he was secure in the job until he was ready to abandon it and because it also meant the end of his political career. But he didn't show his dismay to the world. Instead, he put a positive spin on the move, "The strategy Apple has been pursuing for three years, which Michael [Spindler] and I designed, is coming to fruition. We decided the CEO position is a full-time job." He was correct on both counts.

Though Sculley and Apple put the best face on the firing, the real story came out three months later in one of the strangest episodes in John Sculley's strange tenure at Apple. In late September, Al Eisenstat, Apple's veteran (thirteen years) executive vice president and secretary, furious for having just been squeezed out of the company, filed suit against Apple and its new CEO, Michael Spindler. According to the suit, Eisenstat and Kevin Sullivan, those two hidden powers on the executive team, had secretly spent months preparing Spindler to depose Sculley.

Eisenstat claimed that he had been approached by several outside Apple directors and asked to sound out Spindler about taking over the CEO post. According to Eisenstat, those directors felt Sculley "was not focused on the day-to-day operations of Apple, other than on its technology" and wanted help removing him. Eisenstat did as he was asked, and when Spindler proved amenable, he and Sullivan worked with him to grease the transition. As Sculley's chief adviser, Eisenstat was particularly well placed for treachery. But tied to that service was a quid pro quo—or at least Eisenstat thought. Maybe an employment guarantee. A promotion. Stock.

So the ax fell on Sculley. And Eisenstat, who had sided with Sculley nine years before against Jobs, was in the front row for the execution, knitting his own future Apple. Then—surprise!—Mike Spindler, apparently with little trust for traitors, even his own, concluded that since Al's primary job was as John Sculley's adviser, and since Sculley was gone, Eisenstat was now superfluous. Eisenstat, who had made $911,831 in salary and stock the year before, and who held $6.5 million in company stock, would just have to get by somehow on the gilded executive severance package he'd helped Sculley devise a few years before.

Eisenstat would have none of it. He sued for emotional distress, conspiracy (!), age discrimination and wrongful termination under California "whistle blower" laws. His case was dismissed.

8.25 EXIT STRATEGY

Some optimists predicted that leaving Apple would at last free Sculley to take on Washington; the number two job in Commerce was currently vacant. But the call still didn't come, especially now that he was damaged goods.

Meanwhile, Sculley's old Pepsi skills returned to him one last time. After having done the same for his lieutenants over the years, he held out for the biggest golden parachute he could get, a reward for the quality of his stewardship. The negotiations dragged on, the board trying to get out of this ugly situation with the minimum of bad publicity, Sculley knowing he had the board over a barrel for exactly the same reason. In the midst of this, Art Rock, the grand old man of high-technology venture capital and, in the words of one Apple manager, "the one really adult adult in the whole place," abruptly resigned after thirteen years on the board. He claimed a potential conflict of interest between his directorship at Intel and Apple's involvement with the PowerPC chip. But the timing suggested there was more to it. Certainly the results were far-reaching. With Rock's departure, the board caved, and John Sculley walked away from Apple with a lucrative parting gift: $1 million in severance, $750,000 in "consultant fees" and immediate vesting of all unearned stock options, worth $2.4 million—$4.1 million in all. Sculley also got the rest of his 1993 salary ($1.059 million, plus a bonus of $412,000). Apple agreed to buy Sculley's house in Woodside ($3.95 million) and his Lear 55 jet for "fair market value." It was a deal so munificent that the next day the SEC announced a plan to give shareholders more control over executive bonuses and severance packages. Nothing was too good for *Financial Week*'s CEO of the Year.

For Eric Krugler, a six-year Apple veteran who went on to become CEO of Orbital Concepts Inc., the John Sculley era was bracketed by two company meetings.

The first all-hands meeting, taking place at the Flint Center within days of Krugler's arrival in 1989, was a celebration. "Everybody loved to go. There were demonstrations of great new technologies, then afterward there'd be a party with good food and music. Everybody seemed really excited.

"But I also remember that at that first meeting they showed a videotape of employees talking about the company and their work and how exciting it was. But all through the video they kept cutting to a guy holding up a sign saying 'No More Reorgs.' It was a running joke, which I didn't really get. Then three weeks later, sure enough, there was another reorganization."

Krugler remembers, "Apple in those days was a great place to work. Apple had great furniture, a great work environment, great office space. But it was no way to run a company. There were no financial controls. The audit department couldn't keep up because the rest of the company was simply out of control."

By the autumn of 1993, the high life had finally caught up with Apple and John Sculley. There was yet another company meeting. This time, said Krugler, "instead of talking to the employees, they videotaped a joint speech between Sculley and Spindler in a studio and broadcast it to us. The spin was that John was leaving and handing over the reins to Michael—a kind of amicable separation. But it didn't work because on the tape John was so obviously uncomfortable that it was obvious he wasn't giving up power willingly. We all knew he was being forced into it."

8.26 POSTMORTEM

The Sculley era at Apple was finally over. But how to judge it? On the one hand, in his decade-long tenure, Apple had grown from $800 million in sales to $6 billion. It had also introduced a score of impressive, if not remarkable products. Yet, at the same time, the company had almost continuously lost market share. It had lost the technical leadership of the industry that it had once carried so effortlessly. It had lost the attention of 90 percent of the marketplace and the dreams of the best talents in the industry. And, having begun his stewardship when it was the most dynamic and innovative computer corporation on earth, Apple at the time of his departure had been reduced to a bureaucratic, bloated organization with no obvious direction and no apparent ability to convert a new idea into a real product. The sleek panther roaming the jungle of personal computing had become a fat snail darter in a tiny, and evaporating, puddle.

"John Sculley was extremely bright," said Tim Bajarin afterward. "And when he first arrived at Apple John wisely knew he wasn't a technologist. But toward the end he started thinking of himself as a technical futurist. He got so involved in the future that he lost his effectiveness as a company manager. Then add politics on top of that and a wife who hated being in California. He took his eye off the ball."

There are in the story of high technology a number of men who grew great companies into even bigger companies, but because of mistakes and missed opportunities, ultimately destroyed them, leaving them rotting, sinking hulks. John Young at Hewlett-Packard, John Akers at IBM, Ken Olsen at DEC—and John Sculley at Apple. For them is reserved a special fate. The brilliance of Silicon Valley is that it honors most types of failures. The ambitious start-ups that never get it together, the companies that take enormous risks and lose, the pioneers who cut a new path and are sacrificed in the process—the executives of these companies are held in great esteem and backed in their next business ventures. But not the men who snuff out the spark of great companies. Their fate is to become invisible. Their public comments, the speeches and participation on panels, their honorary positions, are all politely ignored.

In John Sculley's case, he made the right move and headed back East. There he hid out in Maine and Manhattan.

In mid-October, he joined an unknown 200-person Long Island telecom company called Spectrum Information Technologies as its chairman and CEO. Spectrum had only a few million in sales and hadn't turned a profit in five years. Its stock had fallen as low as $1 per share. Days after Sculley's arrival, Spectrum was awarded a major patent. The company's stock jumped $3½ to $11⅛. The result was that, just three weeks after joining his new company, John Sculley had made nearly $63 million on paper. Even high-rolling Silicon Valley was boggled.

Then the little Spectrum house of cards collapsed. Three executives resigned. Then it was discovered that the company had backdated $3.8 million in patent license fees to pump its quarterly financials and give itself a profit. Meanwhile, Spectrum's president had made $8 million in profits selling a million shares of company stock while it was plumped. The SEC announced an investigation.

Innocent, but humiliated, turned into a chump and a dupe, Sculley resigned. This commentary on his skills at judging businesses and people made him the subject of even more derision.

Eventually, he joined up with his brothers to create a venture fund to invest in technology companies. In an effort to rehabilitate himself, he also started an annual conference on the future of technology held each summer in Maine. Slowly, he worked his way back into electronics. He invested in companies in Israel, where his name still had some cachet, and eventually in a multimedia company located just south of Silicon Valley.

But Silicon Valley was not ready to either forgive or forget. There, his name connected with any enterprise was still poison. Still, when Apple was in extremis in 1997, Sculley offered the press his own suggestions about what Apple should do, notably hire Del Yocam. He was ignored.

At the end of 1997, interviewed by *Forbes ASAP*, John Sculley said that he was happier than ever, that people came up to him now and told him how great he looked. But the words were belied by the cadaverous picture of him on the facing page. He closed the interview by saying that in the future "I will continue doing what I've always done. Help people."

Mike Moritz had a different view. In the years since writing *The Little Kingdom*, Moritz had become a successful venture capitalist and, thanks to a brilliant investment in the Internet company Yahoo!, became as rich as Apple's founders. Looking back over the intervening thirteen years, having watched Apple disintegrate and Microsoft take over the computing world, he had his own bitter judgment on John Sculley's career:

"For what he did to Apple, John Sculley deserves to be in the cell next to Charlie Manson."

9.0 STUMP

9.1 DIESEL

If ever a company fit William Carlos Williams's observation about the pure products of America going crazy, it was Apple Computer. And now this most idiosyncratic of American firms was in the hands of a fifty-year-old German CEO with a thick accent whose experience with daily life in the United States could be counted in months.

Even for Apple, it was a reckless move. Sculley's tenure ultimately had been a failure, but at least in hiring him Jobs had set out to find the best marketer in the world to run what he believed was the best company in the world. This time, the board of directors, after a moment of courage in toppling Sculley, reverted to type. As if royal succession was the rule rather than the exception in Silicon Valley, as if the preceding five years at Apple had been a smashing success rather than prelude to disaster, the board simply promoted the president and COO to the top spot. Mike Markkula, the perpetual custodian of the status quo, was named company chairman. John Sculley couldn't have picked a better combination to take the fall.

History, in the fickle form of Apple fanatics, reviles Spindler as at best an incompetent and at worst a cowardly fool. But history is wrong. Spindler is more a tragic figure. And if he made mistakes—and he made many—his biggest was in being, like Mike Scott, Jef Raskin, Burrell Smith and several million customers, a true believer in the Apple myth. Few people have ever given so much for a company and, at least at the executive level, been rewarded with such calumny.

Michael Spindler's short unhappy reign stands as one more reminder of the old saw that no good deed ever goes unpunished. By giving his all to Apple, he inherited the Furies. In Europe, Spindler had thrived. In fact, in terms of market share, customer satisfaction, share of mind and almost every other competitive measure, Apple was more successful in Europe than in the

United States. Spindler had succeeded partly because he was more entrepreneurial than most of his fellow Europeans and partly because he was like a provincial governor: close enough to get the products, marketing tools and support from headquarters, but far enough away to be independent of all the political bullshit that encased Cupertino.

But once at headquarters, Spindler's strengths became his weaknesses. He was wholly unprepared to deal with Cupertino's court intrigue. As president, he could be shielded from much of this by being relatively impotent. As CEO, there was no escape.

It began well enough. Apple employees, investors and even customers were relieved to get the Sculley years behind them, especially with the stock price now having fallen from a high of $70 in 1991 to a low of $22 in mid-1993. The Sculley era was one of those experiences that, while you live it, seems eminently reasonable, but once it's over you suddenly look around and ask, "What the hell were we thinking?" After Jobs's psychoses and Sculley's neuroses, Spindler perversely seemed the perfect antidote to all that was wrong with Apple. No more vainglorious, egomaniacal or self-conscious CEOs risking other people's dreams to fulfill their own.

Spindler was just a meat-and-potatoes kind of guy, without any apparent artifice or hidden emotional problems. He was the Diesel—and though that unfortunate moniker didn't catch the gentleness of the man, he was nevertheless a head-down-and-charge-forward kind of guy who didn't care who got the credit as long as the ball moved forward. It was such a great relief to have somebody prosaic in the top spot that nobody seemed to notice that Spindler was, in his own, wholly different way, utterly unsuited for the job.

Having dealt with the ethereal Sculley for a decade, no group was more thrilled with Spindler's arrival than the press. *Forbes* magazine hailed him as "Mr. Pragmatic":

> That his feet are firmly planted, Spindler has left no doubt. "Pragmatist" is one of his favorite words. He sprinkles his conversation with it. Being pragmatic means dealing with the world as it is rather than as you would like it to be. . . . When speaking in his native German, he frequently uses the word *Mut*. The word means courage, which is what it took to cancel projects and fire thousands of people. But *Mut* also means spirit, which is what Steve Jobs had. Spindler promises to combine the two kinds of *Mut*.
>
> Scrambling his metaphors but speaking with great sincerity, Spindler sums up: "I won't mortgage the company's future by amputating the things that Apple stands for." He leaves his listeners in little doubt

about his determination to keep in Apple that magic mixture of imagination and pragmatism that made it great.

The only problem with this appraisal was that it missed three crucial facts.

First, Apple had lost that "magic mixture" of imagination and pragmatism in about 1989. It was still full of imagination, but pragmatism was hard to find—and those pockets (such as the Star Trek project) in which it survived were well fire-walled to keep them from contaminating the rest of the company.

The second mistake was to believe that even if both traits were still available in equal proportions, Spindler had anywhere near the talent needed to mix them.

And the third mistake was in believing that Spindler's feet were "firmly planted." He was, in fact, at this point in his life, a deeply divided and distracted man. Perhaps at another time he might have been ready to run Apple Computer, Inc. successfully, as he had Apple Europe and Apple Japan. But not now.

The years of devoting himself to Apple's success had taken their toll. Spindler was tired. His blood pressure was elevated. He was frustrated by corporate politics, by Sculley's micromanagement and self-promotion and by Apple's financial roller coaster. In 1987, not long after coming to Cupertino, he'd been talked out from under his desk. Two years later he had a stress attack and his secretary had found him on the floor of his office. On another occasion, he was found passed out at his desk. In the years thereafter, he occasionally had to be raced by ambulance to the hospital—always taken out of the building by the back door, and in an ambulance with the siren off.

Spindler knew that the chief executive's job would be infinitely more stressful. So when Eisenstat and Sullivan approached him about the prospective coup d'état, Mike Spindler should have said no. But his hands were already dirty from having helped boot Yocam years before. Besides, who could turn down a dream of more than fifteen years, the chance to correct all the wrongs that have haunted you for much of your professional career? To justify all your scheming and backstabbing and corporate climbing?

Spindler should have said no. If not during the coup, then right after he took the CEO job, when his wife was diagnosed with lymph cancer and he spent most of the time he needed to rest at Stanford Hospital taking care of her. Or a year after that, when his daughter was in a major car crash that seriously injured the other driver, put her parents into a nasty lawsuit and drove her away to a distant boarding school. Or when his blood pressure kept climbing and he stopped sleeping and eating, and when the waves of depression paralyzed him at his desk. Or when his doctor wrote him that Christmas and warned him that if he didn't quit he'd die.

But most of all Mike Spindler should have quit when he realized that he wasn't the man for the job. That Apple needed some radical decisions that he wasn't healthy enough to make. When he realized that the management techniques that worked out in the field, like leaving subordinates alone and trusting them to do their jobs, didn't work anymore in Cupertino.

But Michael Spindler didn't quit. Even after Regis, now all but out of Apple, warned him, "Quit, or you'll end up dead at your desk and two weeks from now no one will remember who you are."

9.2 TUNNEL VISION

What Mike Spindler *did* have was a profound understanding of everything that had gone wrong with Apple since he had joined the firm. It was the perfect example of the obsessive outsider who has a very precise idea of where a company has made mistakes, and a commitment to fix them, but not a clue about what to do after that. Spindler merely set out to follow his plan, no matter how devastating its effects, no matter how cold-blooded it seemed to everyone else, and worst of all, without ever looking around to see if the world had changed and the strategy still worked. Thus, Mike Spindler's worst moves were often better than his best moves because both were so ill timed.

It was the classic behavior of an engineer. And Spindler, unlike Markkula, Jobs or Sculley, really was an engineer, a graduate of Rheinische Fachhochschule. He couldn't have been more different in terms of personality, than Mike Scott, his only engineering predecessor in the executive office, and yet they had much in common, especially their belief in a rational approach to business leadership. And both suffered the same fate of having their irrational hearts broken (in Spindler's case, literally) by the company.

The Apple Computer that Spindler inherited was in serious trouble. The new Windows-based PCs were coming on fast. Heavy competition was driving down costs in that market, each month making more dramatic the growing gap in price between Macs and everyone else. In some cases PC clones with power comparable to Macs' were selling at half the price. No matter how great the Mac operating system, that was a pretty wide gap to overcome. Apple had to cut prices, further.

But that only underscored the essential dilemma that now lay across the company's path to a viable future. As the sole "other" architecture in the personal computing business (Unix aside), Apple had to go alone against the combined efforts of scores of Wintel machines. The fact that these other companies were competing ferociously among themselves only heightened their push to be more innovative, more powerful and more price-competitive. So, though Apple might see itself as competing piecemeal against Dell, Compaq, Acer and all the rest, it was in fact competing against a single monolithic entity called the Windows PC Market, with hundreds of thousands of employees, a hundred billion dollars in annual revenues and R&D expenditures totaling perhaps $20 billion. Even if many of these efforts were redundant, even contradictory, nevertheless they still totaled far more than anything that could be put together by Apple, an $8 billion company with just $90 million in profits to reinvest.

The company was showing the strain. New competitors, new products and new ideas were busting out all over in the Wintel world—Compaq was becoming an unequaled manufacturer, Dell had put into place a superb distribution system, every month IBM and HP were coming up with new designs for laptops, graphical workstations and peripherals, Gateway 2000 was establishing a new system for fast custom manufacturing and the Japanese and Koreans were bombing the hell out of prices. Wintel trade shows, especially Comdex, which drew 200,000 engineers, executives and reporters to Las Vegas every winter, now dwarfed MacExpo. Hundreds of new applications programs were being introduced every month, all of them for Windows, a few with a token tag line in the announcement release promising to introduce a Mac-compatible version sometime in the next year. And up in Redmond, Gates & Co. were readying a new operating system, code-named Chicago, that was rumored to be its Mac buster. It was slated for introduction in 1993.

So it came down to this: there was no possible way that Apple could keep up with the Wintel world. The company's one hope had been to set the pace and force the others to follow, always remaining far enough ahead to command the maximum price. But Sculley had blown that opportunity. Now Apple was trapped forever selling to its own customer base. But even that infinitely suffering, infinitely loyal base wasn't going to buy such obviously overpriced products as a $5,000 Quadra that didn't have any more speed or memory than a $2,300 Compaq PC.

So prices had to come down. But, once again, when prices fell, margins fell as well. And that in turn meant that the company wouldn't have enough money for R&D to stay in the race. The only solution was to cut costs—and the only way to do that in a knowledge-intensive company was to lay off people. It was a cruel equation. But it was also inescapable, as not only Spindler but his successor would learn to their dismay.

Making matters worse, Spindler's own lieutenants screwed him. They gave him optimistic unit sales projections, which he dutifully presented to the board of directors, then turned around a few days later and revised those numbers down by *100,000* units for the quarter.

So within weeks after taking over Apple, Spindler was forced to announce the layoff of 2,100 employees, bringing the company rolls down to fewer than 11,000. Like all smart new CEOs dealt a bad hand, he quickly consolidated the company's financial problems into a single big $188 million one-time quarterly loss.

If the great Sculley era layoff had been a devastating and traumatic shock to both Apple and the electronics industry, the Spindler era layoff was just ugly. There was a growing sense now that this would be Apple's future: an endless whittling away until there was nothing left. In yet another bit of Apple symbolism, this layoff round took Bill Fernandez, Apple's first employee, the guy whose family name had given Woz and Jobs cover when they'd shopped at Owen Whetzel's store, the young man whom Jobs had refused to reward with stock before the IPO. In the face of everything he'd been through, Fernandez had been a loyal Apple employee for almost twenty years. This was his thanks.

Spindler made no excuses. "When you're hit with something like this," he said, "you have to take action very swiftly." And he was right. To stay competitive, some Apple computer prices were cut by 20 percent or more. That in turn had a devastating effect upon gross profit margins, which fell from 43 percent to 26 percent in a single year. Spindler knew that these weren't enough profits to keep Apple competitive in the long term. Moreover, it seriously hurt the company's stock price, which had shown some signs of renewal with Spindler's arrival and the subsequent layoff. By collapsing again to the mid-20s, the market all but closed the doors on another source of investment capital for Apple.

So, as Spindler saw it, Apple was on the brink of being stuck in a downward spiral of falling prices, tumbling profits and stock prices and endless rounds of layoffs driving away the company's best talent and loyal customers. There were only two ways out of this spin. One was to again produce products so obviously superior to the competition that the company could command high prices once more. The other way was to increase market share by any means necessary and thus capture greater influence with developers and customers, with the resulting jump in revenues (and drop in profits). Best of all would be to do both at the same time.

Spindler set out to do the latter. His first step was to do the unthinkable . . . at least to his predecessors. He licensed the Mac OS. It was the key move John Sculley should have made almost a decade before. Spindler had believed in licensing for years, but his had been a lonely voice at Apple headquarters.

The argument for licensing was straightforward: clones would not only generate licensing revenues for Apple, money it needed desperately for new-product development, but would also create the same competitive fervor that had driven the DOS/Windows world to leadership. That in turn would grow overall Mac OS market share, capture more shelf space for products and draw back the prodigal applications designers.

There was only one downside to this strategy. It was the IBM lesson: if you are going to cede ownership of your market, then you'd better be damn sure you can control it through other means. Big Blue had come down with a bad case of stupidity at the time of the 80286 computers and had surrendered its leadership in innovation, manufacturing, packaging and distribution to its clones. Now it was still playing catch-up. But still, the overall strategy had worked: setting the PC free had enabled it to rule the world. So the trick would be to free the Mac OS while still remaining the strongest competitor in its market.

Spindler thought he had the answer to that too. After all, he was an engineer. All those prima donnas in the labs might have been able to blow fast ones past John Sculley, who never turned down a project he liked and never killed one that was underway, but they weren't going to fool Mike Spindler. He was fully prepared to cancel new products and boot the design team if they couldn't prove their worth.

So, as Apple reeled from the big layoff and the price per share began to climb once again, Spindler took stock of what products he had in his portfolio to begin his assault on the future. Well, for one thing, there was the benighted Newton. As he told *Forbes*: "I won't mortgage the company's future by ampu-tating the things that Apple stands for." And Newton, failure that it was, *was* what Apple stood for: independence, innovative technology, personal creativ-ity. If it had sold just 80,000 units in its first six months, that could be blamed on its price (at $750, it was 50 percent more than the public thought it was worth), the flaws in its first-generation handwriting-recognition software and, most of all, because Sculley and his damn Knowledge Navigator campaign had wildly oversold the technology. Spindler was convinced that Newton could be redeemed through improved software, discounting and better market positioning.

If it worked, Newton would be a safety valve, a market away from the computer wars (and Microsoft) where Apple could hide if things got too hot. But in the meantime, Apple was a personal computer company, fighting the good fight against a giant, many-headed competitor. And here too Spindler thought he had a roster of powerful new weapons in the form of the soon to be introduced PowerPC Macintoshes, the "PowerMacs."

The PowerMacs seemed to have everything going for them. The Motorola PowerPC 601 processor, a 32-bit RISC chip, was not only as fast as Intel's Pentium but less than half the price. And waiting in the wings were some new PowerPCs—the 603, 604, and 620—that outperformed anything Intel had to offer. The 620 was the real beast, a 64-bit processor capable of screaming along at 300 MHz—twice as fast as Intel's best. It also could not only emulate the PC world but actually execute Intel instructions at the chip level. In other words, as Mike Spindler's strategy saw it, with the new line of PowerMacs, Apple would be able to offer computers that were more powerful than their PC counterparts, at about the same price, *and* able to run the entire DOS/Windows applications software library.

Spindler predicted one million PowerMacs sold in the first year, and the numbers to skyrocket thereafter as popular applications programs were rewritten by their developers in order to take full advantage of the PowerPC's speed.

This was heady stuff. For the first time in a decade, Apple would be able to take the battle to the Wintel universe, carving out new market share, instead of trying to defend what it already had. Then, once Apple had regained its market momentum, it would be able to shift into overdrive through the object-oriented software tools in development at subsidiaries Taligent and Kaleida. These tools would allow for quick custom software updates, thus giving Apple the same edge with software designers it expected to soon have in hardware. And that in turn, by the late 1990s, would position Apple to consolidate its gains by advancing its user interface through new versions of the Mac OS (starting with Copland), new functions such as speech recognition and new media such as set-top boxes to turn TVs into computers. Newton was one step in this direction, but much more important was the company's line of PowerBooks. Having screwed up its first laptop, Apple now had a winner in this line. The key was to keep improving the high end, first with a color display, then with the PowerMac processor, all the while dropping prices on the low end to bring in new users.

It was a sound business plan. But it depended upon one crucial factor: Apple had to be able to execute Spindler's strategy. The company had to be able to move fast enough and with enough decisiveness to stay a step ahead of its new clone-maker competitors. That didn't seem too hard, especially given Apple's size, lead and technological prowess. Spindler himself had proven he had the mettle for the job not just with his work in Europe but also as Apple's COO. In his three years as the company's chief operations guy, Spindler had driven the company's notoriously lax product development cycle times down from twenty-four months to just nine months. In any company that would be amazing; at Apple it was nothing short of a miracle. And if the Diesel could do that in product development, just think what he could do with the entire company given the chance.

But if the strategy looked good, it also was very, very fragile. Nobody knew this better than Spindler. One mistake — a delay in the next generation of PowerPC chips from Motorola, a bad distribution or pricing strategy on a major product in Apple's catalog, too many slips or bugs in the new software tools — and the whole edifice could collapse like a house of cards. And if that happened, the company would stall quickly and fall back into its downward spin, a vicious cycle of plummeting prices, margins, market share and stock prices, a growing inability to hire new talent and an abandonment of new-product development projects.

Spindler knew that he was walking on a high wire. The problem was: Did the rest of Apple know it was too? And there lay the mortal flaw in Spindler's plan. After a decade of John Sculley, Apple had become its own worst nightmare: arrogant, bloated, introverted, balkanized, obsessed with office politics and trapped in its own myth. Down in its foxhole Apple had embarked on an extended conversation with itself, its suppliers and its customers and seemed to have forgotten that there was still a war going on.

Rousing Apple out of its lassitude and inertia would require a brilliant leader. Worse, the legacy of Steve Jobs was such that it wasn't enough to *lead* Apple. Now it took *charisma* to awaken the sleeping company. Sculley may have had the charisma of a nervous Unitarian minister, but he was also a demon marketing man. He could fake charisma with theatrically staged events, appeals to the corporate myth and, when all else failed, the Knowledge Navigator video. He could be Virtual Steve for an hour at a time. And, after a few years, he was content to let Apple slumber.

But Spindler no longer had that option. He had to put the company on the march. And no one was less suited for the task. The taciturn Diesel not only hated the limelight; he hid from it at every opportunity. His self-consciousness with the English language only made matters worse. He ducked press interviews, rarely appeared at public events and under the spot-lights in front of Apple employees he couldn't have looked more uncomfort-able than if he'd been a janitor plucked from backstage and pushed out through the curtains.

So why was Mike Spindler, of all people, thrust into this impossible role? The answer went back to Apple's board of directors and most of all to Mike Markkula. Though the sheer inadequacy of the board wouldn't be brought into harsh relief for another few years, it was already woefully ill prepared to advise a company like Apple Computer. Just the list of members should have been enough of a clue: Katherine Hudson, president and CEO of W. H. Brady, a clothing manufacturer; Delano Lewis, president and CEO of National Public Radio; French packaging company executive B. Jurgen Hintz; investment banker Bernard Goldstein of Broadview Associates; venture capitalist Peter Crisp of Venrock Associates (filling for Art Rock); Gil Amelio, CEO of National Semiconductor; and Markkula. It was a dream lineup for a CEO who never wanted to be second-guessed. Sculley had done a masterful job: with the exception of Amelio, all the experienced managers knew nothing about technology, and all the directors who knew anything about technology knew little about management. Divide and conquer. And presiding over it all was Markkula, back as chairman with Sculley's departure.

This toothless board had rubber-stamped Spindler's promotion and now didn't have the insight to recognize that he was the wrong man to direct his own strategy. Besides, there were too many dazzling products to enjoy. And it was so much fun to be part of a such a cool and famous company.

There was another problem as well. By now, Apple had lost just about every talented senior executive who might have taken over Apple's reins. A new generation was now in place: Dan Eilers, who was running Claris; Ian Diery, executive vice president; Joe Graziano, the bonus baby lured back from Sun to become chief financial officer; and Dave Nagel, head of software. None had the experience to run a company the size of Apple, but at least one, Graziano, secretly believed he deserved the top spot and was already plotting to get it. Thus, the board would have had to go outside Apple for a new CEO—something it was unprepared to do.

Like most disasters, the Spindler era started out promising. The new PowerPCs were hailed as impressive new machines, proof that Apple could still do it. Licensing plans moved forward. And even the Newton began to get a little respect. By mid-1994, Apple seemed to be back on its feet. The market was strong and the company's stock price was climbing beyond $40 again for the first time in nearly two years. At the same time, Spindler held hiring down, kept staffing steady at about 11,000 full-time employees and made up the added demand for staffers with contract workers.

Then a huge market break: Microsoft's Mac killer, Chicago software, now generally known as Windows 93, had begun to slip. There was talk of it becoming Windows 94—then, as the new year dawned, word leaked out that it would now be Windows 95.

It was a chance for Apple's survival. The Mac OS had fumbled along now for a decade, being upgraded every couple of years, blowing breakout chances like Pink and Star Trek. Meanwhile, Gates had been laying on the whip hand at Microsoft, driving Windows ever closer to the Mac ideal. He didn't need to catch Apple, only come close, and Microsoft would seal up the market forever. Now was the moment for Copland, years in the works, to roar across the finish line first, steal Microsoft's thunder and put Apple once again a decade ahead of the Boys from Redmond.

But Copland wasn't ready. It wasn't ready in 1993. Or in 1994. Or in 1995. The company had spent hundreds of millions of dollars and it had nothing to show for it. Copland forever remained just around the corner.

Hardware too began to explode. Literally. At a trade show in March 1995, the new model 5300 PowerBooks were a hit . . . until a new type of battery caused them to overheat so much they ignited. An embarrassed Apple had to halt production and order a recall just as the machines were taking off in the marketplace.

That problem fixed, an even greater one emerged. Spindler had entered 1995 forecasting a year of good, but not spectacular growth. It was an uncharacteristically conservative position for the usually wildly optimistic Apple. And it turned out to be the worst possible year to turn careful. In fact, 1995 proved to be one of the greatest years in personal computing history—and Apple, with its new strategy and hot new products, was wonderfully positioned to take advantage of it. Expecting 15 percent market growth, instead of what proved to be twice that, the company terribly underproduced. As a result, by October and the end of its fiscal year, Apple had a $1 *billion* backlog. That meant there were nearly a million customers out there—small companies, giant corporations, loyal private users—who wanted a Mac and now faced the prospect of waiting months to get one. In the already dwindling floor space in computer stores devoted to Apple products, the shelves were stripped bare. Spindler had had his chance to fulfill his strategy and regain five years of lost market share—and he'd blown it.

Spindler well understood his predicament. So did the market, which began to kill Apple's stock value. But no one *understood* Apple's problems more acutely than the CFO, Joe Graziano. In one respect, Graziano was now the key executive at Apple. Since his return, he had forced the company to develop a new and more realistic set of metrics to evaluate its performance. Before, all of Apple's measurement schemes had been, typically, self-centered. The company set its own internal performance goals and tried to meet them. R&D expenditures were held sacred. The company was, in Graziano's accurate description, a fiscal "monastery." Apple, he told *CFO* magazine, "had this belief that it wouldn't be affected by what these other people did."

Graziano, with the power that comes from being not only chief financial officer but the only other employee director besides Spindler, instituted a new, more pragmatic program, one that demanded such market comparison metrics as market share and return on capital employed. "People thought I had my head screwed on backward," Graziano said later. But it worked. "It was like they were monks who never read a newspaper, and all of a sudden they come out of the monastery and saw this new world." This was Graziano playing Plato, but it wasn't far from the truth.

And that truth wasn't a pleasant one for Apple's management team. But it had played a crucial role in moving Spindler to adopt his current strategy.

But for all his brilliance, and his undeniable contributions to the company, the flamboyant Graziano, with his thick curly hair and black mustache, trendy clothes and vintage Ferraris, was also the most dangerous lieutenant a CEO like Spindler could have. Graziano was brilliant enough to see the inadequacies in the company and its top executive, but not wise enough to see the flaws in himself.

Graziano had heard himself called Spindler's heir apparent long enough to actually believe it, not noticing that his vain style was as unlikely for corporate leadership as Spindler's inarticulateness. And now, as the troubles at Apple began to mount, there was no shortage of Apple people whispering in Graziano's ear confirmation of what he already deeply believed: that he was the only man who could save Apple.

At first, it was hard to argue with that appraisal. Graziano seemed to have an easygoing rapport with the press that Spindler could only dream of. He also seemed to have some of Steve Jobs's long-missed gift for turning a disaster into an apparent triumph. For example, way back in early 1985, when Apple was still going strong, the company announced first quarter profits of $73 million on sales of $2.7 billion. That was a fourfold improvement over the disastrous profits of a year before, but still a long way from analysts' predictions of as much as $120 million in profits. So where had the missing $50 million gone? Graziano had lost it in foreign currency hedging as the dollar dropped.

Yet, when the stories about his screwup appeared in the press, Graziano wasn't vilified but lionized. *Business Week* went so far as to applaud him for, of all things, his usually conservative fiscal management. The story went on to credit Graziano with cutting Apple's operating expenses from 36 percent to 19 percent of sales. It talked about him taking care of his dying brother, of growing up in a working-class family and of hauling meat and delivering potatoes to pay his way through college. And accompanying this exercise in hagiography were adoring quotes from peers and industry observers ("He has had a lot to do with making Apple a more competitive company," said Robert Saltmarsh, a former Apple vice president), and a photo of the Man Himself looking kicked back and casual, as if losing $50 million was the kind of thing pros did before lunch.

This was self-promotional genius of the highest order. It made Mike Spindler look like a guy who shoveled coal for a living. And it only made Graziano more certain of his destiny. What he couldn't yet know was that he had already peaked.

So had the company's stock. In the second week of June 1995, Apple stock reached $50 per share. Then it began to fall, slowly at first, then picking up speed with each round of bad news, until by October it sat at $35 per share. Spindler had been given two years to turn Apple's fortunes around. But his good strategy had combined with miserable execution. Some of it, like the inaccurate forecast, was his fault; some of it, like the exploding laptops and the endlessly unfinished Copland, were the fault of others, but his responsibility.

But the most pernicious problem Apple had, the declining quality of Apple employee talent, long preceded him. The 80-20 rule was starting to tell. Like so many successful companies before it, Apple, believing it would stay on top forever, was profligate with talent. Now there were scores of companies all over the Valley (not to mention scores of offices at Microsoft in Redmond) filled with ex-Apple people. They were everywhere you looked: General Magic, MIPS/Silicon Graphics, Sun, Radius, Adobe, HP, Macromedia, WebTV, Intuit, Pixar, Logitech, the venture capital firms in Menlo Park, the U.S. Department of Commerce—everywhere but Cupertino. Apple was beginning to compete with the legendary Fairchild Semiconductor as the mother firm of a whole new generation of Valley start-ups. By the Spindler era, there were more talented ex-Apple people than sterling employees still at the firm. And Apple no longer had the cachet to attract new ones. The best and brightest now were lining up to become Microserfs. And that imbalance in talent was now about to become obvious to the world.

Spindler had not taken this loss into account. No high-tech executive ever does. After all, how do you quantify the fact that your employees aren't as clever as they used to be? If anything, Apple employees now had more advanced degrees than ever before, so how could you test for loss of magic? You can dumb down a machine tool factory, but not a high-tech company. You have to go with your best strategy and hope your staff can pull it off. And Spindler, feeling the growing resentment of the rank and file, was unwilling to leave the tower to visit the troops.

Spindler's plan was good, but Apple could no longer execute. It would be the same frustration felt by his successor. The brain still sent out commands, but the body no longer responded.

Midway through Mike Spindler's tenure as CEO at Apple, one of the company's directors received a visitation from a ghost.

As Gil Amelio would later recount in his memoirs, he was in his office at National Semiconductor, where he was CEO, when he got an unexpected phone call. It was Steve Jobs.

Amelio, of course, knew of the legendary figure, now much in the news with the success of the film *Toy Story*, but had never met him. He took the call.

"I want to come over and see you," said Jobs.

The younger man arrived exactly on time in a long-sleeved sport shirt, dress slacks and, in Amelio's words, "grungy tennis shoes."

After a few minutes of small talk, Jobs cut to the chase. "Apple is on its way out of business. The only thing that can save it is a strong leader, somebody who can rally employees, the press, users and developers."

Amelio was taken aback. But he was also curious. After all, this was Steve Jobs.

Jobs continued his pitch: "The world has changed, the Mac has outlived its usefulness, it's time to go on to something else."

Now Amelio was amazed. After all, the Mac was Jobs's greatest creation. He asked, "If the Mac is dead, what's going to replace it?"

To that Jobs had no real answer. Nor did he have good answers to the questions Amelio then posed, such as "What would you do if you were CEO tomorrow? What would your first decision be?" Instead, according to Amelio, Jobs replied in clichés and evasions. He recalled, "His pitch added up to 'Apple should make a change, I can lead the change, but I don't know what the change will be.'" Nevertheless, Amelio found him charming.

Once Jobs realized that his pitch was going nowhere, the visit began to fall apart. He grew visibly irritated, snapping, "Maybe you have some better ideas." Finally, the conversation lapsed into a long silence, and the meeting was over.

———

Recalled Eric Krugler, "My boss was trying to get in good with Spindler, so one morning I got called in at 7 A.M. to fix some problems and add software to Spindler's computer.

"I get there and turn the machine on. Nothing comes on the monitor. I checked . . . *and it wasn't even plugged in.* Spindler was obviously embarrassed that he'd called somebody in to fix a problem that was so obvious. But he still asked me to come over to his house and set up his home system.

"I was starting to get annoyed. I politely suggested he get someone else.

"But that day, while I was working on Spindler's machine, I noticed something amazing. There was absolutely no security on the main corporate computers. There wasn't even security on the file servers containing all the corporate contacts. *Anybody* could have gone into the corporate files, even Spindler's personal files. It was so indicative of the atmosphere at Apple, even at that late date. There was just a complete lack of control."

9.3 SUITABLE SUITORS

There was one other piece in Mike Spindler's grand strategy. That was to set the turnaround in motion, pump up the stock . . . and then sell off the company. Obviously, he wasn't the first person running Apple to come up with this idea. In fact, it is infinitely telling that, after Mike Scott, *every* Apple CEO tried to unload the company. Protestations to the contrary, big speeches at trade shows announcing that Apple was here to stay, great plans for new products and markets—all fell before the inescapable fact that neither Jobs nor Sculley nor Spindler (and soon Amelio and Jobs again) ever really believed that Apple could survive on its own. Everything else was a pose, a fraud, a worst-case contingency. The company that never really was was also forever the company that wasn't to be.

Spindler had embarked on his search for a sugar daddy almost from the day he arrived at Cupertino. The company he focused on a second time as his savior was none other than IBM, still smarting from its wounding at the hands of Gates and Grove. It was not a bad pick: the courtship of Taligent and foreplay of the PowerPC joint venture both pointed toward a consummation of the relationship he had once initiated. Apple, as it had seven years before, desperately needed IBM's financial firepower, distribution channels and business market cachet. IBM, conversely, would gain from Apple a PowerPC architecture that worked better than its own abortive efforts, and better yet, the jewel in the crown, the Mac OS. Put that baby on the Intel chip, and Microsoft, Compaq, Dell and all the other jumped-up pretenders to the throne could watch Big Blue's dust. IBM would be back on top where it belonged.

At least that was the case that Spindler intended to make with the white-shirt boys in Armonk. And it seemed to work. By the late summer of 1994, negotiations between IBM and Apple were heating up. Finally, IBM was ready to deal. It offered $50 per share for Apple, then selling at about $45. It was a good offer, but not a great one. In retrospect, Spindler should have jumped on the deal and dropped to his knees to thank God for his deliverance. But he was worshipping before a different altar. As one associate would say: "The Macintosh is a religion to Mike, and he wants to see it sustained."

Now Spindler would pay the cost of being Apple's last true believer. The IBM deal would have been perfect for any CEO but one who believed the Mac's true destiny was to rule. But selling to Big Blue would have been consorting with a onetime enemy of the Mac, giving the product to a buyer that would likely junk the beautiful box and tinker with the operating system until it was just another of the tens of thousands of products in the IBM catalog. This wasn't the fate Mike Spindler had worked for all those long years flogging Apple products all over Europe.

Even then, Spindler might have sold, but for the fact that in late 1994 Apple was still on a tear. It was as if the Diesel had developed a strategy whose end play was the sale of the company, then performed the first part of the plan so brilliantly that he forgot why he'd embarked on the strategy in the first place. Apple could no longer survive on its own. In a world where Windows machines held more than 90 percent of the market, Apple was now little more than a rounding error on a pure monopoly.

But the numbers were so damn good that Spindler began to feel some of the old magic again. He grew cocky. Maybe, he asked himself, I really can save this company. And as the quarters of 1994 passed, each of them showing ever-increasing sales growth—5 percent in the first quarter, 17 percent in the second, 27 *percent* during the Christmas selling season—and with profits hovering between 25 percent and 30 percent, and even market share begin-ning to rise, Spindler stopped wondering and began to believe. He was going to save Apple. He would be Apple's savior and redeemer.

Recalled Tim Bajarin of Creative Strategies, who consulted Apple at the time, "Mike's nickname may have been the Diesel, but he had to be moti-vated by something to drive himself into the ground the way he did. I couldn't figure out what it was—until one day I had to leave a meeting to go make a phone call. Mike followed me and pulled me into a private conference room. 'Listen,' he said, 'This next generation of Mac OS is so good that Bill Gates will want it.'

"That's when I finally realized what was motivating Spindler. He wanted to beat Bill Gates at his own game. In operating systems. That's what had destroyed Ray Noorda (of Novell). And that's what almost killed Mike Spindler. Fighting Bill Gates is always bad for your health."

One person who knew better was Graziano. He was the man who ran the meters, and what those gauges showed him was a whole different story. What Graziano saw was that nothing had really changed; the good news of the last year was just a blip, a bit of momentary relief in what was still a growing tragedy. With overpriced products, declining distribution, fewer third-party software and hardware developers and a dwindling share of mind among consumers, Apple was still racing toward oblivion. Apple had merely benefited from a cusp year in the Wintel juggernaut. Microsoft had momentarily stumbled, the world was awaiting the arrival of the new Intel Pentium chips and no radically new boxes had appeared on the scene. That wouldn't last for long.

So Graziano watched in horror as the deal with IBM collapsed. Then a deal Spindler nearly brokered with Philips missed by a single vote of the Philips board. Another deal, with Sun Microsystems (yet another contact brokered by Regis McKenna), was intermittently on and off because Spindler didn't seem to have respect for Sun's boss, Scott McNealy. Then Spindler began to behave as if Apple was no longer interested in a merger or buyout. There were rumors on the street that one hot firm after another—Silicon Graphics, Oracle—was eyeing Apple. Oracle's CEO, Larry Ellison, not known for either subtlety or sanity, almost acted like a humble suitor when he announced that "if Apple should want to merge, we would be honored." But Spindler didn't follow up on any of these hints. Instead, he seemed to dismiss them, saying that, short of an "indecent" proposal, "there's no strategic fit that makes sense." What? Anybody who read the newspaper could identify a half dozen companies that could make good use of Apple—and even if they couldn't, who cared? Apple wasn't buying, it was selling. The employees would get some job security, the technology would survive, customers would, at least for a while, see some product stability and investors would get a nice payoff. Who would lose?

But Spindler plunged on. And glorious 1994 became disastrous 1995. The exploding PowerBooks, the wrong forecast, the missing new operating system. Then the capstone: on August 24, 1995, Microsoft, two years late, finally introduced its second-generation Windows product. It was now called Windows 95, and its formal introduction—taking place with its arrival on computer store shelves throughout the world at exactly midnight—was the biggest media event the personal computing industry had seen since . . . the Macintosh introduction. Hundreds of thousands of PC owners queued up in late-night parking lots in Manhattan, Paris, Bombay, Jakarta and a thousand other sites around the world. Soft-drink and fast-food distributors vied for the right to sell to these masses. It was the single most important mass cultural event between the Gulf War and the death of Princess Diana.

This is what it had come to, two decades after Steve Jobs's perhaps apocryphal moment getting robbed selling blue boxes in a Sunnyvale parking lot. Now it was a kind of robbery on a global scale, not the least of which at the supermarket-sized Fry's department store on the other side of Sunnyvale. Like all mythic occasions, the Windows 95 introduction captured the zeitgeist of the era: unembarrassed millions lining up Soviet style for the chance to buy a second-rate product two years late from the world's richest private citizen . . . and thankful for the opportunity.

Windows 95, the apotheosis of Bill Gates, was inevitable. Until now, the electronics industry had known many great entrepreneurs, a few of them saints, many of them monsters, who had driven their companies to great success and industry dominance. But at some point, all of these men had stopped because they were bored, or distracted by the lure of other types of fame, or exhausted, or just hungry to enjoy their new wealth. But in Bill Gates, high tech had at last met the incorruptible man. Power was Bill Gates's greatest love, and his hunger for it seemed insatiable. The great guessing game of Silicon Valley (and eventually the world) in the 1990s was: What does Bill Gates want? And the terrifying answer was always the same: He wants everything. And one thing Bill Gates had wanted since he was little more than a teenager, was the Apple magic.

Every company bears the stamp of its founder, and Microsoft was no exception. It was filled with young people, many of them made wildly rich by the company, the others hoping to do the same, and all of them without any doubt that Microsoft's success, its endless bullying of every industry near it, was a just cause. Even if it meant destroying the electronics revolution in the process. Microsoft stultified every technology it touched, but it also gave that technology to the world at a low price with a promise of perpetual, if slowed, innovation, and offered the security of knowing that it came from a company that knew how to win.

It was a devil's pact each customer made when signing on with Windows, but that was the point. Unlike Apple, Microsoft seemed to know what it was doing. If it wasn't exciting, it also wasn't unpredictable. Join Microsoft and you joined the Great Mass: designers developed for you; stores set aside their aisles for you; you could swap files with the employee down the hall; and most of all, you didn't have to be a rebel anymore and suffer all the discomforts and humiliations that came with rebellion.

But if Microsoft's run-up to the Windows 95 introduction was predictable—late, arrogant, offering less than it seemed to promise, but available everywhere in good quality at a low price backed by whole libraries of new applications—Apple's response was not. At least not to anyone who still believed the myth. Faced with the biggest single competitive threat in its history, an operating system that duplicated much of what the Mac OS could do and yet offered many things (multiprocessing) it could not, Apple did . . . nothing. Well, almost nothing: there were those pissy bumper stickers seen all over Cupertino that read "Windows 95, Macintosh 84." Cute, accurate, but utterly meaningless because it wasn't 1984 anymore, but 1995, and Microsoft had just produced a perfect cubic zirconium copy of Apple's crown jewel.

In the decade since his departure, Steve Jobs's loss was never felt more acutely than in those days when Microsoft was making front pages all over the world. Since 1990, *five* years, Apple had known Microsoft was coming. It didn't take a rocket scientist to appreciate that, faced with this upcoming event, Apple Computer had only one real priority: come up with its next-generation operating system. If it didn't, relentless Microsoft would eventually catch up and, having achieved parity with Apple in the only place Apple still had an advantage, would quickly crush it with its superior manufacturing, marketing and enormous market base.

Everybody knew that was true. Fourth graders knew it. And yet Apple wasted those years on Newton and upgrades to the current OS, endless hardware permutations, education programs, sponsorships of concerts and television shows . . . everything but getting the damn operating system ready. Copland, the hope of Apple, had turned into a black hole, sucking up money and talent and producing nothing.

Steve Jobs may have been an executive horror and spoiled brat, but nobody ever accused him of missing an opportunity. And as Windows 95 rolled out with totalitarian irresistibility, you couldn't help musing what Apple under Jobs would have done in response. One thing for sure, there would have been a new OS not only in the works but already introduced. And even if it wasn't ready, Jobs would still have announced it just to steal Gates's thunder. One could almost imagine the full-page ad in *The Wall Street Journal* and the *New York Times*: "You Waited Five Years for a Second-Rate Product, How About Waiti ng Six Months More for the Greatest Operating System in History?" in Apple's unmistakable typeface on a white background. That was what playing to win looked like. That was what had made Jobs's Apple, for all of its manifold flaws, so magnificent. Apple had long forgotten what the burn of that fire felt like.

9.4 IAGO

At the October board meeting in Austin, Graziano made his move. He knew that Apple was headed for the rocks; both his business sense and his financial indicators told him so. The company was resting its bloated hulk on a foundation of sand. No one could save Apple but him, and he had spent months building support within the company, finding allies in the likes of Dan Eilers.

Eilers was now the number two man at Apple, having joined the firm as part of the Lisa project way back in 1982—and he had been one of the happiest to see Jobs go. After that, he'd been vice president for strategic planning, president of Claris and, since April, senior vice president for worldwide marketing. Eilers, who had as much institutional memory as anyone left at Apple, also had a bad feeling about the direction in which the company was heading. And despite being the ultimate Apple team player, he too secretly threw in his lot with the CFO.

Now was Graziano's chance to capture the support of his fellow board members. He had the perfect venue—a board of directors meeting, with CEO/director Spindler in attendance—and what he was convinced was a compelling case.

As the board members, and not least Spindler himself, listened with growing uneasiness, Graziano presented his argument: the year-to-year gains Apple was enjoying right now were a smoke screen hiding deep and perhaps mortal problems in the company. Disaster was waiting around the corner. Apple had made a terrible mistake in not selling out to IBM, and it would be making an even greater mistake if it didn't land another corporate buyer right away.

The room was silent, though as the other directors listened they began to twist in their chairs, some even to tremble with anger. One director would say that "the body language was incredible."

Graziano thought he was getting his point across. He never raised his voice, but spoke in measured, intimate, almost funereal tones—as if Apple, enjoying one of the most successful years in its history, was ready to be fitted for a shroud. Over and over during the presentation, Graziano repeated that this was not meant to be a coup against Mike Spindler and that he, Graziano, didn't want the CEO job. When it was over, Graziano thanked his fellow directors and, on Markkula's orders, left the room (as did Spindler) convinced that he had saved Apple and turbocharged his own career. The hero had met his greatest challenge—*veni, vidi, vici!*

But the moment the door closed behind Graziano, the board members caught their breath, then turned to one another with raised eyebrows and shaking heads. A couple even made the thumbs-down sign. Graziano thought he had won over the room, but what the room saw was an ambitious vice president making a devious run at the top job by playing Cassandra. The men in the room saw Graziano's behavior as cowardly, his voice "whining." "If you're there saying you've got to throw the guy out, you've got to throw the guy out," said one.

Katherine Hudson was a bit more sympathetic. She told *CFO* magazine, "He felt morally and ethically obligated to make this pitch because he was a member of the board. I can sympathize with this." But notice that she too said "pitch." Nobody was fooled by Graziano's protestations of his own disinterest.

And there was one thing all the board members agreed upon. It was that Graziano had come woefully unprepared to make his case. He was the CFO for Christ sakes! Where was his evidence? The only financials the directors saw were glowing. Did Graziano have other figures to support his argument? And if he did, had he shown them to Spindler? Had he tried to help Apple or only himself? And how could you trust a guy with the reins of a giant corporation if he couldn't even run a coup d'état without fumbling it?

It was one of those moments, much more common in literature than in real-life business, when a person's greatest moment is also his worst. When Graziano walked out of the boardroom, he was on top of the world. A few hours later that world had fallen on him.

The irony—one more for the long Apple list—is that both sides were right. The message Graziano brought that day was an accurate one, as the board and the world would soon learn. But he also wore his ambition on his sleeve. Given a decision between Spindler, who honestly seemed to put the company first and who had achieved a measurable level of success, and Graziano, who seemed to be leveraging off the company's potential misfortune to improve his own résumé, the decision was clear. Graziano was gone. And if Apple's board of directors shot the messenger, well, some messengers deserve it.

But Graziano was also telling the truth. Had he been more generous and presented his case more selflessly, or more professional and proved his point with charts and graphs, or more cynical and waited until the troubles began, he might have saved Apple. But instead, he had forced the board to stand forthright behind Spindler at the worst possible moment. Now they were committed to keeping the Diesel behind the wheel as the bus went off the cliff. And who better to do the driving than a man heading for a crash himself?

Remarkably, having just been handed his head, Graziano asked Markkula if he might hitch a ride on Mike's jet back to Silicon Valley. Equally remarkably, the third passenger was another director, Gil Amelio.

It was a very strained trip. No one knew what to say. As Amelio remembered: "He must have convinced himself of being right and figured at least a fifty-fifty chance of succeeding. But he had failed miserably, to a degree he must not have foreseen as a possibility. Though he didn't lack for money, he was flying home to no job, no income and, it must have seemed a clouded future."

Inevitably, the stilted conversation came around to what had just happened, and as it did, Graziano became more and more upset. Finally he began to sob. Had any other company caused so many tears?

Mortified, Amelio tried to change the subject. He knew Graziano was a Ferrari fiend, so he asked, "Joe, I've been thinking about buying a sports car. What do you think? Can you give me a recommendation?"

Relieved, Graziano dried his tears and launched into a monologue about the relative merits of different Ferraris.

9.5 AERIE

Graziano's Last Stand, as it came to be called, did more than rob Apple of its smartest internal analyst. It also broke Mike Spindler.

It had been a year of unbearable contradictions, apogees and nadirs. The company had record sales and profits. It had the hottest new products in the industry. But it couldn't get its laptops to work for much of the year. It had made inaccurate market forecasts that had cost it a magnificent opportunity. The company's second tier of top managers had embarked on a failed mutiny that had now cost Apple its superb CFO and soon, thanks to a "reorganization" that was in a fact a punishment for disloyalty, its number two executive, Dan Eilers. Add that to the departure early in the year of Ian Diery and the director of Apple Japan and Spindler had either lost, turned on or been betrayed by and then fired much of his inner circle. And, of course, Microsoft had now introduced a product that essentially negated Apple's last real technological advantage.

Spindler was now left alone in his Cupertino tower, knowing his Grand Strategy had failed. Even at the top of his game, Spindler had been a brusque, isolated, socially inept manager. But now the situation grew bizarre. In public, he ran from reporters, even well-wishers. And there were stories of him hiding behind his desk, ducking unwelcome visitors. He still talked a good game when forced to. But Michael Spindler knew what was coming, and he could only hold on and await its impact.

He didn't have to wait long. The unraveling of high-tech companies usually occurs at a stunning pace. Great companies appear to be rolling along just fine, their employees bustling about, new products in the works, conferences being held, users groups holding meetings—and then everything suddenly implodes. It happened at Wang, Digital Equipment and Atari before Apple, and at Borland, Conner Peripherals and Silicon Graphics after. In an industry where success and technological leadership are worshipped above all and loyalty is an archaic notion among employers, employees and customers, once a great firm stumbles or shows weakness it is quickly abandoned by friends and devoured by enemies.

In personal computing, the situation was only marginally better, primarily because the amount of intellectual and financial capital that users had to invest in hardware, software and training was high enough to make them dread the prospect of switching computer architectures. Also working to Apple's advantage was the growing dread and resentment of the hegemony of Bill Gates and Microsoft. The Windows 95 introduction would prove to be the high-water mark of Microsoft's reputation. From now on, fearful (with good reason) of the rule of a monopoly in computer software—and soon the Internet—the world would begin to turn on Microsoft.

And there was one other factor as well working in Apple's favor as it entered its greatest crisis. There were millions of people who still believed in Apple. Not the company, nor even its products, but the myth of Apple itself. More than the Mac, more than the Apple II and certainly more than the reality of the company itself, Apple had created a vision of a new kind of enterprise, a new way of approaching the world that had resonated now with generations of computer owners. It had proved to be only a minority view, but that only cemented its case. This myth was Jobs's and Woz's greatest invention and it had now long outlived them at the company they founded.

If there weren't enough of these true believers to keep Apple strong, there were enough to keep it alive. And in a few months, Apple, which had turned down a multibillion-dollar offer from IBM just a year before, would be happy to settle for staying alive.

"Apple always had a good athletic program run by the employees and held at Foothill [Junior] College," recalled Eric Krugler, "I played on some softball and volleyball teams there. One person I met there from Apple was a junior financial analyst. He told me that Apple was heading to profit margins under twenty percent. At the time, our margins were thirty-five percent.

"But sure enough, by the next year the margins were twenty percent. I've always wondered: Why did some junior financial analyst know this and senior management didn't?

"There was some critical information being filtered somewhere at Apple. Valuable information that was being ignored or not getting through."

9.6 UNRAVELING

By Christmas, the nightmare scenario Graziano described and Spindler feared was beginning to play itself out.

It went like this: Following the poor forecasts at the beginning of the year, Apple pumped up production by 30 percent in an effort to catch up during the usually strong Christmas season. But the Windows 95 announcement, and the run-up to that announcement, temporarily slowed the company's sales. Faced with the prospect of excess inventory, and simultaneously caught in an unexpected price war on personal computers in Japan, Apple then did what Spindler had feared: it cut prices, reducing the price difference between Macs and comparable PCs from $1,000 to just $320. That made Macs more desirable, but those cuts came at the expense of profit margins.

The cuts were across the board, on nearly every company model, and in some cases were as great as 30 percent. Unfortunately, this discounting didn't have its desired effect—it didn't sell enough entry and mid-level models to new customers. Instead, recognizing a temporary bargain, both new customers and Apple's veteran customers used the opportunity to pick up high-end Macs. Before long, instead of a surplus, there was a shortage of these high-end models, the most profitable computers in the company's catalog. So now, having slashed prices and profits, Apple could no longer make up the difference through volume.

There was no turning back. Graziano's indicators were now going crazy.

The good news was that, for the first time in many years, Apple's market share jumped—from just less than 8 percent in mid-1995 to nearly 10 percent by year's end. Unfortunately, capturing that added market share so quickly had devastated all of the company's other financials. Gross profit margins fell from their 1994 high of nearly 30 percent to just 20 percent, and revenue growth slumped from 28 percent to just 15 percent. Apple was growing, but killing itself in the process. Cash reserves were sinking fast—so low ($200 million) that a week before Christmas both Standard & Poor's and Moody's started reviews of the company's credit.

Needless to say, the stock was in free fall as well. From just kissing $50 per share at the middle of the year, Apple stock by year's end had slumped to less than $30—a figure not much above the company's book value of $23.50 per share. That made the company takeover bait; but at a selling price far less than what it had turned down fifteen months before. To no one's surprise, by year's end rumors were racing around Silicon Valley that Sun Microsystems, that hot-dog computer workstation maker up the road that'd almost run itself into the ground until it all but tripped over the Java programming language for the Internet, was in serious negotiations about purchasing Apple with some of its newfound riches.

Sun was, in fact, in play. But it was a measure of Apple's predicament that Sun's opening bid, when it came in, was in the high 20s—less than Apple's market price!

This was an insult. But it was not made flippantly. The opening bid reflected a sober—and, as would soon be apparent, accurate—appraisal of Apple's future. With Spindler's Grand Strategy in shambles, and no killer hardware or software products waiting in the wings, Apple now had no choice but to become a different company, one that competed on price, manufacturing and product quality—everything the company wasn't good at. Sun's offer said that Apple might not yet be in the commodity business, but it was on its way. Everything had hinged on Apple maintaining its high prices and margins through product differentiation, and now that difference was gone. It would now have to slug it out in the mud with everyone else, and given the company's character and history, few gave it much hope of being able to do so.

And even as all this was happening, Apple had no choice but to keep building market share by undercutting profits. The only chance now was a paradoxical strategy of having to dig a deep enough hole to be able to regain its destiny and climb out. Thus, by the end of the year, Apple was offering added discounts to its largest resellers and slashing prices still further on its PowerBooks and on the top-of-the-line PowerPC Macs it could still deliver in a reasonable time.

9.7 WHIPLASH

There are few things more devastating to a company than to abruptly switch its business model. The torque of that change is felt in every office, and in every career, in the company. Suddenly, nothing works quite right. Every piece of paper the company produces is out of synchronization with where the company is now going. Employees whose skills and talents were uniquely suited to the company now find themselves horribly out of place and disoriented. Meanwhile, some marginal employees who never really fit in the organization, whose jobs were perpetually precarious, now find themselves the ideal people to help lead the company in its new direction. Power shifts back and forth and up and down. Rules of behavior and notions of best business practices are thrown out or revised. The entire process is so dislocating, so unproductive and so destructive that few companies that ever attempt it survive the process. And those that do, emerge as such vastly different enterprises from the ones that entered the tunnel that, but for the logo and name, they might as well be new companies.

Apple went into that tunnel in December 1995, with no idea of how or when it would come out. It entered as the manufacturer of a proprietary computer family sold at a premium. Some, perhaps all, of those characteristics were now untenable. Some, perhaps all, would have to be jettisoned. But how? And what would replace them? After twenty years of intense competition, almost every market niche in personal computing was filled. In every direction, a giant company, many of them as big as Apple, squatted directly in the company's path. Mass-market a Windows clone and Compaq would crush you. Custom-build budget machines and you ran into Dell and Gateway 2000. Laptops? IBM, Toshiba, NEC, Compaq, Hitachi and Acer had every market segment sewn up. Peripherals? Network computers? Hello Hewlett-Packard.

Apple seemed checkmated. And that proximate predicament argued then for an even more radical move. Perhaps specialty machines for education or graphics design, Apple's last two market strengths. But would schools train their kids on computers they wouldn't use as adults? And were there any margins left in that market? As for graphics, going after that tiny market was like declaring yourself a permanent bit player.

There was another market emerging, the Internet, that supposedly was going to explode. And early reports were that all the good Web page designers were doing their development work on Macs. But who knew where that was going?

Then how about something *really* radical? Like getting out of computers altogether. But then where would Apple go? Software? But it had no Copland. Consumer products? Like the *Newton?* There was talk of a new class of hardware emerging, the so-called network computer being stumped by Oracle's Larry Ellison, that would be a low-cost (under $1,000) half-empty box (no disk memory) optimized for cheaply surfing the Internet. An interesting notion, and certainly the talk of that year's Comdex, but no one knew whether it could be built at that price and make any money—or if anyone would even buy it with full-blown PC prices already down to $1,500 and falling.

But as Apple entered 1996 and prepared for its annual meeting, all of those considerations would have to wait. Even if the company made a strategic decision, the impact of that choice wouldn't be felt for a year or more. Right now, the company had to deal with the consequences of the past. It would now have to endure the purifying fire of failure.

9.8 PLUMMET

When the numbers appeared, they were breathtakingly bad. Worse than anyone outside the company had imagined. Sales for the first quarter ended December 31 amazingly were up to $3.15 billion. But it meant next to nothing, because margins had utterly collapsed amid all the discounting. For the quarter, Apple lost $69 million, or 56 cents per share. That was compared to profits of $188 million ($1.55 per share) the year before. This was a quarter-billion-dollar swing in profits for a company with sales of just $9 billion.

And that wasn't even the worst of it. Apple might have been able to justify some of these losses in the name of capturing market share. But Windows 95 had taken care of that. Thus, Apple's market share, which had climbed back to nearly 9 percent in the fourth quarter ended the previous September, had now slumped back to 7.4 percent, two percentage points less than when Spindler had taken over the company. And it wasn't going to get any better. Apple had no important new software or hardware products in the works for at least a year. And this was just the first broadside—it had pulled down a mast and chewed up some sails. The next financial blast, three months from now, would be aimed at Apple's hull.

Spindler now had no real strategy but to react with damage control. He ordered another round of layoffs, the second in his brief career as CEO. This time it was 1,300 people, though everyone knew that would not be enough. Literally risking death, reading the calumny directed toward him in the press and in the eyes of his fellow Apple employees, Spindler soldiered on. He convinced himself that he could still save Apple.

But first he had to save himself. The annual meeting and the board of directors meeting lay dead ahead.

9.9 PILLORY

Everyone was worried about Michael.

It was one thing to fire a guy, another to kill him. And sitting there at the long board table in the Venrock offices on the fifty-fifth floor of Manhattan's Rockefeller Center, his heavy face pale and melted, Michael Spindler looked like a dying man. Word was that on January 8, three weeks before, Spindler had checked into the hospital with heart palpitations.

It wasn't supposed to happen this way. Sure, everybody believed the Apple Computer myth. The users did, the programmers did, even the senior managers. But it was like all childhood myths; one day when harsh reality just became too self-evident, you gave up the fantasy and moved on to a more realistic adulthood. Nobody ever martyred themselves for the Tooth Fairy.

Steve Jobs certainly didn't believe the myth and he invented it. If Jobs believed anything, it was in his own glory. And Sculley believed only in his career. Both were perfectly happy to let the Apple cult thrive so long as it reflected upon them.

But Spindler was supposed to be the businessman, the technology guy, the Diesel. The Teutonic salesmeister who'd turned Apple Europe into a powerhouse. Spindler was the guy who always talked about pragmatism. When he told Forbes, "I'm as much of a dreamer as anyone else, but I'm also a realistic businessman," everybody thought he was just kidding about the first part. He wasn't supposed to believe in the myth.

The nightmare had begun on Tuesday, January 23, 1996, the day of Apple's annual meeting. Behind the scenes, the company had once more been negotiating with Sun Microsystems—and Sun, despite having been blown off by Spindler, was once more acting interested in getting its hands on Apple to fill out the bottom of its product line. Even Sun's chief technologist, Eric Schmidt, one of the canniest press manipulators in Silicon Valley, had been quoted as saying that Apple was a "strong brand."

Negotiating teams were meeting every day now up in Palo Alto in the offices of Valley überlawyers Wilson Sonsini Goodrich & Rosati. Larry Sonsini was a player—the man who had so many IPO Lucite cubes on his shelves that they nearly demolished his office and killed a secretary when they fell during the Loma Prieta quake, the man who saved the MIPS's IPO with a single telephone call to the SEC—so something was going to happen.

Sun would play, and soon. No doubt about it. The company had recently offered $33 a share for Apple stock. Still not enough, of course, but just a few bucks light from where it ought to be at, say, $40 a share. So the trick was to spend a couple of hours doing duck-and-cover with the angry shareholders at the annual meeting, look thoughtful, answer their complaints sincerely and not say anything that might scare off Sun and queer the deal. Just run the gauntlet and keep telling yourself that all will be forgiven and forgotten in a few days when Sun buys everybody's problems away.

The Diesel was the biggest worry. It was he who would have to sit there on the dais and answer for the company's falling margins (down to 15 percent from a peak of 42 percent a decade before ago), slipping market share and $69 million loss in the fourth quarter.

The Copland operating system, the erstwhile savior of Apple, the Windows 95 killer, was still not ready—and now there were rumors it might never be ready.

Worst of all, there was a potential bombshell hiding in warehouses all over the world: $1 *billion* in unsold inventory; computers and peripherals that were supposed to be sold off during the Christmas season, and now might very well end up in that notorious Arizona landfill where Atari bulldozed all of its obsolete products just before that company crashed.

Spindler was a man of enormous pride. He blamed himself for this debacle. And though PR had thoroughly coached him to stay cool as the shareholder lynch mob roared over him, there was grave concern that he might crack under the stress.

But he didn't, even though the meeting was a howling storm of shareholder fury. These were, after all, not just investors in some company from which they expected a predictable return. Those people invested in Compaq or Dell. No, the people who came to the Apple annual meeting to wave their six or fifty or 20,000 shares were stakeholders in the revolution, they had bought into the dream of the Little Kingdom . . . and now not only their bankbooks but their faith had been betrayed.

An hour later, the board's pro forma commitment to a shareholders meeting complete, the gathering was adjourned and the management team staggered off to a nearby meeting room for a press conference. There, at the front table, fielding not only tough questions from the mainstream press but even zingers from the normally lapdog computer magazines, were ex-chairman and co-founder Mike Markkula and Mike Spindler, peeking with frightened eyes around his hands as they folded as if in prayer against his face, looking ready to disintegrate at any moment.

But again, the Diesel, through sheer force of will, survived. Under the pressure, his heart didn't explode. Then word came that the Sun offer had just arrived. Right in front of the assembled press, a relieved Markkula even put his hand on Spindler's shoulder and declared, "I like this guy. He's a very good person."

The directors retired to Apple's boardroom in a state of excitement to review Sun's offer. *God bless Scott McNealy.* An Apple-Sun combination would strike fear into the heart of IBM (again), Hewlett-Packard, Silicon Graphics and just about anyone else who put chips in a box.

The offer was read. Before it was half completed, the board knew that redemption had decided to bump its appointment. *Twenty-five* bucks a share, seven dollars off their offer of just a few days before. Twenty-five bucks! That was the goddamn *book* value. That was what Sun was offering for Apple in a stock swap. They didn't have to read the stock tables in the newspapers beside them to know that Apple that day was selling for a tick over $31. It was an insult. Scott McNealy was trying to fire-sale them. The shareholders, that angry mob just getting into their cars outside, were never going to go for it.

"The board really thought they would come out with a deal and all would be forgiven," an insider told *Business Week.*

Not this time. Now they were stuck with the place. The board called an emergency evening session and the parade began. One manager after another—from sales, from manufacturing, from international, from education, from the labs—marched in and did a core dump of everything that was wrong. Some were defensive, some tried to be optimistic, others were glad to finally get a hearing and blow off.

And the board members just sat stupefied, barely saying a word. *My God, it's even worse than we figured,* each of them thought in one manner or another. *How are we going to fix this and get out alive?*

It was nearly midnight when the board at last adjourned to stagger off to limousines and hotel suites and corporate jets. But even as they did they knew this was no "Thanks for the dinner, see you next quarter" board meeting. This was not going to go away. Whatever their manifold other commitments, the Little Kingdom was going to be foremost in their minds in the weeks to come.

It didn't even take that long. By the next morning, the denunciations had begun. First in the press, and then among major shareholders. It came in waves. First up were the newspapers, which pilloried Spindler and Apple for not only doing nothing about the company's plight but not even having a clue about what to do next.

The rest of the industry took its shot as well. Venture capitalist John Doerr, bitter that his ally in the two-front war against Microsoft was blowing up and abandoning his litter of new Internet start-ups, said with uncharacteristic rancor, "Apple's management ought to be tried for war crimes." Most devastating of all, because of its precise and chilly description by Apple's most veteran reporter of everything that had gone wrong at the Little Kingdom over the last five years, was Kathy Rebello's cover story in *Business Week*. Its devastating title was "The Fall of an American Icon."

Then came the shareholders, especially the big institutional investors. Rumors of the negotiations with Sun had leaked out, and the big shareholders, who had assumed that Apple would take the low-ball offer, were hopping mad. Faxes were coming in. Letters. Phone calls. E-mails. Everybody was shrieking for the board not to take Sun's offer. Well, hell, that was easy: the board didn't want it either. No, we stick with Spindler; Markkula likes him, he says he's got a plan. What other choice is there?

Each day for the rest of the week, new reports of disasters from the front poured in. From every sales region, stories were flying back to Cupertino that key customers weren't reordering, but instead were waiting to see if Apple was going to pull itself out of this newest swamp. Pissed-off shareholders you could deal with—give them good financial news and all is forgiven. But when customers start complaining, then you're on the fast slide to corporate death.

After a long weekend trying to recover, the board was hit with an even harder body blow first thing Monday morning, the 29th: Standard & Poor downgraded a bunch of Apple's debt to junk. In other words, S&P, the arbiter of corporate value, had just announced to every Apple distributor, consultant, supplier and contractor that Apple IOUs were all but worthless. Standard & Poor had just made Apple a corporate leper.

That did it. It was time to forget friendships and start throwing bodies overboard. Time to say adios, Michael Spindler. The Diesel would be making no more long hauls for Apple.

Markkula called an emergency board meeting for Tuesday, January 30, at the St. Regis Hotel and the Venrock offices in Manhattan. Spindler was invited too. He brought his wife along and seemed unaware of the fate awaiting him.

The board members rode together from the St. Regis to Rockefeller Center, no one giving the slightest hint to Spindler of what was to come. Once there, fearful of making Spindler's termination the penultimate one, the board members broke the news gently. Markkula, who had approved the Diesel's hiring sixteen years before and watched as the promising young German salesman had risen up through the ranks, led the meeting. It was touching. Spindler fought heroically to stay on. He had made some mistakes, he said, but his overall strategy had been right. It still was. The key was to focus on the execution.

But the board was firm in its resolve. He was out. Markkula walked his shattered, but proud ex-CEO to the door, then left him to wander back to his wife and home to global humiliation. Apple's last boardroom romantic was gone.

Apple needed a new CEO, and it needed him *now*. With the company's business imploding there was no time to go on a multimonth star search for talent. Nor, given the company's current reputation for management incompetence, was there any possibility of promoting up from inside. Besides, the only Apple executive qualified for the job had been Dan Eilers, head of worldwide marketing. But he had sided with Graziano and Spindler had canned him.

No, it would have to be some near-insider, somebody the chairman already knew, respected and could work with. It would be Markkula's call. Markkula, always invisible, but always there for the big purges. He already knew whom he wanted in the job.

That man, sitting there at the same table, looking like a middle-aged refrigerator repairman, was Gil Amelio.

Amelio, fifty-two, the current CEO of National Semiconductor Corp., was everything Apple wasn't. And that was part of his appeal. He was a friendly, badly dressed, socially awkward, honest, plain-spoken engineer, and thus the very antithesis, in some ways, of every Apple CEO who had come before him.

Amelio also had a reputation as a turnaround artist. He had come out of the second, Les Hogan–Wilf Corrigan, era of Fairchild—a nice little irony when one remembered that Jobs built Apple as a rebuttal to the old Fairchild-Valley way of doing business. Then Gil had spent a dozen years running the semiconductor operations at Rockwell, where he'd turned an obsolete operation into an industry player. And for the last half decade he'd taken on the turnaround of National Semi, an old Valley chip dinosaur with an unsavory reputation. Amelio had pulled that company up from losses of $151.4 million in 1991 to a record profit of $264.2 million by streamlining operations, abandoning old product lines and focusing the firm on peripheral processors and microcontrollers rather than continuing to beat itself to death trying to knock down the impregnable walls of Intel in microprocessors.

Amelio was also a working engineer, with sixteen patents to his credit. He was even a certified jet pilot, just like Mike Markkula, a topic the two discussed nearly as much as Apple on their flight home together in Markkula's plane. Still, they talked enough about business for Markkula to offer Amelio the job. Amelio, despite having been given three warnings about the cost of joining Apple—Graziano's tears, Jobs's scheming visit and Spindler's disintegration—accepted the job.

By 8 A.M., when A Clean Well-Lighted Place for Books opened its doors just a mile down the road from Apple headquarters, employees were already waiting to rush in and buy Amelio's new book, *Profit from Excellence*, a typically dreary, self-congratulations-disguised-as-sober-advice, CEO business tome that had gone largely unnoticed. Now it was flying off the shelves. After all, if you are going to suck up to the new boss, it certainly couldn't hurt to have a suitably well-worn copy of *PFE* on your shelf when the old man happens to walk by.

Both of Apple's CEOs, the newly minted and the newly deposed, went that morning to their respective offices, as if nothing had changed. This, of course, was the traditional Executive Quadrille. *You* knew everything had changed. Everyone around you knew everything had changed. By tomorrow morning the press would be reporting rumors that everything had changed. But until the Securities and Exchange Commission and Nasdaq were properly notified, *nothing* had changed.

That afternoon, Amelio notified National's board—in particular, Charlie Sporck—that he was resigning. The meeting took twenty minutes. Gil told the board that he had not sought the Apple job, but having been offered it, he was going to take it. For America's sake.

The news, to put it mildly, was not taken well.

Charlie had never much liked Amelio. Part of it was that Amelio was from the wrong family of Fairchildren. He wasn't first-generation, like Sporck and Noyce and Sanders, the men who built high tech's most mythical company, then tore it apart to build Silicon Valley. Amelio had been a minor player in Fairchild's second generation, the apostasy of Hogan and Corrigan, the Motorola cabal that had taken over Fairchild and had systematically, and arrogantly, driven it into the ground.

But it went deeper than that. Sporck had run National as his own fiefdom for twenty-five years, taken it from a falling-down little outfit based in New Jersey, moved it to Santa Clara, turned it into a billion-dollar giant, taken the Japanese invasion head-on and, though the company was crippled in the process, managed to hold the place together long enough for the good times. Then Amelio comes along, does a solid job in a rising market and the next thing you know he's a turnaround genius.

The old Valley vets gnawing on steaks and sucking on Camels in Mac's Tea Room in Los Altos laughed at that one. Months later one semiconductor demi-legend would take a pull on his gin on the rocks and say, "How the fuck did Gil Amelio ever get a rep as a turnaround artist. I mean, what did he do? Turn a piece-of-shit, third-rate chip house like Rockwell into a piece-of-shit, second-rate chip house? And all he had to do at National was not fuck it up while the U.S. chip industry came back." He laughed. "Apple thought in Gil Amelio it was getting the second coming."

Publicly, Sporck was polite. Older now, but still more than six feet tall, and still wearing the Zapata mustache of his early National days, his eyes hard as gravel, Sporck managed to say, "I was shocked and annoyed. I'm disappointed that he decided to bag it." For Charlie Sporck, that was diplomatic. Privately, he was furious. At Mac's he would say through gritted teeth, "I cannot believe a professional would behave in such a manner."

National had no choice but to accept Amelio's resignation. By then it was early afternoon. The stock exchanges had closed. Having considerable practice in such matters, the company chose to spend the rest of the day preparing a terse press release, vetted by the board and the corporate lawyers into shaved ice, and then sent it out the next morning.

Thus, at 8:30 A.M. on Friday, February 2, 1996, the world officially learned that Amelio had left National Semiconductor. And though, thanks to CNN, the *New York Times* and the Associated Press, everybody knew where he was going, the announcement of his hiring never appeared.

The day went on. No news. The markets closed for the weekend, and still no news. One by one the key newspapers on the East Coast, the Midwest and finally on the West Coast passed their deadlines and were put to bed. Apple, the company that had invented big-event tech publicity now couldn't even get a simple press release out on time—and when it did the story would already be old news.

The apparent reason for the delay, though Apple refused to comment in reply to the increasingly anxious press calls, was that Spindler and Markkula hadn't come to final agreement on the size of the Diesel's golden parachute. Why compensation negotiations would hold up an exit announcement was never clear. But little about Apple was clear anymore.

While this was going on, Spindler had time to compose and e-mail a message to those embattled survivors he'd left behind.

"Dear Colleagues: The end of a long voyage. A page in my life has turned," it began, followed by a rambling reminiscence of his years at Apple, of the good times and the bad. He blamed himself for all that had gone wrong—a noble sentiment, but exactly the wrong message for the legions of screwups, malcontents, myopics and empire builders at Apple who collectively bore at least as much responsibility for the current disaster as the Diesel.

Then the big, chest-baring finish: "So it's time for me to go! Mistakes or misjudgments made? Oh yes—even plenty. Both in business and personal judgment terms. I take personal responsibility for things that didn't work and should have worked. I tried to give it my best—both intellectually and physically in every corner of the world to carry this cause and its color."

It was just the kind of loopy, overwrought message to remind everybody that Michael Spindler was exactly the wrong person to have run Apple.

At last, at 6:45 P.M., in the closing darkness of the worst business week in Apple's history, the company finally sent out a missive. Michael Spindler had officially resigned as Apple's chief executive officer, replaced by Gilbert Amelio. Then a surprise: Amelio would also assume the title of Apple chairman, with A. C. "Mike" Markkula stepping down to his old title of vice-chairman. Markkula had retired again—and his move signaled that the play was now Gil's. Amelio and Apple would rise and fall together . . . and alone.

9.10 GONE TO GROUND

And alone was how Gil Amelio would play it for the next fourteen weeks. The world, or at least the dwindling part of the world that still shared or cared about Apple's fate, waited for a sign.

But the real sign was that there were no signs. No big press conferences. No massive layoffs. No sweeping pronouncements about the future. Amelio remained out of sight, by all reports quietly and systematically surveying the company, taking technical presentations, talking to outside observers.

No one before had ever been so apparently unaffected by the most famous bully pulpit in high technology. But no one who had run Apple before had been this much of an adult. It was comforting now to come to work in the morning and look up at the big glass double tower with its microprocessor motif on the top floors and know that behind the glass Gil Amelio was working to fix everything.

And the weeks passed. Business, such as it was, went on as usual. The middle managers read and reread and deconstructed *Profit from Excellence*, all the while looking for a puff of white smoke from the tower. The programmers went back to throwing the Frisbee on the lawn at Infinite Loop, eating sushi in the cafeteria and working on their own hermetic corner of the endlessly late Copland operating system. Occasionally a new rumor would pop up on their computer screen and they would laugh or momentarily freeze with dread. Then they would pass it on.

Some of the rumors were fantastic—that Jobs, Ellison and Lotus's Jim Manzi had made an accepted buyout offer—and would be proven untrue. Other rumors that were equally fantastic—that Copland would be killed and its design team fired *(Impossible! We've already spent too much)*—would in time prove true. And still others—the negotiations with Sun had permanently broken down—were quickly confirmed by the press.

But still, there was no word from Gil Amelio. Within hours of his appointment, he had asked for a hundred days to study the company and its problems, and amazingly enough, he actually meant it. For Apple, this consistency was almost breathtaking. Only in late April did he have a serious interview with the press, and then he merely outlined his long-term plans. No grandstanding. No posing. It was almost as if the man didn't have an ego.

Not that he was doing nothing. Like all smart CEOs, before his honeymoon with the public ended, Amelio dumped every obsolete piece of inventory he could find, thus sticking the blame where it belonged, on his predecessors. It was ugly: a $740 million loss in the first quarter of 1996—an amount big enough, had it been profits, to make Apple one of the hundred most successful companies in America. But even this devastating announcement was done ex cathedra, the press release sent out and Gil not available for interviews.

During his disappearance, Amelio also made a bold move: he met with Bill Gates. After six weeks as CEO, Gil decided he knew enough about Apple's predicament to meet with the man largely responsible for it.

Amelio had worked with Gates before, during his National Semiconductor days, so he knew a little of what to expect. Gates even offered to fly down to Cupertino, but Amelio preferred to fly with a small Apple contingent on his own jet to Redmond.

Gates met them graciously like old friends. Then, as the meeting began, and Gates launched into a long presentation on his long relationship with Apple—including old photos of him with Jobs—it seemed clear to the visitors that America's richest man was pained by the turn that relationship had taken in recent years. And since with Bill Gates the personal was also the commercial, part of the pain came from the fact that Microsoft's billion-dollar Mac software business was declining along with the fortunes of Apple.

When he and Gates retreated to the latter's office for a private conversation, Amelio was convinced that he was close to a deal—one in which Microsoft would agree to design its key programs (like Office) specifically for the Mac, not just translate them over from Windows in forms that were slow and unwieldy to load and use.

Gates refused, insisting instead that Amelio and Apple adopt Microsoft's new Web browser, Explorer—without a quid pro quo. The conversation ended there. For the rest of Amelio's time at Apple, the two would continue to talk and negotiate. But it went nowhere. In time, Amelio concluded: "Once he's explained his position, Bill sincerely can't understand why you don't want to do what he wants you to. On the other hand, when you make the point that the best deals are 'I'll scratch your back, you scratch mine,' he's ready with a list of excuses and reasons why that isn't possible in this case. I rapidly came to realize that Bill found it difficult to meet another person halfway."

Amelio came down from the tower on May 14, 1996, almost exactly five-score days since he had arrived at Apple. To a gathering of employees Amelio gave a sort of State of the Company address, which was to be part of the annual Apple Worldwide Developers Conference—a group even more important than Apple's own employees. The venue was to be the quarter-mile-long neo-Quonset hut of the San Jose McEnery Convention Center.

The hall was standing room only as Amelio stepped up to the podium. His chunky, avuncular image, projected on the giant screen above him, drew an audible murmur from large regions of the audience. Was this Apple's new image? Sure, Spindler had been heavyset and sloppily dressed, but at least he was German. An exotic. But think of Sculley and Jobs—both of them lean as whippets, bony and drawn as if the purity of their purpose had mortified their flesh to parchment.

And now . . . *this.* Gil Amelio, with his red tie, his square meat-and-potatoes face, his short wavy hair brushed straight back, looked like a high school shop teacher. Worse, in an era when nine-year-olds practice news bites in front of the mirror, and when corporate CEOs are as smooth in public as movie stars, Amelio behaved like an assistant plant supervisor at Dow Chemical in 1956 giving a presentation to the Wilmington Rotary Club. His hands shook with nerves and adrenaline as he made his first gesture. His voice wavered momentarily at the sight of thousands of anxious faces.

Then something happened. A gravity came into Amelio's face. It was if an iron weight settled into his jaw. Gil smiled. Not a warm grin, but a smile of power. "Can you believe all the press on this thing?" he asked. "You'd think I was going to part the Red Sea." Yes, yes, laughed the audience. That's exactly what we expect you to do.

Another smile. "Actually, it's kind of intimidating to be here in front of four thousand people, all of whom know more about the technical details of our computers than I do." A roar. Was this real humility by the CEO?

A heckler in the audience, no doubt one of those legions of employees who still believed Apple was a philosophy and not a moneymaking enterprise, shouted, "Take off your tie!" to the titters of hundreds of the like-minded throughout the hall. Gil ignored them, but for a millisecond his look said: Laugh now, clown. You are going to disappear long before my tie does.

Like good children, the audience sat up a little straighter in its folding chairs.

After that, the rest of the speech was anticlimax. Copland, the troubled new operating system that had been the Mac's long-awaited savior, would no longer wait to be presented in final form. Instead it would be chopped up, the best pieces currently ready would be part of the upcoming Mac OS 7.6. No more "insanely great" products of the Jobs era. Now we go for revenues whenever anything is ready to sell.

There was also to be a major simplification of Apple's incoherent eighty-product Mac family, a list so convoluted and redundant that few company employees, much less customers, could understand it.

There was also to be a reorganization—SOP for new CEOs—dividing the company into "independently competitive" hardware and software groups. The audience had heard that bullshit many times before and always ignored it. Much better, except to middle managers, was Amelio's announcement that henceforth the company would abandon its tradition of promoting only from within and would seek talent elsewhere: "In order to get the depth we want, we'll have to go outside."

Then even better news. Amelio announced that Apple's new focus for its products would be on the two hottest markets in computing: the Internet and multmedia. *Finally*, thought every developer in the room. Three years late on the former, five on the latter, but at last Apple is finally committing to two industries it helped create. Had the company done this when it should have, Apple would now *own* computing. No Netscape, no Silicon Graphics and only half a Microsoft.

By now the developers were getting aroused. Employees too. The dogs of the press were scribbling furiously. This might be it! The Apple Messiah, disguised as the head of the paint department at Orchard Supply Hardware. Amelio's unslickness, laughable at the beginning, was now a reason for celebration. Here was one guy too boring to lie to us. And too plodding to be anything but consistent.

It had come to this: Apple had sunk so low that the only person anyone believed was the one who obviously didn't belong there.

Feeling the crowd's growing support, Amelio responded by becoming ever more earnestly pedantic as the speech went on. And that only increased the crowd's ardor—until, by the trademark Amelio attenuated dead finish, the convention center had become a giant lovefest. Old Silicon Valley and New had bonded around their two common passions: technology and money.

It was a beautiful thing.

And that meant something was wrong. By this time the hall should have filled with wailing and the gnashing of teeth as the Apple dream died in its thousands of incarnations. Instead, there was applause and cheers. Gil was visibly heartened by this response, the absolutely wrong one from a company that desperately needed the corporate equivalent of shock therapy.

Had Gil Amelio looked down to his left, he would have seen a warning, an omen of the past and future. Sitting on the carpet between the front row and the speaker's platform, was Ben Weiss, Macintosh programming guru, his hair and beard falling on his chest, wearing a sleeveless, low-cut sarong shirt, brown corduroys and Birkenstocks, scrutinizing every bump on Gil's face through a little monocular telescope.

Weiss, like hundreds, maybe thousands, of others scattered throughout the hall, was a ghost of Apple Past. In the months to come, these ethereal keepers of the flame would haunt Amelio and bollix his attempts at change, sometimes by ignoring him, sometimes by fighting him, but most of all by embracing him.

But in the end, the greatest role of these wraiths would be incantatory: summoning back the greatest Apple ghost of them all: Steven Jobs.

On Tuesday, March 26, 1996, while Amelio and Apple were in their self-imposed quiet period, David Packard, Silicon Valley's patriarch, died quietly at age eighty-three.

A deep sadness fell over the Valley. In a rare tribute to a businessman, the news made headlines throughout the world. Thousands filled Stanford Chapel and the Quad for the funeral. The San Jose Mercury News devoted an entire special section in tribute.

It is the strange fate of business titans, the absolute value of their power in life often so much greater than that of entertainers or politicians or novelists, to be forgotten far sooner in death. But not David Packard. If every CEO stands in the shower each morning and dreams of immortality, Packard in life and death gave them a glimpse of what it really looked like. The greatest businessman in the history of the electronics revolution. And, if the sum of an enterprise's success, innovation and respect is the true measure, co-founder of the greatest American company of modern times.

The death of David Packard, and the effusions of tributes that followed, only threw Apple's latest troubles into sharper relief.

If Apple always talked revolution, HP actually lived it. Profit sharing, flex-time, tuition support, telecommuting . . . all HP organizational innovations that had changed the world as completely as its calculators, instruments and computers. In the end, it was always about character at HP, that secret ingre-dient that Apple had always lacked. And that character, made manifest in the famous HP Way, had its roots in the lives of David Packard and Bill Hewlett. Like Woz and Jobs, Bill and Dave had also met in their late teens, drawn together by a mutual interest in technology, in their case electronic test and measurement instruments.

But Bill and Dave were not only business partners but also best friends. They worked together, and played together, for sixty years. In all of those years, neither ever betrayed the other. In fact, there is no record of them ever having fought. Their respect for each other was boundless, and they shared that respect with everyone with whom they worked. In the words of ex-HPer and Valley entrepreneur Bill Krause, Packard was a hardhearted businessman who demanded perfection from everyone in the company, but when it came to his employees' lives, he was the most softhearted of men. In six decades, David Packard was never seen to belittle or humiliate an employee—or any-one else, for that matter. And to cap their magnificent careers, Bill and Dave, now among the richest men in America, joined their wives in creating two of the nation's largest philanthropies.

At the heart of Packard's greatness, of his character, was a rock-hard integ-rity. He did not lie. He did not assume credit for others' work—on the con-trary, he was comfortable giving credit and authority to people he thought more talented or more brilliant than he. And most of all, he was a man of his word, and his word was literally as good as gold. David Packard had always behaved maturely, gravely and with a deep sense of responsibility to those who worked for him and those who bought his products. Largely for these reasons, he and Bill had built a real company, with mass and form, a proud past and a hopeful future—all of the things Apple never had.

There was one other decisive difference between Hewlett and Packard and Wozniak and Jobs. It was that at HP, the founders never left. For a half century, Bill and Dave stayed at their posts, through good times and bad, protecting their people, maintaining the company's philosophy and myths, and defending HP from anyone who would put themselves before the com-pany.

It was this combination of integrity, trust and commitment that led to the extraordinary final act of these two remarkable men. At the beginning of the

1990s, HP, like Apple, was sinking into a decadence of executive perquisites, bloated bureaucracies, departmental fiefdoms and endless meetings. Bill and Dave were now in their eighties and increasingly in ill health. They had long since retired from the daily operations of the company and were now on the brink of retiring from the HP board of directors. But a memo changed all of that: a secretary, buried deep in the bowels of the company, wrote to Packard to tell him what was going wrong at his company.

Only a man like David Packard would have ever gotten such a note from an employee so far down the organization chart, and only a man like David Packard would have read the memo, understood its underlying meaning and taken action. Within a year, Packard and Hewlett had turned HP upside down, reorganized it, slashed away at the fat and replaced deadwood managers with dynamic ones. Two old men in their last hurrah, one of them literally just months away from the end. It was one of the most heroic accomplishments in business history. By Packard's death, Hewlett-Packard not only had regained its old energy but was growing as fast as any company of its size had ever done.

So, on that March day at Stanford, it was easy for one's heart to go out to Bill Hewlett, as he sat feebly in a wheelchair saying goodbye to his lifelong friend, and to the crowds of current and ex-HPers as they mourned the greatest human being they would ever meet. And it was hard to feel much sympathy for the predicament of the arrogant little tribe down the road in Cupertino.

9.11 REEMERGENCE

The Apple that emerged from Amelio's hundred days was a vastly different one from the company that began it. It was already on its way to becoming, if Amelio's strategy worked, a new company.

Amelio, to his credit, went about this reconstruction systematically and relentlessly. First, he changed the company's relationship with its shareholders. On February 12, he suspended the company's program, first begun in 1987, of awarding quarterly stock dividends. This had been a classic bit of Sculley's East Coast mentality. Silicon Valley companies, even wildly successful ones like Intel, didn't give out dividends. You wanna invest in a high-tech company, then you gotta play venture capitalist. You make your money on the stock appreciation; we reinvest the dividends for growth. Done.

Next up, the senior management. On February 29, Amelio announced the new title of chief administrative officer and hired corporate enforcer George

Scalise away from National. Sporck howled. So, soon, would Apple employees. Then, on March 7, Amelio announced the hiring of Fred Anderson, formerly CFO of Automatic Data Processing of Roseland, New Jersey, to take on the same post at Apple. Anderson had a rep for being able, and loyal. Then Amelio hired Ellen Hancock, who had quit National on the morning of Amelio's hundred-day speech. Hancock was one of the highest-ranking women scientists in American industry.

With his new team in place, Amelio turned to the company's operations.

In finance, Amelio recognized that for his turnaround plan to succeed—the process he publicly predicted at the May gathering would take three years—he would need a lot of cash. Cash flow, never a big concern at Apple, now became something of an obsession. And the company was burning cash fast: reserves fell almost by half in the first three months of 1996, from $1.1 billion to $592 million. This wasn't very much money for a company that needed to drive new-product development on multiple fronts *and* was still running in the red.

Next, Amelio went after Apple's products, software in particular. By the time of the speech, he had already killed the pathetic Copland, picking through its entrails for bits he could bolt onto the current System 7 Mac OS. He pushed for the speeded-up development of System 8, with added emphasis on its Internet capabilities. That still left all the pissed-off and alienated developers. As a bone to them, Apple hired, or more accurately, rehired Heidi Roizen. Roizen had been the best developer relations manager Apple had ever known. But like so many others, she had drifted off to try her hand at entrepreneurship. She had successfully co-founded T/Maker Co. in Mountain View, which published clip art programs and children's software.

Roizen knew what it was like to deal with a troubled Apple from within and without—especially without. When T/Maker began to move away from the Mac platform, Roizen had been amazed that Apple never even noticed. Nobody drove the five miles from Cupertino to find out what was going wrong at T/Maker. For a company that had always treated its developers like part of the family, this was like having your parents suddenly stop returning your phone calls.

Needless to say, having been abandoned gave Roizen a special understanding of the needs of the developers she was to manage and motivate. Her friendship with Bill Gates gave her a special understanding of the competition. Roizen's return as vice president for developer relations signaled that Apple was again serious about the $1 billion in Mac software sold annually. As Roizen was willing to admit at the time of her hiring, "In many ways, Apple has been its own worst enemy . . . [it] has forgotten at times to treat developers as a business community and treated them more as religious followers."

Hardware too came under Amelio's scrutiny. Besides moving to consolidate the company's confused Mac desktop line, he also began to knock heads in other parts of the catalog. At about the time of his public reemergence, Apple had to once again suspend production and recall its PowerBooks. This time the problem was buggy software, cracked cases and an often experienced but little reported tendency for the display lid to fall off. The days when Steve Jobs would demand the highest-quality packaging for Apple products was a distant memory. Now, despite being elegant and powerful, Apple's portables were gaining a reputation for being shoddy.

The recall could not have come at a more damaging time. In the first quarter of 1994, Apple PowerBooks had reached a 9 percent market share in an extremely competitive market—then collapsed in the second and third quarters thanks to the exploding keyboards. By the fourth quarter, though, the problem solved, PowerBook market share had climbed back up to 7.5 percent, with shipments reaching a record 200,000 units. And the demand was only expected to get bigger as summer approached and the PowerBook's image got a big goose from its appearance in two blockbuster movies, *Mission: Impossible* and *Independence Day*. In the former the PowerBook did everything but provide the movie with a coherent plot, and in the latter it saved all of mankind.

Even before the recall, the PowerBook division was in trouble. In a market where most competitors rolled out a new model every six months, Apple was still hanging on to its 1995 models as they approached their first birthday. After putting out too many models when the market didn't want it, now Apple wasn't introducing enough when the market did. Not surprisingly, by April, a month before the recall, PowerBook retail sales dropped 31 percent. They fell another 27 percent in May. Then came the recall, and suddenly Apple wasn't selling *any* of the product that accounted for 15 percent—$1.5 billion—of its annual revenue. The company promised to have the machines back on the shelves in a month. But two months went by and still no PowerBooks. Then, to make matters worse, the company quietly announced that it might not have any new models ready until late 1996 at the earliest.

In losing the PowerBook, Apple lost not only its sexiest product but also the allegiance of many of the developers for the PowerBook—the people Heidi Roizen had been hired to hold on to. One of these angry developers was Global Village Communication Inc., a leading supplier of computer modems. When Apple stopped selling its PowerBooks, Global Village's

PowerBook modem business stopped dead. To stay healthy, the company responded by switching its emphasis to the laptop platform that *was* still shipping. "It has certainly caused us to increase investment in the Windows products we do," company president Neil Selvin told the *San Jose Mercury News.* "We took a lot of risks [in launching our PowerBook modem] and decided to do things that were cutting-edge. In the last two years, with all the problems [at Apple], they got cautious. We're not seeing the kind of aggressive risk taking that we'd like to see."

This was the first nonfinancial crisis of Amelio's tenure. He handled it with a welcome decisiveness. The head of the PowerBook division was booted and replaced with Brodie Keast, who had run the division during its good times the year before and had been promoted to corporate marketing. Six weeks later, when the problem still wasn't solved, Amelio allowed Keast to quietly take a two-month sabbatical long due him.

Before he left, Keast uttered a comment that stood not only for the PowerBook division but for Apple Computer itself—and, as time would show, Gil Amelio as well: "If there's anything we've learned over the last year or two, it's that we need to be more humble."

Amelio replaced Keast temporarily with Fred Forsythe, Keast's boss and Apple's vice president for Macintoshes. Eventually the problem resolved itself and PowerBooks began to reappear in stores. But not before the product's reputation and market dominance had been lost. The PowerBook, like the Macintosh before it, had been a trendsetter. It had defined the future of portable computing. Now, like the Mac, it was reduced to a niche product used by a small population of true believers.

The PowerBook division, though its crisis took up considerable portions of his time, wasn't the only hardware operation that Amelio targeted during his first Hundred Days and the weeks thereafter. In the company's bread-and-butter business, he began hacking up the Macintosh's eighty-product catalog, emphasizing especially the overlap between the Performa and Quadra families. When he was done, the Mac had half as many models.

Next came the Newton. There had been considerable talk about unloading the Newton division to a consumer electronics company or other hardware manufacturer, or in the worst case, simply jettisoning it. Jobs was advising the company to get rid of it. Amelio would later say that he spent weeks pondering at what price to sell off the operation, which was generating $200 million per year, but costing $250 million. The sale price, Amelio concluded, was $50 million, but despite serious negotiations with Samsung and Ericsson, neither company's offer was close to that amount.

So, eyeing the (finally) growing market for personal digital assistants, and the lively interest in the future of "thin clients" in the global telecommunications grid, Amelio surprised Apple watchers by sticking with the product synonymous with Apple's current disasters. The Newton, he announced, would become yet another Apple subsidiary.

Amelio also hung in with Pippin, a new $600 television set-top box that combined CD-ROM player technology with Internet search capabilities—a device not far, in theory at least, from Larry Ellison's budget network computer. Helping this decision was the advice of Wozniak, who made a strong case for Apple refocusing on education and young people. Pippin was targeted for late 1997.

That left the matter of clones. Needless to say, licensing the Mac OS had been a decision faced by every Apple CEO except Mike Scott. Jobs and Sculley made the wrong decision for the right reasons. Spindler made the right decision for the wrong reasons. Now the crisis Apple faced pretty much resolved the matter. Jobs and Sculley had, thoughtfully and against the best advice to the contrary, chosen not to clone out of simple arithmetic: why make $85 on every licensed Mac sold when you can make $1,500 selling your own machine? Especially when you lose market share in the process? Only in the latter years of the Sculley era did the equation change and the reclamation of lost market share become first priority for Apple's survival. But by then the anticloning philosophy had locked in.

Spindler, fighting the last war, had decided to license the cloners in the belief that market share rather than profits was now most critical. But by now the marketplace had changed. It had settled in rigid boundaries, in which there was little Apple could do to make serious market share gains. The window (literally) of opportunity for Apple to regain market dominance had closed. Now the best strategy for Apple was to hold on to its unique OS and try to compete against the Wintel world by attacking it on the corners and by diversifying into brand-new markets, such as Internet-dedicated machines. And for that, the company would need the money generated by profits, not licenses. But Spindler, fulfilling a dream, went ahead and licensed anyway. The one consolation was that, typical for Apple in the 1990s, he did it so badly—forcing prospective cloners to use Apple, their chief competitor, as their only source of supply—that clones barely made a dent in the market under his leadership.

When Amelio arrived, the situation had once again changed. Apple was now so deep in extremis that it needed revenues, even licensing fees, anywhere it could find them. That made Amelio's decision easier. By February 19, less than three weeks after his takeover, Apple announced that Motorola had signed a sublicensing agreement that made it a second supplier to clones of Macintosh technology. In May, IBM signed an agreement to license the Mac OS.

The result was an explosion of growth and an efflorescence of exciting new products in the clone community. For the first time in a dozen years, Mac owners now had a choice. In the dark days ahead, the clone companies, notably Power Computing, would become more effective advocates for Apple than Apple itself.

Stock, senior management, developers, hardware and software. Three months into his tenure, Amelio had taken on every part of the company but one: the employees. Until the big coming-out party on May 14, Amelio's only real mass interaction with Apple's staff had been a negative one done by remote control. Like all smart new CEOs, he took the gall with the vinegar as early as possible in his tenure to minimize personal blame: in April, as he announced Apple's $740 million loss for the quarter, Amelio also announced—ex cathedra, of course, the layoff of another 1,500 employees. The first figure was big enough to annihilate 98 percent of the businesses in America; so big that the sidetracking of more than a thousand careers and families was scarcely noticed. After two years of Spindler, Apple employees were becoming used to having their departments regularly purged and to regularly upgrading their own résumés for quick use.

Now, having emerged from his lair, Amelio set about restoring the morale of his people. His results were perversely mixed. Amelio, the corporate dinosaur, proved to have greater rapport with the rank and file at Apple than with management. Senior managers, used to being on the inside of the endless feel-good consensus building at the top of Apple during the Sculley years, were now shocked to find themselves locked out of Amelio's inner circle. Amelio was willing to give them more latitude and freedom to run their operations than ever before. But what Gil gave he also took away: *he* decided what the goals of each operation would be. Managers were now free to get to those targets any way they liked, but by God, they better hit those targets or they were gone.

Not that some senior executives didn't try to skirt the new paradigm and convert Amelio to the Apple Way. Jim Buckley, president of Apple America, gave it a shot. At a staff meeting of the Apple Leadership Team, he suggested to Amelio that the company write letters to all of its customers asking them to hang in with Apple during these tough times. Great, said Amelio, prepare the letters and I'll sign them personally. Buckley disagreed, saying that those are *my* customers, so the letter should come from me. No, said Amelio with finality, the letters will come from *me*.

It was a minor matter, and the participants later insisted it had little importance, but the story of Amelio stomping Buckley sent shock waves through Apple. Here was a real boss, who understood the perquisites and responsibilities of command . . . and did not accept disagreement on the boundaries of his control. From that point on, Apple's managers privately complained about being left out of the loop and not knowing where the company was going, but at the office they deferred to Number One. "He doesn't appear to be into management by committee," gulped Frank Casanova, director of the company's advanced prototyping laboratory.

Upon his arrival, George Scalise, National's enforcer, underscored the difference between the old order and the new, between those in the circle and those outside it, by marching into City Center 3 and taking over the office of Kevin Sullivan, vice president for human resources and the most powerful member of the Old Guard. Sullivan meekly accepted the new rules. He would later claim he offered the office to Scalise, but few believed him.

By comparison, the Apple workforce seemed happy with Amelio's presence. After years of endless reorganizations, misdirected new-product developments and, most of all, flip-flopping management strategies, most were frankly relieved just to have as boss a guy who seemed to have the same consistent plan from one day to the next. "The challenge," said George Everhart, former Apple vice president for U.S. sales, who left to run Fujitsu America, "is if you don't have a feeling where you are headed, it tends to drain energy. It tires out people who are working hard. When you boil it down, that's been the company's problem over the past year."

Amelio seemed to offer the hope that now Apple would have a direction. That even now he was formulating a plan, and then would order the troops to march on the objective. As one engineer told the *San Jose Mercury News*: "Everyone is certainly willing to work around the clock for him, but we want to know on what."

Even the "Skirt Man," engineer Jeremy Bornstein in the advanced technology group, who got his moniker from his choice of skirts and sarongs as work clothes, gave Amelio a thumbs-up: "When I met [him], I could see there were some wheels turning in there. I heard later he talked about doing something about the dress code around here."

9.12 INDIAN SUMMER

As summer turned to autumn in 1996, there was a renewed sense that Apple could indeed be restored to its glory days. Just the fact that there was little news coverage about the company that fall was a welcome relief from the endless run of bad news over the previous eighteen months.

What news there was was mostly good. Morale was up. So was demand, with the company's traditionally strong market sectors—education, desktop publishing, Europe and Japan—showing renewed strength. Good news even came from unexpected quarters. Microsoft, fearing further antitrust actions by the Justice Department of the type that led it to sign a recent consent decree, suddenly showed new interest in helping its old friend.

Microsoft had long been in the odd position of being not only Apple's greatest competitor but the leading independent third-party supplier for Macintosh—to the tune of more than a billion dollars each year. In fact, the combination of Microsoft Word and Microsoft Office for Mac usually led to Microsoft making more money per Macintosh sold than Apple did.

Microsoft was doubly motivated to help its old enemy. Apple was now reduced to the humiliating position of having its triumphant opponent giving it life support. In 1995, as the troubles began, Gates had dispatched a team to Silicon Valley to establish a liaison with Apple. By 1996, as Apple began to collapse, Microsoft strengthened the operation, assigning it the task of helping small software companies write Internet programs for Apple. Since Microsoft was using every machination to crush Netscape and control access to the Net, it could afford to spend millions to help prop up Apple as a cover for its activities. Don Bradford, head of the operation, even admitted that his assignment was to "help make sure that Apple's market share stays between 8 percent and 11 percent"—in other words, not enough to be in any way threatening to Microsoft's hegemony, but yet enough to make Apple a credible competitor Microsoft could point to the next time it was called a monopoly.

Some of the more prescient observers saw in this deal a future quid pro quo: "How would this conversation be any different if I was talking to Satan?" asked Mark Kriegsman, president of ClearWay Technologies Inc. in Boston. "They're saying, 'I'm your friend, here's some money, but don't worry, we'll figure out later how you can help me?'" Apple wouldn't learn what that quid was for another year. But already the company was Bill Gates's cat's-paw.

By the end of 1996, the Microsoft operation in Silicon Valley had several dozen employees. And, at a time when Microsoft bashing by Apple reached a hysterical pitch, the Apple faithful could still attend Mac Expo and see a Microsoft booth filled with arrogant, but nervous people.

So Apple now had an unlikely patron. Further support came from another, equally unexpected direction: the clone makers. The changed rules on licensing had unfettered Mac copycats around the world. The best of these companies, such as Power Computing and Umax, were now starting to bring their products to market. The new machines were everything Apple hoped for—and feared—from clones. They were only adequately designed in terms of packaging, but they were fast, as powerful as their Apple counterparts, and about 30 percent cheaper . . . in other words, about the price the average consumer thought Macs should carry.

But the best thing about the new clone builders was that they were cheeky bastards; brash, full of themselves, willing to take wild risks. In other words, they were Apple back when Apple was the hottest company in the world. None captured that style better than Power Computing Corp.

Power Computing had been founded in the Silicon Valley city of Milpitas in 1993 by a born entrepreneur named Stephen "King" Kahng. Kahng had gotten his nickname as a pioneer in the cloning of IBM PCs a decade before, but he had always seen the Mac as a terrific business opportunity. As Apple began to show signs under Spindler of licensing the Mac OS, Kahng made his move. He incorporated Power Computing in November 1993 and by the spring of 1994 he was deep in negotiations with Apple. He finally got the license in November. By February 1995, with backing from Olivetti, he opened a factory in Austin, Texas, and by May 1995 was shipping his first clones, called the Power family. The Power machines were as powerful as their Apple counterparts and a lot less expensive—as much as 25 percent. By October 1995, Power Computing was shipping its second, more powerful product family, called the PowerWave line.

Umax was a different story. Formed from the purchase of Radius's clone line, Umax was a division of a $3 billion Taiwanese corporation. It got into the business largely to protect its scanners, most of which were used with Macs, but soon found low-cost cloning of the expensive Apple line to be a lucrative business. The vice president for engineering, Peter Mehring, who had come from Radius, argued that "we don't even compete directly with Apple. Rather, we complement its sales. Apple doesn't sell a machine priced at under $1,800. We don't sell anything priced above that. And we sell in places where Apple is now weak, like Taiwan, Japan and Western Europe. I don't see how we can do anything but help Apple."

Amelio knew the key to managing clones was to stay on top of them. They were going to be innovative and audacious—that was the point of having them—but the trick was to never let them get too far ahead. But once they took the risk of finding a price point that generated the best sales and profit margins, the smart big company could then roll in after them and stake out that territory. If the clones came up with a new wrinkle in hardware and software, you watched the market's response. If it was strong, then you adopted the new idea. Clone companies were outliers; you gave them their lead, allowed them good strong growth, you worked with them when it was useful—but you always stayed in command of the market. IBM had forgotten that, and its clones had simply broken their reins, run off and grown rich.

But once again, knowing what had to be done and actually doing it with a self-centered and unwieldy organization were two different things. Power Computing dazzled the Mac world, and infuriated Apple by producing not just better machines but designs a generation ahead of anything being done by the crowd in Cupertino. Thus, the Power line was the first to feature Motorola's new 120 MHz PowerPC chip. Then, as Apple struggled to keep up, Kahng brought out the 150 MHz PowerWave. Six months later, as Apple was bringing out its own 150 MHz models, Power Computing announced its first Power Tower, with 180 MHz speed. Combine that with lower prices, and if you were willing to sacrifice some swanky packaging and the little rainbow logo in the corner, Power Computing looked like a far better buy. Apple didn't even have the traditional advantage of stability. Apple might be shipping 5 million computers per year compared with Power Computing's 50,000. But in May 1996, Power Computing had $250 million in annual revenues, while $11 billion Apple was in the midst of *losing* three times that much. So much for the security of a large, established company.

The same thing happened at the low end of the market. Umax, by producing computers that were the equal of Apple's but at half the price, not only found new customers but (because Apple didn't sufficiently advance its own machines to be worth the premium price) began to carve away at the low end of Apple's business. By 1997, it had global Mac clone sales estimated at $300 million.

Said Umax chairman Frank Huang, "The industry today is very different than it was ten years ago. There are price segments where companies compete on price alone. Apple is a symbol of the American computing industry. They still have a big media and PR presence, but their marketing power has dwindled and they don't have the compelling technological lead they once had. Their advantage is diminishing faster than we can imagine. Our existence makes them more powerful."

Ten years after the success of Compaq and Dell, clones didn't bear the stigma they once had. Even Rush Limbaugh, with the largest radio audience in history and one of the last highly visible Apple fanatics, would proudly announce to his listeners that he had just bought a Power Computing clone.

Kahng was also creating a competing myth for Power Computing. Whereas Apple under Sculley would blow tens of thousands of dollars on airplane logos and its executive would stay in the poshest hotel suites, Kahng's staff became famous for attending a Boston trade show and staying in a $49-per-night motel.

At the January 1996 MacWorld Expo in San Francisco, Power Computing pulled off a coup the industry hadn't seen since Apple hijacked the West Coast Computer Faire in 1977. Apple, in the midst of the Spindler crisis, had all but pulled out of the event. In response, several other companies bailed as well. Power Computing made its move: picking up an abandoned $170,000 booth for just $30,000. Power Computing stole the show. Luck, mixed with audacity, was on Power Computing's side.

And the little company, now with 300 employees, just got more interesting and lovable. Perhaps nothing better captured the style of this brash new start-up than an advertisement run by Power Computing. It was an imitation Roy Lichtenstein comic book painting showing in close-up an All-American blonde in front of an American flag holding a smoking .45 automatic and saying in a talk balloon, "You can take my Mac when you pry my cold, dead fingers off the mouse!" The caption shouted: "Refuse to be a victim! Fight back for the Mac!"

It was thrilling. Power Computing offered a vision for the Macintosh in the 1990s and a road map for Apple to follow, if it dared. And Power Computing wasn't alone. Other clone makers were signing licenses with Apple and building their own Mac knockoffs. It was an interesting, if motley group, including Umax, with it refugees from monitor maker Radius, DayStar Digital, a small workstation builder, Japanese giant Pioneer Electronics Corp., which proposed to sell to the Japanese market, and two American giants, Motorola and IBM.

The last were particularly interesting. Motorola, bigger than Apple, was not only the supplier of the microprocessor for Macs, but also one of the world's best manufacturers of consumer electronics. Thus, it seemed to have Apple bracketed. IBM, meanwhile, under a historic turnaround by Lou Gerstner, had more than regained its old glory. It remained the leading computer maker, but had also become a very aggressive marketer. With these two behemoths on one side, and a plucky start-up like Power Computing and a price bomber like Umax on the other, it wasn't hard to look out a few years into the future and see a sluggish Apple slowly being crushed between them.

But in the meantime, the cloners served Amelio's purpose nicely. During the hard times of 1996, the Macintosh line was in very great danger of simply being buried in all the gossip and speculation about Apple's financial predicament. If Apple really was in danger of dying, what difference did it make how good its new products were? No sane person ever bought an orphan computer. But the clones offered a welcome cognitive dissonance. If the Mac was doomed, why were all these big companies and intriguing start-ups so anxious to build it? Did they know something the rest of the world didn't?

At least for the short term, the Mac clones did what Spindler and Apple's critics had always said they would: raise product visibility, enlarge retail shelf space, open new distribution and marketing channels and ultimately improve market share. They could also (via Motorola and hopefully in time IBM) sell to the corporate world in ways Apple had never been able to duplicate. And they could provide a marketing counterpoint—techie or abrasive or sternly corporate—to Apple's increasingly predictable sleek New Age style.

But in the long term, there was still the question that had scared off Sculley and haunted Spindler. Could Apple still keep up with its copycats? Could it still set the agenda for the market? Was Apple still clever and competent enough to allow the cloners to prospect new territories, then enable Apple to overrun them and consolidate the success?

The thrilling answer came in October. Just six months after Amelio predicted it would take three years for Apple to rise from its woes, the company announced a profit for the final quarter of fiscal 1996. Twenty-five million bucks, 20 cents per share. It wasn't much for an $11 billion company, but it was nevertheless a bombshell. A year before, Apple had enjoyed a $60.1 million profit on revenues of 48 cents per share, but everything in between had been a nightmare. Even with this little profit, losses for fiscal 1996 were $816 million ($6.59 per share), compared to a profit of $424 million ($3.45 per share) in fiscal 1995.

These losses had taken their toll in customer loyalty. In the fourth quarter of 1995, Apple had enjoyed a run rate of a $12 billion company. Now, at the end of the fourth quarter of fiscal 1996, Apple had shrunk to just a $9.3 billion company. There weren't enough clones in the world yet to make up that difference in lost market share. Commensurately, during the fourth quarter, Apple shipped only 932,000 units, down 26 percent from the year before.

Nevertheless, shipments were up 11 percent from the third quarter. And there was no denying the reality that Apple was again profitable. It seemed a miracle. On the day of the announcement, company stock jumped $2.25 to $28, the highest it had been in many months. As for employees, the good news meant that layoffs would now be stopped at just 1,500, instead of the planned 2,800.

Two days later, Apple followed with a counterpunch. It slashed prices on its Performa family, top to bottom. The high-end 6400/200 with 200 MHz speed, 16 megabytes of RAM and a 2.4 gigabyte hard drive had been announced just two months before at $2,799. It was now reduced in price by 20 percent to just $2,199. So it went down the line. But the capper was the introduction at the high end of a 6400/200 model with built-in video editing circuitry for $2,699—proof that Apple understood who its premium customers were—and better yet, a new low-end machine, the Performa 5360 (160 MHz, 16 Mb RAM, 1.6 Gb disk) for just $1,499.

This last was a real breakthrough: now, for probably the first time in its history, Apple had the lowest-price computer for its power on the market. The news was like a blast of trumpets. Apple, which had spent twenty years charging its customers a premium for the right to use the products of the company's genius, was now going to compete on price! It was if the aging heavyweight champ, knocked around for ten rounds and left for dead, had somehow risen off the canvas just before the bell and landed a roundhouse on the stunned opponent. For a company that just a few months before had been given up as doomed, Apple now looked like the supplier to beat during the Christmas buying season.

The hero of the hour was Gilbert Frank Amelio. The retro chip guy with the shy manner and will of iron seemed godlike. Two months before, at the Mac Expo in Boston, one unabashed fan had even run up after his keynote speech and planted a kiss on him. Millions of shareholders were ready to do the same. Amelio, for his part, looked proudly presidential when he added to the financial goodies by saying he "remained confident" that Apple would achieve sustainable profitability by the end of the second quarter of fiscal 1997. The reason, he said proudly, was that under his watch Apple had accomplished two critical goals: increasing revenues from the third quarter and strengthening the company's financial position.

It seemed that Gil Amelio had fixed everything.

9.13 VANITAS

But not everyone was so enraptured by Amelio's apparently successful turnaround of Apple.

Some senior managers at Apple had privately complained, almost from the moment of Amelio's arrival, that they were being left in the dark about company plans and strategies, and that there were no clear lines to Amelio. Others darkly noted that Amelio's technique for team building among his senior managers—bringing them together at places like the Claremont Hotel in Berkeley to create task forces and meet with management training specialists—was just more of the same old "talk about it endlessly, then do nothing" Apple style.

Again, the rank-and-file Apple employees were much more enthusiastic. They loved it when Amelio said, "I'll never be as charismatic as Steve Jobs. And Steve will never be as accomplished an operations manager as I am." Finally, Apple seemed oriented toward results, not good intentions.

Soon after Amelio arrived, one enthusiastic employee told the *San Jose Mercury News*, "People [are] letting him know, 'We are with you.' He has a big magnifying glass and is going around to everyone and looking at everything. We are not going to get the knee-jerk stuff we were expecting. We are going to get a cure."

In the first few months, Amelio reinforced his image of a decisive, competent, employee-oriented CEO by regularly trying to get out and meet employees. He held regular meetings with employees, with his leadership team and one-on-one encounters throughout the company. It was hard work for a man who was obviously awkward and shy, but Amelio seemed intent upon being a people-oriented boss. But tellingly, what proved to be his most effective communications tool with employees was electronic mail. Once employees learned that he was diligent about answering these missives, Amelio was quickly flooded with mountains of crisp complaints, rambling monologues and thoughtful suggestions.

All that changed with the arrival of George Scalise. Scalise had been known at National as Amelio's hatchet man, but like most such reputations, the relationship was much more complex. Scalise was Amelio's alter ego and, at times, his demonic. Extravagant (he once wore a cravat to a "casual dress" meeting at Apple) and voluble, Scalise enjoyed contact with people, whether it was to praise or kick butt. He could be what Gil was not: smooth, glib and fearless in public. Scalise could shout and pound his fist so that Amelio would never have to raise his voice or his hand.

Needless to say, before Scalise had been at Apple more than a few weeks, Amelio began to retreat from the public life at Apple. National Semi folks had called this the good cop/bad cop routine, but it was closer to Mr. Inside/Mr. Outside. As Scalise would later describe it: "I spent a lot of time [at Apple] meeting and talking to people. Gil would spend a lot of time in his office, thinking."

This was not a good sign. And it became even less so once the world realized what Gil Amelio was thinking about.

Behind the hosannahs about Amelio's performance as Apple CEO there had always been an undercurrent of resentment and concern. For one thing, there was his supposedly sterling record at National Semiconductor. Charlie Sporck would later say, "His main drive is an ego drive and money. His biggest legacy [at National] was a corporate jet and that book." But Sporck was bitter. Yet Amelio's reply—"That's bullshit. If you look at that place when I left compared to when I got there, it's obvious. There's not a person on Wall Street who would say I didn't do a terrific job"—had the odd ring of a man judging himself by others' perceptions.

Sporck wasn't alone. Others from the National days noted the difference between what they saw at National under Amelio and the legend he had subsequently created for himself. As National's CEO, Amelio—*Doctor* Amelio, he insisted on being called, even though his doctorate was in solid-state physics—had been a corporate climber who talked a good management game, but who rarely lived up to his own bromides. He was insulated, intensely self-conscious, and on the business side emphasized short-term gains over long-term market power . . . in all, a man who some might say was more interested in his own career success than in the company he worked for, or the people who worked for him.

Narcissism is no stranger to Silicon Valley, and certainly not to Apple Computer. But Amelio was something different. Most of the great egos of high tech are flamboyant, preening or loquacious. Amelio was none of these things. He was the old-fashioned chip nerd who fooled the new cybernerds. And beneath the avuncular, slightly amusing exterior—the moussed hair, the monogrammed custom shirts, the pimpy Cadillac Seville, the uneasy air of a man who thinks he looks great but isn't quite sure—was the soul of a man of enormous ambition.

One member of Apple's executive offices, who watched three CEOs come and go, when asked about why such apparently competent and successful men were so distorted by the presidency of Apple, replied in Latin: "*Vanitas!* The office of CEO is a strange animal anywhere, but at Apple it is especially bizarre. All the publicity, the attention, the fame. If you don't know where you are vulnerable, the office will show you very quickly."

Gilbert Amelio had been a painfully shy child, the son of a contractor, who had found success in the perfectible world of science and mathematics. Through sheer force of will he made himself into a top student. By forcing himself to join social groups and clubs as well as learn public speaking, Amelio made himself into a successful, if uncomfortable, member of the outside world. Like many self-created success stories, Amelio was obsessed with success; it defined his value as a person. As he would recall in his book: "I needed to be a credit to my family, my university and my science."

He was. He earned his undergraduate degree from the Georgia Institute of Technology, then a master's in physics and a PhD in solid-state physics. He was a good enough scientist to land his first job at AT&T Bell Labs in New Jersey, where the transistor had been invented, and the Lourdes of commercial electronics research. He felt unworthy and terrified to be there, but his fear of failure was even greater—"Anything short of success would have been humiliating" he would write. Ultimately, he earned sixteen patents while at Bell.

Crushing self-doubt often is a paradoxical partner with grand illusions. Thus, the frightened young man who joined Bell Labs became, at age thirty-five, an angry veteran annoyed that he hadn't won—and likely never would win—a Nobel Prize. So he decided to play his hand for greatness on a different table: management. If young nineteenth-century romantics threw away their lives, often literally, after reading Goethe's *Young Werther*, engineers and physicists in the 1960s and 1970s often decided to abandon their careers and pursue corporate management after reading Peter Drucker. In Drucker's works they found a mix of scientific reasoning and heroic entrepreneurial independence that appealed to ambitious young men with advanced degrees, like Gil Amelio, stuck in prestigious but unrewarding laboratory jobs.

Fairchild, Rockwell, National Semiconductor. Amelio had risen to the top with a string of successes. Even landing the Apple job was a clever piece of maneuvering. Unlike Graziano, Amelio had waited to hear the cries of distress before he offered to save the day. Now he had the glittering prize: the most visible corporate presidency in the world, the friendship of the famous, the press hanging on his every word.

So overwhelming was his success that Amelio even maintained the pretense of humility for several months. The man of the people, the new Apple CEO who was honest enough to admit that he knew less about technology than his employees. Who joked about being such a square.

But he couldn't maintain the guise for long. Scalise's arrival signaled as well the debut of the real Gil Amelio. He began to be much less accessible not just to managers but to the rank and file. Apple's executive offices became much less accessible too. Those who did get access to Amelio's office quickly noticed a growing shrine to one man's success. There was the framed *Forbes* cover of himself and the embarrassing tendency to hand reporters copies of glowing articles about himself. As Mark Leibovitch of the *Mercury News* recounted about one such occasion, Amelio, in the middle of an interview, handed him a printout of a *Hot Wired* article in which the headline "Amelio Cheered" was highlighted in yellow.

Even Amelio's old friends noticed the change. The old Gil had been a hail-fellow-well-met kind of guy, down to earth, comfortable in his traditional, conservative lifestyle. A jokester. And a man proud to be a scientist. One lifelong, but increasingly estranged friend, Bill Sweet, remembered the two of them taking their kids and a carload of guns up into the mountains and having fun shooting at everything in sight. The "New Gil," as Sweet described him, would never do such a thing. "He would worry about having to read about the CEO of Apple shooting up pinecones in the *San Jose Mercury News.*" When it was discovered that Amelio had bought for his father a replica of George Patton's pearl-handled revolvers, Amelio took great pains to announce on the record that he himself did not own a handgun.

As the year ended, there was a growing disquiet within Apple that instead of a savior, Apple had managed to find yet another martinet. And this time one without any style or charisma. The more cynical suggested that the unexpectedly profitable quarter had merely been a puff job to give Amelio the maximum personal bonus—and a rumor that grew teeth in December, when an SEC filing showed that Apple had awarded him a total of $3 million, just for the interval between February and September. A $655,061 salary and a $2.3 million bonus. Amelio, who already had a house in Silicon Valley, also received from Apple a $5 million loan and, most bizarre of all, the company leased his airplane at $1,695 per hour, for a total of $108,000. The fuddy-duddy hardware store clerk was beginning to look more and more like Cash McCall.

These numbers might have provoked more of a scandal had they not already been ameliorated by the profitable quarter. But what residual resentment remained was quickly forgotten in an even bigger, brasher move by Amelio. Having convinced himself that he had already saved Apple, Amelio did the one thing that would have put a stab of fear in the hearts of his two predecessors:

He brought back Steve Jobs.

9.14 PRODIGAL

In December 1996, Steve Jobs had been out of Apple Computer for more than eleven years. He was no longer the *enfant terrible* of high tech. Now, at forty-one, he was still a striking figure, with an affection for European suits with waist-length jackets and shirts with banded collars—a kind of hybrid between a Nehru jacket and executive power suit in *Blade Runner*. But though he retained his old panache, he was not a young man anymore. His wire-rimmed glasses no longer reflected rebellion but astigmatism. His straight hair was still long and black, but it had noticeably thinned in the front. And his familiar hawklike profile had softened slightly, giving him the look less of a raptor than a Cheyenne chief.

Jobs's decade in the wilderness had, after a rocky start, given him considerable wealth, but not fame. When he had stormed off to get his revenge on Apple by founding NeXT, the entire world watched. It waited for NeXT to bring out its own computer and for the battle with Apple to begin.

But the NeXT computer was a dud. Not that it wasn't a good machine. In fact, it was beautiful, smoky black and sleek, easily the best-looking computer ever built. It had the usual Jobs quirky touch: in this case an optical memory system that was quickly abandoned. But, beginning in 1989, it also had a new object-oriented operating system, NeXTStep, that was even more magnificent than the box. It had a user interface, OpenStep, that was light-years ahead of both the Mac OS and, still in the distant future, Microsoft Windows. With the NeXT computer and operating system, Jobs had proven once again that he was the greatest design team leader in the history of electronics.

But Jobs was trapped in his own infinite loop. The NeXT computer, like the Macintosh before it, failed because a good design was no longer enough. NeXT didn't have the size or distribution to drive the new computer into the marketplace. In a world where MS-DOS was dominant, where Jobs's own Mac OS covered all the lower fringes and Unix-based computers held the high end, there just wasn't any room for a fourth operating system. Especially one being promulgated by a little company, no matter how famous the guy running it. Had Jobs cut a deal with Apple, or gone into the IBM clone business, his high profile and brilliant design sense might have made NeXT into a giant. He might even have beat Gates at his own game by coming out with a DOS-based NeXTStep that would have been five years ahead of Windows 95. But Jobs was already showing his age. Whereas the real visionaries in personal computing now recognized that the future lay in software and microprocessors, Jobs, like an old factory supervisor, still believed success lay in Big Iron.

Meanwhile even as Jobs was embroiled in the Apple/NeXT soap opera, he was still casting about for other business opportunities. So distracting was the bigger story that Jobs's purchase in February 1986 of a little computer graphics company called Pixar Inc. was barely noticed by the public. Computer graphics in those days was still more a wish than a reality, and George Lucas's founding of the firm to help create movie special effects was viewed as a secondary effort, a way to park some of his *Star Wars* money, to his much more famous Industrial Light & Magic.

Pixar slipped out of the public's imagination almost from the day Jobs bought it. Unfortunately, NeXT soon did as well. Once it became apparent that NeXT had not produced the home run everybody expected from Jobs, that the company's orders were a fraction of predictions, the world turned away. NeXT seemed to be the corporate crypt for Steve Jobs's career.

What attention the company did get was almost uniformly negative. Gossips shook their heads to stories about Jobs yelling at caterers and contractors, belittling employees, making arbitrary decisions and acting like the same old jerk they loved to hate. And they clucked when rumors leaked out about the pampered but degraded NeXT employees slowly going mad in such an autocratic, dysfunctional work environment. It served them right for going to work for a lunatic megalomaniac. As for Jobs, let him stay forever in his self-created, elegantly appointed purgatory.

As he sensed impending failure, the darker sides of Steve Jobs began to dominate his personality. When *Upside* magazine published a devastating story about NeXT, its editor, Rich Karlgaard, received a phone call at home one Saturday morning what years later he still recalled as one of the strangest he'd ever experienced. "It was Steve Jobs. He started by telling me how he was going to destroy me. Then how much he liked me. Then what a worthless magazine *Upside* was. Then how he was my friend. And sometimes he would say both things *in the same sentence*. It was eerie."

By 1992, NeXT had fallen down the Silicon Valley memory hole. If its name was mentioned, it was usually accompanied by a knowing snicker. Jobs had gotten his comeuppance. And when, in February 1993, NeXT announced that it was getting out of the hardware business and laying off 500 employees—having burned up an estimated $200 million in the process, the general reaction was: Are they still in business?

But great software never really dies. It just waits for a good application. And great operating systems are like gold—they never really lose their value. Even as NeXT was pulling out of hardware, it was licensing NeXTStep to Sun and to Hewlett-Packard, two firms fighting one another for control of the workstation market. Thus, while most of the world forgot it, NeXT found itself in the unlikely position of having the only personal computer operating system that was fully compatible with five of the world's major computer architectures: Hewlett-Packard's PA-RISC, Sun's SPARCstation, Intel-based PCs, NeXT's own computer . . . and Macintosh.

Meanwhile, with NeXT running itself, Jobs began to spend more time in the East Bay with his other little company, Pixar. Without anyone really noticing, mainly because its products appeared under the Disney label, Pixar had become the world's leading computer animator. Though the image was one of computers doing all the work, the reality of a Pixar film was experienced illustrators working tens of thousands of hours designing images on banks of powerful graphic workstations to produce a few minutes of film stock. The results, awkward at first, grew increasingly beautiful and Pixar began to pick up Oscars and critical raves.

As Jobs was neither an animator nor a programmer, there was little he could do in the actual production process—to the relief of the folks at Pixar, who knew all too well Jobs's reputation. Thus, Steve was reduced to doing what he did best: cheerleading, making connections, creating visions, motivating, building team confidence. It was an almost perfect setting for Jobs. He could lead without managing, direct without running. He excelled.

The result was *Toy Story*, one of the most popular feature cartoons ever, a landmark in the history of animation as the first full-length computer-generated movie—not to mention a terrific story with memorable characters. This time the world wanted to look past the Disney label—and Pixar was happy to oblige, especially since it was ramping up toward its initial public offering of stock.

The happy glow remained all through Pixar's quiet period before the IPO. The company didn't have to promote itself. Its advertisements were on every junior sheet, pair of underpants, lunch box and Halloween costume in the world. And so, in January 1995, Pixar stock opened on its first day in the teens and, buoyed by a strong market, quickly rose to $49 per share. It soon slumped a little as the irrational exuberance calmed to a pragmatic appraisal. Nevertheless, for a few days in January, Steve Jobs was officially a billionaire. Though his net worth wilted with the stock price, the mantle remained. From now on, Jobs would be listed in the Billionaire's Valhalla with his enemy/friend Bill Gates and his new best buddy, Larry Ellison of Oracle.

Interviewed on PBS's *Charlie Rose*, a professorial Jobs would profess to "not really following the computer industry much anymore," and claim that he was dedicated now to the future endeavors of Pixar. It was a convincing act for people in Manhattan, New York, and Manhattan, Kansas. But few believed it in Silicon Valley. They knew that Steve Jobs would burn forever for vindication at Apple. A more accurate clue to how little the Apple wound had healed could be found in a revealing interview with *Wired* magazine soon after the Pixar IPO. There, asked about Apple, Jobs testily replied, "Microsoft dominates . . . That's over. Apple lost."

Meanwhile, though he had all but fallen off the technology world's radar screen, Jobs had never fully left the public eye. Every few years his name popped up—as on the list of key contributors to the Clinton campaign who had spent a night in the Lincoln bedroom. When *Time* ran a list of the 100 most important baby boomers, there he was in the top ten, with the likes of

Steven Spielberg and Gates. When the same magazine ran a cover story on the new young tycoons of Silicon Valley, there was the obligatory sidebar on the most famous young tycoon of them all, telling how he had become a more introspective person, less flamboyant, and best of all, how he had learned to become a loving father to Lisa, now a bright teenager. Neighbors often saw them walking or Rollerblading together. Those who worshipped Jobs during his Apple days had always had to admit that his denial of paternity damned him. Now, even those who despised Jobs had to admit that this quiet rapprochement with his daughter redeemed him.

Even megalomaniacs grow older and wiser. Neighbors reported that Jobs still regularly reamed out caterers and other hired help. But he had mellowed. The suicidal brashness that had destroyed him at Apple in 1985 had been replaced by a more careful, thoughtful style. He was a husband now, having married in 1990. The courtship was classic Steve Jobs: romantic, impulsive and unique. While waiting to give a lecture at the Stanford Business School, he struck up a conversation with the student sitting next to him. By the time he took the stage he had her phone number—but later, rushing to his car to get to a business dinner, he stopped in his tracks: "I was in the parking lot, with the key in the car, and I thought to myself, 'If this is my last night on Earth, would I rather spend it at a business meeting or with this woman?' I ran across the parking lot, asked her if she'd have dinner with me. She said yes, we walked into town and we've been together since."

Steve and Laurene Jobs had two children (Lisa also lived with them until leaving for college), with a third child born in late 1998. He had fully settled into a domestic life as a burgher of Palo Alto, restoring a 1930's house, and this new domesticity seemed to improve his management style. Tom Carlisle, who had left Apple with Jobs and had followed him to NeXT, then Pixar, would say, "At Apple [Jobs] had a difficult time hearing what he didn't want to hear. Now, he's very much more open. He'll say, 'Don't tell me what I want to hear. Tell me the truth.' In reality, it's not always so clear-cut. But he's trying so much harder."

Still, no one believed that the New Steve Jobs was profoundly different than the Old one. So only a naive fool or someone utterly convinced of his own abilities *and* career invulnerability would embrace the most dangerous viper of all to his breast. Gil Amelio was a little of the former and a lot of the latter. He believed his recent success in turning around Apple, combined with superior management skills and Jobs's reputation, would protect him. And if all else failed, there was always the board of directors, especially Markkula, who had an understandable fear of the return of the prodigal son.

But Amelio had one very strong reason for inviting Jobs back: he needed NeXT.

With the collapse of Copland, Amelio faced a serious problem. The Mac OS was getting archaic. And though it still had an almost religious appeal to everyday users, in the cutting-edge applications, Apple's bread-and-butter graphics business, the OS's lack of multitasking and multithreading—the ability to run several different programs, or several different operations within one program, at the same time—was slowly driving long-standing customers into the arms of Microsoft. With the rise of the Internet, with millions of people running Java applets or constructing their own Web pages, this flaw in the Mac OS would soon become pandemic to Apple's entire customer base.

So the company needed a new operating system, fast. The lesson of Copland was that Apple couldn't do the job itself. So that meant licensing. A survey of the market showed there were four candidates: Windows NT, Sun Solaris, Be Inc. and NeXT. Amelio talked with Gates about moving the NT onto the Mac while keeping the Mac user interface—a combination that would give the Mac access to the whole world of Windows. Gates, seeing before him the chance of a complete monopoly of the desktop, was, needless to say, enthusiastic. But Ellen Hancock argued against it, saying that despite Gates's claims to the contrary, such a combination would be extremely difficult to pull off. She, instead, fought for Solaris, a solid, Unix-based operating system with a weak user interface. In the end Amelio turned against both, the former because of the complexity of the task, and the latter because Apple would have to create a whole new interface. With that decision, Apple now turned its full attention to the other two candidates. And with that decision, Apple went back into the irony business, because Be Inc. was founded and run by Jean-Louis Gassée and NeXT by Steve Jobs.

Be Inc. was the most likely candidate. Its Be OS not only worked on the PowerPC chip but had all the advanced features Apple desired. Scalise made the initial approach to Gassée in June 1996. By autumn, the negotiations were taking place in earnest.

But right from the start there was one very big obstacle to a deal. Gassée was greedy. He understood Apple's predicament as well as anyone—after all, he had helped create it. Now he was convinced he had his old company over a barrel. He was almost right. Still, Gassée overplayed his hand. He asked for $400 million for the rights to the Be OS—throwing in the added incentive of his rejoining Apple to run the software program. Apple, stunned (it had concluded that Be's market value was just $50 million), offered $120 million, then slowly lifted the offer to $200 million. But Be, believing it had time on its side, dragged its feet. Bad poker. While Gassée thought he was forcing a desperate Apple to the table, he was instead driving the company into the arms of another. Apple was indeed desperate for a solution, but at that price it was willing to even consider the unimaginable.

Though in many ways the Be OS was a superior, and more modern, operating system, NeXTStep did have its advantages. For one thing, it was more mature; there were hundreds of developers out there who knew how to write for it. There was also that nice connection with Sun and HP, as well as the crossover to the PC world. It would be harder to port NeXTStep over to the Mac OS world, but once you did, a whole universe opened up in the area of enterprise—that is, large-scale corporate network computing. Apple had never been good in that sphere and, seeing the success of companies such as Oracle, coveted some of that business. Finally, one other appealing thing about NeXT was its founder. As Gassée said later: "I think putting [Steve Jobs] back into the company subliminally has a value we should not underestimate."

But the presence of Jobs posed a problem. *He* would never consider approaching Apple. And who at Apple would have the guts to suggest contacting Steven Jobs? Given all the historical bad blood, how could contact between NeXT and Apple be accomplished?

The answer was through a little skulduggery. The people at NeXT were convinced that they held the solution to Apple's software dilemma, if only Apple would listen. The word was out about the Be Inc. negotiations, so time was running short. The move was ultimately initiated by John Landwehr, a product manager, who convinced Mitch Mandich, NeXT's vice president for sales, that it was now or never to approach Apple. But Mandich, reacting like most people at NeXT when discussing fraternization with a blood enemy, decided not to make the call himself, but directed a marketing manager to do it. That manager passed the buck too, to Garrett Rice, NeXT's channel marketing manager.

Rice at last made the call to an engineering contact at Apple—who in turn passed him upward to Hancock, Apple's chief technical officer. This was the week of November 18. By the 26, representatives of both companies met via a conference call. "They wanted to come down here right away and see what we had," said Landwehr. The next day, November 27, the Apple contingent arrived at NeXT. Steve Jobs, busy at Pixar, was told nothing.

The meeting went well. Then, in the middle of it, by eerie coincidence, a call came in from Jobs on some minor business matter. It was only then that he learned what was going on.

He wasn't angry. On the contrary, he told the NeXT wheeler-dealers that he too had been thinking about Apple lately, and had even placed a call to an Apple executive he knew.

After that, things moved quickly. The two teams, now sometimes number-ing thirty people, met almost every day, usually on neutral ground, such as at the offices of the Valley law firm of Wilson, Sonsini, Goodrich & Rosati or at the Garden Court Hotel across from the Stanford Shopping Center. There were some tough technical questions to be addressed; in particular, could NeXTStep, which had shown itself well suited for high-end video and graphic applications, also run the prosaic little programs that were the province of most everyday Mac users? The answer seemed to be yes.

Meanwhile, other parts of Apple raced around doing due diligence on the prospective new business partner. With the kind of care for superfluous details that bureaucracies are gifted at, Apple called nearly everyone who had ever worked for or with NeXT: developers, contractors, current and former custom-ers, past and present employees, trying to find that one fatal bit of evidence that would nix the deal. "They gave us a very thorough scrubbing," said Jobs. But Apple never found that fatal flaw—like all bureaucracies, it devoted mas-sive amounts of time and resources in pursuit of minutiae, while no one seemed to ask the one simple big question: Do we really want Steve Jobs back inside Apple?

The deal came down to a series of CEO blind dates. Jobs and Amelio had met before, first at that strange encounter at National Semi, then at a party held soon after Amelio took over Apple. Now it was time for them to meet more formally. At the first meeting, Jobs performed one of his classic product demonstrations, this time showing how NeXTStep could play five movie clips at the same time. Even for a computer veteran, this was an impressive demon-stration. For a neophyte like Amelio, it was enthralling. Jobs too came away in a good mood about Gil Amelio. "He seems like an awfully nice guy," Jobs said. Soon, Amelio was visiting Jobs at his home. It wasn't a Manhattan aerie this time, but then again, Amelio was a more anxious buyer. Amelio would later say, scarily, that his relationship with Jobs was "like a flower blossoming."

Meanwhile, the financial negotiations continued to pick up speed. Curi-ous to see them up close, Jobs paid a visit to one of the meetings. It just happened to be taking place at Apple itself. And thus, for the first time in many years, Steve Jobs walked on the grounds of the company he had founded. It was a historic moment noticed by only a few people. And it must have been disorienting, if satisfying, for Jobs. The Apple he visited, with its giant twin-towered headquarters and multi-acre research center, was only a block, but also a lifetime, away from the cluster of little buildings he had left behind in 1985. The company that had obsessed him for so many years, the people who had betrayed him, the maverick corporate culture that he had created through the force of his personality—all were gone now, or nearly so. He was the Rip van Winkle of the computer age, and now returning after a long absence to his old village, he found few recognizable touchstones beyond the logo on the wall. To those who saw him that day, Jobs was a myth unexpectedly made incarnate, a Founding Father suddenly emerging out of the misty past.

He was back.

It wasn't long before Be Inc. got wind of the negotiations with NeXT. Realizing that their bluff had been called, Gassée and his team rushed back to Apple with a final counteroffer: $210 million. But it was too late. In its greed, Be had left the door wide open, and now the NeXT deal had taken on enough momentum to be unstoppable. "C'est la vie," said Gassée, showing why he would never be a true Silicon Valley player. He would later rationalize that he had been lucky to have been spared from "hijacking the *Titanic*."

The week before Christmas 1996, the figures were finalized: $425 million, not just for NeXTStep but for the outright purchase of NeXT Inc. Apple would pay $350 million for NeXT, plus assume that company's $50 million debt.

It was an amazing amount—with the added coincidence that this was the same amount that Be Inc. had first proposed and Apple found outrageous. The difference, apparently, was that Apple was not just licensing the NeXT OS but buying the whole company.

But that too raised a disturbing question: What exactly was Apple getting for all that money? Well, there was the NeXTStep operating system. It had the potential to take the Mac into the wide world of multimedia, enterprise computing and Internet development. But it would not be an easy hybridization: at best, it would still take the Mac its usual thirty seconds to boot up (compared with five seconds with Be OS) and even then the question of its being able to run the basic Mac software library wasn't fully resolved. Then there was the user interface for NeXTStep, called OpenStep. It was impressive, but largely redundant to the much more popular Mac icons.

Perhaps it was the company itself. But, a decade old, and with only $50 million in annual revenues and 350 employees, NeXT was hardly an up-and-comer. In fact, it was in bad shape. Despite hundreds of millions of dollars spent, and the support of IBM, HP and Sun, NeXTStep had never caught on with the mass market. By early 1996, the firm was running out of capital to invest in new product enhancements to make NeXTStep more efficient on the Internet. The situation became sufficiently desperate that as late as August, NeXT was shopping NeXTStep around to competitors.

Thus, to the objective observer, NeXT seemed less a hot company with an even hotter product than an aging firm on its last legs looking for a Sugar Daddy to save it. In that light, one could only wonder why Apple didn't wait and force NeXT's hand—or at least bargain as hard as it did with Be Inc.

Jobs had always enjoyed a lot of fans, but he never had as many enthusiastic true believers as he did that day among the NeXT employees. Like the good entrepreneur he was, Jobs had distributed most of NeXT's stock to its employees and now, after years of frustration and hard work, they were about to get the payoff of their lives. Many were now millionaires. It was one promise that Steve Jobs more than fulfilled.

9.15 ODYSSEUS

The news of Steve Jobs's return to Apple rocked the high-tech world. The Beatles were never all going to get back together, but at least one great boomer era estrangement was now about to be mended.

Jobs tried to dampen the cheering, reminding the world that "my job is not savior . . . I'm just a part-time consultant," but no one believed him. Damnit, his job *was* savior. Jobs knew it too, which was why he smiled when he said, "Gil asked me to give him some advice . . . I'd love to help Apple." All Jobs's pretending not to care, of acting indifferent to the company's fate through the years, was shown to be the defensive, hurt lie it had always been. It was great to be back, to know that your predictions about the company without you had all come true. To return even richer than when you left. To still be a household word when all of your enemies were now forgotten. To save Apple as the great third act of your young life.

At the news of the NeXT purchase and Jobs's return, Gil Amelio received a call from Bill Gates. "Do you really think Steve Jobs has got anything there?" Amelio recalled Gates asking. "I know his technology, it's nothing but warmed-over UNIX, and you'll never be able to make it work on your machines." Then Gates grew even angrier: "Don't you understand that Steve doesn't know anything about technology? He's just a supersalesman. I can't believe you're making such a stupid decision."

The rant went on for twenty minutes. "Damnit, Gil," Gates said at one point, "Steve is a pure salesman, that's all he is. He's not an engineer, he doesn't know anything about engineering, and 99 percent of everything he thinks and says is wrong. What the hell are you buying that garbage for?"

Jobs's return was the talk of Silicon Valley through the Christmas holidays. It was such big news that it buried the other big Apple story taking place on store shelves throughout the United States and Europe: despite the profitable quarter, the new pricing policy, the return of the founder, Apple computers weren't selling. A clue that things weren't as good as portrayed could have been found as far back as the beginning of September. Then, *The Wall Street Journal* had kicked off its second-section front, the most widely read newspaper page in high tech, with the headline "Companies Dump Macs as Loyalists Lose Faith." The story went on to recount Apple Computer's worst nightmare, that one by one its big corporate accounts were giving up supporting Macs and surrendering to the comfortable hegemony of Windows. The examples were devastating: 9,000 Macs dropped at Dow Chemical, 3,000 at Northern Telecom Ltd., 7,000 at Eli Lilly & Co., 2,000 at Ernst & Young and on and on. That was just the tip of the iceberg, because for every one of these office Macs dropped, there was at least one compatible home machine that would likely soon be dropped too, as well as thousands of Macs at suppliers and distributors that had been bought to be compatible with the giant corporate client.

It wasn't just the big boys either; the abandonment of Macs was also occurring at those key pivot points and opinion leaders, where the number of computers lost was minuscule, but the influence was enormous. Thus, when Kleiner Perkins, the world's hottest venture capital firm, decided to convert from Apple to Windows, the message to every entrepreneur in Silicon Valley was: Apple is dead; Windows is the future.

The only thing scarier than these facts were the quotes from people who'd made those decisions. All had once been Mac fanatics. They had suffered risks to their careers, censure and jeers from their peers in their lonely missionary work for the Mac. They had fought to bring the maverick Macs into giant companies where the inertia and conservatism had naturally led top management to prefer IBM clones. They had finally won their case . . . and now years later, they seemed to speak for millions of weary, heartbroken Mac owners when they said they were tired of fighting for a company that had been too busy in the last few years dealing with its own arrogance, mismanagement and bureaucratic incompetence to fight for them. Their words were devastating:

"Buy a PC. They're cheaper. And the Mac is going to disappear. . . . It's just not worth fighting for anymore," said Jeffrey Bade of Dow Chemical.

"Once [Windows] NT came out, that was it. . . . I used to tell my bosses that the Mac was like a Ferrari and the PC was a Model T. . . . Now it's the reverse," said Seth Gersch of Montgomery Securities.

"I used to say that it didn't matter if there were more programs available for Windows machines," explained computer consultant Darren Starr, "as long as there was at least one of what I needed running on the Mac. But now there isn't even that."

Throughout the world, not just in great clusters at big corporations and other institutions, but one by one in dens and family rooms, Mac users were making the painful decision to divorce their Mac mate. It was typically an awful experience, because the Macintosh was not just another appliance. It wasn't even the equivalent, say, of a good reliable toaster that had been a trusty tool for twenty years. It was deeper than that. At some point in every Mac owner's career, you made the decision to turn your back on the main parade of the personal computer revolution and follow another, smaller, quirkier group heading off in a different direction. And the cost of making that decision was remeasured almost every day. The seemingly endless stream of Windows users who mocked your use of a "dying" architecture, the long waits for Mac versions of Windows-based applications that sometimes never appeared, the vast mass of exciting new low-cost hardware, peripherals and software for Wintel machines and the volumes of stories about the success of Microsoft and the matching counterpoint stories of the growing disaster at Apple. The hundreds of magazines devoted to the Wintel world, the thousands of creative companies developing new products for it. The millions of people in users groups. The repair shops. The consultants. The aisles and aisles of Windows products at the computer store, compared to the single pathetic, half-empty shelf of Mac products.

Worst of all was the gnawing sense, growing by the year, that you had made the wrong choice, and that history was passing you by.

And then one day, the loyalty, the dissonance and the thousands of hours of experience with the Mac were no longer enough. It often happened the day your old Mac broke down or became too obviously underpowered and you decided it was time to buy a new computer. Then you realized that while it was painful to stay with Apple, it would be madness to re-up with it. Then, though you hated it, though it made you feel like a Quisling, a traitor to your youth and your beliefs, you held your nose and bought a Wintel computer. And after it was over, and you sat there with your new Micron Millennium or Toshiba Satellite Pro, you had the satisfaction of smugly pronouncing to your friends that the Windows 95 interface was "crap" compared to the Mac OS . . . while secretly inside feeling relieved that it was all over and that you would never have to depend upon Apple again.

9.16 DENIAL

It wasn't just among key customers where Apple's cracks began to show in the autumn and winter of 1996. Inside the company there were warning signs as well. In his supreme self-confidence about his management skills, Gil Amelio convinced himself that he really had turned Apple around. An engineer at heart, he knew he had put in place the right systems and that those systems in turn guaranteed that a structural change was now occurring in Apple. It was already, Amelio was certain, a different company.

But he was wrong, fatally so. The systems approach to high-tech management works only if you already have changed the hearts and minds of the people involved. Only then can you use reorganizations, new communications networks and new command and control systems to bring out the best of the staff, clear away bureaucratic roadblocks and streamline and supercharge operations.

Amelio's techniques had largely worked at National Semi because the company he inherited was merely exhausted from fighting the Japanese and frustrated from living under a reactionary, autocratic administration. But the people at National Semiconductor were still "the animals of Silicon Valley," as that ad had once claimed; they were still the tough-minded, hard-charging sumbitches that had taken on everybody from Intel to NEC and lived to tell about it. By opening up the chain of command, clearing away deadwood and establishing a new, more orderly system of communication and measurement, Amelio had allowed the best parts of National to again come to the fore.

But Apple was a different story. Its unique perversity, the greatest legacy of both Jobs and Sculley, was that there was no great gleaming company beneath the tarnish waiting to emerge. The trick was not to let Apple be Apple. It already was, in spades. The trick was to force Apple to become something else, to eradicate those features that Apple thought best about itself—the cleverness, the triumph of image over content, the eminence of philosophy over results—and replace them with those traits, like pragmatism, raw competitiveness and dissatisfaction with anything but results, that many Apple people now considered crass, even evil. This would have taken a great leader, and Gil Amelio was merely a good executive when put in the proper setting.

Even more insidious was the office of the chief executive itself. Steve Jobs had created in the Apple CEO's position a job only he could handle—and even he didn't do it well. Everyone who followed was even less suited to the task. So even as Gil Amelio was working to fix Apple, the Apple CEO position was undoing him.

Amelio never really understood the magnitude of the task before him. If he had, he never would have taken the job. By the autumn of 1996, he had largely revamped Apple's executive team, filling it with the kind of folks who got things done. But there he stopped, convinced that this part of the task was done. He made the mistake of believing the e-mail he got from the rank and file, never realizing that Apple's uniformly brilliant employees were now masters at flimflamming the executive office. They were sabotaging his efforts and reestablishing the old destructive status quo, all while convincing Gil that they had been transformed by his leadership.

A visit to the Infinite Loop campus of Apple early that winter only underlined the stories being whispered around the Valley. Here, in the home of Copland, nearing the end of a year in which the company would lose nearly $900 *million*, nothing seemed to have changed. No one was panicking. On the contrary, there appeared to be ample time to sip lattes, nosh sprouts and throw Frisbees out on the lawn. There was chatter everywhere—Apple people being legendary talkers—but little about the company.

Employees played at Microsoft too, but only because Microsoft was winning; and when they talked it was almost always about Microsoft. Were Gates or Grove running Apple at that moment, there would have been bread and water in the cafeteria, the espresso machines would have been sold off and programmers' heads would have been on poles along the driveway.

But not at Amelio's Apple. It was as if it was 1987 and all was well, not the brink of 1997 and the shadow of death lurking in every corner. It was the Eloi in H. G. Wells's *The Time Machine*—beautiful people gamboling on green lawns, ignoring the fact that Morlocks occasionally appear from underground to drag off some of their numbers for food.

Amidst this surrealistic contentment, the only source of nervous energy in sight was Guy Kawasaki, the prodigal son brought back to help save Mother Apple. But even Kawasaki, who would remain optimistic if the sun went supernova, seemed disoriented. His patented rap about the glories of Apple and the evils of Microsoft contained an unexpected undertone of irony. It was as if he still believed in Bill Gates as the Antichrist, but it was getting tougher and tougher each day to look around him and still believe in his own company as the savior and redeemer of personal computing.

He was interrupted mid-rap by two company managers, who bent his ear for twenty minutes seeking advice on how best to play the politics of getting approval for a project by not really telling top management what they were doing. When Kawasaki got back to the first conversation, he had the look of a man who had returned home to find that nothing had changed, except that his family had become more insincere, backstabbing and incompetent than ever. "This is what it's like here now," he said with a shrug and a touch of sadness. Then he went back to slamming Microsoft.

Chris Braun joined Apple in mid-1996 as an assistant to the director of international marketing. "The first question that I was asked in my interview was 'Are you allergic to dogs?' I said 'No,' which was good because my boss had a German shepherd named Gretyl that followed her everywhere.

"Those I associated with at Apple were some of the most talented, well-traveled and exceptionally intelligent people I have ever been around. There was a lot of stress during those ten months because there were so many reorganizations."

In the end, Braun found himself enlisted in one of the strangest stress-reduction programs Apple ever invented: "Every Friday I would escort an ice-cream deliveryman named Uncle Tommy through four floors of the engineering building. Apparently the idea was to build morale."

In November 1996, at a glitzy Los Angeles press conference, Apple Computer announced a new, and paradoxical, marketing thrust.

With a British firm called Mega Bytes BVI International, Apple planned to create a chain of Mac-based cyber-cafes on the lines of Planet Hollywood and the Hard Rock Cafe. Mega Bytes had already hired the Landmark Entertainment Group to design the eateries, and the first 20,000-square-foot restaurant/Internet surf shop, in L.A., was slated for late 1997. If all went according to plan, future stores would open in San Francisco, New York, London, Paris, Tokyo and Sydney.

The news, meant to thrill the market, instead landed with a nasty thud. What was Apple doing in the restaurant business? Didn't it have enough problems already? And wasn't this just the kind of goofy, tangential activity that Amelio was brought in to stop?

It was a first glimpse that Gil Amelio's Apple Computer was not as clear-headed or as disciplined as the world had been made to think. Nor its judgment in selecting business partners: within a couple of months, Mega Bytes stopped returning phone calls. Nor did it ever make a licensing payment. The project was quietly buried.

9.17 PREMONITION

On December 17, Gil Amelio allowed ten reporters into Apple headquarters for an informal ninety-minute discussion on the state of the company. There he announced that Apple was on the road to recovery. Nineteen ninety-six, he said, had been phase one of the turnaround, fixing the infrastructural problems in the company. Nineteen ninety-seven, he predicted, would be a year spent overhauling all of the company's product lines. Nineteen ninety-eight would then be phase three. "At that point, I think, we'll be ready to start growing again and maybe even getting some market share back." The reporters had heard this before.

Amelio also mentioned that Pippin, the little consumer CD/ROM player/ Internet box for the TV set that many hoped would be Apple's new breakout consumer product, was now dead. Apple had decided not to manufacture the device, but had licensed it to the Japanese company Bandai, which would begin shipping it in March 1997. With that news, Apple essentially admitted that it had failed once again. It had the core of Larry Ellison's $500 Network Computer ready a year before the competition and it had once again failed to follow through.

It didn't go down as well as Gil expected. Desperate, Amelio tried another spin: "There is still enormous sentiment in support of Apple," he argued. "I've had more than one corporate executive tell me that when we have an offering for the purpose of corporate computing . . . they'd be delighted to consider another option." In other words, a maybe on top of a chance of a possibility. Pathetic stuff. And through it all, Amelio nervously twisted his wedding ring and rolled a Styrofoam cup in his hands, like a man sitting on top of a bomb.

It was a bizarre moment. Why call such a gathering at all? One answer is that Amelio already knew what the numbers for the quarter would be, he had already heard the bad news coming from retailers about the disastrous Christmas season—and so now he was trying to do some quick dampening of the expectations raised by the previous quarter's success. But it was already too late for that. He had set the marketplace up for rising expectations with that profitable quarter. Now, no talk of going back to the old three-year plan would be sufficient.

The real answer may have been that Gil Amelio, consciously or not, had a premonition about what was coming and was making one last attempt to tell his own story his own way. In three weeks, unless a miracle happened—and miracles almost never happen in big business—Apple was going to announce quarterly losses of $150 million dollars. This time, especially after the turn-around quarter and his own big bonus, there would be no one to blame but

Amelio himself. That would be ugly enough. But now, the NeXT deal was in the bag. That meant, no matter what his protestations, the return of Steve Jobs. And that spelled doom for the career of Gil Amelio at Apple Computer. Even before the founder arrived, Gil had handed Steve Jobs the fiscal club with which to beat him to death.

9.18 NADIR

The bad financial news arrived on Friday, January 3, 1997, after the close of the market. Analysts had expected a loss, but in the range of $15 million. At ten times that amount, this loss was a slap in the face, a magnitude of error guaranteed to set off cries of fraud and misrepresentation.

It was a long two days that weekend. Was Amelio's reputation sufficient to mitigate the bad news?

The answer was no. As the market opened on Monday, millions of sell orders were already in place. By the end of the day, Monday, January 6, Apple shares had fallen $3.88 to $17.88, a plunge of nearly 20 percent. During that single session, 16.8 million shares were traded—one in every eight outstanding shares of Apple stock—making it the single most active stock that day on Nasdaq. Even Jobs couldn't escape the blast: his 1.5 million shares of Apple stock from the NeXT sale fell $5.8 million in value that day to $26.8 million. Luckily, he had held out for $150 million in cash from the deal as well. Asked about the bad news, an annoyed Jobs replied curtly, "I'm not interested in commenting on that."

Apple's stock was now once again in free fall. It had started 1996 at more than $34 per share and had slumped during the worst of the financial news the following July to just over $17 per share. Since then, the stock had recovered nearly half the loss, peaking at about $27 per share in November. Now it was again heading straight down. The next day it would fall again, to $17.50 per share.

As it happened, that next day, January 7, was the opening of MacWorld Expo in San Francisco. The year before, during the Spindler crisis, Apple had been a wraith at the show, backing off at the last moment from most of its commitments. But this year, to prove that it was alive and still vital, Apple planned to come steaming into Moscone Hall and, dangling a new operating system and Steve Jobs as bait, hold the world's attention for at least a few hours. It was to be a watershed event in Apple's history, the official turning point of the company's fortunes, the moment of inflection between the Old Apple and the New.

In that, Apple succeeded. The January 1997 MacWorld Expo proved to be the second great set piece of the Apple story. It was the other bookend to the Macintosh introduction almost exactly thirteen years before. It bracketed the company's story. Before the 1984 Mac introduction, Apple was a hungry young company struggling for survival and respect. After the 1997 MacWorld Expo, Apple would no longer be Apple, but a kind of Restoration comedy of grand gestures, pompous players and a convoluted plot.

As profoundly different as the two events were, both nevertheless uncannily captured the essence of Apple at that particular moment in its history. The Mac introduction had been improvisational, intimate and cocky. Before that comparatively small crowd, Steve Jobs had set off a revolution. On that day, Apple could do no wrong. Even its mistakes were brilliant. Its attempts at creating an "event" were so crude they were endearing. This was a company that knew it had everything to win and went for it. With just days to prepare, Jobs & Co. constructed a masterpiece, the model for every corporation, private institution and government agency ever after.

If the Mac intro was Jobs as Cortez, the tiny band with nothing to lose capturing an empire, MacWorld Expo was Amelio at the breaching of the Berlin Wall, a bloated, decadent empire knowing it is in collapse but unable to muster even the will to do anything about it. Nine-billion-dollar Apple Computer, with 11,000 employees and access to the best designers, producers and writers on earth, and given six months to prepare for an event upon which the fate of the entire corporation might rest, managed to produce a hollow, overwrought, disjointed and endless extravaganza that was less of a call to arms than a horrifying and unwelcome glimpse into the soul of a dying company. The worst hack journalist in the hall didn't have to work hard to spot the symbolism.

It began well enough. Given all the attention focused on the resurgent Apple, Moscone Hall was jammed to the rafters with 80,000 excited visitors, hundreds of companies showing off their wares, camera crews racing about covering the event for an anxious world.

Be Inc. took its best shot at conquering the show. Its booth was the most crowded at the event, as people swarmed around demonstrations of the losing Mac operating system. Many were blown away, and more than one viewer asked rhetorically, "Why can't my Mac do that?" Power Computing also took its best shot. Its employees in their camos and Humvee would have stolen any other show but this one.

The imminent presentation was the talk at every booth, and in every hallway conversation and pressroom interview. Was Apple doomed? Could

Jobs save the company, or was he an even bigger menace? This was the conversation between two industry veterans:

"So, are you of the school that believes Steve Jobs is a visionary? Or the one that thinks he is a sociopath?"

"I don't think the two are mutually exclusive."

They weren't the only ones who were both thrilled and frightened by the founder's return. A few months before, in a private conversation, one Silicon Valley analyst, when it was suggested that the best thing Apple could do would be to bring back Steve Jobs, rolled his eyes and said, "Good God! That'd be the last thing Apple needs right now." But he was quoted in the paper that morning saying that Apple had made a brilliant move bringing Steve back.

At the appointed time, the crowd of 8,000 true believers and curiosity seekers, as well as those who made a living reporting on both, hurried across the street to the grand ballroom of a nearby hotel. They jammed into a narrow hallway awaiting admission. When at last the doors opened, the crowd swarmed and filled the several thousand seats, and then, in violation of fire marshal restrictions, the believers squeezed into every square inch of floor space in the aisles and wings.

"If Gil doesn't give the speech of his life," muttered the editor of *Mac Home Journal*, "I'll give it for him."

The show literally began with a bang. The giant screen showed the clip from *Independence Day* in which Jeff Goldblum, riding in Air Force One, looks at his Apple PowerBook and realizes that the alien countdown has ended and the White House is about to be destroyed. Then an explosion and a glare of lights . . . and suddenly the spotlight focused on the real actor Jeff Goldblum standing at the podium. The crowd roared and cheered.

Then Gil Amelio stepped out onstage. Wearing chinos and a sport coat, he had made the unbelievable fashion mistake of putting on a collarless dress shirt. Thirty seconds earlier, Apple had once again looked like the coolest company on the planet. And now here stood the CEO, looking exactly like your newly divorced uncle on his first date. The crowd tried to stay pumped up, but Apple's old panache, its legendary hipness, invoked for that one thrilling moment, was now slipping away before their eyes.

It went downhill from there. Amelio's presentation didn't even have the attribute of brevity. Instead it went on for a disastrous, butt-breaking three hours.

Two hours into this marathon, the moment everyone had been waiting for finally arrived. "I'd like to bring a friend out," Amelio said casually, with more showmanship than he'd exhibited in the previous 120 minutes. The expectant rumble rose to a full-throated cry.

Steven Jobs, imperially slim in his dark, tailless suit, emerged from the wings to the explosion of a hundred camera flashes. He winced at the glare. "You guys are going to have to stop making me blind or I'm going to fall off the stage." He responded to the cheers with his little smile—and that set off another round of cheering. There he was. The legend. The one solipsist of his generation who had actually been proven right. At that moment, everyone was indeed merely an agent of his desires. And one suddenly realized the shocking possibility that the entire history of Apple Computer, twenty years of glory and ignominy, brilliant success and embarrassing failure, the parade of fallen captains on the Ship of Fools, even Jobs's passion, crucifixion and now resurrection, had been planned all along by Steven Jobs. And all of us—Apple employees, customers, suppliers, even casual observers—were merely characters in a gigantic epic novel, a *Bildungsroman* Jobs had been writing since he was nineteen years old. Perhaps that had always been the secret behind that ironic little smile.

And this was the latest brilliant chapter. Before the adoring audience, the constituency he needed to fulfill his plans, Jobs managed to accomplish in ten minutes what Apple had been trying to do all day. He gave the company a sense of purpose, a history (". . . that day I went to Xerox PARC"), and, through the new NeXT/Mac hybrid, to be called Rhapsody, a reason to believe in the company's future. That was awesome enough, but even more breathtaking was how he did it. Though he effortlessly owned the hall, Jobs presented himself humbly, as if he was just one more presenter, another, say, director of Pippin keyboard development. It was so disarming, such an unexpectedly clever new form of seduction, that the audience melted. Even those who knew better. And when he left the stage, Jobs left an aching void in the audience's heart.

Amelio should've ended the extravaganza right there, on the perfect emotional note, with the audience ready to climb out of the trenches and attack. But Gil Amelio couldn't stop. He still had a half dozen items on the agenda. Another hour, as the audience, already spent and happy, groaned and begged to be left alone in its afterglow.

Yet, amazingly, in that last hour there was one more transcendent, signifying moment. It came at the end, almost like an afterthought. Jobs was called back onstage, this time with Steve Wozniak. It was their first time together onstage in many years. The old best friends, separated by time, success and betrayals, but forever linked by history. If Jobs was a sleeker version of his old self, Woz was a more avuncular version of his. Rotund now, and dressed in a baggy, violently loud sweater, this middle-aged legend looked uncannily like Norm Abram on *This Old House*.

In the most obvious ways, Wozniak's Wilderness Years had been far less productive and yet more successful than his old partner's. He had not become a billionaire—in fact, he had less money than ever. Nor had he founded a successful company or slept in the White House. On the contrary, these days he was better known for being a has-been and an eccentric—a guy who paid for small items by cutting dollar bills from sheets purchased from the mint. He had become a well-known philanthropist too, his timely gift to the Children's Discovery Museum only the best-known of his donations.

In subtle ways, Woz's victory had been the most satisfying and complete of all. In the intervening years he had followed his own inner compass. It had not begun well, with the failure of CL9 and his second divorce. Bill Graham also reentered his life, this time taking $600,000 of Woz's money for a rock concert in Moscow—to interview the ferocious Graham and the trusting Woz sitting side by side was a chilling experience. Graham later confided to his associates that he thought Wozniak was "a simpleton."

Still, even the predator-prey relationship with Graham eventually bore fruit for Wozniak. The two became partners in the Shoreline Amphitheater, the largest concert venue between San Francisco and San Jose—and for years Woz attended almost every concert, sometimes bringing along a toy laser to draw squibbles on the theater's vast tent roof.

Meanwhile, Woz also learned something about finances: he knew nothing about how to handle his wealth. As he once famously said, "I don't feel attached to my money in normal ways." In the late 1980s, he took the small fraction of what was left of his once-great wealth and put it into tax-free municipal bonds—"safe," wrote *Wired*, "from the depredations of wise guys." The move at last freed Woz to grow up.

He married again, to Suzanne Mulkern, and the marriage seemed a happy one. He shared custody of his three children with Candy Clark. And if he paid too much for his big house in the Los Gatos hills, at least he didn't lose it. Instead, it sat nearly empty, as Woz and Mulkern moved elsewhere in town.

In a *Wired* profile of Woz in 1998, the magazine told how, in true style, Woz had spent years trying to get a phone number with matching digits— impossible in the Bay Area. Then came a new cell phone exchange, 888, and Woz quickly grabbed 888-8888 as his own number. He was soon buried in hundreds of phone calls each day, nearly all of them dead air, the sound of a TV in the background, or gurgles. It turned out to be babies, playing with the phone and endlessly tapping the number eight. As *Wired* noted with irony about the old phone hacker: "The children of America were making their first prank call. And the person who answered the phone was Woz."

It might have all ended badly, except that in 1990 Woz at last found something he could care about as much as he had personal computers: teaching. Using his own money to hire teachers, he volunteered with the Los Gatos school district to teach computers to fifth through eighth graders. The classroom was the three-car garage of the empty mansion, the latest-model computers sharing space with unopened cases of Jolt Cola.

By all accounts, Woz was a wonderful teacher, changing the lives of his young students. The man whose own life had gone sideways into unimaginable worlds when he was thirteen was now dedicating his time left to helping other children through that moment. The legacy of his middle years might not be *Toy Story* and NeXT Computer, but the street leading into the Children's Discovery Museum was officially titled Woz Way. Even Steve Jobs didn't have a city street named for him. And it was Woz who drew the biggest applause of the afternoon.

Wozniak didn't say a word. He didn't have to. His life had now taken him away from the ongoing soap opera of Apple and of Silicon Valley. There was now nothing for him to add to the Apple story—except one fact, revealed without the need for explication. As incredible as it seemed, Woz had won. Like David Packard, he now stood as a model for how not just to succeed in Silicon Valley but how to triumph. The lesson was missed by the assembled cheering thousands, because if Packard's path to victory was impossible, Wozniak's was utterly improbable. He didn't *fit* the image of high-tech success in the 1990s. He didn't look like Larry Ellison or Steve Jobs. He wasn't obsessed with the defeat of everyone else like Bill Gates.

The audience cheered Woz for his technical genius and at the same time pitied him for his irrelevance—and got it exactly backward. He was just a frumpy, poorly dressed middle-aged man who happened to be a legend. That he might also have found happiness in the same way Packard did—through loyalty, integrity, concern for others and doing what he loved most—did not fit the equation. And if he acted sometimes like a child, Woz had nevertheless become more of an adult than the superannuated adolescents who now wrote the narrative of Valley life . . . including the former friend with whom he now shared the stage. For Woz at least, the loop had not been closed, but shattered.

Having reassembled the founding duo, Amelio then announced that he was awarding them the first two models of a special version of the Macintosh. Out they came atop a rolling table, two exquisite machines that looked like a cross between a crystal Baccarat award and a Bang & Olufsen stereo. An upright, rearing flat box bearing a flat panel display, a pair of equally rampant stereo speakers, brushed chrome and Lucite. In their elegance, the two computers were as stunning and standard-setting as the original Macintosh had been all those years before.

Then, in a flicker, they were gone, leaving more than one reporter to ask, "*What the hell was that?*"

It was the visual highlight of the three hours. It seemed to cast in the shade everything in the presentation that came before it. And in perfect symmetry with the rest of the debacle, Amelio had brought it onstage like an afterthought, teased the audience and pulled it away. Computatis Interruptus. Months later, the magnificent box that would have been Apple's new hardware style, if Apple still had style or courage, appeared as the overpriced and rare Mac Special Edition.

Apple, it seemed, could still design interesting products. It could just no longer build them or market them. It really was time for Steve Jobs's return.

The Amelio marathon (or, as *Upside* cheekily called it, Gil Aid '97) ended as it had run, in a minor key on the downbeat. The crowd gleefully tore their free videos of *Independence Day* from under their chair seats and ran. But onstage there was one last telling moment. Wozniak walked to the edge of the stage to meet his friends and admirers. So did Gil Amelio, to accept false congratulations for his unfortunately unforgettable performance. (It was so bad that one attendee on the way out of the hall asked an Apple employee if Amelio had suffered a stroke.)

But the moment the lights came up, Steve Jobs slipped away, refusing to be part of a joint photograph with his old partner. The Wizard stepped behind the curtain and was gone—as if to remind everyone that he was merely a presenter, a *guest*, and that this travesty was not his creation. Thus, while Woz and Amelio stayed behind, Steve Jobs was already racing into the future.

10.0 GREEN SHOOTS

10.1 SERPENT'S TEETH

With the arrival of Steve Jobs, Gil Amelio found himself holding the devil by the tail—and realized that was the worst place to hold him. Not only was the most dangerous threat to his dreams of glory now by his side, but Amelio had invited him there. Steve Jobs not only believed he was brighter than Amelio, that he better understood both Apple and the personal computer industry, but, thanks to the success of a cartoon, appeared to be a better businessman than Amelio too.

This was lethal. The two times in the past, with Scott and Sculley, when Jobs had decided that his apprenticeship was over and that he now knew more than the CEO, a career homicide soon followed. And since Jobs had been the victim the last time, it was a sure bet that he would now strike first.

In the meantime, Amelio was Jobs's Toy Story. Jobs merely had to wait for the right moment. In the meantime, he let Amelio take the fall.

It didn't take long—though it seemed forever to the growing numbers of Macolytes who were convinced that Apple's only hope was for Steve Jobs to take over the company *right now.* For his part, Amelio was in the purgatory of doing exactly what he said he'd do, a strategy which drew cheers just three months before, and now being told that he was a disaster as CEO. That meant that from now on even his successes would be counted as failures. A more pragmatic or clever man might have pumped up the next quarter's profits, declared a victory and bailed out. But Amelio hadn't reached this pinnacle in his career to give it up so easily. He read the reports of his miserable performance at MacWorld Expo, but he dismissed them. After all, everybody knew he was awkward in public. What really mattered wasn't image but results.

No. After Jobs's appearance, Apple lovers everywhere suddenly decided that what they craved most was, in fact, image—and the rush of excitement that came with it. Gil Amelio was in the tragic position of being the only person in that crowded hall who didn't fall for Steve Jobs's charms. Thus, he couldn't even feel the weather changing around him.

The irony in this, a new one for the Apple archives, was that now that he had destroyed his image, Amelio suddenly discovered how to put on a tight, compelling show. The occasion was the Apple annual meeting, held once again at Flint Center at De Anza Junior College, site of the Mac introduction. Everyone walked into the hall that day, February 5, one month after the MacWorld Expo debacle, knowing the news was bad. Not only had Apple lost $120 million for the quarter, but there was an added wrinkle. Apple was now falling even further behind the rest of the personal computer industry. The precise amount had been made public a week earlier by the market research firm Dataquest: while worldwide PC shipments had increased by nearly 18 percent in 1996, Apple's had fallen by 22 percent. Apple's domestic slump was even greater, 30 percent, the biggest drop-off occurring during the Christmas season. That fourth quarter also marked the first time since records had been kept that Apple was not among the top five PC vendors in the United States. "Apple may have a rebound this year," predicted Dataquest, then added dolefully, "What that doesn't mean is that the underlying problems have been fixed."

And the stock kept sliding. By January 28, it had fallen from $26.56 the previous October to just $16.63. In the greatest bull market of modern times, Apple's stock couldn't even hold its value. Meanwhile, the company's business continued to slide, as did its market share. In *The Wall Street Journal*, columnist Walter Mossberg, perhaps the most influential journalist in high tech—and a longtime Apple advocate—stunned the computer world by announcing: "After carefully reading the plan and interviewing top Apple executives, I believe the strategy makes buying a Mac a relatively risky investment for [consumers and small business owners], compared with buying a computer running Microsoft's Windows 95 or Windows NT operating systems."

If Regis McKenna was correct, that only a handful of key opinion makers guided the thinking and buying habits of the entire electronics industry, then this one column was as damaging as the $120 million loss. When it came to making a computer purchase, Mossberg was the Man, and now he had turned his face against Apple. His words echoed millions of other once loyal Macintosh owners.

> I don't say this with any glee. It was Apple's computers that got me
> into computing, and I still own two Macs. . . . Only last year I advised

that it was still safe to buy a Mac, despite Apple's troubles. But this new operating system plan asks for too much waiting and too much blind faith on the part of consumers.

At the heart of Mossberg's rejection was his concern not that the new Rhapsody operating system wouldn't work, but that it would work too well. After all, the NeXT OS had always been a product for large corporate users. No consumer applications library had ever been written for it, and there appeared to be no one signing up for that opportunity now that NeXT was part of Apple. Thus, as Mossberg saw it, there was a very great danger that the Mac's key customers—consumers, small businesses, graphics houses and schools— would find themselves trapped between an obsolete System 7 Mac OS and an unusable Rhapsody. Those who chose the former would end up abandoned by Apple, while those who chose the latter would discover that Rhapsody was in fact Threnody, a hymn for the dead.

It was certainly not a good time for the Apple CEO to be facing the company's shareholders, especially in light of what those same shareholders had done to Mike Spindler at the same event and location a year before. The employees on hand wouldn't be happy either, having received a memo the week before preparing them for even more layoffs. The crowd rumbled and grumbled into the hall loaded for bear.

But then, unexpectedly, amazingly, Amelio rose to the occasion. Commanding and self-assured, he faced the surly crowd.

As you know, I've dealt with troubled companies before. I am well acquainted with what it takes to bring them back to health. When I joined Apple, I said the journey would take about three years. Today, we're a third of the way there. We're working hard to move faster, but unfortunately there are no shortcuts, no magic bullets.

That aside for a moment, let me confess that I have never felt comfortable meeting with shareholders at a time when the stock is declining. I am no happier about that than you. And you have my word, for both institutional and personal reasons, that I am highly motivated to take all the necessary corrective steps to reverse our downward plunge.

Amelio went on to list "five crises" facing Apple when he joined the company and the strategies he had taken to "help the 'patient' get better." It was one of the best overviews of the company ever given:

1. *Liquidity.* "When I came on board, Apple's cash position was precari-

ous. . . . Today we are in much better shape. We ended the first quarter with $1.8 billion in cash. We slashed inventory by 75 percent."

2. *Quality.* "Faulty products were undermining Apple's greatest asset, its loyal customer base. . . . These quality issues, by the end of the year, would cost the company hundreds of millions of dollars. . . . Our PowerBook line was so severely faulted that we had to halt distribution. [Now] the data to date show a 90 percent decrease in warranty claims on our current PowerBook 1400 models."

3. *Copland.* "Our customers and developers demanded—and deserved—a clear road map for how we planned to bring them into the future with System 7 upgrades and with a new, state-of-the-art OS. And we didn't have one. Until we put a viable OS strategy in place, with [a] clear transition path for customers, we could not have a viable future. . . . With regard to Mac OS 7, our response was to plan releases every six months and to have at least three such releases defined at any given time. With regard to a new OS, our response was to identify and define a new architecture and implement that architecture in a timely fashion. We did a thorough and careful exploration of options. NeXT proved to be the answer."

4. *Culture.* "The fourth crisis involved Apple's internal culture. When margins were over 50 percent, the company seemed to move forward on sheer exuberance. But in today's world of competitive pressures and lower or even nonexisting margins, the lack of cohesiveness and discipline was killing us. Apple acted less like a coherent organization than a loose coalition of projects; a collection of tribes instead of a modern industrial enterprise. And perhaps that is a generous description. My response was to build a seasoned management team. . . . We instituted management training at all levels. We welcomed back Steve Jobs and Steve Wozniak in advisory roles. . . . My aim in this is to harness Apple's culture, not stifle it. I want to be clear that there is much I value—and much that you should value here: the incredible passion and resilience of our employees. Our insistence on creativity. And, yes, our sometimes evangelical fervor for the social value of our work. These are jewels you cannot create in management training seminars. I'm confident that they'll shine even brighter with the kind of mature management attention and nurturing we're giving them."

5. *Fragmentation.* "The company was simply doing too much, moving in too many directions—and not enough of it was profitable. . . . [That crisis] is still largely in front of us. And it is the most urgent near-term management issue we face. The lesson we are striving to teach is that the totality of our business is much greater than its individual parts. . . . We have made significant headway over the past year: lowering our break-even point by more than

a billion dollars, reducing head count by 3,565 and selling off facilities. But as our first quarter indicated, we continue to deliver unacceptable results. It will be necessary to be even more disciplined in narrowing our focus. We plan to make further cutbacks in expenses to bring us to a sustainable financial position."

It was both a magisterial presentation and the best argument Gil Amelio had yet mustered for his own continuing tenure as head of Apple Computer. But for all of its understanding of Apple's predicament, on closer inspection it also showed the weaknesses of his approach. For example, unanswered were the doubts about the NeXT OS, and thus about Rhapsody, as a consumer product. And then there was the matter of just how efficiently System 7 users would be able to migrate to Rhapsody. Amelio presented a chart showing a smooth transition from 7.6 to Tempo (late 1997) to new products code-named Allegro (early 1998) and Sonata (late 1998)—but, despite the melodic titles, no intersection with Rhapsody. Did that mean Apple would carry *two* operating systems through the end of the century? Wasn't this fragmentation?

Next there was the matter of corporate culture. The impressiveness of Amelio's acute and honest appraisal of Apple's internal problems was matched only by his breathtaking self-delusion that the problem had been solved by a new executive team, management training and bringing Jobs and Woz back for a cup of coffee. Apple's cultural problems were so vast they even scared the people who worked there and were part of that problem.

Finally, on the matter of fragmentation, the phrase "more disciplined in narrowing our focus" was code for: layoffs. Lots of them. Apple still needed to cut its overhead by another $400 million. And you couldn't do that by cutting back on sashimi and travel budgets. But to the shareholders, Amelio would only say that he would be more precise on the matter in a few days.

So there it was. Financially, the company appeared in worse shape than ever. But against that, Dr. Amelio posited the counternotion that such bad financial news was merely the painful symptom of a company in the process of healing and growing stronger by the day.

"It was pretty damn impressive," said one shareholder, Joe Shane, afterward. "I didn't know Gil had it in him." He immediately placed an order for more shares—and made money on the brief two-point bounce—then sold them. Within a few days, the stock was sliding again.

On the day of the annual meeting, Apple announced yet one more in its endless history of reorganizations. This one divided R&D into hardware and software, and pulled all marketing under one organization, headed by Guerrino De Luca, former chief of Claris. Then, on February 10, the company announced that it expected "substantial" losses in the current, second quarter, in large part because the $400 million deal with NeXT had now risen to about $430 million. Apple added that it also did not expect to be profitable until the fourth quarter. Meanwhile, Apple employees waited for the other shoe, layoffs, to drop.

But before that, there were two more blows. The next day, February 11, Apple's canary decided to fly off before the coal mine collapsed on her. Heidi Roizen resigned, citing a desire to spend more time with her children. No one really believed her explanation. And, in fact, when pressed, Roizen admitted that the reorganization had played a major part in her decision. The departure of Apple's "barometer" warned of a major storm ahead. (In May 1998, she joined Microsoft as a part-time consultant to burnish that company's image in Silicon Valley.)

The same day Roizen resigned, CalPERS, the California Public Employees' Retirement System, a $108 billion pension fund that was one of the most influential investors in America, put Apple at the very bottom of its annual list of America's ten leading "Financial Underperformers." This meant that Apple was now targeted by the organization for close monitoring and governance. And that meant regular meetings with Apple's managers and directors, and demands for structural changes or risk losing the fund's investment—in Apple's case, 710,000 shares. That was less than 1 percent of Apple's outstanding stock, but such was CalPERS's influence that should it pull out an avalanche of other departing investors would soon follow.

CalPERS slammed Apple for the "high salaries" of its top managers at a time of "poor performance and mounting layoffs"; an executive staff that "has not articulated a clear-cut strategy" for financial recovery and too many directors who sat on too many other boards, "thereby diminishing their ability to help the company." In a final insult, Kayla Gillan, chief counsel for CalPERS, said she'd sent a certified letter to Amelio way back in November noting these problems and requesting a meeting, "but they lost the letter."

On February 25, Steve Jobs and Pixar signed a ten-year deal with Disney to provide five more animated films. On the news, Pixar's stock jumped nearly 50 percent in value in a single day, to $21. Newspapers around the country carried the AP photo of him joking with Disney chief Michael Eisner—two titans of American industry having a private laugh over Eisner's Snow White tie. Reading those papers, a million Macolytes, awaiting the impending bombshell from Apple, saw the look of a winner, of the man who might lead them out of this slough of despond.

On March 6, with his inimitable timing, Joe Graziano, now advising new start-ups (and sitting on the board of Pixar), used the moment to kick Apple while it was down. In two long telephone interviews with the *Mercury News*, he recapitulated how, if only Apple's board had listened to him that day in Texas in 1995, he might have saved Apple. Then he savaged everything about the current company, especially Amelio, whom he said "hasn't a clue what he's dealing with." He particularly slammed Amelio's bonus package. As for the profitable quarter, Graziano claimed it was an accounting scam that involved taking back $28 million of previously booked charges. "Only in corporate America can anyone get away with that stuff. It's theft on a grand scale, only it's legal." Finally, with the NeXT deal, Graziano claimed, Apple was now "grasping at straws," adding, "It's good for Steve, and I'm glad for him. But I think it's too late even for Steve to save it. I don't see any scenario where Apple becomes a profit-making company."

For the second time in his strange relationship with Apple, Graziano delivered a message with the ring of truth about it. And once again, he wasted his shot by undermining the point he was trying to make.

The bomb, which had been whistling down over everyone's head for weeks, finally hit on March 14, a Friday—that being the traditional day for layoffs so everyone can be run out of the facility and given a weekend to cool off. Four thousand one hundred jobs cut. That was 31 percent of the company's total payroll. And though the layoffs were fairly equally distributed around the world, 4,100 jobs was almost equal to the number of employees Apple had in Silicon Valley. It was also among the largest mass firings the Valley had ever experienced. From a high of more than 17,500 full- and part-time employees in early 1995, Apple's employment rolls had now slumped to just 9,300.

At the same time, Amelio announced that the company was abandoning a number of new projects, notably OpenDoc, a Java-like framework for building software out of modular software pieces, Cyberdog, a Web browser, and QuickDraw GX, a graphics program. Since most of these were available in alternative, often better versions from other vendors, they weren't a great loss. But two other abandoned projects were much more disturbing. One was Open Transport, the networking software for the Mac, which was to be replaced by the networking system in Rhapsody; the other was any future development of tools—the programs used to write other programs—for the Mac OS. As one software vendor complained: "This is strictly the NeXT mafia trying to wrest control of the operating system from Apple." The news was chilling to Mac customers, especially big corporate customers that purchased hundreds, even thousands, of Apple computers. The announcement said: no matter what it publicly professes, Apple was not going to support its installed base of older machines.

And even with all that, Amelio wasn't yet done with the bad news. He also hinted that, financially, the current quarter was going to be bad. Very bad. Unbelievably, it might even be as bad as the horror of early 1995. The inflated NeXT price was just the start. Sales were still tanking—perhaps for losses as great as $150 million. Now to that the company would have to add another $155 million in severance costs. This suggested losses for the quarter of more than $700 million dollars. If true, that would mean that Apple would have lost, in just eighteen months, a total of nearly $2 *billion*—a loss so vast that a person couldn't count it in two lifetimes; a loss so big that if it were revenues it would make the Fortune 1000. At the same time, Apple's revenues were down by 25 percent, its staff by nearly a third and its total share of the world's personal computer market under 5 percent.

And yet, for all that, there was no indication that Gil Amelio had made Apple into a better company. It was easy simply to blame him—as many did. But the answer lay elsewhere, in a possibility that no one wanted to admit. It was that Amelio's real problem was a lack of imagination. He had followed all the traditional rules of business turnaround: pare back products to those that are or can soon be made profitable. Cut back employment to a central core of productive talent. Hold on to your supply and distribution channels for dear life.

But what if there was no core at Apple? What if the entire company was like a collection of Chinese boxes or Russian nested dolls? What if you kept peeling away layer after layer of superfluousness and then found, to your dismay, that there was nothing left—and that in the process you had turned a hollow, but enticing package into a pile of empty shells?

10.2 PROGENY

That Friday afternoon of the layoff was different from times past. Before, as far back as the Night of the Long Knives, Apple layoffs had been a time of bitterness, acrimony and a seething sense of betrayal. Not this time. The only people now at Apple who were surprised were the ones who *weren't* laid off. Everyone had seen it coming for weeks and had prepared themselves. Work in the offices had nearly stopped. Like soldiers pinning names on themselves before an attack, fresh résumés were copied and secreted into briefcases. And in many offices the prayer was not to keep one's job, but to get a great severance package that would let one hang out for a few months. The prayer even had a name: DSP, for Desperately Seeking Package.

When the pink slip did arrive, many met the news with relief. Apple, the "Graduate School of Silicon Valley" as one employee called it, was no longer seen as a career, much less a calling. It was now where you worked off the last fantasies of adolescent idealism before you moved on to the real-life world of work. Everyone knew there was no future at Apple. But like many young people leaving home for the first time, some needed a push. The layoff did just that. Meanwhile, beyond the lobby, Silicon Valley was enjoying its Golden Age, the most successful period of its already remarkable history. By one estimate, every single day of 1996 minted an average of sixty-four new millionaires. At start-ups like Yahoo! and Siebel Systems, generous stock options meant that *everybody* got rich.

Burke Tyree had just been hired by Apple as a temp. His first job was to go through the many offices of the newly fired and help them clean out their rooms. "They had about an hour to get their things and separate usable office supplies from personal junk. Some people who had just been fired were in shock. But mostly, even people who hadn't been fired were moping around.

"So many people had been laid off that the company seemed empty. There were now something like five hundred empty offices. So we consolidated the people that were still there, moved them closer together, so there wouldn't be so many empty offices between them."

Those who were soon to be fired and those who would soon be unexpectedly still employed walked out of Apple that afternoon and gathered in local restaurants and watering holes. Few were concerned. Many had been fielding calls from headhunters for days. Others found business cards from Aerotek Data Services Group, a recruiting firm, under the windshield wipers of their cars. In a Valley desperate for warm bodies, more so talented computer types, the ex-Apple employees knew they could have a new job in the morning.

So, for the sheer irony of it, they sat in places like the Peppermill, a retro lounge-restaurant full of retirees and waitresses forced to dress like tarts, and raised glasses in a toast to their old employer. As you looked at them, with their ironic smiles and knowing glances, long hair and grunge clothes, you suddenly realized that this entire generation was the bastard child of Steve Jobs. And if, as it was said, Jobs had set out to change the world, while Bill Gates had set out with the more prosaic goal of putting MS-DOS in every computer—then both had, in fact, achieved their goal.

The Apple children laughed the evening away. Some wore Apple decals on their faces. They joked about taking jobs at Microsoft, or having everyone gather around and drink, Jonestown style, a poison Kool-Aid in the colors of the Apple logo—not realizing that was a decade-old joke about working for Steve Jobs. Then, after drinks and appetizers, they broke up and wandered off into their separate lives. Summer camp was over.

For the older, truer believers, the end was much more touching. Said one assistant to a senior executive, "I had my very identity, my social life, my intellectual life, my whole sense of well-being wrapped up in the fabric of the Apple culture. It was a privilege to be part of a society so erotic, so liberating. I'd wake up in the morning and didn't feel I was going to work because I had this incredible sense of excitement. It was like being back in college.

"Then it was like the whole value system of the place shifted. I started to lose respect for the company. It wasn't the same place after Sculley left, and worse after Spindler. Finally one morning, it started to be work.

"I cried the day I quit."

10.3 AUTOPSY

Giving advice on how to save Apple Computer had become something of a cottage industry—one more profitable than its subject. As early as January, at the time of MacWorld Expo, industry leaders, academics, former employees, business theorists and, ultimately, anybody famous who owned a Macintosh was called upon to enlighten mankind on what should be done to turn around Apple's fortunes.

What was intriguing about these considered opinions, and they numbered in the hundreds, was (1) how contradictory they were, suggesting that none of these "experts" really had a clue; and (2) how passionate they were, a reminder that Apple may have lost its market share, but still enjoyed a truly spectacular share of mind. Nobody wept when Compaq had a bad quarter.

The first round of opinion makers, and the advice they gave, was fairly predictable: venture capitalist John Doerr ("Make a major contribution, with NeXT technology, to the development of the Java tsunami"), Esther Dyson ("Support what's already being done on the Mac") and Marc Andreeson ("Concentrate on building and demonstrating momentum"). As if Amelio & Co. hadn't at least considered every one of these platitudes. What was far more interesting was the realization of how the tables had turned. Most of these individuals had been made by Apple or the revolution it kicked off. Now these progeny were as famous as and much more influential than their progenitor.

By March and the big layoff, the Apple opinion factory was running at full capacity on all three shifts. You couldn't turn on the new wave of television business and computer shows on CNBC, MSNBC, CNN and Fox without hearing someone bloviate on Apple's problems and how they could be cured.

The apogee of all this opinion making came with the June 1997 edition of *Wired* magazine. *Wired*, having blown its own IPO a few months earlier, knew a lot about failing companies, and this newfound wisdom gave its article on Apple an edge. The cover was a classic: the Roman Catholic Sacred Heart, beloved in Latin American churches, with its wrapping of thorns dripping blood and starry spikes bursting behind it. Only this time it wasn't the *sacré coeur* within the barbs, but the Apple logo. And a one-word headline: *Pray.*

Inside, *Wired's* editors had compiled "101 Ways to Save Apple." Some were tough ("1. Admit it. You're out of the hardware game." "6. Apologize." "76. Make damn sure that Rhapsody runs on an Intel chip.") Some were thoughtful ("2. License the Apple name/technology to appliance manufacturers." "9. Fire the people who forecast product demand." "15. Dump, or outsource, the Newton, eMate, digital cameras and scanners." "20. Sell yourself to IBM or Motorola." "36. Clone the PowerBook." "50. Give Steve Jobs as much authority as he wants in new product development.") And some— deservedly—were facetious and cruel: ("32. Advice to Gil Amelio: shorter speeches, tighter pants." "57. Bring back John Sculley. He would provide a convenient whipping boy." "69. Change your name to Snapple and see if you can dupe Quaker Oats into buying you.")

Surrounding these suggestions was the collected advice of experts and celebrities, ranging from MIT's Marvin Minsky to film critic Roger Ebert. Even Jef Raskin, now a bald graybeard, weighed in with the same advice of fifteen years before: "[Apple] never rethinks the whole proposition. Throw out the old and clumsy desktop, along with its operating-system-and-applications paradigm, and go for true task-centered design."

But amid all these pronouncements, there was one comment different from the rest. It was devastating in its accuracy. And, in an irony of ironies, it came from Nathan Myhrvold, chief technologist at Microsoft:

At a certain critical point—perhaps five years ago—Apple stopped investing time, effort, brainpower and money in continuing to make a better product. Instead, it dissipated its energy on everything *but* the Macintosh—on Newton, Sweet Pea, Kaleida, Taligent. Meanwhile, the rest of the world caught up. The last great engineering task accomplished on the Mac was the switch to PowerPC. However, no new features went in. The company that had been the leader in operating systems found that it could no longer write an operating system— Copland was a disaster that never shipped. It had to suffer the ultimate ignominy of buying one outside. The NeXT purchase is too little too late. The Apple of the past was an innovative company that used software and hardware technology together to redefine the way people experienced computing. That Apple is already dead. Very adroit moves might be able to save the brand name. A company with the letters A-P-P-L-E in its name might survive, but it won't be the Apple of yore.

It was the epitaph of Apple Computer, written, perhaps appropriately, by its greatest competitor. *Apple is already dead.* It was what Valley veterans had been privately saying to each other for months. No company could emerge the same after what Apple had just been through.

If the death of Apple didn't fit the image of a traditional corporate death— broken men shuffling off into the darkness, padlocks on the gates, boarded windows and weeds in the parking lot—it was because nothing ever really died in high technology. Rather it was sold off in pieces or whole or its patents were licensed away. Even Fairchild, the founding company of modern Silicon Valley, still existed, even though it had been extinguished as a corporation for a decade. It was now a division of National Semiconductor. And even as Apple was laying off its thousands, National Semiconductor, now even more prosperous than it had been under Amelio, sold off the Fairchild division to an East Coast concern—which immediately announced it was bringing the firm back to the Valley.

Technology never really died either. Within most of the major software programs on the market were the kernels, sometimes just a few lines of code, of scores of long-forgotten programs that preceded them from decades past. It was the same with semiconductors. Inside of every new Pentium Plus chip from Intel was the tiny core of the original 8086 microprocessor. And even the little MOS 6502, the processor around which Wozniak had built the Apple I, still survived. Its design, having been licensed to one manufacturer after another over the course of a quarter century—including Synertek and Rockwell—was still regularly upgraded and redesigned by a little ten-person company called Western Design Center of Mesa, Arizona. Now a low-powered microcontroller chip sold for just pennies, the 6502 nevertheless was still being used by the millions by such giants as AT&T, ITT, Sanyo and Siemens.

For the same reason, a great company like Apple could die, and yet still be operating, even selling billions of dollars' worth of products. It could still have buildings and grounds and factory automation equipment and even thousands of employees showing up each day. But it would be a ghost, a phantasm.

The March 1997 layoff was that crossing over, that point of no return—as Apple's young employees instinctively understood. The Children's Crusade was over, ending, a lot like the original, in a massacre. The narrative itself might still go on, but it was now self-reflexive. Henceforth the Apple story would be only about the Apple story. A new company might climb out of the crater, it might even use the same name and logo, sell a few of the same products, even have a familiar face on the first page of the annual report. But it would be a different company. The infinite looping of Apple Computer had finally blown up the machine. Whether the new company would repeat the same deadly cycle was something only the future could tell. In the meantime, a lot of people would fight over Apple's corpse.

10.4 EXILE

In the months that followed, senior management at Apple behaved like a deposed royal family. Still going through the motions, still keeping up appearances, convincing themselves that the blade would never fall, the firing squad would never arrive at the door. And no one was more lost in this self-delusion than the king himself. Gil Amelio, convinced that his strategy was still sound, albeit unfinished, that he had saved Apple and was, as predicted, halfway through the turnaround, acted as if it was business as usual.

But it obviously wasn't. Now events began to pick up speed. On a single day, June 30, Apple's biggest Mac distributor to schools, Education Access, abruptly ended its relationship with Apple and switched to IBM, Compaq and Power Computing. Then Power Computing added to the damage by announcing that it would begin making Windows computers, claiming that to grow it needed to expand beyond the limited Apple market. It added that it was increasingly frustrated by the delays in its dealings with Apple.

Yet, in spite of this, so secure did Amelio feel in his position that, bizarrely, he devoted much of the board of directors meetings to endless discussions of what options and appointments he should have on his new jet.

But this was a different board than the rubber stamp of years past. In response to criticism, a fire breather had been added to the placid body: Edgar S. Woolard, Jr., chairman of E. I. Du Pont de Nemours & Co. Silver-haired, with an elegant nose, Woolard may have looked like a Delaware aristocrat, but he was tough as Kevlar. He'd done his own successful turnaround at Du Pont—his sell-off of $1.8 billion in assets and layoffs of 40,000 employees made even Amelio's efforts seem puny—so he was not a man to be fooled by CEO bombast. So, not surprisingly, it was Woolard who finally had enough and organized a vote over the Fourth of July weekend to remove Gil Amelio. And it was Woolard who delivered the news by phone to Amelio on Saturday, July 5, that the board wanted his resignation. Amelio quickly mounted a flurry of phone calls to press his case, but soon realized he had no chance. On Sunday, after telling his wife the news, he formally tendered his resignation.

He also learned that Steve Jobs had been asked to advise the company during the transition.

To his credit, Amelio not only took the news well but even faced the press a few days later. He was unrepentant, refusing to admit any errors. Instead, Amelio reasoned, the board had decided that he, having successfully completed 90 percent of the task at hand, now needed to get out of the way for someone with a different set of skills to take Apple across the finish line. It sounded good, and let him preserve his dignity.

"I know that I've rescued this company," Amelio said. "This company would not be here at this point in time had I not intervened when I did and done the things I've done. And I have done enough of the right things to lay a foundation so that they can realistically talk about a future that was impossible a year and a half ago. So I leave with the greatest sense of accomplishment that you can have for having done an awful lot in a very short period of time."

Others were not so kind. Pieter Hartsook, a former Apple vice president, said simply, "He was not a visionary leader and he never had the confidence of the employees."

"Gil never got his hands around Apple's culture," said Tim Bajarin afterward. "He didn't penetrate and motivate. His model was Lou Gerstertner of IBM. Gerstertner had started his turnaround of IBM by staying out of the public eye and touring around talking to employees and customers. Gil tried the same thing. But Amelio was no Gerstertner, and Apple was no IBM."

But columnist Mike Barnicle of the *Boston Globe*, speaking for the many nontech Mac owners, was much harsher—and probably more accurate about history's judgment. The column was entitled "Road Kill on the Information Highway":

> . . . Today, as a huge MacWorld convention begins in Boston, Apple is nearly extinct. It is at the edge of existence for a lot of reasons. First, some cement head from Pepsi decided that Apple was so great it didn't have to make its technology compatible with other computers because foolish start-up operations like Microsoft were pathetic pretenders and would soon die.
>
> The stupid soft drink guy was succeeded by someone with a funny name who was afraid to emerge from his office as long as the stock market was open. After he got fired, the Apple board of directors ran right out and got somebody else with a weird name and narrow perspective.
>
> . . . How can these nitwits still draw a paycheck when they took the only computer that didn't frighten people while getting the job

done and turned it into the technological equivalent of the 1987 Red Sox bullpen?

And so Gil Amelio, the rising turnaround star, who saw Apple as his launchpad to fame, who had rushed out to meet the movie stars and powerful politicians almost from the moment he took the job and who dreamed of business immortality, became merely a footnote, a nitwit with "a weird name and a narrow perspective." Apple had done it again.

Meanwhile, many inside Apple and out, saw the hidden hand of Steve Jobs in this latest coup d'état—and predicted that Jobs would soon be running Apple outright. But on that there was only silence . . . except for a denial by Gil Amelio, deluded about Jobs right to the end. Steve, said Gil, is my friend. And he added that one of his finest accomplishments at the helm of Apple was bringing Jobs home.

The next day, another ghost from Apple's past appeared from the mists of history to render his opinion on the matter. Happily out of sight now for nearly three years, Sculley decided to use this inauspicious moment to weigh in. It was his belief that the best person Apple could hire to replace Amelio was Sculley's old number two, Del Yocam, currently running a turnaround at another crippled company, Borland International. "While we will never know," Sculley continued, "I believe if Del had been made CEO seventeen months ago, Apple wouldn't be in its current precarious position." He went on to suggest that Jobs be made Apple's "non-executive chairman of the board"—note the first term. "Together, Steve and Del are a creditable team."

Sculley went on to explain that he was making this suggestion now because "this way it's harder for Apple's board to ignore, since time has run out for more absurdity." But of course, the board did ignore him. Who gave half a fuck what John Sculley thought? He made this mess. Besides, Yocam wasn't interested.

Not to be outdone, Jean-Louis Gassée distributed an essay entitled "I like Apple so much I want two of them," in which he recommended that Apple be split into a hardware company, run by Steve Kahng of Power Computing, and a software business run by current Apple marketing vice president Guerrino De Luca. It received about as much attention as Sculley's idea had.

Meanwhile, in the midst of all this management reshuffling, Apple's stock had now fallen to less than $14 per share. The company, it seemed, was now worth as much for its buildings and capital equipment as it was for its business.

On July 16, Apple announced that its losses for the third quarter were just $56 million. It was a measure of how far the company had fallen that this was welcomed as terrific news. After all, the final tally on the previous quarter had been a $708 million loss. And many analysts were half expecting a similar catastrophe, this one likely fatal for Apple as a corporation. "[It's] not good, but everybody was braced for a Greek tragedy," said J. P. Morgan analyst Daniel Kunstler.

Meanwhile, Apple's revenues fell by 20 percent to $1.7 billion. That meant the company had sold 140,000 fewer computers than it had during the same quarter in 1996. It also meant that Apple had shrunk, since the second quarter of 1996—in order by quarter—by 17 percent, 15 percent, 23 percent, 32 percent, 27 percent, and now 20 percent. It was now a $6 billion company—though it could not break even at anything less than $8 billion. For the quarter, it sold fewer than 700,000 computers. And, showing how its market was changing, half of those computers were entry-level products sold to schools and consumers. Server sales accounted for only 1 percent of the business. And sales of that old standby, the PowerBook, were slumping.

10.5 DICING

Amelio's initial claims to the contrary, it was hard not to see the hand of Steve Jobs in the ouster. Vast conspiracies had been rumbling away in the background at Apple for months now, and though the mechanism still remained hidden, the increasingly Felliniesque nature of the players could only have been the work of one man.

Two of the players were especially intriguing. The first was, of all things, a Saudi Arabian prince. Prince Al-Waleed bin Talai bin Abdul-Azil al-Saud, forty-one, was one of the world's wealthiest and lowest-profile investors. Al-Waleed over the years had shrewdly built a $11.7 billion portfolio, and a $2 billion war chest, largely through a strategy of buying positions in large, struggling retailers (Saks Fifth Avenue), entertainment companies (Euro Disney) and luxury hotels. Those who knew anything about him agreed that Al-Waleed was known for his patience in holding an investment for a long-term recovery.

They also agreed that Al-Waleed's April 1997 investment in Apple—a 5 percent stake (6.25 million shares) for $115 million—was nearly unprecedented. He had never before shown much interest in playing the high-stakes game of technology investment. Now, after American Express, Al-Waleed was Apple's largest shareholder.

There was another departure from Al-Waleed's past investments. Typically he bought a piece of the action based upon a positive impression of the company's management. With Apple, however, his motives seemed to be different. Though in his official statement, he wrote, "I believe there is serious potential for Apple to provide large returns to its stockholders once again, as it did in the past," he privately made it known that if Amelio didn't turn the company around soon, he would support any outside group that could.

So it was not a friendly investment. As the prince told *Business Week*, "Gilbert Amelio extended an invitation to me to go to Apple, to be introduced to management and hear their objectives and see what they're doing. . . . He's saying publicly that recovery is only two, three, four quarters away. But he has to assure me in private that this is the case. Apple has to focus on areas it is strong in. Their biggest problem is that they expanded too much and are fighting on too many fronts. They've got to focus and cut costs."

But why choose Apple? The real clue was an aside by the prince that he was friends with Oracle's Larry Ellison, the man who called Steve Jobs his "best friend."

If the high-tech revolution had produced a few noble billionaires, such as Hewlett, Packard and Moore, it had also produced more than its share of venal, eccentric and scary ones. And the scariest, perhaps most demented of all was Larry Ellison.

Ellison, with his preternaturally smooth skin and Armani suits at the office, his obsession with Japanese samurai (and the kimonos he wore at his Japanese-style home), his yacht and Russian MiG, was like the worst-case scenario of the poor kid who got rich. Success only seemed to ignoble him. Along with his flamboyance, Ellison also had a reputation as a rake, of using Oracle as his private harem. But there was no denying he was a bold, creative and very smart businessman.

When Ellison sprang the $500 Internet computer, the NC, on the assembled throng at the Fall 1996 Comdex in Las Vegas, he managed the unprecedented act of hijacking the show. It was the talk of everyone assembled, instantly rendering obsolete everything on display, and even forcing Bill Gates to devote his speech to a rebuttal. In fact, so compelling was the NC idea that Ellison took the uncharacteristic step of actually following up on it. By Christmas, he had assembled a consortium of major companies committed to build the NC.

But what he didn't have was a real personal computer company, a company with both experience in building and selling computers to consumers and instant brand recognition. In Apple, he saw the perfect opportunity: a struggling company in need of a new product/market thrust and the most famous technology brand name on earth. And in his best friend Steve Jobs (interestingly, Jobs didn't say the same of his relationship with Ellison) found a receptive, if more careful, co-conspirator.

There were two things everyone, even his most loyal fans, agreed was true about Larry Ellison. He was incredibly bright . . . and he was almost inhumanly vain. The first enabled him to come up with brilliant ideas like the NC and superb strategies for implementing it. The second made him organically incapable of not blabbing about his plans the first chance he got.

That chance came on a hike with, incredibly enough, a reporter for the *Mercury News*. Yes, he told her, Steve and I, with the help of the prince and some others, are planning a buyout of Apple.

Needless to say, the story ran on the front page of the newspaper the next morning—complete with disavowals from Jobs. I don't know what Larry's talking about, said Steve defensively. But a few days later, at an informal "fireside chat" with a thousand Mac software developers in San Jose, Jobs, acting as if he now had nothing to lose, proceeded to lay into Apple, especially Amelio's management. He told the crowd what he said he'd already told Gil: Apple should sell off the Newton, make the cloning of Apple software easier but more expensive and, most of all, get into network computers. "Apple has suffered from lousy engineering management," he told the crowd. "I think Apple has had its head in the sand for . . . many years." The audience, which had already nicknamed the event the "pyreside chat" and expressed dread of having to endure the Jobs Reality Distortion Field at 9 A.M., ended up giving him a standing ovation.

But even as he appeared to be closing the door on his relationship with Apple, Jobs still took the time to keep a hand in and tidy up some loose ends. "I still have enough faith in Apple's management," he told the crowd, "that I told Larry Ellison not to try to take over Apple." That took care of the historical record.

A few weeks later, Jobs, his plan apparently exposed, sold off all but one share of the 1.5 million Apple shares he earned in the NeXT buyout. When Amelio demanded to know if the rumors of the sale (Jobs's name was not on the transaction) were true, whether Jobs had broken his promise, made at the time of the NeXT buyout, of not selling his shares, Jobs lied.

Jobs would later say that he prevaricated because he was embarrassed and depressed and that now he felt bad about it. His take, at the depressed price of $15 per share, was just $22 million. Apple was destined to be run by a man who had so much faith in it that he sold off his stock in the company.

Then fortune, which had ignored him for months, once again smiled on its mischievous child. As Jobs watched, the board of directors, led by the swift and efficient Edgar Woolard, did the job for him and tossed Amelio out on his ear. Jobs suddenly found himself in the power seat at Apple without spending a dime or getting a drop of blood on his hands. Even the press, loving the sheer theatricality of it, cheered him on. The past was nearly forgotten, and what little was remembered was treated as a mark of character. A characteristic swoon appeared in the *San Francisco Examiner:*

> Is Steve Jobs really about to hop back into the fray? Is this the case of the simultaneously headstrong and heartfelt fireman who, even as his cohorts warn that running in there means two dead rather than one, just can't stand by idly and watch his baby go up in flames?
>
> Certainly if this weren't playing itself out before our very eyes, it would make awfully good drama—actually the stuff of Greek mythology. How far mighty Apple has fallen. And who better to come to the rescue than its own—spurned—progenitor?

Said Tim Bajarin, "I think Jobs knew from the beginning that Amelio was going to fail."

But the most accurate comment was that of Steve Wozniak, who said simply, "Gil Amelio meets Steve Jobs. Game over."

Having been lurking around Apple now for a half year, privy to all of its inside information on products and markets, combined with the larger strategic planning that came with plotting the aborted coup, put Jobs in a superb position to take over his old company. He was already running; now he merely had to step onto the track. Doing so, Jobs moved so fast that he almost seemed to pull Apple—and the attentive world—along in his wake. Though he was still ostensibly merely an adviser to the company and current head of Pixar—and though Fred Anderson, former chief financial officer, was now officially the interim Apple CEO—there was no question that Steve Jobs was running Apple. He attended meetings, made decisions in the company's name and established the company's new strategy. Memos to employees were signed "Steve and the Executive Team." He also began cleaning house of the entire executive team brought in by Amelio. Scalise, a master of the Silicon Valley game, had left in May, skipping out just before the blast. But Jobs took care of the rest. By mid-September, when marketing chief Guerrino De Luca, the last of the Amelio team, quit, Jobs had run off eight top executives, including Ellen Hancock (she reportedly made the mistake of telling Jobs to stop acting like a child), and replaced them with people of his own. Now he would turn his sights on the board.

Executives weren't the only talented veterans leaving Apple. Even with the excitement created by Jobs's return, Apple was still bleeding good people from every department. Even the coddled Apple Fellows began to flee.

Jobs tried to stanch the flow of talent by completing a project Amelio had begun but never put into action: boosting the value of employee stock options through repricing. It was a good idea, but too late. The Thoroughbreds were already out of the barn. In a devastating appraisal of the company's current condition, executive recruiter Igor Still of Geneva Group International said, "Apple today is not viewed by other companies as having especially innovative technology or executives with superior management skills. Their best people have left over the past 24 months. There is no great interest in their remaining people."

Meanwhile, speculation about a corporate buyer for Apple slowly evaporated. This was despite the fact that the entire company could now be purchased (given the current record low stock price of $13.25) for just $2 billion—and that included the $1.3 billion Apple had in cash on hand. Yet even at this bargain basement price, there were no takers. "It's not as though it hasn't been shopped," said Andrew Neff of Bear, Stearns. Apple was now there for Steve Jobs's asking. It was generally assumed that he would take both jobs, as chairman and CEO, as soon as it was tendered by the board.

Yet, three weeks after Amelio's departure, when that offer finally was made, Jobs turned it down. His explanation was that he had a commitment to Pixar and wanted to spend more time with his family. Instead, he would manage the search to fill those positions. However, it escaped nobody that, title or not, Steve Jobs was running Apple Computer. In fact, even as he made the announcement, Jobs was busily approving Apple's final plans for the next week's MacWorld Expo in Boston—and preparing his own keynote speech.

10.6 IN VITRO

The Boston MacWorld Expo, which began on Wednesday, August 6, 1997, was the first major event of Jobs's second term, the first gathering of the post-Apple era. Jobs, with his magnificent sense of occasion, understood that more than anyone, and from the moment he took control again of Apple, he focused everything the company had on that moment. Sensing even that wouldn't be enough, he also arranged to drop a bombshell so big that no one would be able to ignore it.

Apple may have never really been a company, but now it was no longer even an idea. It had lost its technology, its philosophy and most of its market. All it had left was its outsized grip on the popular imagination—and that came from its story and the symbolism that attached to it. Jobs appreciated the power of that story and those symbols. After all, he had helped create both. But even he must have been amazed by their potency, their seductiveness. What, after all, did Larry Ellison want but to append his own increasingly sordid story to Apple's, and thus elevate it in the process?

Now there was an even greater figure who wanted to be in on the story; someone who had coveted Apple even longer than Steve Jobs. And that man, the most powerful private citizen on earth, wanted to close his own loop with Apple Computer.

MacWorld Expo, like any good Steve Jobs event, began with a crisis. Meeting with a few hundred corporate computer buyers, Power Computing's COO, Joel Kocher, called for a protest at Jobs's keynote speech. The reason was Apple's apparent stalling in signing a deal to let clone makers sell their products equipped with Apple's new OS 8 operating system upgrade. The $99 OS 8 had earned raves from *The Wall Street Journal*'s Walter Mossberg and was helping move Apple computers . . . but not clone machines, which were still forced to use OS 7.6. Only Umax had managed to squeeze out an OS 8 license. It seemed that the clones, which now owned 30 percent of the Mac market, had been a little too successful. And the era of good feelings under Amelio had ended with Jobs's arrival.

There had been considerable speculation in the days before about what Jobs was going to discuss. Some insiders predicted that he would formally dedicate the company to the until now secret Zephyr project, an under $1,000 network computer that would run both Macintosh and Java applications. Other insiders contradicted this by predicting Jobs would talk about Apple's new commitment to high-end servers that would combine multiple Intel processors with the Rhapsody operating system.

Just on these rumors, Apple stock jumped to $19 per share, half again its worth just a month before. Jobs would have made a lot of money had he not sold his stock.

But these product announcements were just news flashes compared to what Jobs had planned for his keynote. He ordered a huge proscenium stage built, complete with a full-sized movie screen and a bank of computer monitors. *Time* magazine, warned about what was coming, sent a photographer and a reporter with hopes for a cover story. The photographer was even allowed into the hall early to scout sight lines. And Jobs, to keep the big mystery intact, even ordered up multiple finishes for his speech.

"He's Hamlet," said one observer at the show. "This is the way Steve Jobs likes it. He's the drama king."

By the morning of August 6, the consensus among the thousands of attendees at the Boston Castle was that Jobs would use the big close to announce Apple's new board of directors, including Larry Ellison. But a few, knowing even this wouldn't be enough for Jobs, still argued that he had something even bigger planned.

Within days after Amelio's exit, Jobs recognized that Apple might well collapse before he could even start fixing it if he didn't make some radical moves and find some cash. He knew where the answer to both lay: in Redmond. He called Bill Gates, and within days a barefoot Jobs was walking around Palo Alto in deep negotiations with Gates's emissary, Microsoft CFO Gregory Maffei.

Maffei had come expecting the worst. Just a year before, on Robert Cringley's popular PBS miniseries *Revenge of the Nerds*, Jobs had looked into the camera and said, "The only problem with Microsoft is they just have no taste. I don't mean that in a small way. I mean that in a big way, in the sense that they don't think of original ideas and they don't bring much culture into their products. I have no problem with their success—they've earned their success for the most part. I have a problem with the fact that they just make really third-rate products."

But Jobs, Maffei told *Time*, was expansive and charming: "We had spent a lot of time with Amelio, and they had a lot of ideas that were nonstarters. Jobs had a lot more ability. He didn't ask for 23,000 terms. He looked at the whole picture, figured about what he needed. And we figured he had the credibility to bring the Apple people around and sell the deal." Thus, Steve Jobs not only got credit for the deal with Microsoft that Gil Amelio had initiated but had given Bill Gates everything he had originally wanted—for only money, not the crucial quid pro quo in software.

If this was a different Steve Jobs and Apple, it was also a different Bill Gates and Microsoft. No one in American history, not even the Gilded Age robber barons like Rockefeller, Vanderbilt and Carnegie whom schoolchildren were taught to revile, had ever owned so complete a monopoly on a major U.S. industry. Even his counterpart, Andy Grove at Intel, had to fight Motorola and the Intel cloners. But Gates essentially owned the operating system of the half billion personal computers on the planet. Even the few computers that didn't run Windows, like Macs, most likely used Microsoft Word or Microsoft Excel as their main application.

Now, in the mid-1990s, Microsoft was moving outward from its secure center, using its mountains of cash and the implied (and sometimes not so implied) blackmail of Windows to envelop and absorb whole new markets.

Windows itself had moved up, as Windows NT, to slowly take over the server software business, and down, as Windows NX, to begin to swallow up the consumer electronics market.

Gates was anything but a fool. He knew his history. Whenever a company was on top in American business, it became a magnet for every antagonism in American life. Companies organized to defeat it, unions and activists plotted against it, columnists used it as a metaphor for all that was wrong in society, psychotics targeted it as the source of their demons—and worst of all, the government used its power under antitrust laws to shatter it. It had happened, each in their turn, to Standard Oil, Ford, IBM and AT&T. Now, Gates knew, it was happening to Microsoft. Venture capitalist John Doerr set up a $200 million investment fund just to create companies to attack Microsoft. Gates himself had stormed out of an interview with Connie Chung when it became too ugly—then had his PR people paint it over the next day by announcing that he planned to someday become a great philanthropist. Most ominously, Microsoft had to sign a consent decree with the U.S. Justice Department not to use the monopoly it held with Windows to force its way into other markets. Now Netscape and others were howling that Microsoft had done just that with the Explorer browser. It would not be surprising if the Justice Department made a major move, perhaps brought suit, very soon. For Gates, whose only goal in life had been to win, victory was turning to ashes.

And then, like the answer to a prayer, Steve Jobs called. For Gates, the offer had everything going for it. By investing just $150 million to prop up Apple, Microsoft, as the largest Apple software developer, would be protecting its $1 billion-plus-per-year Mac software business. And it would get nonvoting shares in the company to boot. There was also an agreement, for an undisclosed amount, to settle Apple's claims against Microsoft for violating its patents. That removed that tiresome little problem.

Gates had also gotten his own concession from the deal: all future Macintosh computers would come bundled with the Microsoft Internet Explorer. And Apple would join with Microsoft to help drive Microsoft's own version of Java. Netscape and Sun were to be left at the altar. Now every PC in the world would be sold with the Microsoft browser and run Microsoft's Java. Each of those concessions alone was worth more than a piddling $150 million to Microsoft.

But the agreement was far more than just the paperwork and the exchange of cash and equity. By keeping his enfeebled last competitor alive, Gates strengthened his argument against the Justice Department. How can you say I'm a monopoly? Apple remains a mighty competitor! Conversely, if Apple nevertheless were to shut its doors, no one could now blame Microsoft. Hey, we helped those guys stay alive!

And there was one other reason, much subtler than the rest. Like Larry Ellison, Bill Gates coveted the Apple story, the love and fidelity it enjoyed not only from its customers but from the general public. The world might buy Windows 95, but it did so without love. Since the Homebrew days, Gates had watched Apple longingly from afar. That was why he wrote the letter, why he hung in with Apple software even though he could easily have pulled out, killed Apple overnight and forced its customers to migrate to Wintel. In 1984, at the time of the Mac's introduction, he had gushed in *MacWorld*'s first issue: ". . . the Mac heralds a major change in how people view and interact with applications programs. That's why I'm so excited about it. There's no question that I'll let my mom try it out."

The toughest businessman of his era was a closet Macolyte, a secret romantic in love with the Apple myth. That wasn't the only reason why he was willing to help the company one more time; but it certainly was why he was willing to come out of his secure bunker in Redmond and make a live television appearance before an audience that was certain he was Satan incarnate. Bill Gates was closing his own loop with Apple Computer.

The final arrangements for the keynote were made the day before. As caught by the *Time* photographer, Jobs paced the stage, making last-minute decisions about the presentation (to be run by Jobs's IBM Thinkpad laptop), all the while talking with Gates in Redmond over a cell phone. The epiphany, the image *Time* put on its cover, came at the end of the conversation: Jobs, dressed all in black like a famous fashion designer, squatting on the stage, signing off on the phone to the world's richest man by saying, "Bill, thank you for your support of this company. I think the world's a better place for it." It was beautiful. Steve Jobs had attached his dead company to the most successful firm in America and somehow made it look not like he'd managed a desperate bailout but instead had performed a selfless act to save all of humanity. He said it was "a little like Nixon going to China. It's the right thing to do." In the process, Jobs had given a mini-lesson in self-promotion to his old friend and enemy. Of course, it was just for such lessons that Bill Gates had signed on.

The keynote itself was as earthshaking as Jobs had planned it to be. And it seemed so effortless—why hadn't he done it with NeXT or Pixar during the last decade? His talk was that unique mix of cockiness, false (and perhaps now even some real) humility and change-the-world optimism that had always been uniquely persuasive. It was a multimedia extravaganza as well, the computers themselves providing their own show—a measure of how far technology had come since the crowd had applauded the first Mac's ability to talk.

Then the first—as it turned out, minor—climax. Apple introduced its new board of directors. Conspicuously evident were Jobs and Larry Ellison. Conspicuously absent was Mike Markkula. His twenty-year side career at Apple was, mercifully, at an end. Jobs had finally taken his last bit of revenge.

On-screen, newly anointed director Larry Ellison, caught on video by a camera crew at the San Jose airport, described his feelings about Apple. He spoke from the heart, and his words unknowingly also captured the feelings of the surprise guest who would soon appear. "Apple is the only lifestyle brand in the industry," said Ellison. "It's the only company people feel passionate about. My company, Oracle, is huge; IBM is huge; Microsoft is huge; but no one has incredible emotions with our companies."

Then, unbelievably, on the giant screen appeared the live image of Bill Gates. The crowd, utterly stunned, was momentarily silent. Then it exploded into cheers, as much for Jobs as for Gates. My God! He even got *Bill Gates* to show up!

But in the midst of the cheers, there was also a chorus of boos. Someone yelled, "You've got to be kidding!" Gates heard this and for an instant was taken aback. He made a small smile of recognition. Normally he had an army of flacks to protect him from this exposure to the real world, and the smile was his acknowledgment that this was the cost of coming out in the open. Jobs was visibly annoyed at what, with no trace of irony, he later called "childish behavior." He added, "I'm sure some people want to cling to old identities. I was a little disappointed at the unprofessional reaction. On the one hand, people are dying to get the latest release of Microsoft Office on their Macs, and on the other hand, they're booing the CEO of the company that puts it out. It seems really stupid to me."

But to the stunned crowd, Jobs was more diplomatic. He told them, "We have to let go of the notion that for Apple to win, Microsoft needs to lose. The era of competition between Microsoft and Apple is over, as far as I'm concerned."

Gates himself spoke in the careful platitudes of a man who knew that nearly $200 billion of stock rested on his every word. "It's very exciting to renew our commitment to Macintosh," etc. etc. But what the crowd saw was something entirely different. It took a few moments, but soon whispers were racing through the multitudes. It was déjà vu. Where had they seen all this before?

Of course.

The famous "1984" commercial. The bespectacled Big Brother on the screen, spouting gibberish. How did it go?

> Each of you is a single cell in the great body of the state. And today, that great body has purged itself of parasites . . . The thugs and wreckers have been cast out . . . our unification of thought is more powerful a weapon than any fleet or army on earth. *We are one people. With one will. One resolve. One cause* . . .

The crowd gasped in realization that it had always been wrong. The "1984" commercial was not an allegory about IBM. It was a *prophecy*. And now that prophecy had come true.

10.7 FAN DANCE

The Gates-Jobs reconciliation stunned and amazed the world. It ran in every newspaper on the planet. It led television news stories. And if *Time* had the exclusive on the story, *Newsweek* countered by devoting its cover story to a feverish debate on whether Microsoft was good for Apple. Only editor Allan Sloan, like the one sober grouch at a really fun drunken party, was churlish enough to note that it didn't really matter. Microsoft had won. And Apple was now too small and too dead to matter anymore except as an antitrust shield for Bill Gates. "Why a company with less than a 4 percent market share gets so much ink is one of life's mysteries," he wrote.

Meanwhile, Jobs, knowing the truth in those comments, but also understanding that now once again, as at the beginning, image meant more than reality, did his best to keep the delirium going—and keep the press focused upon Apple.

The new board quickly got kudos from analysts everywhere. Finally, Apple had a collection of directors with both technical and business experience— and enough reputation not to be buffaloed. There remained two holdovers from the past, both of whom had shown themselves capable of making decisions: Woolard and Gareth C. C. Chang, senior marketing vice president of Hughes Electronics. Then the impressive new four: Jobs (who finally got some Apple stock options again); Ellison; Jerry York, the former CFO of Chrysler and IBM; and Bill Campbell, the onetime head of Apple USA and Claris and now chairman of Intuit, one of the few companies that had ever taken on Microsoft and lived.

It was an amazing collection of names for such a little company, a credit to both Apple's image and Jobs's charms. But the personal dynamics were impossible. Ellison, for example, hated Gates to the point of obsession. How was that supposed to jibe with the new Apple-Microsoft love affair? Then there was the matter of how two giant egos like Jobs and Ellison were going to fit in the same room, much less come to an agreement. And what about all the baggage from the past being brought back by Campbell?

That kept Apple watchers occupied for days. And when that story faded, Jobs had another: Who would Apple choose as its interim CEO? The answer, of course, was a foregone conclusion. But Jobs strung it out for all that it was worth, finally accepting the job only after repeating that he didn't want to be the real CEO because his commitments lay elsewhere.

Then another bombshell. Jobs began to shut down all of Apple's support for its clone makers. Jobs hadn't liked the idea of licensing the OS in 1985 and he still didn't like it. The bitter cloners were left high and dry, scrambling for new survival strategies. Then Jobs drove home his point—*there will be no other Macs before me*—by buying back Power Computing's Apple license for $100 million. Power Computing's management, knowing it had no real choice, gulped and took the offer. As one Macolyte wrote on the Web: "In one fell swoop [Jobs] has alienated the hundreds of thousands of Mac clone buyers." Too bad.

Even as that story was filling the business pages of daily newspapers, Jobs played another card: the search for a new CEO. As early as the end of September there was rumored to be a short list of candidates who had been scrutinized and interviewed. They included, among others, Campbell, IBM senior vice president Samuel Palmisano, Sun senior executive Ed Zander, Pacific Bell CEO/SBC Communications vice president David Dorman, Autodesk CEO Carol Bartz and Cadence Design chief Joe Costello. But Dorman privately told others that the newspaper coverage was the first he'd heard of it, that Apple had never interviewed him and that in his conversations with some of the other candidates they said the same. Besides, said Dorman, "Good God, can you imagine taking a job where you've got Steve Jobs and Larry Ellison looking over your shoulder? You'd have to be out of your mind." Instead, Dorman took over hot little Internet company Pointcast.

The CEO campaign, planned as a nice publicity bridge, now began to backfire. Jobs publicly hinted that the CEO search was not going as well as expected. He said that he had turned the company over "to a bozo" once before, and he was not going to do it again. He told attendees at a Macromedia User Conference that he was considering dropping "interim" from his title at Apple.

It all smelled like a setup. Especially when Jobs announced that he was going to Hawaii—Mount Ararat apparently being too far—to walk on the beach and ponder his future. Everyone was surprised when he did just that, then returned to announce that . . . no, he wasn't going to take the CEO job. Instead, he would direct the interviews of his potential replacement.

The months rolled on. On October 15, 1997, Apple announced a larger than expected $24 million loss. Worse, company sales fell by 31 percent. The stock market, seeing these numbers and watching Apple's market share continue to fall, all the while noting the blank slot in the permanent position at the top of the company's organization chart, began to bail out. On December 23, Apple's stock hit a low of $12.94 per share. For a while, it was rumored that Apple would be able to announce a new CEO—apparently it had settled on a candidate—at the usual big venue of the January MacWorld Expo. But January 1998 passed without any news. Apparently the candidate had balked. The rainy El Niño winter of 1998 turned into a cold spring. Still no word. When asked about the search on CNBC, Jobs announced that there had been an agreement beforehand not to discuss that (there wasn't) and stormed off the set.

"One can only hope," joked the San Francisco Chronicle, "that they'll burn white smoke over Cupertino when the blessed event occurs."

Commenting on his now lifelong nemesis/partner Bill Gates, Jobs said, "I wish him the best, I really do. I just think he and Microsoft are a bit narrow. He'd be a broader guy if he had dropped acid once or gone off to an ashram when he was younger"—a responsible quote from a parent and role model.

John Dvorak, now an industry old-timer, wrote in his column that the best joke around was as follows: Bill Gates and Steve Jobs were playing a friendly game of Frisbee at the Gates estate on the shore of Lake Washington. At one point, Bill accidently sends the Frisbee over Steve's head, and the Frisbee lands in the lake. Steve walks out onto the surface of the lake and retrieves the Frisbee.

The next day, the newspapers report:

GATES' THROW EXCEEDS EXPECTATIONS
APPLE CEO UNABLE TO SWIM

In the last week of December 1997, after eighteen years at the company's headquarters, Apple packed up his museum, with its complete collection of Apple Computers dating back to Woz's Apple I, manuals, photos from company parties and coffee mugs, and shipped it to Stanford University for the school's Silicon Valley archives.

10.8 Resprouting

Then, on January 7, 1998, Jobs thrilled the crowd at MacWorld Expo—and shareholders everywhere—by announcing that though revenues for the quarter would be down slightly (to $1.575 billion), the company would show a $47 million *profit!* Nobody expected Apple to be in the black for another year or two, if ever again. And now Steve Jobs had pulled it off in a matter of months. Given that the company had spent the previous year losing $1 billion, this was a turnaround of almost historic proportions.

That was only the beginning. The company had already introduced a new PowerMac product family, the G3, and it seemed to be doing well. But hardware had never been Apple's problem—it had always been everything else. And so everywhere else was where Jobs attacked next.

He fired 300 workers at the Claris subsidiary, renamed the place FileMaker Inc. and folded it back into Apple. He also blew up Apple's shrinking distribution system, pulling out of every computer retailer except one, CompUSA, which had continued to aggressively sell Apple products. From now on, Jobs announced, Apple would direct-sell over the Internet, a technique successfully pioneered by Michael Dell. "We're coming to get you, buddy," Jobs warned Dell at a public event, talking to a giant poster of the Texas billionaire. Dell's reply was brief: "Having our picture on the wall isn't going to help them with the problem of their legacy."

Apple sold $30 million in computers the first day of its new Web retail site. Meanwhile, the company's share of the education market, the historic heart of Apple's business, dropped to 27 percent, compared with 61 percent four years before.

In January 1998, Gordon Thygeson, a one-time Apple contract employee, published *Apple T-Shirts: A Yearbook of History at Apple Computer.*

Thygeson explained the book by saying that he had been looking for a compelling way to tell the Apple story "when it hit me one day that it really was T-shirts."

There in the pages, was the other side of the Apple story. Not the great events and great men and women who led the company through them, but the witty voices of the Apple employees, T-shirt warriors for the great crusades, cannon fodder for the disasters. It was all there: from psychedelia (a photo of Steve Jobs: "This is Apple"; a photo of John Sculley: "This is Apple on drugs . . . any questions?") to power business in the 1990s (from the Power Macintosh group: "I helped save the company and all I got was this lousy T-shirt."). It was a reminder that no technology company had ever been so identified with the culture, had so changed the culture, or been changed by it in return, than Apple Computer.

Jonathon Martin, the first Apple baby, was now twenty years old. His father, Gary Martin, after serving as company treasurer and controller, had left Apple in 1982 and gone on to a successful career at several high-tech companies. He still stayed in touch with Mike Scott and looked back on his Apple days fondly as "the best of times and the worst of times."

Young Jonathon, a third-generation Valleyite, not surprisingly was a computer fan. His machine of choice was a Compaq.

Geoff Chatterton joined Apple in 1994 after graduating from MIT and a stint in the Navy. In his three years at Apple, most of them spent in a software engineering group for high-end Macs, Chatterton had worked for three different CEOs and suffered through six reorganizations. "I once spent eight months trying to put together some specs on a licensing deal, only to have them thrown out when Apple changed its strategy."

Chatterton had initially put a lot of hope in Gil Amelio straightening out the mess at Apple. But he was quickly disappointed. "Amelio went through an MBA 101 book to figure out how to run Apple. Everybody trusted him at first because he was a real engineer. But he turned out to have less charisma even than Spindler, had no insight into the business and ultimately added no value to the firm." As for Ellen Hancock: "Everybody was singing praises about her technical ability, but she understood broad concepts—that was all. People cheered when she left."

Now the boss was Steve Jobs. Chatterton admired his style, if he wasn't quite sure of his character. "Some people think he is good for Apple; others don't trust him," Chatterton said. What he liked was the man's decisiveness. "If he sees something that's screwed up, he makes a decision."

Decisiveness, and the consistency it created, had long been the missing factor in his time at Apple. His group, though it had been a major contributor to Apple's bottom line, had long been a victim of changing corporate strategies, especially in licensing. "It distracted a lot of time and energy from our work. Every time Apple licensed its technology to cloners, and they came up with some little improvement, Apple then felt compelled to respond to it. It was an incredible time sucker."

So why did he stay at Apple? Because he loved the Mac, the autonomy and most of all the camaraderie of his group. "A lot of people have been here a long time. They don't care about the CEO—they've seen them come and go. At one time, the three levels of management above us were all vacant. It didn't make any difference. They just keep doing their work."

Lubricating that camaraderie was plentiful quantities of beer. For a while, Apple bought the beer to stock the group's refrigerators. "It's not unusual to see people drink at any time of the day," says Chatterton. "You see guys drinking at 10 A.M. As long as we get our work done."

But, as an austerity measure during the hard times at the end of Amelio's term, Apple stopped supplying the beer, forcing the employees to bring their own. "That's their way of cutting costs."

10.9 GHOSTS

On March 2, 1998, Apple killed the Newton. Steve Jobs had now eliminated every trace of John Sculley from Apple. The explanation was that in its current condition Apple needed to focus on a much more narrow product line. Personal digital assistants were no longer in the business strategy.

The tragedy of the Newton was that, at the end, it was a superb little machine, better than anything on the market. But it still bore the stigma of its disappointing beginnings, and it had never escaped that curse. Apple might have been able to burnish that image. But it had been too distracted by two years of nightmares to pay much attention.

On the day after the announcement, the standard Apple protest crowd of a hundred appeared on the company lawn. Few knew the grass they walked on had been well trod. The group waved a few signs and spoke to a few bored reporters, but mostly they swapped business cards and programs and promised to stay in touch. Then they went on with their lives.

On the day the Newton was exterminated, John Sculley was invited to be Neil Cavuto's guest on the Fox news channel.

The segment was entitled "The Perils of Being Ahead of the Technological Curve." John Sculley had finally gotten his wish—at least on the East Coast, he was seen now as a great technological visionary, and, in Cavuto's words, "one of the classiest acts in corporate America."

In his eulogy for the Newton, Sculley described one of the most expensive failures in high-tech history (though far short of his disastrous Copland) as a noble failure. "In retrospect," he said, "the Newton shot too high," whereas the wildly successful Palm Pilot was "more pragmatic." Still, Sculley added wistfully, "the DNA of Apple is to be out on the leading edge of invention. The first versions [of Apple's products] were often not successful, but the second versions always were . . . [We] had to keep improving on them."

In other words, the Newton wasn't a multihundred-million-dollar disaster that had contributed to the meltdown of one of the most successful companies in America, but a great product on the brink of a magnificent victory . . . if only given a second chance.

Sculley was then asked about the return of Steve Jobs. "He should," Sculley replied. "It's his company. Only he can run it."

A few weeks later, yet another Apple ex-CEO was heard from. Gil Amelio was promoting his new book, *On the Firing Line*, subtitled *My 500 Days at Apple*. It was one of the oddest, and most memorable, memoirs ever written by the head of a major U.S. corporation, and tangible proof of the adage that nobody ever left Apple the same person.

Amelio's argument, presented as a Shakespearean tragedy (even the chapter heads were quotes from *Hamlet*, *Macbeth*, etc.) was that he had done a great job at Apple and had been in full command of the situation. As with Sculley's Newton, Amelio argued he needed only a little more time to turn things around.

But then he supported his case by, perversely, showing that he was neither competent nor in control of the company. In essence, CEOs have two tasks: make the company successful and identify any competitive threats to the company when they appear. Under Amelio's command, Apple had lost $1.6 billion and thousands of employees. Moreover, he had invited into the executive offices a dangerous and brilliant individual that everybody but Amelio (despite more than fair warning) knew would soon hijack the firm.

Thus, instead of the triumphant revisionism Gil Amelio imagined his book to be, it was in fact a revealing—and pathetic—look into the life of a successful businessman lost in a cultural phenomenon he still didn't understand. Slate.com called it "a work of colossal petulance."

In the book, Amelio whined about how he lost precious time because the CEO didn't have a reserved parking place (then noted that Jobs merely parked in the handicapped zone). He dropped celebrity names ("Michael Crichton's carefully expressed contribution was memorable and Richard Dreyfuss poignantly described the importance of saving Apple . . ."). He carefully blamed himself for what happened, but then accused subordinates of stupidity, cupidity or selfishness. He kvetched about the size of his golden parachute. He attacked some of the best reporters in the business for being inaccurate, cynical, disrespectful or irresponsible—then lauded some of the most notorious softballers in the media. In all, it was, in the words of one Valley veteran, "the kind of kiss-off book you write when you've got enough money not to worry about ever working again."

But Amelio saved most of his bile for Steve Jobs. In that meeting at National, Jobs had not only warned Amelio he wanted the CEO's seat again at Apple, but let him know what he would do to get it. Now, after Jobs had done exactly that, Amelio was bitter. "Betrayal, assassination, [and] trashing of reputations are part of the everyday tool kit of a person obsessed with power, control, or revenge," he wrote. "I was in Steve's way and had to be eliminated."

At a book-signing party in Silicon Valley after the publication of the book, Gil Amelio showed up in his standard dress suit. Looking around the room at the casual crowd, he ended his story with Apple perhaps as he might have begun.

He took off his tie.

10.10 Going Home

As the weeks of Jobs's return turned into months, observers increasingly began to complain that there appeared to be no rhyme or reason to Steve Jobs's leadership of Apple, that he seemed to be making it up as he went along, changing his mind almost every time he changed his socks.

But that was the point: Jobs *was* making up Apple as he went along. He always had. Then and now he understood that until the company found solid ground (if it ever did) he would have to keep dancing, bluffing, fighting for attention. Because if the world ever stopped looking or, more accurately, stopped believing in the fantasy, Apple would shrivel away to its true self: a tiny, dead company trying desperately to reincarnate itself. For fiscal 1997, Apple's total share of the world personal computer market was just 3.1 percent, down from 5.2 percent the year before. By February 1998, and the end of the company's first quarter, that number had slumped to just 2.6 percent.

But there was an even more mysterious question behind the first one. What does Steve Jobs want? Why was he back at Apple? He was already rich, famous beyond imagining, involved with another highly successful, wildly popular company. He hobnobbed with the rich and famous of Hollywood, Washington and Silicon Valley. He was reconciled with his daughter, happily married and blessed with two new children. He could have let Apple fade away and the blame would have fallen on Sculley, Spindler and Amelio. He seemed to have nothing to gain and much to lose by returning to the blasted remains of his former glory. What did Steve Jobs want with Apple?

A clue appeared not long after the Boston MacExpo. Steve Jobs requested a permit from the city of Palo Alto to allow him to purchase the property next door to his own, bulldoze the house and plant a fruit tree orchard.

The request provoked considerable mirth in Silicon Valley. But at its heart was a devastating image. The man who had probably done more than anyone else to bury verdant Santa Clara Valley, the "Valley of Heart's Delight," under the steel, asphalt and concrete of Silicon Valley, was now trying to restore a tiny corner of that lost world of his childhood. As any old orchardist could have told him, it wouldn't work. Fruit trees need virgin soil. But that probably still wouldn't have stopped him. The man with all the success any person could ever dream of was now looking back to that strange little boy who had begun this journey.

Then in October it became clear. The occasion was to announce a new advertising campaign for Apple. Its ungrammatical title was "Think Different" and it featured old black-and-white footage of famous mavericks: Einstein, Gandhi, Hitchcock, Bob Dylan, Martha Graham, Cassius Clay, the Dalai Lama (the last cravenly pulled in the Far East when China objected), and Ansel Adams. In downtown New York, on Fifth Avenue, a four-story-tall image of Joan Baez, Jobs's old girlfriend, appeared on the side of a building in all her folk era glory.

It was the whole pantheon of boomer heroes: the authors of the Penguin paperbacks you carried in your knapsack in 1969, the famous faces on the posters in your dorm room and at the art film house you hung out at in Palo Alto. The images would soon appear on billboards, in giant posters hung from the sides of the Infinite Loop facility and in television commercials featuring a voice-over by Richard Dreyfuss that sounded uncannily like Steve Jobs. It was a strange campaign, anachronistic in the 1980s and seemingly ill-suited for Apple at this moment in its history. As Umax Fred Huang said, "Apple's campaign is exactly wrong at this moment in history. In computing, nobody wants to think differently anymore. They want standardization. They all want to think the same way."

Huang was exactly wrong, for all the right reasons. If "Think Different" was preaching to the choir, it was also uniquely Steve Jobs. And these were his heroes. Once again, he was mapping his own inner world on to the one he was forced to share with the rest of us. The message was: These were the people you dreamed of growing up to be. And now, even if you have grown up to be only a department IT manager or an ad agency art director, you can still own the computer most of these people might have used if they weren't dead.

This oddly compelling campaign held yet another clue. Standing at the press conference before a giant projected image of Picasso—one sacred monster paying tribute to another—Steve Jobs looked as happy as he'd been in years. It was all there now, a recreation of the best days of his life: the tiny band, facing impossible odds, living by wit and pluck, fighting nobly to convince the world to dream its dream, and Steve Jobs standing before them, leading them on by the sheer force of his personality.

The journey is the reward, Steve Jobs had once famously said. And that reward had proved to be a second chance, a repeat journey. The opportunity to do it all over. And maybe not to just do it well this time, but also to do it right. No betrayals, no deceits, no victories at any cost.

10.11 SEMPER FI

As before, Steve Jobs found his fanatical followers. His return was a catalyst for all the true believers, the Macolytes, to finally release all the pent-up frustration of years of apology and shame.

In early 1998, Rich Karlgaard, now the editor of Forbes ASAP, included an article on Apple in the issue about "Failure." Recalled Karlgaard, "Within days we were buried in dozens of e-mails calling us traitors and stooges for Microsoft and all kinds of obscenities. And most of them came from members of something called 'the Mac Marines.'"

Forbes ASAP responded in a later issue by running a parody of the "Think Different" ad, showing a picture of "Do," the leader of the suicidal Heaven's Gate cult.

10.12 REVISIT

Could Steve Jobs regain the future by recreating the past?

The world had, after all, changed profoundly since he was touring computer stores along El Camino trying to sell the Apple I. Almost every person he had worked with or competed against in those days was now either dead, retired or long out of the industry. That too had been the seventies, with its economic recessions, antiestablishment hangover from the sixties, contempt for corporate life and its cult of individual satisfaction. It was the last hurrah of the baby boomers as a youth movement, and perhaps the last time small undercapitalized entrepreneurial start-ups could carve out a new hardware industry.

This was the nineties, one of the most prosperous epochs in American economic history. Corporate success stories, not lone rebels, were now the heroes of the age.

Technology, following the dictates of Moore's Law, had profoundly changed as well—so much that it belonged in a different universe from that of the Homebrew years. On March 17, 1998, Apple introduced a new PowerMacintosh G3 model. With 400 megahertz processing speed, more than a billion bits of disk memory, a built-in modem and stereo sound, a single one of these new computers was as powerful as all the computers in America when Jobs and Wozniak were first learning about data processing at Homestead High.

When Woz built the Apple I, the entire U.S. electronics industry was smaller than just Hewlett-Packard in 1998. Electronics was now, in fact, America's largest industrial employer, the linchpin of the current economic boom. Not only was Bill Gates, at $50 billion in personal worth, the richest private citizen in the world, but one company now had a market capitalization greater than the entire U.S. automobile industry. By century's end, it was predicted that one billion people would regularly be surfing the Internet. From David Packard's garage, and Steve Wozniak's garage and the halls of Fairchild Semiconductor had emerged one of the great social and economic revolutions in human history.

Could Steve Jobs really do it all again?

Certainly his luck seemed to have returned. Just six months before, Microsoft had seemed an unstoppable juggernaut—so dominant in high tech that new start-ups were now putting "sell to Microsoft" as the last step in their business plans. Now Microsoft found itself embroiled in one of the nastiest antitrust battles of the century. Bill Gates was appearing before congressional subcommittees, touring the country doing good PR works and marshalling support from cowed customers.

But arrayed against him was a Justice Department SWAT team and half the country's state attorney generals. There was talk of stopping the sale of the new Windows 98. Even of breaking up the company. Microsoft, which had never been defeated by a competitor, had now met the one force even greater than itself: the law and its enforcers.

That was only half of it. Despite its near-monopoly, until now Gates and Co. had escaped the calumny that usually surrounds monopolies. Until an extraordinarily late date, Bill was still seen by the general public as a benign nerd and his company an asset to modern life. That was crucial because Microsoft depended upon that reputation to recruit the best, brightest young people to become self-sacrificing "microserfs," to overrun new markets without fear of government interference and to sell its products to happy millions of eager customers.

Now all of that was at risk. Even if Microsoft survived the legal challenge, it was obvious that the image of the company would never be the same again. Microsoft was now the Evil Empire in many minds, a pernicious force in high tech—and perhaps soon in every other part of daily life. Against this backdrop, Apple suddenly once again seemed appealing. It was no longer an anachronism, a remnant of the past, but a refreshing alternative to Microsoft's totalitarianism.

Suddenly and serendipitously, Steve Jobs was back in vogue.

For those who believed he had changed over the previous two decades, they were soon disabused of that notion by reports coming out of Apple. Jobs, it seemed, was as manipulative and unpredictable as ever. If Jobs had intended to be different this time around, he had already failed. Jim Carlton presented a memorable image of the new/old Jobs on the cover of *The Wall Street Journal*.

In the profile, Jobs arrives at an interview with five prospective new engineering hires. He is wearing shorts and a T-shirt. One of the engineers asks what, after selling his stock and refusing to take the permanent CEO's post, is Jobs own commitment to Apple?

"Mr. Jobs starts out by tensely explaining how he is devoting so much time to Apple that he is sacrificing his family life. 'I'm working here eighteen hours a day,' he says. Then he quickly builds up to an obscenity-laced tirade, thundering, 'To the people who ask me that question, I say, "Fuck you! Fuck you!" ' "

When asked a similar question on a cable news show, Jobs announced,

"We agreed not to discuss that," yanked off his microphone and stormed off the set. The stunned reporter then informed the viewers there had been no such agreement.

The belittlement and abuse portions of the Jobs Reality Distortion Field were also back in regular use. Sculley and Amelio were publicly pronounced "bozos," with Amelio getting the added honor of having a stupidity gauge—the "Gil-o-meter"—named after him by Jobs: "two Gils" being twice as stupid as the man who had brought Jobs back to Apple. Wozniak, meanwhile, was informed he was no longer welcome.

The sweeping indictment was also restored. Not only did Jobs obviously favor his old NeXT employees at Apple, but even told visitors that Apple had "10,000 mediocre employees that have to be cleaned out." And, as always, there was the vengeance. After Jobs took over, he sent out a series of company-wide e-mails announcing everything from austerity measures to a new rule against bringing pets to work. When some employees, harkening back to the first Jobs era, responded by sending around a fake Jobs e-mail denouncing all Apple employees as lazy and reserving the handicapped parking only for himself, Jobs sent out yet one more e-mail making fake company e-mails a firing offense.

It was as if, after the decade-long absence, marriage, parenthood and independent success, Steve Jobs had not changed. He was as awful as ever. Yet, the same behavior that had driven him out of the company in 1985 was now met with a shrug, even a cheer. What had changed? One answer was Apple: The arrogant but troubled company of 1985, though now several times larger, was humbled and deeply in trouble. Even among the true believers there was a sense that this was the company's last chance. That it had nothing to lose by taking a final fling with the greatest, but most frightening, figure of its past.

There was also the myth itself. After ten years, there was almost no one left at Apple who recalled the Jobs era as it really had been. Rather, they remembered it from once-removed, from the stories they had heard and read of that time . . . and those tales had a frisson of excitement and danger. Better to reign in a thrilling corporate Hell than serve in a boring, dying Heaven.

They made the right choice—as had everyone who ever had the patience, the courage and the masochism to stick with Steve Jobs all the way through to the end. Somehow, as inexplicably as the first time, Apple Computer once again began to act like a winner—then became one. On April 15, the company announced yet another profitable quarter: $55 million. Sales were again down, $1.4 billion for the quarter, compared to $1.6 billion the year before, but operating expenses were also down (despite the new advertising campaign) and profit margins were up. The market responded by pushing Apple stocks to $28 per share, its highest point since the Sculley era, and adding $1.6 billion to the company's value. Better yet, the newest surveys showed Apple's market share back above 4 percent.

Profits up, market share up, stock up, hot new products rolling out the door, customer pride once again strong, Steve Jobs had once again pulled off a miracle at Apple Computer. The company was back from the dead.

And yet, like a new shoot from an old stump, the odds were against Apple this time ever becoming but a poor imitation of its former self. As much as one might cheer the company doubling its market share, that share was still less than 5 percent of the market—and the rest was almost entirely owned by the Wintel standard. The new G3's might be great machines, but the vast majority of the hardware and software was still being designed for Windows computers. Even if the Justice Department broke up Intel and Microsoft, that reality would not change.

Way back in the early 1980s, Mike Markkula had privately told Dave Martin, the Apple CFO, that the company had to maintain a 50 percent market share or it would lose control over its own destiny. Markkula had been prescient. When Apple crossed that line the year before the introduction of the Macintosh, its fate had been sealed. And no matter how many great new products the company introduced, how much attention it received in the press, how loyal its camp followers, the subsequent fifteen years had been one long slide.

In that light, for all of his success, all Steve Jobs had really accomplished was a temporary pause in Apple's long-term decline. Valley watchers understood this, seeing the recent two quarters of good news from Apple not as a rebirth, but as a perfect time to sell—for Jobs to repeat the successful final act of NeXT, the big payoff for loyal employees and shareholders—this time with his most famous creation. He had brought Apple into the world; now he was on hand to take it out.

Rumors ricocheted around the Valley in May 1998. Some thought the perfect buyer would be a content provider, such as Disney. Others guessed an appliance maker, such as GE. Still others suggested an infrastructure firm, such as cable giant TCI. Chris Nolan, tech gossip columnist at the *Mercury News*, reported rumors from inside Apple that the most ardent suitors were Japanese: Sony and Fujitsu. But the company denied any such reports.

10.13 INFINITE LOOP

But before the final fate of Apple Computer was determined, Steve Jobs still had one more unfinished item left on his agenda.

On May 7, 1998, Apple put on one more new product introduction. It was held, as long ago, at Flint Center on the campus of De Anza College. It was a disorienting sight. It seemed the same adoring crowd, the same press corps and camera crews as at the original Macintosh introduction 172 months before. Yet only Steve Jobs was the same. This was no longer a bid to control the future, but a long shot to save the past.

As on that first rainy afternoon, Jobs appeared onstage in a suit beside an object hidden beneath a velvet drape. With a flourish, Steve Jobs pulled away the cloth to reveal: the iMac, a stylish new G3 in a self-contained box of translucent "Bandai blue" plastic. In design, it was the sum of all of Steve Jobs's experiences in his first tenure at Apple, a cross between the Apple II, the Mac and the old Beehive terminals on which he and Woz had first learned about minicomputers. In style it was, like so much about Jobs's life, sixties redux, Jetsons meets the new Volkswagen Beetle. It was throwback artful enough to be cool. Some reviewers, including the reviewer for the on-line magazine *Salon*, hated it, suggesting that it looked like a sixties Japanese plastic toy. But he was buried in a tidal wave of adoration for the cute new Apple computer.

For ninety days, the world waited anxiously for the iMac to hit the shelves. With a mastery not seen in the computer industry since, well, the Macintosh, Apple nurtured the hysteria. Thanks to a $150 million advertising campaign (NOT AVAILABLE IN BEIGE read one Menlo Park billboard just a mile from the site of the first Homebrew meeting), consumers were brought to a near-frenzy of anticipation.

Amid the excitement, it was hard to get past the noise and spin and note that the iMac was, in fact, a pretty mediocre computer by the standards of the day. On the plus side, it did have a 233 MHz PowerPC G3 chip that made Jobs crow, "Faster than the fastest Pentium II money can buy"—an accurate statement for a few weeks at least. It also had a 4 GB hard disk, stereo speakers and a 33.6 modem—everything you needed for surfing the Net—all for just $1,299.

But it also didn't have a floppy disk drive, a decision made by Jobs to save money and justified by his belief that in the age of e-mail people didn't need floppies anymore. (As with the Mac and the Next computer, memory had always been Steve Jobs's biggest blind spot.) Adding an external floppy drive boosted the price a couple hundred bucks—a much less impressive price tag in a world where equivalently powered PCs (with 56K modems) were selling for $999.

Finally there was the design itself. Cute as a button, but the fixed screen and the circular mouse were a denial of fifteen years of accumulated experience in the ergonomics of personal computing. The iMac screamed repetitive stress injuries.

But none of that mattered in the least. What really mattered was that, in a dreary world of predictable, boring beige personal computers, Steve Jobs had brought style back to the computer industry. He had regained the perfect pitch in PCs he had enjoyed so many years before. Once more, he knew what the market wanted before the market itself knew.

If the iMac was more of a price and packaging breakthrough than a technological revolution, well, damn it, these weren't revolutionary times. If it represented a triumph of style over substance, so, it seemed in that dreary summer and autumn, did most things, including the U.S. presidency, the stock market and, in light of the impending Year 2000 Crisis, the technology revolution itself. Now that we knew that computers weren't going to save the world, why not just buy a cute one?

On August 14, 1998, the iMac was officially shipped to the world. The Apple I had made its first appearance in the little Mountain View Bytes Shop, one of a half-dozen computers in a store the size of a tract house living room. Twenty-two years later the iMac arrived in Silicon Valley at places like Fry's Electronics in Sunnyvale, giant 180,000-square-foot high-tech supermarkets that were commercial temples to the new religion invented by Woz and Jobs.

The iMac's arrival wasn't as earthshaking as Windows 95 had been—no midnight riots this time—but it was impressive nevertheless. All through the day, and for many days thereafter, customers parked in the giant parking lot and made their way past a huge inflated iMac balloon beside the front door and on into the noisy maw of Fry's in its full retail frenzy. Once inside, with scores of others, they crossed the crowded floor, past the espresso shop and the racks of hundreds of trade magazines, to the single aisle that offered Apple products.

Usually a lonely afterthought in the sea of PCs, the Apple aisle was now the target of all eyes. One after another, boxes bearing the blue iMac image were loaded into shopping carts and proudly rolled to the fifty checkout registers at the front of the store. And as the iMacs and their proud new owners made the transit across the store, they passed a small lucite pyramid, a museum in miniature, containing an original Apple I, the printed circuit board still bearing Woz's original solders.

Thousands of shopping carts were filled with iMacs in the next few weeks.

At the end of August, the iMac was declared the second bestselling personal computer in the world (behind the budget HP Pavilion 6330) during the month—despite the fact that it had been available only for two of the four weeks. The iMac had captured 7.1 percent of total sales for the month, despite being the most expensive of the top five (the other three were Compaq Presario versions). Analysts were now predicting that Apple might sell 400,000 to 600,000 iMacs by year's end—spiking Apple's sales by 120 percent in August alone and adding a predicted $400 million to the company's sales for the quarter on a base of $1.5 billion.

And the news only got better. Of the iMac's purchasers, only 82 percent were current Apple owners—meaning that the new computer was hardly cannibalizing the company's current customer base. Meanwhile, an incredible 16 percent of iMac buyers were either first-time computer purchasers or owners of Windows machines—the first serious turnaround in Apple's downward market share slide in twenty years. Better yet, one in five iMac purchasers were fifty years or older—meaning that the iMac was now penetrating markets even Microsoft couldn't reach. In the graphics and publishing world, the gains were even more significant, as the trade press for those industries reporting that firms were junking their multi-PC networks for comparable iMac configurations. By late September, to the world's appreciation but Silicon Valley's chagrin, even the unlamented old Apple arrogance could be seen in cafes and shops around Cupertino. On October 14, 1998, the company announced its first profitable year since 1995.

It was, by any measure, an extraordinary coup for Apple, perhaps the last great victory in the story of personal computing. Steve Jobs had kicked off the personal computer revolution, and now he had likely pulled down the curtain on the final act. For all the excitement generated by the iMac, it had about it the air of a twilight act.

The personal computer industry, long the embodiment of youthful enterprise, was growing old. Worse, it was growing stable. Despite the tiny revolts in the provinces, Bill Gates and Microsoft had won. The market itself, once unstoppable, had begun to plateau, the battle now largely between the big price-bombing mass manufacturers like Compaq, Dell and Gateway. By Christmas 1998, the world would likely see the first $600 PCs. As early as October, a Korean firm had announced a $995 laptop. In this low-budget, commodity computer world Apple could never compete. Even as the iMac was setting sales records, rumors were rife in Silicon Valley that Apple would soon surrender at last and introduce a Windows-based computer.

What once seemed heresy now seemed merely good business. Even reports that Apple was moving out of computers and seeking a Japanese game maker as a strategic partner in the marketing of a new TV set-top Web-surfer/ game machine—code-named Columbus—didn't set off any anguished cries. It was enough that Steve Jobs had brought back the magic one last time.

And he certainly did. Once more he had drawn the world's attention to Apple; the company he had formed out of sheer will. Once more he had asserted his personality, his style, upon the entire computing world—a world that now stretched around the globe and numbered 500 million people.

Whatever came next in the Apple story, for good or bad, Steve Jobs would always have this moment, the capstone of the great second act of his career. He would forever have that moment, before the crowd at the iMac introduction. Standing there, Steve Jobs had grinned—not the twisted, ironic, but a true and sincere grin of joy—as the crowd watched and cheered. And then, on the iMac's screen, like a punchline that had been waiting fourteen years, appeared the words

hello
AGAIN

And with that, Steve Jobs closed the greatest and most enduring Apple loop of them all.

NOTES ON SOURCES

There is no shortage of source material on the story of Apple. On the contrary, for nearly twenty years we have been awash in it. Even with the recent attention afforded Microsoft, it can still reasonably be claimed that no company in history has earned such intense press and public scrutiny over the entire course of its existence.

The real challenge is to wade through these mountains of reporting, commentary and gossip, and try to extract the true story of Apple Computer. It isn't easy, not in the least because Apple itself has been an effective co-conspirator in this myth-making. Nowhere is the fog of myth thicker than in the official stories about the beginnings of the company, that shadowy world in which the young Steve Jobs and Stephen Wozniak skirted back and forth across the boundaries of the law.

All successful companies attempt to rewrite their histories, promoting those who stayed and erasing others who left, downrating losers in corporate purges and honoring the often ignoble winners. But always there is a patina of glory that is gilded onto these official histories. Every decision made was brilliant, every victory heroic, and every failure due to forces beyond the company's control. That's why official corporate histories are so excruciatingly awful. Not a whiff of failure, of human complexity or cupidity, is ever allowed to arise from the endless empty pages.

But Apple Computer is different. In its official story, the principals often seem to vie for the most outrageous story, for the behavior most deviant from the traditional business norm. And when they aren't boasting of their antisocial behavior, as in the case of the founders, they seem to be acting out their deepest psychological impulses and fears. Looking back over the manuscript of this book, I was struck by how many grown men, when faced with a serious career obstacle, collapse into tears. It's hard to imagine a book about Bethlehem Steel or Boeing Aircraft or Dow Chemical containing so many lachrymose moments.

Yet, all of this corporate soul-bearing is itself a form of propaganda—especially in the hands of we baby boomers. And especially at Apple Computer, the emblematic company of that generation. In the story of Apple, sensitivity has often been used as a bludgeon, and heady talk of changing the world as a smokescreen for the exploitation of employees, customers and outsiders.

Yet, opposed to this, there is always that other, larger, more magical story. Of the little company founded in a garage by kids with a dream—that went on to change the world and turn thousands of people into multimillionaires. It is the seminal entrepreneurial myth of our time, and one that will be told for generations.

When writing about Apple, you must approach the subject warily, because nothing—good or bad—is what it seems. Nothing. Read an expose about some corporate misadventure or stunning success, and with a little digging you're likely to find a "true" story behind it that presents the opposite conclusion. Then, six months later you'll encounter another company veteran who'll tell you the "real inside story" that somehow contradicts both.

Having grown up with Apple and its founders, and at times in its history having been inside the company, I at least knew enough not to trust any of the accepted stories, nor to believe anything I heard just once. It proved to be a good strategy.

I also faced another challenge. Every book ever written about Apple has been obsolete from the day it arrived on the bookstands. Inevitably, the company has gone sideways right after the latest corporate history has gone to press. This was true for *The Little Kingdom* (1984), the first major Apple history, which appeared just after the Macintosh was introduced and paled its story, right up to Jim Carlton's *Apple* (1997), which ended just before Steve Jobs hijacked the company and turned it around.

That last turn nearly caught me as well. Luckily I was running behind—and thus have been able to capture all of Jobs's great turnaround year, as well as the introduction of the watershed iMac. Nevertheless, I have little doubt that between the time I write this at the end of October 1998 and the time you read it, Apple will have surprised us again.

As I noted in the Foreword, I chose not to footnote *Infinite Loop*. Some of my books, especially those of business theory, have included hundreds of notes. But I felt they would be distracting to this kind of narrative. Moreover, the Internet has transformed the very nature of research by allowing high-speed quote checking.

Nevertheless, I want to use this Note to recognize all of those authors and reporters on whose hard work this book rests. I truly stand on the shoulders of dozens of giants. I will begin with listing key texts, then magazines and newspapers, and then individual sources. I have tried to cite individual sources in the text itself; what follows are sources for dozens of quotes and facts.

BOOKS

One of the impressive things about the books written on Apple is their universally high quality. One reason, no doubt, is that the Apple story is just so crazy that it almost writes itself. On top of that, the company is also such a big story that it attracts the very best business writers. Finally, I think the overachieving nature of the company, especially in its early years, has brought out the best talents in those covering the firm.

Here, in chronological order, are some of the most useful books on Apple:

1. *The Little Kingdom* by Michael Moritz (Morrow, 1984)—Though long out of print (and out of date), still the best book ever written about Apple. Good reporting teamed with fine writing and filtered through a tough reporter's sensibility. Almost no factual errors—an amazing achievement given the corporate smokescreen the author had to cut through. At the time, Moritz was the San Francisco bureau chief for *Time*. Afterward, he became a very successful venture capitalist. His lead investment in Yahoo! made him richer (except for Jobs) than anyone at Apple he wrote about.

2. *Fire in the Valley* by Paul Freiberger and Michael Swaine (Osborne, 1984)—A paperback that has become something of a Silicon Valley cult classic. The seminal text on the early, early years of the personal computing industry. Identifies all the players. Great photos, too. A great reminder that there was a personal computer industry before the Apple II.

3. *Odyssey* by John Sculley (Harper & Row, 1987)—A standard self-promoting executive autobiography; in light of subsequent events almost amusing. Yet the first half of the book is an unusually revealing memoir of a Steve Jobs seduction, the second half a glimpse of Sculley's obsession with coming up with the Next Big Thing (the Knowledge Navigator).

4. *West of Eden* by Frank Rose (Viking, 1989)—Rose had the misfortune of having one tiny factual error (the location of a room in an Apple exec's

house) blown up into a scandal by Guy Kawasaki in the latter's book. *West of Eden* didn't deserve that fate, nor its subsequent disappearance from memory. It is, in fact, a terrific piece of reporting, covering the purge of Jobs from Apple. A crucial text.

5. *The Macintosh Way* by Guy Kawasaki (Doubleday, 1990)—Kawasaki is one of the Valley's more memorable characters—a human dynamo, a brilliant speaker and a tongue-in-cheek true believer. No one read this book expecting anything but a cheerleading session about Apple Computer. Yet, the book is surprisingly tough-minded about many of the company's flaws. As always, Guy is full of surprises.

6. *Accidental Millionaires* by Robert X. Cringely (Addison-Wesley, 1992)—The pseudonymous Cringely is notorious for his sloppy way with facts (and his lifting, without credit, of other reporters' stories). No sane person would ever use this book—or to a lesser degree the popular PBS miniseries, *The Revenge of the Nerds*, based upon it—as a sole source of information. But if Bob often gets the little stuff wrong, he gets the big stuff right more often than anybody in tech reporting. And, he is one hell of an entertaining writer. The Apple section of this book can make you laugh out loud.

7. *Insanely Great* by Steven Levy (Viking, 1994)—Essentially a paen to the Macintosh on its tenth anniversary, this book does a good job at capturing the milieu into which the Mac exploded. A real weakness to researchers is the book's lack of an index. Levy, who was writing for *MacWorld* at the time, has gone on to the prestigious and influential post of top computer writer at *Newsweek*.

8. *Apple* by Jim Carlton (Times Books, 1997)—Carlton, a terrific reporter at *The Wall Street Journal*, is the unluckiest of all the Apple historians. His topic is the Spindler/Amelio era—the least interesting part of the entire Apple story. Moreover, as noted, the book appeared just as Jobs took over and rendered his two predecessors superfluous. Despite this, the book is the critical missing link in the Apple canon, and Carlton's reporting is the best ever done about Apple—almost too much, some reviewers complained, the facts all but burying the narrative. Perhaps, but for researchers it is a dream.

9. *On the Firing Line* by Gil Amelio (Harper Business, 1998)—A rather sad attempt at explanation and revenge by Apple's ousted CEO. Amelio attempts to justify his tenure and trash Jobs as a Judas, but instead undermines his own case. After all, if Amelio was as clever as he claims to be, how come he didn't see Jobs coming? Everybody else sure did. Still, a good source for gossip about the great Apple collapse.

Needless to say, there are dozens of other books about Apple, ranging from hardcore tech manuals to coffee-table design books to novelty items such as a book on company T-shirts. The serious fan or student will find useful material in nearly all of them. A few of particular interest are *The Mac Bathroom Reader* and *The Macintosh Reader*, two compendia of trivia about that momentous product; Jeffrey Young's biography *Steve Jobs: The Journey Is the Reward*, a look at Jobs during the Next era; and Doug Garr's *Woz*.

MAGAZINES

Apple Computer has led the march of technology stories out of the trade press, where such coverage began in the late 1960s, into business magazines and then into general interest magazines. It is telling these days that such publications as *Newsweek* and *Time* not only have computer and technology sections, but regularly devote covers to the topic. The revolution is now over; technology won. We all live in Woz's world.

A number of magazines were important sources in the preparation of *Infinite Loop*. The following is a list of them, and, in parentheses, the names of especially influential reporters:

Among the mainstream business magazines, the most important were *Business Week* (Kathy Rebello, perhaps the best—and most enduring—of all the journalists covering Apple), *Fortune* (Brent Schlender), and *Forbes* (Julie Pitta). One often overlooked magazine, but one that I have always found incredibly useful for any technology story, is *Industry Week*.

Among technology business magazines, the most important source has long been *Upside* (Eric Nee, Richard Brandt, Tish Williams, Dave Coursey, Paulina Borsook, and numerous others), which has covered Apple in almost every issue since the magazine's founding a decade ago. *Upside* has never been popular with Apple, and it is despised by Steve Jobs—which underscores the fine job it has done. Other useful tech-business sources on Apple include *Forbes ASAP*, *Red Herring*, and most of all, *Wired* (James Daly), whose June 1997 sacred Apple heart cover is one of the classics of the genre.

The electronics trade magazines that have educated me about Apple over the course of the last quarter-century are too numerous to mention, and include the various Apple-related magazines (*MacWorld*, etc.), PC magazines (*PC*, *Dr. Dobbs*, *Infoworld*), and newsletters (*Release 1.0*). I would like to note, though, two unlikely but very useful sources. First, *Computer Currents* is a thick, free publication handed out in Silicon Valley at places like Fry's. It offers a surprisingly extensive level of editorial coverage on computer-related topics. Second, the source for Jef Raskin's myth-demolishing memoir is Kip Crosby's *The Analytical Engine*, the journal of the Computer History Association of California.

NEWSPAPERS

The primary source for this book, especially from 1984 to the present, was daily newspapers. Several generations of newsies have covered the Apple beat, most of it through hard work under tight deadlines with little lasting recognition. The phrase about journalists writing "the first draft of history" was never more accurate.

The three national newspapers that have done the best job covering Apple are *USA Today* (especially Kathy Rebello, in an earlier incarnation), the *New York Times* (the two veterans Andrew Pollack and John Markoff), and *The Wall Street Journal* (Walter Mossberg, Jim Carlton and G. Pascal Zachary). All have done an excellent job over the last decade in keeping the Apple story in its proper perspective.

But the real heavy lifting in the daily coverage of Apple has always been done by the newspapers of the San Francisco Bay Area: the *San Francisco Examiner*, the *San Francisco Chronicle* (Peter Sinton, Herb Greenberg, Tom Abate, Jon Swartz, David Einstein) and most of all, the *San Jose Mercury News*. Over the years, an army of Merc reporters have given Apple almost unprecedented attention, capturing nearly every nuance of that company's operations. At least one hundred quotes in this book come from the *Mercury News*'s twenty-plus year coverage of Apple. Here are the names of some of the reporters who did the work: Bruce Entin, Mike Cassidy, David Plotnikoff, G. Pascal Zachary, Nancy Marx Better, Ron Wolf, Jim Bartimo, Steve Kaufman, Evelyn Richards, Jim Mitchell, Rory O'Connor, Kathy Holub, Mark Shwanhausser, Lee Gomes, Alex Barnum, Mary A. C. Fallon, Kathleen Parker, Jodi Mardesich, Miranda Ewell, David Sylvester, Lisa Raleigh, Debra Hauser, Jonathan Greer, Ray Alvareztorres, Denis Collins, Leigh Weimers, Valerie Rice, Tom Schmitz, Christopher Pummer, Laurie Flynn, Michelle Levander, Dan Gillmor, Chris Nolan, Miguel Helft, Oanh Ha, Mark Leibovich, Tom Quinlan, Adam Lashinsky and Mike Langberg.

To all of these folks, history (and I) owe an enormous debt of gratitude.

INDEX

ABOUT THE AUTHOR

Michael S. Malone grew up in Silicon Valley and joined the *San Jose Mercury News* as one of the nation's first daily high-tech reporters. He has written for *The Wall Street Journal,* the *New York Times* and other national publications. He is currently editor of *Forbes ASAP.* Among his books are *The Big Score, The Virtual Corporation* and *Intellectual Capital.* He also hosts *Malone,* an interview series now in its ninth season on public television.